THE ESSENTIAL KALDOR

The Essential Kaldor

edited by

F. Targetti and A.P. Thirlwall

HM

HOLMES & MEIER

New York

Published in the United States of America 1989 by
Holmes & Meier Publishers, Inc.
30 Irving Place
New York, NY 10003

Library of Congress Cataloging-in-Publication Data

Kaldor, Nicholas, 1908-1986.
    The essential Kaldor / edited by F. Targetti and A.P. Thirlwall
        p.   cm.
    Includes index.
    ISBN 0-8419-1235-1 (alk. paper)
    1. Economics.   2. Keynesian economics.   3. Economic development.
4. Equilibrium (Economics)   I. Targetti, Ferdinando.
II. Thirlwall, A. P.   III. Title.
HB171.K286   1989
330—dc20
                                                                        89–34890
                                                                        CIP

CONTENTS

To Bogna
with love

INTRODUCTION

Professor Lord Kaldor (1908-1986) had a long and distinguished career as an academic economist and policy adviser. This book brings together a selection of twenty-three of his most innovative, influential and important papers written over a span of fifty years (from a total output of close to two hundred journal articles and pamphlets). Kaldor made original and lasting contributions to the theory of the firm, to Keynesian economics, to growth and distribution theory, to equilibrium economics, and to thinking about domestic and international economic policy; and the essays are organised under these heads. The book is designed to give students and teachers alike easy access to Kaldor's writings in these fields.

The firm, equilibrium and welfare

This section includes papers on the theory of the firm, the concept of equilibrium and welfare economics. All were written while Kaldor was a young lecturer at the London School of Economics (LSE) in the 1930s when his interests were almost exclusively theoretical, and he was participating in the theoretical controversies of the time. The first, "A Classificatory Note on the Determinateness of Equilibrium", was published in 1934. It was first presented at the famous Robbins-Hayek LSE Seminar when he was still a follower of the Austrian neoclassical school. It is designed to clarify the assumptions of static theory necessary to make equilibrium determinate, and to classify the various causes of 'indeterminateness" under the headings of existence, uniqueness and stability. The clarity of exposition enhances the pedagogic usefulness of the paper. The main theoretical contribution is the discussion of stability conditions. Kaldor coins here for the first time the term "cobweb" theorem to describe oscillatory movements to and from equilibrium when adjustment is continuous.

The second paper, "The Equilibrium of the Firm", was published in the same year and contributes to the debate, started by Sraffa, concerning the incompatibility of long-period static equilibrium and perfect competition if there is a tendency for the size of the firm to grow relative to the size of the industry. Kaldor seeks a flexible factor of production for the industry, but fixed for the firm, which will produce an upward sloping supply curve for the competitive firm and at the same time determine firm size. Marshall focused on entrepreneurship. Among the three functions of the entrepreneur—risk taking, supervision and co-ordinating ability—Kaldor argues that only the last has the required properties. However, in the long-run static equilibrium the task of co-ordination is transformed into a mere supervision task: the co-ordination as a fixed factor disappears and becomes a free good. The contradiction between perfect competition and long-run equilibrium is solved by Kaldor by dropping the assumption of perfect competition.

Kaldor extends the arguments in his classic paper "Market Imperfection and Excess Capacity", 1935. Here he shows formally that free entry into an industry will only lead to perfect competition if there are constant returns to scale. If there are increasing returns, free entry, increasing the number of producers, will raise their costs per unit of output and eventually halt the entry of new firms. Firms will end up with excess capacity in the sense of each producing and selling less than the "optimum" output. It had never previously been admitted that free competition might raise costs and prices. It followed also from this analysis that if at the point of equilibrium productivity increases and costs decrease, serious problems arise for neoclassical price and distribution theory. Hicks admitted in *Value and Capital* (1939) that if the assumption of increasing marginal costs is abandoned "the basis on which economic laws can be constructed is shorn away", causing "wreckage of the greater part of economic theory". Kaldor also shows that, if economies of scale exist, pure profit may exist even in a state of equilibrium because the minimum size of new entrants may reduce the demand for each firm's product so much as to involve all firms in losses, thus deterring entry. This will prevent tangency of the demand curve and the average cost curve. Only if average costs are constant is perfect competition possible. Kaldor remarks: "Mathematical economists in taking perfect competition as their starting point weren't such fools after all. For they assumed perfect divisibility of everything; and when everything is perfectly divisible, and consequently economies of scale are completely absent, perfect competition must necessarily establish itself solely as a result of the free play of market forces." It is this line of thinking that has been influential in the argument that imperfect competition is a necessary condition for involuntary unemployment, because if constant returns prevailed, every unemployed person could become self-employed with no barriers to entry.[1] At one time Kaldor seemed to endorse this position,[2] but a fundamentalist Keynesian should not agree that this is the *ultimate* source of involuntary unemployment in Keynes's own system of thought.

Kaldor drew no welfare implications from his analysis of market imperfections and excess capacity except to say that under imperfect competition there can be a conflict between the minimisation of costs and the maximisation of social welfare, because without barriers to entry the number of producers and products is larger, and with barriers to entry the products are more standardised but are sold at a lower price. Kaldor was interested in welfare economics, however, and in 1939 he made a seminal contribution to the subject in his paper "Welfare Propositions in Economics and Interpersonal Comparisons of Utility", which launched the "new welfare economics". Kaldor was reacting against the nihilism of the Pareto doctrine that, since individual utilities cannot be compared, an economic change cannot be pronounced "good" or "bad" if some people are affected favourably and others unfavourably. As a solution to the impasse, Kaldor suggested compensation tests. If the

---

[1] See M. Weitzman, "Increasing Returns and the Foundations of Unemployment Theory", *Economic Journal*, December 1982.

[2] "Keynesian Economics After Fifty Years" in J. Trevithick and G.N.D. Worswick (eds.), *Keynes and the Modern World* (Cambridge University Press, 1983).

gainers could *potentially* compensate the losers and still be better off, the policy change must be for the better in the sense that physical productivity must have increased. The distribution of the gains is, of course, a separate issue, which Kaldor recognised, to which there is no objective answer without the specification of a social welfare function with explicit distributional weights. This paper of Kaldor generated an enormous secondary literature, involving Hicks, Scitovsky, Baumol, Samuelson and Little, among others, but without resolution of the distributional issue.

Contributions to Keynesian economics

Kaldor was in the United States on a Rockefeller Research Scholarship when Keynes's *General Theory* first appeared. He was prepared for it, however, and outside Cambridge he was one of the first converts to Keynesian ways of thinking. Throughout his life, he remained faithful to the fundamental message of the *General Theory*, but was critical of some of its assumptions, and also sought to extend Keynesian modes of thinking in various directions. The first two papers in this section show how Kaldor helped to seal the Keynesian revolution. "Pigou on Money Wages in Relation to Unemployment", published in 1937, convinced Pigou that he was wrong to believe that a cut in money wages could increase the level of unemployment independently of a fall in the rate of interest. That was a notable victory. "Speculation and Economic Stability", published in 1939, was described by Sir John Hicks in private correspondence with Kaldor as the "culmination of the Keynesian revolution in theory. You ought to have had more honour for it."[1]

After the *General Theory* was published, Pigou was quick into print to defend the classical view of a direct inverse relation between the level of money wages and the aggregate level of unemployment. Pigou maintained that "it is enough for my purpose to show that a money wage cut is not simply a piece of ritual that enables the real cause of employment expansion—a

[1] Letter dated 20th May 1986.

fall in the rate of money interest—to take effect".[1] Kaldor took issue, and showed that a fall in the rate of interest must be implied owing to the effect of falling prices on the real value of the money supply—what was later called the "Keynes Effect". Pigou conceded "in the sense that [a cut in money wages] would not entail an increase in employment *unless* it entailed a reduction in the rate of interest, we may properly say that it works on the volume of employment *through* the rate of interest".[2] Both Keynes and Kaldor always maintained that there are simpler, less destabilising, ways of reducing interest rates than by cutting money wages.

"Speculation and Economic Stability" (and its Appendix "Keynes's Theory of the Own-Rates of Interest", published separately in 1960)[3] was the paper that gave Kaldor most intellectual satisfaction. It generalised the *General Theory*, and provided an original theory of the term structure of interest rates. Kaldor's explanation of why the classical supposition is wrong that saving will lead to investment is the stabilising influence of speculators which dampens fluctuations in interest rates. In the extreme, if the influence of speculation in the market for long-term bonds is infinite, output will do all the adjusting when there is disequilibrium in the goods market. Keynes seemed to accept this argument as the foundation of his multiplier analysis. On the question of the determination of interest rates, it will be remembered that Dennis Robertson accused Keynes of leaving the rate of interest on long-term bonds "hanging by its own bootstraps" (i.e. with no base). Kaldor provides what might be called a "bottom up" theory of the rate of interest in which the short rate is determined by monetary policy in the money market, and this anchors the edifice. The structure of interest rates is then determined by the risk premium on assets of different maturities. Section II of the original Appendix, which deals more extensively with the relation between short- and long-term rates of interest, is reprinted in this volume.

[1] A.C. Pigou, "Real and Money Wage Cuts in Relation to Unemployment", *Economic Journal*, September 1937.
[2] A.C. Pigou, "Money Wages in Relation to Unemployment", *Economic Journal*, March 1938.
[3] *Collected Economic Essays*, Volume 2 (Duckworth, 1960).

The third paper in this section is Kaldor's famous and unique "A Model of the Trade Cycle" published in 1940. Kaldor taught trade cycle theory at the LSE in the 1930s. He had already appeared in print as a strong critic of Hayek and Austrian theories of the trade cycle based on the influence of monetary policy on the length of the production period. He also realised that the newly expounded theories of Frisch, Tinbergen and Kalecki based on a linear accelerator could not explain oscillations betwen a low- and high-level equilbrium. A shifting non-linear investment function, however, could produce a 'limit' cycle. Kaldor was the first to argue (subsequently followed by many others, notably Goodwin) that investment is likely to be a non-linear function of output because at low levels of output there is excess capacity and at high levels of output there are physical constraints on further output growth. The savings function is also likely to be non-linear in relation to output. Kaldor shows how these functions can produce multiple equilibria with the economy oscillating between two stable limits as forces develop which cause the curves to shift up and down. Kaldor also addresses the periodicity of the cycle. The appeal of the model is that it can generate self-sustaining cycles without the need for time lags, shocks or the rigid specification of parameters which characterise most other trade cycle models.

The last paper in this section, "Keynesian Economics After Fifty Years", was prepared for the centenary celebrations in Cambridge of Keynes's birth in 1883. After the war Kaldor made very few direct contributions to static Keynesian employment or monetary theory, although there is no doubt that a Keynesian vision inspired his work on growth and distribution. In this paper, looking back, he takes issue with some basic assumptions and limitations of the Keynesian model of the economy; particularly the short-run Marshallian assumption of diminishing returns to labour; the treatment of the money supply as exogenously determined, and the assumption of a closed economy. Relaxing the assumption of increasing marginal cost means that employment and the real wage can be positively correlated. Relaxing the assumption of an exogenous money supply has profound implications for the predictions and interpretation of the equations representing the quantity theory of money. And relaxing the assumption that the economy is closed brings to the fore the importance of the balance between exports and imports as a more important determinant of the level of activity in an open economy than the "Keynesian" emphasis on the balance between savings and investment in the closed economy.

Distribution, growth, technical progress and 'cumulative causation'

During the war, and immediately after, Kaldor worked mainly on applied economics issues particularly connected with the war effort and with post-war reconstruction at home and abroad. Between 1947 and 1949 he was Director of Research for the Economic Commission for Europe in Geneva. On return to academic life in Cambridge in 1950, he turned his attention once again to economic theory—to the old preoccupations of the classical economists of growth and the functional distribution of income between wages and profits. Since the marginalist revolution of the late nineteenth century, marginal productivity theory was the prevailing theory of distributive shares. And in the field of growth economics, neoclassical theory, based on the notion of an aggregate production function, was also beginning to grip the economics profession in response to the challenge thrown up by Harrod in his essay on dynamic economics in 1939.[1] The task that Kaldor embarked on in the 1950s, which was not finished until the mid-1960s, was to explain the dynamics of the capitalist system in the Keynesian tradition, both to undermine the growth pessimism of classical theory and at the same time to provide an alternative to the neoclassical theory of growth and distribution. Kaldor simply could not accept the neoclassical assumptions of perfect competition and constant returns to scale as an adequate description of the real world on which to base a long-run theory of equilibrium growth and distribution.

"Alternative Theories of Distribution" gives a lucid resumé of

---

[1] R.F. Harrod, "An Essay on Dynamic Theory", *Economic Journal*, March 1939.

previous theories of distribution, including a beautiful exposition of the Ricardian system that Kaldor learnt from Sraffa. In this pathbreaking paper, first published in 1956, he presents his own macro-theory of distribution which derives from the insight of Keynes in his *Treatise on Money* (1930), and Kalecki's "Theory of Profits" (1942) that profit is the *result* of investment by entrepreneurs, not its cause. Capitalists can only make profits if there is spending in excess of the costs of employing workers (which may not even be covered by workers' consumption if workers save). If investment determines saving, and the propensity to save out of profits is higher than out of wages, the investment ratio must be associated with a unique distribution of income between wages and profits. The theory is in stark contrast to the neoclassical theory of distribution, based not on the relative scarcity of factors of production but on the dynamism of accumulation. It also contrasts with Ricardian and Marxian distribution theory, in which the rate of profit is a residual, whereas in Kaldor's theory it is the real wage that plays the passive role. Kaldor's theory is beautiful in its simplicity and has survived largely unscathed from the attacks made upon it. In its original form the model assumes full employment so that the Keynesian multiplier only affects the relationship between prices and wages (not output), but subsequent work has shown that the model can be generalised to less than full employment states.[1]

Changes in the distribution of income also provide a mechanism for equilibrating the warranted and natural rates of growth, which was the challenge thrown up by Harrod's essay on dynamic economics. The neoclassical response was to rely on variations in the capital-output ratio through the substitution of labour and capital for the achievement of equilibrium growth with the full employment of labour and capital. Changes in the savings ratio brought about by a change in the distribution of income is an alternative mechanism. Kaldor's distribution theory is an integral part of his model of economic growth which is designed to explain what he calls the "stylised facts" of

---

[1] *E.g.* A. Wood, *A Theory of Profits* (Cambridge University Press, 1975).

economic history, namely: a steady trend rate of growth of labour productivity; a steady increase in the amount of capital per worker; a steady rate of profit on capital; the relative constancy of the capital-output ratio; a fairly constant share of wages and profits in national income, and lastly, wide differences in the rate of growth of output and labour productivity between countries (associated with different levels of investment).

Kaldor's 1961 paper "Capital Accumulation and Economic Growth" (originally written in 1958) provides a complete non-neoclassical model to explain the above-mentioned tendencies and trends. It followed on the heels of an earlier paper "A Model of Economic Growth"[1] which not only uses his distribution theory but also introduced for the first time the novel concept of the technical progress function to overcome the artificial distinction between movements along a production function (as a result of capital deepening) and shifts in the function (as a result of technical progress). In Kaldor's model capital accumulation and technical progress are interconnected by the technical progress function which relates the rate of growth of output per worker to the rate of growth of capital per worker. The relation is direct; however, the rate at which technical progress is introduced falls as accumulation grows. Given an investment function in relation to the expected profit, the accumulation of capital will reach a rate which is equal to the rate of growth of labour productivity. The flexibility of distributive shares between profits and wages supplies the necessary saving to match the investment which the economy needs to grow at that rate, which represents the long-run equilibrium growth rate of the model. As the accumulation of capital and labour productivity grow at the same rate, the capital-output ratio is constant in long-run equilibrium. Given the constant capital-output ratio and a constant share of profits, the model shows that the long-run rate of profit is uniquely and directly determined by the rate of growth of output (which is determined by the parameters of the technical progress

---

[1] *Economic Journal*, December 1957.

function) and inversely determined by the propensity to save out of profits.

This result, which is often labelled the "Cambridge equation", has been challenged by neoclassical Keynesians such as Modigliani, Meade, Tobin, Hahn, Solow and Samuelson, and it has been defended by Joan Robinson, Richard Kahn and above all Luigi Pasinetti, who demonstrated that it holds even when workers save, provided that their propensity to save is less than the share of investment in income. On these matters, and related issues on the theory of capital, the debates between Cambridge, England and Cambridge, Massachusetts, mesmerised the economics profession for close on twenty years.

Another paper in this period which must be mentioned is one written with J. Mirrlees in 1961.[1] Here Kaldor brings to the extreme the consequences of his theory of technical progress. It is one of the earliest examples of a vintage model in which only the new capital goods bring about a higher productivity of labour. The capital goods are different and competition equalises the rate of return only on the new capital goods. On this issue, Kaldor's approach is different from the other Cambridge economists involved in the debate on the theory of capital.

By the mid-1960s, however, Kaldor had lost interest in growth theory. He became increasingly interested in the applied economics of growth, partly as a result of being a Special Adviser to the British Chancellor of the Exchequer from 1964, and particularly as a resident of a country with the slowest post-war growth rate of any of the major industrialised countries. He was particularly concerned with the search for empirical regularities, related to inter-country and inter-regional growth-rate differences, and with the question of why growth-rate differences persist instead of narrowing as equilibrium theory would predict.

These questions were first addressed in two sets of lectures in 1966: the Frank Pierce Memorial Lecture at Cornell University (published under the title of *Strategic Factors in Economic*

---

[1] "A New Model of Economic Growth", *Review of Economic Studies*, Vol. XXXIX, No. 3, 1962.

Development), and his inaugural lecture in Cambridge on *Causes of the Slow Rate of Economic Growth of the United Kingdom*, reprinted here. In these two publications he presents three empirical regularities or "laws". First, that manufacturing growth is the "engine of growth" in the sense that the greater the excess of manufacturing growth over GDP growth the faster GDP growth seems to be. He attributes this to two major factors which constitute the two other "laws": namely, that output growth in industry induces productivity growth in industry through static and dynamic returns to scale (what Kaldor labels Verdoorn's Law), and that output growth in industry induces productivity growth outside industry by the absorption of unemployed or low-productivity resources. Kaldor draws inspiration from Adam Smith, and from his early LSE teacher Allyn Young, with his emphasis on increasing returns as a macro-economic phenomenon and a characteristic primarily of manufacturing industry where the elasticities of supply and demand are much higher than for primary products and many service activities.

Kaldor's original contention was that Britain's slow rate of economic growth could be attributed to a labour-supply constraint as a result of the "early" contraction of agriculture before industry had reached a high level of productivity (a state of "premature maturity"—as he called it). But he soon changed his mind, and then laid the blame for Britain's poor growth performance on the weakness of the tradeable goods sector, i.e. poor export performance relative to the propensity to import. Kaldor revived the doctrine of the Harrod trade multiplier, which in its dynamic form makes the rate of growth of output equal to the ratio of the growth rate of exports to the income elasticity of demand for imports. This ratio defines a country's growth rate consistent with balance of payments equilibrium, assuming that relative prices measured in a common currency remain unchanged. Kaldor's explanation of why growth-rate differences persist between regions is then related to the "virtuous circle" set up within countries resulting from successful export performance. Exports are the major component of autonomous demand in an open economy to which other components of demand adapt, and the induced productivity growth from faster output growth maintains a country's competitiveness which sustains its export performance. A process of "circular and cumulative causation", as Myrdal once called it, is set in train.

These ideas are presented in the fourth and fifth papers reprinted here on "The Case for Regional Policies" (1970) and "The Role of Increasing Returns, Technical Progress and Cumulative Causation in the Theory of International Trade and Economic Growth" (1981). In the latter Kaldor also addresses the question of the gains from trade and casts doubt on the mutual profitability of trade when one of the partners specialises in diminishing-returns (primary-product) activities which may suffer unemployment in the process of resource reallocation because there is a subsistence limit below which wages cannot fall.

For more than twenty years Kaldor was an adviser to less developed countries on development policies and taxation. He saw clearly that development must ultimately imply industrialisation, and that industrialisation requires an initial short period of protection of domestic industry, followed by a stage of growth led by manufacturing exports. The last paper in this section is an historical one, "Capitalism and Industrial Development: Some Lessons from Britain's Experience" (1975), which contains some important messages for countries currently in the throes of development. The initial industrial revolution resulted from a combination of fortunate circumstances which led Britain to the introduction of the factory system. Subsequent industrial development took place mainly as the result of the acquisition of new markets abroad due to the market superiority of British goods. But this process of "cumulative causation" had not only a polarisation effect, but also a decentralisation effect, which led to the decline of British industry. In fact, the European countries, importing British capital goods and protecting their domestic industry, started from about 1870 to increase their share of world manufacturing exports: consequently, the growth of British exports fell, import penetration grew, and, as a consequence, Britain's growth rate

fell below that of the countries of the "second industrialisation".
This long-run trend, only briefly interrupted by protectionist
policies between the two wars, continued even more adversely
after the Second World War, exacerbated by inappropriate
domestic policies which encouraged consumption at the
expense of exports.

The challenge to equilibrium theory

Kaldor was a long-standing critic of neoclassical value theory
based on Walrasian general equilibrium analysis. It was not the
notion of equilibrium he objected to, but neoclassical modes of
thinking, based on unreal assumptions, with their static
emphasis on substitution and allocation (a "tangential"
economics, as Allyn Young once called it) to the neglect of the
dynamic process of growth and change based on increasing
returns. The framework of competitive equilibrium he believed
to be "barren and irrelevant as an apparatus of thought to deal
with the manner of operation of economic forces, or as an
instrument for non-trivial predictions concerning the effects of
economic changes".[1] His first attack was a challenge to
Samuelson and Modigliani in 1966: "it is high time that the
brilliant minds of MIT were set to evolve a system of
non-Euclidian economics which starts from a non-perfect,
non-profit maximising economy where ... abstractions [neces-
sary for the existence of a competitive equilibrium] are initially
unnecessary."[2] The assault was renewed in two powerful papers
reprinted here, "The Irrelevance of Equilibrium Economics"
and "What is Wrong with Economic Theory", and culminated
in his 1983 Okun Lectures[3] and his 1984 Mattioli Lectures.[4]
Kaldor's critique of what he calls for short "equilibrium
economics" has three major strands. The first is methodological; the second relates to the lack of realism

---

[1] *Collected Economic Essays*, Volume 5 (Duckworth, 1978).

[2] "Marginal Productivity and the Macro-Economic Theories of Distribution: Comment on
Samuelson and Modigliani", *Review of Economic Studies*, October 1966.

[3] *Economics Without Equilibrium* (University College Cardiff Press 1985).

[4] *Causes of Growth and Stagnation in the World Economy*.

concerning how markets function and the third to the implications of the neglect of increasing returns. The methodological attack is simply that, if economics is to be a useful science, models must be based on realistic and empirically verifiable assumptions, not on *a priori* assumptions which are empirically false or cannot be tested. On the question of the functioning of markets, Kaldor wants to highlight the creative function of markets and the complementarities that exist in the real world between the demand for products, the demand for factors of production and activities in general, in contrast to equilibrium theory in which goods and factors of production are regarded as competitive and nothing can be done except at the expense of something else. The emphasis on the price mechanism as the *deus ex machina* of the economic system is also attacked as if agents act on prices and nothing else. In the real world agents are not simply price takers and quantity makers; on the contrary, in industrial economies quantity signals are frequently more important than price signals in the determination of producer behaviour. Kaldor's third critique relates to the implications and consequences of increasing returns. First, there cannot be a competitive equilibrium with increasing returns unless they are "small" relative to the scale of the economy. Kaldor asks what is the meaning of "general equilibrium" when increasing returns will cause everything in the equilibrium system to change—resource availabilities, technology, tastes, prices and so on? Secondly, once increasing returns are admitted, the concept of an optimum allocation of resources loses meaning since the position of the production possibility curve will itself depend on the allocation of resources. Thirdly, the existence of increasing returns undermines the notion that at any moment of time output must be resource-constrained, since the process of production will generate its own resources. Finally, if supply and demand interact in the presence of increasing returns, there can be no guarantee that once a disequilibrium occurs there will necessarily be a return to equilibrium. There is no reason why factor prices should equalise with free trade; why migration should equalise factor prices or unemployment between regions or countries, and no reason why growth rates between regions or countries should necessarily converge.

In "What is Wrong with Economic Theory", and in the third paper in this section, "Equilibrium Theory and Growth Theory", Kaldor gives the outlines of a two-sector closed-economy model of industry and agriculture which he lectured on in Cambridge for many years but never formalised.[1] The purpose of the model is twofold: to explore the constraints on industrial growth in a closed system such as the world economy, and to give an interpretation of the stagflationary bias of the world economy based on the asymmetric adjustment of industrial prices to the prices of primary commodities. We discuss this matter later. On the first point, the model highlights the importance of achieving an equilibrium terms of trade between the two sectors, and shows that growth in the long run is dependent on the rate of land-saving innovations in agriculture as an offset to diminishing returns. The products of land-based activities are the only true long-run constraints on industrial growth; certainly not labour, as in neoclassical theory.

Domestic and international economic policy

This section includes a miscellany of papers primarily addressed to important policy issues concerned with taxation, monetary policy, general economic management and the instability of the world economy.

The first paper on the expenditure tax looks again at an idea that Kaldor revived and forcefully propagated in a classic book in 1955.[2] The principle of progressive taxation rests on the concept of taxable capacity or ability to pay. The question that occupied Kaldor when he was a member of the Royal Commission on the Taxation of Profits and Income 1951-4 was whether measured income is a good measure of taxable capacity. Kaldor had three main worries: first, income by itself is not an unambiguous concept; secondly, in practice, the actual

---

[1] For separate formalisations, see F. Targetti, "Growth and the Terms of Trade: A Kaldorian Two Sector Model", *Metroeconomica*, February 1985, and A.P. Thirlwall, "A General Model of Growth and Development on Kaldorian Lines", *Oxford Economic Papers*, July 1986.

[2] *An Expenditure Tax* (Allen and Unwin 1955).

definition of income for tax purposes can introduce major inequities into the system by some receipts being treated as income and others not; and thirdly, income is only one measure of taxable capacity because it ignores ability to pay that resides in property. In other words there are sources of spending power other than income, but it is not easy to express them all in a single measure of taxable capacity. All this convinced Kaldor that expenditure itself should be used as a measure of spending power, and that an expenditure tax would provide the basis for a more equitable tax system than income tax. An expenditure tax was implemented in India and Ceylon (Sri Lanka) where Kaldor was a tax adviser in the late 1950s, but it was later abandoned in both countries. Kaldor admits that he underestimated the complexities of administering such a tax and exaggerated the conceptual ease of defining expenditure as the basis for taxation in comparison with income.

The next two papers are on money and monetarism. The first represents his evidence to the influential Radcliffe Committee on the Working of the Monetary System which is important because it heavily influenced the conclusion of the Committee's Report.[1] Monetary policy in the United Kingdom had been revived in 1951, but there was increasing disquiet concerning its efficacy. This was the origin of the Radcliffe Inquiry, and its overriding conclusion was that there is no direct link between the supply of money and the level of demand in the economy, first on account of changes in the velocity of circulation of money, and secondly because, as far as spending is concerned, it is not the quantity of money that is important but the wider structure of liquidity. Kaldor in his submission treats the money supply as if it were exogenous, and gives evidence to show the variability of velocity. He then goes on to enumerate the reasons why expenditure may be insensitive to changes in the rate of interest. He warns against pronounced interest rate variability to control expenditure because this will increase the degree of risk in the bond market and tend to raise the average rate of interest and hence the required rate of profit at which

[1] Cmnd. 827 (London, HMSO, August 1959).

investment in physical assets is attractive. Kaldor also questions the relevance of monetary policy for coping with cost inflation and the balance of payments. He argues strongly the case for demand inflation as a stimulus to investment by raising the rate of profit: a theme he took up later in two lectures at the LSE in 1959.[1] He also puts forward an alternative explanation of the inverse relation between the rate of inflation and unemployment (i.e. the so-called Phillips Curve), arguing that unemployment stands as a proxy for profits, and that the real source of rising money wage demands is rising profits when unemployment is low. This theory has come into its own again in recent years.

The second paper, "The New Monetarism", is Kaldor's first major assault on the doctrine of monetarism associated with Professor Milton Friedman: "The new monetarism is a Friedman revolution more truly than Keynes was the sole fount of the Keynesian revolution." Kaldor highlights three essential elements of the doctrine: first, reaffirmation of the classical dichotomy that only money matters in determining money variables, and that in long-run equilibrium money is neutral as far as real variables are concerned; secondly, money supply changes preceding income changes is "proof" that money is exogenous and causal in the process of money-income determination, and thirdly the ineffectiveness of monetary policy in the short run and the case for a non-discretionary monetary growth rule in the long run. For inflation to be "always and everywhere a monetary phenomenon" in a causal sense requires that money is the determinant of the system not the determinate, and that the demand to hold money is a stable function of income. Kaldor is adamant that in modern industrial economies with extensive finance and credit mechanisms, the money supply cannot be considered as exogenously determined, but rather as endogenous responding to the needs of trade (including the need to finance autonomous wage increases). There are two concepts of endogeneity in Kaldor's work on money which, unfortunately,

[1] "Economic Growth and the Problem of Inflation", Parts I and II, *Economica*, August and November 1959.

he never fully specified. The first is a long-run process which deals with what might be called technical progress in the financial sector: the growing demand for money (for "finance", to use Keynes's terminology of the *Treatise*) induces the creation of new money substitutes and new financial intermediaries.[1] The second is a short-run process related to the behaviour of the Central Bank whose essential task is to provide some stability to the financial system by stabilising interest rates and acting as lender of last resort. Monetarists deny the endogeneity of the money supply with two kinds of evidence: first because peaks and troughs of the money supply apparently precede peaks and troughs of money GNP, and secondly because banks, it is claimed, are always fully loaned-up so that bank deposits vary closely with high-powered money which the Central Bank can control. On the first point, as Kaldor notes, since money is demanded in anticipation of expenditure, the lagged relation between money and money income cannot be "proof" that money is causal. On the second point, it is simply not true that there is invariably a high correlation between the monetary base and the money supply, but in any case the monetary base is not exogenously determined because the monetary authorities generally desire stable interest rates in the interests of government debt financing.

With regard to the demand for money, Kaldor argues that the reason why the demand for money may appear stable is precisely because the supply of money is unstable responding to demand at a constant rate of interest. Thus the interest inelasticity of the demand for money is not "proof" of the potency of money (and monetary policy) in determining money income but the exact opposite, namely evidence of the difficulty of controlling the supply of money. In responding to Friedman, Kaldor attributed large variations in the money supply in the UK to variations in the Public Sector Borrowing Requirement (PSBR) (since before 1970 deficits were financed by the banking

---

[1] See N. Kaldor and J. Trevithick, "A Keynesian Perspective on Money", *Lloyds Bank Review*, January 1981.

system). In later writings[1] he was to demolish one of the planks of the Thatcher government's monetarist experiment, by showing no relation between the PSBR and changes in M_3 money in the post-1975 period. Friedman replied to the Kaldor critique "if the relation between money and income is a supply response ... how is it that major differences among countries and periods in monetary institutions and other factors affecting the supply of money do not produce widely different relations between money and income?"[2] Kaldor answered curtly that they do![3] The international evidence shows wide differences in the velocity of circulation of money.

The next paper, "Conflicts in National Economic Objectives", is Kaldor's Presidential Address to Section F of the British Association for the Advancement of Science in 1971 which addresses the topic of the conduct of British economic policy. He is highly critical of the consumption-led growth policies of successive governments, to the neglect of the foreign trade sector. In 1971 Kaldor still believed in the efficacy of exchange rates as an efficient balance of payments adjustment mechanism, and did not lose faith until the experience of floating exchange rates post-1972 showed otherwise.[4] Kaldor was the inspiration behind the so-called New Cambridge School that for a time wanted to reverse the traditional use of policy instruments and to assign monetary and fiscal policy to external balance and exchange rate adjustment to internal balance. There was alleged to be a direct causal relation between the size of the budget deficit and the deficit on the current account of the balance of payments which was not amenable to devaluation. The theory was based on several assumptions relating to the stability of the private sector and its net acquisition of financial assets. But the relation was to break down. Kaldor then embraced import controls during his period

---

[1] *E.g.* in his Memorandum of Evidence on Monetary Policy to the Select Committee on the Treasury and Civil Service, HMSO 17th July 1980, reprinted as "Monetarism and United Kingdom Monetary Policy", *Cambridge Journal of Economics*, December 1980, and in *The Scourge of Monetarism* (Oxford University Press 1982).

[2] *Lloyds Bank Review*, October 1970.

[3] *Ibid.*

[4] See his essay "The Effect of Devaluations on Trade in Manufactures" in *Collected Economic Essays*, Vol. 6.

as Special Adviser to the Chancellor of the Exchequer from
1974 to 1976. At the same time, the rationale of such a policy
was extensively argued by colleagues in the Department of
Applied Economics at Cambridge. It should be emphasised,
however, that the aim of the policy was not to reduce the
absolute level of imports, but the ratio of imports to national
income. In the long run, however, as Kaldor argues in the
paper included here, there is no substitute for export-led
growth. Exports are the only component of demand that can
provide the foreign exchange to pay for imports as output
expands, and the only component of demand that can solve the
dilemma of a reduction in consumption being necessary to
release resources for investment yet an increase in consumption
being necessary to stimulate investment. With export growth,
both consumption and investment can rise together. In this
paper, Kaldor also expresses concern over Britain's economic
performance if she entered the Common Market on the
proposed terms.

"Inflation and Recession in the World Economy" is Kaldor's
Presidential Address to the Royal Economic Society in 1976 and
addresses both domestic and international issues. Kaldor had a
long-standing interest in the topic of inflation, from the age of
fifteen when he witnessed first-hand the German hyper-
inflation of 1923 while on holiday with his parents in the
Bavarian Alps.[1] He identified several sources, and put forward
several explanations, of the inflationary process, unrelated to
monetary impulses, including: a wage-price (or wage-profit)
spiral in the growing economy; a wage-wage spiral in a dual
economy; structural imbalances and bottlenecks in industrialising countries, and the international transmission of inflation
through supply shocks. In the paper included here, the basic
thesis put forward is that to understand world inflationary
tendencies it is necessary to distinguish between primary
production on the one hand and secondary (manufacturing)
production on the other. In the markets for primary products,
prices are demand (market)-determined; in manufacturing

---

[1] "Recollections of an Economist", *Banca Nazionale del Lavoro Quarterly Review*, March 1986.

prices are cost-determined. When primary-product prices rise, industrial costs and prices rise, and governments depress demand to avoid inflation. When primary-product prices fall, purchasing power over manufactured goods falls, leading to recession. Hence Kaldor's conclusion that fluctuations in primary-product prices are a recipe for stagflation. He blames the behaviour of commodity prices for the stagflation experienced in the world economy post-1972. He finds the inflation between 1968 and 1971 more difficult to explain, but if trade union militancy was to blame, there is still the puzzle of why the explosion should have occurred more or less simultaneously in several countries.

Kaldor's views on commodity prices as a source of inflation and instability in the world economy are well outlined in the final paper on "The Role of Commodity Prices in Economic Recovery". The volatility of primary product prices poses a number of problems. First, it leads to a great deal of instability in the foreign-exchange earnings and balance of payments of the producing countries which makes investment planning and economic management much more difficult than otherwise would be the case, particularly in LDCs which are heavily dependent on the production and export of primary commodities. Secondly, because of asymmetries in the economic system, volatility imparts inflationary bias combined with tendencies toward stagnation, as described above. Thirdly, the volatility of primary-product prices leads to volatility in the terms of trade which may not reflect the equilibrium terms of trade between primary products and manufactured goods in the sense that supply and demand are equated in both markets, which then may cause growth either to be supply-constrained (if the industrial terms of trade are too low) or demand-constrained (if the industrial terms of trade are too high). This was an issue that greatly concerned Keynes, who advocated in 1942 a Commod-Control scheme that would have been administered as a buffer stock for individual commodities financed by international money issued by a world Central Bank (the International Clearing Union). Kaldor, with Hart and Tinbergen in 1964,[1] put forward a proposal for a new international reserve currency backed by thirty principal commodities which would have served three purposes. First, it would have eliminated the fragility of the gold exchange standard instituted at Bretton Woods, and provided the world with a new international reserve asset. Secondly, it would have prevented ups and downs in the world economy by linking the supply of money to the production of commodities. Thirdly, it would have provided a bulwark against inflation. No action was taken. In the paper published here, Kaldor, in effect, endorses Keynes's Plan for Commod Control which could be financed by the issue of Special Drawing Rights (SDRs). In Kaldor's words the purpose of the scheme would be "to secure the highest sustainable rate of growth of world industrialisation which the growth of availabilities of primary products permits". The output growth of the primary and secondary sectors would be kept in line not through primary product price variations, but through variations in the rate of investment in stocks by a newly created International Commodity Control Authority which would buy and sell commodities in exchange for SDRs to keep price within, say, a 5 per cent margin of their value in terms of SDRs. Net purchases would give a boost to world liquidity when needed and *vice versa*. The price stability would also give the incentive to invest in, and expand, the production of primary commodities, the supply of which, in Kaldor's view, is the only true long-run constraint on industrial growth.

Conclusion

Nicholas Kaldor's influence on the economics profession was pervasive, both theoretically and at the policy level.[2] In Britain he was a dominant influence for fifty years, surpassed only by Keynes this century in the ability to mix theoretical and policy analysis. In many respects Kaldor's interests were even wider

---

[1] N. Kaldor, A.G. Hart and J. Tinbergen, *The Case for an International Commodity Reserve Currency*, Memorandum submitted to UNCTAD, Geneva, 1964.

[2] For a full description of the life and work of Kaldor see A.P. Thirlwall, *Nicholas Kaldor* (Brighton: Wheatsheaf Books Limited 1987), and F. Targetti, *Nicholas Kaldor* (Milan, Il Mulino, 1989).

than Keynes's, and his policy advice extended far beyond the shores of Britain to many developing countries. Keynes and Kaldor had many academic characteristics in common. Both were primarily interested in policy first and theory second; they both treated economics as a moral science, and both possessed that intuition and insight which enabled them to distinguish the important from the unimportant and to understand complex economic relationships in a simple, but often novel, way. Both men also shared the rationalist belief in the power of intelligence to triumph over economic barbarism and absurdity, and to devise schemes to make the world a more civilised and humane place in which to live.

Notwithstanding his pre-eminence, it is our view that Kaldor's contribution to economic thinking has been under-valued by the wider profession, and the selection of essays offered here is a small attempt to redress that bias.

F. Targetti & A.P. Thirlwall

PART I

THE FIRM, EQUILIBRIUM AND WELFARE

1

THE DETERMINATENESS OF STATIC EQUILIBRIUM[1]

A MORE rigorous formulation of the conditions under which it is possible to make generalisations about the factors determining economic equilibrium may be regarded as one of the main achievements of theoretical development during the last fifty years. The growing realisation both of the difficulties confronting the use of the analytical method and of the usefulness of its application have led to a gradual "purification" of theory; to a more and more precise statement of the conditions under which its generalisations can be applied.

Hence the evolution of "static" theory: the economics of that abstract world in which it is possible to give an exact account of the course of events solely by the aid of scientific generalisations. Hence, also, the concept of a "determinate" equilibrium: an equilibrium whose nature can be rigorously determined from a few self-evident postulates alone. All this has helped, of course, to make economics more technical and incomprehensible to the layman; but no one who studies it seriously would maintain that in advancing along this path economics has gradually lost its "relevance to facts"; or that economists, in their anxiety to preserve the validity of their "laws" have come increasingly to neglect the operation of those forces which "really matter". For in any analytical study, forces whose laws of operation are known must clearly be separated from others in whose behaviour no such "uniform principles" have yet been detected; and the only satisfactory way to detect and account for the influence of the latter in the real world is by assuming them away and examining what events would be like in their absence. It is, moreover, only by employing this "method of difference" that we can hope gradually to extend the range of phenomena over which we can make generalisations.

The assumptions of static theory are, therefore, nothing else than the conditions necessary to make equilibrium "determinate":

[1] Originally published in *Review of Economic Studies*, February, 1934.

the conditions under which we can give a scientifically precise description of the actual course of economic phenomena. Once these assumptions have been specified and have gained general acceptance as the limits within which deductive speculation must proceed, any new elements subsequently discovered which play a rôle in shaping the course of events are likely to be put down as "causes of indeterminateness", since the human mind finds it easier to alter the conclusions arrived at within an accepted framework, than to alter the framework itself. Whenever, therefore, new causes of "indeterminateness" are said to be detected this is merely another way of saying that a new set of determining forces has been found: forces whose behaviour and manner had not hitherto been reducible to uniformities and whose influence must therefore also be assumed absent if the existing body of generalisations is to be regarded as valid. Once the existence of these additional forces has been incorporated in the main body of assumptions, the "indeterminateness" disappears (it has been buried in the assumptions) and the "abstractness" of pure theory has advanced one stage farther.

All this is clearly in accord with the main canons of scientific analysis; it is the only possible procedure to adopt if we aim at a clarification of the intricate inter-relationship of events by investigating the causal sequence of phenomena.

The assumptions under which modern economics has found it possible to determine the position of equilibrium from the "system of data" (a set of independent variables whose behaviour can be described by a "law", i.e. by a uniform principle) namely, the utility functions of individuals and the production functions of goods, are the following:

1. A closed economy (either an isolated individual or a completely self-sufficient community, with a given volume of human and natural resources).
2. "Perfect knowledge": all the relevant prices quoted in all markets are known to all individuals.
3. "Perfect competition": all exchanges are carried out in markets so large that no individual can influence any of the prices with which he is confronted.

4. "Direct exchange": all goods, services, etc., are exchanged directly for one another, while all prices are expressed in one of the goods serving as a unit of account.

Finally, if account is taken of the time-dimension, i.e. of the fact that all economic phenomena take place in time, some additional assumptions have to be introduced, regarding (i) the behaviour of the independent variables, the data, in time; (ii) people's expectation of this behaviour or, more precisely, people's expectation of the future course of prices. The simplest assumptions in these respects and those which have been implicit in static analysis are the following:

5. All independent variables remain constant through time.
6. All individuals expect the prices actually ruling to remain in force permanently: no price-changes are anticipated.[1]

These assumptions we may thus regard as the "accepted framework" of static theory:[2] and it is the sufficiency of this framework which is, in fact, contested when the "determinateness" of equilibrium is called into question. Investigations of such "causes" of indeterminateness have become only too frequent in recent theoretical literature; though in many cases no clear formulation has been given of the conditions which would cover them, i.e. the precise change of framework which they necessitate. The following note attempts to remedy for this deficiency and, by classifying the various "causes", at the same time to clear up the confusion which has arisen over the concept of indeterminateness itself. We shall make the above enumerated assumptions as the

---

[1] Just because the dependence of equilibrium on anticipations is not always clearly realised, this assumption is hardly ever expressly stated although it is inherent in any type of static analysis which aims at demonstrating the tendency towards equilibrium independently of the degree of foresight. The only alternative assumption consistent with the degree of abstractness necessary for the generalisations of pure theory would be the assumption of *complete foresight*: that everybody foresees correctly the future course of prices. In this latter case, however, there is no need to assume constancy of the independent variables in order to show the determinateness of equilibrium: and consequently this latter assumption can be more conveniently adopted as the basis of "dynamic" as distinct from a "static" type of analysis. Cf. Hicks, "Gleichgewicht und Konjunktur," *Zeitschrift für Nationalökonomie*, Vol. IV, No. 4.

[2] Or rather a rough summary of them; a precise enumeration would have to include assumptions in regard to the legal system (e.g. the institution of private property, the freedom and sanctity of contract) and a number of other things which, though essential for other purposes, are irrelevant to the following analysis.

"accepted framework" of static theory, our starting-point, ignoring consequently all those complications (such as indeterminacy due to the use of money or the absence of perfect competition) which were eliminated by them and with which static theory in general is not directly concerned.

I

The objections which have been raised concerning the sufficiency of static analysis can be summarised under three main headings:

(i) It has been pointed out that static analysis only succeeds in deriving the *conditions of equilibrium* from its "system of data", but not the *position of equilibrium*; i.e. it can point to a system of prices which, *if established*, would secure equilibrium, but it cannot determine the system of prices which will actually be in operation once equilibrium has been established. For the mere fact that there is, in any given situation, at least one system of prices which, if established, would secure equilibrium, does not imply that this particular set of prices will also be put into operation immediately; and if any other set of prices is established, not only will further price-changes become necessary, but the equilibrium system of prices (i.e. that particular set of prices which does *not* necessitate further changes in prices) will itself be a different one. It is not possible, therefore, to determine the position of equilibrium from a given system of data, since every successive step taken in order to reach equilibrium will alter the conditions of equilibrium (the set of prices capable of bringing it about) and thus change the final position—unless the conditions are such that either (1) an equilibrium system of prices *will* be established immediately, or (2) the set of prices actually established leaves the conditions of equilibrium unaffected (in which case the final position will be independent of the route followed).

(ii) An altogether different type of objection is that the system of data may itself be of such a nature as to admit of *more than one* position of determinate equilibrium from a given situation, i.e. that there may be more than one system of prices capable of securing equilibrium. This objection refers to the problem whether the *conditions* of equilibrium (as already defined) are unequivocally determined by the data or not; and arises, therefore, also in those

cases—moreover, it only becomes important in those cases—
where the position of equilibrium is otherwise determinate (i.e.
where from the conditions of equilibrium we can derive the
equilibrium position).

(iii) Finally, it has been pointed out that not only may equilibrium be "indeterminate" (in the sense that the process of adjustment itself alters the conditions of equilibrium), but that
furthermore, if the various forces do not react instantaneously on the
incentive of price changes, the economic system need not tend
towards a position of equilibrium at all. The successive alterations
of prices will then merely represent a constant or an expanding
range of fluctuations.

We shall examine these objections in turn by enumerating, in
each case, the conditions which are necessary to make them inoperative (or in the absence of which they would be operative).
We shall call an equilibrium "determinate" or "indeterminate"
according as the final position is independent of the route followed,
or not;[1] we shall call equilibrium "unique" or "multiple" according
as there is one, or more than one, system of equilibrium-prices,
corresponding to a given set of data; and, finally, we shall speak
of "definite" or "indefinite"[2, 3] equilibria, according as the actual
situation tends to approximate a position of equilibrium or not.[4]

---

[1] In using the word "indeterminateness" in this sense we are merely following
traditional terminology, since this is the sense in which both Marshall and Edgeworth
have employed the term. Since, however, both had demonstrated it in the example of
a barter-exchange, this type of indeterminateness is often associated with the absence
of perfect competition though, as we shall see below, it is not really eliminated by
any of the customary definitions of a "perfect market".

[2] It is questionable how far the term "equilibrium" is justified in connection with
"indefiniteness", i.e. divergent fluctuations which do not lead to a position of equilibrium at all. The main reason for employing the term "indefinite" in the present
paper—as will be apparent to the reader—is to preserve the symmetry of the classification.

[3] We shall use the terms "indefiniteness" and "instability" interchangeably in the
last section of this paper, just because neither of these expressions conveys with
sufficient precision the meaning desired. The word "unstable" would really be more
suitable than "indefinite", but for the fact that it is generally used in a different
sense—to denote a "passing equality of supply and demand" which does not represent
equilibrium (when, for example, a "forward falling" supply curve cuts the demand
curve from above—this is the sense in which Walras and Marshall use the term) or
a "minimum" rather than a "maximum" position (see p. 39 below).

[4] The relations between determinate and indeterminate (definite and indefinite)
equilibria can be illustrated on the diagram on next page. Let us assume there are only
two goods; then the price system will consist of only one price (one exchange-ratio).
Let us measure this price on the vertical axis and let us measure time on the horizontal
axis, t_0 being the "base period", the starting-point of the investigation. Then the

Since the problem of "multiple equilibria" only becomes of interest, if the position of equilibrium is otherwise determinate, while the problem of "indefiniteness" only arises in cases where equilibrium is indeterminate, we shall first examine the conditions necessary to make equilibrium determinate; then the conditions under which this determinate equilibrium will also be "unique"; and finally the conditions under which an indeterminate equilibrium will be definite.

II

(*a*) Since the "indeterminateness" of equilibrium[1] on the above definition can only arise through the disturbing influence of intermediary situations, equilibrium will always be determinate, if the position of equilibrium is *immediately* reached. This implies the presence of certain conditions which will vary according to the nature of the general situation contemplated:

line A will represent the condition of equilibrium at t_0; it will also represent the conditions of equilibrium at any other point of time, if equilibrium is determinate; and it will represent the position of equilibrium from t_0 onwards, if the equilibrium is "established immediately". Curve B represents the actual course of prices in case

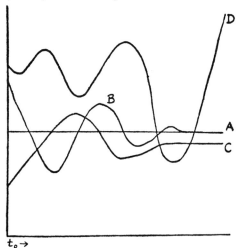

$t_0 \rightarrow$

Fig. i

equilibrium is determinate, but "not immediately reached"; curve C the case of an indeterminate but definite equilibrium; while curve D the case of an indefinite equilibrium. The case of "multiple equilibria" (not shown in the diagram) could be represented by the presence of several A lines.

[1] The word "equilibrium" is always used in this article in the sense of a "full equilibrium", as meaning the "long-period equilibrium" of Marshall.

α. In the case of the isolated individual we must assume either that Robinson Crusoe possesses "full experience" before he undertakes any economic activity and thus starts his activities with an equilibrium system of dispositions; or else that he accidentally places himself at the very beginning in such a situation that every successive acquisition of experience merely serves to confirm him in his existing dispositions, but does not induce him to change these dispositions. (The word experience merely relates to Crusoe's knowledge of his own tastes and preferences and his knowledge of environmental conditions. It excludes any accumulation of knowledge which represents a change in the technical terms at which he can obtain various things.)

β. In the case of the closed community we must have in addition to full experience on everybody's part (i.e. full knowledge of all individuals in regard to their own tastes and abilities)[1] the condition that *all* exchange transactions will be undertaken at the *same* system of prices.[2, 3] This will be the case if either:

(i) Buyers and sellers, meeting simultaneously in the market, go on "crying" prices, revising and re-revising their list of offers, but not entering into any actual exchange, until they hit upon a system of prices which secures equilibrium for everybody and in all parts of the market (Walras' assumption)[4]; or

(ii) buyers and sellers, knowing that all sellers can re-contract with all the buyers, and vice versa, make only *provisional* contracts until a system of prices is reached where no re-contracts could be made with advantage to all the re-contracting parties. (Edgeworth's assumption.[5])

[1] Which is something more than what we already assumed under "perfect knowledge": namely that all individuals know all the relevant prices quoted in the market.

[2] Since under a given "constellation" of data, there will be one system of prices only at which *all* transactions can be concluded (as any other price system will necessitate further transactions at *different* prices) this is merely another way of saying that the process of exchange should *start* at equilibrium prices.

[3] This was first explicitly stated by Jevons. He erroneously assumed, however, that the realisation of this condition follows from his own "Law of Indifference": namely that there can be only one price in one market at the same time. Cf. *Theory of Political Economy*, 4th ed., p. 94.

[4] *Elements*, 6th ed., pp. 129-30.

[5] *Mathematical Psychics*, pp. 17, 35 ff., Appendix IV. Also *Papers*, Vol. II, pp. 311-12.

Both these assumptions come to much the same thing; they should both be considered as attempts to formulate the conditions under which buyers and sellers are able to find out the true "equilibrium price" *before* they undertake any exchange activity—but Edgeworth also thought that this state of affairs followed from the "principle of re-contract" and is thus a property of "perfect competition". Whether it is so considered or not is irrelevant, so long as it is made clear that this is *not* the same thing as either the condition (*a*) that prices should be given to all individuals (that no individual should be able to influence, by his own actions, the prices of the market), or (*b*) that there should be "perfect inter-communication" and thus only one price for the same good *at the same time*—both of which are used as definitions of a "perfect market". While Edgeworth's analysis may be slightly obscure and Walras' assumption slightly ridiculous, the main idea stands clear: in a really perfect market (in a market which is sufficiently perfect to make equilibrium determinate) it is not by trial and error that prices are established; in so far as there is any initial higgling and bargaining this should be done by playing with chips and not with hard cash (by making only provisional and not final or irrevocable contracts). The formation of prices must *precede* the process of exchange and not be the result of it.[1]

(*b*) Equilibrium will be determinate, however, even if it is only gradually established, so long as the position of equilibrium is independent of the actual path followed:

α. This will be true for Robinson Crusoe, if his system of data (his tastes and obstacles), in any one period of time is not affected by his actions in the previous period. It must either be assumed that there is no carry-over of goods from one period to the next, or that there is a constant carry-over; and that his effective scale of preferences in any one period of time is unaffected by his want-satisfying activities in the previous period.[2] Then at the beginning of every period Crusoe is confronted with the same initial situation; his only inheritance from the past is his gradually accumulated

---

[1] The only (otherwise imperfect) market in the real world where this condition is fulfilled is the auction-sale.

[2] The actual length of time chosen as the time unit is irrelevant so long as there is a *definite period of time* for which the above conditions are satisfied and we are only interested in the total of his activities for that period.

experience. We can assume that he has no experience at the beginning; his initial actions will then be accidental or "irrational"; but the gradual accumulation of experience will lead him, through a process of relative valuation, to a gradual change of his daily dispositions until he reaches a situation where no further accumulation of experience will induce him to change his dispositions any further—so long as the initial data (the independent variables) remain unchanged. It can then be shown that this final position will be the same as the one he might have reached at the beginning if, by some accident, he placed himself in equilibrium straight away; in other words, that corresponding to a given set of data, there is always at least one system of dispositions which would merely be confirmed, not altered, by the gradual accumulation of experience.

It seems to be this problem of the effects of experience with which the "causal-genetic approach" of the Austrian School has been mainly concerned.[1] The aim of the latter is to exhibit, not so much the conditions of equilibrium under a given situation (the task assumed by the "functional" theories), but to show how, in a given situation, a position of equilibrium is reached—the problem of how prices come into being rather than what system of prices will secure equilibrium. It is, however, only under our present very rigid assumptions that a causal-genetic theory can reach the same conclusions concerning the nature of equilibrium as are evolved, by using a different method, by the "functional" theories. In the absence of these conditions it is only by means of a "theory of the path" (a theory showing what determines the actual path followed) that a causal-genetic approach can arrive at generalisations concerning the nature of equilibrium—and such a theory has not hitherto been forthcoming, although the necessity for it has frequently been emphasised by writers of the Austrian School.

β. For the closed community, substantially the same conditions will be required as in the case of Crusoe: that tastes and obstacles, on each day, for everybody, should be unaffected by the events of the previous day. It is here, however, that Marshall's famous

[1] Cf. especially, Hans Mayer, *Der Erkenntniswert der funktionellen Preistheorien*, *Wirtschaftstheorie der Gegenwart*, Vol. II, *passim*.

assumption[1] of the constancy in all exchanges of the marginal utility of one of the goods exchanged, must be introduced. Unless the "marginal utility of money" is constant, the condition of "no-carry-over" is insufficient in itself to secure determinateness *within any one period*, if exchanges do not begin at equilibrium prices. For the mere fact that with the gradual accumulation of experience everybody moves towards an equilibrium system of *individual* dispositions will not necessarily bring about a tendency towards a "continuous equilibrium" in the *market* situation: i.e. the market will not necessarily acquire an ability to hit upon the equilibrium prices at the beginning of each period. If it does not, it is only under Marshall's assumption that the final rates of exchange will be independent of the terms on which the first exchanges were made.[2]

Further reflection shows, however, that the necessity for introducing this condition depends on the interpretation of the words "gradual accumulation of experience". If we assume that individuals accumulate experience relating not only to their own system of data but also to the tastes and obstacles of others, they will gradually acquire an ability to judge the equilibrium prices of a given market;[3] and, therefore, the proportion of the total amount exchanged, within any period, which will be exchanged at the "final rates of exchange" will continuously grow until it equals the whole—since it will then be in the long-run interest of

---

[1] *Principles*, esp. Appendix F. Marshall's assumption is generally classed as an alternative to Walras' and Edgeworth's; which in a sense it is. From our point of view, however, the one tries to formulate the circumstances in which all exchanges will be concluded at the *same* price; while the other tries to demonstrate how equilibrium can be determinate *without* this condition being fulfilled. (The value of Marshall's analysis consists in showing that in a large number of cases—where only a small part of an individual's resources are spent on the commodity in question—the indeterminacy introduced by this case is not likely to be very important.)

[2] There is, of course, no inconsistency between our initial assumption of "direct exchange" (absence of money as a medium of exchange) and the assumption of a constant marginal utility of "money". For the validity of Marshall's assumption is not dependent upon the use of money, as is often mistakenly assumed (an error for which Marshall himself is partly responsible) but upon the question whether the single commodity does or does not "use up" a considerable proportion of our total resources. Nor is there any need to assume either the "measurability" or the "independence" of utilities in order to attach a precise meaning to Marshall's notion. (Cf. Hicks, "A Reconsideration of the Theory of Value", *Economica*, February, 1934, p. 64, for the expression of this condition in terms of the modern, "relative-utility" analysis.)

[3] In our view, it is the absence of any need for this sort of knowledge, and not the absence of inter-personal exchange as such, which explains why the sort of difficulty which Marshall's fiction attempts to eliminate does not arise in the case of Crusoe.

every individual that he should make as many exchanges as possible at equilibrium prices.[1]

It may be objected, however, that this alternative assumption— that individuals will be able to judge equilibrium prices before any transactions are made—is inconsistent with one of our initial assumptions since it means that they are influenced by expected future prices rather than by prices already ruling. It all depends on how rigidly this assumption is interpreted, and it can easily be shown that under our present assumption of a "constant carry-over" a *very rigid* interpretation would lead, by a different route, to the same result. For a rigid interpretation in this case would imply that the final rate of exchange on any day is generally expected to be the ruling price of the following day—which means that it would *become* the initial rate of that day. Now, it follows from Marshall's analysis (in the Appendix on Barter), that though the final rate will always deviate from the true equilibrium price, if the latter is not hit upon at the beginning, it *can never deviate so much* as the initial rate;[2] i.e. prices must move *towards* the true equilibrium price during the day. Consequently, if the final rate of Day One always becomes the initial rate of Day Two, then the final rate of Day Two will show less deviation from the true equilibrium rate than the final rate on Day One. On successive days, therefore, the deviation will become less and less until it finally disappears (or as we stated it above, the proportion of the total transactions made at the final rate of exchange on any day will become greater and greater on successive days). This leaves the condition of a "constant carry-over" (which implies that the conditions of supply and demand on any day should be the same as those on every other day) as the sole condition of determinateness, under our static assumptions.

III

This closes our investigation of the conditions under which the position of equilibrium is determinate. We must next enquire under

[1] On this point cf. Wicksteed's analysis in *Common Sense of Political Economy*, Vol. I, Chapter VI, pp. 219-26.

[2] Except in the case where one of the goods has no "marginal utility" at all to one of the parties, and thus the market-supply of that good, as distinct from the volume available, is "fixed".

what conditions this position will be "unique", i.e. what are the possibilities of *multiple* positions of determinate equilibrium?

(i) Hitherto we have tacitly assumed that the nature of the initial data is such that they yield what might be called "normal-shaped" basic curves.[1] The principle of an "increasing marginal rate of substitution"[2] being applicable to both utility and production functions, psychological indifference curves will be convex downwards throughout, while the production indifference curve will be concave downwards throughout. Under these conditions there is only one equilibrium position possible for Robinson Crusoe, and normally there will be only one position of equilibrium for the community as a whole. In the case of the community, however, the possibility of multiple equilibria is never completely eliminated thereby. For if the owners of resources have *any* demand for the use of their own resources (if these resources represent a "good" in their own utility functions), the supply curve for such resources (which is the owners' aggregate demand curve for all other resources) must turn backwards at a certain price; and then there is always a possibility that this "backward-rising" supply curve should cut the demand curve in more than one, and so at least in three, points.[3] This is Walras' well-known case of multiple equilibria,[4] and the assumption necessary to eliminate it as a possibility is that the owners should have no *immediate* use for their own resources, i.e. that not only the volume of resources available but also the market supply of those resources should be a given quantity.

A similar case of multiple equilibria which is compatible with the assumption of normal-shaped utility and production functions, is the case of a "backward-falling" demand curve—when the elasticity of the demand curve becomes zero, and then negative, *before* the price reaches zero. It then also becomes possible for this

[1] We use the expression "basic curves" for curves denoting the properties of the basic utility and production functions; as distinct from the "derived curves" (such as the supply and demand curves) which are derived from those functions and from the actual quantitative magnitudes in each individual's initial possession.

[2] Cf. Hicks, "A Reconsideration of the Theory of Value", *Economica*, February, 1934, p. 55.

[3] One of these points must be "unstable" (in the Marshallian sense) representing merely a "passing equality of supply and demand", but not equilibrium. The first and the third points will be stable, however, i.e. these will be real equilibrium positions.

[4] *Elements*, 6th ed., pp. 68-70. Also Wicksell, *Über Wert Kapital und Rente*, pp. 61 ff.

backward-falling demand curve to cut the supply curve in more than one, and so at least in three, points. But since backward-falling demand curves (unlike the backward-rising supply curves) only occur in very rare cases,[1] this case of multiple equilibria should not be regarded as more than a curiosum.

(ii) We may assume, however, that the basic curves are not "normal-shaped", i.e. either (a) that the principle of an increasing marginal rate of substitution does not obtain for either the utility or the production functions *throughout* (as a general rule) or (b) that this principle, for one or the other of these functions, does not obtain *at all*.

In the second case (b), clearly no equilibrium is possible. If either the psychological indifference curves are concave throughout or the production indifference curve convex throughout, an "equilibrium position" (characterised by the parallelism of the tangents of these curves) could at best be regarded as a position of minimum satisfaction but not a position of maximum satisfaction.[2]

The situation, however, is different if the condition of convexity and concavity, respectively, is only partially broken. Here we shall limit ourselves to the case where the production indifference curve is thus "queer-shaped": since the consideration of the other case (where the psychological indifference curves are aberrant) is both more complex and of much more dubious significance.

A production indifference curve[3] in which sections of concavity are interspersed with sections of convexity always involves multiple equilibria, in the sense that there is always more than one point at which the tangent of this curve is parallel to the tangents of the psychological indifference curves. In the terms of the Marshallian, particular equilibrium analysis, the multiple equilibria in this case are due to "forward-falling", as distinct

---

[1] Cf. Hicks, *op. cit.*, p. 68, for the conditions necessary for a backward-falling demand curve (in his terminology, a rising demand curve).

[2] *Ibid.*, p. 57.

[3] The term is not really suitable (since it implies an "indifference" which in this case has no meaning) and has only been chosen to emphasise the fact that it is a counterpart to the psychological indifference curves. It has also been called the "curve of obstacles" or the "co-efficient of transformation", neither of which is more attractive than the one given in the text. What the curve really shows is the technical rate of substitution between various goods at the margin, under varying distributions of production.

from "backward-rising", supply curves.[1] But whereas backward-rising supply curves merely involve the possibility, but not the necessity, of multiple equilibria, in the case of forward-falling supply curves multiple equilibria will always be present,[2] i.e. there will always be more than one arrangement which satisfies the conditions of equilibrium. This, however, cannot be shown with the aid of the particular equilibrium analysis, since the position of the demand curves will be different in the alternative situations.

If, however, the situation is one where equilibrium is reached immediately (case (*a*) above), normally only one of these positions will be a true position of equilibrium, since one of these points will be generally preferred to all the others. Only if the production indifference curve becomes tangential at more than one point to the *same* indifference curve (and this condition has not much sense in the case of the community!) will it be a true case of multiple equilibria.[3]

If, however, the position is only gradually reached (case (*b*) above), the possibility of multiple equilibria will always be present whenever the production curve has more than one peak (irrespective of whether these peaks touch the same indifference curve or not) because once a start has been made along one road there will be no tendency to reverse the route even if the peak towards which another road is leading is higher. In these cases, therefore, multiple equilibria will always be present whenever there are states of increasing returns to single industries, i.e. whenever there are stages of diminishing technical marginal rates of substitution. In these cases, therefore, the final situation will be "indeterminate" in the sense that it will depend upon the direction which happens to be adopted initially; though equilibrium may still be

[1] Similarly it could be shown that "queer-shaped" psychological indifference curves yield "forward-rising" as distinct from "backward-falling" demand curves. The terms "backward-rising", "forward-falling" and "forward-rising", "backward falling," respectively, are taken from Mr. Kahn (*Review of Economic Studies*, Vol. I, No. 1, pp. 71 ff).

[2] Except in cases where the psychological indifference curves are not asymptotic to the axes but turn away from them after a certain point. In this case multiple equilibria do not necessarily follow from queer-shaped production curves.

[3] It will, of course, be equally true in cases where the multiple equilibria are due to "backward-rising" supply curves, that in so far as one of these positions is preferred to the others, only one of them will be a "true position" in cases where "equilibrium is reached immediately".

determinate on our definition of the term, since all the possible equilibrium positions may still be deduced from the data of the initial situation.

IV

If, however, the conditions enumerated above in Section II, under (*a*) and (*b*), are not satisfied, equilibrium will always be indeterminate, as the successive moves undertaken in order to reach equilibrium will influence the nature of the final position. The situation, of course, may still be one which is tending towards an equilibrium, i.e. towards a system of prices which in the absence of independent changes, will maintain itself indefinitely; but the point at which price-movements ultimately come to rest can no longer be deduced from the data of the initial situation.

The question which we now have to answer is whether this will be necessarily so; whether, if the equilibrium system of prices is not put in operation immediately, the succeeding price-changes will necessarily end up in reaching some equilibrium position.

As we have already pointed out, it follows from Marshall's analysis that if the initial price differs from the true equilibrium price, changes will become necessary (a further set of transactions will take place at a different price); but these price-changes will always be in the *direction* of the equilibrium price and there will always be some final price which "brings about equilibrium", i.e. which puts an end to the process of exchange. This, however, relates to the case of "market equilibrium", i.e. to a given period of time in which there are a given volume of goods available and given wants to be satisfied. When we were dealing with "long-period normal equilibrium", however (i.e. given rates of supply of the ultimate resources, and given structure of wants recurring in every period), we were assuming a "constant carry-over" from one period to the next, and thus postulated the same initial situation at the beginning of every period.

This assumption of a "constant carry-over" conceals another assumption (which it includes, but with which it is not identical), namely that the quantities (demanded and supplied) react instantaneously on price changes; since if the quantitative reaction to a certain price change of a certain "day" only takes place on the next day or the day after, we can no longer postulate the same initial situation at the beginning of every day. This problem of the time-lag between quantitative and price-changes does not arise, therefore, at that stage of the enquiry. It must be examined, however, as soon as the assumption of a "constant carry-over" is dropped. And once allowance is made for the fact that in the real world functional adjustments take time and different forces in the system may operate with different velocities of adjustment, it may become possible to construct cases—*under the assumption that ruling prices are always expected to remain in operation*, which is assumed throughout the present article—where the successive reactions lead away from, rather than approach, an equilibrium position.[1]

The question, therefore, whether in any given case, equilibrium will be "definite" or "indefinite" (i.e. whether it will be approximated to or not) appears to depend on the velocities of adjustment of the factors operating in the system. It is this factor, therefore, which we have to examine in some detail.

The "velocity of adjustment" may be alternatively defined as the time required for a full quantitative adjustment to take place (either on the supply side or on the demand side) corresponding to a given price-change[2]—i.e. the time elapsing between the establishment of a certain price and the full quantitative adjustment to that price—or the rate at which the quantities (demanded or supplied) change per unit of time in response to price-changes. (The first may conveniently be termed the "adjustment period", and the second the "unit-velocity" of adjustment.) Given this rate (the unit-velocity), given the magnitude of the initial price-change and given the elasticities of the curves,[3] the time required

---

[1] On the place of the 'factor "velocity of adjustment" in the general theory of equilibrium, cf. Rosenstein-Rodan, "Das Zeitmoment in der mathematischen Theorie des wirtschaftlichen Gleichgewichtes", *Zeitschrift für Nationalökonomie*, Vol. I, No. 1. Also, "The Rôle of Time in Economic Theory", *Economica*, February, 1934. Cf. also Fasiani, *Velocita delle variazione della demanda e dell' offerta e punti di equilibrio stabile e instabile, Atti della R. Acad. de scienze di Torino*, 1932.

[2] Which is not the same thing as the reaction of price to an initial change in supply or demand. (Cf. Rosenstein-Rodan, *op. cit.*, p. 89.) But since these latter velocities, although different from, yet depend on the velocities of the quantity reactions to initial price-changes (the velocity of price-reactions to supply-changes being the reciprocal of the velocity of demand-reactions to price-changes and vice versa), they are not separately treated in the present analysis. Cf. also p. 44 note 2 below.

[3] By elasticities we mean here the elasticities of "long-period-curves", i.e. curves showing the quantities supplied or demanded, per unit of time, corresponding to each price, after *all* adjustments have been made to that price.

for full adjustment (the adjustment period) will also be determined. Allowance should be made, however, for the possibility that these unit-velocities may themselves be interdependent—i.e. the rate at which quantities change per unit of time may itself depend on the magnitude of the initial price-change.

An analysis which makes full allowance for all these factors would necessarily be very complex. We can simplify it considerably, however, by making certain assumptions. We may either assume that the unit-velocity is always the same, whatever the magnitude of the initial price-change; or, alternatively, that the unit-velocity is always directly proportional to the magnitude of the initial price-change—in which case the adjustment period will be independent of this factor.

We shall also neglect the fact that the curves themselves shift during the process of adjustment (if they did not, the final position in so far as it is definite, would also be determinate, i.e. independent of the path followed). But the introduction of this factor would only complicate the analysis, without altering the nature of the results.

Finally, we have to take account of the fact that adjustments always proceed at more or less frequent intervals—that they are more or less continuous. The quantity of anything demanded or supplied may change once a day, once a week, a month, or a year —depending on such factors as the technical period of production, etc. We shall call an adjustment *completely discontinuous* if the full quantitative adjustment to a given price-change occurs all at once, at the end of a certain period. (E.g. a change in the price of rubber may not influence the rate of supply for a period of seven years, at the end of which the full quantitative reaction may take place at once. Or a change in the price of corn, by inducing farmers to change the area sown, will make its effect felt a year later when the new harvest comes to the market.)[1] Similarly, we shall call an adjustment *completely continuous* if it proceeds at a steady rate in time, or if the time-lags between the appearance of successive quantitative changes are such as can be neglected. The latter will always be the case when the degree of discontinuity—

[1] If, therefore, there are differing elasticities for the Marshallian long and short periods, this always implies that adjustments are continuous, or, at any rate, less than completely discontinuous.

the length of the time-lags—is the same on the demand side as on the supply side. In the following analysis we shall treat only these two cases of complete discontinuity and continuity.

I. Where the adjustments are completely discontinuous, stability (or "definiteness") of equilibrium will depend on the relative elasticities of demand and supply; according to what may be called "the cobweb theorem" of Professor Henry Schultz and Professor U. Ricci.[1]

Let us assume that a shift in demand from DD to $D'D'$ changes the price from P to P_1, which is not an equilibrium price, since

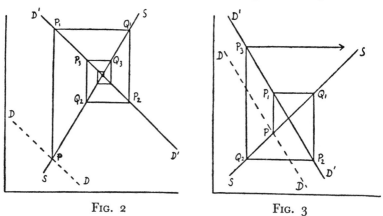

FIG. 2   FIG. 3

the true long run supply corresponding to this price is Q_1. After a time, depending on the adjustment period, supply will therefore change to Q_1, and price will then change from P_1 to P_2.[2]

---

[1] Schultz, *Der Sinn der statistischen Nachfragekurven*, p. 34, and Ricci, "Die synthetische Ökonomie von Henry Ludwell Moore", *Zeitschrift für Nationalökonomie*, 1930, p. 649. It is evident that this theorem is only applicable to cases of "completely discontinuous adjustments", or to the case (which Professor Schultz had in mind) where adjustments are completely discontinuous on the side of supply and instantaneous on the side of demand.

[2] Under our present assumptions that ruling prices are always expected to remain in operation, and thus no stocks for future sale will be carried, the price-reaction to changes in supply must always be instantaneous; since we can either assume that (1) *demand* reacts instantaneously to price-changes, in which case price will also react instantaneously to changes in supply: or (2) that demand-reactions take time, in which case the *immediate price-reaction* to changes in supply will be greater than the ultimate price-reaction. Under the assumption that adjustments are completely discontinuous, the slowness of demand-reactions to price-changes manifests itself in reducing the elasticity of the demand curve, and thus alters the situation in the direction of instability—since the relevant demand curve is the one which shows the amounts taken at various prices *immediately* after the (rate of) supply has changed. Whether the true (long period) demand curve will then have any relevance or not,

Again, after a time, supply will move from Q_1 to Q_2 (the supply corresponding to P_2) and price from P_2 to P_3. The successive stages of adjustment present the appearance of a cobweb (see Figs. 2 and 3), which will be contracting or expanding according as the demand curve is more elastic than the supply curve or vice versa. From this the following propositions can be derived:

(i) If demand is elastic relatively to supply, the cobweb will be contracting; equilibrium will be "definite".

(ii) If supply is elastic relatively to demand, the cobweb will be expanding; equilibrium will be "indefinite".

(iii) If the elasticity of supply and demand are the same, there will be a constant range of fluctuations.[1]

It is easy to see why this proposition is true only in cases where adjustments are completely discontinuous. For if quantities move slowly but steadily in response to price, the successive movements of quantities will change price and thus the direction of the movement, *before* the full adjustment has been made to the previous price. In this case the elasticities of the long-period curves will have little or no influence in determining the question of stability.

II. In the case of continuous adjustments the question of stability will depend not on the relative elasticities but on the relative velocities of adjustment of demand and supply. This can be seen from the following simple consideration. Let us divide the

will depend on whether the adjustment period on the demand side will be less, or greater, than the adjustment period on the supply side. In the former case the price will alter *befo re* the supply-reaction has taken place; and will thus diminish the range of succeeding fluctuations in supply.

[1] [The above conditions refer to the special case where the elasticity of both the demand and the supply curves is constant throughout their length. In other cases the necessary conditions cannot be expressed in terms of a simple general rule. (i) In the case of straight line demand and supply curves (such as those shown in Figs. 2 and 3), contraction or expansion is a matter of the relative *slopes* of the two curves, and not of their elasticities. The cobweb will be contracting when the demand curve is flatter than the supply curve, and *vice versa*. (ii) In the case of non-linear curves of varying elasticity, the cobweb will be contracting or expanding when the elasticity of the demand curve is *consistently* higher or lower than that of the supply curve, for all prices. (iii) In all other cases no general rule can be formulated, and it is possible that the cobweb could be an expanding one within certain ranges of price-fluctuations and a contracting one outside that range, so that the movement approaches a limit cycle, whatever the nature of the initial disturbance. It is also conceivable that the opposite should be the case; then the stability condition will be satisfied for small disturbances and not for large ones.]

"period of adjustment" (the period during which prices and quantities move in response to an initial price-change) into a series of sub-periods which are small enough to make quantitative adjustments completely discontinuous within that sub-period. Suppose that the smallest period to register any quantitative change in demand or supply is a "day"—then one day is the period within which adjustments can be regarded as "completely discontinuous", within which, therefore, prices must be steady, or rather can only change once, at the end of the day. We can then construct such "ultra-short-period" demand and supply curves which show the quantity demanded or supplied at any price, assuming that this price has been in operation only for a day. There will always be one point on these short-period curves which will correspond to the long-period demand (or supply) at this price;[1] but, otherwise, the elasticity of these curves will depend not on the elasticity of the long-period curves but on the velocities of adjustment. That factor whose unit-velocity is greater will have the more elastic curve. Applying, then, Professor Schultz's theorem to each of these sub-periods separately, we get the following results:

(i) If the velocities of adjustment are greater on the demand side than on the supply side, movements will lead towards an equilibrium, i.e. equilibrium will be "definite".

(ii) If the velocities of adjustment are greater on the supply side than on the demand side, movements will lead away from equilibrium, i.e. equilibrium will be "indefinite".

Since on general grounds we may expect supply reactions rather than demand reactions to be slow, and since cases of completely discontinuous adjustments are rare, inherent instability (in so far as the above conclusions are correct) may rather be regarded as a special case—so long as the fundamental data are such that they yield stable situations (i.e. so long as the basic curves are not completely "queer-shaped"). And it may not be out of place to emphasise once more the fact that all these conclusions have been

[1] Since any such curve can only be drawn from a given long-period price as the starting-point, i.e. one such short-period curve can be drawn from every point of the long-period demand (or supply) curve.

derived on the assumption that all economic decisions are made on the basis of ruling prices alone, without any regard to future price-changes; though in any actual situation, the presence oı some foresight may always be expected. The existence of foresight, however incomplete, will always change the situation in favour of stability so long as the expectations of price-changes are in the right direction (in the direction in which prices actually move), though it will change the situation in favour of instability if expectations are in the wrong direction. Once, however, the assumption of the constancy of fundamental data is removed and allowance is made for the fact that the data change, and often change unexpectedly, there is no longer any reason to assume that the expectation of future price-changes will generally be in the right direction. Instability in the real world[1] then appears as the result of *wrong* anticipations.

---

[1] Whether in any actual case anticipations will be in the right direction or not, will depend partly on the nature of the change and partly on the efficiency of the institutions of the market whose function it is to anticipate future price movements. Given the forecasting ability of a speculative market, anticipations of future price-changes are as a general rule much more likely to prove correct when they are due to localised causes than when they are of a more general "monetary" character. Cf. Dr. Hicks' analysis in *Gleichgewicht und Konjunktur, loc. cit.*, esp. pp. 446 ff.

THE EQUILIBRIUM OF THE FIRM[1]

1. THE exploration of the conditions of equilibrium of the individual firm has in recent times occupied to an increasing degree the attention of economists. This, as should be evident, was a necessary development of the so-called "particular equilibrium" method of analysis developed by Marshall and especially of the concept of the "supply curve": the postulation of a definite functional relationship between price and rate of supply in the various industries. The latter, though an integral part of the Marshallian system, was by no means such a straightforward self-evident concept as its counterpart, the demand curve. The reasons for this asymmetry are not far to seek. The assumption that buyers respond to price stimuli in a definite and unequivocal manner (which is all that the demand curve implies) can be deduced from the general proposition that they have a definite system of wants and act in accordance with it; that is to say, it can be directly derived from the general postulates of the subjective theory of value. But the assumption that sellers do the same is a much more complex affair—at any rate in a world where production is carried on on a co-operative basis. It implies that there exists a mechanism which translates technical and psychological resistances into cost computations in such a way that a definite amount of a commodity will be offered by each producing unit in response to any price. It implies, therefore, that there is a definite relationship between the costs incurred and the amount produced for each individual source of supply and between price and the number of such producing units; and finally between price and some derivative of the cost function of the individual producing unit. Briefly, then, it assumes two things: perfect competition[2] and the existence of a definite cost function

---

[1] Originally published in *Economic Journal*, March, 1934.

[2] Under "perfect competition", here and in the following, we simply mean a state of affairs where all prices are given to the individual firm, independently of the actions of that firm.

for each firm. (The assumption of perfect competition is, of course, also necessary in the case of the demand curve. But on the demand side this can more or less be treated as a "datum"—at least in so far as the demand for consumers' goods is concerned[1]—for it follows from the facts that in buying individuals act alone[2] and that the contribution of a single individual to the social income and, thus, his individual spending power, is relatively small. But the nature of the conditions of competition on the supply side, as is now increasingly realised, is itself something to be explained.) In order to arrive at the supply curve for an industry, therefore, it must be shown that corresponding to each price there will be a definite number of firms in the industry and a definite amount produced by each *when all firms are in equilibrium.*[3]

Moreover, the importance attached to the nature of the supply function in post-Marshallian economics, the division of industries into those of increasing, constant and diminishing supply-price, and the distinction between external and internal economies, which postulated different cost functions for individual firms and for the aggregate of firms composing the industry, made it more than ever necessary to analyse the conditions of equilibrium for the individual firms *before* any postulates were made about the supply function of an industry. For only when the necessary functions are found which determine the behaviour of individual firms and some formal conclusions have been arrived at about the forms which these functions can actually take and when the inter-relations of these cost functions have been analysed, only then can

[1] The demand for producers' goods (derived demand functions), on the other hand, are more like supply functions in this and the following respects.

[2] This is not to be interpreted as saying that "co-operative buying" is not feasible. But the advantages of buyers' co-operation consist solely in marketing advantages (in "exploiting" sellers), while the advantages of sellers' (producers') co-operation follow from the principle of the division of labour and exist independently of any additional marketing advantage which can thereby be gained.

[3] Both Marshall and Professor Pigou appear to argue that an "industry" can be in equilibrium without all the firms composing it being simultaneously in equilibrium. This is true in one sense but not in another. If it is assumed that firms have a finite life like individuals, that they gradually reach their prime and then decline, it is, of course, not necessary that all the firms' outputs should be constant when the industry's output is constant. But if the growing output of young firms is to cancel out the declining output of old ones on account of something more than a lucky coincidence, it is necessary to assume that all firms are in equilibrium, i.e. that they produce the output appropriate to the ruling prices, to their costs and *to their age.* The introduction of a third type of "variable" (i.e. the firm's age) merely implies that equilibrium must also be established with respect to this; it certainly does not imply that equilibrium need not be established with respect to the other variables.

we derive those supply curves of various shapes which the simple two-dimensional diagram at once suggests to the mind.[1]

2. Marshall realised that it was necessary to describe the mechanism with the aid of which the reactions, which the supply curve exhibits, actually come about; and this, I believe, was the reason which led him to the concept of the "representative firm". His purpose was therefore not the establishment of a concept which has analytical significance as such, but rather the construction of a mental tool with the aid of which the reaction-mechanism postulated by the supply curve can be, if not analysed, at least rendered plausible. The representative firm was therefore meant to be no more than a firm which answers the requirements expected from it by the supply curve. In the words of Mr. D. H. Robertson: "In my view it is not necessary . . . to regard it (i.e. the representative firm) as anything other than a small-scale replica of the supply curve of the industry as a whole."[2] In this sentence, I believe, Mr. Robertson has admirably summarised the real weakness of the Marshallian concept; perhaps more so than he would himself care to admit. It is just because the representative firm was meant to be nothing more than a small-scale replica of the industry's supply curve that it is unsuitable for the purpose it has been called into being. Instead of analysing at first the conditions of equilibrium for individual firms and then deriving from them, as far as possible, the conditions of equilibrium for an industry, Marshall first postulated the latter and then created a *Hilfskonstruktion* which answered its requirements.

Professor Robbins has shown[3] that Marshall's concept of the representative firm (apart from the defect that it is nowhere in the *Principles* adequately defined) is open to the *prima facie* objection that it introduces elements which are not consistent with the

[1] With the growing realisation of the difficulties confronting any attempt at a workable definition of the concept "commodity", doubts arose concerning the legitimacy of the concept of a single "industry" which are probably more important and fundamental than the objections raised in the present article. But as the results of our investigation do not depend upon the validity of this concept, while its use considerably simplifies the analysis, we shall assume for the purposes of the present article that production can be divided up between a definite number of "standardised" commodities, each of which is sufficiently unlike the other to justify the use of the word "industry" applied to it.

[2] "Increasing Returns and the Representative Firm", *Economic Journal*, March. 1930, p. 89.

[3] "The Representative Firm", *Economic Journal*, September, 1928.

general assumptions upon which economic theory is based. We are here asked to concentrate our attention upon a particular firm, which, whether it is conceived as one selected from a large number of actual firms or merely some sort of average of all existing firms, is supposed to fulfil a special rôle in the determination of equilibrium in a way which other firms do not. "There is no more need for us to assume a representative firm or a representative producer than there is for us to assume a representative piece of land, a representative machine or a representative worker."[1] Professor Robbins' criticism only affects Marshall's particular solution, however, and shows that the kind of short cut Marshall attempted will not do. It enhances rather than obviates the necessity for analysing the conditions of firm-equilibrium as such.

Since Marshall's time the analysis of the equilibrium of the firm has been carried to a much higher stage of refinement. In one respect, however, later constructions suffer from the same deficiency as Marshall's. They also assume cost-conditions for the individual firms which *fit in* with the postulates made about equilibrium rather than prove how the cost functions of individual sources of supply make possible, under a given system of prices, a determinate equilibrium for the industry. Explicitly or implicitly the equilibrium of the firm is made dependent upon the equilibrium of the industry rather than the other way round.[2] And although, in this particular branch of economics, attention has more and more concentrated upon the equilibrium of the individual firm,[3]

[1] *Ibid.*, p. 393.

[2] Cf. especially the definition of the "equilibrium firm" by Professor Pigou, ". . . whenever the industry as a whole is in equilibrium in the sense that it is producing a regular output y in response to a normal supply price, p, [it] will itself also be individually in equilibrium with a regular output x_r" (*Economics of Welfare*, 3rd ed., p. 788). Professor Pigou does not, however, make clear whether (*a*) the concept of the "equilibrium of the industry" necessarily involves the concept of the "equilibrium firm" (he merely says that "the conditions of the industry are compatible with the existence of such a firm"), and (*b*) whether the existence of an equilibrium firm is a sufficient condition for the equilibrium of the industry. In our view, the conception of an "equilibrium of the industry" has no meaning except as the simultaneous equilibrium of a number of firms; and consequently the conditions of the latter must be analysed before the concept of the "equilibrium of the industry" and the categories of industries of increasing, constant and diminishing supply-price can be established.

[3] Cf. especially the writings of Professor Pigou, Mr. Shove, Mr. Harrod, Mr. and Mrs. Robinson in England, Professor Viner, Professor Yntema and Professor Chamberlin in the United States, Dr. Schneider and Dr. von Stackelberg in Germany, Professor Amoroso in Italy.

it has never been called into question, so far as the present writer is aware, whether the assumption of a determinate cost schedule (upon which the whole theory of supply rests) can be derived from the premises upon which static analysis, in general, is based. It is the purpose of the present paper to show that the conception of such a determinate cost function, obvious and elementary as it may seem, involves unforeseen difficulties as soon as an attempt is made to analyse the factors which actually determine it.

3. We propose to start in a roundabout way, by postulating at first the two assumptions on which the Marshallian supply curve is based: namely, perfect competition[1] and the existence of a definite functional relationship between the costs incurred and the amount produced by the individual firm;[2] and then to examine whether it is possible to find a form for this cost function which will make these two assumptions compatible with each other. We shall see that an analysis of the factors which determine the form of this cost curve will lead us to doubt the legitimacy of the concept itself. We shall also see later on that our results retain some interest even after the assumption of perfect competition is dropped.

As is well known, the requirement of the firm's cost curve under perfect competition is that it must slope upwards after a certain amount is produced[3]—an amount which is small enough to leave a sufficiently large number of firms in the field (for any given total output of the industry) for the conditions of perfect competition to be preserved. For the short-run analysis this presents no difficulties. In the short-run (by definition) the supply of some factors is assumed to be fixed, and as the price of the other

---

[1] If competition is imperfect, only the amount produced *under given conditions of demand* can be determined, but there is no definite relation between *price* and supply. Mrs. Joan Robinson employs the concept of the supply curve even under conditions of imperfect competition (*The Economics of Imperfect Competition*, Chapter VI), but a perusal of her book shows that she merely retains the name of the latter for an analysis of the former.

[2] We ought to start, in an analysis of this sort, by attempting to define a "firm". This, however, would render the treatment unnecessarily complicated and, as will be seen later on, a definition, sufficient for the purpose, emerges by itself in the course of the analysis (see below).

[3] This was first pointed out by Cournot (*Researches*, p. 91). Marshall's remarks in a footnote (*Principles*, 8th ed., p. 459) concerning Cournot's alleged error on this point were wholly unjustified. I am indebted to Dr. J. R. Hicks for this point.

(freely variable) factors is given, costs per unit[1] must necessarily rise after a certain point.[2] (This follows simply from the assumption, frequently styled "the law of non-proportional returns", that the degree of variability of the technical coefficients is less than infinite—which is just another way of saying that there are different kinds of factors.) But such a short-run curve will be hardly sufficient for our purpose. Unless we can assume that the "fixed factors" are fixed by Nature and not as a result of a previous act of choice (and it is hardly legitimate to make such an assumption in the case of an individual firm), we must again enquire why the fixed factors came to be of such a magnitude as they actually are. The problem of equilibrium again presents itself.

We must start, therefore, at the beginning, i.e. the problem is essentially one of long-run equilibrium. All factors which the firm employs are therefore assumed to be freely variable in supply and all prices to be given. What will be the shape of the cost curve? Will costs per unit vary with output, and if so, how?

(i) If the assumption of complete divisibility of all factors is dropped we know that cost per unit, for some length at any rate, must necessarily fall. This is due to the fact that with increasing output more and more indivisibilities (actual and potential) are overcome, i.e. *either* the efficiency of the actually employed factors increases *or* more efficient factors are employed whose employment was not remunerative at a smaller output.[3] Given

---

[1] Under "costs" here and in the following we include only such payments for the factors which are necessary in order to retain those factors in their actual employment, at a given efficiency. The remuneration of "fixed" factors (i.e. factors which are rigidly attached to the firm) form, therefore, no part of costs. (Fixity of supply implies both (*a*) that the factor is available to the firm irrespective of its remuneration, and (*b*) that its efficiency is not a function of its remuneration.)

[2] They must also necessarily fall up to a certain point if the fixed factors are also indivisible. Indivisibility and fixity of supply are, however, two entirely distinct properties which are frequently not kept apart, as both give rise to fixed costs, i.e. costs which do not vary with output. But on our definition of costs, only the remuneration of indivisible factors whose supply is not fixed enters into costs; while indivisible factors of fixed supply, although no part of costs, influence costs (through changing the physical productivity of the other factors) in a manner in which factors of fixed supply which are not indivisible do not. (Factors of the latter category can only influence costs *upwards*, not *downwards*.) The relevance of this distinction in connection with the present paper will become clear later on (see § 7, pp. pp. 61-2 below).

[3] It appears methodologically convenient to treat all cases of large-scale economies under the heading, "indivisibility". This introduces a certain unity into analysis and makes possible at the same time a clarification of the relationship between the different kinds of economies. Even those cases of increasing returns where a more-than-proportionate increase in output occurs merely on account of an increase in the amounts

the state of knowledge, however, a point must be reached where all technical economies are realised and costs of production therefore reach a minimum. Beyond this point costs may rise over a certain range, but (if, in accordance with our assumptions, factors continue to be obtainable at constant prices) afterwards they must again fall until they once more reach their minimum at the same level as before. The optimum point can then only be reached for certain outputs, but there is no reason why the successive optimum points should not be on the same level of average costs. Indivisibilities, causing rising costs over certain ranges, thus do not explain the limitation upon the size of the firm so long as *all* factors are freely variable and all prices are constant.

(ii) It has been suggested, alternatively, that there are external diseconomies under which (as pecuniary diseconomies are ruled out by definition) must be meant the limitation upon the supply of such factors as the firm does not directly employ but only indirectly uses. (Cf. Pareto's example of the rising costs to transport agencies owing to traffic congestion.) But such external diseconomies (assuming that they exist) are again not sufficient for our purpose. By definition, they affect all firms equally,[1] and therefore do not explain why the output of the individual firm remains relatively small (the number of firms in the industry relatively large), as they only give a reason why the costs of the industry should be rising, but not why the costs of the individual firm should be rising *relatively to the costs of the industry*. The diseconomies, therefore—in order that they should account for the limitation upon the size of the firm—must be *internal*.

(iii) It follows clearly from these considerations that (as diminishing returns to *all* factors together are not conceivable) the technically optimum size of a productive combination cannot be determined if only the prices of the factors and the production function of the commodity are known. Knowledge of these only

---

of the factors used, without any change in the proportions of the factors, are due to indivisibilities; only in this case it is not so much the "original factors", but the specialised functions of those factors, which are indivisible.

[1] If external diseconomies affect different firms unequally, this merely explains why some firms should expand relatively to others, but not why their size should be limited. (Similarly in the case where different firms have different access to external economies.)

enables us to determine the optimum proportions in which to combine the factors but not the optimum amounts of these factors. In order to determine, therefore, the optimum size of the combination it is necessary to assume that the supply of at least one of the factors figuring in the production function should be fixed— in which case the optimum size (or at any rate the maximum amount of the product which can be produced at minimum costs) becomes determinate as a result of the operation of the law of non-proportional returns.[1]

Moreover, it is necessary that the factor whose supply is "fixed" for the firm should at the same time have a flexible supply for the industry—otherwise the industry would have to consist of one firm or at least a fixed number of firms. It is not the case, therefore, of a factor which is rent-yielding for an industry (a special kind of land, for example, which, though its supply for the industry is fixed, must have under the assumption of perfect competition a definite supply-price for the individual firm!), but rather the reverse: a factor which *is* rent-yielding (price-determined) for the firm but has a definite supply-price for the industry. In this case, therefore, the fixity of supply must arise, not from a natural limitation of the amount available, but from a special peculiarity of the firm's production function; that is to say, there must be *a* factor, of which the firm cannot have "two" units— just because *only one unit* can do the job.

It has been suggested that there is such a "fixed factor" for the individual firm even under long-run assumptions—namely the factor alternatively termed "management" or "entrepreneurship". As it follows from the nature of the entrepreneurial function that a firm cannot have two entrepreneurs, and as the ability of any one entrepreneur is limited, the costs of the individual firm must be rising owing to the diminishing returns to the other factors when applied in increasing amounts to the same unit of entrepreneurial ability. The fact that the firm is a productive combination under a single unit of control explains, therefore, by itself why it cannot expand beyond a certain limit without encountering increasing costs. The rest of this paper will be taken up by a

---

[1] It would be sufficient for the determination of the optimum size if one of the factors had a rising supply curve to the firm. This, however, is not compatible with the assumption of perfect competition.

discussion of the problems arising out of this suggestion: what is meant by entrepreneurship as a factor of production? Is its supply really fixed in the long run? And finally, does it justify the construction of a determinate long-run cost curve of the required form?

4. The term "entrepreneurship" as a factor of production is somewhat ambiguous—or rather more than ambiguous, possessing as it does at least three distinct meanings. What is generally called the "entrepreneurial function" can be either (1) risk—or rather uncertainty-bearing; or (2) management, which consists of two things: (*a*) supervision, (*b*) co-ordination. The latter two are not generally kept separate, although, in the writer's view, to distinguish between them is essential to an understanding of the problem. Supervision is necessary in the case of co-operative production (where several individuals work together for a common result) in order to ensure that everybody should do the job expected of him—in other words, to see that contracts already entered into should, in fact, be carried out. Co-ordination, on the other hand, is that part of the managerial function which determines what sort of contracts should be entered into: which carries out the adjustments to the given constellation of data. Which of these three functions can be considered as having a "fixed supply" in the long run?

The first of these functions—uncertainty-bearing—can be dismissed offhand, from our point of view. Because whatever measure of uncertainty-bearing it will ultimately be found most convenient to adopt—the theory of risks and expectations is as yet too undeveloped for us to talk about a "unit" of uncertainty-bearing—it is highly unlikely that it will be found to have a fixed supply for the individual firm. The mere fact that with the rise of joint-stock companies it was possible to spread the bearing of uncertainty over a great number of individuals and to raise capital for an individual firm far beyond the limits of an individual's own possession, excludes that possibility.

Nor is it likely that management possesses these unique characteristics—in so far as this term refers to the function of supervision. Supervising may require a special kind of ability, and it is probable that it is a relatively indivisible factor. It may not pay to employ a foreman for less than fifty men and it may be most economic to employ one for every seventy-five; but is there any reason why it should not be possible to double output by doubling both, foremen and men? An army of supervisors may be just as efficient (provided it consists of men of equal ability) as one supervisor alone.

This is not true, however, with regard to the co-ordinating factor: that essential part of the function of management which is concerned with the allocation of resources along the various lines of investment, with the adjustment of the productive concern to the continuous changes of economic data. You cannot increase the supply of co-ordinating ability available to an enterprise alongside an increase in the supply of other factors, as it is the essence of co-ordination that every single decision should be made on a comparison with all the other decisions already made or likely to be made; it must therefore pass through a single brain.

This does not imply, of course, that the task of co-ordination must necessarily fall upon a single individual; in a modern business organisation it may be jointly undertaken by a whole Board of Directors. But then it still remains true that all the members of that Board will, in all important decisions, have to keep all the alternatives in their minds—in regard to this most essential mental process there will be no division of labour between them—and that it will not be possible, at any rate beyond a certain point, to increase the supply of co-ordinating ability available to that enterprise merely by enlarging the Board of Directors.[1,2] The efficiency

[1] The essential difference between supervising and co-ordinating ability is that in the case of the former, the principle of the division of labour works smoothly: each supervisor can limit his activities to a particular department, or a particular sub-department, and so forth. In the case of a Board of Co-ordinators, each member of that Board will have to go through the same mental processes, and the advantages of co-operation will consist solely in the checking and counter-checking of each other's judgments. If the Board consists of men of equal ability, this will not materially improve the quality of their decisions; while if the abilities of the different members are markedly unequal, the supply of co-ordinating ability could probably be enlarged by dismissing the Board and leaving the single most efficient individual in control. In practice, of course, a certain amount of co-ordinating activity will be undertaken by Departmental Managers alone in large businesses, but this will always refer to such "infra-marginal" cases where the weighing of *all* alternatives is manifestly superfluous. Only such decisions, however, which affect the "margins" fall under the heading of co-ordination, properly defined. (Cf. Professor Knight's distinction between the "important decisions" always reserved for the entrepreneur, and the "routine work" of management. *Risk, Uncertainty and Profit*, Chapter X *passim*. For a fuller treatment of "marginal" and "infra-marginal" acts of choice, cf. Rosenstein-Rodan, art. "Grenznutzen", *Handwörterbuch der Staatswissenschaften*, 4th ed., Vol. IV, pp. 1198 ff.)

[2] Cf. the analysis on the problem of co-ordination in E. A. G. Robinson, *The Structure of Competitive Industry*, pp. 44 ff.

of the supply of co-ordinating ability can be increased by the introduction of new technical devices, e.g. by a better system of accounting; but given the state of technical knowledge and given the co-
ordinating ability represented by that enterprise, the amount of
other factors which can be most advantageously employed by that
enterprise will be limited, i.e. the supply of co-ordinating ability
for the individual firm is fixed.

It follows from these considerations that for theoretical purposes
the most satisfactory definition of a firm is that of a "productive
combination possessing a given unit of co-ordinating ability"
which marks it off from productive combinations (such as an
industry) not possessing this distinguishing peculiarity. It is the
one factor which in the long run is "rigidly attached to the firm",
which, so to speak, lives and dies with it; whose remuneration,
therefore, is always price-determined.[1, 2] On this definition, firms
whose co-ordinating ability changes, while preserving their legal
identity, would not remain the same firms; but then all the
theoretically relevant characteristics of a firm change with
changes in co-ordinating ability. It might as well be treated,
therefore, as a different firm.

5. We have found, therefore, that the firm's long-run cost
curve is determined by the fixity of supply of the co-ordinating
ability represented by it. Further considerations, however, so
far from lending support to the usual representation of this cost
function and the supply function which is based upon it, lead to

---

[1] The case of the salaried General Manager of modern joint-stock companies
presents difficulties which the present writer by no means professes to have solved.
Professor Knight (*op. cit.*) seems to take the extreme view that control always rests
with those who bear the ultimate risks; while the salaried managers are only concerned
with routine work. This is manifestly untrue in certain cases, if "control" is to be
interpreted as the "making of important decisions". Also, we have to take into account
the possibility that the efficiency of a given unit of co-ordinating ability should vary
with the amount of profits it receives—though just in the case of the entrepreneur this
is very unlikely. In so far as it does, however, the supply of co-ordinating ability will
be variable and the entrepreneur's remuneration (or rather that proportion of it
which is necessary to maintain him in a given degree of efficiency) will enter into costs.
All these, however, though they put difficulties in the way of the definition we have
chosen, do not affect the rest of the argument.

[2] Which does not imply, of course, that co-ordinating ability is rigidly attached to
an industry—as a given unit of co-ordinating ability (and thus a firm) can always
leave one industry and turn to another. Similarly, there are factors which are rigidly
attached to the industry, but not to the firm: specialised kinds of machinery, for
example, which can only be used by the industry in question, but which a firm will
not continue to employ if they yield a greater product in combination with a different
unit of co-ordinating ability than they do for the firm which originally possesses them.

the conclusion that this very fact renders the cost function of the individual firm indeterminate. For the function which lends uniqueness and determinateness to the firm—the ability to adjust, to co-ordinate—is an *essentially dynamic function*; it is only required so long as adjustments are required; and the extent to which it is required (which, as its supply is fixed, governs the amount of other factors which can be most advantageously combined with it) depends on the frequency and the magnitude of the adjustments to be undertaken. It is essentially a feature, not of equilibrium but of disequilibrium; it is needed only so long as, and in so far as, the actual situation in which the firm finds itself deviates from the equilibrium situation. With every successive adjustment to a given constellation of data, the number of co-ordinating tasks still remaining becomes less and the volume of business which a given unit of co-ordinating ability can most successfully manage becomes greater; until finally, in a full long-period equilibrium (in Marshall's stationary state), the task of management is reduced to pure supervision, co-ordinating ability becomes a free good and the technically optimum size of the individual firm becomes infinite (or indeterminate). There is thus no determinate ideal or equilibrium position which a firm is continuously tending to approach, because every approximation to that situation also changes the ideal position to which it tends to approximate. It is not possible, therefore, to derive the firm's cost function from the economic data—i.e. from a given system of prices and a given production function: because the nature of that production function, or, rather, the relative position which the factor "co-ordinating ability" occupies in that production function, is not given independently of equilibrium, but it is part of the problem of equilibrium itself.[1]

It is possible, of course, that if the frequency and the magnitude of the adjustments to be undertaken remain the same (in other words, the degree to which economic data are changing per unit of time is constant), the theoretically optimum size of the individual firm might remain constant. But even if it were possible

[1] Similar ideas are expressed by Professor Chamberlin concerning his curve of selling costs (*The Theory of Monopolistic Competition*, p. 137). Professor Chamberlin, however, does not draw the consequences which, in our view, follow from these in regard to his own analysis.

to formulate a kind of theory of "static-dynamics" where, having once found a suitable measure of economic change (a kind of compound variable made up of the degree of variation of all the different data and weighted according to some arbitrary standard), the magnitude of the latter could be assumed to remain constant, the above conclusion by no means follows necessarily. For the optimum size would still be dependent upon the nature of the change and upon the degree to which adjustments to each given constellation of data can be made in a given time (in other words, the degree to which the path actually followed deviates from the equilibrium path).[1] Thus the mere introduction of dynamic change does not render the situation any more determinate than it was without it. It might mean, however, that in the actual world, the average size of individual firms will remain more or less the same because the inherent tendency of the size of the firm to expand will be continuously defeated by the spontaneous changes of data which check it.

6. What conclusions follow, from a theoretical point of view, from these considerations? It follows, first, that under static assumptions[2] (i.e. a given constellation of economic data) there will be a continuous tendency for the size of the firm to grow and therefore *long-period static equilibrium and perfect competition are incompatible assumptions.* Even if conditions of perfect competition obtain in any given situation, that situation cannot become one of equilibrium so long as the conditions of perfect competition remain preserved. It follows, secondly, that the existing organisation of the economic system, the division of the productive organisation into a great number of independent units under a single control, is essentially one adapted to the existence of dynamic change and imperfect foresight; and therefore the institutional pattern borrowed from a dynamic world cannot readily be applied

[1] Only if all future changes, and the consequences of these changes, are completely foreseen by everybody, will the situation be different; but then it will be analogous to a continuous long-run equilibrium and co-ordinating ability will be unnecessary. For the conception of a dynamic equilibrium with complete foresight see Hicks, "Gleichgewicht und Konjunktur", *Zeitschrift für Nationalökonomie*, Vol. IV, No. 4.

[2] The sole significance of static assumptions in this connection is that in this case the tendency to equilibrium is not dependent on the degree of foresight. All our conclusions also apply to a dynamic world with complete foresight. (Cf. also Knight, *op. cit.*, p. 287: "To imagine that one man could adequately manage a business enterprise of indefinite size and complexity is to imagine a situation in which effective uncertainty is entirely absent.")

to a theoretical static society where every kind of dynamic change is absent. It follows, lastly, that all concepts which are derived from the twin assumptions of a determinate static equilibrium and perfect competition (such as that of a determinate, reversible supply function) are open to the *prima facie* objection that they are derived from assumptions which are mutually inconsistent. In fact, the idea of a determinate equilibrium corresponding to each given constellation of "tastes" and "obstacles" becomes questionable in a world where the existence of indivisibilities offers advantages for co-operative production.[1]

7. We started off by enquiring into the cause which makes the cost curve of the individual firm rise relatively to the costs of the industry and thus makes a determinate equilibrium under perfect competition possible. We came to the conclusion that there is no such thing. We now have to drop the assumption of perfect competition and assume, in accordance with the conditions in the real world, that a firm can, at any rate beyond a certain point, influence by its own action the prices of the goods it is buying and selling. The limitation upon the size of the firm no longer presents any problem. It is sufficiently accounted for by the supply and demand curves with which it is confronted. But the element of indeterminateness, which the isolating assumption of perfect competition enabled us to detect, still continues in force when the basic assumption is removed. In so far as the relative place of co-ordinating ability is still not given by the production function, but depends on, and changes with, the relation of the

---

[1] It is at least questionable whether the same conclusions would hold in a world of perfect divisibility, where *all* economies of scale are absent; and it is to be remembered that it was under this assumption that the conception of equilibrium of the Lausanne School was elaborated. We have seen that the extent to which co-ordination is needed, in any given situation, depends on the volume of business (i.e. the scale of operations of the individual producing unit); and in a world where the scale of operations offers no *technical* advantages, economies could be gained by reducing that scale further and further until the need for co-ordination (i.e. the need for a specialised function of control, of decision-making) was completely eliminated. (This is not to be interpreted as saying that each "infinitesimal" unit would not have to co-ordinate its own activities —in the sense of "equalising its alternatives on the margin"—but these would be completely similar to the co-ordinating activities undertaken by each individual on the side of consumption. There would be no need for co-ordinators, i.e. factors of production specialised in the function of co-ordination. It was with this idea in mind that we found it legitimate to assume earlier in this article [cf. p. 49, especially footnote 2] that in buying, individuals act alone and thus treat perfect competition on the demand side as a datum.) In such a world, therefore, there would be no organisation of production into firms, or anything comparable to it; and perfect competition would establish itself merely as a result of the "free play of economic forces".

actual situation to the equilibrium situation, it still remains true that the cost curve of the individual firm, and consequently its position of equilibrium in relation to a given system of supply and demand curves, is indeterminate.

On closer scrutiny, however, there appears a line of escape for those who believe that the position of equilibrium under imperfect competition is otherwise determinate. Co-ordinating ability may be regarded as a fixed factor, but it is not, or at least it need not be, regarded as an indivisible factor.[1] Although it is not possible to increase the amount of factors applied to a unit of co-ordinating ability beyond a certain limit without loss of efficiency, there is no ground for assuming that there will be increasing returns to the other factors if they are applied in less than a certain amount to a unit of co-ordinating ability.[2] A certain business manager may not be able to manage more than a certain volume of business, in a certain situation, with undiminished efficiency, but why should he not be able to manage *less* equally well?[3] Thus the indeterminateness in the amount of co-ordinating ability required per unit of product does not affect the downward-sloping portion of the cost curve, it merely affects the upward-sloping portion. Now, under conditions of imperfect competition, only the downward-sloping section of the firm's cost curve is relevant from the point of view of the determination of equilibrium, as in equilibrium the firm's average cost curve must be falling.[4]

On further consideration, however, this point turns out not to be very serious. The costs which, in equilibrium, must be falling are average total costs, including the remuneration of uncertainty and co-ordinating ability (including, therefore, all profits which cannot be eliminated by the forces of competition); it is not a condition of equilibrium that marginal costs or even average costs,

---

[1] Cf. footnote 2 on p. 53 for the distinction between "fixed" and "indivisible" factors.

[2] There might be increasing returns for other reasons (if the factors themselves are indivisible), but this does not concern us here.

[3] "Co-ordinating ability" can also be assumed to be an indivisible factor if the type of decisions which entrepreneurs have to make varies in accordance with the volume of business and if an individual entrepreneur is better fitted for the making of some kinds of decisions than other kinds. If this assumption is preferred, the rest of the argument in the present paragraph becomes irrelevant.

[4] Cf. Chamberlin, *The Theory of Monopolistic Competition*, Chapter V, and Joan Robinson, *The Economics of Imperfect Competition*, Chapter VII.

in our definition of the term,[1] should be falling[2] while those sections of the cost curve, where these are rising, will be indeterminate. Moreover, it is possible to argue that changes in the amount of co-ordinating ability required per unit of product will affect "normal profits" in Mrs. Robinson's definition[3] (i.e. the amount of profits necessary to induce new firms to come into the industry), and thus change the position of the demand curves with which existing firms are confronted. In case this is true, not only the equilibrium amount produced by a given firm will be indeterminate, but also the number of firms in the industry, given the conditions of the demand for goods and the supply of factors.

8. There remains, finally, a more practical question to be answered: What is the effect of the elements of indeterminateness above analysed on the actual world? How can their influence be evaluated in terms of what some writers call "the instability of capitalism"? And here we can conclude our investigation with a more reassuring note.

In relatively "quiet" times, i.e. in times when tastes and the rate of saving are steady, technical innovations rare and changes in the population small, we may expect the actual size of "representative" firms to expand. If the system is one in growth (i.e. if capital and population are increasing), this will probably take place without a diminution in the number of existing firms. It is in any case questionable how far this tendency for the individual firms to expand can actually lead to a diminution in the number of firms. Although if "relatively static conditions" prevail long enough the number of firms existing must fall, and fall rapidly, it is very questionable whether in any actual case the process could be carried far. In the first place, the fall in the scarcity of co-ordinating ability represents, from the point of view of society as a whole, a reduction in real costs. It implies an increase in the "bundle of utilities" which can be produced out of a given amount of resources. It is quite possible, therefore, that the increase in the amount produced by the representative firm should run *pari passu* with an increase in the social product and should not

[1] Cf. footnote 1, p. 53. The importance of choosing this definition lies in the fact that it draws attention to the purely tautological nature of the conclusions arrived at by including price-determined remunerations under the cost-items.

[2] On this point cf. Mr. Harrod's note on "Decreasing Costs", *Economic Journal* June, 1933.   [3] *The Economics of Imperfect Competition*, p. 92.

necessitate any diminution of production elsewhere. In the second place (and this seems more important), the growth in the size of some firms, due to the fact that they periodically revise their ideas of their own cost curves (which is what the change in co-ordinating ability comes to), throws new co-ordinating tasks upon other firms (to whom this must appear as a change of data), and even if it does not oblige them to reduce their output, at least it will check their growth. For this reason alone it is not to be expected that the process of expansion will be smooth and continuous, even under purely static conditions.

The reverse is true in times of "disquietude", when changes of data become more frequent and more far-reaching. But while the tendency to expand in quiet times mainly acts in the long run through changing the supply of the long-period variable factors (because so long as plant, machinery, etc., are given, the tendency to expand is effectively blocked by the limitation upon the amount of other factors which can be combined with them),[1] the tendency to contraction may affect short-period output, by raising the prime costs (marginal costs) curve.

All this must in no way be construed as an attempt by the present writer to put forward yet another theory of the trade cycle. Although if all major causes of fluctuations were absent there would exist a certain range of fluctuations due to the causes above analysed, in the author's view these are completely covered up in the real world by the more violent fluctuations which emanate from other causes—just as the ripples on the sea which emanate from the movement of ships (and which would make their effect felt over wide ranges if the sea were absolutely quiet) are fully absorbed by the more powerful waves which are due to the winds and the movements of the moon. When compared with the instabilities due to the monetary system, the rigidities of certain prices and the uncertainty of international trading conditions, the instability caused by the vagaries of the factor "co-ordinating ability" must appear insignificant.

---

[1] Save in the case where the long-period factors are divisible, i.e. consist of small units, and where, therefore, their supply can be expanded, though not contracted, within a short period. For example, in a factory which uses a great number of highly durable machines it is always possible to increase their number in a short period, but it may not be possible to diminish it until some of them wear out.

MARKET IMPERFECTION AND EXCESS CAPACITY[1]

I

OF all the doctrines emerging from recent work on the economics of imperfect competition, none appears more intellectually striking or more significant from a practical point of view than the doctrine of "excess capacity". It is intellectually striking, because it admits possibilities which the traditional "laws of economics" seem to have excluded: e.g. that an increase in "supply" may be followed by a rise in price.[2] And it is practically significant, because if the main contentions of the theory are found to be correct, it affords some reasons for interfering with the "free play of competitive forces" on grounds upon which traditional economic theory would have dismissed the case for interference. The theory envisages a situation where, on the one hand the market facing a group of competing firms is, for one reason or another, not absolutely "perfect", while on the other hand the entry of resources into the "industry" is free, and it shows that under such conditions "competition" (i.e. the free flow of resources into uses where they expect to obtain the largest net remuneration) will drive each producer to a situation in which he is not using its resources to the best advantage; and it will thus lead to a reduction of the physical productivity of resources all round. In a sense, it thus reverses the old argument about increasing returns and monopoly; it not only says that falling costs will lead to monopoly but that a monopolistic or rather a pseudo-monopolistic situation[3] will automatically lead each firm to a position where it is faced

---

[1] Originally published in *Economica*, February, 1935.

[2] Since Marshall, we are aware of the fact that, given certain cost conditions, an increase in demand may be followed by a fall in price. But neither the Marshallian nor, so far as the present writer is aware, any other theoretical system left room for the possibility that, under certain market conditions, an increase in the number of sources of supply (an inflow of resources into the industry) could lead to a rise in prices.

[3] We shall see later what precisely the term "monopolistic" implies in this connection.

with falling average costs.[1] It is a highly ingenious and one might almost say revolutionary doctrine: it shows up "free competition" (i.e. the freedom of entry into any trade or industry) not in the traditional and respectable rôle as the eliminator of the unfit but in the much more dubious rôle as the creator of excess capacity. It affords an excellent theoretical background for the age-old cry of business-men about the "wastes of competition"—so far completely neglected by the economists. It is worth while therefore to examine this theory in some detail.

The theory is put forward both in Professor Chamberlin's recent work and also in Mrs. Robinson's book.[2] Closer inspection reveals, however, that Mrs. Robinson's version possesses a merely formal similarity with Professor Chamberlin's theory. For Mrs. Robinson includes in her "cost curves" such profits which are not competed away by the entry of new producers; and in the circumstances, her statement that "demand curves will be tangential to cost curves" and that firms will be of "less than their optimum size" is merely a statement of a tautology.[3] It does not imply "excess capacity" or anything of that sort. In the subsequent analysis we shall follow therefore mainly Professor Chamberlin's statement of the theory.

II

The main argument can be stated briefly. Although not stated so explicitly, it is really based on four assumptions. First, it is

[1] "Falling average costs", if they are to be regarded as the criterion of excess capacity, should be interpreted that in the relevant output, costs are falling *in a state of long-period equilibrium* (after *all* adjustments have been made to that output), which also implies that *variable costs* are falling (since in the long run the supply of all factors— even the resources supplied by the entrepreneur himself—can be assumed variable and consequently there are no fixed costs). Since in a state of full equilibrium short-run cost curves must be tangential to the long-run cost curve, falling long-period costs also imply that short-run total costs are falling. But the converse is not necessarily true; falling short-run total costs (the fixed costs being calculated on a "historic" basis) need not involve falling long-run costs, for the same output, and consequently these are no safe criteria for establishing the prevalence of excess capacity.

[2] Chamberlin, *The Theory of Monopolistic Competition*, Chapter V. Mrs. Robinson, *The Economics of Imperfect Competition*, Chapter 7. The theory, of course, is by no means completely new. Wicksell had already stated it (*Lectures*, p. 86) and it is also to be found, in essentials, in Cairnes' *Political Economy*, p. 115. It was outlined in P. Sraffa's well-known article ("The Laws of Returns under Competitive Conditions", *Economic Journal*, 1926). The first systematic exposition is, however, Chamberlin's.

[3] Cf. on this point G. F. Shove, "The Imperfection of the Market" (*Economic Journal*, March, 1933) an article which, in the present writer's view, contains one of the most penetrating analyses so far published on this whole subject.

assumed that there are a large number of independent producers, each selling one product only, which is "slightly different" from the products of the rest of the producers. The words "slightly different" imply, that while the demand for the product of any of the producers is highly sensitive to the prices charged by the others, yet this sensitiveness is never so great as to compel all producers to sell at the same price. It implies that a producer, by lowering his price relatively to his competitors' prices, will attract away some, but not *all* of their customers; or alternatively, that he will lose some, but not all of his own customers, if he raises his price relatively to the rest.[1] It is assumed, secondly, that *"consumers' preferences are fairly evenly distributed among the different varieties,"*[2] and since there are a large number of them "any adjustment of price or of 'product' by a single producer spreads its influence over so many of his competitors that the impact felt by any one is negligible and does not lead him to any readjustment of his own situation."[3] Thus, given the prices of all the others, a "demand curve" can be drawn up with respect to the product of each.[4] Thirdly, it is assumed that no producer possesses an "institutional monopoly" over any of the varieties produced and thus the entry of new producers "into the field in general and every portion of it in particular is free and unimpeded". Fourthly, the long-run cost curves of all producers are assumed to be falling up to a certain rate of output; in other words, it is assumed that up to a certain output, there are economies of scale. (Professor Chamberlin's cost curves are U-shaped, i.e. they begin to rise

[1] In technical terms this implies that the consumer's elasticity of substitution between the different producers' products is large, but not infinite; which is the same thing as saying that the cross-elasticities of demand (the elasticity of demand for one producer's product with respect to another producer's price) are considerable but not infinite. Looking at it in this way, monopoly and perfect competition appear as the two limiting cases, where the cross-elasticities are zero or infinite, respectively; and there can be little doubt that the large majority of industrial producers in the real world are faced with imperfect markets in this sense.

[2] Which implies, in the above terminology, that the cross-elasticity of the demand for the product of any producer is of the same order of magnitude with respect to the price of *any* of his competitors. Cf. my article, "Mrs. Robinson's Economics of Imperfect Competition", *Economica*, August, 1934, p. 339.

[3] Chamberlin, p. 83. Mrs. Robinson does not state this so definitely, but her analysis is implicitly based on the same assumptions. Professor Chamberlin states (pp. 82-3) that he only makes these assumptions temporarily in order to facilitate the exposition, and removes them later on (pp. 100-11). But, as I shall try to show, the theory in its rigid form at any rate, really stands or falls with these assumptions.

[4] In the absence of these assumptions one can speak of a demand curve only in the sense of an "imagined demand curve", cf. below.

after a certain point. But while the legitimacy of the latter assumption in the case of long-run curves appears doubtful,[1] it does not affect his argument, which merely requires that costs should be falling over a certain range.) The elasticity of the demand curve, and the cost curve of each producer, are also assumed to be the same, but this, as I shall try to show, is not essential to the main argument so long as institutional monopolies are assumed to be absent. Now, given these two curves, each producer will try to produce that output which will maximise his own profits, i.e. equate marginal revenue with marginal cost. But since marginal revenue is less than price, price will be higher than average cost (including under the latter the displacement cost of the resources supplied by the entrepreneur himself) unless average cost is also, and to a corresponding degree, higher than marginal cost (which it can only be if average costs are falling). Let us assume that this is not the case initially. Entrepreneurs in the industry will then make "monopoly profits", i.e. remuneration for their own resources will be higher than that which similar resources could earn elsewhere. This will attract such resources into the industry; new firms will come in, producing new substitutes, which will reduce the demand for all existing producers; and this process will continue, until profits are reduced to normal, i.e. the difference between the actual earnings and the displacement costs of the entrepreneur's own resources is eliminated. In the position of final equilibrium not only will marginal cost be equal to marginal revenue, but average cost will also be equal to price. The demand curve will thus be tangential to the cost curve. The effect of the entry of new competitors will not necessarily reduce the price of existing products; it may even raise them. The profits which the entrepreneur no longer earns will thus not be passed on to the consumer in the form of lower prices but are mainly absorbed in lower productive efficiency. The producers, *as a body*, could of course prevent this from occurring by reducing their prices *in anticipation* of the entry of new competitors. But since the appearance of any *single* new producer will only affect the demand of a *single* existing producer very slightly,

---

[1] Cf. my article, "The Equilibrium of the Firm", *Economic Journal*, March, 1934, p. 70 [pp. 58-9 above].

while similarly the reduction of price of a *single* existing producer will only slightly affect the profits which a potential producer can expect, no producer could take these indirect effects on his own price policy into consideration.

There can be little doubt that given these assumptions the theory is unassailable. Any criticism therefore must be directed against the usefulness and the consistency of the assumptions selected.

III

1. The first of these concerns the assumptions made about the interrelations of the demand for the products of various producers (which are substantially the same as those underlying Mrs. Robinson's concept of an "imperfectly competitive industry").[1] No doubt, in most cases, the products of various producers selling the same sort of goods are not perfect substitutes for each other in the sense that the slightest price difference would eliminate all demand for the products of higher-price producers. The reasons for such market imperfection may be classed under one of three headings. There may either be slight differences in the products themselves (as in the case of motor cars, wireless sets, etc., the absence of "standardisation"); or differences in the geographical location of producers in cases where the consumers themselves are distributed over an area; or finally, there may exist a certain inertia on behalf of the buyers themselves who will require either some time, or a certain magnitude in the price-difference, before they make up their minds to buy from another seller—even if they are quite indifferent as between the products of different sellers.[2]

---

[1] Cf. *The Economics of Imperfect Competition*, Chapter 1. Cf. on this point my review, *op. cit.*, p. 339.

[2] It might be objected that anything which causes a lack of indifference between buyers will make the products imperfect substitutes in relation to each other (since the consumers' attitude is the final criterion for classifying "products") and consequently no distinction can be made out between "buyers' inertia" and "product-differentiation" as causes of market imperfection. There is, however, a very good reason for keeping them separate. Whereas in the ordinary case of imperfectly substitutable commodities the consumers' elasticity of substitution between two products is symmetrical (i.e. a given change in the price ratio will cause a given change in the relative quantities demanded, whichever of the two prices has moved relatively to the other) this is by no means the case when the lack of indifference is merely due to the inertia of buyers. In the latter case, one cannot even speak of a given "marginal rate of substitution", since this rate will be different according to the direction of the change.

Whatever the cause, the effect, from the analytical point of view, will be the same: the cross-elasticities of demand will have a positive finite value. But is there any justification for the further assumption that they will also be of the same order of magnitude with respect to the prices of *any* group of rival products? Can we say that any adjustment of price or of "product" by a single producer will spread its influence evenly over all his competitors? No doubt, cases are conceivable when it would. When the imperfection of the market is due to sheer buyers' inertia *and nothing else*, we could invoke the law of large numbers and say that the buyers who no longer buy from A, will pair themselves more or less evenly with B, C, D. . . . But buyers' inertia, though an important factor in practice, is rarely found in isolation as a cause of market-imperfection. It is generally coupled with either or both of the other causes.[1] And in these cases, it is clear that the different producers' products will never possess the same degree of substitutability in relation to any particular product. Any particular producer will always be faced with rivals who are nearer to him, and others who are farther off. In fact, he should be able to class his rivals, *from his own point of view*, in a certain order, according to the influence of their prices upon his own demand (which will not be necessarily the same order as that applying to any particular rival of his). This is clear in the case where market-imperfection is merely due to differences in the geographical location of producers. It is equally true in cases of "product-differentiation". Savile Row tailors will be most influenced by Savile Row prices; they will be less concerned with fluctuations in the price of East-End clothes.[2]

"Pseudo-monopolists"—distinguished from the old-fashioned "real monopolists" merely by the fact that the cross-elasticities of demand for their product is large—thus cannot be grouped

[1] Moreover, the case where market-imperfection is *merely* due to buyers' inertia is not a very good one from the point of view of this theory: since it always implies the presence of institutional monopoly as well. Cf. p. 77.

[2] It is conceivable that the "scale of preferences" of different consumers should differ in just that degree as to eliminate the differences in the degree of substitutability of different products for the body of consumers as a whole. (If individual X regards product B as a nearer substitute to A than either C or D, but Y regards C as a nearer substitute than either B or D, while Z regards D as the nearest substitute to A, then the prices, B, C, D may have the same influence on the demand for A.) But this is a rather improbable supposition.

together in a lump but can at best be placed into a series. Each "product" can be conceived of as occupying a certain position on a scale; the scale being so constructed that those products are neighbouring each other between which the consumers' elasticity of substitution is the greatest (a "product" itself can be defined as a collection of objects between which the elasticity of substitution of all relevant consumers is infinite). Each producer then is faced on each side with his nearest rivals; the demand for his own product will be most sensitive with respect to the prices of these; less and less sensitive as one moves further away from him. "Product variation" by an individual producer can then itself be represented as a movement *along* the scale; and, given the position of all other producers, each producer will tend to settle at that point on the scale where his anticipated profits are the greatest. New entrants must also occupy a position on that scale, and will thus necessarily make the chain of substitutes "tighter".

The idea of such a scale can best be envisaged in the case of the simplest type of market-imperfection, the distribution of consumers over an area. Let us assume that all consumers are situated along a road (a kind of "ribbon development"), they are evenly densely spread, and all of them have an equal desire to buy. They are completely indifferent as between the products of different sellers; or rather the only difference consists in respect to transport costs (which can be equally regarded to be borne either by the buyers or the sellers). Under such conditions, sellers will tend to settle at equidistant points from each other along the road,[1] and thus they are all "pseudo-monopolists", since no two producers sell from the same spot.[2] Looked at from the point of view of any seller, a change of price by any other particular seller (the prices of the rest being assumed as given) is less and less important for him, the further away that particular seller is situated.

[1] If only there are more than two of them, cf. Chamberlin, p. 196, where Professor Hotelling's relevant theorem is corrected.

[2] The assumption that institutional monopolies are absent implies, in this case, that any seller *could*, if he wanted to, move to the same spot as that occupied by any other seller (or so near to it as to eliminate differences in transport costs) and thus make his own product "indistinguishable" from that of the other. Neglect to distinguish between these two cases of "monopolies" has been the source of much confusion in the past.

It follows from this, first, that even when the number of producers is large (the chain of substitutes tight) it cannot be assumed that the effect of a single producer's action will spread itself *evenly* over a large number of his rivals and will be negligible for each of them individually. The other producers' prices and "products" thus cannot be assumed as given in drawing up the demand schedule for the first; and the real demand curve for a single producer's product is thus indeterminate (depending on any of the large numbers of possible reactions in which his rivals might indulge).[1] The problems of "duopoly" are thus not merely concomitants of a situation where there is a "small number of producers", but arise in all cases where producers are selling substitute products, since the fact of imperfect substitutability necessarily involves the presence of the scale, and thus of the "small number". "Duopoly" is thus seen not as a special class by itself but rather as "the leading species of a large genus".

Secondly, it can just as little be assumed that "new products" (the products of new or prospective entrants) will stand in the same or similar relation with *all* existing products. A new product must necessarily be placed in between two existing products; and will thus make considerable inroads into the markets of its nearest neighbours. Thus a producer, if far-sighted, will take the effect of his own actions not merely on his existing competitors into consideration but also on his *potential competitors*.[2] He will act on the basis of an "imagined demand curve" which shows the amount he can sell at different prices *in the long run*, under the assumption that his competitors' products, prices and the number of his

---

[1] This does not imply that each producer will not base his policy upon certain ideas concerning the relation between the demand for his product and its price. But this "imagined demand curve" is based on certain expectations concerning his rivals' behaviour as a result of changes in his own policy; irrespective of whether these expectations are correct or not. Such an imagined demand curve is always determinate (since something must always exist in the producer's own mind). But it is a different sort of thing from the demand curves of traditional analysis which always implied an *objective* relationship between price and the quantity demanded. For a fuller treatment of the distinction between a real and an imagined demand curve, cf. my previous article quoted above, *Economica*, August, 1934, p. 340.

[2] If a producer takes into account the consequences of his own policy on his *existing* competitors, this will probably induce him to charge a higher price than otherwise (will make his imagined demand curve less elastic). But if he takes *potential competition* into account, this will probably induce him to charge a price lower than otherwise (make his imagined demand curve more elastic). "Potential competition" implies both (*a*) the appearance of a new rival, (*b*) the possibility of product-adjustment rather than price-adjustment by an existing rival.

competitors are all adjusted to his price. If a producer knows that if he charges a high price to-day a competitor will appear to-morrow whose mere existence will put him in a *permanently worse position*, he will charge a price which will afford him only a low profit, if only he hopes to secure this profit permanently; i.e. he will act in a manner *as if* his own demand curve were very much more elastic than it is. And this "foresight" will, or at any rate may, prevent him from being driven to a state of excess capacity.[1]

2. Moreover, it can be shown that even if none of the producers takes the indirect effects of his own policy into consideration,[2] "potential competition" will never succeed in making the individual demand and cost curves tangential, if economies of scale exist; while the possibility of product-differentiation will by itself never prevent the establishment of perfect competition if economies of scale are completely absent. Demand curves and cost curves therefore will only become necessarily tangential to each other when "demand curves" have also become horizontal.

In order to prove this, let us again take the simplest case of market imperfection which is at the same time the one most favourable to the "excess capacity" theory—when it exists solely on account of the spreading of consumers over a large area. Let us again assume that consumers are evenly distributed over the whole area; that they have no preferences whatever as between the different sellers; and that the cost functions of all producers are identical. The demand curves of individual sellers will be downward-sloping solely on account of the increase in transport costs as more is sold. Let us assume that producers are situated at equal distances from each other and that they all make profits (sell at prices which more than cover average displacement costs).

---

[1] Whether it will do so or not, will depend on the relative willingness and ability to bear losses—on behalf of the existing producer and the new entrant. For let us assume that a producer reduces his price in anticipation of the entrance of new competitors. If the new producer comes in nevertheless, *at the ruling price*, both will be involved in losses. But there will be some higher price at which both will make some profits; and if the new entrant can induce the old producer to raise his price to that level he can thereby secure his place on the "scale" permanently. If, on the other hand, the old producer persists in charging the low price, one of them will have to drop out. (In so far as buyers' inertia is present at all, there is always a presumption that such a price-war will cost less to the old producer than the new one.)

[2] I.e. they all act on the basis of an imagined demand curve which corresponds to a real demand curve drawn on the assumption that the prices and products of all other producers remain the same, irrespective of what the first producer is doing (which is the assumption underlying Professor Chamberlin's demand curves).

Let us assume that new producers enter the field. Each producer's market will be smaller; the elasticity of demand, at any price, higher than before. But if we assume that economies of scale are completely absent (i.e. long-run cost curves are horizontal) profits will never be eliminated altogether so long as the elasticity of demand is less than infinite. For each producer can always recover some of his lost profits by reducing output up to the point where marginal revenue equals marginal cost (which in this case, also equals average cost). The inflow of new producers will continue, leading to a continuous reduction in the output of existing producers and a continuous increase in the elasticities of their demand until the latter become infinite and prices will equal average costs. There the movement will stop. But each firm will have reduced his output to such an extent that he has completely lost his hold over the market.

We see therefore that the mathematical economists in taking perfect competition as their starting point, weren't such fools after all. For they assumed perfect divisibility of everything; and where everything is perfectly divisible, and consequently economies of scale completely absent, perfect competition must necessarily establish itself solely as a result of the free play of economic forces. No degree of product-differentiation and no possibility of further and further product-variation will be sufficient to prevent this result, so long as all kinds of institutional monopolies and all kinds of indivisibilities are completely absent.

Let us now introduce indivisibilities and economies of scale. The movement of new firms into the field will then not continue until the elasticities of demand for the individual producers become infinite; it will be stopped long before that by the increase in costs as the output of producers is reduced. *But there is no reason to assume that it will stop precisely at the point where the demand and cost curves are tangential.* For, on account of the very reason of economies of scale, the potential producer cannot hope to enter the field profitably with less than a certain magnitude of output; and that additional output may reduce demand, both to his nearest neighbours and to him, to such an extent that the demand curves will lie *below* the cost curves and all will be involved in losses. The interpolation of a third producer in between any two producers may thus transform profits into losses. *The same reason therefore which prevents competition from becoming perfect—i.e. indivisibility—will also prevent the complete elimination of "profits".* It will secure a "monopolistic advantage" to anybody who is first in the field and merely by virtue of priority. The ultimate reason for this is that it is not the original resources themselves, but the various uses to which they are put that are indivisible—you can divide "free capital" but you cannot invest *less* than a certain amount of it in a machine—and consequently the investment of resources cannot be so finely distributed as to equalise the level of marginal productivities.[1]

The above argument does not hold if we assume, as Professor Chamberlin assumed at the start, that consumers' preferences are *evenly distributed* over the whole field; and consequently the entry of a new firm affects *all* existing firms to an equal degree. Then the demand for each is only reduced by an insignificant amount by a single new entrant; and consequently the number of firms could increase with impunity until profits are completely wiped out and the demand curves become tangential.

That Professor Chamberlin is aware of our first objection is clear from his analysis of chain-relationships on pp. 102-4 of his book. That he is also aware of the second is clear from certain remarks in connection with spatial competition on p. 199. It would be most unfair therefore to criticise him on a point of logic —since the logic of Professor Chamberlin's analysis is indeed excellent. What he does not seem to be aware of is the degree of unreality involved in his initial assumptions, and the extent to which his main conclusions are dependent on those assumptions.

3. So far we have not mentioned the most frequent and conspicuous objection against the "excess capacity" theory: that it assumes "identical cost and demand curves" for the different producers. In our view, this is no valid criticism on Professor Chamberlin's assumptions. The identity of the demand curves

---

[1] This brings out clearly also the objection against Mrs. Robinson's "normal profits". We see how the level of profits in each firm—the difference between its actual remuneration and the displacement cost of its earnings—is determined by the degree of indivisibility which acts as a "protective shield" against intruders. There is no more reason to assume these profits to tend to a normal level than there is to assume that the extent of indivisibilities is the same in all cases.

merely ensures that the *prices* of different producers will be identical. But since producers are free to vary the quality of their product as well as their price, differences in elasticity will not save producers from being driven to a position of "tangency"— although they may reach this position by selling at different prices. The identity of the cost curves—*in the required sense*—follows on the other hand from the assumption of the absence of any institutional monopoly. It is assumed, that is to say, that every producer *could*, if he wanted to, produce commodities completely identical to those of any other producer—if he does not, this is merely because he would not find it profitable to do so.[1, 2] Such institutional monopolies may consist of patents, copyrights, trade-marks or even a trade-name. They may be conferred by law, by ownership, or merely by the will of the public. If the public *prefers* to buy from Messrs. Smith and Robinson and thus the name of the seller becomes part of the "quality of the product", then Messrs. Smith and Robinson have an institutional monopoly of their products. They possess something which others cannot possess. Similarly, if the entrepreneur *owns* resources which are *relatively* better fitted for the production of some varieties than the resources over which other entrepreneurs have command, he has exclusive control over resources which to that extent are unique: and this also implies the presence of some institutional monopoly.[3] Consequently, in the absence of these, since the relative costs of producing different varieties must be the same for the different producers, their cost curves, *for each single variety*, must also be identical.

It might be objected that "institutional monopoly", thus defined, covers a much larger number of cases than what is generally understood by this term. Indeed, one could make out a nice distinction between the possession of an "absolute"

---

[1] Professor Chamberlin does not state this explicitly; but this is the only logically consistent interpretation one can give to his assumption that "the entry of new producers into the field in general and every portion of it in particular is free and unimpeded".

[2] This implies in our terminology that every producer is free to move along and settle at any point of the "scale"; he can get therefore "as near to" the products of any other producer as he wants without incurring higher *relative* costs.

[3] In order to avoid misunderstanding it must be pointed out that the absence of institutional monopoly does not imply that the abilities of each entrepreneur, and consequently the *absolute levels* of their costs, are identical.

monopoly (when no other producer is able to produce a completely identical product at *any* cost) or a comparative or "partial" monopoly (when no other producer is able to produce the same product at the same relative cost). But as all products are more or less close substitutes for one another, this distinction becomes analytically unimportant since it comes to the same thing whether producer B can produce merely a "more or less close substitute" to A—or whether he can produce the *same* product but only at a higher cost than A.[1] Anything therefore which imposes higher costs on one producer than another (whether it is due to the possession of unique resources by one entrepreneur or whether it is merely due to buyers' inertia[2] imposing a special cost of entry on new producers) implies, to that extent, the presence of institutional monopoly.

Such institutional monopolies of course are never completely absent. Their presence—though, as we have seen in the last section, by no means essential—may even be directly responsible for a large part of market imperfection, as Professor Chamberlin himself so convincingly shows in his appendix in favour of "unfair trading". They cannot therefore usefully be assumed absent when a situation is analysed which is often largely bound up with them. And what does the situation look like when they are not absent?

If the "scale of differentiation" of the consumers can be regarded as given (as e.g. in the previous example, when the degree of substitutability of different products was rigidly determined by the level of transport costs) institutional monopoly, to the extent to which it is present, will prevent the generation of excess capacity—since, to that extent, profits earned by one producer cannot be competed away by another producer. Many types of institutional monopolies, however, by themselves increase the degree of market imperfection, and to that extent are favourable

---

[1] In both cases producer B will obtain smaller total receipts for the same total outlay.

[2] What we designated above as "sheer buyers' inertia" (i.e. that consumers require either a certain lapse of time, or a certain minimum of price-difference before they change over from one seller to another, even if they are otherwise completely indifferent between the different sellers' products) is merely a special case of institutional monopoly; since it always imposes a differential advantage on the existing producer relatively to the new entrant. The mere existence of specialised durable plant, however, does not imply such a differential advantage in the long run, although it may prevent adjustments being undertaken in the short run.

to the generation of excess capacity.[1] The sudden appearance of buyers' inertia, for example, has the double effect of reducing the elasticity of demand for the individual products and of imposing a cost of entry on potential competitors; these two opposing tendencies may cancel out, or the net effect may go in either direction.

To sum up the results of the above argument. The extent to which excess capacity may be generated as a result of "free competition" (under the assumption that the existence of economies of scale will prevent this competition from becoming perfect) will depend: (1) on the degree of "short-sightedness" or "far-sightedness" of producers (how far they take potential competition into account in deciding upon their price- and product-policy). This is a question of business psychology rather than economics. (ii) The extent to which institutional monopolies are present. This, as we have seen, will tend to prevent the generation of excess capacity if it leaves the scale of differentiation unaffected; while it will have an uncertain effect if it increases the scale of differentiation as well. (iii) The extent to which the market-situation resembles a "chain relationship" (in Professor Chamberlin's terminology), i.e. the extent to which the various cross-elasticities of demand differ in order of magnitude. Only in the special case when they are all of the same order of magnitude will Professor Chamberlin's conclusion (that demand curves will be tangential to cost curves) necessarily follow. At the same time, there is a presumption that some degree of excess capacity will be generated even if profits will not be completely competed away since "indivisibilities", by themselves, will not offer a strong enough shield to prevent *some* rise in costs as a consequence of the intrusion of new competitors. Many of the objections therefore which can be brought against the theory if put forward in its

---

[1] The difference between these two types of institutional monopolies (the one which affects merely the relative costs of different producers, and the other which affects the elasticities of the demand curves for products as well) can best be elucidated by examples. A legal patent for a certain cheap process of producing ordinary window glass will not lead the consumers to differentiate between glass produced by one process or another. It will merely have the effect of imposing higher costs upon anybody who does not possess the patent. A trade-mark protecting a certain soap or medicine, however, may lead the consumers to differentiate between different soaps or medicines; and thus reduce the elasticity of demand for the products of each producer.

rigid form (that demand curves will tend to become tangential with the cost curves), do not affect the fundamental proposition that the effect of the competition of "new entrants" and consequent reduction of the level of profits earned may take the form of a rise in costs rather than a reduction of prices.[1]

4. So far we have not touched upon another abstract assumption which Professor Chamberlin has made, i.e. that each producer produces only a single product. In reality the majority of producers produce a series of different products, if products are to be defined by the same rigid market-criteria as were applied in the earlier parts of this paper. And at first sight at any rate, it does appear as if the spreading of production over a series of different products is the way in which producers can overcome the effect of those indivisibilities which form the *conditio sine qua non* of imperfect competition. If there is not a sufficiently great demand to produce one product on an "optimal scale", the producer may still utilise his plant fully by producing two or more products, rather than building a smaller, sub-optimal plant or leaving his existing plant under-employed. In this way, indivisibilities will be overcome; and consequently excess capacity will not make its appearance either. The effect of "competition from outside" will be to induce producers to produce a larger series of products, rather than to reduce the scale of output as a whole.

In our view this line of reasoning is not strictly accurate; for even if it is admitted that varying the number of different kinds of products produced provides one line of adjustment for the entrepreneur, this does not imply that the essential consequences of this type of situation (that increased competition will lead to an increase in costs) can thereby be avoided. Whether they will or

[1] Professor Chamberlin's analysis is most valuable also in throwing light upon the probable consequences of all monopolistic agreements which refer to selling prices rather than quantities produced. It explains why, if a uniform taxi-fare is imposed, one will find too many empty taxis about. Or if the code of "professional etiquette" prevents doctors and lawyers from undercutting each other, sooner or later they will all complain that they are "under-employed". Or if manufacturers' cartels or trade associations impose a uniform price or a uniform "profit-margin" on retailers, one will find too many tobacco shops round the streets. It should also make us very sceptical about any remedying of the evils of imperfect competition by compulsory rationalisation, cartellisation, or any type of interference with price-competition. For measures which intend to prevent the alleged evils of "price-cutting" not infrequently tend to aggravate the real evils which they are supposed to remedy.

not, will depend on the nature of the cost function of the jointly produced products.

Commodities, of course, will only be produced jointly if it is cheaper to produce them jointly than separately. For certain commodities (such as wheat and straw) this is always the case: whatever is the amount produced of each (or rather whatever is the amount of resources engaged in producing them); irrespectively therefore of whether the economies due to scale are attained or not. These are the cases of "by-products" where more than one commodity emerges as a result of a single productive process. Certain other commodities, however, may be jointly produced simply because the demand for any of them is not large enough to be produced on a scale which should enable the realisation of the economies of scale; while some of these economies can be retained by utilising a larger plant for the production of several commodities. For such commodities joint production will only be profitable at certain outputs, and will become unprofitable as soon as the demand for each or any of them is sufficiently large to enable the economies of scale to be secured in the case of separate production. This is the case simply because the indivisible factors (buildings, machinery, etc.) which are responsible for these economies, are never completely specialised; and can be used, more or less effectively, for the production of several things simultaneously.

Since, however, in most cases, indivisible factors are not completely unspecialised either, such a "spreading of production" is always attended with some cost; i.e. the physical productivity of a *given* quantity of resources calculated in terms of *any* of the products will always be less, the greater the number of separate commodities they are required simultaneously to produce. That this is the case for a large proportion of jointly produced commodities is shown by the fact that the development of an industry is always attended by "specialisation" or "disintegration", i.e. the reduction of the number of commodities produced by single firms.[1]

Assuming that the cost functions of jointly produced commodities are of this nature, how does the equilibrating process

---

[1] Cf. Allyn Young, "Increasing Returns and Economic Progress", *Economic Journal*, 1929.

work itself out under our previous assumptions? For simplicity, we can postulate that there is a given number of firms, and initially each of them produces only one product and all are making profits (not necessarily to the same degree). Let us suppose that one of them finds it profitable to produce another commodity, highly competitive with the products of some other producers. These latter producers will now find the demand for their products reduced; and *this* may make it profitable for them to engage in the production of a second, or even a third, commodity —even if this was not profitable before. This in turn will induce other producers (possibly our "first" producer) to do the same, which in turn will lead to a further "spreading of production" by competing producers. Assuming always that producers merely take the *direct* effects of their actions into consideration (i.e. act upon an imagined demand curve which regards the prices and the products of all other producers as given)[1] this process will continue, so long as producers continue to make some profits; and so long as the loss caused by a reduction in the amount of resources engaged (if the reduction in the output of one commodity were not compensated by an increase in the output of another) is greater than the loss caused by a further "spreading of output". A precise formulation of this process would require either some very cumbrous language or some rather involved mathematics; but without resorting to either, it is easy to see what conditions the final equilibrium will involve. The demand curve for each single product will have become very much more elastic[2] (since each producer now produces a very much smaller share of each product, or "type of product"); profits will have been wiped out and the general level of costs of each product, or type of product, will have become higher. There will not be much "excess capacity" in the sense that, given the *number* of different products produced simultaneously by each firm, an increase in the output of all of them would reduce costs per unit. Yet there

[1] This implies in this case that producers ignore not only any adjustment of price or of product by other producers as a result of their own policy, but also any effect upon the demand for some of the other commodities produced by themselves.

[2] It can become infinitely elastic only when the "spreading of output" involves *no* additional cost at all. In this case the "economies of scale" refer to the amount of resources used by single firms rather than those engaged in the production of certain products; and for each single product, conditions of perfect competition might be brought about even if the total number of firms is small.

will be a "technical wastage", since the physical productivity of resources will be less than what it would be if each producer produced a smaller number of products and a larger proportion of the total output of each; a policy they undoubtedly would prefer if all of them could foresee the ultimate, as distinct from the immediate, consequences of their actions.[1]

IV

We have seen therefore that in all cases where economies of scale are present over certain ranges of output and where market imperfection exists (in the sense that highly and yet imperfectly substitutable commodities are on sale), "increased competition" (i.e. an increase in the number of firms in a particular industrial field) might lead to a reduction of technical efficiency rather than to a reduction in price or an increase in aggregate output; while in cases where firms can vary the number of different products produced, this might come about even without an inflow of "new firms". In both cases this result was seen to depend on a certain "short-sightedness" of producers who act on the basis of the immediate industrial situation confronting them rather than following out the further consequences of their own policy. The prevalence of such short-sightedness can be sufficiently accounted for, however, partly by the producers' ignorance of those further consequences and partly by the uncertainty as to the extent of far-sightedness with which their actual and potential competitors are endowed.

It is extremely difficult to deduce any general conclusions from the above analysis as to the effect of the generation of excess capacity upon economic welfare in general—in whatever arbitrary way this concept may be defined. If the money-value of the National Dividend is to be made its criterion (calculated on the basis of some *given* price-level), then no doubt, it could be increased, in some fields quite considerably, by compulsory "standardisation", cartel-agreements, the restriction of entry or any similar measure enabling producers to realise more fully the

---

[1] There may be another reason, apart from this type of "short-sightedness", why producers would prefer a policy of many-product production: and this is the reduction of risk, especially important in cases of fashionable articles, where they cannot calculate with any precision how the public will take any particular variety.

"economies of scale". The recognition of this fact, however, as yet far from warrants the advocacy of such measures. Apart from the ill-effects on distribution (and in a world of wage-rigidities, upon employment) which such processes of monopolisation inevitably involve, the public would be offered finally larger amounts of a smaller number of commodities; and it is impossible to tell how far people prefer quantity to diversity or vice versa.

Neither is it permissible to argue, on the other hand, that the generation of excess capacity is itself the result of consumers' choice; since it only comes about by creating a greater diversity of commodities: and consequently that its emergence is evidence that the public, to that extent, prefers "variety" to "cheapness". This line of reasoning would only be permissible if consumers were actually confronted with the choice of having *either* a smaller range of commodities at lower prices *or* a larger range at higher prices. In fact, they never are in a position to choose between these alternatives: they are offered either the one or the other, but never both. To expect the consumers to be so "far-sighted" as to concentrate on the purchase of a few varieties merely in the hope of thereby reducing prices in the future, is an assumption which even the highest level of abstraction should avoid.

WELFARE PROPOSITIONS IN ECONOMICS[1]

IN the December 1938 issue of the *Economic Journal* Professor Robbins returns to the question of the status of interpersonal comparisons of utility.[2] It is not the purpose of this note to question Professor Robbins' view regarding the scientific status of such comparisons; with this the present writer is in entire agreement. Its purpose is rather to examine the relevance of this whole question to what is commonly called "welfare economics". In previous discussions of this problem it has been rather too readily assumed, on both sides, that the scientific justification of such comparisons determines whether "economics as a science can say anything by way of prescription". The disputants have been concerned only with the status of the comparisons; they were—apparently—agreed that the status of prescriptions necessarily depends on the status of the comparisons.

This is clearly Mr. Harrod's view. He says: "Consider the Repeal of the Corn Laws. This tended to reduce the value of a specific factor of production—land. It can no doubt be shown that the gain to the community as a whole exceeded the loss to the landlords—*but only if individuals are treated in some sense as equal.* Otherwise how can the loss to some—and that there was a loss can hardly be denied—be compared with the general gain? If the incomparability of utility to different individuals is strictly pressed, not only are the prescriptions of the welfare school ruled out, but all prescriptions whatever. The economist as an adviser is completely stultified, and unless his speculations be regarded as of paramount aesthetic value, he had better be suppressed completely."[3] This view is endorsed by Professor Robbins: "All that I proposed to do was to make clear that the statement that social

---

[1] Originally published in *Economic Journal*, September, 1939.

[2] "Interpersonal Comparisons of Utility: A Comment", *Economic Journal*, December, 1938, pp. 635-91.

[3] "Scope and Method of Economics", *Economic Journal*, September, 1938, pp. 396-7. (Italics mine.)

wealth was increased [by free trade] itself involved an arbitrary element—that the proposition should run, *if* equal capacity for satisfaction on the part of the economic subjects be assumed, *then* social wealth can be said to be increased. Objective analysis of the effects of the repeal of duties only showed that consumers gained and landlords lost. That such an arbitrary element was involved was plain. It seemed no less plain, therefore, that, here as elsewhere, it should be explicitly recognised."[1]

It can be demonstrated, however, that in the classical argument for free trade no such arbitrary element is involved at all. The effects of the repeal of the Corn Laws could be summarised as follows: (i) it results in a reduction in the price of corn, so that the *same* money income will now represent a higher real income; (ii) it leads to a shift in the distribution of income, so that some people's (i.e. the landlord's) incomes (at any rate in money terms) will be lower than before, and other people's incomes (presumably those of other producers) will be higher. Since aggregate money income can be assumed to be unchanged, if the landlords' income is reduced, the income of other people must be correspondingly increased. It is only as a result of this consequential change in the distribution of income that there can be any loss of satisfactions to certain individuals, and hence any need to compare the gains of some with the losses of others. But it is always possible for the Government to ensure that the previous income-distribution should be maintained intact: by compensating the "landlords" for any loss of income and by providing the funds for such compensation by an extra tax on those whose incomes have been augmented. In this way, everybody is left as well off as before in his capacity as an income recipient; while everybody is better off than before in his capacity as a consumer. For there still remains the benefit of lower corn prices as a result of the repeal of the duty.

In all cases, therefore, where a certain policy leads to an increase in physical productivity, and thus of aggregate real income, the economist's case for the policy is quite unaffected by the question of the comparability of individual satisfactions; since in all such cases it is *possible* to make everybody better off than before, or at any rate to make some people better off without

[1] *Loc. cit.*, p. 638.

making anybody worse off. There is no need for the economist to prove—as indeed he never could prove—that as a result of the adoption of a certain measure nobody in the community is going to suffer. In order to establish his case, it is quite sufficient for him to show that even if all those who suffer as a result are fully compensated for their loss, the rest of the community will still be better off than before. Whether the landlords, in the free-trade case, should in fact be given compensation or not, is a political question on which the economist, *qua* economist, could hardly pronounce an opinion. The important fact is that, in the argument in favour of free trade, the fate of the landlords is wholly irrelevant: since the benefits of free trade are by no means destroyed even if the landlords are fully reimbursed for their losses.[1]

This argument lends justification to the procedure, adopted by Professor Pigou in *The Economics of Welfare*, of dividing "welfare economics" into two parts: the first relating to production, and the second to distribution. The first, and far the more important part, should include all those propositions for increasing social welfare which relate to the increase in aggregate production; all questions concerning the stimulation of employment, the equalisation of social net products, and the equalisation of prices with marginal costs, would fall under this heading. Here the economist is on sure ground; the scientific status of his prescriptions is unquestionable, provided that the basic postulate of economics, that each individual prefers more to less, a greater satisfaction to a lesser one, is granted. In the second part, concerning distribution, the economist should not be concerned with "prescriptions" at all, but with the relative advantages of different ways of carrying out certain political ends. For it is quite impossible to

---

[1] This principle, as the reader will observe, simply amounts to saying that there is no interpersonal comparison of satisfactions involved in judging any policy designed to increase the sum total of wealth just because any such policy *could* be carried out in a way as to secure unanimous consent. An increase in the money value of the national income (given prices) is not, however, necessarily a sufficient indication of this condition being fulfilled: for individuals might, as a result of a certain political action, sustain losses of a non-pecuniary kind—e.g. if workers derive satisfaction from their particular kind of work, and are obliged to change their employment, something more than their previous level of money income will be necessary to secure their previous level of enjoyment; and the same applies in cases where individuals feel that the carrying out of the policy involves an interference with their individual freedom. Only if the increase in total income is sufficient to compensate for such losses, and still leaves something over for the rest of the community, can it be said to be "justified" without resort to interpersonal comparisons.

decide on economic grounds what particular pattern of income-distribution maximises social welfare. If the postulate of equal capacity for satisfaction is employed as a criterion, the conclusion inescapably follows that welfare is necessarily greatest when there is complete equality; yet one certainly cannot exclude the possibility of everybody being happier when there is some degree of inequality than under a régime of necessary and complete equality. (Here I am not thinking so much of differences in the capacity for satisfactions between different individuals, but of the satisfactions that are derived from the prospect of improving one's income by one's own efforts—a prospect which is necessarily excluded when a régime of complete equality prevails.) And short of complete equality, how can the economist decide precisely how much inequality is desirable—i.e. how much secures the maximum total satisfaction? All that economics can, and should, do in this field, is to show, given the pattern of income-distribution desired, which is the most convenient way of bringing it about.

PART II

CONTRIBUTIONS TO KEYNESIAN ECONOMICS

5

PROF. PIGOU ON MONEY WAGES IN RELATION TO UNEMPLOYMENT[1]

1. In an article in the last issue of the *Economic Journal*[2] Professor Pigou attempts to demonstrate the proposition that a general all-round reduction in the rate of money-wages, assuming that the reduction does not set up the expectation of further wage-cuts, must necessarily lead to an increase in output and employment in the short run (and independently whether it occurs with or without a reduction in the rate of interest), given certain reasonable assumptions about the attitude of the public towards cash-holdings and the policy of the banking system as regards the creation of money. The demonstration is made only in regard to a highly simplified model; but, as Professor Pigou suggests in conclusion, "the elements of actual life excluded from the model are probably irrelevant; what is true of the model is probably true—with a fair degree of probability—of actual life."[3] It is not the purpose of this note to dispute this last contention, but to show that Professor Pigou's results do not follow from the assumptions of his own model, or rather that they would follow only as a result of additional assumptions which are not explicitly stated. It is hoped that the analysis will also enable us to set out the results following from Professor Pigou's model in a more general form; in particular, to show the conditions under which an increase in employment would result from the money-wage reduction, the factors determining the extent of this increase, and the relation of Professor Pigou to those writers who hold the contrary opinion (which can be reduced to a difference in assumptions.)

2. It is best to begin by restating Professor Pigou's argument

---

[1] Originally published in *Economic Journal*, December 1937.

[2] "Real and Money Wage Rates in Relation to Unemployment", *Economic Journal*, September 1937, pp. 405 ff. The present paper merely deals with Professor Pigou's propositions relating to money wages, in § II, especially §§ 6-10.

[3] *Loc. cit.*, p. 422.

in a brief form. The significant elements of his model are, first, that "land and fixed capital (i) last for ever, so that no element of depreciation enters into prime cost; and (ii) consist of things of which it is impossible to make any more"; and secondly, that "each sort of consumption good has exactly the same period of production which period cannot be altered."[1] Thus it is impossible to make any investments other than the strictly temporary investment arising out of an increase in working capital associated with a larger rate of output. In equilibrium, therefore, investment must be zero; and since investments are zero, saving must also be zero.[2] In other words, in equilibrium individuals must spend on the purchase of current output no more and no less than their current income. If they did either one or the other, forces of adjustment would be set up (via changes in prices, the rate of interest and real income) which would eliminate the difference. This can also be expressed by saying that the receipts obtained from the sale of goods, at any period, must equal the current outlay on production— including expected profits under outlay—otherwise entre- preneurs would not maintain their scale of operations.[3]

The operation of the model depends on three equations which are set out in §§ 7 and 8 of the article. The first relates to banking policy, and regards the quantity of money in circulation as an increasing function of the rate of interest.[4] This can be written in the form: $M = f(r)$, where $f'(r)$ is positive. The second of these equations relates the rate of interest to the public's rate of discount of future income—the rate of

---

[1] *Ibid.*, p. 406. There are a number of other assumptions which are not material in connection with the present argument, *i.e.* the assumption of homogeneous labour, perfectly mobile between different industries; the perfect similarity of demand and supply conditions in all industries, so that a change in total output leaves relative prices unaffected; perfect competition so that in equilibrium price is everywhere equal to marginal prime cost. (This last assumption is removed in a later section, with which the present paper is not concerned.) And last, but not least, of course, that there is a sufficient amount of unemployed labour.

[2] This is thus the one obvious difference between Professor Pigou's model of the "short-run" and other "models" which merely assume investment to be constant, but not necessarily zero. It will be shown, however, that this difference is not significant; propositions obtained under the assumption of zero-investment can be applied to cases where investment is assumed to be constant and positive, and vice versa.

[3] This is not explicitly stated by Professor Pigou, but obviously follows from his assumptions.

[4] It is also assumed—which we take for granted—that there is no "rationing of credit": "at any ruling rate of interest, the banking system allows that quantity of money to be outstanding which at that rate the public desires to hold" (p. 408).

time-preference, ρ—which could be written in the form: $r = \rho$. This equation, which might cause difficulties to some readers, can be interpreted in the following way. There must be some rate of interest—at any rate if total real income and its distribution are given—at which the public as a whole have no desire to convert assets into current income, or current income into assets, and, in equilibrium, the ruling rate of interest must correspond to this rate. In other words, when savings are zero—though not otherwise—the rate of interest must correspond to the rate of time preference,[1] which for the present purposes merely amounts to savings. This equation, therefore, could equally be written in the form $S = \psi(r) = 0$, where $\psi(r)$ is the amount of savings as a function of the rate of interest. Finally, there is the equation expressing the demand for money, which, given its quantity, determines the velocity of circulation:

$$V = \phi\{r, \frac{I}{wx}\},^2 \text{ where } \frac{\delta V}{\delta r} \text{ is positive and } \frac{\delta V}{\delta \frac{I}{wx}} \text{ negative.}$$

The inclusion of r in this equation takes account of "liquidity-preference". It is thus the great merit of Professor Pigou's demonstration, as compared with previous demonstrations of the same proposition, that it expressly allows for the dependence of the demand for money on the liquidity-preference function.

Given these functions, the actual demonstration is simple. If money wages are cut, equilibrium at the same level of employment as the previous one could obtain only if prices fall in the same proportion as money wages. This requires that money income, MV, should fall in the same proportion as money wages. But is that possible? If employment is unchanged, the rate of interest must remain unchanged, since nothing has happened to change the equation $S = \psi(r) = 0$. But if r is unchanged, M must also be unchanged; this follows from

[1] Cf. Ramsey, "A Mathematical Theory of Saving", *Economic Journal*, December 1928.

[2] *I* stands for total money income, w for the rate of wages and x for the volume of employment (which is uniquely related to the level of real income). The velocity of circulation will, in fact, depend both on the size of real income *and* its distribution; but since $\frac{I}{wx}$ is a single-valued function of x, x can be neglected.

the assumptions on banking policy: M = $f(r)$. Further, if r and x are unchanged, V must necessarily remain unchanged, for V depends on r and $\dfrac{1}{wx}$ and the equilibrium value of $\dfrac{1}{wx}$ only depends on x. Therefore, *at an unchanged level of employment the equilibrium level of money income must also remain unchanged.* This does not imply that money income cannot fall as a result of the wage-cut; merely that a fall in money-income can only occur *pari passu* with an increase in employment. An unchanged level of employment is not consistent therefore with a position of equilibrium.

3. In order to criticise this argument, it is necessary to start with the reverse assumption—that a fall in money wages does lead to an increase in employment—and investigate under what conditions, an increased level of employment can become a position of equilibrium. If it can similarly be shown that in certain cases this could not become an equilibrium-position either, we shall at any rate have something to go on.

The critical function, on which Professor Pigou's demonstration depended, was the one relating the rate of interest to the rate of time preference. We have already attempted to show that this is merely the old-fashioned savings-function in disguise, or rather, it stands for that point of this function at which savings are zero.[1] It is now, however, fairly generally agreed, at any rate since the publication of Mr. Keynes's *General Theory*, that savings cannot be regarded as a function of the rate of interest alone.[2] Professor Pigou carefully refrains from asserting that it is—even indirectly—since, in the critical passage (p. 409), he merely says if "real income is unaltered ρ (the rate of time preference) must be unchanged." If we want to be inclusive, we ought to say that savings depend on the rate of interest, the size of real income and its distribution. But since, in accordance with the assumption of perfect competition, the

---

[1] Or some other given amount, if it is assumed that investments are not constant and zero, but constant and positive.

[2] It is interesting to note that the assumption that savings are largely a function of real income has not been questioned by any of Mr. Keynes's critics. Yet, in the present writer's view, it is this assumption, more than any other, which is responsible for the "revolutionary" innovations of Mr. Keynes's system.

distribution of income $\dfrac{I}{wx}$ is a single-valued function of total employment (x), it is sufficient to write S = ψ{r, x}. We know that $\dfrac{\delta S}{\delta x}$ is necessarily positive; and it will be all the larger the smaller is the elasticity of the marginal productivity function for labour (*i.e.* the larger is $\dfrac{d\dfrac{I}{wx}}{dx}$). About the nature of $\dfrac{\delta S}{\delta r}$ there have occasionally been doubts; but since it is essential for Professor Pigou's own demonstration that it should be positive, we might assume it so for the moment.

The inclusion of *x* in Professor Pigou's re-formulated second' function makes a considerable difference to the situation. For we do know now that an increase in real income will lead to savings; and savings, under the framework of our model, must lead to a fall in prices,an increase in the size of real balances, and thus to a fall in the rate of interest. This must continue until savings are again reduced to zero, either because (i) prices have fallen so far that real income and employment fall back to the previous level; or (ii) the rate of interest falls so far that the incentive to save, due to a larger income, is exactly offset by the opposite incentive due to the lower interest rate. In other words, assuming that $\dfrac{\delta S}{\delta r}$ is positive, there is zero-savings rate of interest (or time-preference-rate of interest) corresponding to each different level of employment; and the actual equilibrium level of employment at any given level of money wages will be determined by the additional "Keynesian" condition that the rate of interest must also equate the demand for money with its supply.

Professor Pigou is therefore right in asserting that a fall in money wages will lead to an increase in employment if, and only if, $\dfrac{\delta S}{\delta r}$, $\dfrac{\delta V}{\delta r}$ and $\dfrac{dM}{dr}$ are all positive and finite. He is clearly wrong in thinking, however (p. 411), that his result does not depend on the reduction of the rate of interest; or that "if the money rate of wages is reduced, after a *temporary* fall in the rate of interest, we shall have employment standing *permanently* above the original level" (my italics). So long as $\frac{\delta S}{\delta x}$ is assumed positive, the increase in employment can occur only if the rate of interest falls, and last only so long as it remains reduced. The opposite conclusion—that a reduction of money wages *cannot* increase employment—requires either the assumption that $\frac{\delta S}{\delta r}$ is zero or negative, in which case the fall in the rate of interest cannot raise the propensity to consume, or that the elasticity of the banking-policy or of the velocity-of-circulation functions with respect to the rate of interest is infinite, in which case the rate of interest cannot change.

Professor Pigou's view, on the other hand, that an increase in employment necessarily follows, irrespective of whether the rate of interest is reduced or not, or whether such reduction is merely temporary, clearly assumes a 'special case', where $\frac{\delta S}{\delta x}$ is zero.

4. Our argument so far has left Professor Pigou's own demonstration in §§ 7 and 8 of his paper formally intact. It still remains true that if $\frac{\delta S}{\delta r}$ is assumed to be positive, a unique rate of interest is associated with every given level of employment—in other words, there is only one rate of interest which secures zero savings for every real income. Given the level of employment and real income, the rate of interest cannot change, whatever happens to money wages. And if $\frac{dM}{dr}$, $\frac{\delta V}{\delta r}$ are assumed to be positive and finite, total money income (MV) cannot change if the rate of interest is given. The re-establishment of equilibrium must therefore require an increase in employment. But in the light of the preceding it is easily seen that too much importance must not be attributed to this demonstration. For the resulting inrease in employment might be very small—so small, indeed, as to be negligible—if $\frac{\delta S}{\delta r}$ is only mildly positive, while $\frac{\delta S}{\delta x}$, $\frac{dM}{dr}$ or $\frac{\delta V}{\delta r}$ are relatively large. The resulting increase in employment will therefore be all the larger, the larger is $\frac{\delta S}{\delta r}$ and the smaller is

$\dfrac{\delta S}{\delta r}$, $\dfrac{dM}{dr}$ and $\dfrac{\delta V}{\delta r}$. On realistic grounds there are reasons for supposing that the elasticity of savings with respect to changes in the interest rate is not very large.

If, on the other hand, $\dfrac{\delta S}{\delta r}$ is zero, Professor Pigou's demonstration formally breaks down, since this is tantamount to assuming the condition of zero savings, for any given level of real income, can be satisfied at various rates of interest. There is no determinate rate of "time-preference". In this case the reduction of money wages can neither lead to an increase in employment nor can it leave the rate of interest unchanged. On the contrary, the rate of interest will continue to fall up to the point where MV becomes reduced to the same extent as money wages.

If, however, $\dfrac{\delta S}{\delta r}$ is negative, a reduction of money wages must actually lead to a reduction of employment.[1] For the reduction in wages must lead to a fall in interest, which in turn induces savings; and this in turn leads to a reduction of real income until savings are again eliminated. Moreover, under these conditions equilibrium at a given level of output will be unstable unless $\dfrac{dM}{dr}$ or $\dfrac{\delta V}{\delta r}$ is sufficiently large. For the reduction in real output might induce a further reduction in interest, thus creating a further incentive to save, leading to a further reduction in income. Hence if the supply curve of savings (as a function of interest) is "backward-rising", a banking policy which aims to keep the rate of interest constant in the short run is much more conducive to stability than a policy which aims to keep the quantity of money constant.[2]

---

[1] It could be argued on *a priori* grounds that at the point of zero savings $\dfrac{\delta s}{\delta r}$ is necessarily positive since a supply curve cannot actually cut the *y* axis negatively inclined. This does not affect the argument in the more general case where investment is not zero but positive.

[2] This is only in apparent contradiction to Mr. Harrod's view (*The Trade Cycle*, p. 120) that fluctuations in the rate of interest are conducive to stability. Mr. Harrod is thinking in terms of the period of the investment-cycle; while our argument runs in terms of a short-run model where investment is assumed to be constant. Cf. below.

Thus in the "general case" (assuming $\frac{dM}{dr}$, $\frac{\delta S}{\delta x}$ and $\frac{\delta V}{\delta r}$ to be positive and finite) the effect of a general wage reduction on employment depends solely on the relation of savings to the rate of interest. A general and proposed reduction in money wages will increase, leave unchanged, or reduce unemployment, according as a rise in the rate of interest increases, leaves unchanged, or reduces savings.

5. So far we have assumed, in accordance with Professor Pigou's model, that investments are actually zero in short-period equilibrium. But it is easily shown that the argument is equally applicable to the more general case where investment is assumed to be constant and positive. In that case the critical rate of interest, for any given level of output, will be the one which secures a volume of savings equal to the volume of investments. The rest of the argument follows automatically.

6. In the "longer run",[1] when the rate of investment can vary, the situation is rather more complicated. Investment will be stimulated both by the reduction in interest and by the increase in real output. The effect on employment of a given reduction in money wages will certainly be enhanced by the reaction upon investment. It is sometimes argued[2] that even if the rate of interest does not change, a reduction in money wages increases the inducement to invest. Hence it is urged that even if the reduction in money wages involves some reduction in the money rate of interest, it leads to a greater increase in investment and real income than would be brought about by the same reduction in the rate of interest without any accompanying fall in money wages.

But this is not so. Both savings and investment depend on the rate of interest and on the level of real output, the only difference being that in the case of savings $\frac{\delta S}{\delta x}$ and $\frac{\delta S}{\delta r}$ can both be assumed positive, in the case of the investment function,

[1] I use the term "longer run," since the analysis that follows is still a short-period one in the Marshallian sense; it is not assumed that the period in question is long enough for a change in the existing stock of productive capacity. Professor Pigou introduces the investment factor in his last section (p. 421) on "long period effects"; but here he deals both with changes in the rate at which equipment is produced as well as with the true long period effects, *i.e.* changes in the stock of equipment. The two should be treated quite separately.

[2] Cf. Viner, *Quarterly Journal of Economics*, November 1936, p. 162. Also Pigou *loc. cit.*, p. 241.

$(I = \chi\{r, x\})$, $\dfrac{\delta I}{\delta x}$ is positive and $\dfrac{\delta I}{\delta r}$ is negative. Under our assumption that the stock of equipment is given, the distribution of income is a unique function of real income. Hence there is no way in which a change in money wages could affect either the savings function or the investment function. It cannot alter therefore the level of real output which secures equality between savings and investment at a given rate of interest. Hence if the rate of interest is given, the equilibrium level of employment is also given, irrespective of the level of money wages.[1]

It is possible that an increase in real income raises the demand for investment by more than it raises the supply of savings (*i.e.* $\dfrac{\delta S}{\delta x} > \dfrac{\delta I}{\delta x}$) in which case it will raise the equilibrium rate of

[1] This proposition could be best illustrated by the type of diagram used by Dr. Hicks (*Econometrica*, April 1937, p. 157). Measuring real output (or employment) along OX, and the rate of interest along OY the curve IS (determined by the I and S functions) shows the various levels of real output at which savings are equal to investment, at different rates of interest. The

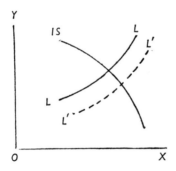

LL curve, depending on the M and V functions, shows the money rates of interest consistent with different levels of output. A reduction in money wages cannot affect the position of the IS curve, but it will shift the LL curve to the right; for, by reducing the size of "working balances" at a given level of real income, it enhances the size of "idle balances", and thus reduces the interest rate consistent with that level of output. Its effect therefore is exactly the same as that of an increase in the quantity of money or a reduction in liquidity preference. It is, in fact, nothing more than an alternative way of increasing the quantity of money in terms of wage-units (cf. Keynes, *General Theory*, p. 267). If the banking system pursues a policy aiming to keep the rate of interest constant, the LL curve will be horizontal and the effect on employment will be nil. If $\dfrac{dM}{dr}$ is large, the effect on employment of any reduction in wages can only be small.

A *general subsidy* on wages (financed by taxation), on the other hand, will alter the equilibrium-distribution of income at a given level of output (*i.e.* the distribution that obtains when prices are equal to marginal costs): it will therefore shift the IS curve to the right. It will operate on the "real factors" as well as on the "monetary factors."

interest.[1] Under these conditions a reduction in wages will lead to a rise in interest. But these are precisely the conditions under which an increase in the quantity of money or a reduction in liquidity preference will also lead to a rise in interest; where, in fact, a reduction in interest can only be secured temporarily, at the cost of a cumulative increase in the quantity of money. It will still be true that the effect of a wage-reduction on employment will depend upon its effect on the size of "idle balances"; and that the result on employment and on the rate of interest will be exactly the same as if the real value of these balances had been increased by the same amount in some other way.[2]

Thus Professor Pigou's view that a "money wage cut is not simply a piece of ritual that enables the real cause of employment expansion—a fall in the money rate of interest—to take effect" cannot be upheld. If the above analysis is correct, it is indeed such a piece of ritual; although, if we want to be quite accurate, the increase in the size of idle balances, rather than simply the fall in the money rate of interest, should be regarded as the ultimate cause of employment expansion.

---

[1] *I.e.* the *IS* curve of the diagram opposite, is upward sloping (cf. Hicks, *loc. cit.*, note 8). Equilibrium is only possible, in this case, if the *LL* curve is steeper than the *IS* curve. Under these assumptions a banking policy which aims to keep the rate of interest constant is not consistent with equilibrium.

[2] It will be true, furthermore, if we assume that the amount of money individuals want to hold at a given rate of interest varies in inverse proportion with the purchasing power of money, that a reduction in wages in a given proportion will have the *same* effect on employment as the same proportionate increase in the quantity of money maintained by the banking system at any given rate of interest.

SPECULATION AND ECONOMIC STABILITY[1]

1. THE purpose of the following paper is to examine, in the light of recent doctrines, the effects of speculation on economic stability. Speculation, for the purposes of this paper, may be defined as the purchase (or sale) of goods with a view to re-sale (re-purchase) at a later date, where the motive behind such action is the expectation of a change in the relevant prices relatively to the ruling price and not a gain accruing through their use, or any kind of transformation effected in them or their transfer between different markets. Thus, while merchants and other dealers do make purchases and sales which might be termed "speculative", their ordinary transactions do not fall within this category. What distinguishes speculative purchases and sales from other kinds of purchases and sales is the expectation of an impending change in the ruling market price as the sole motive of action. Hence "speculative stocks" of anything may be defined as the difference between the amount actually held and the amount that would be held if, other things being the same, the price of that thing were expected to remain unchanged; and they can be either positive or negative.[2]

2. The traditional theory of speculation viewed the economic function of speculation as the evening out of price-fluctuations due to changes in the conditions of demand or supply. It assumed that speculators are people of better than average foresight who step in as buyers whenever there is a temporary excess of supply over demand, and thereby moderate the price-fall; they step in as sellers, whenever there is a temporary deficiency of supply, and

---

[1] Reprinted from *The Review of Economic Studies*, October, 1939. It incorporates a revised version of § 4.

[2] The expectations of different individuals composing the market are normally different, of course. But it is permissible to speak of a single expectation for the market as a whole, since *cet. par.* there is always a definite amount of any good that would be held, at any particular expectation, if all individuals' expectations were the same.

thereby moderate the price-rise. By thus stabilising prices, or at any rate, moderating the range of price-fluctuations, they also automatically act in a way which leads to the transfer of goods from uses where they have a lower utility to uses where they yield a higher utility. (If future conditions of demand and supply were generally foreseen, this transfer would no doubt be effected without the agency of speculators. But in a world of perfect foresight nobody could make a speculative gain; speculators would be non-existent. In a world of imperfect foresight, the existence of speculators enables the system to behave with more foresight than the average individual in the system possesses.) Hence speculative gains are very much of the same order as other kinds of entrepreneurial gains; they are earned, similarly to the profits of wholesalers or retailers, as a result of the transference of goods from less important to more important uses.

The possibility that speculative activity might cause the range of price fluctuations to become greater rather than narrower, and that it might lead to the transfer of goods from more to less important uses, was not seriously contemplated in traditional theory. For this would imply that the speculators' foresight, instead of being better than the average, is worse than the average; such speculative activity would be attended by a loss, and not a gain; and such speculators would be speedily eliminated. Only the speculator with better than average foresight can hope to remain permanently in the market. And this implies that the effect of speculative activity must be price-stabilising, and in the above sense, wholly beneficial.

This argument, however, implies a state of affairs where speculative demand or supply amounts only to a small proportion of total demand or supply, so that speculative activity, while it can influence the magnitude of the price-change, cannot at any time change the direction of the price-change. If this condition is not satisfied, the argument breaks down. It still remains true that the speculator, in order to be permanently successful, must possess better than average foresight. But it will be quite sufficient for him to forecast correctly (or more correctly) the degree of foresight of other speculators, rather than the future course of the underlying non-speculative factors in the market.[1] If the proportion of speculative transactions in the total is large, it may become, in fact, more profitable for the individual speculator to concentrate on forecasting the psychology of other speculators, rather than the trend of the non-speculative elements. In such circumstances, even if speculation as a whole is attended by a net loss, rather than a net gain, this will not prove, even in the long-run, self-corrective. For the losses of a floating population of unsuccessful speculators will be sufficient to maintain permanently a small body of successful speculators; and the existence of this body of successful speculators will be a sufficient attraction to secure a permanent supply of this floating population. So long as the speculators differ in their own degree of foresight, and so long as they are numerous, they need not prove successful in forecasting events outside; they can live on each other.

But the traditional theory can also be criticised from another point of view. It ignored the effect of speculation on the general level of activity—or rather, it concentrated its attention on price-stability and assumed (implicitly perhaps, rather than explicitly) that if speculation can be shown to exert a stabilising influence upon price, it will *ipso facto* have a stabilising influence on activity. This, however, will only be true under certain special assumptions regarding monetary management which are certainly not fulfilled in the real world. In the absence of those assumptions, as will be shown below, speculation, in so far as it succeeds in eliminating price fluctuations will, in many cases, generate fluctuations in the level of incomes. Its stabilising influence on price will be accompanied by a destabilising influence on activity. Hence the question of the effect of speculation on price-stability and its effect on the stability of employment ought to be treated, not as part of the same problem, but as separate problems.

In the subsequent sections of this paper we shall deal first with the conditions under which speculation can take place, secondly, with the effect of speculation on price-stability, and finally, with the influence of speculation on economic stability in general.

---

[1] Cf. Keynes, *General Theory*, Chapter 12 on "Long Term Expectations". "We have reached the third degree [in the share markets] where we devote our intelligences to anticipating what average opinion expects average opinion to be." (p. 156.)

I. The Pre-requisites of Speculation

3. Not all economic goods are the objects of speculative activity; in fact the range of things in which speculation, on any significant scale, is possible is rather limited. The two main conditions which must be present in normal circumstances in order that a particular good or asset should be the object of speculation, is the existence of a *perfect, or semi-perfect, market* and *low carrying cost*. For if carrying costs are large, and/or the market is imperfect, and thus the difference between buying price and selling price is large, speculation becomes far too expensive to be undertaken—except perhaps sporadically, or under the stress of violent changes.[1]

The presence of these two conditions presupposes, on the other hand, a number of attributes which only a limited number of goods possess simultaneously. These attributes are: (1) The good must be fully standardised, or capable of full standardisation; (2) It must be an article of general demand; (3) It must be durable; (4) It must be valuable in proportion to bulk.

The first two conditions are indispensable for anything resembling a perfect market to develop in exchange.[2] The last two ensure low carrying cost. For the greater the durability the less is the wastage due to mere passage of time, the greater the value in proportion to bulk the less the cost of storage.

These last two factors make up what might be called carrying costs *proper*. But *net* carrying cost also depends on a third factor: the yield of goods. In normal circumstances, stocks of all goods possess a yield, measured in terms of themselves,[3] and this yield

[1] In conditions of hyper-inflation—as in Germany in 1923—the range of goods in which speculation takes place is, of course, very much extended.

[2] In particular the degree of standardisation required is very high. For the difference between the simultaneous buying price and selling price can only be small when there is a large and steady volume of transactions, in the same article, per unit of time, so that it pays individuals to undertake purchases and sales through the agency of an organised market. It is necessary for this that the commodity in question should have but few attributes of quality (that it should be simple) so that a specification of standard qualities ("grades") can be drawn up without difficulty. In the organised exchanges of the world this standardisation is carried so far that buyers rarely see the article they are actually buying—contracts are made between buyers and sellers with reference to standard grades and places of delivery. It is also necessary that the amount bought by the representative individual in a single transaction should represent considerable value. Nobody would go to the trouble of buying, say, cigarettes, through the agency of a central market, even if this would imply some saving.

[3] By defining yield as that return which goods obtain when measured in terms of themselves, we exclude here any return due to appreciation of value (in terms of some standard) whether expected or unexpected.

which is a compensation to the holder of stocks, must be deducted from carrying costs proper in calculating net carrying cost.[1] The latter can, therefore, be negative or positive.

From the point of view of yield, it is important to distinguish between two categories of goods: those which are used in production and those which are used up in production. (There is no convenient English equivalent for the German distinction between *Gebrauchsgüter* and *Verbrauchsgüter*, both of which can refer to durable goods.) Stocks of goods of the latter category also have a yield, *qua* stocks, by enabling the producer to lay hands on them the moment they are wanted, and thus saving the cost and trouble of ordering frequent deliveries, or of waiting for deliveries.[2] But the important difference is that with this latter category, the amount of stock which can be thus "useful" is, in given circumstances, strictly limited; their marginal yield falls sharply with an increase in stock above "requirements" and may rise very sharply with a reduction of stocks below "requirements".[3] When redundant stocks exist, the marginal yield is zero.[4] With the other category of goods, items of fixed capital, the yield declines much more slowly with an increase in stock, and it is normally always positive. Hence as we defined "speculative stocks" as the *excess* of stocks over normal requirements (i.e. that part of stocks which is only held in the expectation of a price-rise and would not be held otherwise) we may say that with working-capital-goods (*Verbrauchsgüter*) carrying costs are likely to be positive, when speculative stocks are positive, and negative when they are negative; with fixed-capital-goods (*Gebrauchsgüter*), carrying costs are normally negative, irrespective of whether "speculative stocks" are positive or negative.

[1] Our definition of net carrying cost is, therefore, the negative of Mr. Keynes' "own-rate of own-interest" in Chapter 17 of the *General Theory*—except that no allowance is made here for the factor termed "liquidity premium". Our reason for deducting the yield from the carrying cost, and not the other way round, is because (as will be clear below) from the point of view of speculation, net carrying cost is the significant concept rather than the own-rate of interest.

[2] There is, of course, in addition, the stock of goods in the course of production (goods in process) which depends on the length of the production process, but with this we are not here concerned (since they are not standardised).

[3] This, as we shall see below, is equally true of stocks of money, as of other commodities.

[4] Mr. Keynes, in the *Treatise on Money*, uses the term "working capital" for stocks which have a positive yield, and "liquid capital" for those which have a zero yield. (Vol. II, p. 130.)

It would follow from this that fixed-capital-goods like machines or buildings, whose carrying cost is negative and invariant with respect to the size of speculative stocks, ought to be much better objects of speculation than raw materials, whose carrying costs are so variable. The reason why they are not, is because the condition of high standardisation, necessary for a perfect market, is not satisfied, and hence the gap between buying price and selling price is large. It is not that machines, etc., by being used, become "second-hand", and thereby lose value, since the depreciation due to use is already allowed for in calculating their net yield. The reason is that all second-hand machines are to some extent de-standardised; it is very difficult to conceive a perfect market in such objects.[1, 2] The same lack of standardisation accounts for the comparative absence of speculation in land and buildings.

This explains, I think, why in the real world there are only two classes of assets which satisfy the conditions necessary for large-scale speculation. The first consists of certain raw materials, dealt in at organised produce exchanges. The second consists of standardised future claims or titles to property, i.e. bonds and shares. It is also obvious that the suitability of the second class for speculative purposes is much greater than that of the first. Bonds and shares are perfect objects for speculation; they possess all the necessary attributes to a maximum degree. They are perfectly standardised (one particular share of a company is just as good as any other); perfectly durable (if the paper they are written on goes bad it can be easily replaced); their value is very high in proportion to bulk (storage cost is zero or a nominal amount);

[1] I.e. the seller of a second-hand machine must not only allow for a reduction of value due to depreciation, but also an extra loss due to the fact that he is selling the machine and not buying it.

[2] Mr. Keynes, in certain parts of the *General Theory*, appears to use the term "liquidity" in a sense which comes very close to our concept of "perfect marketability"; i.e. goods which can be sold at any time for the same price, or nearly the same price, at which they can be bought. Yet it is obvious that the attribute of goods is not the same thing as what Mr. Keynes really wants to mean by "liquidity". Certain gilt-edged securities can be bought on the Stock Exchange at a price which is only a small fraction higher than the price at which they can be sold; on this definition, therefore, they should have to be regarded as highly liquid assets. In fact it is very difficult to find a satisfactory definition of what constitutes "liquidity"—a difficulty, I think, which is inherent in the concept itself. As will be argued below, what appears to be the result of a preference for "liquidity" may be explained as the consequence of certain speculative activities in which "liquidity preference" in any positive sense, plays a very small part.

and in addition they (normally) have a yield, which is invariant (in the short period at any rate) with respect to the size of speculative commitments. Hence their net carrying cost can never be positive, and in the majority of cases, is negative.

4.[1] If expectations were quite certain, speculative activity would so adjust the current price that the difference between expected price and current price would be equal to the sum of interest cost and carrying cost. For if the difference is greater than this, it would pay speculators to enlarge their commitments; in the converse case, to reduce them. The interest rate relevant in calculating the interest cost is always the short term rate of interest, since speculation is essentially a short period commitment.[2] The carrying cost, as mentioned above, is equal to the sum of storage cost and "primary depreciation",[3] minus the yield.

If expectations are uncertain, the difference between expected price and current price must cover, in addition, a certain risk premium, which will be the greater (1) the greater the dispersion of expectations from the mean (the less the standard probability); (2) the greater the size of commitments. Given the degree of uncertainty, marginal risk premium is an increasing function of the size of speculative stocks.

It will be useful to re-state the relationship between expected price and current price in algebraical form. We denote marginal interest cost by i, the marginal risk premium by r, the marginal yield by q, the marginal carrying cost proper by c (so that carrying cost $=c-q$); and the current price and expected price by CP and EP respectively. The following relationship must then be satisfied:

$$EP - CP = i + c - q + r$$

[1] [This section is a revised amalgam of § 4 as published in the original version of the article, *Review of Economic Studies*, 1939-40, pp. 5-7, and of my contribution to the Symposium, "A Note on the Theory of the Forward Market", *Review of Economic Studies*, 1939-40, pp. 196-201.]

[2] If there is a difference between the speculators' borrowing rate and their lending rate, one or the other will be relevant, according as the marginal unit of commitment is made with borrowed funds or not. Hence when speculators reduce their commitments, interest costs may fall, and this has (even if the market rate is unchanged) a similar effect as a fall in carrying cost (rise in yield).

[3] The term "primary depreciation" is Mr. Hawtrey's (*Capital and Employment*, p. 272), and is used to denote that part of depreciation which inevitably arises through the mere passage of time.

For certain problems in the theory of speculation, the concept of the "representative expectation" is perfectly legitimate; it enables us, as do other similar constructions, to simplify the problem without materially affecting the result. From the point of view of the theory of the forward market, however, it may not be legitimate; for the determination of the futures price, and in particular, the relation of the futures price to the expected price, will not be the same in the case where everybody's expectations are the same as in the case where the "representative expectation" is an average of divergent individual expectations. It will be convenient therefore to divide the analysis into two stages: in the first stage, to assume that all individuals have the *same* expectations at any one time, and to deal afterwards with the consequences of differences in individual expectations.

In both cases, individuals participating in the forward market can perform three different functions: "hedging", "speculation" and "arbitrage". "Hedgers" are those who have certain commitments independent of any transactions in the forward market, either because they hold stocks of the commodity, or are committed to produce the commodity, or are committed to produce, in the future, something else for which the commodity is required as a raw material; and who enter the forward market in order to reduce the risks arising out of these commitments. "Speculators", in general, have no commitments[1] apart from those entered into in connection with forward transactions; they assume risks by entering the market. Both hedgers and speculators can be, in particular circumstances, buyers or sellers of "futures",[2] but in both cases, it is the speculators who assume the risks and the hedgers who get rid of them.

The possibility of arbitrage, i.e. buying spot and selling futures simultaneously and holding the stock until the date of delivery,

---

[1] Ordinary stockholders and producers of the commodity may of course also indulge in speculation, in so far as they carry extra stocks in the expectation of a rise in price.

[2] I use the term "futures" here as equivalent to a forward purchase or sale; in other words, I assume that the commodity dealt in is completely standardised—as in the case of the foreign exchange market—and hence there is no difference in the obligations assumed in a spot contract or a futures contract. If there are differences then as Mr. Dow has shown, they can be introduced as an additional element causing some further deviation in the futures price from the spot price. Cf. J. C. R. Dow, "A Theoretical Account of Futures Markets", *Review of Economic Studies*, Vol. VII, 1939-40, pp. 185-95.

arises when the relationship between the futures price and the current price ensures a riskless profit. An arbitrage operation differs from an ordinary hedging operation only in that the ordinary hedger enters the futures market in order to reduce a risk arising out of a commitment which occurs independently of the existence of the forward market; whereas the arbitrageur assumes risks which he would not have assumed if the facilities of the forward market did not enable him to pass them on, on advantageous terms. Hence, any ordinary holder of stocks of a commodity becomes an "arbitrageur" in so far as the existence of the futures market tempts him not only to hedge the stocks he would ordinarily hold, but to enlarge his stocks in relation to turnover owing to the advantageous terms on which they can be "hedged".

The possibility of arbitrage sets an upper limit to the futures price in relation to the spot price. While there is no limit, apart from expectations, to backwardation, i.e. to the extent to which the futures price may fall short of the current price, there is a limit to contango, in that the futures price cannot exceed the current price by more than the cost of arbitrage, i.e. by more than the sum of interest plus carrying costs. Since, as explained above, ordinary holders of stock automatically become arbitrageurs whenever the relation between the futures price and the spot price tempts them to do so, the carrying cost consists of the costs of storage and wastage *minus the yield*, so that the net cost of arbitrage is $i + c - q$.[1] Denoting the futures price by FP, we have

$$FP - CP = i + c - q$$

and since, in all cases

$$EP - CP = i + c - q + r$$

it follows that

$$FP = EP - r$$

Thus, arbitrage prevents the futures price from rising above $EP - r$, while speculation (see below) prevents it from falling

[1] We must bear in mind however that the marginal convenience yield of stocks varies (in some cases fairly rapidly) with changes in the size of stocks in relation to turnover, so that even a moderate enlargement of stocks for arbitrage purposes might be sufficient to reduce q to zero.

below this amount. This conclusion is quite general,[1] and it is consistent with both contango and backwardation, i.e. with the futures price being either above or below the current price. When the yield is one of convenience, the marginal yield (q) varies inversely with the size of stocks in relation to turnover. When speculative stocks are zero, the expected price equals the current price (the stocks of ordinary holders are "normal"), and therefore $-(c-q)=i+r$, i.e. the negative of carrying cost must be equal to the sum of interest cost and risk premium. Since i and r are always positive, the carrying cost must be negative—the yield must exceed the sum of storage cost and primary depreciation by the required amount. In this case, $FP=CP-r$, and the futures price falls short of the current price by the amount Mr. Keynes called "normal backwardation".[2]

If stocks are sufficiently large in relation to turnover, q declines to zero, though it cannot become negative. It follows that, given an expectation of a rise in price, the upper limit to contango is $i+c$. In this case $FP-CP=i+c$, but as $q=0$, $EP-CP=i+c+r$; FP again equals $EP-r$. This upper limit to contango is likely to appear at times when the market is unduly depressed by the prevalence of excessive stocks in relation to current consumption; and when, as a result of this, the spot price has fallen to such low levels that there is a definite expectation in the market that the price will recover in the future, with the gradual absorption of excessive stocks. This is another way of saying that when the stocks carried are excessive in relation to turnover (so that q is zero), the current price must be below the expected price, since only the expectation of a rise in price can induce the market to carry the outstanding volume of stocks.

On the other hand, when stocks are scarce, the marginal yield is large so that abnormal backwardation must appear, i.e. $q>i+c+r$. In this case, the high marginal convenience yield

---

[1] [In the original article and again in the Symposium, *Review of Economic Studies*, 1939-40, I held that where the yield was one of convenience, arbitrageurs may not obtain it (since the convenience yield accrues only to those who hold stocks as part of their normal course of business), so that the upper limit to contango is $i+c$ even in cases where q is positive, and $FP=EP-r+q$. I ignored, however, the fact that when the futures price exceeds the current price by more than $i+c-q$, it will pay ordinary holders to enlarge their stocks and hedge by selling futures at the same time.]

[2] J. M. Keynes, *Treatise on Money*, Vol. II, pp. 142-4.

ensures that the spot price rises to abnormally high levels and, as a result, the market expects a fall in price in the future as stocks are restored to more normal levels. Just as it is impossible for the market to expect a rise in prices in the (foreseeable) future when stocks are scarce in relation to current consumption (since the spot price will have to rise sufficiently to eliminate any such expectation), so in the absence of an expectation of a change in price (i.e. when stocks are normal and the underlying factors are considered stable) there must always be backwardation.[1]

We have seen that arbitrage prevents the futures price from rising above $EP-r$. It remains to be shown that speculation prevents the futures price from falling below $EP-r$. Hedgers, in principle, could be either sellers or buyers of futures, though normally, hedging will be predominantly on the selling side.[2] Since transactions between hedgers who are sellers and hedgers who are buyers cancel out, it is the net sale of futures by hedgers (i.e. the excess of hedging on the selling side) which requires to be taken up by speculators. The hedgers will *sell* futures if the futures price is *equal to or higher than* $EP-r$; whilst speculators will *buy* futures if the futures price is *equal to or lower than* $EP-r$ (where r is

[1] The reason why this is not the case in the forward transactions of the Stock Exchange is due to the convention that the yield is credited to the forward buyer (from the date of the contract) and not to the forward seller who actually holds the stock. Hence the forward price is equal to the current price plus interest cost and there is contango (since in this case $c=0$, $FP=EP-r+q=CP+i$). Backwardation can only arise on the Stock Exchange if a fall in price is expected, and this expected fall, on account of a shortage of stock for immediate delivery which is known to be purely temporary, cannot be adequately reflected in the current price (e.g. in the case of trans-Atlantic stocks, when arbitrageurs run out of stock and have to wait for fresh supplies to be sent across the Atlantic). It is always a sign, therefore, of the current price not being in equilibrium in relation to the expected price.

[2] This is because the risk normally hedged against is the risk of a fall in the prices of the commodities actually carried by the manufacturer or trader, i.e. the risk of an inventory loss. The opposite risk of a future rise in the prices of the materials which the manufacturer uses, with its attendant possibility of a lower profit on fabrication (or at least the sacrifice of the inventory profit he would have made if he had bought earlier) is not normally compensated by buying futures, simply because manufacturers are less afraid of making losses on account of rising raw material prices than on account of falling prices (since in times of rising raw material prices the increase in cost can normally be passed on to the buyer). A failure to make a profit on account of the failure to make an investment is not considered as contributing the same kind of "risk" as that of a loss on the capital actually invested. In exceptional cases, however, e.g. where the manufacturer works on long-term contracts, and does not expect to be able to pass on the higher prices of materials by raising his selling price, or where the futures price is abnormally low in relation to the spot price (due to temporary shortages of stock), manufacturers may well allow their stocks to be run down below normal levels, and compensate for the risks arising therefrom by becoming buyers in the futures market.

the individual marginal risk premium in both cases).[1] If every-body's expectations are the same, futures transactions between hedgers and speculators can only arise owing to differences in the marginal risk premium, i.e. in the marginal willingness to bear risks among the different individuals in the two groups, and would proceed until these differences are eliminated. Since the marginal risk premium varies, not only with individual psychological propensities to bear risks, but also with the size of commitments, i.e. with the amount of the possible loss relatively to the individual's total assets, we need not assume any variation in psychological propensities in order to account for such differences. When hedgers are predominantly sellers of futures, the buying of futures by speculators therefore prevents the futures price from falling below $EP-r$, whilst arbitrage, as we have seen, prevents it from rising above this level.

The above theory of "normal backwardation" (according to which the futures price must be below the spot price when stocks in relation to turnover are normal, while contango can only develop in times of excess stocks and abnormally low spot prices) is subject however to an important qualification when we allow for the fact that the expectations of different individuals comprising the market are not uniform.[2] Transactions will now take place not only between hedgers and hedgers, between hedgers and specula-tors, and hedgers and arbitrageurs, but also between speculators and speculators; and transactions of the latter type may swamp all others. We now have to divide speculators into two groups: bulls and bears. Bull speculators will be *buyers of futures*, and their demand price is $EP-r$ (where both EP and r are subjective terms and refer to the mean value of the individual speculator's expecta-tion, and his individual risk premium, respectively); bear specu-lators will be *sellers of futures* and their supply price is $EP+r$.

[1] If hedgers are buyers of futures on balance, they will buy futures if FP is equal to or lower than $EP+r$; whilst the speculators will sell futures if FP is equal to or higher than $EP+r$. However, with uniform expectations, this will not establish the futures price at $EP+r$ on account of the fact that it will be the arbitrageurs and not the speculators who provide the supply of futures to match the excess hedging on the buying side. Arbitrage, as we have seen, will always bring the futures prices to $CP+i+c-q$ which, on the assumption of unanimous expectations, equals $EP-r$. Speculation on the selling side can only appear as a result of differences in expecta-tions.

[2] [I am indebted to Mr. R. G. Hawtrey's criticism of the original version of this paper for the conclusions that follow.]

It should be clear at once that if by "expected price" we mean not the expectations either of bulls or of bears, but some kind of average expectation for the market as a whole, the price which will tend to get established as the outcome of transactions between bulls and bears is neither $EP+r$, nor $EP-r$, but something in between the two. We cannot say that the futures price will *correspond* to this average "expected price"; this would only be true if the marginal risk premia of different speculators were equal; and when the expectations themselves are different, there is no reason to assume that the marginal risk premia will be the same. But it is clear that the opposite risks assumed by bulls and bears will tend to cancel each other out—leaving the futures price if not equal to, at any rate fairly near, the "expected" price.[1] In a market where bulls predominate, the futures price will tend to exceed the "expected" price and vice versa, when bears predominate. Hedging on the selling side and arbitrage will act in the same fashion as a strengthening of bearish sentiment, while hedging on the buying side will act in the same fashion as a strengthening of bullish sentiment.

Thus, in addition to the factors mentioned above, the determination of the futures price will also depend, in the real world, on *divergence of opinion*; this factor will be all the more important the greater the degree of divergence and the more equally bulls and bears are divided. In markets where this divergence is important, and where transactions between speculators dominate over hedging transactions, we cannot say that the futures price will either be above, or below, the expected price, but simply that it will reflect the "expected" price; always subject, of course, to the provision that it cannot exceed the current price by more than the cost of arbitrage.

[1] The more favourable relationship between the futures price and the expected price resulting from this will mean however that the market will carry larger stocks than it would have carried otherwise. For, as we have seen, when expectations are uniform and the expected price is the same as the current price, the futures price will necessarily be *below* the current price. In a market where the bullish sentiment expecting a rise in price and the bearish sentiment expecting a fall are equally strong, the futures price may well establish itself in the neighbourhood of the current price, as being the only price capable of bringing speculative supply and demand into equilibrium. In that case, however, ordinary traders will enlarge their stocks in connection with arbitrage operations until the marginal convenience yield falls sufficiently to eliminate the profitability of such operations. This action by arbitrageurs may not depress the futures price significantly, when the speculative demand and supply is large in relation to the non-speculative demand for holding stocks.

5. The elasticity of speculative stocks may be defined as the proportionate change in the amount of speculative stocks held as a result of a given percentage change in the *ratio* of the expected price to the current price.[1] This elasticity will obviously depend on the variations in the terms i, c and r, which are associated with a change in speculative stocks, in other words on the elasticity of marginal interest cost, marginal carrying cost, and the marginal risk premium, with respect to a change in speculative commitments.

Of these three factors the marginal interest cost, as we have seen, may be subject to discontinuous variation if the "marginal speculator", in a particular market turns from a lender of money into a borrower, or vice versa, but apart from this its elasticity is likely to be fairly high, if not infinite.[2] The marginal risk premium is normally rising, and its elasticity probably differs greatly between different markets. The more numerous are speculators in a particular market, and the more steady the price on the basis of past experience[3] the higher this elasticity is likely to be. Finally, the marginal carrying cost, as we have seen, can be assumed to be constant in the case of securities, while it will rise sharply (at any rate over a certain range) in the case of raw materials and primary products. Hence, taking all factors together, the elasticity of speculative stocks is likely to be much higher in the case of long-term securities than in the case of raw materials.

The higher the elasticity of speculative stocks, the greater the dependence of the current price on the expected price. In the limiting case when this elasticity is infinite, the current price may be said to be entirely determined by the expected price; changes in the conditions of non-speculative demand or supply can then

---

[1] [In the original version this elasticity was defined with reference to the percentage change in the *difference EP—CP*. It was pointed out by E. Rothbarth in 1942 and recently by Mr. Streeten that to be consistent with the formula on p. 33, the elasticity should be defined in terms of the *ratio* of the two prices. The latter definition is correct in cases where the items $(i+c+r-q)$ are proportional to CP, whilst the former definition is appropriate when $(i+c+r-q)$ is fixed in money terms and hence varies, as a percentage, with a change in CP. The correct formula corresponding to the former definition is that given by Streeten in equation (3*a*). (*Review of Economic Studies*, October, 1958, p. 67.)]

[2] In certain markets the lending rate only is normally relevant, and not the borrowing rate. In this case the elasticity of interest cost can be taken as infinite.

[3] In other words, the elasticity of the marginal risk premium is likely to vary inversely with the amount of the risk premium. When the risk premium is low, its elasticity is also likely to be high. Cf. § 10, below.

have no direct influence on the current price at all (since speculative stocks will immediately be so adjusted as to leave the price unchanged); any change in the current price must be the result of a change in price-expectations.[1]

In the opposite limiting case, when the elasticity of speculative stocks is zero, changes in the expected price have no influence upon the current price; the latter is entirely determined by the non-speculative factors.

II. Speculation and Price Stability

6. We can now attempt to analyse the question of the effect of speculation on price-stability. We have seen in § 2 that the argument that speculation *must* exert its influence in a price-stabilising direction in order to be successful presupposes that speculative purchases (or sales) make up only a small fraction of total transactions, and does not hold otherwise. But this still leaves the question of whether the effect of speculation is price stabilising or destabilising open.

We have seen that in all circumstances speculation must have the effect of narrowing the range of fluctuations of the current price *relatively to the expected price*. Hence, if the expected price is taken as given, speculation must necessarily exert a stabilising influence: a rise in the current price will be followed by a fall in speculative stocks, and vice versa.

In order that speculation should be price destabilising, therefore, we must assume one of two things: either (*a*) that changes in the current price lead to a change in the expected price by *more* (in proportion) than the current price has changed; or (*b*) that there are spontaneous changes in the expected price which are speculative in origin and are not justified or not fully justified in the movement of non-speculative factors.

The second of these needs further elucidation. It may be that an impending change in data is foreseen by speculators, but exaggerated in importance and, therefore, creates price movements greater than those which would have occurred in the

---

[1] This does not imply, of course, that the current price must be *equal* to the expected price; this would only be the case if in addition, the sum of $i+c-q+r$ were zero. Nor does it imply that changes in the non-speculative factors can have no influence upon price at all, for changes in these factors may influence price-expectations.

absence of speculation. E.g. a good harvest which, in the absence of speculative activity would have caused a 10% reduction in price, will involve a price movement which is both smoother and smaller in extent, if it is correctly foreseen by speculators. But if speculators foresee a 50% price reduction, in consequence of the expected harvest, the resultant price oscillation will be much greater than if they had not foreseen it at all. It may be also that the speculators expect that a certain event will react, favourably or unfavourably, upon a particular price, though in the absence of the expectation no such reaction would have occurred at all. The day-to-day movements on the Stock Exchange, where considerable changes in prices occur in accordance with the day's political news, could hardly be accounted for on any other ground but on the attempt of speculators to forecast the psychology of other speculators. If one is selling this is because he thinks the other would do likewise. If speculators combined and formed a monopoly, these price-movements could not take place at all.

The first of these factors—i.e. the reaction of expectations to *changes* in the current price—may be measured by Professor Hicks' concept of the "elasticity of expectations".[1] This elasticity is defined as unity when a change in the current price causes an equi-proportionate change in the expected price. Hence, if the elasticity of expectations is positive, but less than unity, speculation will still have a stabilising influence, though, of course, a weaker one than if the elasticity is zero. The case of unit elasticity of expectations is, as Professor Hicks has said, on the borderline between stability and instability.

Thus the elasticity of expectations and the elasticity of speculative stocks *together* determine what may be termed "the degree of price-stabilising influence of speculation": the extent to which price-variations, due to outside causes, are eliminated by speculation. This may be measured by the proportionate change in stocks in response to a given change in the *current* price, since the larger this change, the smaller the extent to which any given change in outside factors (a shift in demand or supply) can affect the price. If we denote the degree of price-stabilising influence by σ, the elasticity of speculative stocks (as above defined) by e,

---

[1] *Value and Capital*, p. 205.

and the elasticity of expectations by η, their relation is as follows:

$$\sigma = -e\,(\eta - 1)$$

Since e cannot be negative, the expression is negative or positive according as η is greater or less than 1.

7. It is not possible, however, to express the behaviour of expectations at any given moment in terms of a single elasticity. For what this elasticity will be, on a particular day, will depend on the magnitude of the price-change on that day, the price-history of previous days, and on whether the price expectation refers to next day, next month, or next year. This elasticity is thus likely to be both large and small, at the same time, according as the price-change has been large or small, and according as the expectation refers to the near future or the more distant future. It will vary, moreover, with the *cause* of the price-change. For it is permissible to assume that in most markets, speculators regard price-changes merely as indicators of certain forces at work, and that they attempt to form some idea as to the nature of these forces before adjusting their expectations. A given change in price will react differently on speculators' expectations according as they regard it as the result of speculative forces, or of "outside" demand or "outside" supply and so on.

If any generalisation can be made it is that expectations are likely to be less elastic as regards the more distant future than as regards the near future, and as regards larger changes in price than as regards smaller changes. These two factors moreover are not independent of each other. For the expectations as regards the more distant future are likely to be more and more influenced by the speculators' idea as to the "normal price"—this "normal price" is determined by different factors in different markets, but as we shall see below, it is likely to function in most—and *the larger the deviation of the current price from the normal, the longer must the period be which speculators expect to elapse before the price reverts to normality.* Beyond a certain point, therefore (whether the word "point" is understood to be a distance of time in the future or a magnitude of price-change), expectations become insensitive; the elasticity of expectations becomes zero or may even become negative.

Speculation, therefore, is much more likely to operate in a de-stabilising direction when we consider price-fluctuations within smaller ranges, than larger ranges; and when we consider the movements over a shorter period, than over a longer period. This is so not only because it is the short-period expectations which are most *elastic* (show the strongest reaction to price-changes), but also because it is these short-period expectations which are most *flexible* (are most liable to spontaneous changes). Those changes in expectations which are caused by the speculators' own attempts to anticipate each other's reactions, and thus set up purely spurious price-movements, are essentially short-period expectations; and they are responsible for short-period movements.

Hence to our question: does speculation exert a price-stabilising influence, or the opposite? the most likely answer is that it is neither, or rather that it is both simultaneously. It is probable that in every market there is a certain range of price-oscillation *within which* speculation works in a destabilising direction while *outside* that range it has a stabilising effect. Where markets differ, is in the magnitude of this critical range of price-oscillation. In some markets (among which the market for long-term bonds is conspicuous) this range is in normal circumstances relatively small, the stabilising forces of speculation dominate over the others. In other cases (and here one may count perhaps the markets for certain classes of ordinary shares) the range is large and the stabilising forces are relatively weak. The explanation of these differences lies in the varying degree of influence exerted by the idea of the "normal price" in the different markets. It is to this factor that we must now turn.[1]

8. In the case of many commodities, and in particular, non-agricultural raw materials, the elasticity of supply is rather high if the period of adjustment is allowed for, though supply is inelastic for periods shorter than this period of adjustment.[2] The upper limit of the expected price, for periods longer than this

---

[1] The following owes much to Hicks, *Value and Capital*, pp. 270-2.

[2] This period of adjustment varies, I believe, for different commodities from six months to anything up to two years, though it is likely to be between six and twelve months in the majority of cases. The case of rubber and tin, where the period is several years, is exceptional. But in these last two cases, the short-period elasticity (through more or less intensive "tapping" or "plucking") is considerable.

period of adjustment, is given by this supply price. The stability, therefore, depends on the general belief that the normal supply price in the future will not be very different from the normal supply price of the past; it is ultimately a belief in the stability of money wages.[1] It is in this way that the rigidity of money wages contributes to the stability of the economic system, by inducing the forces of speculation to operate in a much more stabilising fashion than they would do if money wages were flexible.

If the current price is in excess of the normal supply price, the future date at which the price is expected to return to the normal is given by the period of adjustment. If the current price is below the normal supply price, the date at which the price is expected to return to the normal is determined by the speculators' expectations as to the period of absorption of excessive stocks. Hence in markets where the belief in the existence of a normal supply price is strong, and where speculators are in a position to form a reasonable opinion as to the size of redundant stocks, we should expect speculation to work mainly in a stabilising direction.

Such is the case with the main industrial raw materials; and yet we find that here price-fluctuations are more violent than in most other markets.[2] The explanation for this, however, lies in the sudden changes to which the yield of stocks of such raw materials is liable, combined with the low elasticity of speculative stocks. Traders' requirements of such stocks, as stated before, are a fairly fixed proportion of the expected turnover; and a relatively slight reduction in the expected turnover is sufficient to bring their marginal yield down to zero. But this necessitates a very sharp reduction in the current price, since net carrying costs, which were negative before, have now become positive. Assuming that previously the price was equal to the normal supply price, so that the forward price fell short of the current price by the amount of the "normal backwardation", the price must fall far enough for the backwardation to turn into a contango, sufficient

---

[1] For it is the level of money wages which governs money supply prices if the elasticity of supply is high.

[2] Mr. Keynes stated in the *Economic Journal*, September, 1938, p. 451, that the difference between the highest and lowest price, in the same year, in the case of rubber, cotton, wheat and lead amounted in the average to 67% over the last ten years.

to cover interest plus carrying costs. If the "normal backwardation" (i.e. the marginal risk premium) was equal to 10% per
annum[1] and the interest cost plus carrying cost (when the yield is
zero) is also equal to 10% per annum, the current price must fall
by 20% if the excess stocks are expected to be absorbed in one
year, and 40% if they are expected to be absorbed in two years.[2]
In the converse case, where owing to a rise in turnover, stocks fall
below the normal proportion, there might be an equally sharp
rise in price due to the rapid rise in the yield of stocks. According
to Mr. Keynes[3] it is easy to quote cases where the backwardation
amounted to 30% per annum; and this implies that the marginal
yield of stocks must have risen to 40%. Hence the explanation
for the wide fluctuations in raw material prices need not be sought
in any inelasticity of supply (except, of course, in the short
period), or in the destabilising influence of speculative activities,
but simply in instability of demand and the low elasticity of
speculative stocks.

9. In the case of agricultural crops, the supply curve is much
less elastic and is subject to frequent and unpredictable shifts, due
to the weather. It is impossible to foretell the size of the crop a
year ahead, and it is not possible to say when prices will revert to
normal. Hence, in this case, the effect of speculation on price-
stability is much more doubtful. If, nevertheless, the recorded
range of price-fluctuations is no greater than in the case of
industrial raw materials, the explanation might be sought in the
fact, as an article in *The Economist* recently suggested,[4] that these
goods are mostly foodstuffs the demand for which is much more
stable than the demand for raw materials.[5] The fluctuations in
the size of stocks are caused by changes in the supply side; and
since the Southern Hemisphere became an important source of
supply, the extent of the annual fluctuation in world output is
much less considerable. It would probably be found, however,

---

[1] In markets where the range of price-fluctuations is large, the marginal risk premium is also likely to be large, thus making the range of fluctuations still larger.
10% is a "normal" figure in the case of seasonal crops; 1 to 2% may be regarded as
the appropriate figure in the case of long-term government bonds.

[2] Keynes, *Treatise on Money*, Vol. II, p. 144.   [3] *Ibid*, p. 143.

[4] *The Economist*, August 19th, 1939, p. 350.

[5] Industrial crops, such as cotton, have shown in the past more violent price-
fluctuation than either foodstuffs or industrial raw materials.

that in the case of agricultural crops the *same* percentage changes in stocks are associated with greater variations of prices than in the case of industrial raw materials (not because the elasticity of speculative stocks is less, but the elasticity of expectations is probably greater).

10. In the market for securities (bonds and shares) there is no such "external" determinant of normal price as the producers' supply price in the case of commodities. Yet in the market for long-term bonds the notion of a "normal price" operates very strongly; only thus can the remarkable stability of the long-term rate, relatively to the short-term rate, be explained. Since the elasticity of speculative stocks, in this case, is very large, the current price is largely determined by the expected price; if the current price is stable, this must be because the expected price is insensitive to short-period variations of the current price. But how is this expected price determined?

The simplest explanation which suggests itself is that the expected price is determined by some average of past prices. The longer the period in the past which enters into the calculation of this average, the less sensitive is the expected price to movements in the current price.

This hypothesis, however, taken by itself, is not very satisfactory. In the first place, as Professor Robertson has pointed out, it appears to leave the long-term rate of interest "hanging by its own bootstraps". If the current price of consols is determined by the expected price, and the expected price by an average of past prices, how were these past prices determined? How did the rate of interest come to settle at one particular level rather than at some other level? In the second place, why should expectations be so inelastic in the long-term bond market in particular? The fact that the price of many industrial shares moves fairly closely with fluctuations in current earnings, does not suggest that this is a characteristic attribute of security markets in general.

These difficulties can be resolved, however, if account is taken of the dependence of the current long-term rate on the expected future short-term rates. A loan for a particular duration, say for two years, can be regarded, as Professor Hicks has shown,[1] as

---

[1] *Value and Capital*, pp. 144-5. Cf. also Pigou, *Industrial Fluctuations*, pp. 230-2.

being made up of a "spot" short-term loan (say for three months) *plus* a series of "forward" short-term loans; a short-term loan renewed so many times, and contracted forward. Hence the existence of a long-term loan market *implies* the existence of a series of forward markets in short-term loans. And since the forward price of anything, if uncertainty is present, must be below the expected price, this implies that the current rate of interest on loans of any particular duration, must be above the average of expected future short-term rates, over the same period.

This explains why the yield of bonds with a currency of, say, twenty years or over is so stable. For it depends on the expected average of short-term rates over the next twenty years and we need not suppose that the elasticity of expectations with respect to the short-term rate is small in order that this average should be stable. E.g. if the current short-term rate is half the "normal rate", and is expected to remain in operation for as long as five years, this will only reduce the average over the next twenty years by one-eighth. Thus the explanation is not that interest-expectations are particularly inelastic; the expectations regarding the short-term rate would need to be extremely elastic in order that the expected long-term rate should be responsive to changes in the current rate.[1]

This also answers the objection that the expectation-theory leaves the structure of interest rates, current and expected, hanging in the air by its own bootstraps. For while the current long rate depends on the expected short rates, the current short rate is *not* dependent either on the expected short rates or the expected

---

[1] We can regard the current long-term rate as being determined either by the expected future long-term rate, or the average of expected future short-term rates. The two come to the same thing since the expected long-term rate also depends on the average of short rates.

If R_1 is the current yield of a bond repayable in ten years' time and R_2 is its expected yield next year, r_1 is the short-term rate this year, r_2 . . . etc., are the "forward" short-term rates in subsequent years (i.e. the expected short-term rates plus the risk premium), their relation is given by the following equations:

$$(1+R_1)^{10} = (1+r_1)\,(1+r_2)\; . \; . \; . \; (1+r_{10})$$
$$(1+R_2)^9 = (1+r_2)\,(1+r_3)\; . \; . \; . \; (1+r_{10})$$

Hence,

$$(1+R_2)^9 = \frac{(1+R_1)^{10}}{1+r_1}$$

Thus the expected long-term rate will exceed the current long-term rate if the current short-term rate is below its expected average, and vice versa. (Cf. Hicks, *op. cit.*, p. 152; also Hicks, "Mr. Hawtrey on Bank Rate and the Long-Term Rate of Interest", *Manchester School*, 1939.)

long rate.[1] The latter is not dependent on expectations at all (or only to a very minor extent) but only on the current demand for cash balances (for transaction purposes) and the current supply. And since the elasticity of supply of cash with respect to the short-term rate is normally much larger than the elasticity of demand, the current short-term rate can be treated simply as a datum, determined by the policy of the central bank.[2]

[1] The current short rate is not dependent on the expected *short rates*, simply because the life-time of short-term bills is much too short for expectations to have much influence. The expected rate on bills next year can have no influence in determining the rate on a three-months' bill to-day; while the expected rates for the next three months are very largely determined by the current rate. It is only in exceptional circumstances that the market expects a definite change in the short-term discount rates within the next few months. It is just because the elasticity of expectations for very short periods is generally so near to unity, that the short-term interest market is largely non-speculative.

Similarly, a change in the long-term rate (either the current or the expected rate) cannot react back on the short-term rate except perhaps indirectly by causing a change in the level of income and, hence, in the demand for cash. For, supposing the change in the long rate causes speculators to sell long-term investments, this could only affect the short rate if they substituted the holding of cash for the holding of long-term bonds; it cannot affect the short rate if the substitution takes place in favour of short-term investments other than cash (savings deposits, etc.). But there is no reason to expect, in normal circumstances at any rate, that the substitution will be in favour of cash. "Idle balances"—i.e. that part of short-term holdings which the owner does not require for transaction purposes—can be kept in forms such as savings deposits, which offer the same advantages as cash (as far as the preservation of capital value is concerned) and yield a return in addition. It is only when the short rate is so low that investment in savings deposits is no longer considered worth while (see footnote below) that there can be a *net* substitution in favour of cash; but precisely in those circumstances the elasticity of substitution between cash and savings deposits is likely to be so high that this cannot have any appreciable effect on the short-term rate.

Thus, while the current short rate does determine the relation between the current long rate and the expected long rate, this is not true the other way round.

[2] The nature of the equilibrium in the short-term interest market is shown in the accompanying diagram, where the quantity of cash is measured along Ox, the short-term interest rate along Oy. DD and SS stand for the demand and supply of money, respectively. The demand curve is drawn on the assumption that the volume of money transactions (i.e. the level of income) is given. This demand curve is inelastic, since the marginal yield of money declines fairly rapidly with an increase in the proportion of the stock to turnover. Below a certain point (g) the demand curve becomes elastic, however, since the holding of short-term assets other than money is always connected with some risk (and, perhaps, inconvenience), and individuals will not invest short term if the short-term rate is lower than the necessary compensation for this.

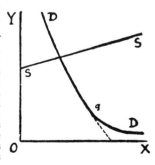

There is a certain minimum, therefore, below which the short-term rate cannot fall, though this minimum might be very low. (The dotted line shows what the demand curve would be if this risk were entirely absent.) Hence, when the short-term rate is very low, it can be said to be determined by the risk premium attaching to the holding

How is this related to Mr. Keynes' theory of the long-term rate of interest being determined by liquidity-preference? It leads to much the same result (i.e. that the rate, in the short period, is *not* determined by savings and investment), but the route by which it is reached is rather different. The insensitiveness of the long-term rate to "outside" influences (i.e. the supply and demand for "savings") is not due to any "liquidity premium" attached to money or short-term bills; in fact, the notion of a "liquidity premium" appears entirely absent. It may be objected that it is merely *replaced* by the notion of a marginal risk premium, and that Mr. Keynes' "liquidity premium" on the holding of short-term assets is merely the *negative* of our marginal risk premium on the holding of long-term bonds. But in this case, the peculiar behaviour of the long-term interest rate is certainly not explained by the existence of this risk-premium.[1] For let us suppose that subjective expectations are quite certain, so that this risk premium is completely absent. In this case the current long-term rate, instead of being above the average of expected short-term rates, will be equal to that average. But "the elasticity of demand for idle balances with respect to the long-term interest rate", in the sense in which Mr. Keynes employs this concept, would certainly not be removed thereby; on the contrary, it would be rendered infinite. For in the absence of uncertainty, when the marginal risk premium is zero, the elasticity of speculative stocks in the bond market would be infinite (since the other factors determining the elasticity of speculative stocks, i.e. interest costs and carrying costs, are, in this case, also infinitely elastic). The current price of bonds would be entirely governed by the expected price; if we assume the expectations concerning future interest rates as given,

---

of the safest short-term asset; otherwise it is determined by the supply-price of money (i.e. banking policy) and changes in the short-term rate are best regarded as due to shifts in this supply price. (The elasticity of the supply of money in a modern banking system is ensured partly by the open market operations of the central bank, partly by the commercial banks not holding to a strict reserve ratio in the face of fluctuation in the demand for loans, and partly it is a consequence of the fact that under present banking practices a switch-over from current deposits to savings deposits automatically reduces the amount of deposit money in existence, and vice versa.)

[1] Moreover, the long-term rate is never *equal* to this risk premium (or liquidity premium); this only accounts for the difference between the long-term rate and the expected average of short-term rates. Professor Hicks has calculated this risk premium to have been about 1% in Great Britain before the last war, and 2% after the war (*Manchester School*, Vol. X, No. 1, p. 31).

the current long-term rate would be uniquely determined.[1] Changes in the rate of savings or in the marginal efficiency of capital could not affect the long-term rate at all, except through the slow and dubious channel of changing the level of incomes, and, hence, the demand for cash; this reacting on the short-term rate of interest, and this, in turn, gradually affecting the interest expectations for the future.

It is therefore not so much the *uncertainty* concerning future interest rates as the *inelasticity* of interest expectations which is responsible for Mr. Keynes' "liquidity preference function", i.e. which causes the demand for short-term funds to be elastic with respect to the long-term rate.[2] The uncertainty of expectations works rather in the opposite direction. For when uncertainty is high not only is the amount of the marginal risk premium high, but the elasticity of the marginal risk premium curve (and hence the elasticity of speculative stocks) is low; speculators are much less willing to extend their commitments or to reduce them. It is in such periods that variations in the "outside" demand or supply can be expected to have the most marked effect on bond prices.[3]

Nor is it quite accurate to represent the forces determining the long-term rate as the demand for liquid funds (money + bills) *vis-à-vis* the supply of such funds. We have seen that the proposition that "the rate of interest is the agency which equates the supply and demand for money" is true if under "rate of interest" is meant the short rate of interest, and under "money" the sum total of things which mainly serve as a means of payment (i.e. bank notes and current deposits).[4] But in the case of the long-term

---

[1] To assume that subjective expectations are *certain* is not the same thing, of course, as assuming "perfect foresight" or assuming that the expected prices are the *same* as current prices. Suppose e.g. that, despite the current short-term rate being 2%, speculators are absolutely certain that a year hence, and for ever afterwards, the rate will be 4%. The existence of this expectation will not cause any change in the current short-term rate; but it will invariably fix the level of the current long-term rate at 3·92%.

[2] Mr. Keynes appears to be aware of this, when he speaks of the influence of the notion of the "safe rate" of interest in determining the current rate. (*General Theory*, p. 201.) But in the general statement on the liquidity preference function he relies on the factor of uncertainty of which money is free and, hence, commands a "premium".

[3] It is well known that in periods of great political uncertainty it becomes impossible either to buy or to sell gilt-edged in large amounts without thereby directly affecting the price.

[4] The proposition is true, partly because both the demand and the supply of money vary with the rate of interest and also because any factor influencing the short-term rate can do so only by affecting the demand or the supply of cash. As mentioned

rate, we are not really confronted with a demand curve for liquid funds but with a supply curve of long-term assets by speculators;[1] and the two methods of representation do not always yield the same conclusions. It is not clear, for example, why an increase in the aggregate amount of liquid funds should have any direct effect on the speculators' willingness to hold long-term assets, other than through the change in the short-term rate. An increase in the supply of money will directly reduce the short-term rate (unless it is already so low that it cannot fall further); this will have a minor effect on the long-term rate (for the current price of bonds will now be higher relatively to the expected price); a major effect will only come about slowly as expectations are affected.[2]

To sum up. In the market for long-term bonds, the elasticity of expectations is normally small, and the elasticity of speculative stocks is large, both absolutely and relatively to the elasticity of the non-speculative demand and supply (i.e. the elasticity of supply of savings, and the elasticity of the producers' demand for long-term funds, as a function of the rate of interest). Hence the price in the short period is largely determined by speculative influences. It would not be correct to say that these outside factors have *no*

before, emphasis should be placed on the elasticity of the supply of money (with respect to the short-term rate) rather than on the elasticity of demand. The latter, except when the rate is very low, is relatively small: which is shown by the fact that the short-term rate can be varied within fairly wide limits without these changes being associated with equally significant variations in the quantity of money in existence or in the level of incomes.

[1] If the price of bonds is regarded as determined by the supply and demand for liquid funds, the price of any other thing which is subject to the price stabilising influence of speculation could be equally regarded as such. In all these cases it is the speculators' willingness to undertake commitments in a particular direction, and not their preference for avoiding commitments in general (i.e. their preference for "liquidity") which is relevant.

The "liquidity premium" on money and savings deposits, etc., in the sense in which Mr. Keynes employs this concept, may be regarded as 2% per annum if the market for consols is chosen as the standard with reference to which this liquidity premium is measured. But it will be 10% per annum if, say, the market for wheat is chosen as a standard, and something else again if the tin market is chosen. But is there any particular reason for selecting the gilt-edged market as the standard?

[2] It might be argued that an increase in the proportion of short-term assets in the total of assets will reduce the marginal risk premium on long-term assets and, hence, lower their yield. But it is doubtful whether this effect could be appreciable, unless the change in this proportion is large; and since short-term assets amount in any case only to a small proportion of total wealth, a *large* change in their amount can only cause a *small* change in this proportion. In the case of banks and other financial institutions, however, which keep a *large* proportion of their assets on short term, the effect may be considerable.

influence upon price;[1] only that this influence is largely over-shadowed by speculative forces. And for reasons given in the next section, the inability of these forces to influence the price in the short period will much weaken their price-determining influence in the long period as well.[2]

11. There remains to examine the situation in the market for shares; and after what has been said above, it should not be difficult to account for the apparent contrast between the stability in the gilt-edged market and the instability of the share market. Shares are also subject to the same influences as bond prices; changes in the expectations regarding future interest rates should affect the one just as much as the other. But in addition they are also subject to changes in the expectations concerning the expected level of profits. And here experience suggests that the elasticity of expectations concerning the future level of profits is fairly high; share prices correlate fairly well with fluctuations in current earnings.

There are several explanations for this. In the first place, the course of profits of any particular company is likely to exhibit a *trend*, in addition to fluctuations; and this trend may make it impossible for the expectation of a long-run "normal level" to develop such as is formed in the case of the short-term interest rate where there is no such trend. In the second place, owing to the absence of any means of information concerning the more distant future, the profits relating to the more distant periods are likely to be heavily discounted for uncertainty; thus the profits relating to the near future are more heavily weighted than would follow from the mere fact of discounting at compound interest. And, lastly, just because the short-period price fluctuations are large, investors are likely to concentrate attention on the short-period expectations concerning capital value, rather than the long-period prospects of enterprise; speculative motives get in-separably mixed up with other motives and it is no longer possible to distinguish between speculative demand and non-speculative

[1] Here I am not thinking of the day-to-day fluctuations in gilt-edged prices which are, of course, also due to speculative influences—they either reflect genuine variations in the degree of certainty with which expectations are held, or the expectation of such variations on behalf of others—but changes which sometimes follow from the pressure of new issues.

[2] Cf. §§ 15-16 below.

demand. It is in such circumstances that the destabilising influence of speculation will dominate over a wide range of price oscillation.

III. Speculation and Income-stability

12. There remains, finally, to examine the effects of speculation on the stability of the general level of economic activity. Speculation affects the level of activity through the variations in the size of speculative stocks held. We have seen above that if there is speculation, any change in the conditions of the outside demand or supply will be followed by a change in the amount of stock held; if speculation is price-stabilising (the elasticity of expectations less than unity), a reduction in demand or an increase in supply will be followed by an increase in stocks; if speculation is price-destabilising (elasticity of expectations greater than unity) a reduction in demand or increase in supply will be followed by a decrease in stocks, and vice versa.

An increase in speculative stocks of any commodity implies an increase of investment in that commodity, or, to use Mr. Hawtrey's expression, a "release of cash" by the market. (Conversely, a reduction of stocks implies an absorption of cash.) Unless this increase is simultaneously compensated by a decrease in the amount of stocks held in other commodities, it must imply a corresponding change in the level of investment for the system as a whole. Such compensation can take place in two ways. (i) If there are several goods whose markets are speculative, an increase in speculative stocks in one market may, in certain cases which we shall analyse below, involve a consequential decrease in speculative stocks in other markets. (ii) If the monetary authorities raise the short-term rate of interest they can induce a reduction in stocks in the system as a whole. Without making some assumptions about monetary policy, it is impossible, therefore, to make any generalisations about the effects of changes in the amount of speculative stocks. In the present section we shall assume that the monetary authorities maintain the short-term rate of interest constant. In the last section we shall deal with the question of how far the instabilities due to speculation can be counteracted if a different monetary policy is adopted.

13. Before proceeding further we must introduce the distinction between "income goods" and "capital goods". There are certain categories of goods in the case of which it can be assumed that *spontaneous* changes in the amount of money spent on them (per unit period) will be associated with equivalent and opposite changes in the amount of money spent on other goods. There are other categories of goods for which this is not (or not necessarily) the case. The first category may be said to consist of goods which are ordinarily bought "out of income", the second category, of goods bought "out of capital" (i.e. whose purchase is charged to a capital account, and not to an income account). For under the assumption that *all* the income of individuals is spent one way or another,[1] and the level of income is given,[2] any change in the amount of money spent on anything must be associated by an opposite change in the amount of money spent on something else. In the case of goods purchased on a capital account this is not so, for variations in the amount of money spent on them may represent variations in the total volume of borrowing. Thus our distinction between "income goods" and "capital goods" comes close to the usual distinction between "consumption goods" and "capital goods", though we must remember that in our case, it is not the character or the destination of the goods which is at the basis of the distinction but simply whether spontaneous changes in the amount of money spent on them imply simultaneous changes in the total amount of expenditure or not.

14. In the case of income goods, a change in speculative stocks, which has a stabilising effect on price, must exert a destabilising influence on the level of economic activity, irrespective of whether the change was due to a change in the conditions of demand or supply. For an increase in the demand (a shift in the outside demand curve to the right), by causing a reduction in speculative stocks, also entails a reduction in the level of incomes,

---

[1] Income *saved* is also spent on something in so far as it is spent on the purchase of securities or other income-yielding assets. What we are assuming here, therefore, is that there is no attempt to "hoard"; that changes in the disposition of incomes between the different lines of expenditure do not involve changes in the demand for money.

[2] This is the meaning of the word "spontaneous" in the above definition. If there is a change in the amount spent as a result of a change in the level of incomes, there need not be, of course, any reduction in the amount spent on other things.

since the increase in the demand is associated with a reduction in the amount spent, and thus of incomes earned, in the production of other things, without any compensating increase in incomes earned in the particular commodity in question. Conversely, a reduction in demand will involve an increase in the level of incomes, for the same reason. An increase in supply on the other hand (a shift in the outside supply curve to the right) will involve an increase in speculative stocks and thus an increase in the level of incomes; a reduction in supply a reduction in incomes. None of these changes in incomes could have taken place in the absence of speculation; and the extent of the change in incomes, following upon a given shift in supply or demand, will be the greater the larger the price-stabilising influence of speculation as above defined.[1]

We can conclude, therefore, that in the case of income goods, an increase in demand or a reduction of supply will cause a reduction in incomes, and vice versa, the magnitude of which depends, *inter alia*, on the degree of price-stabilising influence. When this is negative (speculation is price-destabilising) a reduction in demand or an increase in supply will cause a reduction in incomes, and an increase in demand or a reduction in supply an increase in incomes. Only when the degree of price-stabilising influence is zero will a shift in demand or supply leave the level of incomes unchanged.

15. It might be objected that this effect of speculative activity on incomes will be purely temporary; for while a discrepancy between "outside" demand and "outside" supply lasts, speculative stocks must increase (or decrease, as the case may be) continuously and this process cannot go on for ever. There is no market which has either resources or the inclination to go on "absorbing cash" or "releasing cash" indefinitely; sooner or later, the elasticity of speculative stocks and, hence, the degree of price-stabilising influence, must become zero. This is true, but it does not follow from this that either the price-stabilising or the income-raising (or income-lowering) effect of speculation is purely temporary. For in certain cases the change in incomes itself provides a mechanism which brings the discrepancy between

---

[1] Cf. pp. 116-17 above.

demand and supply gradually to an end. For commodities whose income-elasticity of demand is greater than zero (or to use another terminology, where the marginal propensity to consume is positive) an increase in incomes will involve an expansion in demand, and vice versa. And since we have seen that if the price-stabilising influence of speculation is positive, an excess of supply over demand must lead to an increase in incomes, and an excess of demand over supply to a reduction in incomes, in both cases the discrepancy between demand and supply will tend to get adjusted through the variations in demand caused by the change in incomes.[1]

This is nothing else but the well-known doctrine of the Multiplier put forward in a generalised form. The latter, strictly speaking, assumes that the degree of price-stabilising influence is infinite, so that the price can be regarded as constant. In that case the increase in incomes created by a given increase in supply (or a given reduction in demand) will be (ultimately) as many times the value of the original increase in supply (or reduction in demand) as the reciprocal of the proportion of marginal income spent on the commodity in question. This is so because so long as the excess of supply over demand continues, stocks are accumulated and entrepreneurs' receipts continue to rise. When income has risen in the ratio stated above, the discrepancy between demand and supply disappears (owing to the adjustment in demand) and the accumulation of stocks ceases.

The doctrine of the Multiplier could therefore be restated as follows. The demand and supply of anything always tend towards equality. In normal cases this equality is secured by adjustments in the price of that commodity. But if changes in the price of a particular commodity are attended by variations in the amount of stocks held, the equality may be secured—to a greater or lesser extent—by adjustments in the level of incomes. Only if the stabilising influence of speculation is infinite and the income-elasticity of demand greater than zero can the adjustment come about entirely through a change in incomes. In general, following upon a change in the demand or the supply schedule, the

[1] These equalising forces operate if (a) σ (the price-stabilising influence) is positive and (b) the income-elasticity of demand is positive. If the income-elasticity of demand is negative, the equalising forces operate if σ is negative.

mechanism of adjustment is all the more likely to operate through a change in incomes, rather than a change in price:—(i) the greater the degree of price-stabilising influence of speculation; (ii) the greater the proportion of marginal income spent on the good; (iii) the less is the elasticity of the (outside) demand and supply schedules.

16. This doctrine is subject, however, to an important qualification. If there is more than one good whose price is stabilised, or quasi-stabilised, through speculative activities, the mechanism of the demand-and-supply equalisation through a change in incomes will not operate in the same way as in the case of only a single good. Suppose that out of a large number of things on which consumers spend their incomes, coffee is the sole good whose price is stabilised by compensatory stock-variation. In that case, whenever there is, say, an increase in the supply of coffee, stocks of coffee will increase, incomes will rise, and this process will go on until the demand for coffee, in consequence, has risen in the same proportion in which the supply has increased. But if the price of sugar is also subject to the same influences, and consumers spend part of their increased incomes on that commodity, then whenever there is an increase in the stocks of coffee and a consequent increase in incomes there will also be a decrease in the stocks of sugar, which will act as a brake on the rise in incomes. In this case the level of incomes can never rise sufficiently (as a consequence of the increase in the supply of coffee) to adjust demand fully to the increase in supply. Hence, the existence of more than one "multiplier" weakens the operation of any one of them.

In the real world the most important case of "income goods" whose prices are stabilised through speculation are long-term bonds dealt in the capital market. On our definition the things bought and sold in the capital market are not "capital goods", but "income goods", for the outside or non-speculative demand for securities consists of savings, savings are "paid" out of income; a change in the rate of savings out of a given income must imply an opposite change in the amount spent on other income goods. And since both the proportion of marginal income going to savings and the elasticity of speculative stocks for bonds is large, it is in the case of the long-term investment market that one would expect disequilibria due to changes in supply or demand (i.e. in the propensity to save or in the investment-demand schedule) to be adjusted through variations in the level of incomes, rather than in the long-term rate of interest.

This, however, cannot be entirely true, except for a closed system. In the case of an individual country which is on the Gold Standard, or where the price of foreign exchange is stabilised through the operation of an Exchange Equalisation Fund, the price of foreign exchange, and, hence, the price of imported goods, behaves in much the same manner as the prices of goods stabilised by speculation. Hence, in addition to the "savings-investment multiplier" there exists a "foreign trade multiplier", and the operation of the latter must weaken the price-stabilising forces operating in the former (and vice versa).

This can be best elucidated by an example. Let us suppose that for the community as a whole, 25% of additional income is saved, and that there is an increase in the rate of long-term investment (financed through the sale of securities) by £1 million per week. This will immediately increase incomes in the investment goods industries by £1 million and savings by £250,000. Thus, while in the first "week" the investment market was required to furnish the whole of the additional expenditure of £1 million out of its speculative funds, in the second week it only has to furnish three-quarters of that amount; one quarter will be furnished through the additional savings.[1] If we suppose that all the income which is not saved is spent on home-produced goods, there will be a further increase in incomes by £750,000 in the second week, and £562,500 in the third week, and so on.[2] Similarly, the outside demand for securities will expand by £187,500 in the third week, £140,625 in the fourth week, and so on. As a result, after a certain number of "weeks", total incomes will have expanded by £4 millions per week, and total savings by £1 million; the outside demand for securities will ultimately have increased in

[1] On the assumption, of course, that all increase in "genuine savings" is directed at the purchase of long-term assets.

[2] Abstracting from any involuntary reduction in stocks in the hands of retailers and wholesalers, which is purely temporary; this will merely delay adjustment not prevent it.

the same rate as the outside supply. The size of speculative commitments has increased, of course, during this process, but this
increase will come to a halt once the increase in outside demand
has caught up with the increase in the rate of supply; the contribution which the speculative resources of the market have to
make is limited. Provided that the total required increase in the
size of speculative stocks is not too large relatively to the resources
of the market (i.e. provided it does not impair the degree of price-
stabilising influence) there will be no pressure on the price of
securities (i.e. no tendency for the rate of interest to rise) either
in the long run, or in the short run.

Let us suppose now, however, that not three-quarters, but only
a half of the marginal income is spent on home-produced goods;
and while 25% is saved, another 25% is spent on additional
imports. In that case the "multiplier" will not be 4, but only 2;
the ultimate increase in incomes, following upon a £1 million
increase in the rate of investment, will be £2 millions (per week)
and of savings £500,000. Hence, even after incomes have been
fully adjusted to the change in the level of investment the rate of
outside demand for securities will have only increased by one-half
of the increase in the rate of supply; if the rate of interest is to
remain unchanged, speculators will have to furnish £500,000 per
week, *indefinitely*.

It is true that in this case the increase in speculative stocks in
the securities market is attended by a decrease in stocks (of gold
and foreign exchange) in the foreign exchange market; while in
the first market speculators continuously borrow (on short term)
in the second market they will continuously lend; and since the
one must be numerically equal to the other, there can be no
tendency for the short-term interest rate to change.[1] In Keynesian
terminology one might also say that Investment and Savings will
be equal; for if the export surplus is added to Investment, the net
increase in the rate of Investment will not be £1,000,000, but
only £500,000. Yet the situation will obviously not be one of

[1] There will be an initial increase in the demand for short-term funds with the
increase in incomes; but provided this demand is satisfied by the banking system, no
further contribution is required to keep the short-term rate stable. The continuous
increase in the short-term indebtedness of the speculators in securities will be exactly
offset by the decrease in the short-term borrowings of the foreign exchange market.

equilibrium: it could not be indefinitely maintained. As the stocks of gold and foreign exchange continuously decrease, and the speculative commitments in the long-term investment market increase, one of two things must happen: either the price of gold (and foreign exchange) must rise, thus raising the prices of imported goods and thereby the home-investment multiplier, or the price of securities must fall (the long-term rate of interest rise) and thus the level of home investment will be reduced. Whether equilibrium is finally reached through a rise in the price of foreign exchange, or of the rate of interest, will depend on the relative elasticity of speculative stocks in the two markets (or rather on the range over which, in the two markets, speculative stocks are elastic). Assuming that it takes place through the second and not the first, it would be wrong to attribute the rise in the interest rate to any shortage of *cash*. In the situation contemplated there is no shortage of cash, and no pressure on the short-term rate of interest. The long-term rate rises *relatively* to the short-term rate simply because, owing to a shortage of savings, speculators are required to expand continuously the size of their commitments: and there are limits to the extent to which this is possible.

It is not quite accurate, therefore, when Mr. Keynes says that "the investment market can be congested on account of a shortage of cash. It can never be congested on account of a shortage of savings."[1] This proposition would only hold if it were assumed, in addition to the degree of price-stabilising influence being infinite, that the long-term investment market is the only market which is subject to such speculative influences; in other words, that $\frac{dC}{dY}$ (the marginal propensity to consume) which is relevant for calculating the home-investment multiplier, is necessarily equal to $1 - \frac{dS}{dY}$ (where $\frac{dS}{dY}$ is the marginal propensity to save). This, as we have seen, need not be the case.[2]

---

[1] "The Ex-Ante Theory of the Rate of Interest", *Economic Journal*, December, 1937, p. 669.

[2] Mr. Keynes' own proof of this proposition is that there must "always be *exactly* enough ex-post saving to take up the ex-post investment and so release the finance which the latter had been previously employing" (*ibid.*, p. 669). Ex-post investment and ex-post saving will always be equal if "ex-post investment" is so defined as to include consequential changes in stocks (in our example, foreign exchange balances). But in order that the funds released through the reduction in stocks should be available

Mr. Keynes' General Theory, therefore, in so far as it concerns his theory of the rate of interest and the theory of the multiplier, is rather in the nature of a "special case"; strictly it only holds if σ is infinite in the case of long-term bonds and zero in the case of everything else. But if we abstract from the case of foreign exchange under a gold standard or quasi-gold-standard régime, it is true that the degree of price-stabilising influence, though not perhaps infinite, is very much larger in the case of long-term bonds than for any other commodity; and this means that the Keynesian theory, though a "special case", gives, nevertheless, a fair approximation to reality.

17. In the case of "capital goods", a change in speculative stocks which has a stabilising effect on price will also have a stabilising influence on activity, if the change in stocks was due to a shift in demand, and a destabilising influence, if it was due to a change in supply. This difference is due to the fact that changes in the demand for capital goods are not (normally) associated with opposite changes in the demand for other goods; they represent variations in the investment-demand schedule (in the marginal efficiency of capital) and such variations, in a régime where the long-term interest rate is itself subject to the price-stabilising influence of speculation, and/or where the short-term rate of interest is held constant, must imply variations in the total scale of expenditures. Hence, an increase in the demand for capital goods involves an increase in the level of incomes, when σ is zero (in the absence of speculation); in so far as σ is positive (the increase in demand is associated with a reduction in stocks), the increase in incomes will be less than it would be otherwise. Thus, the existence of speculation in capital goods, if price-stabilising, damps down the multiplier and hence the range of

for the finance of long-term investment somebody must perform the "arbitrage operation" of borrowing on short term and re-lending it on long term; and the willingness to perform this arbitrage must necessarily depend on the total amount of such transactions already undertaken. Sooner or later this willingness must fall off; which in our own terminology, is expressed by saying that the marginal risk premium by which the current long-term rate exceeds the average of expected short rates, must rise But no stretching of the meaning of words could describe this situation as one of a "shortage of cash" or one which could be remedied through an increase in cash. Temporarily, the banks might prevent the long-term rate from rising by *reducing* the short-term rate; but however much they inundate the system with cash, sooner or later the long rate must rise.

income fluctuations, in much the same way as the existence of a stabilised price for foreign exchange in our previous example. But whereas in the case of foreign exchange, there can be "spontaneous" changes in demand which themselves set up income-variations (when, e.g., there is a spontaneous change in the propensity to consume foreign goods) the changes in demand for capital goods are always "induced"; they reduce the magnitude of other multipliers but do not have a multiplier-effect of their own.

It follows from this that in a world where the long-term rate of interest is a "conventional phenomenon" (to use Mr. Hawtrey's phrase) the existence of price-stabilisation schemes for raw materials which are mainly used for the production of capital goods, and operated by means of compensatory stock-variation[1] (and *not* by the restriction of supply) will have a beneficial effect on economic stability; it will reduce the instability arising from the operation of the savings-investment market. We must remember however that this conclusion only holds if the price-variation which the stabilisation scheme is designed to eliminate, arises wholly or mainly from fluctuations in demand, rather than fluctuations in supply. In the case of agricultural crops, where it is supply, rather than demand, which is unstable, such price-stabilisation schemes must have a destabilising influence on activity.[2]

18. We may now summarise the argument of this section. Speculation in any good, by creating uncompensated variations in the amount of stocks held, is responsible for variations in the general level of activity. If the effect of speculation is price-destabilising (a rise in price being associated with an increase in speculative stocks, and vice versa) an increase in demand or a decrease in supply will be followed by an increase in the level of activity, and vice versa. If the effect of speculation is price-stabilising (a rise in price is associated with a decrease in speculative stocks) an increase in demand or a decrease in supply will be

---

[1] As recommended by Mr. Keynes in the *Economic Journal*, September, 1938, pp. 449-460.

[2] Apart from the case, of course, where the price fluctuations are themselves created or enhanced by speculation (i.e. when σ is negative) in which case the elimination of such price variations is always income-stabilising.

followed by a reduction in activity, a fall in demand or an increase in supply by a rise in activity.

If there is more than one good which is subject to speculation of the price-stabilising type, and if the income elasticity of demand of such goods is positive, changes in the amount of speculative stocks in any one market will set up compensatory changes in the amount of stocks held in other markets, and thereby make the variations in the level of activity smaller than they would be otherwise. This compensatory effect will be all the stronger the more alike is the degree of price-stabilising influence in the different markets. Hence, while the introduction of speculation in any particular market in a system which is otherwise free from speculation is bound to have an unsettling effect on economic activity (quite irrespective of whether it is price-stabilising or price-destabilising) the extension of speculation over *further markets*, if price-stabilising, may reduce the instability in the level of incomes. It is not so much therefore the existence of speculation as such but its widely differing incidence between the different markets—the fact that while in some markets speculation plays such a dominating rôle, in others it has only an insignificant influence—which is responsible for the instability of our economic system.

IV. Monetary Policy and Stability

19. The analysis of the previous section was based on the assumption that the monetary authorities hold the short-term interest rate constant, despite the fluctuations in the level of money incomes. Suppose that the monetary authorities raise the short-term rate whenever there is an expansion of activity, and lower it when there is a contraction, would this not secure stability of incomes, despite the destabilising influences emanating from speculative markets? Mr. Hawtrey, who more than anyone else regards economic stability as a matter of bank rate policy, himself admits that the *sources* of inflationary and deflationary tendencies may lie in markets other than the market for short-term credit.[1]

---

[1] *Capital and Employment*, p. 66. *A Century of Bank Rate*, p. 38. He still regards the fluctuations in short-term investment as the prime mover of the Trade Cycle, and the inflationary (or deflationary) influences emanating from the capital market as subsidiary. But he would concede, I think, that this need not *necessarily* be the case.

But he argues that it is the business of the monetary authorities to counteract such tendencies by appropriate adjustments of the bank rate.

There are, of course, serious practical difficulties confronting a policy of this kind: the difficulty of determining the correct timing and the appropriate magnitude of the changes that are required. For if the changes in the bank rate are incorrectly timed, or if they are greater than necessary, the instrument of the bank rate becomes a source of further instability and not a stabiliser. But apart from these practical difficulties, there are also certain theoretical limitations to the extent to which stability can be secured by monetary policy; and the remaining part of this paper may be devoted to a discussion of some of these limitations.

20. The instrument of the bank rate operates through its effect on the amount of stocks held of commodities in general. Hence, if any particular market becomes a source of inflation (i.e. begins to accumulate stocks) it is never possible to eliminate the source of the disturbance *directly* through the changes in the short-term rate; all that can be achieved is to offset the accumulation of stocks in the one market by enforcing a reduction in stocks held in all the other markets. There is, of course, always *some* rate of interest which, if enforced, would be sufficient to stop the inflationary tendency emanating from any particular market. But unless this rate of interest is confined to lenders and borrowers in that particular market, its effect would be clearly deflationary; for in addition to preventing the accumulation of stocks in the "inflationary" market, it would involve a decumulation of stocks in all the others. Hence, the "appropriate" short-term rate (the one which leaves the level of incomes unchanged) is one which balances the accumulation of stocks by a decumulation elsewhere, not one which prevents it.

The effect of any change in the short rate of interest on activity is purely temporary. It operates by causing an adjustment in the size of stocks to the new interest rate; once stocks have been adjusted to the new rate, its effect is exhausted. A 6% bank rate, provided it has been in operation long enough, is no more "deflationary" than a 4% rate or a 2% rate (apart from its effect on the long-term rate, which we shall discuss below). It is not the absolute level of the short-term rate, therefore, but its change from some previous level which acts as a stimulant (or the reverse). Hence, if a particular market becomes the source of an inflationary tendency, and continues to do so, even after the effect of the rise in the bank rate has exhausted itself, a further rise in the bank rate becomes necessary, and so on. An expanding or contracting tendency in the level of incomes may not be counteracted, therefore, by a single change of the bank rate, but only by a series of changes.

21. The instrument of the bank rate is subject, moreover, to a great constitutional weakness: it cannot operate equally freely in both directions. It should always be possible to stop an expansion of activity by a rise in the short-term rate of interest, whatever the strength of the forces of expansion. As Mr. Hawtrey says: "If a rate of, say, 6% were found to be negligible, the rate could be raised indefinitely. No one would regard a rate of 60% as negligible."[1] But it is not equally possible to prevent a contraction of activity through a reduction in the rate. For the rate can never be below zero; and as we have seen, there is a certain level, above zero, at which the power of the monetary authorities to determine the rate (by varying the quantity of money) ceases to function.[2] In order that the bank rate mechanism should be efficacious in the downward direction, as well as in the upward direction, its *average level* must be kept high so as to leave sufficient "elbow room" for reductions, as well as increases. For if, after a period of stable activity, a deflationary process develops, it is much easier to counteract it by monetary measures if the short-term rate stood previously at 10% or 6% than if it stood at 4% or 3%. The effectiveness of a reduction in the bank rate from 4% to 2% is no greater than that of a reduction from 10% to 8%; and so far, Central Banks have never found it practicable to reduce the official rate of discount below 2%.

---

[1] *A Century of Bank Rate*, p. 195.
[2] Cf. the diagram on p. 123 above. When the rate falls below the point *g* the demand for cash balances becomes elastic and this makes further reductions in the rate difficult or impossible. It is only when the short-term rate is at this point that "idle balances", in the sense of idle *cash* balances, really exist; and it is only then that the short-term rate reflects "liquidity preference", in any significant sense. (When the rate is above this level, the marginal demand price for cash is determined by the marginal yield of money-stocks in terms of convenience, and not by the risk premium attached to alternative forms of investment.)

We have seen above that as far as the short-term rate of interest is concerned, it is the change in the rate, and not its absolute level, which has an influence on activity. Hence, if the average long-run level of the short-term rate is kept at 10% this is no more detrimental to activity than if the average rate is 3%. This is not so, however, when the effect on the long-term rate is taken into account. In the short period, as we have seen, changes in the short-term rate have only a minor effect on the long-term rate, because the latter depends on the *average* of short-term rates expected over a long period in the future,[1] and this average is but little affected by the changes in the current rate. But if the monetary authorities, in their long-period policy, regulate the short-term rate in such a way as to keep its average level high, then it is this average level which will come to be regarded as the "long period normal" and thus govern the level of the long-term rate. If over considerable periods in the past the monetary authorities varied the bank rate between 2% and 10% and maintained it on the average at 6% (thus allowing for a 4% elbow room in each direction) the long-term rate will settle at a level which is *above* 6%.[2] This in turn, by restricting long-term investment, will have a considerably depressing effect on the *average* level of activity.

In the long run, therefore, the monetary authorities are not free to vary the short-term rate as they like; if they want to maintain activity at a satisfactory level, they must keep the mean level of the short-term rate sufficiently low so as to secure a long-term rate which permits a sufficient amount of long-term investment. Alternatively, if they want to secure stability by means of monetary policy, they must allow the average level of employment to fall to a low enough level to permit the mean level of the short-term rate to be sufficiently high. Thus the two main aims of monetary policy, to secure a satisfactory level of incomes, and

---

[1] We need not suppose, of course, that people have any definite expectation as to what the short-term rate is going to be at any particular date in the future, other than the immediate future. If the theory depended on there being such a definite expectation, it would clearly be wrong. But all that is necessary to suppose is that people have certain ideas as to what constitutes the "normal" level of the short-term rate of interest, and that they consider deviations from this normal level as temporary. Their idea as to the normal is based, of course, on past experience, and reflects the average level which ruled over some period in the past.

[2] Ignoring the lag between the official discount rate and the market rates.

to secure stability of incomes, may prove incompatible: the one may only be achieved by sacrificing the other.

Assuming that the monetary authorities regard the achievement of a satisfactory level of activity as their paramount consideration, we must expect the bank rate mechanism, as an instrument of economic policy, to become increasingly ineffectual. As real incomes increase, savings rise, and the available investment opportunities become smaller, the bank rate, though still available for dealing with an occasional boom, becomes more and more ineffective as a safeguard against the ravages of deflation.

Mr. Hawtrey is well aware of this constitutional weakness of the bank rate mechanism; and he calls the state of affairs where the mechanism is put out of action through the bank rate having reached its minimum level a "credit deadlock". But he is too much inclined, I think, to attribute the emergence of a "credit deadlock" to past mistakes in banking policy—to the Central Bank not having lowered the rate sufficiently soon, or sufficiently suddenly —rather than to the inherent causes connected with the long-term rate.[1] If Professor Hicks' calculations are right,[2] and 2% is now to be regarded as the necessary marginal risk premium by which the current long-term rate exceeds the average savings deposit rate, then a 3% rate on consols presupposes a 1% average on deposits; and a 1% rate on deposits is perilously near its absolute minimum level. If "full employment" requires a long-term rate which is below 3%, and this is what the monetary authorities aim at, the "credit deadlock" becomes a more or less permanent state of affairs.

In a world of perpetual or semi-perpetual credit deadlock, stability cannot be achieved by monetary policy (in the sense in which this term is ordinarily understood); nor can fluctuations in the level of activity be regarded as a "purely monetary phenomenon". For in those circumstances monetary factors can neither be said to have caused the fluctuations, nor have they the power to prevent them.

[1] This is because he is sceptical of any influence of the short-term rate on the long-term rate (either the current short rate or the average of past short rates) and regards the two rates as independently determined. But it is difficult to see how the long-term rate can remain below the short-term rate, once the prevailing level of the short-term rate comes to be accepted as "normal". The supply of long-term funds comes from savers, and why should savers place any money in long-term investments if they expect a higher return on savings deposits?

[2] *Manchester School*, Vol. X, No. 1, p. 31.

APPENDIX

THE RELATION BETWEEN
THE SHORT AND LONG TERM
RATES OF INTEREST

[This Appendix is taken from "Keynes's Theory of the Own-Rates of Interest", *Essays on Economic Stability and Growth*, Collected Essays, vol. II.]

*

To explain the relationship between short and long rates of interest, it is best to start with a bond which carries a definite redemption date, so that its redemption yield (consisting of the annual interest payment and the appreciation to the redemption date) can be elicited from its current market price, and included in q while the a-term can again be treated as zero. The redemption yield of this bond, Q, can be looked upon as being a function of the current short rate of interest, the short rates expected during the remainder of the currency of the bond and a risk premium depending on the uncertainty of those expectations.

Alternatively, as Professor Hicks suggested,[1] a loan of any

---

[1] *Value and Capital*, p. 144.

particular duration can be looked upon as consisting of a spot loan transaction for the current "year", plus a series of forward loan transactions, each renewing the loan for some successive "year". A capital market where bonds of all durations are traded simultaneously (i.e. where it is possible to borrow or lend for any particular length of time) *implies* the existence of a series of future markets in loans of short duration, since an individual can lend "forward" for one year t years hence by lending for t years (i.e. buying a bond of t years' maturity) and simultaneously borrowing for $(t-1)$ years (i.e. selling bonds of $(t-1)$ years' maturity). Hence if we denote by $Q_1 \ldots Q_t$ the current yield of bonds of $1 \ldots t$ years' maturity, i_1 as the current short rate of interest, $i_2 \ldots i_t$ the "future" short rates, currently ruling in the market, i_{10} the current "future" short rate 10 years hence can be elicited from the difference in yields between bonds of 9 years' maturity and bonds of 10 years' maturity according to the following formula:

$$i_{10} = \frac{(1+Q_{10})^{10}}{(1+Q_9)^9} - 1$$

Assuming simple interest in the first approximation this reduces to the following:

$$10 \, Q_{10} = i_1 + i_2 + \ldots + i_{10}$$
$$9 \, Q_9 = i_1 + i_2 + \ldots + i_9$$
$$\therefore i_{10} = 10 Q_{10} - 9 Q_9$$

These future short rates, $i_2 \ldots i_t$, are in turn the expected short rates *plus* the risk premium, in accordance with our general formula concerning the relationship of the futures price to the expected price.[1] Since expectations are more uncertain for the more distant future than for the nearer future, the risk premium, up to a point at any rate, will tend to be all the higher the more distant the future period to which it relates. Hence if one postulates that the expected short rates of interest, for all future periods,

[1] The risk premium is an addition to the expected *yield*, which is consistent with the formula which treats it as a deduction from the expected *price* of bonds or bills. As was shown (p. 112 above) this formula only applies, strictly speaking, in the case where expectations are uniform. The existence of a normal yield curve (see below) is some indication that the existence of divergent expectations does not normally cause much difference to market price formation.

are identical with q_2, the currently ruling short rate of interest, the current yield of bonds of t years' maturity, Q_t (again, ignoring compound interest) will be equal to

$$Q_t = q_2 + \frac{\sum_{t2}^{t} \bar{r}}{t}$$

where $\bar{r}$ stands for the series of risk premia embodied in the "futures" short rates i_2 to i_t.

The second term on the R.H.S. of the above equation is the nearest to Keynes' "liquidity preference"—i.e. it measures the amount by which the yield of a long-term bond of a definite maturity-date exceeds the short-term interest rates expected to rule during the currency of the bond. And since $\bar{r}$ rises with the distance of time, the current yield of a long-term bond of t years' maturity will be below the "futures" short rate for the tth year.

It may be assumed, however, that the risk premia on "future" short rates will cease to rise past a certain time-horizon, so that with lengthening maturity, the yield of bonds will approximate to that of the highest future short rate of interest: i.e. to the future rate for that particular future year for which the rate, as shown by the above formula is the highest. It follows also that the yield of irredeemable bonds (or "perpetual annuities") will be governed by the yield of those redeemable bonds whose redemption date is sufficiently far distant for their yield to have approached this ceiling level.

The expected future short rates of interest can be assumed to be the same as the current short-term rate, when the latter itself is at its "normal" level—i.e. when the current short rate is around its long-term average level, and the current short rate is not considered to be either abnormally low or abnormally high. In that case the structure of yields for bonds of varying maturities will exhibit the properties of the normal yield curve, shown by A in Fig. 1 (where bonds of lengthening maturities are measured along Ox, and interest rates (yields) along Oy. The current short rate of interest is thus indicated by the point on the curve where it intersects the y-axis). When the short rate of interest is either abnormally high or abnormally low, the yield curve will be distorted in shape in the manner suggested by curves B and C; at times when the short rate is very high, it is even possible for the yield on long-term and irredeemable bonds to stand lower than the current short rate of interest. This must reflect the

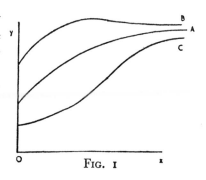

Fig. 1

expectation that the short rate will fall in the future, and with the fall in the short rate, the yield of bonds of any particular maturity will also fall—i.e. the *price* of bonds will rise, quite apart from any "normal" appreciation due to the gradual approach of the redemption date (which latter has already been allowed for in calculating the "yield"). In times, therefore, when the short rate of interest is abnormally high the *expected* yield of bonds (for the current period or some subsequent periods) will exceed their *apparent* yield, so that the gap between the apparent yield of bonds and the current short rate of interest will be abnormally narrow, and vice versa when the short rate of interest is abnormally low. In times, however, when the short rate of interest is normal, and the market has no specific reason to expect an impending change in the short rate in the near future, the structure of interest rates for loans of various durations will exhibit the characteristic of the normal yield curve: of yields increasing with lengthening maturity-dates up to a certain ceiling. This, as we have seen, is the consequence of the increasing uncertainty of interest expectations and the increasing risk premia demanded as a compensation for this uncertainty: the long rate of interest will thus exceed the *normal* short rate for much the same reasons as, in the case of the commodity markets, the futures price will stand below the spot price by the amount of "normal backwardation". For in the case of the long-term loan market, it is the "true" (outside) borrowers who are in the nature of hedgers willing to pay an extra price for getting rid of the risk of unfavourable changes in the cost of borrowing, by borrowing on long term in order to cover long-term commitments; whilst the lenders are in the nature of speculators who assume additional risks by entering into long-term commitments.[1]

The theory of "normal backwardation" strictly holds, as we have seen, only in the case where expectations are uniform, or if not uniform, there is a predominant or "representative" expectation for speculators as a group. If there is sufficient divergence of expectations in the market, so that "speculators" enter in large numbers both as buyers and sellers, this theory need no longer hold, since the "futures price" in that case need not stand below the "expected price" (or the current price, in so far as the current price can be taken to reflect the *average* of expected prices by bulls and bears). In the same way, if there is sufficient divergence of expectations concerning future interest rates there is no longer any necessary reason to suppose that the long-term rate will be above the average of past short rates; and the theory underlying our "normal yield curve"—which makes the yield of long-term bonds a function of the "normal" short rate, derived from the average of past short rates, and of a risk premium varying with the duration of the particular loan—will break down. Conversely, if the behaviour of the capital market lends support to the existence of a "normal yield curve", this affords evidence that the existence of divergent expectations is not a critical factor in determining the relationship between interest rates for loans of varying length.

---

[1] There is a class of long-term lender who looks for certainty of income rather than of capital value (i.e. the trustees of widows and orphans) who may be said to be "hedging" by lending on long term. So long, however, as the lenders are not exclusively of this category this will merely serve to reduce the gap between the long and short rates; for the balance of "hedging" will still be on the borrowing side, and not the lending side. Moreover, in a world where the preference for long-term lending by the "savers" exceeded the preference for long-term borrowing by the "investors" (because, e.g., the "investors" were mainly interested in covering short-term commitments in stocks, etc., whereas the "savers" were predominantly widows and orphans) there would arise a special class of "arbitrageurs" to restore the balance—i.e. those who ordinarily wish to keep a part of their assets in liquid form, and who could thus satisfy their desire for liquidity by borrowing long and re-lending the money in the short-term market, in much the same way in which a predominance of hedging on the buying side will be balanced by arbitrage in the case of the commodity markets.

A MODEL OF THE TRADE CYCLE[1]

1. THE following pages do not attempt to put forward any "new" theory of the trade cycle. The theory here presented is essentially similar to all those theories which explain the trade cycle as a result of the combined operation of the so-called "multiplier" and the investment demand function as, e.g., the theories put forward in recent years by Mr. Harrod and Mr. Kalecki.[2] The purpose of the present paper is to show, by means of a simple diagrammatic apparatus, what are the necessary and sufficient assumptions under which the combined operation of these two forces inevitably gives rise to a cycle.

2. The basic principle underlying all these theories may be sought in the proposition—a proposition that is really derived from Mr. Keynes' *General Theory*, although not stated there in this form—that economic activity always *tends* towards a level where Savings and Investment are equal. Here the terms Savings and Investment are used, of course, in a sense different from the one according to which they are always and necessarily equal— in the *ex-ante*, and not the *ex-post* sense. Investment *ex-ante* is the value of the *designed* increments of stocks of all kinds (i.e. the value of the net addition to stocks plus the value of the aggregate output of fixed equipment), which differs from Investment *ex-post* by the value of the undesigned accretion (or decumulation) of stocks. Savings *ex-ante* is the amount people intend to save—i.e. the amount they actually *would* save if they correctly forecast their incomes. Hence *ex-ante* and *ex-post* Saving can differ only in so far as there is an unexpected change in the amount of income earned.

If *ex-ante* Investment exceeds *ex-ante* Saving, *either ex-post* Investment will fall short of *ex-ante* Investment, *or ex-post* Saving will exceed *ex-ante* Saving; and both these discrepancies will induce an expansion in the level of activity. If *ex-ante* Investment

[1] Reprinted from the *Economic Journal*, March, 1940.
[2] Harrod, *The Trade Cycle*; Kalecki, "A Theory of the Business Cycle", *Review of Economic Studies*, Feb., 1937, reprinted in *Essays in the Theory of Economic Fluctuations*.

falls short of *ex-ante* Saving *either ex-post* Investment will exceed *ex-ante* Investment, *or ex-post* Saving will fall short of *ex-ante* Saving, and both these discrepancies will induce a contraction. This must be so, because a reduction in *ex-post* Saving as compared with *ex-ante* Saving will make consumers spend less on consumers' goods, an excess of *ex-post* Investment over *ex-ante* Investment (implying as it does the accretion of unwanted stocks) will cause entrepreneurs to spend less on entrepreneurial goods; while the total of activity is always determined by the sum of consumers' expenditures and entrepreneurs' expenditures. Thus a discrepancy between *ex-ante* Saving and *ex-ante* Investment must induce a change in the level of activity which proceeds until the discrepancy is removed.

3. The magnitudes of both *ex-ante* Saving and *ex-ante* Investment are themselves functions of the level of activity, and both vary positively with the level of activity. Thus if we denote the level of activity (measured in terms of employment) by x, both S and I (*ex-ante* Savings and Investment) will be single-valued functions of x[1] and both $\frac{dS}{dx}$ and $\frac{dI}{dx}$ will be positive. The first of these expresses the basic principle of the multiplier (that the marginal propensity to consume is less than unity),[2] and the second denotes the assumption that the demand for capital goods will be greater the greater the level of production.[3]

---

[1] S and I are, of course, both functions of the rate of interest in addition to the level of activity. But the rate of interest, at any rate in the first approximation, could itself be regarded as a single-valued function of the level of activity, and thus its influence incorporated in the $S(x)$ and $I(x)$ functions. (It is not necessary to assume, in order that $\frac{dI}{dx}$ should be positive, that the rates of interest—short and long term—are *constant*. We can allow for *some* variation in the rates of interest, to be associated with a change in investment and incomes, provided this variation is not large enough to prevent the change in incomes altogether. All that we are excluding here is a banking policy which so regulates interest rates as to keep the level of incomes constant.)

[2] $\frac{dS}{dx}$ is, of course, the reciprocal of Mr. Keynes' investment multiplier, which is defined as $\dfrac{1}{1 - \dfrac{dC}{dx}}$, where $\frac{dC}{dx} = 1 - \frac{dS}{dx}$.

[3] This assumption should not be confused with the "acceleration principle" (of Professor J. M. Clark and others), which asserts that the demand for capital goods is a function of the *rate of change* of the level of activity, and not of the level of activity itself. The theory put forward below is thus not based on this "acceleration principle" (the general validity of which is questionable), but on a much simpler assumption— i.e. that an increase in the current level of profits increases investment demand.

If we regard the $S(x)$ and $I(x)$ functions as *linear*, as in the absence of further information one is inclined to do, we have two possibilities:

(i) $\dfrac{dI}{dx}$ exceeds $\dfrac{dS}{dx}$, in which case, as shown by Fig. 1,[1] there can be only a single position of unstable equilibrium, since above the equilibrium point $I > S$, and thus activity tends to expand, below it $S > I$, and hence it tends to contract. If the S and I

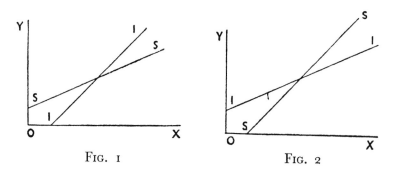

Fig. 1   Fig. 2

functions were of this character, the economic system would always be rushing either towards a state of hyper-inflation with full employment, or towards a state of complete collapse with zero employment, with no resting-place in between. Since recorded experience does not bear out such dangerous instabilities, this possibility can be dismissed.

(ii) $\dfrac{dS}{dx}$ exceeds $\dfrac{dI}{dx}$, in which case, as shown in Fig. 2, there will be a single position of stable equilibrium. (This, I believe, is the assumption implied in Mr. Keynes' theory of employment.) If the economic system were of this nature, any disturbance, originating either on the investment side or on the savings side, would be followed by the re-establishment of a new equilibrium, with a stable level of activity.[2] Hence this assumption fails in the opposite direction: it assumes *more* stability than the real world appears, in fact, to possess. Also, if there is any justification

[1] In Fig. 1, as in all subsequent diagrams, the level of activity is measured along Ox and the corresponding value of *ex-ante* Investment and Saving along Oy.

[2] Except in so far as the existence of time-lags of adjustment might prevent, on certain assumptions, the new equilibrium from being reached. Cf. Appendix below.

in the contention of the "accelerationists", the possibility of $\frac{dI}{dx}$ being greater than $\frac{dS}{dx}$, at any rate for certain values of x, cannot be excluded. For $\frac{dI}{dx}$ could be many times greater than I, while $\frac{dS}{dx}$ can never be more than a fraction of I.

4. Since thus neither of these two assumptions can be justified, we are left with the conclusion that the $I(x)$ and $S(x)$ functions cannot both be linear, at any rate over the entire range. And, in fact, on closer examination, there are good reasons for supposing that neither of them is linear.

(*a*) In the case of the investment function it is probable that $\frac{dI}{dx}$ will be *small*, both for low and for high levels of x, relatively to its "normal" level. It will be small for low levels of activity

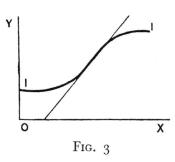

FIG. 3

because when there is a great deal of surplus capacity, an increase in activity will not induce entrepreneurs to undertake additional construction: the rise in profits will not stimulate investment. (At the same time, the level of investment will not be zero, for there is always some investment undertaken for long-period development purposes which is independent of current activity.) But it will also be small for unusually high levels of activity, because rising costs of construction, increasing costs and increasing difficulty of borrowing will dissuade entrepreneurs from expanding still faster—at a time when they already have large commitments. Hence, given some "normal" value of $\frac{dI}{dx}$, appropriate for "normal" levels of activity, the $I(x)$ function will deviate from linearity in the manner suggested in Fig. 3.

(*b*) In the case of the savings function, the situation appears to be exactly the other way round: $\frac{dS}{dx}$ is likely to be relatively *large,* both for low and high levels of activity, as compared with its normal level. When incomes are unusually low, savings are cut drastically, and below a certain level of income they will be negative. When incomes are unusually high, people are likely to save not only a higher amount, but also a larger proportion of their income.[1] These tendencies, for society as a whole, are likely to be reinforced by the fact that when activity is at a low level, an increasing proportion of workers' earnings are paid out of capital funds (in the form of unemployment benefits); while when activity is at a high level, prices will tend to rise relatively to wages, there will be a shift in the distribution of incomes in favour of profits, and thus an increase in the aggregate propensity to save. Hence $\dfrac{dS}{dx}$ will deviate from its normal level in the manner suggested in Fig. 4.

In what follows it will be assumed that the two functions conform to these criteria. But, as the reader will note, our analysis would remain valid even if only *one of the two* functions behaved in the manner suggested, while the other was linear.

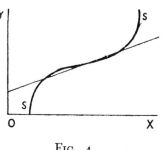

Fig. 4

5. Given these assumptions about the behaviour of the savings and investment functions, and assuming further that the normal value of $\dfrac{dI}{dx}$ *is greater than* the normal value of $\dfrac{dS}{dx}$, the situation will be one of multiple equilibria, as shown in Fig. 5. *A* and *B* (in the diagram) are both stable positions, for at points below *A* or *B*, $I>S$, hence activity tends to expand; above it $S>I$, hence activity tends to contract. *C* is an unstable position in both directions, and hence not a possible position of equilibrium. The significance of point *C* is simply that if activity happens to be

---

[1] Thus there is something like a "customary standard of living" based on the "normal level" of incomes, and, corresponding to it, there is a certain normal rate of savings. If incomes are much below it, individuals will attempt to maintain their standard of living by consuming capital; if incomes are much above it, they will tend to save a disproportionate amount.

above *C*, there will be a process of expansion which will come to a halt at *B*; if it happens to be below *C*, there will be a process of contraction until equilibrium is reached at *A*.

Hence the economic system can reach stability either at a certain high rate of activity or at a certain low rate of activity. There will be a certain depression level and a certain prosperity level at which it offers resistance to further changes in either direction. The key to the explanation of the trade cycle is to be found in the fact that each of these two positions is stable only *in the short period*: that as activity continues at either one of these levels, forces gradually accumulate which sooner or later will render that particular position unstable. It is to an explanation of the nature of these forces that we must now turn.

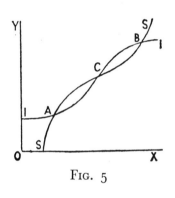

FIG. 5

6. Both $S(x)$ and $I(x)$ are *short-period* functions—i.e. they assume the total amount of fixed equipment in existence, and hence the amount of real income at any particular level of activity, as given. As these factors change in time, the *S* and *I* curves will shift their position; but according as activity is high or low (equilibrium is at *B* or at *A*) they will shift in different ways.

(i) When activity is high (equilibrium at *B*), the level of investment is high, the total amount of equipment gradually increases, and so, in consequence, the amount of consumers' goods produced at a given level of activity. As a result the *S* curve gradually shifts upwards (for there will be more consumption, and hence more saving, for any given activity); for the same reason the *I* curve gradually falls. (The accumulation of capital, by restricting the range of available investment opportunities, will tend to make it fall, while new inventions tend, on the whole, to make it rise. But the first of these factors is bound to be more powerful after a time.) As a result, the position of *B* is gradually shifted to the left and that of *C* to the right, thus reducing the level of activity somewhat and bringing B and C nearer to each other (see Fig. 6, Stage II).

The critical point is reached when, on account of these movements, the I and S curves become tangential and the points B and C fall together (Stage III). At that point equilibrium becomes unstable in a downward direction, since in the neighbourhood of the point $S > I$ in both directions. The level of activity will now fall rapidly, on account of the excess of *ex-ante* Savings over *ex-ante* Investment, until a new equilibrium is reached at A where the position is again stable.[1, 2]

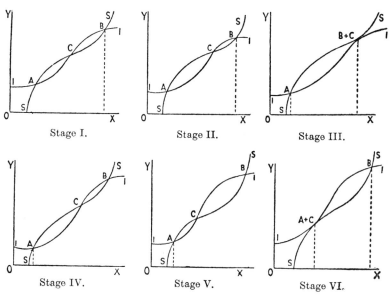

FIG. 6. THE TRADE CYCLE

(ii) When activity is low, the movement of the I and S curves will tend to be in the opposite direction. For if at the level of investment corresponding to A investment is not sufficient to

[1] The route followed in the transition from B to A might be either along the I curve or the S curve, according to whether *ex-post* Saving is adjusted to *ex-ante* Investment, or *ex-post* Investment to *ex-ante* Saving—i.e., according as the disappointment of expectations occurs on the side of incomes, or in the level of entrepreneurial stocks.

[2] The fall in the rate of activity during the transition need not be very rapid, and may even take some years. This is because both entrepreneurs and consumers take some time to adjust their scale of purchases to their changed rate of earnings. If the process is at all prolonged, the two curves will be back at their "normal" position (as shown in Fig. 5 or Stage IV in Fig. 6) by the time point A is reached.

cover replacement, so that *net* investment in industrial plant and equipment is negative,[1] investment opportunities gradually accumulate and the *I* curve will shift upwards; and this tendency is likely to be reinforced by new inventions. For the same reason, the gradual decumulation of capital, in so far as it causes real income per unit of activity to fall, will lower the *S* curve.[2] These movements cause the position of *A* to shift to the right and that of *C* to shift to the left (thus separating *B* and *C* and bringing *A* and *C* nearer to each other), involving a gradual improvement in the level of activity (Stages IV and V). This will proceed until *A* and *C* fall together (the two curves again become tangential), when a new critical situation is reached; the position becomes unstable in an upward direction, since *I>S* on either side of the equilibrium point; an upward cumulative movement will follow which can only come to rest when position *B* is reached (Stage VI). Thereafter the curves gradually return to the position shown in Stage I, and the cyclical movement is repeated.

7. The necessary and sufficient assumptions under which the combined operation of the saving and investment functions inevitably generate a cyclical movement which nowhere tends to come to rest, can therefore be set out as follows:

(1) The "normal value" of $\frac{dI}{dx}$, valid for normal levels of activity, must be *greater* than the corresponding value of $\frac{dS}{dx}$.

(2) The "extreme values" of $\frac{dI}{dx}$, valid for abnormally high or abnormally low levels of activity, must be *smaller* than the corresponding values of $\frac{dS}{dx}$.

(3) The level of investment at the upper equilibrium point must be sufficiently large for the $I(x)$ function to *fall* (in time) relatively to the $S(x)$ function; and at the lower equilibrium point

---

[1] It is not necessary, of course, that *total* net investment should be negative, since investment can take forms (such as armaments, etc.) whose construction does not reduce the available opportunities for the future.

[2] It is possible that even if net investment is negative, real output per head should gradually rise in time (on account of the introduction of superior or more "capitalistic" processes of production during the depression), as a result of which *S* would tend to rise rather than fall. But this makes no difference so long as the *I* curve rises faster than the *S* curve.

it must be sufficiently small for the $I(x)$ function to *rise* (in time) relatively to the $S(x)$ function. In other words, the position of zero net investment must fall within the limits set by the levels of investment ruling at $B+C$ and $A+C$, in Stage III and Stage VI, respectively.

If condition (1) did not obtain, equilibrium at C (which is in fact the "normal" equilibrium position) would be stable, instead of unstable; equilibrium would tend to get established there, and, once established, the shifts in the I and S curves, due to capital accumulation or decumulation, would merely lead to gradual changes in the level of activity until a position of stationariness is reached; they would not generate cyclical movements. If condition (2) were not satisfied (at any rate as regards *low* levels of activity)[1] the system, as we have seen, would be so unstable that capitalism could not function at all. Finally, if condition (3) did not obtain, the cyclical movements would come to a halt at some stage, owing to a cessation of the movements of the $S(x)$ and $I(x)$ functions.

This is not to suggest that in the absence of these three conditions cyclical phenomena would be altogether impossible. Only they would have to be explained with the aid of different principles; they could not be accounted for by the savings and investment functions alone.

8. In fact, conditions (1) and (2) are almost certain to be satisfied in the real world; doubt could only arise in connection with condition (3). It can be taken for granted, of course, that net investment will be *positive* while equilibrium is at position B; but it is by no means so certain that net investment will be *negative* while equilibrium is at position A.[2] It is quite possible, for example, that savings should fall rapidly at a relatively early stage of the downward movement, so that position A is reached while net investment is still positive. In that case the S and I

---

[1] It is possible that the point B should be situated *beyond* the position of full employment—i.e. that in the course of the upward movement the state of full employment should be reached before *ex-ante* Savings and Investment reach equality. In that case the upward movement would end in a state of cumulative inflation, which in turn would, sooner or later, be brought to a halt by a rise in interest rates sufficient to push the point B inside the full-employment barrier. From then onwards the cyclical movement would proceed in exactly the same manner as described.

[2] The term "net investment" here is used in the sense defined in § 6 (ii).

curves will still move in the same direction as at B, with the result that the position A is gradually shifted to the left, until net investment becomes zero. At that point the movements of the I and S curves will cease; the forces making for expansion or contraction come to a standstill. Alternatively we might assume that net investment at A is initially negative, but in the course of the gradual improvement, the position of zero net investment is reached before the forces of cumulative expansion could come into operation—i.e. somewhere during Stages IV and V, and *before* the cycle reaches Stage VI. In this case, too, the cyclical movement will get into a deadlock.

Hence the forces making for expansion when we start from a state of depression are not so certain in their operation as the forces making for a down-turn when we start from prosperity; the danger of chronic stagnation is greater than the danger of a chronic boom. A boom, if left to itself, is certain to come to an end; but the depression might get into a position of stationariness, and remain there until external changes (the discovery of new inventions or the opening up of new markets) come to the rescue.

9. The preceding analysis offers also certain indications regarding the determination of the period and the amplitude of the cycle. The period of the cycle seems to depend on two time-lags, or rather time-rates of movement: (i) on the rate at which the S and I curves shift at any particular level of investment (this, of course, will vary with the level of investment, and will be faster when investment is high or low, than in the middle); (ii) on the time taken to complete a cumulative movement— i.e. the time required for the system to travel from $B+C$ to A or from $A+C$ to B (Stages III and VI).

The second of these factors obviously depends on the velocity with which entrepreneurs and consumers adjust their expectations and thus their buying plans to unexpected changes in the situation. The first factor, on the other hand, seems to depend on technical data, on the construction period and durability of capital goods. The shorter the construction period, the greater will be the output of capital goods, per unit period, at a given rate of investment; the shorter the life-time of capital goods, the larger will be the percentage addition to total equipment represented by a given output of capital goods. Hence the shorter the construction period, and the lower the durability, the faster will be the rate of shift of the S and I curves at any given rate of investment: the shorter the length of the trade cycle.[1]

As regards the amplitude, this depends on the *shapes* of the I and S curves, which determine the distance between A and B, at their normal position (i.e. at Stages I and IV). The amplitude will be all the smaller the shorter the range of activity over which the normal values of $\frac{dI}{dx}$ and $\frac{dS}{dx}$ are operative. Variations in the amplitude of successive cycles, on the other hand, seem to depend entirely on extraneous factors, such as new inventions or secular changes in habits of saving. There appears to be no necessary reason why, in the absence of such factors, the amplitude should be gradually decreasing or vice versa.[2]

10. Our model should also enable us to throw some light on problems of economic policy. Here I confine myself to two points. (i) It appears that measures taken to combat the depression (through public investment) have much more chance of success if taken at a relatively early stage, or at a relatively late stage, than at the bottom of the depression. If taken early, the problem is merely to prevent that gradual fall in the investment function relatively to the saving function which carries the cycle from Stage II to Stage III. But, once Stage III is passed, nothing can prevent the switch-over from the B-equilibrium to the A-equilibrium, and then the problem becomes one of raising the investment

---

[1] If the "capital intensity" of investments varies in the different phases of the cycle in an *inverse relation* to the rate of investment (i.e. is less in boom periods than in depression periods), this will tend to reduce the period of the cycle, as compared with a situation where the capital intensity is constant, since it will increase the rate of shift of the S and I curves. Conversely, if capital intensity varied *in direct relation* with the rate of investment, this would lengthen the period. Finally, if capital intensity showed a *steady increase* throughout the cycle, this would lengthen the boom periods and shorten the depression periods.

[2] At first sight one might think that this question also depends on *endogenous* factors: that the cycle will be "damped" (amplitude of successive cycles decreasing) if the point of zero net investment is so situated that there will be net capital accumulation over the cycle as a whole, and vice versa. But this is not so. If there is net accumulation over the cycle as a whole (i.e. the accumulation over the boom period exceeds the decumulation during the depression), then in the absence of extraneous changes, the position B at the corresponding stages of successive cycles will be situated more and more to the left; but the position A will also be situated more to the left, with the result that, though there will be a gradual fall in the average level of activity, there need be no decrease in the deviations around the average. The same holds, *mutatis mutandis*, if there is net decumulation over the cycle as a whole.

demand schedule sufficiently to lift the position to Stage VI (at which the forces of expansion come into operation). The amount of public investment required to achieve this is obviously much greater in the early phase of the depression (at Stage IV) than in the later phase (at Stage V). Thus just when the depression is at its worst the difficulty of overcoming it is the greatest. (ii) The chances of "evening out" fluctuations by "anti-cyclical" public investment appear to be remote. For if the policy is successful in preventing the downward cumulative movement, it will also succeed in keeping the level of private investment high; and for this very reason the forces making for a down-turn will continue to accumulate, thus making the need for continued public investment greater. Thus, if, on the basis of past experience, the Government Authority contemplates a four years investment plan, in the belief that thereby it can bridge the gap between one prosperity period and the next, it is more likely that it might succeed in *postponing* the onset of the depression for four years than that it will prevent its occurrence altogether.[1] If the trade cycle is really governed by the forces analysed in this paper, the policy of internal stabilisation must be conceived along different lines.

Appendix

It may be interesting to examine the relations of the model here presented to other models of the trade cycle based on similar principles. The one nearest to it, I think, is Mr. Kalecki's theory, given in Chapter 6 of his *Essays in the Theory of Economic Fluctuations*. The difference can best be shown by employing the same type of diagram and the same denotation as used by Mr. Kalecki. Let income be measured along OY, and the rate of investment decisions along OD. Let $D_t = \Phi e(Y_t)$ represent the rate of investment decisions at time t, given the quantity of equipment available. Let the family of curves Φe_1 . . . etc.,

---

[1] This argument is strictly valid only for a closed system; it is not valid in the case of a country which receives its cyclical impulses from abroad. For in that case the cyclical variations in the demand for exports can be taken as given irrespective of what the Government is doing; the chronological order of the "lean years" will not be altered by the attempt at suppressing them. Thus a policy of this type is much more likely to be successful in a small country, like Sweden, than in large countries, such as Britain or the United States, which themselves generate cyclical forces and transmit them to others.

represent this function for different quantities of available equipment, where e_1 represents a *smaller* quantity of equipment than e_2, and so on. Let $Y_{t+\tau}=f(D_t)$ be the level of income at time $t+\tau$ as a function of investment decisions at the time t. This is the same as our savings function, which, for simplicity,

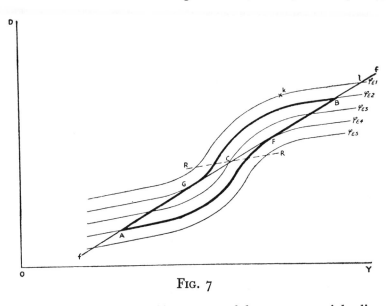

FIG. 7

and following Mr. Kalecki, we regard here as a straight line, independent of the amount of equipment. (τ represents the time lag between investment decisions and the corresponding income, which, as Mr. Kalecki has shown, depends partly on the construction period of capital goods, and partly on the lag between income and consumption.) The meeting points of Φe curves and the f curve are positions of short-period equilibrium, where Savings=Investment; the equilibrium is stable when the Φe curve cuts the f function from above, it is unstable when it cuts it from below. Let RR represent the locus of points on the Φe curves where the level of investment decisions corresponds to replacement so that *net* investment is zero. This curve is slightly *rising*, from left to right, since the higher the amount of equipment in existence, the greater the amount of investment needed for replacement. The point C represents the position of long-period or stationary equilibrium, where Savings=Investment *and* net investment is zero.

Under our assumptions, where $\dfrac{d\Phi}{dY}$ exceeds $\dfrac{1}{\dfrac{df}{dD}}$ for certain values of Y, there must be certain levels of equipment at which the Φ curves cut the f function not once, but three times. In our diagram this will be the case if equipment is greater than e_2 and less than e_4. Given this assumption, and assuming further that the replacement level, *for the critical amounts of equipment*, falls between the limits of stability—i.e. between points F and G in the diagram—the system can never settle down to a stationary equilibrium, but moves around it in a cycle. If we assume that the time-lag τ is small relatively to the time needed to reach successive Φ curves (i.e. relatively to the rate at which the total quantity of equipment is increasing), so that a position of short-period equilibrium can be reached *before* significant changes occur in the amount of equipment in existence, the cyclical movement of the system will be indicated by the trajectory $AGBF$. For if we start from any arbitrary point, such as k, the cumulative forces will increase income and investment decisions until the system reaches l, and thereafter activity will move downwards (owing to the gradual accumulation of equipment) along the f line until it reaches F. At that point equilibrium becomes unstable, and a downward moving cumulative process is set up which lands the system at A. Here investment is less than replacement, and the gradual reduction in available equipment will increase activity until the system reaches G, at which the situation again becomes unstable, an upward cumulative movement follows which lands the system at B. Thus if we start from any point outside the trajectory, the system will move on to it, and the same follows if we start from any point inside. Hence, even if we started from the position of stationary long-period equilibrium (C), the instability of the situation there must generate forces which set up a cycle.

It follows, further, that if all the fundamental data which determine the Φ and f functions—i.e. tastes, technique, population, monetary policy, the elasticity of expectations, etc.—remain unchanged, the cycle would continue indefinitely with constant amplitude and period and the trend (the accumulation of capital between successive cycles) would be zero. Hence changes in the nature of successive cycles would have to be explained by dynamic changes.

In Mr. Kalecki's model $\dfrac{d\Phi}{dY}$ is supposed to be smaller than $\dfrac{1}{\dfrac{df}{dD}}$ throughout, hence all his positions of short-period equilibrium are *stable* positions. In this case, on our assumptions, no cycle would be generated at all; the system would gradually approach stationary equilibrium. He assumes, however, that the time-lag between investment decisions and the corresponding income is large relatively to the rate at which the amount of equipment is increasing—i.e. the movements *along* a Φ curve and the movement *between* Φ curves are of comparable speed—in which case the movements towards a stationary equilibrium may "overshoot the mark"—i.e. the rate of investment decisions can continue to fall, even after it is less than what corresponds to replacement, simply because the fall in income lags behind. Thus the introduction of the time-lag between investment decisions and the corresponding income could explain a cyclical movement even if the underlying situation is a stable one: though, in order that this cycle should not be highly damped (i.e. that it should not peter out quickly in the absence of new disturbing factors), it is necessary to suppose (i) that the effect of current investment on total equipment should be relatively large, so that the equipment added during the period of the time-lag has a considerable influence on the rate of profit, and hence on investment decisions; (ii) that the angle enclosed by the f and Φ functions should be small—i.e. that $\dfrac{1}{\dfrac{df}{dD}}$ should but slightly exceed $\dfrac{d\Phi}{dY}$.[1]

Previous attempts at constructing models of the trade cycle —such as Mr. Kalecki's or Professor Tinbergen's—have thus mostly been based on the assumption of statically stable situations, where equilibrium would persist if once reached; the existence of the cycle was explained as a result of the operation of certain time-lags which prevented the new equilibrium from being reached, once the old equilibrium, for some external cause, had been disturbed. In this sense all these theories may be regarded as being derived from the "cobweb theorem". The drawback of such explanations is that the existence of an undamped cycle can be shown only as a result of a happy coincidence, of a particular

[1] Hence the positions of equilibrium in Mr. Kalecki's model, though formally stable, possess only a *low* degree of stability.

constellation of the various time-lags and parameters assumed. The introduction of the assumption of unstable positions of equilibrium at and around the replacement level provides, however, as we have seen, an explanation for a cycle of *constant amplitude* irrespective of the particular values of the time-lags and parameters involved. The time-lags are only important here in determining the *period* of the cycle, they have no significance in explaining its existence.

Moreover, with the theories of the Tinbergen-Kalecki type, the amplitude of the cycle depends on the size of the initial shock. Here the amplitude is determined by endogenous factors and the assumption of "initial shocks" is itself unnecessary.

8

KEYNESIAN ECONOMICS AFTER FIFTY YEARS[1]

INTRODUCTION

Keynes's *General Theory of Employment, Interest and Money* is undoubtedly regarded as the most important book on economics in the twentieth century, and this view would be shared, I think, by those who are wholly opposed to its teaching as well as by its adherents. Nearly 50 years after its appearance controversy still rages around its basic ideas and prescriptions, and I do not think that any major economist in the West would regard the issues raised by Keynes as finally settled. In this respect Keynes's *General Theory* is in sharp contrast to all the previous pathbreaking books on economics—such as Adam Smith's *Wealth of Nations* or Ricardo's *Principles* or Marshall's *Principles*—whose main tenets have not given rise to violent controversies in the same way as Keynes's. The possible exception is Karl Marx's *Capital*, but then Marx was a revolutionary which Keynes was certainly not—Keynes's avowed purpose was to save the capitalist system, not to destroy it.

Why then all this turbulence? We have authors who have written several fat books on Keynes (and I presume still keep on writing them) the main message of which is that Keynes said nothing new, and others who spent the better part of their life-time in demonstrating (unsuccessfully in my view) that Keynes was entirely wrong.

I cannot point to any single dominant reason for this—I believe there must be several.

The first and perhaps the most important is that Keynes's main message ran counter to the basic tenet of respectable

---

[1] Paper delivered to the Keynes Centenary Conference in Cambridge June 1983, and published in J. Trevithick and G.N.D. Worswick (eds.) *Keynes and the Modern World* (Cambridge University Press 1983).

practitioners of the art which always has been that production in general was confined by the scarcity of human and material resources; that human welfare can be improved only by "economising" in the use of scarce resources (whether of land, labour or capital) which means securing the best allocation of what is available. This meant that an "economy"—a term which implied a community who satisfy their wants by mutual cooperation between their members—was necessarily constrained in its activities by its resource endowment: it was the poverty (or insufficiency) of resources which limited the satisfaction of wants. Since the endowment of resources available to a "community" was supposed to be determined exogenously, the welfare of the community could be maximised (or its misery minimised) only by the free play of market forces under a free enterprise system, with the minimum of government interference and regulation.

Keynes asserted the contrary. His main proposition was that in normal circumstances, production in general was limited by effective demand which determined *how much* of potential resources were effectively utilised. Hence there was scope (in normal circumstances) for securing greater material welfare through the purposeful direction of the economy by a combination of fiscal and monetary policies which could secure full employment whilst avoiding inflation.

In order to explain how this could be done Keynes put forward a model of the interaction of a limited number of strategic variables operating on the economy which serve to explain how, in given circumstances, the level of output as a whole and its movement were determined. This gave birth to a new branch of economics, macro-economics, distinguished by the fact that unlike the prevailing economic theory it made empirical hypotheses concerning the behaviour of groups or categories of individuals, the validity of which could be refuted, by observation if not by experiment, and which made it possible to make quantitative forecasts of how the "economy" would behave in response to either policy changes introduced by the government, or to external changes due *e.g.* to new inventions or spontaneous changes in expectations.

Thus the main reason why Keynes's book found such a widespread echo so soon after its publication was that it brought economics "back to earth"—back to its original purpose of being an instrument for formulating rational policies concerning the economy.

Though the initial reaction of the economics profession was almost uniformly adverse—as shown by the reviews of the book by leading economists in English or American journals—the new ideas made rapid strides among academic economists of the younger generation, and also among civil servants, advisers to Ministers and even financial journalists. No doubt the outbreak of the war greatly lessened the normal resistance to new ideas. Thus in Britain in 1941 Keynes (by that time an adviser to the Chancellor of the Exchequer) managed to embody the new principles in the Budget, which meant aiming at the "right amount" of fiscal deficit—a notion which only made sense in terms of a Keynesian model of the economy. From then on, and until the end of the 1970s, the annual "Budget judgement" meant that the primary function of taxation was regarded as the avoidance of inflationary pressures whilst securing the right climate for expansion in the economy. And well before the end of the war, the Coalition Government gave a solemn undertaking that henceforth "the maintenance of a high and stable level of employment" would be one of the government's principal obligations and responsibilities.[1] Much the same intellectual change occurred in the United States where the new principles of economic management were embodied in the Employment Act of 1946. They were also embodied in the new French Constitution of 1946, in Article 55 of the Charter of the United Nations, and Article 104 of the Treaty of Rome. None of this would have occurred without the appearance of Keynes's *General Theory*—since "maintaining full employment" would not have occurred to economists or politicians as a feasible policy objective.

---

[1] This obligation was formally abandoned only with the arrival of Mrs. Thatcher's Government in 1979—some 36 years later; although in practice it was abandoned after 1973 for various reasons (mentioned later), one of which was that Keynesian demand management proved incompatible with our membership of the Common Market.

In the following quarter of a century—up to 1973—the Western world did in fact experience an unprecedented period of economic expansion, combined in most countries with full employment or even "over-full employment" in the sense that the demand for labour could only be satisfied through the various States allowing a considerable immigration from the surplus labour areas of less developed countries—whether from overseas dependencies or ex-dependencies (as in the case of Britain or France) or from the less developed countries of Europe (as in the case of Germany, Holland, Switzerland, Austria, etc.). How far this was the result of the adoption or the deliberate pursuit of Keynesian policies, or how far it would have happened in any case as a consequence of a prolonged economic boom is a complex question which admits of no simple answer. There were some countries (such as France) where the acceptance of Keynesian ideas led to State investment planning in the form of a succession of five year plans, carried out in cooperation between the state and private enterprises—with the result that France became the fastest growing country in Europe. The results for Britain were not nearly as good (mainly I think because there was too little investment at home and too much abroad; and a strong inborn resistance, absent in France, to the State "meddling" in the affairs of business). Nevertheless the 25 years 1948-73 recorded a higher rate of progress than any earlier period of comparable length in British history, and, except for the last few years of that period, unemployment remained consistently low (well below Beveridge's 3 per cent target) despite considerable immigration.[1]

In the 1970s this happy era came to an end with a rapid inflation of both commodity prices and industrial wages; as a result of which the Governments of industrial countries became preoccupied with the dual problem of inflation and balance of

[1] R.C.O. Matthews (*Economic Journal*, September 1968) tried to demonstrate that all this owed little to Keynesian fiscal management, since it was the increase in *private* investment (in relation to the national income) which filled the pre-war gap in effective demand. However, as I argued (*Economic Journal*, March 1971, p. 9) the main effect of the Government's fiscal policy was to ensure a continued *growth* in demand, which *induced* the increase in investment. (Investment is very dependent on the actual (and expected) rate of growth of demand.)

payments deficits, both of which they believed could be corrected by monetary and fiscal policies. Hence the international conditions which Keynes had always regarded as essential for national full employment policies ceased to hold, and the cumulative process of credit contraction which he had much dreaded was finally unleashed in the post-war world.[1]

Hence recession hit a number of countries and it became generally believed (rightly or wrongly) that "Keynesian" instruments of economic policy were unavailable for coping with this situation. At the same time the anti-Keynesian school of economists, the "new" monetarists, rapidly gained followers among influential people more or less simultaneously in a number of countries and this was combined by widespread and rapidly growing antagonism to Keynesian ideas. The reason for this antagonism, not openly acknowledged, was the change in the power structure of society which the pursuit of Keynesian policies had brought about. This was foreseen well before the adoption of Keynesian methods of demand management. Thus in an article in *The Times* in January 1943 on post-war Full Employment it was stated:

"Unemployment is not a mere accidental blemish in a private-enterprise economy. On the contrary, it is part of the essential mechanism of the system, and has a definitive function to fulfil. The first function of unemployment (which has always existed in open or disguised forms) is that it maintains the authority of masters over men. The master has normally been in a position to say: 'If you don't want the job, there are plenty of others who do.' When the man can say 'If you don't want to employ me there are plenty of others who will' the situation is radically altered."[2]

[1] See in particular his remarkable speech in the House of Lords on 23 May 1944, reproduced in J.M.K., XXXVI, p. 16.
[2] The doctrine is usually associated with Karl Marx who argued that capitalism can only function with a "reserve army" of unemployed labour. But Marx himself owes these ideas (though he never seems to have acknowledged it) to Adam Smith, who wrote in the *Wealth of Nations* that normally there is always a scarcity of jobs relative to job-seekers: "There could seldom be any scarcity of hands nor could the masters be obliged to bid against one another in order to get them. The hands, on the contrary, would in this case, naturally multiply beyond their employment. There would be a constant scarcity of employment and the labourers would

"The change in the workers' bargaining position which should follow from the abolition of unemployment would show itself in another and more subtle way. Unemployment in a private enterprise economy has not only the function of preserving discipline in industry, but also indirectly the function of preserving the value of money. If free wage bargaining as we have known it hitherto, is continued in conditions of full employment, there would be a constant upward pressure upon money wage-rates. This phenomenon also exists at the present time, and is kept within bound by the appeal of patriotism. In peace-time the vicious spiral of wages and prices might become chronic."[1]

The second main point is that whereas the main proposition of Keynes's *General Theory*, concerning the critical role of demand in determining aggregate output and the possibility or likelihood of an "underemployment equilibrium" with involuntary unemployment, withstood the attacks launched against it, many of the theoretical constructs which he invented or employed by way of proof or explanation did not. In other words his famous passage on Marshall (written on the occasion of his obituary of Marshall in the *Economic Journal* of 1924) sounds almost prophetic since it appears to be far more applicable to his own future work than to that of his great teacher:

"It was an essential truth to which he held firmly that those individuals who are endowed with a special genius for the subject and have a powerful economic intuition will often be more right in their conclusions and implicit presumptions than in their explanations and explicit statements. That is to

be obliged to bid against one another in order to get it. If in such a country the wages of labour had ever been more than sufficient to maintain the labourer and to enable him to bring up a family, the competition of the labourers and the interest of the masters would soon reduce them to the lowest rate which is consistent with common humanity" (Book 1, ch. VIII, p. 24).

[1] "Planning Full Employment—Alternative Solutions of a Dilemma", *The Times*, 23 January 1943. (A "turnover" article; the article was unsigned but its authorship is generally attributed to Joan Robinson.)

say, their intuitions will be in advance of their analysis and their terminology."

To this should perhaps be added the famous concluding paragraph to the Preface of the *General Theory* written in December, 1935:

> "The composition of this book has been for the author a long struggle to escape, and so must the reading of it be for most readers if the author's assault upon him is to be successful—a struggle of escape form habitual modes of thought and expression ... The difficulty lies, not in the new ideas, but in escaping from the old ones which ramify, for those brought up as most of us have been, into every corner of our minds."[1]

The result was an extraordinary paradox in that while Keynes took every opportunity to emphasise the novelty of his approach, and his rejection of the "fundamental postulates" of the "classical economists" (by which he meant everybody who figures in "mainstream" economics from Adam Smith to Marshall) this merely disguised the extent to which his theory suffered from an almost slavish adherence to prevailing (Marshallian) doctrine—to which his own ideas were "fitted" more in the manner of erecting an extra floor or balcony here or there, while preserving the pre-existing building. This, I hope to show, applies to Keynes's most radical novelties, such as the principle of effective demand, the liquidity preference theory of interest, his "revision" of the quantity theory of money as well as his retaining the fiction of a "closed economy" which prevented him from analysing the more basic (or intriguing) question of why unemployment looms so much larger in some countries than in others.

In the following section I shall deal with each of these aspects in turn.

---

[1] *General Theory*, p. viii.

THE PRINCIPLE OF EFFECTIVE DEMAND

The core of Keynes's theory is the principle of effective demand which is best analysed as a development or refinement of Say's law, rather than a complete rejection of the ideas behind that law. Say, like Ricardo or John Stuart Mill (or later Walras), takes as his starting point the proposition that ultimately all economic activity consists in the exchange of goods and services between different "agents", hence "demand" and "supply" are merely different aspects of the same thing; when two economic agents exchange two commodities, x and y between them, the supply of x by A is at the same time A's demand for y; the supply of y by B is B's demand for x. If, for sake of convenience, prices are expressed in a common medium the *numéraire*, the situation is not fundamentally altered; the money value of things sold is equal to the money value of things bought for *each* individual and *therefore* for all individuals taken together. Hence the total value of the things sold in terms of money is identical to the total value of things bought; or, as Mill put it, "could we suddenly double the productive powers of the country, we could double the supply of commodities in every market; but we should by the same stroke, double the purchasing power".[1] Hence "Supply creates its own demand".

However the application of this idea takes different forms at different stages of economic development. In a simple barter economy, when goods are exchanged against goods but each commodity is valued in terms of a common unit, the value of the initial bundle of commodities of each participant is no greater or less than the value of the final bundle—at any rate if we abstract from the "tâtonnement" problem, the possibility that some of the commodities are exchanged at "false" prices. When however we go a step further and allow for the existence of money as a medium of exchange this equivalence no longer holds—or not necessarily, because some of the money obtained by sellers may not be used for the purchase of goods of equivalent value on the *same day*; the peasant who brought a

---

[1] Mill, *Principles of Political Economy*, Book III, ch. XIV, para. 2.

bundle of produce to the market may end up with a smaller bundle of goods (in terms of value) and with some unspent money (i.e. with some "savings", even if only from one market day to the next); conversely, some participants may buy things with money left over from the trading of earlier days, and which supplement their purchases from current sales. The existence of durable money which can be stored thus destroys the necessary equivalence between demand and supply in the aggregate—on a particular "market day" the one can be larger or smaller than the other.[1]

All this applied to what Keynes called, in an early draft, a "co-operative economy"—where different producers satisfy at least some of their needs through exchanges of their own produce with those of others. He distinguished this sharply from the "entrepreneur economy"[2] which corresponds to what Marx called "capitalism", where production is carried on in large-scale units by hired labour, with the entrepreneur deciding how much to produce (*i.e.* how many people to employ) in the light of their expectation of sales-proceeds from different levels of output. In other words the entrepreneurs incur costs which become "factor incomes" in the hands of the recipients[3] and which are the primary source of purchasing power for the goods produced. To that extent it is true to say that "supply creates its own demand". But the two are not (or need not be) equivalent to one another; demand generated by supply may not be enough to satisfy the expectation of entrepreneurs for two primary reasons (as we shall see, there can be several others): *first*, because the recipients of incomes may not devote all of it to the purchase of goods (or not immediately); *second*, even if they spent it fully and on the same day, the entrepreneur would only succeed in recovering his

---

[1] Neo-classical economists would argue that the existence of durable money necessarily leads to a "money market" where those with surplus money lend it out to those who are deficient of it for a consideration which takes the form of interest. It is Keynes's contention however that the mere existence of a market of "loanable funds" will not suffice to restore the overall equality of demand and supply at all levels of output.

[2] See J.M.K., XXIX, pp. 66-8.

[3] Each individual entrepreneur incurs costs in buying goods or services from other entrepreneurs, as well as hiring labour. However these are also resolvable into "factor incomes", once double counting is eliminated.

costs, leaving nothing over for his own remuneration. To induce entrepreneurs to stay in business the sales proceeds must exceed the costs incurred in production—in other words firms must make a profit—and profits cannot be treated as part of "factor incomes", fixed in advance; they reflect the *outcome* of the whole operation, and they can be negative as well as positive. One can say (as Keynes does) that entrepreneurs require a larger total profit for large output; but if so, such profits form part of a *minimum* "supply-price" which can be smaller (as well as larger) than the realised sales-proceeds. If realised sales proceeds are inadequate, the entrepreneur will be induced to contract operations. Supply will be reduced, but this in turn, by reducing factor-incomes, will reduce demand, thus leading to a further reduction of supply, etc.[1]

The originality in Keynes's conception of effective demand lies in the division of demand into two components, an endogenous component and an exogenous component. It is the endogenous component which reflects (*i.e.* is automatically generated by) production, for much the same reasons as those given by Ricardo, Mill or Say—the difference is only that in a money economy (*i.e.* in an economy where things are not directly exchanged, but only through the intermediation of money) aggregate demand can be a *function* of aggregate supply (both measured in money terms) without being *equal* to it—the one can be some fraction of the other. To make the two equal requires the addition of the exogenous component (which could be one of a number of things, of which capital expenditure— "investment"—is only one) the value of which is extraneously determined. Given the relationship between aggregate output and the endogenous demand generated by it (where the latter can be assumed to be a monotonic function of the former), there is only one level of output at which output (or employment) is in "equilibrium"—that particular level at which the amount of exogenous demand is just equal to the difference between the value of output and the value of the endogenous

---

[1] Major Douglas, who saw this point but was not able to see further, derived from this the conclusion that a capitalist economy necessarily tends to shrink with more and more unemployment unless factor incomes were supplemented by a "social dividend".

demand generated by it. If the relationship between output and endogenous demand (which Keynes called "the propensity to consume") is taken as given, it is the value of exogenous demand which determines what total production and employment will be. A rise in exogenous demand, for whatever reasons, will cause an increase in production which will be some multiple of the former, since the increase in production thus caused will cause a consequential increase in endogenous demand, by a "multiplier" process. How large this secondary increase will be will depend on a lot of things such as the distribution of the additional output between wages and profits, and the change in productivity (or in costs per unit of output) associated with the increase in production, etc.

The critical role played by exogenous demand in the process of income generation has another aspect, less frequently emphasised—*i.e.* that given the basic behavioural relationships (such as the consumption function) an increase in resources, whether of labour or capital (or in their efficiency due to technical progress, etc.) will not serve to increase actual production unless the exogenous component of demand is increased at the same time. In many cases the same factor may operate on both but this is not necessarily so, nor is there any presumption that the rate of growth of the one will be closely geared to the rate of growth of the other. A capitalist economy (for reasons explained below) is not "self-adjusting" in the sense that an increase in potential output will automatically induce a corresponding growth of actual output. This will only be the case if exogenous demand expands at the same time to the required degree; and as this cannot be taken for granted, the maintenance of full employment in a growing economy requires a deliberate policy of demand management.

This was the chief message which Keynes intended to convey. It was also the message which economists found most difficult to accept—at least all those who regarded the Walrasian model of the economy as the valid paradigm of the functioning of a market economy (and they comprised a far wider group than those who actually studied Walras). Walras' general equilibrium model presupposes the universal rule of perfect competition and constant returns to scale, the twin assumptions necessary to ensure that all markets "clear" (*i.e.* that all resources are fully utilised and the production of each commodity is at its attainable maximum, given the production of all other commodities.[1])

But in the absence of these twin assumptions the mere existence of competition between sellers ("firms") will not in itself ensure the full utilisation of resources unless all firms *expand in concert*. Any one firm, acting in isolation, may find that the market for its own products is limited, and will therefore refrain from expanding its production even when its marginal costs are well below the ruling price. Under these conditions involuntary unemployment could only be avoided if something—the growth of some extraneous component of demand—drives the economy forward.

Keynes was no student of Walras. However, there was enough in Marshall (particularly in Book v, the short period theory of value) to raise the same kind of qualms—*why* don't all markets behave in such a way to *compel* the full utilisation of resources? Marshall's own theory suggested that saving represents an indirect demand for commodities in the same way as consumption which sets up direct demand. Savings provide the supply of "loanable funds" which, given an efficient capital market which equates supply and demand, governs the amount of capital expenditure incurred. This amounts to a denial of the whole idea of an exogenous source of demand—the latter notion presupposes that the supply and demand for savings are brought into equality by changes in income and employment and not by the "price" of savings in the capital market, which is the rate of interest. In order to explain why the market for loans is not "market-clearing" in the same sense as other markets, Keynes introduced the liquidity-preference theory of interest—which, as is evident from his own later writings, was added more or less as an afterthought.[2]

---

[1] For a simple demonstration of this, see my paper, "What is Wrong with Economic Theory", *Quarterly Journal of Economics*, August 1975.

[2] "Alternative Theories of the Rate of Interest," *Economic Journal*, June 1937, pp. 241-52, reprinted in J.M.K., XIV, pp. 201-15: "As I have said above, the initial novelty lies in my maintaining that it is not the rate of interest, but the level of incomes which ensures equality

But for Keynes's critics it was the key assumption needed for showing why the Rate of Interest does *not* behave in the manner required to generate capital expenditure that equals full employment savings. In other words, but for the downward rigidity of interest rates, involuntary unemployment would not exist, and classical economics would be vindicated.

This was the origin of the view that Keynesian economics depended on a "liquidity trap" which could be effectively countermanded by an appropriate policy on interest rates.[1] It was the basis of the post-war "neo-classical synthesis" according to which the notion of general equilibrium (of producers and consumers) guided automatically by the price-mechanism remains valid provided only that monetary policy (which meant interest rate policy) is so directed as to make the market for savings "market-clearing" just like all the other markets. The "micro-foundations of macro-economics" appeared to have shown that so long as one sticks to neo-classical micro-economics, Keynesian macro-economics amounts to very little.

However the *main* attributes of Keynes's "under-employment equilibrium" cannot be ascribed to the "liquidity-trap"—to liquidity preference holding up interest rates. For the very notion of production in the aggregate being limited by demand presupposes a state of affairs in which the production of individual firms in industries of all kinds is limited by lack of orders and not by productive capacity. "Keynesian" unemployment, as numerous writers have pointed out,[2] as distinct from "classical" or "Marxian" unemployment presupposes unutilised or under-utilised capacity as well as involuntary unemployment of labour. The existence of excess capacity on

---

between savings and investment. The arguments which lead up to this conclusion are independent of my subsequent theory of the rate of interest, and in fact I reached it before I reached the latter theory ... But the result of it was to leave the rate of interest in the air ... It was only when the search [for a productivity explanation] led repeatedly to what seemed to be circular reasoning that I hit on what I now think to be the true explanation ... the rate of interest has to be established at the level which ... equalises the attractions of holding idle cash and of holding a loan. It would be true to say that this does not carry us very far. But it gives us firm and intelligible ground from which to proceed ... To speak of the 'liquidity-preference Theory' of the Rate of Interest is indeed to dignify it too much. It is like speaking of the professorship theory' of Ohlin or the 'civil-servant theory' of Hawtrey."

[1] The term "liquidity trap" was first used by D.H. Robertson.

[2] See *e.g.* Malinvaud, *The Theory of Unemployment Reconsidered*, Oxford, 1977.

the other hand implies that the individual producer faces a *limited* demand for his product—not an infinitely elastic demand curve.

The discovery that competition in a capitalist economy does not conform to the assumption of pure or perfect competition was, just as Keynes's *General Theory*, the product of the intellectual ferment of the 1930s.[1] But for reasons that have never been satisfactorily explained, these latter discoveries were never properly integrated—though not because they were found either unimportant or irrelevant. In a paper published in early 1935[2] I showed that imperfect competition requires the assumption of falling long-run cost curves (increasing returns to scale) up to some minimum level of output which is significant in relation to the size of the market as a whole. Given this fact, the competition of potential new producers will come to a halt when any benefit gained from selling a smaller output at a higher price is offset, or more than offset, by the higher cost per unit of the smaller output—when the demand curve for the products of the firm becomes "tangential" to the cost curve. If on the other hand the long run cost curves are horizontal (*i.e.* there are constant returns to scale over the whole range—however small or however large the production) the process of the inflow of new producers (or new "substitute" products—these come to the same thing since the products of different producers are never *wholly* identical with each other) will not come to a halt until the output of the typical producer becomes small enough for the elasticity of demand to become infinite—when prices become equal to *both* average and

[1] As is often the case, the original work in this field was done by economists such as A.A. Young at Harvard and G.F. Shove in Cambridge (England) who never published a systematic exposition of their ideas developed in their lecture courses; instead they left this task to their pupils, E.H. Chamberlin, the author of *The Theory of Monopolistic Competition* and Joan Robinson, the author of the *Economics of Imperfect Competition*, two books independently written which were published more or less simultaneously. However, just because the implications of the imperfect competition and oligopoly proved too difficult to incorporate into traditional theory, these doctrines (unlike Keynes's theory of employment) were gradually ignored and forgotten; the massive post-war work on the theory of general economic equilibrium—by Samuelson, Debreu, Arrow, Hahn and innumerable others—simply assumed away their existence (without attempting to justify this procedure either on empirical grounds or by showing that it is a harmless simplifying assumption which makes no difference to the conclusions).

[2] "Market Imperfection and Excess Capacity", *Economica*, February 1935, reprinted in *Essays on Value and Distribution*, pp. 62-80, and as Chapter 3 of this book.

marginal costs. Hence constant returns to scale (a consequence of an infinite divisibility of all factors) is sufficient to create perfect competition. I concluded "We see therefore that the mathematical economists, in taking perfect competition as their starting point, weren't such fools after all. For they assumed perfect divisibility of everything; and where everything is perfectly divisible, and consequently economies of scale are completely absent,[1] perfect competition must necessarily establish itself solely as the result of the free play of economic forces. No degree of product differentiation and no possibility of further and further product variation will be sufficient to prevent this result, so long as all kinds of institutional monopolies and all kinds of indivisibilities are completely absent."[2]

I *should* have added that under these conditions the "free play of economic forces" will necessarily *also* establish (and maintain) a state of full employment. Unfortunately the above was published a year before the appearance of the *General Theory*, and the notion of a macro-economic "under-employment equilibrium" was as yet unknown.[3] However, more recently, Mr M.L. Weitzman has demonstrated[4] that constant returns to scale, strictly interpreted, are a sufficient condition for the absence of "involuntary unemployment'. The latter arises because a worker who is not offered a job cannot turn himself into his own employer (in the manner originally suggested by Wicksell) since he cannot compete effectively with firms organised for large-scale production.[5] But under these

[1] I have since changed my mind on the question whether perfect divisibility is a sufficient (as distinct from a necessary) condition of constant returns to scale (see "The Irrelevance of Equilibrium Economics", Appendix on Indivisibilities and Increasing Returns, *Economic Journal*, December 1972, reprinted below, pp. 393-8).

[2] *Ibid.* p. 71.

[3] The most widespread explanation for unemployment at that time was that put forward by Pigou in the *Theory of Unemployment* (1933) which is best summed up by saying that unemployment was caused by the downward rigidity of money wages resulting from trade unions and collective bargaining, but which did not indicate (or not necessarily) that real wages correspond to the real supply price (or marginal disutility) of labour.

[4] "Increasing Returns and the Foundations of Unemployment Theory", *Economic Journal*, December 1982, pp. 781-809.

[5] "On the other hand with perfect divisibility, when unemployed factor units are all going about their business spontaneously employing themselves or being employed, the economy will automatically break out of unemployment. While the simple story of supply creating its own demand can be told in a closed barter economy, I do not see the existence of money, savings, investment or international trade *per se* invalidating the basic proposition that a logical inference

conditions no single firm finds it profitable to hire more workers and to produce more output, even though the marginal cost is well below the price set by the firm (but which is strongly dependent upon the prices set by other firms). If all firms acted in collusion, in *all* industries, it would be a different matter, since the increased output of all firms would increase the demand for every one of them sufficiently to justify the increased output. But in the absence of such co-ordinated action the system can be in equilibrium at *any* level of employment and output; Keynes has shown that it will gravitate to a level set by the exogenous components of demand. "There is a sense therefore in which the natural habitat of effective demand macroeconomics is a monopolistically competitive micro-economy. Analogously, perfect competition and classical macroeconomics are natural counterparts."[1]

The implication of this analysis however is that most of the debate around the legitimacy of Keynes's notion of "underemployment equilibrium" was misplaced. It is the notion of a "full employment equilibrium" which is an artificial creation, the consequence of the artificial assumption of constant returns to scale in all industries and over the whole range of outputs which implies infinite divisibility of everything. Once the artificial assumption of pure (or perfect) competition is abandoned, a Walrasian equilibrium with market-clearing prices in every market becomes a mirage, not in any way descriptive as a "first approximation" of the conditions obtaining in the real world.

Hence in my view, most of the voluminous literature concerning the reconciliation of Keynesian analysis with

---

of strict constant returns to scale and perfect competition is full employment. With sufficient divisibility of production, each unemployed factor unit has an incentive to produce itself out of unemployment and market the product directly. In fact the unemployed are induced to create on their own scale an exact replica of the full employment economy from which they have been excluded" (Weitzman, *op. cit.* p. 793). It is not necessary of course that increasing returns with price-*making* firms should be the rule in every single industry. It is quite possible that some sectors of the economy (like parts of agriculture or mining) should conform to the rules of perfect competition, where sellers are price-*takers*, and where equilibrium output involves price = marginal cost. However the demand for their products will largely be determined by the incomes earned in the rest of the economy and provided that in the aggregate there is insufficient pressure for a balanced and simultaneous expansion in all markets—*i.e.* in other words, provided that the forces making for self-generated expansion are too weak, the economy will conform to the same characteristics as if increasing returns extended to every branch of the economy.

[1] *Ibid.*, p. 801.

Walrasian general equilibrium—in terms of "disequilibrium" economics, inverted velocities of price and quantity adjustments, absence of the "heavenly auctioneer", etc.—is beside the point. The two kinds of theory cannot be reconciled, simply because one concerns a purely artificial world of perfect competition, etc., while the other attempts to generalise about the real world.

Keynes himself was by no means fully conscious of this contrast. He accepted neo-classical theory (in its Marshallian version) as regards micro-economics—he assumed that prices of individual commodities are equal to or determined by, marginal costs; that (real) wages reflect the marginal productivity of labour and that marginal productivity declines with increasing employment, so that, as he believed in the *General Theory*, there is an inverse relationship between real wages and employment. There is no mention of imperfect competition or its consequences in the *General Theory*. This prompted Jean de Largentaye, the French translator of the *General Theory*, to say that the acceptance of Marshallian micro-economics by Keynes made it possible for his opponents "to invoke the authority of the *General Theory* in favour of views directly contrary to its essential teaching".[1] Clearly the assumption of the prevalence of involuntary unemployment (which implies that the real wage is in excess of the marginal disutility of labour) is less plausible, or less intuitively obvious, when one assumes that increased employment is associated with lower real wages than when one assumes, on the contrary, that a larger volume of production and employment would be associated with *higher* real wages.

In an important article published in 1939,[2] written in response to the criticisms of Tarshis, Dunlop and Kalecki, Keynes retracted his earlier views concerning real wages and employment, saying that his assertions in the *General Theory* were based on Marshall's empirical findings (and not just on the theoretical requirements of neo-classical value theory) which

---

[1] Jean de Largentaye, "A Note on the General Theory", *Journal of Post-Keynesian Economics*, Vol. 1, No. 3, p. 9. (This is an English translation of the *Introduction* to the second French edition of the *General Theory*, published by Payot, Paris 1968.)

[2] "Relative Movement of Real Wages and Output", *Economic Journal*, March 1939, pp. 34-51, reprinted in J.M.K., VII, pp. 394-412.

however related to a succession of boom and depression periods prior to 1886. Investigating the cyclical variation in real wages since that date he found that the relationship was reversed; real wages were higher in periods of high employment than in depression periods, and he attributed this to the practical workings of the laws of "imperfect competition in the modern quasi-competitive system" characterised by the fact that the individual producer "is normally operating subject to decreasing average costs".[1]

However while this 1939 article was a laudable attempt to rectify erroneous statements (both empirical and theoretical) in the *General Theory*, it would be an exaggeration to say that Keynes even then showed full awareness of the critical importance of increasing returns and imperfect competition to his general theory of employment. Had he done so, a great deal of the post-war controversy concerning the *nature* of Keynesian theory might have been avoided. And as de Largentaye pointed out in the paper referred to above, by the time his 1939 article appeared the harm was done, and there were a number of influential writers who maintained, in line with Milton Friedman later, that the increase in employment associated with a Keynesian policy of demand management was both inflationary and temporary: the policy depended for its effectiveness on a misperception of future prices and hence in over-estimation of the expected real wage relatively to the money wage and the *actual* real wage. Such doctrines could not have gained a foothold had the existence of increasing returns in industry been appreciated and had it been recognised, in consequence, that any "misperception" arising out of the expansion of demand and of employment is more likely to consist of an under-estimation rather than an over-estimation of the expected real wage relative to the actual wage.[2]

Mr Weitzman also shows that "in an increasing return system, the equilibrium trade-off between real wages and employment

---

[1] *Ibid.*, pp. 46 and 406-7.

[2] It is in this respect that Kalecki's original model of unemployment equilibrium (read at the Leyden meeting of the Econometric Society in 1933 and published in *Econometrica*, 1935) which takes monopolistic competition as its starting point, is clearly superior to Keynes's. I heard Kalecki's exposition at Leyden but it was not until Keynes published his *General Theory* that I understood the notion of effective demand.

will tend to make ordinary wage adjustment mechanisms ineffective or unstable". Indeed "a successful attempt to depress real wages would actually *increase* the equilibrium level of unemployment. The implication would seem to be that aggregate wage and price flexibility cannot make this kind of economy self-correcting. Under such circumstances wage stickiness may actually be a blessing."[1]

This is very much in line with the spirit of the *General Theory* and, indeed, it is expressly stated in Chapter 19 on "Changes in Money Wages" (p. 267) that "money wage flexibility is not capable of maintaining full employment". However the argument leading up to this conclusion is by no means as decisive and clear-cut as the conclusion itself, and no doubt Keynes would have been very grateful for Mr Weitzman's support had it been available to him—the more so since the latter's argument (unlike Keynes's) relates to *real* wages and not merely to money wages.

THE MONETARIST COUNTER-ASSAULT

The controversy over the question whether a capitalist economy is necessarily "resource constrained" or whether it can be in underemployment equilibrium constrained by effective demand, is related to, though not identical with, another controversy concerning the role of money in the economy. This second controversy (or rather the second aspect of the controversy) has become far more vociferous and virulent in the past fifteen to twenty years and it has raised the question of alternative economic policies in a far more acute form.

It would be impossible to give a comprehensive review of the various issues raised by this controversy within the confines of a conference paper. I am handicapped also by the fact that I have published a number of papers in this field in the last few years[2] so that most of my views are fairly well-known—at least in those

---

[1] *Ibid.* pp. 800-1.
[2] See (with James Trevithick), "A Keynesian Perspective on Money", *Lloyds Bank Review*, January 1981; *Origins of the New Monetarism* (the Page Lecture, Cardiff, 1981; *Limitations of the General Theory* (a British Academy lecture published by OUP, 1973), all reprinted in *Collected Economic Essays*, vol. 9 (Duckworth, 1989); as well as *The Scourge of Monetarism* (OUP, 1982), which includes my evidence to the Treasury and Civil Service Committee of July 1980.

aspects of the controversy which fall within a realm of discourse that I feel confident of understanding. These relate to what Tobin called Monetarism Mark I—which concerned the question whether changes in prices are the consequence of *prior* changes in the amount of money in circulation, or whether, on the contrary, it is changes in incomes and prices caused by other factors which cause an accommodating change in the "money-supply" in consequence. Monetarism Mark II, on the other hand, raised far more subtle issues that are only relevant in a kind of super-neo-classical world where markets are continuously clearing, and where they also have the additional property that they enable "economic agents" to foresee the future correctly and thereby neutralise the effects of governmental economic policies—as, for example, the effects of switching from taxation to borrowing.

Leaving aside the Rational Expectations Hypothesis, as something which does not belong to the same universe of discourse, we are still left with the issue whether money is "important" or "unimportant" as a factor determining output, employment and prices.

To understand how this controversy developed, two things need to be borne in mind. First, the fact that during most of his working life Keynes (along with other Cambridge economists such as D.H. Robertson) was a true follower of the Quantity Theory of Money in the form developed by Marshall, on which he lectured for many years, and which he wished to develop further, both in the *Tract on Monetary Reform* in 1923 and in the *Treatise on Money* in 1930. Second, that the years in which the *General Theory* was written were years of easy money, with very low interest rates, and where the rate of credit expansion was far more effectively limited by a lack of credit-worthy borrowers than by the Bank's inability or unwillingness to expand the base of bank credit. Hence the question of how the equation determining the equilibrium level of demand, looked at as the sum of business expenditures on investment and personal expenditure on consumption, was reconciled with aggregate demand as determined by monetary factors, *MV*, had never really occurred to him; the liquidity preference theory of interest, as we have seen, served the function not of reconciling the quantity theory with the effective demand theory but of explaining what determines the money rate of interest. Its function as "underpinning" Keynes's concept of underemployment equilibrium (which lent it such importance in the eyes of Dennis Robertson and other writers) was not one that would have naturally occurred to Keynes himself.

Nevertheless it is possible to show in terms of a few equations how monetary and "real" factors relate to each other in both pre-Keynesian and post-Keynesian economics.

The first equation is the traditional Fisher equation $MV = PT$ substituting output Q for Fisher's T (which includes transactions in stock and shares, etc., as well as in newly produced goods and services).
Hence

$$P = \frac{MV}{Q} \tag{1}$$

where $P =$ the price level
$M =$ quantity of money
$V =$ velocity of circulation
$Q =$ output or income in real terms

The second is the "Pigou amendment" to the quantity theory (so named because of its original appearance in Pigou's *Theory of Unemployment*)

$$P = (1 + \eta) \frac{dL}{dQ} w \tag{2}$$

where $L =$ labour
$w =$ the money wage rate per unit of L
$\eta =$ the reciprocal of the elasticity of demand facing the individual producer

Taking these two equations alone, we have two dependent variables, P and Q, while all other terms (including w, the money wage rate) are assumed to be given extraneously. Formally, the two equations jointly determine both P and Q; in fact it will depend on the elasticity of the short-period cost function—the variability of dL/dQ or simply L/Q with respect to changes in Q—whether P is *mainly* determined by equation (1) and Q *mainly* determined by equation (2) or *vice versa*.

The difference between the above system of two equations and the original quantity theory, equation (1), is that the above takes the level of money wages as an extraneous factor (*i.e. not* determined by the requirements of a market-clearing price in the labour market).[1]

This system of two equations summarised the prevailing view on unemployment which amounted to saying that as the demand curve for labour in the aggregate is falling, the amount of unemployment depended on a level of money wages, w, which exceeded the level compatible with full employment.

Keynes introduced a new concept, effective demand, which can be represented by an equation in *real* terms. To represent his theory of real demand in terms of a simple equation we assume that consumption, C, is a simple linear fraction of income $(C = cQ)$ and the condition of equilibrium $I = S$ (investment equals savings) can be written as $I = (1 - c)Q$ (since the model also assumes $S = sQ$ and $s = 1 - c$). Hence

$$D \equiv Q = \frac{1}{1-c} \, I \tag{3}$$

This equation introduces two new exogenous variables $(1 - c)$ and I, but no new dependent variables. The question now is can equation (3) be reconciled with the "Pigou" model, represented by equations (1) and (2)?

Keynes's solution was to introduce a further equation, the "liquidity preference relation" which he put as

---

[1] Hence the two equations provide for an under-employment equilibrium due to excessive wages relatively to the demand for labour—the unemployment however is not "involuntary" in Keynes's sense.

$M = L_1(Y) + L_2(r)$ but which can be expressed more generally in the form

$$M = L(Y,r) \qquad \text{where } Y \equiv PQ \tag{4}$$

which makes the demand for money a function both of income and the rate of interest. This implies that the quantity theory equation (equation (1)) should be re-interpreted in the form of

$$V(r) = \frac{Y}{M} \tag{4a}$$

where $V(r)$ is an alternative form of the liquidity preference function ($L = 1/V$ is the demand for money as a proportion of income).

The replacement of a constant V in equation (1) with $V(r)$ adds in fact two new dependent variables, since V will vary with r, and r must be such as to satisfy equations (4) and (4a), *i.e.* it must equate the demand for money with the supply. However, apart from P and Q, all other variables are exogenous—including M.

The consequence of this interpretation of Keynes (which was the generally accepted one, following Hicks's 1937 article, by Keynesians and non-Keynesians alike) was the whole burden of making equation (1) consistent with equation (3)—the quantity theory of money with the Keynesian theory of employment—fell on $V(r)$; on the change in the velocity of circulation which adapts itself to changes in aggregate demand due to (3).[1]

It fell to a young economist, Milton Friedman, to discover that this model makes Keynes's theory one that can be refuted (or confirmed in the sense of not refuted) by empirical investigations based on time series. For the model predicts on the above presentation that there should be a high correlation between variations in V and variations in Y, which in turn *implies* the absence of any correlation between M and Y. So Friedman

---

[1] Hence the statement by H.G. Johnson, James Tobin, G. Akerlof and numerous others that the difference between the "Keynesian" and the monetarist position turns on an empirical question, the interest-elasticity of the demand for money.

went to work on this with all possible speed, and lo and behold! he found the very opposite—that M and Y were invariably highly correlated (subject only to a variable time lag) whereas V was far more stable and its variations were, if anything, positively correlated with M and not negatively. He then pronounced against Keynes and in favour of the quantity theory, and kept on supplying more and more "proofs" of this kind from 1956 to the present day.

The obvious point that correlation says nothing about the direction of causality was raised of course very early in the controversy; Friedman put forward at different times a whole series of points in "evidence", of which the time lag was the most famous (and also the most hotly contested). Moreover he had written a book with Anna Schwartz[1] of some 800 pages in support of the view that changes in the money supply in the U.S. were exogenous, but as several reviewers pointed out, there is nothing in the book that would really support this, and quite a lot that would support the contrary.[2] He attributed (in his Presidential address to the American Economic Association in 1967) the Great Contraction of the U.S. 1929-1933 to the *deflationary* policies of the Federal Reserve System "which *forced*

---

[1] Milton Friedman and Anna Schwartz, *A Monetary History of the United States, 1867-1960*, Princeton University Press, 1963

[2] The book was subjected to a scathing attack by an American economic historian, Robert R. Russel, in *Fallacies of Monetarism* (Western Michigan University, 1981) who also pointed out that "the basic statistical tables in the appendixes of the *History* do not confirm the authors' findings" (*ibid.* p. 17). He also points out (p. 11) that at the end of the book (on p. 695)—the fifth from the final page of the text—they made a wholly unexpected ambivalent statement about causality: "While the influence running from money to economic activity has been predominant, there have clearly also been influences running the other way, particularly during the shorter-run movements associated with the business cycle ... Changes in the money stock are therefore a *consequence* as well as an independent source of change in money *income* and *prices*. *Mutual interaction*, but with money rather clearly the senior partner in longer-run movements and in major cyclical movements, and more nearly an equal partner with money income and prices in shorter-run and milder movements—*this is the generalization suggested by our evidence*." (Italics in the original.)

It is worth quoting Prof. Russel's comment which follows the above quotation:

"Now I find the above statement pretty hard to parse. What explanation of business cycles does it imply? What explanation of price changes? If changes in the money stock cause the longer-run movements and the big booms and busts, why do they not also cause the shorter-run and milder movements and the little business expansions and milder recessions? And, if changes in prices, wages, profits, interest, and rents can cause mild changes in the money stock, why can they not also cause big changes in the money stock? And what, by the way, is a long-run *movement* or a shorter-run *movement*? Movement of what? And why after 694 pages of evidence and positive thinking must we be content with a 'generalization *suggested* by the evidence' when we had been led to expect a Q.E.D.? It looks very much like a hedge or a cop-out."

or *permitted* a sharp reduction in the monetary base". The facts are that the Federal Reserve *increased* the monetary base in a vain attempt to stimulate the economy, as indeed Friedman's own statistics show.[1]

The extraordinary feature of all the monetary writing in this century both in Britain and in the U.S. has been that the exogenous character of the money supply was almost never questioned, despite the fact that most money assets originate in bank credit—through borrowing either by the public sector or the non-bank private sector. It was assumed by most writers that ultimately the total amount of money held by the public (*i.e.* outside the banking system) is determined by the monetary authorities, independently of the demand for money (or the demand for credit). The monetary authorities have wide powers through fixing the Bank Rate (or the discount rate) supplemented by open market operations, to provide the banking system with the particular amount of "liquidity" which conforms to the authorities' policy. Yet there was plenty of evidence to show that the supply of bank credit was elastic (it responded to fluctuations in demand) and the monetary authorities' power to counteract such fluctuations was severely circumscribed by their function of "lender of last resort"—a function that became all the more important the more the business of banking was concentrated in fewer hands. In addition, under the British banking system, an automatic increase in bank credit is provided in the form of guaranteed overdraft facilities, while the commercial banks have plenty of means at their disposal to replenish their reserves through the creation of inter-bank loans which give rise to negotiable paper in the form of "certificates of deposit" that can be discounted in the discount market.

Moreover the whole mechanism by which changes in the quantity of money will cause a rise in prices postulates a world of commodity money (where gold or silver are the main forms of money and convertible bank notes a subsidiary form): in that world, an increase in the amount of gold in circulation may

---

[1] *Op. cit.*, Table B-3, pp. 800-8.

cause the "supply" of gold, at the existing gold price level, to exceed the demand for it; and since all the gold which is anywhere must be somewhere, the only way the "excess supply" can be eliminated is through a rise in prices (*i.e.* a fall in the value of gold in terms of other commodities). As a result of, say, the discovery of a new gold mine, the circulation of gold will be accelerated until gold has lost enough of its value so that the new amount is no longer regarded as excessive in relation to the amount of real purchasing power which individuals wish to hold in the form of money.

But there is no analogy to any such process in the case of credit money. Since credit (and hence bank money) varies in response to the demand for bank loans, the "money supply" cannot be assumed to vary *relatively* to the money demand; the supply of money can never be in excess of demand for it; if there was such an excess (say, on account of an unexpected fall in business turnover or in incomes and prices) the excess supply would automatically be extinguished through the *repayment* of bank loans, or what comes to the same thing, through the purchase of income yielding financial assets from the banks.[1] It was for this reason that Friedman and his followers were never able to give an intelligible account of how an increase in the "money supply" will lead to an equi-proportionate rise in money incomes eighteen months to two years later. This "transmission mechanism" remains a "black box".

In Britain, monetarism of the Friedmanite type became extremely fashionable in the late 1970s; however since a new "monetarist" government of Mrs Thatcher came into power, these beliefs have fairly quickly evaporated among intellectuals. For the money supply, on the Government's chosen definition, £M3, rose nearly twice as fast as formerly, and it became clear to everyone that the monetary authorities had no direct means at their disposal of controlling its movement, but only indirect means through influencing the growth in the *demand* for money through deflationary fiscal policies. At the same time, a rigid

---

[1] The commercial banks always hold a large proportion of their assets in "investment" (Government bonds) which is the marginal employment of their assets, and which enables them to expand credit, or to repay deposits by corresponding variations in their investment portfolio.

pay policy in the public sector combined with strong pressure on business profits (caused by the over-valuation of the pound) have greatly reduced both the rate of increase in money wages and of prices of imported commodities. Hence the rate of inflation fell from 22 per cent in their first year in office to 5.3 per cent in 1983. But this very fact puts paid to the orthodox monetarists, according to whom the money explosion of the first two years should have caused a *high* rate of inflation of around 20 per cent or more.

Most of the stir created by Friedman's activities might have been avoided if Keynes had explicitly recognised that the quantity of money M is also an *endogenous* variable; at any given rate of interst it is determined by demand. This could have been incorporated in the model by a slight change in the liquidity preference function, writing

$$M(r) = L(Y,r) \qquad (4)'$$

or

$$Y = \frac{M(r)}{V(r)} \qquad (4a)'$$

Since this adds another variable $M(r)$ it requires another equation, which in its simplest form could be put

$$r = \bar{r} \qquad (5)$$

when $\bar{r}$ is the rate of interest as determined by monetary policy.[1] $\bar{r}$ can change of course with changes in policy, but for any given $\bar{r}$ the supply of money is infinitely elastic—or rather it cannot be distinguished from the demand for money; whereas the quantity theory asserts, *per contra*, that it is changes in the supply of money *relative* to the demand which are the sole cause of changes in the general price level.

---

[1] Diagrammatically, the difference in the representation of the supply and demand for money, is that in the original version (with M exogenous) the supply of money is represented by a vertical line, in the new version by a horizontal one, or a set of horizontal lines, representing different stances of monetary policy.

Once this is seen, the importance attached to the interest elasticity of demand for money (reflecting "liquidity preference") disappears. If this elasticity is small or non-existent (as recent experience suggests with regard to M3) this does not argue in favour of the efficacy of monetary controls but of the very opposite—of the impotence of the authorities to vary the quantity of money otherwise than in response to a variation in demand. Of course interest policy may be effective in influencing the level of investment (though hardly as powerful, in my view, as Keynes thought) and in this way would influence the level of incomes generated in the economy; and this in turn would influence the demand for money. In that case, however, monetary policy does nothing more than fiscal policy; it is a particular instrument of demand management in the Keynesian sense.

In a Keynesian model the price level of an industrial society depends on the money costs of production of commodities which, in a closed economy, depends on the level of efficiency wages—on money wages relative to output per head. At any given moment these factors are given exogenously, as a heritage of the past. But there is nothing in the model to determine the rate of change of money wages relative to the rate of change in productivity. It has been the universal experience of industrial countries in the present half century that the former invariably rises faster than the latter, though the gap is habitually greater in some countries than in others. This is a problem which Keynesian methods of demand management leave unresolved—except perhaps in the suggestion that wage-induced inflation would be more serious and show a stronger tendency to accelerate in boom periods with fast-rising profits and high employment than in slack periods with low profits and high unemployment.

The solution of this problem may require far-reaching changes in the institutional arrangements concerning the division of the national product between the different groups and classes which contribute to its formation.

THE TERRITORIAL ASPECT

Though Keynes was only too conscious of the role of foreign trade in Britain's unemployment problem—one need only refer to his opposition to the gold standard, to his numerous pamphlets and papers (of which *The Economic Consequences of Mr Churchill*[1] is justly the most famous)—in the *General Theory* he wished to concentrate on the domestic causes of unemployment, and for this purpose he adopted the traditional fiction of a closed economy.[2]

The analysis of the properties of a closed economy could in principle be applied to a region (such as, say, Scotland) or to a country in the sense of a sovereign entity with its own laws and customs, a common currency, and a single central authority deciding on how economic policy should be conducted—whether this concerns interest policy, public investment, etc. Or it could be related to the economy of a whole world—which is the only definition of a closed system that is literally true.

However, Keynes recognised and emphasised that his analysis relates to an advanced industrial society, such as Britain, which is dependent on imports of food and raw materials and exports manufactured goods to pay for them (or used to); and that its main propositions could be equally applied to other "entrepreneurial economies" such as the U.S. or Germany or France. He believed however (in company with all classical economists or their successors) that the labour supply of each "economy" can be taken as given—in other words, there is no *international* mobility of labour (and capital?), whereas *within* the "economy" space presents no problems, and limitations on the internal mobility of resources which might cause labour bottlenecks in some industries and under-employment in others could, in the first approximation, also be left out of account.

---

[1] J.M.K., IX, pp. 207-30.

[2] There are rare references (as for example on p. 270 of the *General Theory*) that his conclusions relating to "a closed system" may also be applicable to an "open system", "provided equilibrium with the rest of the world can be maintained by means of fluctuating exchanges", but this was no more than an indication that the important issues concerning the causes and cure of unemployment must arise within the system and not be brought in from outside.

There is certainly no indication to suggest that foreign trade can be a cause of a failure of effective demand, even when, thanks to fluctuating exchange rates or other causes, exports and imports are in balance. In his chapter on Mercantilism (chapter 23) he retracted his earlier extreme views on the free trade question, according to which "If there is one thing Protection can *not* do, it is to cure Unemployment. There are some arguments for Protection, based upon its securing possible but improbable advantages, to which there is no simple answer. But the claim to cure Unemployment involves the Protectionist fallacy in its grossest and crudest form."[1]

In the *General Theory*, he quotes the above passage as an example of how wrong he was when—in company with all other economists—he asserted that foreign trade is irrelevant to the problem of unemployment. But the "element of scientific truth" which he then (in 1936) conceded to mercantilism was the proposition (which followed directly from the effective-demand theory) that *net* foreign investment, as reflected in the surplus of the current account of the balance of payments, constitutes "investment" in much the same way as "home investment", and hence, for a country suffering from insufficient investment opportunities, foreign investment (in this sense) can serve as a useful adjunct to home investment in raising production to the full employment level. He pointed out however that this concession to the mercantilist view is full of pitfalls and dangers, since foreign investment, by raising interest rates, can make home investment less attractive; also an export surplus by one country is an import surplus of another: the gain in employment is thus a "beggar-my-neighbour" policy of curing unemployment (though the actual expression "beggar-my-neighbour" is of later origin).

But there is no hint of an indication that the *volume* of exports and their rate of growth (irrespective of whether they represent a current account surplus or not) are powerful factors determining the level of employment—more powerful perhaps than investment. (There was no mention in the *General Theory* of

---

[1] *The Nation and Athenaeum*, 24 November 1923 (quoted in the *General Theory*, p. 334. Italics in the original).

R.F. Harrod's "Foreign trade multiplier", despite the fact that the latter made its first appearance three years earlier in a Cambridge Economic Handbook of which Keynes was the General Editor.)[1] In so far as exports can be regarded as an *exogenous* component of demand (which they certainly can, so long as they are not in the nature of a direct payment for goods and services imported from abroad) they have very much the same kind of multiplier effects as domestic investment; with the important difference that in calculating the multiplier, the marginal propensity to import has to be taken into account and not (or not only) the marginal propensity to save. Assuming that the two propensities stand in the same relation to each other as the value of the two exogenous components of demand (*i.e.* that I/s is the same as E/m) and ignoring any autonomous element (not geared to income) either in savings or in imports, the action of the multiplier will result both in an equality of (home) investment with (home) savings and also in a zero current balance—in an equality of exports and imports. If the two ratios are not equal (say $E/m > I/s$) the process will yield a positive current account balance and a corresponding shortfall of domestic investment over domestic savings; with $E/m < I/s$ the opposite will occur. The latter situation is likely to impose a more binding constraint on employment than the former since it is easier to deal with a chronic tendency towards a balance of payments surplus than to find finance for a chronic deficit.

There is moreover a further important point which Keynes (as distinct from his followers, from Harrod onwards)[2] failed to take into account. Business investment is only partly an exogenous factor; partly it arises from the need, in a *growing* economy, to keep productive capacity growing in line with sales.[3] Such "induced investment" which is often expressed in

---

[1] *International Economics*, by R.F. Harrod, 1933, ch. 6, pp. 104-20.

[2] See Harrod, *The Trade Cycle*, Macmillan, 1938.

[3] Under increasing returns each firm attempts to maintain capacity at a level that is more than adequate for current sales, or sales expected for the immediate future, partly because the unit cost of a plant that is somewhat larger than that required for optimal use may have lower costs than the "optimal" plant; partly also because (for reasons first explained by Marx) each firm is striving to enlarge its market share and thereby gain a cumulative advantage over its rivals; the ready availability of surplus plants alone puts it in a position to exploit any chance increase in its selling power.

the form of the acceleration principle is no different from other induced elements of demand such as consumption; in the view of some writers, such as Hicks, the two ought to be lumped together, in the notion of a "super-multiplier" to gauge the true effect of an increase in exogenous demand.[1]

The final reason which makes exports, and not the export surplus, the important factor for employment and prosperity is that in a growing world economy (where growth may be ultimately governed by increases in the availabilities of primary products, such as foodstuffs, industrial materials or sources of energy) exports emanating from a particular country or region may be the governing factor in determining, not just the *level* of employment, but the growth of employment and productivity in the secondary and tertiary sectors (*i.e.* industry and services) over longer periods.

In most countries (if not all) there are latent reserves in agriculture and in traditional services industries so that it is not possible to say that any recorded level of employment (or unemployment) conforms to the full-employment assumption, in the sense that the general level of output is the maximum attainable in the short period. This may be true in the *very* short period since labour mobility takes time, though it is much accelerated in times of buoyant industrial demand; moreover, since the growth of industrial productivity is highly correlated with the growth of output, the *effective* supply of labour is itself enlarged beyond the growth in actual numbers. Internal mobility, moreover, is supplemented by international mobility—as post-war experience has shown, political barriers to international migration are almost automatically lifted whenever a growth-area becomes congested—and, taking the world as a whole, the magnitude of disguised unemployment is such that it is safe to assume that, from the point of view of any particular industrial growth-region, there are potentially unlimited supplies of labour; this means that it is not the *supply* of labour which is given to an "economy", however defined, but only the *supply price* of labour (or rather the *minimum* supply

---

[1] J.R. Hicks, *A Contribution to the Theory of the Trade Cycle*, Oxford, 1950, p. 50.

price—for the extent of migration depends not so much on earnings-differences as on the availability of jobs in the immigrant areas).[1]

As increasing returns are a prominent feature of manufacturing industries, and because they operate more as a consequence of *large* production than of *large-scale* production, they take the form of an ever-increasing differentiation of processes and of specialisation of human activities—which in turn depends for its success on easy communication of ideas and experience, and the constant emergence of new market opportunities, features emphasised in the famous paper by A.A. Young.[2] For these reasons industrialisation is invariably connected with urbanisation; industrial development tends to get polarised in certain growth points or in "success areas" which become centres of vast immigration either from surrounding or from more distant areas. This process of polarisation—what Myrdal calls "circular and cumulative causation"—is largely responsible for a growing division of the world between rich and poor areas as well as for the persistent differences in growth rates between different industrial countries. Countries which succeed in increasing their share of the world market—because they are relatively more successful in introducing innovations, etc.—impose an increasing handicap on those whose market share is diminished in consequence.

Thus the introduction of the "territorial aspect" or "space aspect" does not diminish, but on the contrary serves greatly to enhance, the emphasis to be placed on demand as a factor determining not just the short-run level of employment, but the long-run development of particular regions of the globe. However, in contrast to the framework of assumptions of neo-classical theory, the actual line of progress is not predictable—except perhaps for short periods in which the range of possibilities is severely circumscribed by whatever exists at a given moment, as a heritage from the past. But with

---

[1] This is amply shown by the enormous cyclical variation in the rate of labour migration from Europe to the U.S.A. in the period 1865-1914 without any corresponding change in earnings differentials.

[2] "Increasing Returns and Economic Progress", *Economic Journal*, December 1928.

each step that modifies the environment, new opportunities for change open up which make the future less and less predictable—owing to a powerful feed-back mechanism the events of each period of historical time can only be explained in terms of the actual sequence through which the system has progressed.

The main stimulus to growth and prosperity is not just more investment—though faced with the alternative of idleness, and its psychological frustration, the kind of investment programme advocated by Keynes in 1929 (in his pamphlet *Can Lloyd George Do It?*) would undoubtedly have meant a very considerable improvement in the performance of the British economy. But it would not have facilitated (or at least not nearly so much) an export-led growth which alone could ensure the long-run prosperity of these islands.

The latter would have required instruments which go beyond those needed for the maintenance of the pressure of demand by ordinary fiscal and monetary policies. It would have involved the deliberate encouragement of industries with a high export potential and a high technological potential, requiring a policy of positive guidance and direction of private as well as public investment (like Japan's "administrative guidance" and France's post-war five-year plans). Unfortunately, the dominance of *laisser-faire* philosophy in Britain for 100 years or more ensured that this kind of State guidance was universally regarded as distasteful and inefficient.

But whatever criticism can be made of the limitations imposed by the intellectual method of "equilibrium economics" (which Keynes inherited and was unable to discard) there can be no question of the greatness of his achievement. Perhaps it is fitting to quote one of his best known critics, Don Patinkin, for a final word:

"One need only study the literature which preceded the *General Theory* to appreciate both the novelty and importance of the message of the equilibrating role of changes in output generated by discrepancies between aggregate demand and supply at the time when Keynes presented it. And the force of that message is not much diminished by the existence of errors or confusion about the exact nature of the demand and supply curves and of the related dynamic process."[1]

[1] Don Patinkin, "Keynes's Theory of Effective Demand", *Economic Inquiry*, Vol. 17 (1979), p.175.

PART III

DISTRIBUTION, GROWTH AND CUMULATIVE CAUSATION

ALTERNATIVE THEORIES OF DISTRIBUTION[1]

ACCORDING to the Preface of Ricardo's *Principles*, the discovery of the laws which regulate distributive shares is the "principal problem in Political Economy". The purpose of this paper is to present a bird's-eye view of the various theoretical attempts, since Ricardo, at solving this "principal problem". Though all attempts at classification in such a vast field are necessarily to some extent arbitrary, and subjective to the writer, in terms of broad classification, one should, I think, distinguish between four main strands of thought, some of which contain important sub-groups. The first of these is the Ricardian, or Classical Theory, the second the Marxian, the third the Neo-Classical or Marginalist Theory and the fourth the Keynesian. The inclusion of a separate "Keynesian" theory in this context may cause surprise. An attempt will be made to show, however, that the specifically Keynesian apparatus of thought could be applied to the problem of distribution, rather than to the problem of the general level of production; that there is evidence that in its early stages, Keynes' own thinking tended to develop in this direction—only to be diverted from it with the discovery (made some time between the publication of the *Treatise on Money* and the *General Theory*) that inflationary and deflationary tendencies could best be analysed in terms of the resulting changes in output and employment, rather than in their effects on prices.

The compression of a whole army of distinguished writers, and schools of thought, between Ricardo and Keynes (Marx aside) under the term of Neo-Classical or Marginalist Theory is harder to justify. For apart from the marginalists proper, the group would have to include such "non-marginalists" or quasi-marginalists (from the point of view of distribution theory) as the Walrasians and the neo-Walrasians,[2] as well as the imperfect competitionists,

[1] Originally published in the *Review of Economic Studies*, Vol. XXIII, No. 2, 1955-6.
[2] By the term "neo-Walrasians" I mean the American "linear programming" and "activity analysis" schools, as well as the general equilibrium model of von Neumann

who though marginalist, do not necessarily hold with the principle of Marginal Productivity. But as I shall hope to show, there are important aspects which all these theories have in common,[1] and which justifies bringing them under one broad umbrella.

Ricardo prefaced his statement by a reference to the historical fact that "in different stages of society the proportions of the whole produce of the earth which will be allotted to each of these (three) classes under the names of rent, profit and wages will be essentially *different*".[2] To-day, a writer on the problem of distribution, would almost be inclined to say the opposite—that "in different stages of (capitalist) society the proportions of the national income allotted to wages, profits, etc., are *essentially similar*". The famous "historical constancy" of the share of wages in the national income and the similarity of these shares in different capitalist economies, such as the U.S. and the U.K.—was of course an un-suspected feature of capitalism in Ricardo's day. But to the extent that recent empirical research tends to contradict Ricardo's assumption about the variability of relative shares, it makes the question of what determines these shares, more, rather than less, intriguing. In fact no hypothesis as regards the forces determining distributive shares could be intellectually satisfying unless it succeeded in accounting for the relative stability of these shares in the advanced capitalist economies over the last 100 years or so, despite the phenomenal changes in the techniques of production, in the accumulation of capital relative to labour and in real income per head.

Ricardo's concern in the problem of distribution was not due, or not only due, to the interest in the question of distributive shares *per se*, but to the belief that the theory of distribution held the key to an understanding of the whole mechanism of the economic system—of the forces governing the rate of progress, of the ultimate incidence of taxation, of the effects of protection, and so on. It was

(*Review of Economic Studies*, 1945-6, Vol. XIII (1)) whose technique shows certain affinities with Walras even though their basic assumptions (in particular that of the "circularity" of the production process) are quite different. From the point of view of distribution theory, however, the approach only yields a solution (in the shape of an equilibrium interest rate) on the assumption of constant real wages (due to an infinitely elastic supply curve of labour); it shows therefore more affinity with the classical models than with the neo-classical theories.

[1] With the possible exception of the "neo-Walrasian" group referred to above.
[2] Preface (my italics).

through "the laws which regulate distributive shares" that he was hoping to build what in present-day parlance we would call "a simple macro-economic model".[1] In this respect, if no other, the Ricardian and the "Keynesian" theories are analogous.[2] With the neo-Classical or Marginalist theories, on the other hand, the problem of distribution is merely one aspect of the general pricing process; it has no particular theoretical significance apart from the importance of the question *per se*. Nor do these theories yield a "macro-economic model" of the kind that exhibits the reaction-mechanism of the system through the choice of a strictly limited number of dependent and independent variables.

I. The Ricardian Theory

Ricardo's theory was based on two separate principles which we may term the "marginal principle" and the "surplus principle" respectively. The "marginal principle" serves to explain the share of rent, and the "surplus principle" the division of the residue between wages and profits. To explain the Ricardian model, we must first divide the economy into two broad branches, agriculture and industry and then show how, on Ricardo's assumptions, the forces operating in agriculture serve to determine distribution in industry.

The agricultural side of the picture can be exhibited in terms of a simple diagram (Fig. 1), where Oy measures quantities of "corn" (standing for all agricultural produce) and Ox the amount of labour employed in agriculture. At a given state of knowledge and in a given natural environment the curve p—Ap represents the product per unit of labour and the curve p—Mp the marginal product of labour. The existence of these two *separate* curves is a consequence of a declining tendency in the average product curve—i.e. of the assumption of diminishing returns. Corn-output

---

[1] "Political Economy", he told Malthus, "you think is an enquiry into the nature and causes of wealth—I think it should rather be called an enquiry into the laws which determine the division of the produce of industry amongst the classes who concur in its formation. No law can be laid down respecting quantity, but a tolerably correct one can be laid down respecting proportions. Every day I am more satisfied that the former enquiry is vain and delusive, and the latter only the true object of the science." (Letter dated 9 October, 1820, *Works* (Sraffa edition), Vol. VIII, pp. 278-9.)

[2] And so of course is the Marxian: but then the Marxian theory is really only a simplified version of Ricardo, clothed in a different garb.

is thus uniquely determined when the quantity of labour is given:[1] for any given working force, OM, total output is represented by the rectangle $OCDM$. Rent is the difference between the product of labour on "marginal" land and the product on average land, or (allowing for the intensive, as well as the extensive, margin) the difference between average and marginal labour productivity which depends on the elasticity of the p—Ap curve, i.e. the extent to which diminishing returns operate.

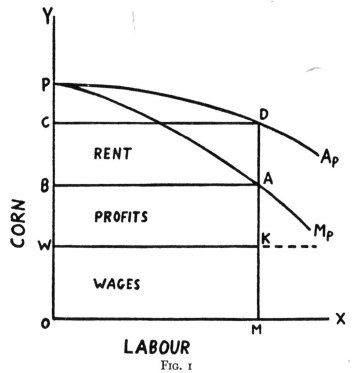

FIG. 1

The marginal product of labour (or, in classical parlance, the "produce-minus-rent") is not however equal to the wage, but to the sum of wages and profits. The rate of wages is determined quite independently of marginal productivity by the supply price of labour which Ricardo assumed to be constant in terms of corn.

[1] This abstracts from variations in output per head due to the use of more or less fixed capital relative to labour—otherwise the curves could not be uniquely drawn, relative to a given state of technical knowledge. As between fixed capital and labour therefore the model assumes fixed coefficients; as between labour and and, variable coefficients.

In modern parlance, the Ricardian hypothesis implies an infinitely elastic supply curve of labour at the given supply price, OW.[1] The demand for labour is not determined however by the p—Mp curve, but by the accumulation of capital which determines how many labourers can find employment at the wage rate OW. Hence the equilibrium position is not indicated by the point of intersection between the p—Mp curve and the supply curve of labour, but by the aggregate demand for labour in terms of corn —the "wages fund".[2] As capital accumulates, the labour force will grow, so that any addition to the total wage fund, through capital accumulation—the *agricultural* wages fund is indicated by the area $OWKM$—will tend to be a horizontal addition (pushing the vertical line KM to the right) and not a vertical one (pushing the horizontal line WK upwards).[3]

For any given M, profits are thus a residue, arising from the

[1] The basis of this assumption is the Malthusian theory of population, according to which numbers will increase (indefinitely) when wages are above, and decrease (indefinitely) when they are below, the "subsistence level". In Ricardo's hands this doctrine had lost its sharp focus on a biologically determined quantum of subsistence to which the supply price of labour must be tied; he emphasised that habits of restraint engendered in a civilised environment can permanently secure for labour higher standards of living than the bare minimum for survival. Yet he retained the important operative principle that in any given social and cultural environment there is a *"natural"* rate of wages" at which alone population can remain stationary and from which wages can only deviate temporarily. The hypothesis of an infinitely elastic supply curve of labour thus did not necessarily imply that this supply price must be equal to the bare minimum of subsistence. Yet this assumption was inconsistent with another (implied) feature of his model discussed below, that wages are not only *fixed* in terms of "corn" but are entirely (or almost entirely) *spent* on corn.

[2] Total wages depend on—and are "paid out of"—capital simply because production takes time, and the labourers (unlike the landlords) not being in the position to afford to wait, have their wages "advanced" to them by the capitalists. This is true of fixed as well as circulating capital but since, with the former, the turnover period is relatively long, only a small part of annual wages is paid out of fixed capital; the amount of circulating capital was therefore treated as the proper "wages fund". Despite his analysis of the effect of changes in wages on the amount of fixed capital used relative to labour, i.e. on the proportions of fixed and circulating capital employed in production (Professor Hayek's celebrated "Ricardo effect"), for the purpose of his distribution theory this ratio should be taken as given, irrespective of the rate of profit.

[3] The feature which the modern mind may find most difficult to swallow is not that capital accumulation should lead to a rise in population but that the reaction should be taken as something so swift as to ignore the intervening stage, where the increase in the wages fund should raise the rate of wages rather than the numbers employed. The adjustment of population to changes in the demand for labour would normally be treated as a slow long-run effect whereas changes in the demand for labour (caused by capital accumulation) may be swift or sudden. Ricardo, however, conceived the economy as one which proceeds at a more or less steady rate of growth in time, with the accumulation of capital going on at a (more or less constant) rate; while he conceded that *changes* in the rate of capital accumulation will temporarily raise or lower wages, he assumed that the rate of population growth itself is adapted to a certain rate of capital accumulation which had been going on for some time.

difference between the marginal product of labour and the rate of wages. The resulting ratio, $\dfrac{\text{Profits}}{\text{Wages}}$ determines the rate of profit % on the capital employed; it is moreover *equal* to that ratio, on the assumption that the capital is turned over once a year, so that the capital employed is equal to the annual wages-bill. (This latter proposition, however, is merely a simplification, and not an essential part of the story.)

In a state of equilibrium, the money-rate of profit % earned on capital must be the same in industry and in agriculture, otherwise capital would move from one form of employment to the other. But it is the peculiarity of agriculture that the money-rate of profit in that industry cannot diverge from the rate of profit measured in terms of that industry's own product, i.e. the corn-rate of profit. This is because in agriculture both the input (the wage outlay) and the output consist of the same commodity, "corn". In manufacturing industry on the other hand, input and output consist of heterogeneous commodities—the cost per man is fixed in corn, while the product per man, in a given state of technical knowledge, is fixed in terms of manufactured goods. Hence the only way equality in the rate of profit in money terms can be attained as between the two branches is through the prices of industrial goods becoming dearer or cheaper in terms of agricultural products. The money-rate of profit in manufacturing industry therefore depends on the corn-rate of profit in agriculture;[1] the latter, on the other hand, is entirely a matter of the margin of cultivation, which in turn is a reflection (in a closed economy and in a given state of technical knowledge) of the extent of capital accumulation. Thus "diminishing fertility of the soil", as James Mill put it, "is the great and ultimately only necessary cause of a fall in profit".

To make the whole structure logically consistent it is necessary to suppose, not only that wages are fixed in terms of "corn" but that they are entirely spent on "corn", for otherwise any change in the relation between industrial and agricultural prices will

---

[1] The analytical basis for this conclusion, given above, was never, as Sraffa remarks, stated by Ricardo in any of his extant letters and papers though there is evidence from Malthus's remarks that he must have formulated it either in a lost paper on the Profits of Capital or in conversation (cf. *Works*, Vol. I, Introduction, p. xxxi).

alter real wages (in terms of commodities in general) so that the size of the "surplus", and the rate of profit on capital generally is no longer derivable from the "corn-rate of profit"—the relationship between the product of labour and the cost of labour working on marginal land. Assuming that agricultural products ("corn") are wage-goods and manufactured products are non-wage-goods (i.e. ignoring that *some* agricultural products are consumed by capitalists, and *some* non-agricultural products by wage-earners), the whole corn-output (the area $OCDM$ in the diagram) can be taken as the annual wages fund, of which $OWKM$ is employed in agriculture and $WCDK$ in the rest of the economy. Any increase in $OWKM$ (caused, e.g., by protection to agriculture) must necessarily lower the rate of profit (which is the source of all accumulation) and thus slow down the rate of growth.[1] Similarly all taxes, other than those levied on land, must ultimately fall on, and be paid out of, profits, and thus slow down the rate of accumulation. Taxation and agricultural protection thus tend to accelerate the tendency (which is in any case inevitable—unless *continued* technical progress manages to shift the p—Ap and p—Mp curves to the right sufficiently to suspend altogether the operation of the Law of Diminishing Returns) to that ultimate state of gloom, the Stationary State, where accumulation ceases simply because "profits are so low as not to afford [the capitalists more than] an adequate compensation for their trouble and the risk which they must necessarily encounter in employing their capital productively".[2]

II. THE MARXIAN THEORY

The Marxian theory is essentially an adaptation of Ricardo's "surplus theory". The main analytical differences are : (1) that Marx paid no attention to (and did not believe in) the Law of Diminishing Returns, and hence made no analytical distinction between rent and profits; (2) that Marx regarded the supply price of labour (the "cost of reproduction" of labour) as being fixed,

---

[1] The evil of agricultural protection is thus not only that income is reduced through the transfer of labour to less productive employments, but that owing to the reduction in the rate of profit, industrial prices fall in terms of agricultural prices; income is thus transferred from the classes which use their wealth productively to classes which use it unproductively.

[2] Ricardo, *Principles*, p. 122 (Sraffa Edition).

not in terms of "corn", but of commodities in general. Hence he regarded the share of profits (including rent) in output as determined simply by the surplus of the product per unit of labour over the supply price (or cost) of labour—or the surplus of production to the consumption necessary for production.[1]

There are important differences also as between Marx and Ricardo in two other respects. The first of these concerns the reasons for wages being tied to the subsistence level. In Marx's theory this is ensured through the fact that at any one time the supply of labour—the number of workers seeking wage-employment—tends to exceed the demand for labour. The existence of an unemployed fringe—the "reserve army" of labour—prevents wages from rising above the minimum that must be paid to enable the labourers to perform the work. Marx assumed that as capitalist enterprise progresses at the expense of pre-capitalistic enterprise more labourers are released through the disappearance of the non-capitalist or handicraft units than are absorbed in the capitalist sector, owing to the difference in productivity per head between the two sectors. As long as the growth of capitalist enterprise is at the cost of a shrinkage of pre-capitalist enterprise the increase in the supply of wage labour will thus tend to run ahead of the increase in the demand for wage labour.

Sooner or later, however, the demand for labour resulting from accumulation by capitalist enterprise will run ahead of the increase in supply; at that stage labour becomes scarce, wages rise, profits are wiped out and capitalism is faced with a "crisis". (The crisis in itself slows down the rate of accumulation and reduces the demand for labour at any given state of accumulation by increasing the "organic composition of capital", so that the "reserve army" will sooner or later be re-created.)

The second important difference relates to the motives behind capital accumulation. For Ricardo this was simply to be explained by the lure of a high rate of profit. Capitalists accumulate voluntarily so long as the rate of profit exceeds the minimum "necessary compensation" for the risks and trouble encountered in the

---

[1] Ricardo himself abandoned in the *Principles* the idea that wages *consist* of corn (to the exclusion of manufactures), but whether he also abandoned the idea that the agricultural surplus is critical to the whole distribution process through the fixity of wages in terms of *corn only* is not clear. (Cf. Sraffa, *op. cit.*, pp. xxxii-xxxiii.)

productive employment of capital. For Marx, however, accumulation by capitalist enterprise is not a matter of choice but a necessity, due to competition among the capitalists themselves. This in turn was explained by the existence of economies of large-scale production (together with the implicit assumption that the amount of capital employed by any particular capitalist is governed by his own accumulation). Given the fact that the larger the scale of operations the more efficient the business, each capitalist is forced to increase the size of his business through the re-investment of his profits if he is not to fall behind in the competitive struggle.

It is only at a later stage, when the increasing concentration of production in the hands of the more successful enterprises removes the competitive necessity for accumulation—the stage of "monopoly capitalism"—that in the Marxian scheme there is room for economic crises, not on account of an excessive increase in the demand for labour following on accumulation, but on account of an insufficiency of effective demand—the failure of markets resulting from the inability of the capitalists either to spend or to invest the full amounts of profits (which Marx called the problem of "realising surplus value").

Marx has also taken over from Ricardo, and the classical economists generally, the idea of a falling rate of profit with the progressive accumulation of capital. But whereas with the classicists this was firmly grounded on the Law of Diminishing Returns, Marx, having discarded that law, had no firm base for it. His own explanation is based on the assumed increase in the ratio of fixed to circulating capital (in Marxian terminology, "constant" to "variable" capital) with the progress of capitalism; but as several authors have pointed out,[1] the law of the falling rate of profit cannot really be derived from the law of the "increasing organic composition" of capital. Since Marx assumes that the supply price of labour remains unchanged in terms of commodities when the organic composition of capital, and hence output per head, rises, there is no more reason to assume that an increase in "organic composition" will yield a lower rate of profit than a higher rate. For even if output per man were assumed to increase more slowly than ("constant" plus "variable") capital per man, the "surplus

---

[1] Cf., in particular, Joan Robinson, *An Essay in Marxian Economics*, pp. 75-82.

value" per man (the excess of output per man over the costs of reproduction of labour) will necessarily increase faster than output per man, and may thus secure a rising rate of profit even if there is diminishing productivity to successive additions to fixed capital per unit of labour.

While some of Marx's predictions—such as the increasing concentration of production in the hands of large enterprises—proved accurate, his most important thesis, the steady worsening of the living conditions of the working classes—"the immiseration of the proletariat"[1]—has been contradicted by experience, in both the "competitive" and "monopoly" stages of capitalism. On the Marxian model the share of wages in output must necessarily fall with every increase in output per head. The theory can only allow for a rise of wages in terms of commodities as a result of the collective organisation of the working classes which forces the capitalists to reduce the degree of exploitation and to surrender to the workers some of the "surplus value".[2] This hypothesis, however, will only yield a constant share of wages on the extremely far-fetched assumption that the rate of increase in the bargaining strength of labour, due to the growth of collective organisation, precisely keeps pace with the rate of increase in output per head.

III. The Neo-classical Theories

(A) Marginal Productivity

While Marx's theory thus derives from Ricardo's surplus principle, neo-classical value and distribution theory derives from another part of the Ricardian model: the "marginal principle" introduced for the explanation of rent (which explains why both Marx and Marshall are able to claim Ricardo as their precursor). The difference between Ricardo and the neo-classics is (1) that whereas Ricardo employed the "principle of substitution" (or

[1] It is not clear, in terms of Marx's own theoretical model, why such a progressive immiseration should take place—since the costs of reproduction of labour appear to set an *absolute* limit to the extent to which labour can be exploited. Some parts of *Das Kapital* could, however, be construed as suggesting that wages can be driven below the (long run) reproduction cost of labour, at the cost of a (long run) shrinkage in the labour force: and with the increasing organic composition of capital, and the rise of monopolies, the demand for labour may show an equally declining tendency.

[2] Marx himself would have conceived a reduction in the "degree of exploitation" in terms of a reduction in the length of the working day rather than a rise in real wages per day. In fact both have occurred side by side.

rather, the principle of "limited substitutability"—which is the basic assumption underlying all marginal analysis) only as regards the use of labour relative to land, in neo-classical theory this doctrine was formalised and generalised, and assumed to hold true of any factor, in relation to any other;[1] (2) whereas Ricardo employed the principle for showing that a "fixed" factor will earn a surplus, determined by the gap between the average and marginal product of the variable factor, neo-classical theory concentrated on the reverse aspect—i.e. that any factor variable in supply will obtain a remuneration which, under competitive conditions, must correspond to its marginal product. Thus if the total supply of *all* factors (and not only land) is being taken as given, independently of price, and all are assumed to be limited substitutes to one another, the share-out of the whole produce can be regarded as being determined by the marginal rates of substitution between them. Thus in terms of our diagram, if we assumed that along Ox we measure the quantity of any particular factor of production, x, the quantities of all the others being taken as fixed, p—Mp will exhibit the marginal productivity function of the variable factor. If the actual employment of that factor is taken to be M, AM will represent its demand price per unit, and the rectangle $OBAM$ its share in the total produce. Since this principle could be applied to any factor, it must be true of all (including, as Walras and Wicksell have shown, the factors owned by the entrepreneur himself) hence the rectangle $BCDA$ must be sufficient, and only just sufficient, for remunerating all other factors but x on the basis of their respective marginal productivities. This, as Wicksteed has shown,[2] requires the assumption that the production function is homogeneous of the first degree

---

[1] As well as of any particular commodity in the sphere of consumption. The utility theory of value is really Ricardian rent-theory applied to consumption demand. In fact, as Walras has shown, limited substitutability in consumption might in itself be sufficient to determine distributive shares, provided that the proportions in which the different factors are used are different in different industries. His solution of the problem of distribution, based on "fixed coefficients" of production (intended only as a first approximation) is subject, however, to various snags since the solution of his equations may yield negative prices for the factors as well as positive ones and it cannot be determined beforehand whether this will be the case or not. If the solution of the equations yields negative prices the factors in question have to be excluded as "free goods"; and the operation (if necessary) successively repeated until only factors with positive prices are left. Also, it is necessary to suppose that the number of different "factors" is no greater than the number of different "products", otherwise the solution is indeterminate.   [2] *The Co-ordination of the Laws of Distribution* (1894)

for all variables taken together—an assumption which he himself regarded as little more than a tautology, if "factors of production" are appropriately defined.[1] From the point of view of the theory, however, the *appropriate* definition of factors involves the elimination of intermediate products and their conversion into "ultimate" or "original" factors, since only on this definition can one assume the properties of divisibility and variability of coefficients. When factors are thus defined, the assumption of constant returns to scale is by no means a tautology; it is a restrictive assumption, which may be regarded, however, as being co-extensive with other restrictive assumptions implied by the theory—i.e. the universal rule of perfect competition, and the absence of external economies and diseconomies.

The basic difficulty with the whole approach does not lie, however, in this so-called "adding-up problem" but in the very meaning of "capital" as a factor of production.[2] Whilst land can be measured in acres-per-year and labour in man-hours, capital (as distinct from "capital goods") cannot be measured in terms of physical units.[3] To evaluate the marginal product of labour it is necessary to isolate two situations containing identical "capital" but two different quantities of labour, or identical amounts of labour, and two differing quantities of "capital", in precise numerical relationship.[4]

[1] *The Co-ordination of the Laws of Distribution* (1894), p. 53. "We must regard every kind and quality of labour that can be distinguished from other kinds and qualities as a separate factor; and in the same way, every kind of land will be taken as a separate factor. Still more important is it to insist that instead of speaking of so many £'s worth of capital we shall speak of so many ploughs, so many tons of manure, and so many horses or footpounds of power. Each of these may be scheduled in its own unit." Under these conditions it is true to say that "doubling all factors will double the product", but since these "factors" are indivisible in varying degrees, it does not mean that the production function is a linear and homogeneous one in relation to incremental variations of output. Also a change in output may be associated with the introduction of *new* factors of production.

[2] For a general equilibrium system, capital goods cannot be regarded as factors of production *per se* (in the manner suggested by Wicksteed), otherwise the same things are simultaneously treated as the parameters and the unknowns of the system.

[3] Measurement in terms of value (as so many £'s of "capital") already assumes a certain rate of interest, on the basis of which services accruing in different periods in the future, or costs incurred at different dates in the past, are brought to a measure of equivalence.

[4] The product of the "marginal shepherd" is the difference in terms of numbers of sheep, between 10 shepherds using 10 crooks and 11 shepherds using 11 slightly inferior crooks, the term "slightly inferior" being taken to mean that the 11 crooks in the one case represent precisely the same amount of "capital" as the 10 crooks in the other case. (Cf. also Robertson, "Wage Grumbles", in *Economic Fragments*, 1931).

Marshall, without going into the matter in any detail, had shown in several passages that he was dimly aware of this; and in carefully re-defining marginal productivity so as to mean "marginal *net* productivity" (*net* after deduction of all associated expenses on other "factors") he shied away from the task of putting forward a general theory of distribution altogether.[1]

In fact, in so far as we can speak of a "Marshallian" theory of distribution at all, it is in the sense of a "short period" theory, which regards profits as the "quasi-rents" earned on the use of capital goods of various kinds, the supply of which can be treated as given for the time being, as a heritage of the past. The doctrine of the "quasi-rent" assimilates capital as a factor of production to Ricardian land: the separate *kinds* of capital goods being treated as so many different kinds of "land". Here the problem of the measurement of capital as a factor of production does not arise: since, strictly speaking, no kind of change or reorganisation in the stock of intermediate products is permitted in connection with a change in the level or composition of production. It was this aspect of Marshall which, consciously or sub-consciously, provided the "model" for most of the post-Marshallian Cambridge theorising. Prices are equal to, or determined by, marginal prime costs; profits are determined by the difference between marginal and average prime costs; prime costs, for the system as a whole, are labour costs (since raw-material costs, for a closed economy at any rate, disappear if all branches of industry are taken together); ultimately therefore the division of output between profits and wages is a matter depending on the existence of diminishing returns to labour, as more labour is used in conjunction with a *given* capital equipment; and is determined by the elasticity of labour's average productivity curve which fixes the share of quasi-rents.

Marshall himself would have disagreed with the use of the quasi-rent doctrine as a distribution theory, holding that distributive

---

[1] "The doctrine that the earnings of a worker tend to be equal to the net product of his work, has by itself no real meaning; since in order to estimate the net product, we have to take for granted all the expenses of production of the commodity on which he works, other than his own wages." Similarly, the doctrine that the marginal efficiency of capital will tend to equal the rate of interest "cannot be made into a theory of interest, any more than a theory of wages, without reasoning in a circle". (Cf. *Principles*, 8th edition, Book VI, Chapter I, paras. 7-8.)

shares in the short period are determined by long-period forces.[1] Clearly even if one were to hold strictly to the assumption that "profit margins" are the outcome of short-period profit-maximisation, this "short-period" approach does not really get us anywhere: for the extent to which diminishing returns operate for labour in conjunction with the capital equipment available to-day is itself a function of the price-relationships which have ruled in the past because these have determined the quantities of each of the kinds of equipment available. The theory does not therefore really amount to more than saying that the prices of to-day are derived from the prices of yesterday—a proposition which is the more true and the more trivial the shorter the "day" is conceived to be, in terms of chronological time.

For the true neo-classical attempt to solve the general problem of distribution we must go to Wicksell who thought that by integrating the Austrian approach to capital with Walrasian equilibrium theory he could provide a general solution, treating capital as a two-dimensional quantity, the product of time and labour. The "time" in this case is the investment period or waiting period separating the application of "original" factors from the emergence of the final product, and the marginal productivity of capital the added product resulting from an extension of "time". This attempt, again, came to grief (as Wicksell himself came near to acknowledging late in life):[2] (i) owing to the impossibility of measuring that period in terms of an "average" of some kind;[3] (ii) owing to the impossibility of combining the investment periods of different "original" factors in a single measure.[4]

In fact the whole approach which regards the share of wages and of profits in output as being determined by the marginal rate of substitution between Capital and Labour—with its corollary,

---

[1] Cf., in particular, *Principles*, 8th edition, Book V, Chapters V and VI, and Book VI, Chapter VIII, para. 4.

[2] Cf. the concluding passage of his posthumous contribution to the Wieser Festschrift. *Die Wirtschaftstheorie der Gegenwart* (1928), Vol. III, pp. 208-9; also his "Analysis of Åkerman's Problem", reprinted in *Lectures*, Vol. I, p. 270.

[3] Since owing to compound interest, the weights to be used in the calculation of the average will themselves be dependent on the rate of interest.

[4] For a more extended treatment cf. my articles on capital theory in *Econometrica*, reprinted in *Essays on Value and Distribution* (1980), pp. 153-205; also Joan Robinson, "The Production Function in the Theory of Capital", *Review of Economic Studies*, Vol. XXI (1953-4), p. 81, and "Comment" by D.G. Champernowne, *ibid.*, p. 112.

that the constancy of relative shares is evidence of a unit-Elasticity of Substitution between Capital and Labour[1]—is hardly acceptable to present-day economists. Its inadequacy becomes evident as soon as it is realised that the "marginal rate of substitution" between Capital and Labour—as distinct from the marginal rate of substitution between labour and land—can only be determined once the rate of profit and the rate of wages are already known. The same technical alternatives might yield very different "marginal rates of substitution" according as the ratio of profits to wages is one thing or another. The theory asserts, in effect, that the rate of interest in the capital market (and the associated wage rate in the labour market) is determined by the condition that at any lower interest rate (and higher wage rate) capital would be invested in such "labour-saving" forms as would provide insufficient employment to the available labour; whilst at any higher rate, capital would be invested in forms that offered more places of employment than could be filled with the available labour.

Quite apart from all conceptual difficulties, the theory focuses attention on a relatively unimportant feature of a growing economy. For accumulation does not take the form of "deepening" the structure of capital (at a given state of knowledge) but rather in keeping pace with technical progress and the growth in the labour force. It is difficult to swallow a theory which says, in effect, that wages and profits are what they are for otherwise there would be too much deepening or too little deepening (the capital/output ratios would be either too large or too small) to be consistent with simultaneous equilibrium in the savings-investment market and in the labour market.

(B) The "Degree of Monopoly" Theories of Distribution

Monopoly profit was always regarded as a distinct form of revenue in neo-classical theory, though not one of any great quantitative importance since the mass of commodities was thought of as being produced under competitive conditions. But the modern theories of imperfect competition emphasise that monopoly profit is not an isolated feature. Profits in general

[1] Cf. Hicks, *The Theory of Wages* (1932), Chapter VI, passim.

contain an *element* of monopoly revenue—an element that is best defined as the excess of the actual profit margin in output over what the profit margin would have been under perfectly competitive conditions. Under Marshallian "short-period" assumptions the perfectly-competitive profit margin is given by the excess of marginal cost over average prime costs. The additional monopoly element is indicated by the excess of price over marginal cost. The former, as we have seen, is a derivative of the elasticity of labour's productivity curve where capital equipment of all kinds is treated as given. The latter is a derivative of the elasticity of demand facing the individual firm. The novel feature of imperfect competition theories is to have shown that the increase of profit margins due to this element of monopoly need not imply a corresponding excess in the rates of profit on capital over the competitive rate; through the generation of excess capacity (i.e. the tendency of demand curves to become "tangential" to the cost curves) the latter may approach a "competitive" or "normal" rate (as a result of the consequential rise in the capital/output ratio) even if the former is above the competitive level.

Kalecki[1] built on this a simplified theory of distribution, where the share of profits in output is shown to be determined by the elasticity of demand alone. This was based on the hypothesis that in the short period, labour and capital equipment are largely "limitational" and not "substitutional" factors, with the result that the short-period prime cost-curve is a reverse L-shaped one (prime costs being constant up to full capacity output). In that case marginal costs are equal to average prime costs; the ratio of price to prime costs (and hence, in a closed economy, the ratio of gross profits to wages) is thus entirely accounted for by the elasticity of the firm's demand curve.

On closer inspection, however, the elasticity of the demand curve facing the individual firm turned out to be no less of a broken reed than its counterpart, the elasticity of substitution between factors. There is no evidence that firms in imperfect markets set their prices by reference to the elasticity of their

[1] The original version appeared in *Econometrica*, April, 1938. Subsequent versions appeared in *Essays in the Theory of Economic Fluctuations* (1938), Chapter I, *Studies in Economic Dynamics* (1943), Chapter I, and *Theory of Dynamic Economics* (1954) Part I.

sales-function, or that short-period pricing is the outcome of any deliberate attempt to maximise profits by reference to an independent revenue and a cost function. Indeed the very notion of a demand curve for the products of a single firm is illegitimate if the prices charged by different firms cannot be assumed to be independent of each other.[1]

In the later versions of his theory Kalecki abandoned the link between the "degree of monopoly" and the elasticity of demand, and was content with a purely tautological approach according to which the ratio of price to prime costs was *defined* simply as the "degree of monopoly". Propositions based on implicit definitions of this kind make of course no assertion about reality and possess no explanatory value. Unless the "degree of monopoly" can be defined in terms of market relationships of some kind (as, for example, in terms of the cross-elasticities of demand for the products of the different firms)[2] and an attempt is made to demonstrate how these market relationships determine the relation between prices and costs, the theory does not provide a hypothesis which could be affirmed or refuted.

There is no need, of course, to follow Kalecki in the attempt to lend spurious precision to the doctrine through implicit theorising —a vice which afflicts all theories which we grouped together as "neo-classical" in varying degrees. Fundamentally, the proposition that the distribution of income between wages and profits depends on market structures, on the strength or weakness of the forces of competition, is not a tautological one; it asserts *something* about reality (which may in principle be proved false) even if that "something" cannot be given a logically precise formulation. Just as the positive content of the marginal productivity theory can be summed up by the statement that the rate of profit on capital (and the margin of profit in output) is governed by the need to prevent the capital/output ratio from being either too

[1] The theory of the "kinked" demand curve is in fact no more than a recognition of the fact that the demand curve of the firm (in the sense required for the purpose of deriving price from the postulate of profit maximisation) is non-existent. Since the position of the "kink" *depends* on the price, it cannot *determine* the price; it thus leaves the profit margin completely undetermined.

[2] The "cross-elasticities" of demand indicate the degree of interdependence of the markets of different firms and are thus inversely related to monopoly power in the usual sense of the word.

large or too small, the positive content of the "degree of monopoly" theory can be summed up in the sentence that "profit margins are what they are because the forces of competition prevent them from being higher than they are and are not powerful enough to make them lower than they are". Unfortunately neither of these statements gets us very far.

Dissatisfaction with the tautological character and the formalism of the "marginal revenue-equals-marginal cost" type of price theory led to the formulation of the "full cost" theories of pricing,[1] according to which producers in imperfect markets set their prices independently of the character of demand, and solely on the basis of their long-run costs of production (including the "normal" rate of profit on their own capital). If these theories asserted no more than that prices in manufacturing industry are *not* determined by the criterion of short-run profit-maximisation, and that profit margins can be fairly insensitive to short-period variations in demand[2] (the impact effect of changes in demand being on the rate of production, rather than on prices), they would provide a healthy antidote to a great deal of facile theorising. When, however, they go beyond this and assert that prices are determined quite independently of demand, they in effect destroy existing price theory without putting anything else in its place. Quite apart from the fact that a "full cost" theory is quite unable

---

[1] Cf. Hall and Hitch, *Oxford Economic Papers*, 1939; P. W. S. Andrews, *Manufacturing Business* (1949).

[2] This, I believe, was the intention of the original Hall-Hitch article. Cf. Marshall, *Principles*, Book VI, Chapter VIII, paragraph 4: "We see then that there is no general tendency of profits on the turnover to equality; but there may be, and as a matter of fact there is, in each trade and in every branch of each trade, a more or less definite rate of profits on the turnover which is regarded as a 'fair' or normal rate. Of course these rates are always changing in consequence of changes in the methods of trade; which are generally begun by individuals who desire to do a larger trade at a lower rate of profit on the turnover than has been customary, but at a larger rate of profit per annum on their capital. If however there happens to be no great change of this kind going on, the traditions of the trade that a certain rate of profit on the turnover should be charged for a particular class of work are of great practical service to those in the trade. Such traditions are the outcome of much experience tending to show that, if that rate is charged, a proper allowance will be made for all the costs (supplementary as well as prime) incurred for that particular purpose, and in addition the normal rate of profits per annum in that class of business will be afforded. If they charge a price which gives much less than this rate of profit on the turnover they can hardly prosper; and if they charge much more they are in danger of losing their custom, since others can afford to undersell them. This is the 'fair' rate of profit on the turnover, which an honest man is expected to charge for making goods to order, when no price has been agreed on beforehand; and it is the rate which a court of law will allow in case a dispute should arise between buyer and seller." Cf. also Kahn, *Economic Journal*, 1952, p. 119.

to explain why some firms should be more successful in earning profits than others, the level of the "normal profit" on which the full cost calculations are supposed to be based is left quite undetermined. The very fact that these full cost theories should have received such widespread and serious consideration as an alternative explanation of the pricing process is an indication of the sad state of vagueness and confusion into which the neo-classical value theory had fallen.

IV. THE KEYNESIAN THEORY

Keynes, as far as I know, was never interested in the problem of distribution as such. One may nevertheless christen a particular theory of distribution as "Keynesian" if it can be shown to be an application of the specifically Keynesian apparatus of thought and if evidence can be adduced that at some stage in the development of his ideas, Keynes came near to formulating such a theory.[1] The principle of the Multiplier (which in some ways was anticipated in the *Treatise* but without a clear view of its implications) could be alternatively applied to a determination of the relation between prices and wages, if the level of output and employment is taken as given, or the determination of the level of employment, if distribution (i.e. the relation between prices and wages) is taken as given. The reason why the multiplier-analysis has not been

---

[1] I am referring to the well-known passage on profits being likened to a "widow cruse" in the *Treatise on Money*, Vol. I, p. 139. "If entrepreneurs choose to spend a portion of their profits on consumption (and there is, of course, nothing to prevent them from doing this) the effect is to *increase* the profits on the sale of liquid consumption goods by an amount exactly equal to the amount of profits which have been thus expended. . . . Thus, however much of their profits entrepreneurs spend on consumption, the increment of wealth belonging to entrepreneurs remains the same as before. Thus profits, as a source of capital increment for entrepreneurs, are a widow's cruse which remains undepleted however much of them may be devoted to riotous living. When on the other hand, entrepreneurs are making losses, and seek to recoup their losses by curtailing their normal expenditure on consumption, i.e. by saving more, the cruse becomes a Danaid jar which can never be filled up; for the effect of this reduced expenditure is to inflict on the producers of consumption-goods a loss of an equal amount. Thus the diminution of their wealth as a class is as great, in spite of their savings, as it was before." This passage, I think, contains the true seed of the ideas developed in the *General Theory*—as well as showing the length of the road that had to be traversed before arriving at the conceptual framework presented in the latter work. The fact that "profits", "savings" etc. were all defined here in a special sense that was later discarded, and that the argument specifically refers to expenditure on consumption goods, rather than entrepreneurial expenditure in general, should not blind us to the fact that here Keynes regards entrepreneurial incomes as being the resultant of their expenditure decisions, rather than the other way round—which is perhaps the most important difference between "Keynesian" and "pre-Keynesian" habits of thought.

developed as a distribution theory is precisely because it was invented for the purpose of an employment theory—to explain why an economic system can remain in equilibrium in a state of under-employment (or of a general under-utilisation of resources), where the classical properties of scarcity-economics are inapplicable. And its use for the one appears to exclude its use for the other.[1] If we assume that the balance of savings and investment is brought about through variations in the relationship of prices and costs, we are not only bereft of a principle for explaining variations in output and employment, but the whole idea of separate "aggregate" demand and supply functions—the principle of "effective demand"—falls to the ground; we are back to Say's Law, where output as a whole is limited by available resources, and a fall in effective demand for one kind of commodity (in real terms) generates compensating increases in effective demand (again in real terms) for others. Yet these two uses of the Multiplier principle are not as incompatible as would appear at first sight: the Keynesian technique, as I hope to show, can be used for both purposes, provided the one is conceived as a short-run theory and the other as a long-run theory—or rather, the one is used in the framework of a static model, and the other in the framework of a dynamic growth model.[2]

We shall assume, to begin with, a state of full employment (we shall show later the conditions under which a state of full employment will *result* from our model) so that total output or income (Y) is given. Income may be divided into two broad categories,

[1] Although this application of Keynesian theory has been implicit in several discussions of the problem of inflation. (Cf. e.g. A. J. Brown, *The Great Inflation*, Macmillan, 1955.)

[2] I first thought of using the Multiplier technique for purposes of a distribution theory when I attempted to analyse the ultimate incidence of profits taxation under full employment conditions in a paper prepared for the Royal Commission on Taxation in 1951. The further development of these ideas, and particularly their relationship to a dynamic theory of growth, owes a great deal to discussions with Mrs. Robinson, whose forthcoming book, *The Accumulation of Capital*, contains a systematic exploration of this field. I should also like to mention here that I owe a great deal of stimulus to a paper by Kalecki, "A Theory of Profits" (*Economic Journal*, June-September, 1942) whose approach is in some ways reminiscent of the "widows' cruse" of Keynes' *Treatise* even though Kalecki uses the technique, not for an explanation of the share of profits in output, but for showing why the *level* of output and its fluctuations is peculiarly dependent on entrepreneurial behaviour. (In doing so, he uses the restrictive assumption that savings are entirely supplied out of profits.) I have also been helped by Mr. Harry Johnson and Mr. Robin Marris, both in the working out of the formulae and in general discussion.

Wages and Profits (W and P), where the wage-category comprises not only manual labour but salaries as well, and Profits the income of property owners generally, and not only of entrepreneurs; the important difference between them being in the marginal propensities to consume (or save), wage-earners' marginal savings being small in relation to those of capitalists.[1]

Writing S_w and S_p, for aggregate savings out of Wages and Profits, we have the following income identities:

$$Y \equiv W+P$$
$$I \equiv S$$
$$S \equiv S_w+S_p.$$

Taking investment as given, and assuming simple proportional savings functions $S_w=s_wW$ and $S_p=s_pP$, we obtain:

$$I = s_pP+s_wW=s_pP+s_w(Y-P)=(s_p-s_w)P+s_wY$$

Whence

$$\frac{I}{Y}= (s_p-s_w)\frac{P}{Y}+s_w \qquad \ldots \text{(1)}$$

and

$$\frac{P}{Y} = \frac{1}{s_p-s_w} \frac{I}{Y} - \frac{s_w}{s_p-s_w} \qquad \ldots \text{(2)}$$

Thus, given the wage-earners' and the capitalists' propensities to save, the share of profits in income depends simply on the ratio of investment to output.

The interpretative value of the model (as distinct from the formal validity of the equations, or identities) depends on the "Keynesian" hypothesis that investment, or rather, the ratio of investment to output, can be treated as an independent variable, invariant with respect to changes in the two savings propensities s_p and s_w. (We shall see later that this assumption can only be true within certain limits, and outside those limits the theory ceases to hold.) This, together with the assumption of "full employment", also implies that the level of prices in relation to the level of money wages is determined by demand: a rise in investment, and thus in total demand, will raise prices and profit

[1] This may be assumed independently of any skewness in the distribution of property, simply as a consequence of the fact that the bulk of profits accrues in the form of company profits and a high proportion of companies' marginal profits is put to reserve.

margins, and thus reduce real consumption, whilst a fall in investment, and thus in total demand, causes a fall in prices (relatively
to the wage level) and thereby generates a compensating rise in
real consumption. Assuming flexible prices (or rather flexible
profit margins) the system is thus stable at full employment.

The model operates only if the two savings propensities differ
and the marginal propensity to save from profits exceeds that
from wages, i.e. if:

and
$$s_p \neq s_w$$
$$s_p > s_w$$

The latter is the stability condition. For if $s_p < s_w$, a fall in
prices would cause a fall in demand and thus generate a further
fall in prices, and equally, a rise in prices would be cumulative.
The degree of stability of the system depends on the *difference* of
the marginal propensities, i.e. on $1/(s_p - s_w)$ which may be
defined as the "coefficient of sensitivity of income distribution",
since it indicates the change in the share of profits in income
which follows upon a change in the share of investment in output.

If the difference between the marginal propensities is small, the
coefficient will be large, and small changes in I/Y (the investment/
output relationship) will cause relatively large changes in income
distribution P/Y; and vice versa.

In the limiting case where $s_w = 0$, the amount of profits is equal
to the sum of investment and capitalist consumption, i.e.:

$$P = \frac{1}{s_p} I.$$

This is the assumption implicit in Keynes' parable about the
widow's cruse—where a rise in entrepreneurial consumption
raises their total profit by an *identical* amount—and of Mr.
Kalecki's theory of profits which can be paraphrased by saying
that "capitalists earn what they spend, and workers spend what
they earn".

This model (i.e. the "special case" where $s_w = 0$) in a sense is
the precise opposite of the Ricardian (or Marxian) one—here
wages (not profits) are a residue, profits being governed by the
propensity to invest and the capitalists' propensity to consume,
which represent a kind of "prior charge" on the national output.

Whereas in the Ricardian model the ultimate incidence of all taxes (other than taxes on rent) falls on profits, here the incidence of all taxes, taxes on income and profits as well as on commodities, falls on wages.[1] Assuming however that I/Y and s_p remain constant over time, the share of wages will also remain constant —i.e. real wages will increase automatically, year by year, with the increase in output per man.

If s_w is positive, however, total profits will be reduced by $S_w \dfrac{I}{s_p}$, i.e. by more than the amount of workers' savings, S_w; the sensitivity of profits to changes in the level of investment will be greater, total profits rising (or falling) by a greater amount than the change in investment, owing to the consequential reduction (or increase) in workers' savings.[2]

The critical assumption is that the investment/output ratio is an independent variable. Following Harrod, we can describe the determinants of the investment/output ratio in terms of the rate of growth of output capacity (G) and the capital/output ratio, v:

$$\frac{I}{Y} = Gv \qquad \cdots \text{ (3)}$$

In a state of continuous full employment G must be equal to the rate of growth of the "full employment ceiling", i.e. the sum of the rate of technical progress and the growth in working population (Harrod's "natural rate of growth"). For Harrods' second equation:

$$\frac{I}{Y} = s$$

we can now substitute equation (1) above:

[1] The ultimate incidence of taxes can only fall on profits (in this model) in so far as they increase s_p, the propensity to save out of *net* income after tax. Income and profits taxes, through the "double taxation" of savings, have of course the opposite effect: they reduce s_p, and thereby make the share of *net* profits in income larger than it would be in the absence of taxation. On the other hand, discriminatory taxes on dividend distribution, or dividend limitation, by keeping down both dividends and capital gains, have the effect of raising s_p. (All this applies, of course, on the assumption that the Government *spends* the proceeds of the tax—i.e. that it aims at a balanced budget. Taxes which go to augment the budget surplus will lower the share of profits in much the same way as an increase in workers' savings.)

[2] Thus if $s_p = 50\%$, $s_w = 10\%$, $I/Y = 20\%$, P/Y will be 25%; but a rise in I/Y to 21% would raise P/Y to $27 \cdot 5\%$. If on the other hand $s_w = 0$, with $s_p = 50\%$, P/Y would become 40%, but an increase in I/Y to 21% would only increase P/Y to 42%. The above formulae assume that average and marginal propensities are identical. Introducing constant terms in the consumption functions alters the relationship between P/Y and $\cdot I/Y$, and would reduce the *elasticity* of P/Y with respect to changes in I/Y.

$$\frac{I}{Y} = (s_p - s_w)\frac{P}{Y} + s_w.$$

Hence the "warranted" and the "natural" rates of growth are not independent of one another; if profit margins are flexible, the former will adjust itself to the latter through a consequential change in P/Y.

This does not mean that there will be an *inherent* tendency to a smooth rate of growth in a capitalist economy, only that the causes of cyclical movements lie elsewhere—not in the lack of an adjustment mechanism between s and Gv. As I have attempted to demonstrate elsewhere[1] the causes of cyclical movements should be sought in a disharmony between the entrepreneurs' *desired* growth rate (as influenced by the degree of optimism and the volatility of expectations) which governs the rate of increase of output capacity (G), and the natural growth rate (dependent on technical progress and the growth of the working population) which governs the rate of growth in output over longer periods (let us call this G'). It is the excess of G over G'—not the excess of s over $G'v$—which causes periodic breakdowns in the investment process through the growth in output capacity outrunning the growth in production.[2]

Problems of the trade cycle however lie outside the scope of this paper; and having described a model which shows the distribution of income to be determined by the Keynesian investment-savings mechanism, we must now examine its limitations. The model, as I emphasised earlier, shows the share of profits P/Y, the rate of profit on capital P/vY, and the real wage rate W/L,[3] as functions of I/Y which in turn is determined independently of P/Y or W/L. There are four different reasons why this may not be true, or be true only within a certain range.

(1) The first is that the real wage cannot fall below a certain

---

[1] *Economic Journal*, March, 1954, pp. 53-71. [See my *Essays on Economic Stability and Growth*, pp. 213-32.]

[2] I/Y will therefore tend to equal Gv, not $G'v$. It may be assumed that, taking very long periods, G is largely governed by G' but over shorter periods the two are quite distinct, moreover; G' itself is not independent of G, since technical progress and population growth are both stimulated by the degree of pressure on the "full employment ceiling", which depends on G. The elasticity of response of G' to G is not infinite however: hence the greater G, the greater will be G' (the *actual* trend-rate of growth of the economy over successive cycles) but the greater also the ratio G/G' which measures the strength of cyclical forces.   [3] Where L=labour force.

subsistence minimum. Hence P/Y can only attain its indicated value, if the resulting real wage exceeds this minimum rate, w'. Hence the model is subject to the restriction $W/L \geqslant w'$, which we may write in the form:

$$\frac{P}{Y} \leqslant \frac{Y - w'L}{Y} \qquad \ldots \quad (4)$$

(2) The second is that the indicated share of profits cannot be below the level which yields the minimum rate of profit necessary to induce capitalists to invest their capital, and which we may call the risk "premium rate", r. Hence the restriction:

$$\frac{P}{vY} \geqslant r \qquad \ldots \quad (5)$$

(3) The third is that apart from a minimum rate of profit on capital there may be a certain minimum rate of profit on turnover —due to imperfections of competition, collusive agreements between traders, etc., and which we may call m, the "degree of monopoly" rate. Hence the restriction:

$$\frac{P}{Y} \geqslant m \qquad \ldots \quad (6)$$

It is clear that equations (5) and (6) describe *alternative* restrictions, of which the higher will apply.

(4) The fourth is that the capital/output ratio, v, should not in itself be influenced by the rate of profit, for if it is, the investment/output ratio Gv will itself be dependent on the rate of profit. A certain degree of dependence follows inevitably from the consideration, mentioned earlier, that the value of particular capital goods in terms of final consumption goods will vary with the rate of profit,[1] so that, even with a *given technique*, v will not be independent of P/Y. (We shall ignore this point.) There is the further complication that the relation P/Y may affect v through making more or less "labour-saving" techniques profitable. In other words, at any given wage-price relationship, the producers will adopt the technique which maximises the rate of profit on capital, P/vY; this will affect (at a given G) I/Y, and hence P/Y. Hence any rise in P/Y will reduce v, and thus I/Y, and conversely,

---

[1] Cf. p. 212 above. In fact the whole of the Keynesian and post-Keynesian analysis dodges the problem of the measurement of capital.

any rise in I/Υ will raise P/Υ. If the sensitiveness of v to P/Υ is great, P/Υ can no longer be regarded as being determined by the equations of the model; the *technical* relation between v and P/Υ will then govern P/Υ whereas the savings equation (equation (2) above) will determine I/Υ and thus (given G) the value of v.[1] To exclude this we have to assume that v is invariant to P/Υ,[2] i.e.:

$$v = \bar{v} \qquad \ldots \quad (7)$$

If equation (4) is unsatisfied, we are back at the Ricardian (or Marxian) model. I/Υ will suffer a shrinkage, and will no longer correspond to Gv, but to, say, γv where $\gamma < G$. Hence the system will not produce full employment; output will be limited by the available capital, and not by labour; at the same time the classical, and not the Keynesian, reaction-mechanism will be in operation: the size of the "surplus" available for investment determining investment, not investment savings. It is possible however that owing to technical inventions, etc., and starting from a position of excess labour and underemployment (i.e. an elastic total supply of labour) the size of the surplus will grow; hence I/Υ and γ will grow; and hence γ might rise above G' (the rate of growth of the "full employment ceiling", given the technical progress and the growth of population) so that in time the excess labour becomes absorbed and full employment is reached. When this happens (which we may call the stage of *developed* capitalism) wages will rise above the subsistence level, and the properties of the system will then follow our model.

If equations (5) and (6) are unsatisfied, the full employment assumption breaks down, and so will the process of growth; the economy will relapse into a state of stagnation. The interesting conclusion which emerges from these equations is that this may be the result of several distinct causes. "Investment opportunities"

---

[1] This is where the "marginal productivity" principle would come in but it should be emphasised that under the conditions of our model where savings are treated, not as a constant, but as a function of income distribution, the sensitiveness of v to changes in P/Υ would have to be very large to overshadow the influence of G, of s_p and of s_w on P/Υ. Assuming that it is large, it is further necessary to suppose that the value of P/Υ as dictated by this technical relationship falls within the maximum and minimum values indicated by equations (4)-(6).

[2] This assumption does not necessarily mean that there are "fixed coefficients" as between capital equipment and labour—only that technical innovations (which are also assumed to be "neutral" in their effects) are far more influential on the chosen v than price relationships.

may be low because *G* is low relatively to *G'*, i.e. the entrepreneurs' expectations are involatile, and/or they are pessimistic; hence they expect a lower level of demand for the future than corresponds to potential demand, governed by *G'*. On the other hand, "liquidity preference" may be too high, or the risks associated with investment too great, leading to an excessive *r*. (This is perhaps the factor on which Keynes himself set greatest store as a cause of unemployment and stagnation.) Finally, lack of competition may cause "over-saving" through excessive profit margins; this again will cause stagnation, unless there is sufficient compensating increase in *v* (through the generation of "excess capacity" under conditions of rigid profit margins but relatively free entry) to push up *Gv*, and hence *I/Y*.

If, however, equations (2)-(6) are all satisfied there will be an inherent tendency to growth and an inherent tendency to full employment. Indeed the two are closely linked to each other. Apart from the case of a developing economy in the immature stage of capitalism (where equation (4) does not hold, but where $\gamma < G$), a tendency to continued economic growth will only exist when the system is only stable at full employment equilibrium— i.e. when $G \geqslant G'$.

This is a possible interpretation of the long-term situation in the "successful" capitalist economies of Western Europe and North America. If *G* exceeds *G'*, the investment/output ratio *I/Y* will not be steady in time, even if the *trend* level of this ratio is constant. There will be periodic breakdowns in the investment process, due to the growth in output capacity outrunning the possible growth in output; when that happens, not only investment, but total output will fall, and output will be (temporarily) limited by effective demand, and not by the scarcity of resources. This is contrary to the mechanics of our model, but several reasons can be adduced to show why the system will not be flexible enough to ensure full employment in the short period.

(1) First, even if profit margins are assumed to be fully flexible in a downward, as well as an upward, direction the very fact that investment goods and consumer goods are produced by different industries, with limited mobility between them, will mean that profit margins in the consumption goods industries will not fall

below the level that ensures full utilisation of resources in the consumption goods industries. A *compensating* increase in consumption goods production (following upon a fall in the production of investment goods) can only occur as a result of a transfer of resources from the other industries, lured by the profit opportunities there.

(2) Second, and more important, profit-margins are likely to be inflexible in a downward direction in the short period (Marshall's "fear of spoiling the market") even if they are flexible in the long period, or even if they possess short period flexibility in an upward direction.[1]

This applies of course not only to profit margins but to real wages as well, which in the short period may be equally inflexible in a downward direction at the *attained* level,[2] thus compressing I/Y, or rather preventing an *increase* in I/Y following upon a rise in the entrepreneurs' desired rate of expansion. Hence in the short period the shares of profits and wages tend to be inflexible for two different reasons—the downward inflexibility of P/Y and the downward inflexibility of W/L—which thus tend to reinforce the long-period stability of these shares, due to constancy of I/Y, resulting from the long period constancy of Gv and $G'v$.

We have seen how the various "models" of distribution, the Ricardian-Marxian, the Keynesian and the Kaleckian are related to each other. I am not sure where "marginal productivity" comes in, in all this—except that in so far as it has any importance it does through an extreme sensitivity of v to changes in P/Y.

---

[1] Cf. the quotation from Marshall, note 2, page 218 above.

[2] This operates through the wage-price spiral that would follow on a reduction in real wages; the prevention of such a wage-price spiral by means of investment rationing of some kind, or a "credit squeeze", is thus a manifestation of downward inflexibility of W/Y.

CAPITAL ACCUMULATION AND
ECONOMIC GROWTH[1,2]

I. INTRODUCTION

A theoretical model consists of certain hypotheses concerning the causal inter-relationship between various magnitudes or forces and the sequence in which they react on each other. We all agree that the basic requirement of any model is that it should be capable of explaining the characteristic features of the economic process as we find them in reality. It is no good starting off a model with the kind of abstraction which initially excludes the influence of forces which are mainly responsible for the behaviour of the economic variables under investigation; and upon finding that the theory leads to results contrary to what we observe in reality, attributing this contrary movement to the compensating (or more than compensating) influence of residual factors that have been assumed away in the model. In dealing with capital accumulation and economic growth, we are only too apt to begin by assuming a "given state of knowledge" (that is to say, absence of technical progress) and the absence of "uncertainty", and content ourselves with saying that these two factors—technical progress and uncertainty—must have been responsible for the difference between theoretical expectation and the recorded facts of experience. The interpretative value of this kind of theory must of necessity be extremely small.

Any theory must necessarily be based on abstractions; but the type of abstraction chosen cannot be decided in a vacuum:

[1] A paper prepared for the Corfu meeting of the International Economic Association in August 1958 and published in *The Theory of Capital* (ed. F. Lutz), London, Macmillan, 1961.

[2] The author is indebted to L. Pasinetti and F. H. Hahn for assistance in setting out the models in algebraic form.

it must be appropriate to the characteristic features of the economic process as recorded by experience. Hence the theorist, in choosing a particular theoretical approach, ought to start off with a summary of the facts which he regards as relevant to his problem. Since facts, as recorded by statisticians, are always subject to numerous snags and qualifications, and for that reason are incapable of being accurately summarised, the theorist, in my view, should be free to start off with a "stylised" view of the facts—i.e. concentrate on broad tendencies, ignoring individual detail, and proceed on the "as if" method, i.e. construct a hypothesis that could account for these "stylised" facts, without necessarily committing himself to the historical accuracy, or sufficiency, of the facts or tendencies thus summarised.

As regards the process of economic change and development in capitalist societies, I suggest the following "stylised facts" as a starting-point for the construction of theoretical models:

(1) The continued growth in the aggregate volume of production and in the productivity of labour at a steady trend rate; no recorded tendency for a *falling* rate of growth of productivity.

(2) A continued increase in the amount of capital per worker, whatever statistical measure of "capital" is chosen in this connection.

(3) A steady rate of profit on capital, at least in the "developed" capitalist societies, this rate of profit being substantially higher than the "pure" long-term rate of interest as shown by the yield of gilt-edged bonds. According to Phelps Brown and Weber[1] the rate of profit in the United Kingdom was remarkably steady around $10\frac{1}{2}$ per cent in the period 1870–1914, the annual variations being within $9\frac{1}{2}$–$11\frac{1}{2}$ per cent. A similar long-period steadiness, according to some authorities, has shown itself in the United States.

(4) Steady capital-output ratios over long periods; at least there are no clear long-term trends, either rising or falling, if differences in the degree of utilisation of capacity are allowed for. This implies, or reflects, the near-identity in the percentage rates of growth of production and of the capital stock—i.e. that for

[1] *Economic Journal*, 1953, pp. 263–88.

the economy as a whole, and over longer periods, income and capital tend to grow at the same rate.

(5) A high correlation between the share of profits in income and the share of investment in output; a steady share of profits (and of wages) in societies and/or in periods in which the investment coefficient (the share of investment in output) is constant. For example, Phelps Brown and Weber found long-term steadiness in the investment coefficient, the profit share and the share of wages in the U.K., combined with a high degree of correlation in the (appreciable) short period fluctuations of these magnitudes.[1] The steadiness in the *share* of wages implies, of course, a rate of increase in real wages that is proportionate to the rate of growth of (average) productivity.

(6) Finally, there are appreciable differences in the *rate* of growth of labour productivity and of total output in different societies, the range of variation (in the fast-growing economies) being of the order of 2–5 per cent. These are associated with corresponding variations in the investment coefficient, and in the profit share, but the above propositions concerning the constancy of relative shares and of the capital-output ratio are applicable to countries with differing rates of growth.

None of these "facts" can be plausibly "explained" by the theoretical constructions of neo-classical theory. On the basis of the marginal productivity theory, and the capital theory of Böhm-Bawerk and followers, one would expect a continued *fall* in the rate of profit with capital accumulation, and not a steady rate of profit. (In this respect classical and neo-classical theory, arguing on different grounds, come to the same conclusion— Adam Smith, Ricardo, Marx, alike with Böhm-Bawerk and Wicksell, predicted a steady fall in the rate of profit with economic progress.) Similarly, on the basis of the neo-classical approach, one expects diminishing returns to capital accumulation which implies a steady *rise* in the capital-output ratio *pari passu* with the rise in the capital-labour ratio, and a diminishing rate of growth in the productivity of labour at any given ratio of investment to output (or savings to income). Finally, the fluctuations in the

[1] *Op. cit.* Fig. 7.

B

share of profits that are associated with fluctuations in the rate of investment cannot be accounted for at all on the basis of the marginal productivity theory—if we assume, as I believe we must, that the fluctuations in the level of investment are the causal factor, and the fluctuations in the share of profits consequential, rather than the other way round.

My purpose here is to present a model of income distribution and capital accumulation which is capable of explaining at least some of these "stylised" facts. It differs from the prevailing approach to problems of capital accumulation in that it has more affinities with the classical approach of Ricardo and Marx, and also with the general equilibrium model of von Neumann, than with the neo-classical models of Böhm-Bawerk and Wicksell, or with the theories which start off with the Cobb-Douglas type of production function. It differs from the classical models in that it embodies the basic ideas of the Keynesian theory of income generation, and it takes the well-known "dynamic equation" of Harrod and Domar as its starting-point.

II. THE CHARACTERISTIC FEATURES OF THE CLASSICAL APPROACH

The peculiarity of classical models as against the neo-classical theories is that they treat capital and labour as if they were complementary factors rather than competitive or substitute factors. Of course Ricardo was well aware that the use of capital is not only complementary to labour but also a substitute for labour— hence the famous "Ricardo effect".[1] This demonstrates that with a rise in wages more machinery will tend to be employed per unit of labour, *because* the price of machinery will fall relatively to labour with any rise in the share of the produce going to labour —but he did not accord this substitution-aspect any major rôle in his distribution or growth theory. As far as his distribution theory is concerned he treated the amount of capital per unit of labour as something given for each industry (and similarly, the distribution of labour between different industries as given by the "structural requirements" of the system). He solved the

[1] *Principles,* ch. i, sec. v.

problem of distribution between wages and profits (after deduction of the share of rent which is determined quite independently of this division) by assuming that the amount going to one of these two factors, labour, is determined by its supply price, whereas the share of the other is residual—the share of profits is simply the difference between output per man (after deduction of rent) and wages per man, the latter being treated as constant, governed by the "natural price" of labour at which alone the working population *can remain* stationary.

Since profits were assumed to be largely saved and invested, whilst wages are consumed, the share of profits in income also determines the share of investment in total production, and the rate of accumulation of capital. The rate of accumulation of capital in turn determines the rate of increase in the employment of labour (since employment was assumed to increase at the same rate as capital, there was no scope for any consequential change in the amount of capital per unit of labour) without enquiring very closely where this additional labour comes from. The model is consistent with the assumption that there is an unlimited labour reserve, say, in the form of surplus population in an under-developed country (the assumption favoured by Marx) or with assuming that the rate of increase in population is itself governed by the rate of growth in the demand for labour (the assumption favoured by Ricardo).

Von Neumann's general equilibrium model,[1] though on a very different level of sophistication, explicitly allowing for a choice of processes in the production of each commodity, and abstracting from diminishing returns due to the scarcity of natural resources to which Ricardo accorded such a major rôle, is really a variant of the classical approach of Ricardo and Marx. Von Neumann similarly assumes that labour can be expanded in unlimited quantities at a real wage determined by the cost of subsistence of the labourers, and that profits are entirely saved and re-invested. These two assumptions enable him to treat the economic problem as a completely circular process, where the outputs of productive processes are simultaneously the inputs of the pro-

---

[1] *Review of Economic Studies*, 1945–6; originally prepared for a Princeton mathematical seminar in 1932.

ductive processes of the following period; this is achieved by treating not labour, but the commodities consumed by labour, as the inputs of the productive processes, and by treating the surviving durable equipment as part of the outputs, as well as of the inputs, of the processes of unit length. Von Neumann is concerned to show that on these assumptions an equilibrium of balanced growth always exists, characterised by the equiproportionate expansion in the production of *all* commodities with positive prices: and that this rate of expansion (under perfect competition and constant returns to scale for each process) will be the maximum attainable under the given "technical possibilities" (the real wage forming one of the given "technical possibilities"), and will be equal to the rate of profit (= rate of interest) earned in each of the processes actually used.[1]

The celebrated Harrod-Domar equation can be applied to the Ricardian model and the von Neumann model as well as to other models.[2] Though it can be interpreted in many ways (according to which of the factors one treats as a dependent and which as an independent variable) it is fundamentally a formula for translating the share of savings (and investment) in income (s) into the resulting growth rate of capital (G_K), given the capital-output ratio, $v \left(\equiv \dfrac{K}{\Upsilon} \right)$[3]

---

[1] Von Neumann was only concerned with demonstrating the *existence* of such an equilibrium solution. Later Solow and Samuelson (*Econometrica*, 1953) have shown that on certain further assumptions this solution will be stable both "in the large" and "in the small"—i.e. the balanced-growth equilibrium will be gradually approached from any given set of initial conditions; and it will restore itself if it is disturbed for any reason.

[2] In von Neumann's formulation, where the surviving equipment at the end of each period is treated as a part of the output, v is $1/1+g$, when Υ is defined as the gross output of the period (since then K_t and Υ_{t-1} are identical) whilst s is unity if Υ is defined as the *net* output (since the wage bill forms part of the commodities consumed in the process of production) so that the net-output/capital ratio is equal to g, the rate of growth of the capital stock. It is possible, however, within the framework of the model, to define Υ in the usual way as being the sum of profits and wages—in which case the output-capital ratio (in a state of balanced growth) is identical with the net rate of expansion of the system multiplied by the ratio of Υ (thus defined) to net output (i.e. the ratio by which the sum of wages and profits exceeds profits). Given a fixed real wage, and the possibility of expanding the rate of employment at the rate dictated by the requirements of a balanced-growth economy, the ratio of wages to profits is itself determined by the relative input-intensities of labour and non-wage commodities when (at the given wage and with the given range of available processes) the rate of expansion of the system is maximised.

[3] Time subscripts are omitted, except in the formal presentation of the models.

$$G_K = \frac{s}{v}, \tag{1}$$

which can also be written

$$s = \frac{I}{\Upsilon} = G_K v. \tag{1a}$$

It further follows that when $s = \frac{P}{\Upsilon}$, i.e. all profits are saved and all wages are consumed,

$$\frac{P}{\Upsilon} = G_K \frac{K}{\Upsilon}.$$

But since

$$\frac{P}{K} \equiv \frac{P}{\Upsilon} \cdot \frac{\Upsilon}{K}$$

$$\frac{P}{K} = G_K \tag{2}$$

the rate of profit on capital is the same as the rate of growth of capital.

As far as Ricardo and von Neumann are concerned, this is really the end of the story, for they do not introduce any limit to the *speed* with which additional labour can be introduced into the system, so that the rate of growth of employment, and hence of income, is fully determined by the rate of growth of capital. Supposing, however, that even if the supply of labour can be increased to an indefinite extent *ultimately*, there is a maximum to the rate of increase of population and/or of employment per unit of time, determined by biological or institutional factors. Writing L for the quantity of employment, this gives us another equation

$$G_n = l, \text{ where } l = \frac{1}{L} \cdot \frac{dL}{dt}. \tag{3}$$

The Ricardo-Marx-von Neumann model clearly does not work when $G_K > G_n$ since in that case the rate of growth of production cannot be determined by G_K alone.

In a progressive economy the labour potential increases, however, not only on account of the rise in numbers, but also on account of the rise in the productivity of labour due to technical progress. Hence, allowing for technical progress,

$$G_n = l + t, \text{ where } t = \frac{1}{Y/L} \cdot \frac{d(Y/L)}{dt}, \tag{3a}$$

which is Harrod's formula for the "natural" rate of growth.

Harrod realised that balanced-growth equilibrium is only conceivable when his "warranted rate of growth" equals the "natural rate",

$$G_K = G_n,$$

in other words $\qquad \dfrac{s}{v} = l + t.$

Since he assumed, however, that s, v, l and t are all independently given and invariant in relation to each other, such an equality, on his theory, could only be the result of a fortunate accident. Moreover, he thought that any discrepancy between $\dfrac{s}{v}$ and $(l+t)$ must set up cumulative forces of disequilibrium, so that a moving equilibrium of steady growth, even if momentarily attained, is necessarily unstable.

The problem takes on an entirely different aspect, however, once we recognise (as we must) that these variables are not mutually invariant, but that there are certain inter-relationships between them. Thus, as will be shown, the proportion of income saved s, is by no means independent of $(l+t)$; nor is the rate of increase in productivity, t, independent of the rate of capital accumulation, $\dfrac{s}{v}$.[1]

III. THE NATURE OF GROWTH EQUILIBRIA

In order to exhibit the rôle of these various factors it is best to start from a model based on a number of artificial assumptions which together produce the simplest solution to the problem of growth equilibrium. We shall afterwards remove these assumptions one by one (with the exception of the first assumption

---

[1] In the above equation, in deference to the generally accepted use of symbols, we have denoted the rate of growth of labour by l and the rate of growth of output per man by t. In the rest of this paper, however, we shall denote the *maximum* rate of population growth by λ, and the rate of growth of productivity by G_0; reserving the letter t to denote time

listed below) in the reverse order in which they are presented here. The six critical assumptions of our "basic model" are:

(1) Constant returns to scale in any particular process of production; natural environment does not impose any limitation to expansion (i.e. there are two factors of production, Capital and Labour (K and L), and two kinds of income, Profits and Wages (P and W)).

(2) The absence of technical progress—i.e. the function relating the output of various commodities to the input-coefficients of production remains unchanged over time.

(3) General rule of competition: the prices of commodities in relation to the prime costs of production settle at the point where the market is cleared. Capital earns the same rate of profit, and labour the same rate of wages, in all employments.

(4) All profits are saved and all wages are consumed; the division of output between equipment goods (or "input goods") and wage goods ("consumption goods") is the same as the division of income between Profits and Wages.

(5) There is strict complementarity between Capital and Labour (or commodity-inputs and labour-inputs) in the production of both equipment goods and wage goods; there is therefore a single kind of "equipment good" for the production of each wage good, and the different kinds of wage goods are also complementary in consumption.

(6) There is an unlimited supply of labour at a constant wage in terms of wage goods.[1]

Under these assumptions the rate of growth of the capital stock, G_K, will govern the rate of growth of the economy, G_Y; and G_K in turn depends on the proportion of output saved, s, and the capital-output ratio, v. The proportion of output saved is determined by the condition that the wage rate cannot fall below a certain minimum determined by the cost of subsistence,

$$w = w_{\min} \qquad (4)$$

[1] These six assumptions are identical (except (5)) with those underlying von Neumann's model; they are substantially the same as those implicit in Ricardo's theory (except for (1)); and Marx's theory (except of course in its "dynamic" aspect, assumptions (2) and possibly (5)).

so that the excess of output per head over the subsistence wage alone determines the share of profits. Output per head (O), the capital-output ratio (v), and hence capital per head, are given technical constants; and in addition the total amount of capital at some arbitrary point of time, $t = 0$, is taken as given.

These assumptions yield a model which can be formally stated as follows. Using our previously introduced notation[1] and denoting output per worker by O, we obtain a system of six relationships, of which four represent assumptions, one is a definitional identity and one equation the equilibrium condition.

$$
\left.
\begin{aligned}
O(t) &= \overline{O} \\
v(t) &= \overline{v} \\
w(t) &= w_{\min} \\
s(t) &= \frac{P(t)}{Y(t)}
\end{aligned}
\right\} \text{for all } t \geqslant 0
$$

$$\text{(i)}$$
$$\text{(ii)}$$
$$\text{(iii)}$$
$$\text{(iv)}$$

$$P(t) \equiv Y(t) - w(t)L(t) \tag{v}$$

$$s(t)Y(t) = \frac{dK(t)}{dt} \text{ for all } t \geqslant 0 \tag{vi}$$

which are sufficient to determine the six basic variables $O(t)$, $v(t)$, $s(t)$, $P(t)$, $Y(t)$ and $w(t)$ given the initial values. From (vi) and (ii) we have

$$G_Y = \frac{s(t)}{\overline{v}} \text{ or } \overline{v}G_Y = s(t).$$

From (v) it follows

$$\frac{P(t)}{Y(t)} = \left[1 - \frac{w_{\min}}{\overline{O}} \right]$$

and hence the share of profit is independent of t. And so, by (iv), $s(t)$ is also independent of t, and hence

$$G_K = \frac{s}{\overline{v}}$$

[1] This notation may be summarised as follows:

$$G_K = \frac{dK}{dt}\frac{1}{K} \qquad G_Y = \frac{dY}{dt}\frac{1}{Y} \qquad v = \frac{K}{Y} \qquad O = \frac{Y}{L}$$

and the symbols K, Y, L, w and s represent the stock of capital, output (or income), labour employed, wage per worker, and the proportion of income saved respectively.

$$G_K = G_Y$$

$$\frac{P}{K} = G_K$$

$$\frac{P}{Y} = G_K \bar{v}. \tag{I}$$

IV. FULL EMPLOYMENT GROWTH

The first modification I shall introduce is the removal of assumption (6), that of an unlimited supply of labour. We may suppose that there is a certain maximum rate of population growth, λ, determined by fertility rates; so that (abstracting from technical progress) this rate determines the long-run "natural rate of growth". Hence

$$G_n = \lambda.$$

If we suppose, further, that initially

$$G_K > G_n,$$

i.e. the rate of capital accumulation, as determined by the conditions of our previous model, exceeds the maximum rate of growth of population, the economy can only grow at the rate G_K as long as there are reserves of unemployed labour to draw upon. But just because the economy grows at a higher rate than λ, sooner or later capital accumulation must overtake the labour supply. According to Marx this is precisely the situation which leads to a crisis. When the labour reserves are exhausted, the demand for labour will exceed (or tend to exceed) the supply of labour, since the amount of capital seeking profitable employment will be greater than the number of labourers available to employ them with. Owing to the competition between capitalists, this will cause wages to rise and profits to be wiped out, until, in consequence, capital accumulation is reduced sufficiently to restore the labour reserve and thus restore profits.

However, there is no inherent reason why this situation should involve a crisis; nor does it follow from the assumptions that the maintenance of accumulation requires the continued existence of a labour reserve. Indeed there is no reason why this situation should not result in a neat balanced-growth equilibrium with a higher rate of wages and a lower share of profits, and with a correspondingly lower rate of capital accumulation that would no longer exceed, but be equal to, the rate of increase in the supply of labour. All that is necessary is to bear in mind that every increase in wages (in terms of commodities) lowers the share of profits in income, and every reduction in the share of profits lowers the rate of accumulation of capital and hence *the rate of increase* in the demand for labour. Hence the situation will lead to a balanced-growth equilibrium in which employment at some arbitrary point of time $t = 0$ is taken as given by the size of the working population at that point of time, and where the rate of growth of population λ is also taken as given.

This gives us an alternative model of seven relationships of which four define the assumptions, one is an identity as before and two are equilibrium conditions. Using, in addition, the notation $L^*(t)$ for the maximum amount of labour available at time t, the relationships are as follows:

$$L^*(t) = L^*_{(0)}e^{\lambda t}$$ (i)
$$v(t) = \bar{v}$$ (ii)
$$O(t) = \bar{O} \qquad \text{for all } t \geqslant 0$$ (iii)
$$s(t) = \frac{P(t)}{Y(t)}$$ (iv)

$$P(t) \equiv Y(t) - w(t)L(t)$$ (v)

$$s(t)Y(t) = \frac{dK}{dt} \qquad \text{for all } t \geqslant 0$$ (vi)
$$L(t) = L^*(t)$$ (vii)

subject to the inequality

$$w(t) \geqslant w_{min}$$

which are sufficient to determine the seven basic variables $O(t)$, $v(t)$, $s(t)$, $P(t)$, $Y(t)$, $w(t)$ and $L(t)$, given the initial conditions.

It follows from (i) and (vii) that

$$G_Y = \lambda.$$

From (vi), $s(t) = \lambda v(t)$ and so, by (i) and (ii), $s(t)$ is independent of t. Hence by (iv)

$$G_K = \frac{s}{v}$$

$$G_K = G_y$$

$$\frac{P}{Y} = \lambda \bar{v}$$

$$\frac{P}{K} = \lambda$$

Also, by (v), $\qquad w(t) = (1 - \lambda \bar{v})\overline{O},$

subject to the inequality stated. (II)

The difference between this model and the previous one is that while in both, output per man and capital per man are constant (over time), in this model the rate of profit on capital and the share of profit in income (given v, which is here as a technical constant) are uniquely determined by λ, the population growth rate, which on our present assumptions will alone determine the uniform expansion rate of the economy. There is an equilibrium wage, w, which will exceed the subsistence wage, w_{min}, by the amount necessary to reduce the share of profits to λv. But despite the similarities, this second model is the inverse of the Ricardian (or Marxian) one; for here it is not profits which form a residual after deducting subsistence-wages, but wages form the residual share after deducting profits, the amount of profits being determined independently by the requirements of the (extraneously given) balanced growth rate.[1]

Ricardo did say, in various places scattered around in the

---

[1] This situation is incompatible also with von Neumann's model, which, as mentioned before, implicitly assumes that the effective supply of labour can be increased at the required growth rate, whatever that rate is. But if one introduced labour explicitly as one of the "commodities" into the von Neumann model (instead of the goods consumed by labour) and assumed that the supply of labour was growing at some autonomous rate that was lower than the maximum potential expansion rate of commodities other than labour, the same result would be reached. For then the equilibrium price system which equalised the rate of profit earned in all the "chosen" processes would be the one which made the price of labour in terms of other commodities such as to reduce the rate of profit earned in the production of commodities (other than labour) to the expansion rate of labour.

Principles, that as capital accumulation runs ahead of population, or the reverse, wages will rise above the "natural price of labour" or may fall below it. But he never drew the immanent conclusion (though in several places he seemed almost on the point of saying it) that the rise or fall in wages resulting from excessive or insufficient rates of accumulation *will itself change the rate of accumulation of capital through changing the profit share*, and thereby provides a mechanism for keeping the rate of accumulation of capital in step with the rate of increase in the labour supply—i.e. that there is an "equilibrium" level of wages which maintains the increase in the demand for labour in step with the increase in supply. (Had he said so, with some emphasis, one cannot help feeling that the subsequent development of economics, both Marxist and orthodox, might have taken a rather different turn.)

Marx's view that where excessive accumulation leads to a crisis due to the scarcity of labour there is nothing to stop wages from rising until profits are wiped out altogether, clearly assumes a *constant* supply of labour over time. If population is rising, profits cannot fall below the level which provides for a rate of accumulation that corresponds to the rate of growth in the supply of labour; and once "full employment" has been reached (i.e. the "reserve army" is exhausted) there is no reason why wages should not settle down to a new equilibrium level, divorced from the cost of subsistence of labour.

There is one other important assumption implicit in this, and in the other growth models, which may be conveniently introduced at this stage. In a capitalist economy continued investment and accumulation presupposes that the rate of profit is high enough (in the words of Ricardo) to afford more than the minimum necessary compensation to the capitalists "for their trouble, for the risk which they must necessarily encounter in employing their capital productively".[1] Hence growth-equilibrium is subject to a further condition which can be written in the form

$$\frac{P}{K} \geqslant r + \rho, \qquad (5)$$

i.e. the rate of profit as determined by the model (under our

[1] *Principles*, Sraffa edition, p. 122.

present assumption by λ alone) cannot be less than the sum of the "pure" rate of interest on financial assets of prime security, and the additional premium required for the risks involved in productive employments of wealth.

We know, since Keynes, that there is a minimum below which the pure long-term rate of interest cannot fall, and that this is determined by the minimum necessary compensation for the illiquidity risk entailed in holding long-term bonds as against cash (or other short-term financial assets which are close substitutes for cash). We also know (though this has received far less emphasis in the literature) that the risks (whether illiquidity risks or other risks) associated with the direct investment of capital in business ventures are quantitatively far more important than the risks entailed in holding long-term financial assets of prime security. (The rate of profit on business investments in fixed capital (in plant and equipment) in the U.S., for example, is generally taken to be 20 per cent gross, or say 10 per cent net, of taxation, when the "pure" long-term rate of interest is around 4 per cent.)

The (expected) marginal return on investments in circulating capital (which, by universal convention, are treated as part of the "liquid assets" of a business) is much more in line with the money rates of interest, though here also, the expected return is likely to be appreciably higher than the (pure) short-term rate of interest. It is indeed highly unlikely that in an economy *without* technical progress, and where *all* profits are saved and re-invested, the rate of profit (as determined by population growth) could be anywhere near high enough to satisfy the above condition. If it is not, there cannot be a moving equilibrium of growth, though this does not mean that the economy will lapse into perpetual stagnation. Accumulation could still take place in periodic spurts, giving rise to a higher-than-trend rate of growth for a limited period.

We must now proceed with the relaxation of the various simplifying assumptions made. As we shall see, until we come to technical progress, none of these introduces a vital difference to our results.

V. NEO-CLASSICAL GROWTH

We can allow for variable proportions, instead of strict complementarity, between capital and labour, by postulating that there is a choice of processes of production involving differing quantities of capital per man (i.e. a differing ratio between "commodities" and "labour" as inputs). Thus output per man, O ($O \equiv Y/L$), will be a function of K/L, capital per man, the increase in the former being less than proportionate to the latter, if the production function for labour and capital together is homogeneous and linear. Hence

$$O \equiv Y/L = f_1(K/L), \text{ where } f_1' > 0, f_1'' < 0. \qquad (6)$$

Assuming that each entrepreneur at any one time has a limited amount of capital at his disposal, the amount of capital per man employed will be such as to maximise the rate of profit; and this optimum amount of capital per man will be all the greater the higher are wages in terms of commodities, hence

$$K/L = f_2(w), \text{ where } f_2' > 0, f_2'' < 0. \qquad (7)$$

(6) in combination with (7) also implies that the capital-output ratio in the "chosen" process will be all the greater, the higher the rate of wages, hence

$$v \equiv \frac{K}{Y} = f_3(w), \text{ where } f_3' > 0, f_3'' < 0. \qquad (8)$$

Further, it also follows that output per man will be the greater the higher the capital-output ratio

$$O = f_4(v), \text{ where } f_4' > 0, f_4'' < 0. \qquad (9)$$

Hence as wages rise (with the approach to full employment and the slowing down of the rate of accumulation) v will rise as well; this in turn will increase the share of investment in output $\left(\dfrac{I}{Y}\right)$ at any *given* rate of growth of output, and hence the share of profits. It *may* also slow down the rise in wages in terms of commodities, but since the rise in v will increase output per man, as well as the share of profits, this does not necessarily follow. However, on the assumption of diminishing returns (which, as we shall argue later, comes to much the same as the assumption that there is no technical progress) $f_1'' < 0$, the rise in the investment ratio and in the share of profits will not be sufficient to prevent a continued fall in the rate of growth of capital with the continued increase in v. Hence this process of adopting more labour saving techniques by increasing capital per head will come to an end when the rate of growth of capital declines sufficiently to approach the rate of increase in the supply of labour, λ. From then onwards the system will regain a balanced-growth equilibrium with unchanging techniques and capital per head and proceeding at the uniform expansion rate λ.

Thus the introduction of a choice of processes permitting the substitution of capital for labour will mean that there will be an intermediate stage between the equilibrium of Model I (where G_Y was determined by G_K) and of Model II (where G_Y was determined by G_n, and G_K by G_Y), characterised by the condition

$$G_K > G_Y > G_n,$$

i.e. where the actual rate of growth is greater than the natural rate, as determined by population growth, and lower than the rate of capital accumulation. In other words, the rate of growth of capital will be higher than that of output, and the latter will be declining. The difference thus introduced is best shown in a diagram (Fig. 1) where output (Y_t) is shown vertically (on a

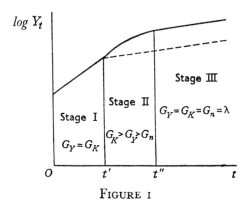

FIGURE I

logarithmic scale) and time horizontally. Assuming that from $t = 0$ onwards the economy is in a growth equilibrium with unlimited supplies of labour with $G_Y = G_K$, G_K being determined by the ratio of savings to income when wages are at the minimum subsistence level; and assuming further that the labour reserves are exhausted at the point of time t', then, in the absence of a choice of "techniques" of a more or less labour-saving character, wages will immediately rise to the point where the share of profits is cut down to the level where the rate of accumulation is brought down to $G_n = \lambda$ and the system attains a new balanced-growth equilibrium at this lower rate. If we assume, however, that there are technical possibilities for increasing output per head by using more capital per unit of labour, the transition will be gradual. Wages will rise more gradually, and accumulation will be maintained (temporarily) at a higher rate, serving both the requirements of the growing working population and the increasing amount of capital per unit of labour. But since during this stage the rate of growth of production will be declining, and will be constantly smaller than the rate of capital accumulation, balanced-growth equilibrium will be regained at a certain point (shown by t'' in the diagram). This will occur when wages have risen to the point at which accumulation is brought down to the rate corresponding to the rate of growth of population, and from then onwards the economy will attain the same constant growth rate, determined by λ.[1]

Given the range of alternative processes represented by our f functions, it follows that there is a unique relationship between output per worker and the capital-output ratio (as stated in equation (9) above) and also between the *desired* capital-output ratio and the rate of profit on capital. Hence for balanced-growth equilibria (where the actual capital-output ratio corresponds to the desired ratio) we have the further relationship

$$v = \phi\left(\frac{P}{K}\right), \text{ where } \phi' < 0, \; \phi'' > 0. \tag{8a}$$

---

[1] The first of our three stages may be termed the "classical" stage, the second the "neo-classical" stage (since it will be characterised by rising capital per man, a rising capital-output ratio, and a declining rate of growth and profit) and the third stage, for reasons set out below, the "Keynesian" stage.

Writing these relationships in this form, this model will be characterised by seven relationships, of which three are equilibrium conditions.

$$\left.\begin{array}{l} L^*(t) = L^*(o)e^{\lambda t} \\ O(t) = f(v(t)), f' > 0, f'' < 0 \\ s(t) = \dfrac{P(t)}{\Upsilon(t)} \end{array}\right\} \text{for all } t \geqslant o \qquad \begin{array}{l} \text{(i)} \\ \text{(ii)} \\ \text{(iii)} \end{array}$$

$$P(t) \equiv \Upsilon(t) - w(t)L(t) \qquad \text{(iv)}$$

$$\left.\begin{array}{l} s(t)\Upsilon(t) = \dfrac{dK(t)}{dt} \\ L(t) = L^*(t) \\ v(t) = \phi\left(\dfrac{P(t)}{K(t)}\right) \end{array}\right\} \text{for all } t \geqslant o \qquad \begin{array}{l} \text{(v)} \\ \text{(vi)} \\ \text{(vii)} \end{array}$$

where
$$\phi' < 0, \ \phi'' > 0$$

subject to the inequalities

$$w(t) \geqslant w_{\min}$$
$$\frac{P(t)}{K(t)} \geqslant r + \rho.$$

By the same argument as employed in Model II above it follows that

$$G_Y = \lambda.$$

Hence by (v), $\dfrac{s(t)}{v(t)}$ is independent of t. By (iii) we have $\dfrac{P(t)}{\Upsilon(t)} = \lambda v(t)$ and so

$$\frac{P}{K} = \lambda$$

and using (vii) we obtain $\quad \dfrac{P}{\Upsilon} = \lambda\phi(\lambda).$ \qquad (III)

As a comparison with the corresponding equations for Model II shows, the introduction of a "production function" which makes the capital-output ratio dependent on the rate of profit will not affect the equilibrium growth-rate, or the rate of profit on capital.

But it will have an influence on the share of profits, and hence on the savings coefficient, s, for any given rate of growth, since λ and $\phi(\lambda)$ are inversely related to one another: the higher the value of λ, the lower the equilibrium value $\phi(\lambda)$. In the special case where the function $\phi(\lambda)$ is one of constant unit elasticity (i.e. when doubling the rate of growth and the rate of profit involves halving the capital-output ratio, etc.) the investment coefficient, $\lambda\phi(\lambda)$, will be invariant with respect to any change in the rate of growth and the rate of profit on capital, and, in that sense, the share of profits and wages can be said to be uniquely determined by the coefficients of the production function. But the assumption of constant unit elasticity for the ϕ function is by no means implicit in the assumption of homogeneous and linear production functions, and indeed it cannot hold in all cases where there are limits to the extent to which any one factor can be dispensed with. If, in the relevant range, the elasticity of this function is appreciably smaller than one, the share of profit will predominantly depend on the rate of economic growth (and on the propensities to save out of profits and wages discussed below) and only to a minor extent on the technical factors, the marginal rates of substitution between capital and labour (which determine the elasticity of the ϕ function).[1]

VI. THE PROPENSITIES TO SAVE

We can now relax our fourth assumption, the one implicit in all "classical" models, that there is no consumption out of profits and no saving out of wages. We can allow both for the fact that profits are a source of consumption expenditure and that wages may be a source of savings—provided that we assume that the proportion of profits saved is considerably greater than the proportion of wages (and other contractual incomes) saved.[2]

[1] Empirical evidence, such as it is, lends little support to the supposition that the capital-output ratio is smaller in fast-growing economies than in slow-growing economies, or in economies where the amount of capital per head is relatively small as against those where it is large. But the reason for this, as we shall argue later, is not the lack of substitutability between capital and labour, but the unreality of the postulate of a ϕ function which abstracts from all technical progress.

[2] I am assuming here, purely for simplicity, that the savings functions for both profits and wages are linear (with a zero constant) so that the average and marginal propensities are identical. If this were not so, it would be the difference in marginal propensities which was critical to the theory.

This assumption can be well justified both by empirical evidence and by theoretical considerations. Thus, on U.S. data, gross savings out of gross (company) profits can be put at 70 per cent, whereas savings out of personal incomes (excluding unincorporated businesses) are only around 5 per cent. Statistical evidence from other countries yields very similar results. On theoretical grounds one can expect the propensity to save out of business profits to be greater than that of wage and salary incomes (i) because residual incomes are much more uncertain, and subject to considerable fluctuations, year by year; (ii) because the accumulation of capital by the owners of the individual firms is closely linked to the *growth* of the firms: since a firm's borrowing power is limited to some proportion of its equity capital, the growth of the latter is a necessary pre-condition of the growth in its scale of operations. Apart from this, it could be argued on Keynesian considerations that it is precisely this difference in savings-ratios which lends stability to a capitalist system, under full employment or near-full employment conditions. For if these differences did *not* exist, any chance increase in demand which raised prices would bring about a cumulative tendency: a rise in prices is only capable of eliminating the disequilibrium in so far as the transfer of purchasing power from "contractual" to "residual" incomes which it represents reduces effective demand in real terms.

If we denote by a the proportion of profits saved and β the proportion of wages saved,

$$I = aP + \beta W, \text{ where } 1 > a > \beta \geqslant 0 \tag{10}$$

$$s \equiv \frac{I}{Y} = (a - \beta)\frac{P}{Y} + \beta \tag{10a}$$

and

$$\frac{P}{Y} = \frac{1}{a - \beta}\frac{I}{Y} - \frac{\beta}{a - \beta}. \tag{10b}$$

If, in the first approximation, we assumed that βW is zero the equilibrium relationships will remain the same as in Model III, with the exception of (ii) which becomes

$$s(t) = a\frac{P(t)}{Y(t)}$$

This modification implies that in equilibrium

$$\frac{P}{K} = \frac{\lambda}{a}$$

$$\frac{P}{Y} = \frac{\lambda}{a} \cdot \phi\left(\frac{\lambda}{a}\right). \tag{IV}$$

In other words, the rate of profit on capital will now exceed the rate of growth by the reciprocal of the proportion of profits saved. Similarly, the share of profit in income will also be raised, except in so far as the rise in $\dfrac{P}{K}$ will reduce v, and hence the investment-output ratio at any given rate of growth.

VII. COMPETITION AND FULL EMPLOYMENT

Before examining the implications of assumption (3), the general rule of competition, I should like to translate our results into terms that are in accord with the Keynesian techniques of analysis. So far we have assumed that the level of production at any one time is limited not by effective demand but by the scarcity of resources available; which meant in the case of Model I that it was limited by the amount of capital (i.e. physical capacity) and in the case of Model II by the available supply of labour. In the "Keynesian" sense, therefore, the equilibrium in both cases is one of "full employment". This is ensured, in the case of Model I, through the assumption, implicit in the model, that it is the "surplus" remaining after the payment of subsistence wages which determines the rate of accumulation. In the case of Model II, where investment demand per unit of time is independently determined by the accrual of new investment opportunities resulting from the given rate of increase in the labour supply, it is ensured through the fact that the level of wages in real terms, and thus the share of profits, is assumed to settle at the point where savings out of profits are just equal to the required rate of investment. This latter presumes in effect a "Keynesian" model where investment is the independent variable, and savings are the dependent variable: but the process of adjustment is assumed to take place not in a Keynesian but in a classical manner through forces operating in the labour market. An excess of savings over investment manifests itself in an excess of the demand for labour over the supply of labour; this leads to a rise in wages which reduces profits, and thus savings, and hence diminishes the rate of increase in the demand for labour. There is therefore some particular real wage at which the rate of increase in the demand for labour, resulting from capital accumulation, keeps in step with the rate of increase in the supply of labour, and which therefore is alone capable of maintaining the labour market in equilibrium.

But we are not *obliged* to look upon the equilibrating mechanism in this way; we could equally describe the equilibrating process in the "Keynesian" manner, through the forces of adjustment operating not in the labour market, but in the commodity markets. In the Keynesian system an excess in the demand for labour in the labour market can only cause a rise in *money* wages, not of *real* wages, since a rise in *money* wages, *ceteris paribus*, will raise monetary demand, and thus prices, in the same proportion. To explain movements in *real* wages (output per man being assumed as given) we need to turn to the commodity markets and examine the conditions of equilibrium for the demand and supply of commodities. It is the most significant feature of Keynes' theory to have shown that equilibrium between savings (*ex ante*) and investment (*ex ante*) is secured through forces operating in the commodity markets. When investment exceeds savings, the demand for commodities will exceed the supply. This will lead *either* to an expansion of supply (assuming the prevalence of "Keynesian" unemployment and hence a state of affairs where production is less than the short-period maximum) *or* to a rise in prices relatively to costs (assuming "full employment" in the Keynesian sense, i.e. that supply is limited by physical bottlenecks). In both cases an increase in the demand for commodities will lead to an increase in savings; in the first case, because savings are an increasing function of real income, at any *given* relationship of prices to costs (or of profits to wages); in the second case, because the rise in prices relative to costs implies a rise in profits and a fall in wages (in *real* terms) which increases savings.

Keynes, in the *General Theory*, writing in the middle of the big slump of the 1930s, concentrated on the under-employment case, and conceived of the mechanism which equates savings with investment as one which operates through variations in the general level of employment. But in his previous book, *A Treatise on Money* (written in the late 1920s), he described essentially the same mechanism as determining the relationship of prices to costs, with output and employment as given.[1]

To illustrate the nature of this process and to analyse the conditions under which the forces equalising savings and investment determine the price-cost relationship at full employment, rather than the level of employment at some *given* relationship of prices to costs, I should like to make use of the time-honoured device of the "representative firm" which is assumed to behave like a small-scale replica of the economy as a whole. I shall assume, in other words, that variations in the output of the "representative firm" reflect equivalent variations in total production, and that the firm employs a constant fraction of the total employed labour force.

I shall ignore falling average prime costs in the short period and shall assume that average and marginal prime costs are constant up to the point where the optimum utilisation of capacity is reached and begin to rise afterwards, as shown by the curves APC and MC in Fig. 2. I shall assume that our representative firm is fully integrated vertically, so that its average and marginal prime costs consist only of labour cost. (The rate of money-wages is assumed to be given.) And I shall further assume, as is appropriate for a "developed" economy under conditions of imperfect competition, that the effective bottleneck setting an upper limit to production is labour rather than physical capacity: there is more than enough capacity to employ the available labour force. Hence, since our firm accounts for a constant fraction of total employment, it cannot produce at a rate higher than that indicated by the full-employment position (as shown by the dashed line in Fig. 2.)[2]

---

[1] *A Treatise on Money* (London, 1930), vol. I, p. 139.
[2] The assumption that physical capacity is more than sufficient for the employment of the available labour force in "developed" capitalist economies is empirically supported by the fact that even in times of very low unemployment, double or treble

Finally, I shall assume that whatever the state of demand, our firm will not be forced to reduce prices to the bare level of prime costs; there is a certain *minimum margin of profit* which competition cannot succeed in eliminating. We can call this minimum profit margin the "degree of monopoly", or the "degree of market imperfection", remembering, however, that it does not necessarily *set* the price (in relation to costs), it merely sets a rock-bottom to prices. (In Fig. 2 the dot-and-dash line indicates the minimum price at the given level of prime cost per unit of output.) The greater the intensity of competition the lower will be this minimum margin of profit.

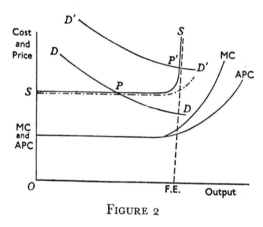

FIGURE 2

The assumption that prices cannot fall below some minimum determined by the degree of market imperfection, and that production cannot exceed a certain maximum determined by full employment, yields a short-period supply curve (the curve *S–S* in Fig. 2) which exhibits the familiar reverse L-shaped feature: the curve is horizontal up to a certain point (when the supply price is set by the minimum profit margin) and well-nigh vertical afterwards (when production is limited by full employment).

We can now introduce the Keynesian demand function which shows the demand price for each level of output—i.e. it shows for

---

shift utilisation of capacity is fairly rare. And it is the existence of considerable spare capacity under conditions of imperfect competition which alone explains the absence of diminishing productivity to labour with increasing employment in the short period, despite the co-existence of physical equipment of varying degrees of efficiency.

any particular output (and employment) that excess of price over prime cost which makes the effective demand in real terms equal to that output. (The excess of price over prime cost is of course the same thing, on our assumptions, as the share of profits in output.) Assuming that investment, I, is an independent variable invariant with respect to changes in output, this demand curve will be falling from left to right, much like the Marshallian demand curve, and its equation, according to the well-known multiplier formula, will be

$$D = \frac{1}{(a - \beta)\dfrac{p - c}{p} + \beta} I, \qquad (11)$$

where D represents aggregate demand in real terms, $\dfrac{p-c}{p}$ the margin of profit over selling price (which, for the representative firm, is the same as $\dfrac{P}{Y}$, the share of profits in income), I the amount of investment (also in real terms), and a and β the co-efficients of savings for profits and wages respectively. The higher is I, and the lower are the coefficients a and β, the higher the position of the curve; the greater the difference, $a - \beta$, the greater elasticity of the curve. If $\beta = 0$, the curve approaches the APC curve asymptotically; if $a = \beta$ the curve becomes a vertical straight line.

Depending on the relative position of the two curves, this intersection can yield either an under-employment equilibrium (when the demand curve cuts the supply curve in the horizontal segment of the latter, as shown by $D - D$, with the point of intersection P) or a full-employment equilibrium (as shown by $D' - D'$, with the point of intersection P'). In the former case the price-cost relationship (the distribution of income) will be independently given by the degree of market imperfection (marginal productivity plays no rôle in this case since the average productivity of labour is assumed to be constant) whilst the level of output is determined by the parameters of the demand function (the savings-investment relationship). In the latter case, output is independently given, and it is the price-cost relationship which will be determined by the demand function, i.e. by the savings-investment relationship.[1]

However, our demand curve has so far been based on the postulate that the rate of investment is invariant with respect to changes in output. In fact, it is the rate of growth of output which governs investment demand; and, in addition to the growth of output due to the natural rate of growth of the economy, investment in the short period will also vary with the change in output reflecting a change in the level of unemployment. Such "induced" investment will only come into operation, however, when the degree of utilisation of capacity permits a normal rate of profit to be earned; in other words when receipts cover, or more than cover, *total* costs, including "normal" profits on the capital invested.

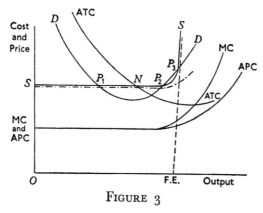

FIGURE 3

In Fig. 3 the curve *ATC* indicates average total costs (including "normal" profits) and the point N (where the curve *ATC* intersects the *S–S* curve) the level of production which yields a "normal" profit on the existing capital equipment. Beyond N, any further increase in production will "induce" investment in the shape of additions to productive capacity, and it is reasonable to suppose that the increase in investment associated with an

---

[1] It follows also that in so far as β (savings out of wages) is zero or negligible, under-employment equilibrium necessarily presupposes some degree of market imperfection; for if competition were perfect and the minimum profit margin were zero, the intersection of the demand curve with the supply curve would necessarily fall on the vertical section of the latter.

increase in output will exceed the increase in savings for any *given* distribution of income. Hence the savings-investment relationship will yield a U-shaped demand curve; the curve will be falling up to N (when induced investment is zero)[1] and will slope upwards to the right of N (when induced investment is positive). As shown in Fig. 3 this will yield multiple positions of equilibrium, P_1, P_2 and P_3, of which only P_1 and P_3 are stable positions whereas P_2 is unstable (since at P_2, where the demand curve cuts the supply curve from below, a small displacement in either direction will set up cumulative forces away from P_2 until either P_1 or P_3 is reached).

It follows that an under-employment equilibrium is only *stable* under slump conditions when induced investment is zero.

It also follows that it is impossible to conceive of a *moving* equilibrium of growth being an under-employment equilibrium. Such an equilibrium is necessarily one where productive capacity is growing, and where therefore induced investment is positive, and hence the $D-D$ curve slopes upwards and not downwards. It therefore postulates the equilibrium of the P_3 type and not of the P_1 type. In that situation the profit margin must be above the minimum level, and the distribution of income will tend to be such as to generate the same proportion of income saved as the proportion of investment in output.

In a balanced-growth equilibrium, the level of investment must of course also correspond to the rate of accumulation appropriate to the rate of growth of the economy, in other words (in terms of Model II) to $(\lambda v)\Upsilon$. This is not necessarily the rate of investment reflected by our (short-period) demand curve at the point P_3; if it is not, the adjustment takes the form of a change in capacity in relation to output (a shift in point N in the diagram) and a consequent change in the investment "induced" by the excess of actual output over N sufficient to make the volume of induced investment equal to $(\lambda v)\Upsilon$.

It further follows that a moving equilibrium of growth is only possible when, given the savings propensities, the profit margin

[1] Up to point N, the position of the demand curve may be regarded as being determined by the existence of some "autonomous" investment which is independent of the current level of activity, or else by a negative constant in the savings functions, which makes savings zero at some positive level of income and employment.

resulting from the equilibrium rate of investment is higher than the minimum profit margin indicated by the height of the horizontal section of the S–S line; and there must be sufficient competition to ensure this. If this were not so, the point P_3 would lie below the S–S line, and the only equilibrium conceivable in that case would be that of the P_1 type at which, as we have seen, induced investment is zero, and the level of output remains stationary over time, irrespective of the growth in population. *It is only under conditions of "Keynesian" full employment that the growth-potential of an economy (indicated by its "natural" rate of growth) is exploited in terms of actual growth.*

We must therefore add a further restriction to our models which can be written (putting m for the minimum profit margin, reflecting the degree of market imperfection):

$$\frac{P}{Y} \geqslant m \tag{12}$$

which, under the assumption of Model II where $\dfrac{P}{Y} = \lambda v$, can be written in the form

$$m \leqslant \lambda v. \tag{12a}$$

If this condition is not satisfied, the economy will lapse into stagnation.

So far we have not mentioned marginal productivity. Clearly, the equilibrium real wage cannot *exceed* the short-period marginal product of labour: for if it did, the position of full employment could not be reached. Under our present assumptions, where the full-employment position falls within the range of the horizontal section of the average prime cost curve (or very near it), this does not impose any further restriction. For when productivity is constant, the marginal product of labour is the same as the average product, and the condition therefore is necessarily satisfied, so long as the equilibrium wage is lower than output per head (i.e. so long as the equilibrium share of profits is positive). In order to generalise our results, however, to cover the case of diminishing (short-period) returns (i.e. when the full-employment line in Figs. 2 and 3 cuts the average prime cost curve in the *rising* section of the latter and marginal costs exceed average prime costs), we need to introduce a further restriction to the effect that the share of wages cannot exceed the marginal product of labour. Writing for a *given* value of K,

$$\Upsilon = \Psi(L), \text{ where } \Psi' > 0, \Psi'' \leqslant 0$$

for the *short-period* relationship between output and employment (L denoting the amount of employment) the condition is

$$\frac{W}{\Upsilon} \leqslant \frac{L\Psi'(L)}{\Psi(L)}. \tag{13}$$

Under conditions of our Model II, where $\dfrac{P}{\Upsilon} = \lambda v$, this could

also be written in the form

$$\frac{\Psi(L) - L\Psi'(L)}{\Psi(L)} \leqslant \lambda v, \tag{13a}$$

i.e. the equilibrium share of profits, as determined by the "dynamic" conditions, cannot be less than the excess of the average product of labour over the marginal product. We can assume, however that the system will tend to generate sufficient excess capacity (in relation to the labour supply) for this condition to be satisfied.

These two restrictions, (12) and (13), together with that given in (5), are not additive but alternative, and only the higher of them will apply. For our minimum margin of profit in (12) is not the same thing as the "optimum" monopoly profit of the text-books, which is the outcome of short-period profit-maximisation with reference to some given marginal-revenue schedule to the individual firm. It is more akin to Marshall's notion of a minimum margin of profit on turnover below which producers refuse to go "for fear of spoiling the market",[1] but which tends to be the lower, the more intense the competition among producers. As such it is related to the average cost of production and not to marginal cost; and as an obstacle to a fall in the profit-share, it overlaps with the technical barrier set by the excess of short-period marginal cost over average prime cost.

---

[1] *Principles* (8th ed.), Book V, ch. 5, section 5, pp. 374–6.

VIII. TECHNICAL PROGRESS

We must now proceed to remove the most important of our "simplifying" assumptions, the absence of technical progress. A moving equilibrium of growth involves continued increase in the productivity of labour and not only in the working population, *pari passu* with a continued increase in the amount of capital per worker; though in the absence of any reliable measure of the quantity of capital (in a world where the technical specification of capital goods is constantly changing, new kinds of goods constantly appear and others disappear) the very notion of the "amount of capital" loses precision. The terms "income" or "capital" no longer have any precise meaning; they are essentially accounting magnitudes, which merely serve as the basis of calculations in business planning; the assumption that money has a stable value in terms of some price index enables us to think of "income" and "capital" as *real* magnitudes only in a limited, and not precisely definable, sense.[1]

Orthodox theory attempts to deal with these problems in terms of the traditional tools—the assumption of a linear and homogeneous production function, coupled with the assumption that with the changing state of knowledge this function is continually shifting upwards and outwards. As depicted in Fig. 4

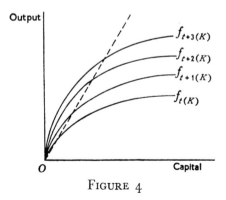

FIGURE 4

---

[1] These problems do not appear in a von Neumann type of model of balanced-growth equilibrium with constant technical functions, precisely because the technical specification of goods, their relative composition and their relative values remain unchanged through time; everything remains the same, except for the actual quantities of goods, and there is no problem involved in aggregation.

at any one *point* of time, *t*, there is assumed to be a unique relationship between capital and output, which conforms to the general hypothesis of diminishing productivity, but this relationship is constantly shifting with the passage of time. The assumption of "neutral" technical progress means that the production curve shifts in such a manner that the slope of the tangents of the functions f_t, f_{t+1}, f_{t+2}, etc., remain unchanged along any radius from the origin. This hypothesis is necessary in order to make it possible for a constant rate of profit over time to be consistent with a constant rate of growth and a constant relationship between capital and output (since the rate of profit on capital is uniquely related to the slope of the production function).

There are, however, several basic faults in this procedure—quite apart from the inherent improbability that technical progress should obey any such rigid rules.

(1) In the first place the production function assumes that the capital stock in existence at any one time is perfectly adapted to any given capital-labour ratio—that there is a particular assortment of equipment goods corresponding to each successive point of the production curve which is different from the assortment associated with any neighbouring point. (This will be true even in the absence of "technical progress" so long as the substitution of capital for labour implies the use of different *kinds* of equipment, and not merely the use of relatively greater quantities of the *same* equipment.) Hence the successive points on this curve represent alternative states of long-period stationary equilibrium any one of which could be actually attained only when any given state of capital endowment (i.e., any given capital-output ratio) has obtained unchanged for a long enough period for the actual assortment of capital goods to have become optimally adapted to it. The production curve thus represents a kind of boundary indicating the maximum output corresponding to each particular "quantity" of capital, a maximum which assumes that the whole productive system is fully adapted to each particular state of accumulation. In an economy where capital accumulation is a continuous process this boundary is never attained—since the actual assortment of capital goods at any one time (even with a *constant* state of knowledge, whatever that assumption may be

taken to mean) will consist of items appropriate to differing states of accumulation, and the output corresponding to any particular "quantity" of capital will be less than the equilibrium (or maximum) output associated with that quantity. This is only another way of saying that in a society which is *not* in continuous long-run stationary equilibrium, output cannot be regarded as a unique function of capital and labour; and the slope of the production curve cannot be relevant to the pricing process, since the system does not move *along* the curve, but *inside* it.

(2) In the second place (and quite independently of the first point) the assumption that there is a curve which continually shifts upwards means that technical progress is treated as a variable of the function in a manner perfectly analogous to a second factor of production, like labour (or land). This is evident from the consideration that if, instead of postulating rising technical knowledge and a constant labour force, we postulated a constant state of technical knowledge and a rising labour force, the nature of the shift of the curve (under the hypothesis of a homogeneous and linear function) would be exactly the same. A given rate of shift of the curve, along any radius from the origin, could equally well result from a given percentage increase in the labour supply as from the same percentage increase in the state of "knowledge". But unlike labour, the state of knowledge is not a quantifiable factor. A *given* or a *constant* state of knowledge is only capable of being defined implicitly: there is no possible way in which, comparing two different positions, at two different points of time, the change due to the movement along the curve could be isolated from the change due to the shift of the curve. The whole procedure by which this separation is attempted is purely circular: since the *slope* of the curve (under the additional hypothesis that the function is not only homogeneous and linear but a constant-elasticity function *à la* Cobb-Douglas!) is supposed to determine the share of profits in income, the share of profits is taken to be an indication of its slope, and the residual is then attributed to the shift of the curve! There could be no better example of *post hoc ergo propter hoc*.

(3) The hypothesis that the *slope* of the curve determines the share of profits, in accordance with the marginal productivity

principle, despite the continued shift in the curve, presumes of course that the factor responsible for the shift is itself rewarded on the same principle, since it is the marginal product of *all* factors taken *together* which exhausts the total product. This condition can be satisfied when the shift of the curve is due to, say, a certain rate of increase in the quantity of labour, since that part of the increase in the product which is due to the shift is definitely imputed to labour in the form of wages. But knowledge, just because it is not a quantifiable factor which can be measured, or brought under exclusive ownership, or bought and sold, cannot receive its *own* marginal product. It is like other scarce but un-appropriated agents of production (like the sea in the case of the fishing industry) whose existence causes divergences between the private and the social product of the *other* factors. This is only another way of saying that we are not free to elevate to the rôle of a "factor of production" anything we like; the variables of the production function must be true inputs, and not vague "background elements", like the sun or the sea or the state of knowledge, any of which may be thought to cause the results to diverge from the hypothesis of the homogeneous-and-linear production function. In terms of the *true* variables, Capital and Labour, the production function will not be linear-homogeneous but will be a function of a higher order, when technical knowledge is increasing over time.[1] It is therefore illegitimate to assume that factor rewards are allocated in accordance with their mar-ginal productivities, since the sum of the marginal products of the factors will exceed the total product. When, the quantity of labour being given, an increase in capital by a given pro-portion yields an increase in output in the same proportion, the "true" marginal product of capital will *alone* exhaust the total product.[2] For this reason any postulate derived from the

---

[1] It is a well-known dodge that any function whatsoever in n variables can be converted into a homogeneous-and-linear function of $n+1$ variables by adding a further variable which is *implicitly* defined. But as Samuelson has pointed out (*Foundations of Economic Analysis*, p. 84), any such procedure is illegitimate, since factor rewards will not conform to the partial differentials of this wider function.

[2] Supporters of the neo-classical approach would argue that the increase in product in this case is not *due* to the change in the quantity of capital alone—it is the joint result of the change in the quantity of the "factor" capital, and the shift in the "state of knowledge" which is presumed to have occurred in the interval of time during which the increase in capital occurred. But this is precisely the point: since the accumu-

hypothesis of diminishing productivity (such as our $v = \phi\left(\dfrac{P}{K}\right)$ function, given in equation (8a) above) is illegitimate when productivity, for whatever reason, is *not* diminishing. Given the fact of constant or increasing productivity to capital accumulation, the share of profit must necessarily be *less* than the marginal product of capital, and there is no reason why a given capital-output ratio should be associated with a particular rate of profit, or indeed, why the two should be functionally related to each other on account of any technical factor.

(4) Added to this is the further complication that the rate of shift of the production function due to the changing state of "knowledge" cannot be treated as an independent function of (chronological) time, but depends on the rate of accumulation of capital itself. Since improved knowledge is, largely if not entirely, infused into the economy through the introduction of new equipment, the rate of shift of the curve will itself depend on the *speed of movement* along the curve, which makes any attempt to isolate the one from the other the more nonsensical.[1]

The most that one can say is that whereas the rate of technical improvement will depend on the rate of capital accumulation, any society has only a limited capacity to *absorb* technical change in a

---

lation of capital is necessarily a process in time, and cannot be conceived of in a time-less fashion, a movement *along* the curve cannot be isolated from the shift of the curve; indeed it is illegitimate to assume the existence of a "curve" independently of its shift, since there is no conceivable operation by which the slope of this "curve" could be identified.

[1] None of the above strictures against the postulate of a "production function" which continually shifts with technical progress invalidates the assumption of a *short-period* relationship between employment and output, which takes the character and composition of fixed equipment of all kinds as given. This short-period production function (as employed in equations (13) and (13a) above) implies that for any given volume of employment a definite "marginal product" can be imputed to labour, which, as we have seen, sets an *upper limit* to the share of wages in output (the "rents" to be imputed to capital being the residual, i.e. the difference between the average and the marginal product of labour). This limit, however, only becomes significant when diminishing returns prevail, so that an increase in production is associated with a more-than proportionate increase in employment—with constant or increasing returns, the marginal product of labour will be equal to, or exceed, the average product, and the former *cannot* therefore be the governing factor determining distributive shares. Whether diminishing returns prevail or not will predominantly depend on the output capacity represented by the existing capital stock and its degree of utilisation when labour is fully employed. Under conditions of imperfect competition it is perfectly compatible with "profit-maximising behaviour" to suppose that the representative firm will maintain a considerable amount of spare capacity even in relation to the output attainable under full-employment conditions.

C

given period. Hence, whether the increase in output will be more
or less than proportionate to the increase in capital will depend,
not on the state of knowledge or the rate of progress in knowledge, but on the *speed* with which capital is accumulated, relatively to the capacity to innovate and to infuse innovations into
the economic system. The more "dynamic" are the people in
control of production, the keener they are in search of improvements, and the readier they are to adopt new ideas and to introduce new ways of doing things, the faster production (per man)
will rise, and the higher is the rate of accumulation of capital
that can be profitably maintained.

These hypotheses can, in my view, be projected in terms of a
"technical progress function" which postulates a relationship
between the rate of increase of capital and the rate of increase
in output and which embodies the effect of constantly improving
knowledge and know-how, as well as the effect of increasing
capital per man, without any attempt to isolate the one from the
other.

It is the shape and position of this "technical progress function"
which will exhibit features of diminishing returns. If we plot percentage growth rate of output per head, $\dot{Y}/Y$, along the abscissa
and percentage growth rate of capital per head, $\dot{K}/K$, along the
ordinate (Fig. 5), the curve will cut the y-axis positively (since
a certain rate of improvement would take place even if capital
per head remained unchanged) but it will be convex upwards,
and reach a maximum at a certain point—there is always a maximum beyond which a further increase in the rate of accumulation

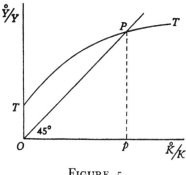

FIGURE 5

will not enhance further the *rate* of growth of output (Fig. 5). This means that the increase in capital (per head) will yield increasing or diminishing returns in terms of output according as the rate of accumulation is relatively small or large. If the rate of accumulation is less than *Op*, output will increase faster than capital, and vice versa.

The *height* of the curve expresses society's "dynamism", meaning by this both inventiveness and readiness to change or to experiment. But the convexity of the curve expresses the fact that it is possible to utilise as yet unexploited ideas (whether old ideas or new ideas) more or less fully; and it is always the most profitable ideas (i.e. those that raise output most in relation to the investment which they require) which are exploited first. Some are old ideas; some are new ideas; most of the technical improvement that takes place embodies both. We cannot isolate the element of pure novelty in a world where knowledge is constantly improving, and where the techniques actually used constantly lag behind the very latest techniques that would be selected if everything were started afresh. When capital is accumulated at a faster rate (and technical improvement goes on at a faster rate), productivity will also increase at a faster rate, but the growth in the latter will lag behind the growth in the former, and beyond a certain point a further increase in the rate of accumulation ceases to be "productive"—it is incapable of stepping up the rate of growth of productivity any further.

There is therefore no *unique* rate of technical progress—no *unique* rate at which alone a constant rate of growth can be maintained. There is a whole series of such rates, depending on the rate of accumulation of capital being relatively small or large.

On this analysis, it is the "technical dynamism" of the economy, as shown by the height or position of our technical progress curve, which is responsible, in a capitalist economy, both for making the rate of accumulation of capital and the rate of growth of production relatively small or relatively large. It explains why there is no long-run tendency to a *falling* rate of profit, or for a continued increase in capital in relation to output, either in slow-growing or in fast-growing economies. In economies whose technical dynamism is low, both the rate of accumulation and the growth of production will be relatively low, but in either case, growth can go on at a steady rate, without any necessary tendency to diminishing returns and thus to a gradual approach to a stationary state.

On the assumption that this function cuts the y-axis positively (i.e. that there would be some positive rate of growth in output per man, even if capital per man remained unchanged—an assumption which is justified by the fact that even a zero rate of net investment implies a certain rate of infusion of new techniques or new designs, through the replacement of worn-out capital; and that there are always *some* improvements which may require no investment at all) and that the curve is convex upwards, there is necessarily a certain point on the curve at which it is intersected by a radius of 45 degrees from the origin—i.e. where the rate of growth of output is equal to the rate of growth of capital (P in Fig. 5). At that point *all* the conditions of "neutral" technical progress are satisfied: the capital-output ratio will remain constant at a constant rate of growth, constant distributive shares, and a constant rate of profit on capital.

In order to "close" our model—that is, to produce a model that would account for the empirical features of the growth process as summarised by our "stylised facts" at the beginning—it is necessary to show, not merely that such a point exists, but that in a capitalist system there is a tendency to move towards this point, which thus represents a long-run equilibrium rate of growth, and which is also stable in the sense that displacements due to shifts in the curve, etc., set up forces to re-establish it.

The hypothesis that *given* the technical progress function, the system tends towards that particular rate of accumulation where the conditions of "neutral progress" are satisfied, cannot of course be justified on *a priori* grounds; it must be based on empirical evidence—at least in the sense that it can be shown to be consistent with facts which are more difficult to explain on any alternative hypothesis. Supposing that the statisticians were to agree that the capital-output ratio tends to be constant in periods in which the rate of growth of production is constant (in which therefore the rate of technical progress is neither increasing nor decreasing) whilst the capital-output ratio tends to decrease in periods of accelerating growth and vice versa. This would support the hypothesis that the system *tends* towards *P*: and variations in the rate of growth, and in the movements in the capital-output ratio, are then to be explained in terms of the unequal incidence of technical progress—i.e. in terms of shifts of our technical progress function. If, on the other hand, the statisticians were to agree that there is no correlation between these magnitudes, that periods of steady growth are just as likely to be associated with a steadily decreasing or a steadily increasing ratio of capital to output, this would support the hypothesis that the system tends towards some point on the curve—to some equilibrium rate of growth of output and of capital—which is not necessarily the one at which the two growth rates are *equal*.

IX. ASSUMPTIONS ABOUT INVESTMENT BEHAVIOUR

In either event, to obtain an equilibrium solution—to assert, in other words, that there is some particular equilibrium rate of growth of output and of capital towards which the system is tending—we need to introduce an "investment function" based on entrepreneurial behaviour. Since we *cannot* say that the rate of capital accumulation depends on the community's propensity to save (since the latter is a dependent variable, depending on the share of profits, and thus on the share of investment) nor on the requirements of the "natural rate of growth" (because one of the two constituents at least of the natural rate of growth, the rate of growth of productivity, is a dependent variable, depending on the rate of accumulation of capital and thus on the share of investment), we need to introduce, in order to close our model, an independent function describing the investment decisions of entrepreneurs. There are various alternative assumptions that can be made about investment behaviour which lead to divergent results; and at the present stage we cannot say that our knowledge of entrepreneurial behaviour is sufficient to rule out any particular assumption in preference to some other. Hence our final choice of assumption must be based on the admittedly weaker procedure of its yielding results that are more in conformity with the facts of experience than its alternatives.

(1) One hypothesis, originally advanced by Kalecki,[1] is that the subjective risks assumed by entrepreneurs are an increasing function of the rate of capital accumulation (or, as Kalecki put it, the rate of investment decisions is an increasing function of the gap between the prospective rate of profit and the rate of interest). This assumption, at any rate for a given market rate of interest, makes the rate of capital accumulation a single-valued function of the rate of profit on capital, and since the latter, in a state of balanced-growth equilibrium, is a single-valued function

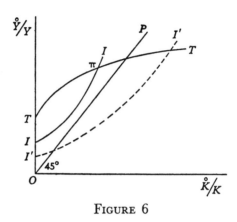

FIGURE 6

of the rate of growth, it makes the desired rate of accumulation a single-valued function of the rate of economic growth. Such an "inducement to invest" function is shown by the curve *I–I* in Fig. 6. The height of this curve (i.e. the point at which it cuts the *y*-axis) reflects the market rate of interest, while the slope of the curve reflects increasing marginal risk. This postulate yields an equilibrium position at point π where the rate of economic growth resulting from the given rate of capital accumulation coincides with the rate of economic growth that is required in order to induce entrepreneurs to accumulate capital at that particular rate. On this hypothesis the equilibrium rate of growth can be anywhere on the *T–T* curve, depending only on the position of the risk preference function (governing the inducement to invest) relatively to the technical progress function (governing

---

[1] "The Principle of Increasing Risk", *Economica*, 1937, p. 440.

the rate of growth resulting from varying rates of accumulation). Thus if π is to the left of P, the equilibrium rate of growth will involve a constantly falling capital-output ratio, and if it is to the right of P (as with the dotted line $I'-I'$ in Fig. 6) it involves a constantly rising capital-output ratio. In both cases the rate of growth will be constant over time, but in the first case the equilibrium will involve a steadily falling share of profit in income and in the second case a steadily rising share of profit. On this hypothesis therefore the "neutral" position at P will only be reached as a result of a coincidence—of the $I-I$ curve cutting the $T-T$ curve at that point.

(2) An alternative hypothesis, which is a variant of the one put forward in my paper "A Model of Economic Growth",[1] makes the principle of increasing risk applicable, not to the volume of investment decisions as such, but only to that part of investment which is in excess of that required to maintain a constant relationship between output capacity and prospective output. Whenever sales are rising, entrepreneurs will in any case increase the capital invested in the business by the amount necessary to enable them to increase their productive capacity in line with the growth of their sales—there are no greater risks involved in a larger business than a smaller one; and no greater risks are entailed in a higher rate of growth of employed capital, if this proceeds *pari passu* with a higher rate of growth of turnover. Hence if their actual sales are rising at the rate of g (where g may be any particular point on the $T-T$ curve in Fig. 6) we may suppose, in accordance with the "acceleration principle", that the growth in output in itself will "induce" sufficient investment to enable that rate of growth of production to be maintained, without requiring a higher prospective rate of profit. As far as this "induced investment" is concerned, any particular point on the curve could be an equilibrium point. But if a particular rate of growth of output and capital involves the expectation of a *rising* rate of profit in the minds of investors, it will induce an acceleration in the rate of accumulation and hence will cause the system

[1] *Economic Journal*, 1957, p. 604. The form of the "investment function" given in that paper was justly criticised; the present version, I hope, meets the objections raised against the earlier version by Professor Meade, Mr. Hudson and others.

to move to the right (on the curve); if it involves the expectation of a falling rate of profit, it will cause it to move to the left.

The *prospective* rate of profit in the minds of entrepreneurs is based on two things: on the amount of capital required per unit of output, and on the expected profit margin per unit of output. If we assume that all savings come out of profits (i.e. $\beta = 0$) then, given constant rates of accumulation and growth, the realised rate of profit on capital will also be constant over time, irrespective of whether capital per unit of output is constant, rising or falling (since any reduction in the capital-output ratio will be matched by a corresponding reduction in the share of profits in output, and vice versa). But we cannot assume that the *prospective* rate of profit on current investment will be the same as the *realised* rate of profit on existing capital—the prospective rate of profit will be higher, precisely because the capital required for producing a unit-stream of future output is less than the amount of capital that was (historically) invested in producing a unit-stream of current output. Nor can it be assumed that the prospective rate of profit on new investment will be the same as the actually realised rate of profit in future periods, since the latter magnitude will itself depend on the investment decisions currently made by entrepreneurs. Thus if at some particular rate of accumulation the trend of progress causes a continued fall in the amount of capital required per unit of output,

$$\frac{P}{K} \equiv \frac{P}{Y} \cdot \frac{Y}{K}$$

will remain constant if the rise in Y/K is offset by a corresponding fall in P/Y. This would occur if the fall in K/Y involved a corresponding reduction in I/Y; if, in other words, it left the rate of expansion of capacity unchanged. But if this consequential fall in profit margins is *not* foreseen, or not sufficiently foreseen, the rise in Y/K will involve the expectation of a higher prospective rate of profit, which by increasing the rate of investment may prevent the fall in P/Y from occurring at all. This is a case, therefore, where the movement of the economy, and the nature of the final equilibrium, cannot be predicted independently of the nature of the expectations of entrepreneurs. The assumption of "static foresight" (i.e. the projection of existing prices, costs and output levels to the future) leads to a different result from the assumption of "perfect foresight"; the latter assumption moreover leaves the situation indeterminate since the expectations that are capable of being actually realised are by no means unique. It is only in the "neutral" equilibrium case (at point P) that the two kinds of assumptions (static foresight and perfect foresight) lead to consistent results.

Expectations are invariably based on past experience, and in that sense, are of the "static" rather than of the "perfect" kind. In addition, they can be defined as being more or less "elastic" according as the projections into the future are based on the events of the very recent past, or on the average experience of a longer interval of elapsed time. Expectations are likely to be the more elastic the less past experience justifies the assumption of some norm around which short-term movements fluctuate; the more, in other words, past movements have been subject to a trend. For that reason, business expectations are far more likely to be elastic with respect to volume of sales than with respect to the margin of profit on turnover; the future expectation concerning the margin of profit per unit of sales, which is taken as the basis of business calculations, is far more likely to reflect some standard, or norm, than the experience of the most recent period alone. This provides a further reason for supposing that in situations in which production rises faster than the stock of capital, the prospective rate of profit will be rising relatively to the realised rate of profit; and if, in response to this, the rate of accumulation is accelerated, the rate of growth of production, and the realised rate of profit, will rise as well.

Hence the tendency of the system to move towards a position where output and capital both grow at the same rate, and where therefore the rate of profit on capital will remain constant at a constant margin of profit on turnover, can be justified by the suppositions (i) that the prospective rate of profit on investments will be higher than the currently realised rate of profit on existing capital whenever production is rising faster than the capital stock; (ii) that a rise in the prospective rate of profit causes an increase in the rate of investment, relative to the requirements of a state of steady growth, and vice versa.[1]

X. THE FINAL MODEL

The equilibrium relationships of this final model can thus be set out as follows. It is based on three functions: first, on a savings function on the lines of equation (10) above, which can be written in the form

$$\frac{S}{Y} = (a - \beta)\frac{P}{Y} + \beta, \qquad (10a)$$

where $\qquad 1 > a > \beta \geqslant 0.$

Second, on a technical progress function showing the relationship between the rate of growth of output per worker (G_0) and the rate of growth of capital per head $(G_K - \lambda)$, and which (using a linear equation for the sake of convenience)[2] can be written in the form

$$G_0 = a' + \beta'(G_K - \lambda), \text{ where } a' > 0, 1 > \beta' > 0. \qquad (14)$$

---

[1] In the first version of the present growth model (published in the *Economic Journal*, December 1957 and reprinted in *Essays on Economic Stability and Growth*, pp. 259–300) I postulated an investment function which made current investment depend (*inter alia*) on the change in the *realised* rate of profit as compared with the previous period. This was unsatisfactory in that it failed to take into account the fact that the inducement to invest depends on the prospective rate of profit, and not on the actual profit earned on existing capital; and that quite apart from the question of expectations, the prospective rate of profit will differ from the currently realised rate whenever (owing to technical progress, etc.) the "productivity" of capital on new investment (i.e. the amount of investment required per unit of future output capacity) differs from the existing capital-output ratio.

[2] It has been pointed out to me by Professor Meade, Mr. Hahn and others that whilst, in general, the technical progress function cannot be integrated in terms of a production function with a particular rate of time shift, a *linear* technical progress function as given in (14) can be integrated to obtain

$$Y_t = Be^{at}K_t{}^\beta \qquad (14a)$$

which appears to be the same as the Cobb-Douglas function (remembering that Y_t and K_t refer to the output and the capital *per unit* of labour). However, as was pointed out to me by H. Uzawa of Stanford University, in integrating the technical progress function, the constant of the integral $B = B(Y_0, K_0)$ is a function dependent on the initial amount of capital K_0 and of output Y_0, whereas a production function of the type

$$Y_t = f(K_t, t) \qquad (14b)$$

requires that the function should be independent of the initial conditions.

Apart from this, the aggregative production function of the type (14b), a special case of which is the Cobb-Douglas function, implies the assumption that at any given time t, the output Y_t is uniquely determined by the aggregates, K_t and L_t, irrespective of the age-and-industry composition of the capital stock. However,

Third, on an investment function based on the assumptions already described, and which makes investment a combination of two terms. The first term of the equation relates to the amount of investment *induced* by the change in output the previous period, and assumes that this investment will be such as to make the growth in *output capacity* in period $(t + \theta)$ equal to the growth in output in period t. Since in view of (14), the rate of capital accumulation per worker $(G_K - \lambda)$, which is required to increase output capacity by G_0 will not (necessarily) be equal to G_0 but to

$$\frac{G_0 - a'}{\beta'}$$

and since

$$G_K \equiv \frac{I}{K},$$

the rate of *induced* investment in period $(t + \theta)$ and which is the first term of our investment equation, will be equal to

$$(G_0(t) - a')\frac{K(t)}{\beta'} + \lambda K(t).$$

The second term of our investment equation depends on the change in the prospective rate of profit which, on our assumptions concerning the expected margin of profit turnover (i.e., that the *expected* value of P/Y is based on an average past values), will be a rising function of the *change* in Y/K over time. Assuming this latter relationship to be linear for the sake of convenience the whole function can be expressed in the following form:

---

when the technical progress of an economy depends on its rate of capital accumulation (when, in other words, the improvements in techniques require to be embodied in new equipment before they can be taken advantage of), no such functional relationship exists. To describe the relationship between capital, labour and output we require a function in the form

$$Y_t = \phi(A_t) \tag{14c}$$

where A_t specifies the distribution of capital according to age as well as (in a multi-commodity world) the distribution of both capital and labour between industries and firms. In that case the postulate of a linear technical progress function is perfectly consistent with the ϕ function being neither homogeneous in the first degree nor of constant elasticity. In the short run the age-and-industry distribution is of course given as a matter of past history. But even in a long-run growth equilibrium with technical progress, A_t could not be treated as a unique function of K_t and L_t, since it will also depend on λ and (in view of the varying incidence of obsolescence at differing rates of progress) on γ', the equilibrium value of G_0.

$$I(t + \theta) = (G_0(t) - a')\frac{K(t + \theta)}{\beta'} + \lambda K(t + \theta) + \mu\frac{d}{dt}\left(\frac{Y(t)}{K(t)}\right), \quad (15)$$

where $\mu > 0$.

The first term of this equation gives rise to an amount of investment at any given rate of growth of output that is sufficient to maintain that rate of growth of output—i.e. sufficient to keep the system on any particular point on the T–T curve. It can also be seen immediately that when

$$G_Y > G_K,$$

the second term of the expression is positive, hence G_K will be rising over time. A rise in G_K, in accordance with (14), will raise G_Y but less than proportionately, and hence lead to a further rise in investment in accordance with the first term at the same time as it diminishes the second term. Hence, whatever initial position we start from (defined by given values of K, L, and O at some initial point $t = 0$), this process will gradually lead to a situation in which the second term of equation (15) dependent on $\frac{d}{dt}\left(\frac{Y(t)}{K(t)}\right)$ vanishes to zero and where therefore

$$\frac{dv(t)}{dt} = 0. \quad (16)$$

This implies that

$$G_0 = \frac{a'}{1 - \beta'} = \gamma', \quad (17)$$

and

$$G_Y = G_K = \lambda + \gamma'. \quad (18)$$

Hence this model, like the earlier ones, also yields a state of moving equilibrium, where the rate of growth, the capital-output ratio and the distributive shares are constant over time—the main difference being that the output per worker, capital per worker and wages per worker are now no longer constant but rising at the equilibrium rate of growth productivity, γ'. However, these assumptions are not yet sufficient to set out a full equilibrium model. The reason is that since we no longer have a technical equation for v on the lines of equation (8a) which was incorporated in Models III and IV, the actual value of v is here left undetermined. From this model it only follows that at the position of equilibrium v will be constant (since this is implicit in equation (15), as shown by (16)); but this is consistent with any particular value for v—or rather v could only be determined in this model historically, if we assumed that it had a certain initial value at some particular point of time, and followed its resulting movement through the successive steps to final equilibrium.

Hence, in order to close the model, we shall introduce two more variables and three additional relationships. These are strictly "Keynesian"—since they are, on the one hand, necessary to ensure that the reaction-mechanism of the model follows the Keynesian system in which the inducement to invest is independent of the propensities to save; and on the other hand because they incorporate Keynesian notions of the rate of interest and the supply price for risk capital based on liquidity preference and the aversion to risk taking.

We have already argued in connection with (5) above[1] that the inequality

$$\frac{P}{K} \geqslant r + \rho$$

is a necessary boundary condition of the model in the sense that the continued accumulation of capital cannot go on unless the ruling rate of profit is *at least* as high as the necessary compensation for risk and illiquidity involved in the productive employment of wealth.[2] Further consideration shows that in order that the investment equation in (15) should hold, it is not enough to make equation (5) into a boundary condition; for so long as P/K is higher than the supply price of risk capital, there is no reason to suppose that investment outlay will be confined to that necessary for the increase in output capacity (i.e. to that given by "the acceleration principle") or to that resulting from a given increase in the prospective rate of profit in a particular period.

[1] P. 243 above.
[2] A more precise statement of this condition would break down $r + \rho$ further into its component elements, distinguishing between the expected average of short rates of interest and the premium of the long rate over the expected average short rate on the one hand, and the additional lenders', borrowers' and speculative risks, etc., involved in direct investment, on the other hand, but this is not necessary for our present purposes.

Indeed, unless the rate of profit actually corresponds to the supply price of risk capital, one cannot assume that the investment of each period will be confined to the *new* investment opportunities accruing in that period—an assumption necessary for an equilibrium of steady growth. Hence equation (5) should be converted into an equilibrium condition

$$\frac{P}{K} = r + \rho. \tag{19}$$

The second relationship concerns the behaviour of the rate of interest, r, and here we shall follow orthodox Keynesian lines in assuming that the rate of interest is determined by the liquidity preference function and/or monetary policy (summarised in the function $\pi\left(\dfrac{M}{Y}\right)$, where $\pi' \leqslant 0$ and M is the real quantity of money), subject to the condition that there is a minimum ($\bar{r}$) determined by the risk premium associated with the holding of long-term financial assets, below which the rate of interest cannot fall. This relationship can therefore be expressed in two alternative forms

$$r \geqslant \bar{r}$$

when $r > \bar{r}$, $$r = \pi\left(\frac{M}{Y}\right). \tag{20}$$

The third relationship concerns the behaviour of ρ, and though this equation can be fully supported on *a priori* grounds, it is put forward here more tentatively, as at present there is insufficient empirical evidence available to support it. It is based on the following considerations.

(1) First, as explained earlier in this paper,[1] it may be assumed that at any given rate of interest the minimum rate of profit necessary to provide inducement for any particular kind of investment will be higher the riskier (or the more "illiquid") that investment is considered to be;

(2) Second, as was also argued,[2] investment in "fixed assets" (plant and equipment, etc.) is considered to be far more risky or

---

[1] Pages 268-70 above.
[2] *Ibid.*

illiquid than either investment in financial assets or in working capital;

(3) Third, it may be assumed that the turnover-period of circulating capital is invariant (or practically invariant) with respect to changes in the techniques of production, so that circulating capital stands always in a linear relationship to output; hence any increase in the ratio of fixed to circulating capital involves an increase in the capital-output ratio.

It follows as a joint result of (2) and (3) that a higher capital-output ratio (including both fixed and circulating capital in the capital employed) requires for any given rate of interest a *higher* minimum rate of profit. Hence when the stage of accumulation is reached in which the actual rate of profit becomes *equal* to this minimum, the capital-output ratio will be uniquely related to the rate of profit; and, as we have seen, it is only under these conditions that the actual investment in each period is limited by the "new" investment opportunities becoming available in that period (through λ and γ').

Writing F for fixed capital and C for circulating capital, k for the turnover-period of circulating capital, ρ_F and ρ_C for the marginal risk premium on the two types of investments respectively, and ρ for the marginal risk premium on investment in general, we thus have the following additional assumptions and relationships:

$$K \equiv F + C$$

$$C = kY$$

$$v \equiv \frac{K}{Y} \equiv \frac{F + kY}{Y}$$

$$\rho_F > \rho_C$$

$$\therefore \rho \equiv \frac{\rho_F F + \rho_C kY}{F + kY} = \xi_1\left(\frac{F}{Y}\right)$$

$$\rho = \xi_2(v), \text{ where } \xi_2' > 0. \tag{21}$$

It will be noted that the relationship expressed in (21) operates in a reverse manner to equation (8a) which determines v in the "neo-classical" model; since in the case of (8a), ϕ' is negative, not positive.

We have argued at some length that equation (8a) can no longer be assumed to hold when technical progress is a continuing process and there is *no* unique function relating output to the capital stock, in which case, depending on the factors determining the rate of growth, varying shares of profit in income and varying rates of profit on capital can be associated with any *given* capital-output ratio. It is now seen that when equation (21) holds, equation (8a) *cannot* hold—at least not within the framework of a model which assumes that the money rate of interest is determined by "monetary" factors and that there is a minimum below which the rate of interest cannot fall.[1]

We can now set out our final Model V in a formal manner. It contains ten equations and ten variables—$T(t)$, $O(t)$, $L(t)$, $P(t)$, $v(t)$, $s(t)$, $w(t)$, $G_0(t)$, $\rho(t)$ and $r(t)$. We shall continue to assume for simplicity that β is zero (there are no savings out of wages) and we shall take the simpler form of (20), treating the money rate of interest as a constant. We shall also bring together the various boundary conditions that emerged in the course of the analysis (cf. equations (4), (12) and (13) above, including a further one that is implicit in the relationship expressed in (21)).

Assumptions

$$L^*(t) = L^*(0)e^{\lambda t} \tag{i}$$

$$G_0(t) = \alpha' + \beta'(G_K(t) - \lambda) \tag{ii}$$

$$s(t) = \alpha\frac{P(t)}{T(t)} \tag{iii}$$

$$\frac{dv(t)}{dt} = 0 \qquad \text{for all } t \geqslant 0 \tag{iv}$$

$$r(t) = \bar{r} \tag{v}$$

$$\rho(t) = \xi(v(t))$$
$$\xi' > 0 \tag{vi}$$

---

[1] It might be argued that the two equations could be made compatible with one another by an appropriate movement of the money price level which brought the "real" rate of interest (*à la* Fisher) into an appropriate relationship with the other factors. But the movement of the price level depends on the behaviour of money wages (relatively to the change in productivity, γ') and this factor cannot, in turn, be treated as a function of the other variables.

Identity

$$P(t) \equiv Y(t) - w(t)L(t) \tag{vii}$$

Equilibrium Conditions

$$s(t)Y(t) = \frac{dK(t)}{dt} \tag{viii}$$

$$L(t) = L^*(t) \qquad \text{for all } t \geqslant 0 \tag{ix}$$

$$\frac{P(t)}{K(t)} = r(t) + \rho(t) \tag{x}$$

subject to the inequalities

(a) $$w(t) \geqslant w_{\min}$$

(b) $$\frac{P(t)}{Y(t)} \geqslant m$$

(c) $$\frac{W(t)}{Y(t)} \leqslant \frac{\dfrac{dY(t)}{dL(t)}(Lt)}{Y(t)}$$

(d) $$\rho_F + \bar{r} > \frac{\lambda + \gamma'}{a} > \rho_C + \bar{r}. \tag{V}$$

It is readily seen that the above yields a determinate system provided that the solutions fall within the limits indicated by the boundary conditions (a)–(d). By (ii) and (iv) we have

$$G_0 = \frac{a'}{1 - \beta'} \equiv \gamma' \text{ (say)}.$$

Hence by (i) and (ix) $G_Y = \lambda + \gamma'$.

But by (vii) $$G_Y(t) = \frac{s(t)}{v(t)} = \lambda + \gamma' \equiv N \text{ (say)}.$$

By (iii), (v), (vi) and (x)

$$\frac{P(t)}{K(t)} = \frac{s(t)}{av(t)} = \frac{N}{a} = \bar{r} + \xi(v(t)).$$

Hence by solving the last equality for $v(0)$, we can obtain all the remaining unknowns of the system.

If inequality (a) does not hold, $\dfrac{P}{Y}$ will be compressed below

its equilibrium level, and hence the rate of accumulation and the rate of growth will be less than that indicated. As long, however, as we abstract from diminishing returns due to limited natural resources, and assume continuous technical progress, so .that $G_0(t)$ rises over time, sooner or later the point must be reached where this inequality becomes satisfied.[1]

If, on the other hand, any one of the inequalities (b), (c) or (d) is not satisfied, $\dfrac{P}{Y}$ will be larger than its equilibrium value,

and full-employment growth equilibrium becomes impossible. As regards (c) we may assume that there is always some degree of excess capacity (i.e., some relationship between output capacity and the full-employment labour supply) which satisfies this condition, and the system will tend to generate the required amount of excess capacity, if it did not obtain initially.[2] It is possible however, that the conditions (b) or (d) represent genuine obstacles to the attainment of balanced-growth equilibrium.[3] In that case the system cannot grow at a steady rate. This does not mean, however, that the economy will lapse into permanent stagnation. As investment opportunities accumulate during periods of stagnation (owing to continued technical progress and population growth), it becomes possible for the system to grow, for a limited period, at a rate appropriately higher than $(\lambda + \gamma')$, thus generating the required value of $\dfrac{P(t)}{K(t)}$.

Finally, if condition (d) is not satisfied, a steady rate of growth is incompatible with the assumed rate of interest $\bar{r}$. Two

---

[1] Allowing for diminishing returns, however, it is possible that (depending on the relative values of λ, α' and β') balanced-growth equilibrium will necessarily settle at the point where the fall in $G_0(t)$ due to λ is precisely offset by the rise in $G_0(t)$ due to γ'; where, in other words, constancy of $G_0(t)$, and $w(t)$ over time, becomes a necessary condition of equilibrium. (This case seems to have application for many of the underdeveloped countries.)

[2] Page 256 above. One may assume that the reaction mechanism here operates via the in- and out-flow of new firms as well as the investment behaviour of the representative firm.

[3] It is evident that these two restrictions are alternatives, of which only the higher one will apply.

cases are possible. If $\dfrac{\lambda+\gamma'}{a} > \rho_F + \bar{r}$, equilibrium requires a higher money rate of interest. If $\dfrac{\lambda+\gamma'}{a} < \rho_C + \bar{r}$, and the money rate of interest is already at its minimum level, it requires a rate of increase in money wages that would permit a rate of increase in the price level which reduced the real rate of interest to the appropriate figure.

Of all the relationships assumed in this model, that represented by (vi) and the inequality (d) are perhaps most open to doubt. Yet it can be shown that the assumption that ρ is a variable of v is the only one which makes the condition expressed in (x)—that the rate of profit is *equal* to the supply price of risk capital—consistent with the rate of profit being also determined by the growth factors, λ and γ' and by a. Equation (x) taken alone is incompatible with the rest of the model if the money rate of interest is assumed to be determined independently. But as indicated earlier, until there is more empirical evidence available to show that ρ_F is *appreciably* higher than ρ_C (or alternatively, that ρ_F itself is a rising function of the fixed-capital-output ratio, $\dfrac{F}{\gamma}$) and in consequence, the rate of profit is higher in industries and/or economies where the capital-output ratio is higher, I hesitate to put forward the relationship expressed in (vi) as more than a tentative suggestion, which I would be prepared to discard in favour of a better alternative, if such could be found.[1]

---

[1] For the reasons given I regard Kalecki's assumption

$$\rho = \theta(G_K), \text{ with } \theta' > 0$$

as a worse alternative, apart from the fact that in the context of the present model it serves as a substitute for equation (15), not for equation (21), and hence is not sufficient for closing the model.

11

CAUSES OF THE SLOW RATE OF ECONOMIC GROWTH IN THE UNITED KINGDOM[1]

I

One of the basic economic facts which has increasingly entered into national consciousness is the relatively slow rate of economic growth of Britain. Thanks to the work of various international organisations, there is now ample material on the comparative growth records of different countries, and in such comparisons Britain appears almost invariably near the bottom of the league-tables. Thus if we take the decade 1953–4 to 1963–4, the rate of growth of our gross domestic product is estimated to have been 2·7 per cent a year, as against 4·9 per cent in France, 5·6 in Italy, 6 per cent in Germany, and no less than 9·6 per cent in Japan. If we take a more recent period, say the five years 1960–5, our rate of economic growth at 3·3 per cent a year looks distinctly better, but our inferiority, in relation to the other advanced countries, appears even more pronounced, since some countries, such as the United States, Canada or Belgium, which previously grew at around 3–3½ per cent a year have all shown much higher growth rates in the more recent period. Indeed every other member of the "Paris Club" of advanced countries has chalked up a growth rate of at least 4½ per cent in the last five years; Japan remained outstanding with a rate of growth of almost 10 per cent a year.

As these facts became more generally known, the minds of our economists and men of affairs, and the public generally, have become increasingly preoccupied with finding the basic cause, or causes, of this phenomenon. There has been no shortage of

[1] Originally delivered as an Inaugural Lecture at the University of Cambridge, November 2nd 1966, and published by Cambridge University Press in 1966.

explanations. Some put the blame on the inefficiency of our business management; some on the nature of our education giving too little emphasis to science and technology, and too much to the humanities; some on the general social milieu which deprecates aggressive competitiveness and looks down on mere money-making as a career; some on over-manning and other restrictive practices of trade unions; some on the alleged national dislike of hard work; some on the insufficiency of investment, or of the right kind of investment; some on the economic policies of successive governments, being either too inflationary, or too deflationary, or both; and no doubt one could cite many other such "explanations".

There may be truth in some, if not all, of these contentions. The difficulty about them is that with one or two possible exceptions, they are not capable of being tested, and there is no way in which their individual role could in any way be quantified. Another basic difficulty with explanations of this kind is that while they may seem *plausible* in relation to some countries, they look implausible in relation to others, whose relatively poor performance equally calls for explanation. (Thus in the decade 1953–63, though *not* in the five years 1960–5, the rate of economic growth of the United States was almost as low as Britain's. Yet no one suggested that the same kind of factors—inefficiency of business management, slowness in introducing innovations, restrictive labour practices, etc.—were likely to have been the causes of *her* slow rate of progress.)

However, the purpose of my lecture today is not to dispute the possible validity of such explanations, nor to argue in favour of one or another, but to suggest an alternative approach which seeks to explain the recorded differences in growth rates in terms of the *stage* of economic development attained by different countries rather than in the realm of personal (or rather individual) abilities or incentives. Put briefly, the contention that I intend to examine is that fast rates of economic growth are associated with the fast rate of growth of the "secondary" sector of the economy—mainly the manufacturing sector—and that this is an attribute of an intermediate stage of economic development: it is the characteristic of the transition from "immaturity" to "maturity"; and that the trouble with the British economy is that it has reached a high stage of "maturity" *earlier* than others, with the result that it has exhausted the potential for fast growth before it had attained particularly high levels of productivity or real income per head. The meaning of the term "maturity" will, I hope, become evident in the course of this lecture; it is mainly intended to denote a state of affairs where real income per head has reached broadly the same level in the different sectors of the economy.

On this diagnosis the basic trouble with the British economy is that it suffers from "premature maturity". This may sound no less pessimistic a conclusion than the alternative view which attributes our failures to some basic deterioration in the national character—such as working too little, spending too much, too little initiative, vitality or incentive—but at least it has the advantage that if the diagnosis were correct, and if it came to be generally accepted, steps could be taken to ameliorate the situation through instruments more powerful than mere exhortation.

I shall begin by examining the empirical evidence in favour of my contention; I will then discuss the theoretical reasons to justify it; and finally its implication in terms of potential growth rates of Britain and other advanced countries.

II

Let us then begin with the evidence. If we take the twelve industrially advanced countries for which figures are available, as shown in Table I (there are a few countries, such as Sweden and Switzerland, which had to be omitted for lack of comparable data), we find that there is a very high correlation between the rate of growth of the gross domestic product and the rate of growth of manufacturing production, and what is more significant, we find that the faster the overall rate of growth, the greater is the *excess* of the rate of growth of manufacturing production over the rate of growth of the economy as a whole.

This is indicated by the regression equation shown at the bottom of the table which, in terms of all the usual tests, shows a

Table 1

RATE OF GROWTH OF G.D.P. AND RATE OF GROWTH OF MANUFACTURING
PRODUCTION (TWELVE INDUSTRIAL COUNTRIES, AVERAGE 1953–4 TO
AVERAGE 1963–4): EXPONENTIAL GROWTH RATES

	Annual rate of growth of G.D.P.[1]	Annual rate of growth of manufacturing production[1]
Japan	9·6	13·6[2]
Italy	5·6	8·2
West Germany	6·0	7·3
Austria	5·4	6·2
France	4·9	5·6
Netherlands	4·5	5·5[3]
Belgium	3·6	5·1
Denmark	4·1	4·9
Norway	3·9	4·6
Canada	3·6	3·4
U.K.	2·7	3·2
U.S.A.	3·1	2·6

[1] Derived from National Accounts Data of G.D.P., and G.D.P. in manufacturing, at constant prices.
[2] Index of manufacturing production.
[3] G.D.P. in industrial production (including mining).

Sources. National Accounts Statistics, O E.C.D.; National Accounts Yearbooks, U.N.

Regression. Growth of G.D.P. (Y) on growth of manufacturing output (X),
$$Y = 1·153 + 0·614X, \quad R^2 = 0·959.$$
$$(0·040)$$
Standard error of residuals as a proportion of mean value of $Y = 0·0825$.

highly significant relationship between the rate of growth of the G.D.P. and the rate of growth of manufacturing production. On the basis of this one can predict fairly accurately the rate of growth of an economy—at least over a run of years—if one knows the rate of growth of its manufacturing production.

Of course, the mere fact that the growth of manufacturing output correlates with the growth of the G.D.P. is not in itself surprising, since the manufacturing sector is a fairly large component of the latter—somewhere between 25–40 per cent for the countries considered. But the regression equation asserts more than this. The meaning of the positive constant in the equation and of the regression coefficient which is significantly less than unity is that rates of growth above 3 per cent a year are found only in cases where the rate of growth in manufacturing output is in excess of the overall rate of growth of the economy. In other words, there is a positive correlation between the overall rate of economic growth and the *excess* of the rate of growth of manufacturing output over the rate of growth of the non-manufacturing sectors. I have not investigated how far this has been true of earlier historical periods, but in a study on historical growth rates since the nineteenth century published some years ago, Miss Deborah Paige found the same kind of relationship.[1]

Assuming, for the moment, that this relationship exists, is there some general hypothesis which is capable of explaining it? We must beware of attributing causal significance to a statistical relationship unless it can be shown to be consistent with some general hypothesis, which can be supported by other evidence. Since the differences in growth rates are largely accounted for by differences in the rates of growth of productivity (and not of changes in the working population), the primary explanation must lie in the technological field—it must be related to the behaviour of productivity growth. Is there some general reason which makes the rate of increase of output-per-man, for the economy as a whole, dependent on the rate of growth of manufacturing production? It has been suggested that because the *level* of productivity in manufacturing activities is higher than in the rest of the economy, a faster expansion of the high-productivity manufacturing sectors pulls up the average; and also that the incidence of technical progress—as measured by the *rate of growth* of productivity—is higher in manufacturing activities than in the other fields, so that a greater concentration on manufacturing increases the overall rate of advance.

However, neither of these suppositions seems capable of explaining the facts. The differences in the level of output per head between different sectors, as Beckerman has recently shown,[2] are quite incapable of explaining more than a small part of the observed differences in productivity growth rates, in terms of inter-sectoral shifts. The second proposition, if it were factually correct, would relate the rate of economic growth to the *size* of the manufacturing sector (in relation to the whole economy)

---

[1] "Economic Growth: The Last Hundred Years", *National Institute Economic Review*, July 1961, p. 41.
[2] *The British Economy in 1975* (Cambridge University Press, 1965), pp. 23–5.

rather than to its rate of expansion: it would make the rate of economic growth the highest in those countries whose industrial sector, as measured by the proportion of total manpower engaged in it, is the largest. On this test, therefore, Britain ought to come out near the top, not at the bottom of the league-table. But quite apart from this, the proposition is factually incorrect: technological progress and productivity growth is by no means confined to manufacturing; in many of the countries examined, productivity growth in agriculture and mining has been higher than in manufacturing, or in industrial activities taken as a whole.

There is, however, a third possible explanation—the existence of economies of scale, or increasing returns, which causes productivity to increase in response to, or as a by-product of, the increase in total output. That manufacturing activities are subject to the "law of increasing returns" was of course a well-known contention of the classical economists. One finds the origin of this doctrine in the first three chapters of the *Wealth of Nations*. Here Adam Smith argued that the *return* per unit of labour—what we now call productivity—depends on the division of labour: on the extent of specialisation and the division of production into so many different processes, as exemplified by his famous example of pin-making. As Smith explained, the division of labour depends on the extent of the market: the greater the market, the greater the extent to which differentiation and specialisation is carried, the higher the productivity. Neo-classical writers, with one or two famous exceptions, like Marshall and Allyn Young, tended to ignore, or to underplay, this phenomenon. As Hahn and Matthews remarked in a recent article "the reason for the neglect is no doubt the difficulty of fitting increasing returns into the prevailing framework of perfect competition and marginal productivity factor pricing".[1]

However, Adam Smith, like both Marshall and Allyn Young after him, emphasised the interplay of static and dynamic factors in causing returns to increase with an increase in the scale of industrial activities. A greater division of labour is more pro-

[1] "The Theory of Economic Growth: A Survey", *Economic Journal* December, 1964, p. 833.

ductive, partly because it generates more skill and know-how; more expertise in turn yields more innovations and design improvements. We cannot isolate the influence of the economies of large-scale production due to indivisibilities of various kinds, and which are in principle reversible, from such changes in technology associated with a process of expansion which are not reversible. Learning is the product of experience—which means, as Arrow has shown,[1] that productivity tends to grow the faster, the faster output expands; it also means that the *level* of productivity is a function of cumulative output (from the beginning) rather than of the rate of production per unit of time.

In addition, as Allyn Young emphasised, increasing returns is a "macro-phenomenon"—just because so much of the economies of scale emerge as a result of increased differentiation, the emergence of new processes and new subsidiary industries, they cannot be "discerned adequately by observing the effects of variations in the size of an individual firm or of a particular industry". At any one time, there are industries in which economies of scale may have ceased to be important. They may nevertheless benefit from a general industrial expansion which, as Young said, should be "seen as an interrelated whole". With the extension of the division of labour "the representative firm, like the industry of which it is a part, loses its identity".[2]

III

This, in my view, is the basic reason for the empirical relationship between the growth of productivity and the growth of production which has recently come to be known as the "Verdoorn Law", in recognition of P. J. Verdoorn's early investigations, published in 1949.[3] It is a dynamic rather than a static relationship—between the rates of change of productivity and of output, rather than between the *level* of productivity and the *scale* of output—primarily because technological progress enters into it, and is not just a reflection of the economies of large-scale pro-

---

[1] "The Economic Implications of Learning by Doing", *Review of Economic Studies*, June 1962, pp. 155–73.

[2] "Increasing Returns and Economic Progress", *Economic Journal*, December 1928, pp. 538–9.

[3] "Fattori che regolano lo sviluppo della produttivitá del lavoro", *L'Industria*, 1949.

duction. Since Verdoorn's work it has been investigated by many others, among them Salter,[1] and more recently by Beckerman,[2] though none of these authors (to my knowledge) has given sufficient emphasis to the fact that it is a phenomenon peculiarly associated with the so-called "secondary" activities—with industrial production, including public utilities, construction, as well as manufacturing—rather than with the primary or tertiary sectors of the economy.

Table 2

RATES OF GROWTH OF PRODUCTION, EMPLOYMENT AND PRODUCTIVITY IN MANUFACTURING INDUSTRY (TWELVE COUNTRIES, AVERAGE 1953–4 TO AVERAGE 1963–4): ANNUAL EXPONENTIAL GROWTH RATES

	Production[1]	Employment[2]	Productivity[3]
Japan	13·6	5·8	7·8
Italy[4]	8·1	3·9[5]	4·2
West Germany	7·4	2·8	4·5
Austria[7]	6·4	2·2	4·2
France[6]	5·7	1·8	3·8
Denmark[6]	5·7	2·5[5]	3·2
Netherlands[8]	5·5	1·4	4·1
Belgium	5·1	1·2[5]	3·9
Norway	4·6	0·2	4·4
Canada	3·4	2·1	1·3
U.K.	3·2	0·4	2·8
U.S.A.[7]	2·6	0·0	2·6

[1] Gross domestic product in manufacturing, at constant prices.
[2] Wage and salary earners adjusted for changes in weekly manhours.
[3] Output per manhour, derived from first two columns.
[4] 1954–5 to 1963–4.
[5] Incorporates estimated change in weekly manhours.
[6] 1955–6 to 1963–4.
[7] 1953–4 to 1962–3.
[8] Industrial production and employment (including mining).

Sources. National Account and Manpower Statistics, O.E.C.D. Statistical Yearbook, U.N.

Regressions.
(1) Rate of growth of productivity (*P*) on the rate of growth of manufacturing production (*X*),

$$P = 1.035 + 0.484X, \quad R^2 = 0.826.$$
$$(0.070)$$

(2) Rate of growth of employment (*E*) on rate of growth of manufacturing production (*X*),

$$E = -1.028 + 0.516X, \quad R^2 = 0.844.$$
$$(0.070)$$

Its application to the case of the manufacturing industries of the twelve countries in the period 1953–4 to 1963–4 is given in Table 2, which shows for each country the growth rates of pro-

[1] *Productivity and Technical Change* (Cambridge University Press, 1960).
[2] *Ibid.* pp. 221–8.

duction, productivity and employment. The results are summarised in two regression equations, productivity on output, and employment on output—which are two different ways of looking at the same relationship[1]—and which suggest that the growth of output must have played a major role in the determination of productivity growth rates. Again, the relationships by the usual tests are shown to be highly significant and they suggest that apart from an "autonomous" rate of productivity growth of around 1 per cent a year, the latter is a function of the growth in total output: each percentage addition to the growth of output requires a 0·5 per cent increase in the growth of employment in terms of manhours, and is associated with a 0·5 per cent increase in the growth of productivity. These coefficients are very close to those found by Verdoorn and other investigators.

There are some economists who, whilst admitting the statistical relationship between productivity growth and production growth, argue that it says nothing about cause and effect: the Verdoorn Law, according to this view, may simply reflect the fact that faster growth rates in productivity induce, via their effects on relative costs and prices, a faster rate of growth of demand, and not the other way round.

This alternative hypothesis is not, however, fully specified— if it were, its logical shortcomings would at once be apparent. If the rate of growth of productivity in each industry and in each country was a fully autonomous factor, we need some hypothesis to explain it. The usual hypothesis is that the growth of productivity is mainly to be explained by the progress of knowledge in science and technology. But in that case how is one to explain the large differences in the *same* industry over the *same* period in different countries? How can the progress of knowledge account for the fact, for example, that in the period 1954–60, productivity in the German motor-car industry increased at 7 per cent a year and in Britain only 2·7 per cent a year? Since large segments of the car industry in both countries

---

[1] One is a mirror-image of the other. The regression coefficients of the two equations add up to unity and the two constants (but for a small discrepancy caused by rounding) add up to zero.

were controlled by the same American firms, they must have had the same access to the improvements in knowledge and know-how. This alternative hypothesis is tantamount to a denial of the existence of increasing returns which are known to be an important feature of manufacturing industry, quite independently of the Verdoorn Law and one which is frequently emphasised in other contexts—as for example, in analysing the effects of economic integration.

Moreover, to establish this alternative hypothesis, it is not enough to postulate that productivity growth rates are autonomous. It is also necessary to assume that differences in productivity growth rates between different industries and sectors are fully reflected in the movement of relative prices (and not in relative movements of wages and other earnings) and further, that the price-elasticity of demand for the products of any one industry, or for the products of manufacturing industry as a whole, is always greater than unity: none of this, as far as I know, has been submitted to econometric verification.

Once the relationship between productivity growth and production growth is recognised the large differences in the recorded productivity growth rates do not appear so remarkable, and we can take a rather different view of the "efficiency-ranking" of various countries. We can award marks to each country, not on the usual basis of simple productivity growth, but on a more sophisticated basis of the deviation of its productivity growth from the Verdoorn regression line: in other words, by relating its actual performance to what it could be expected to be, on the basis of the growth rate of total manufacturing production. On this test, we find that there was one outstandingly good performer— Norway—whose recorded productivity growth was one-third higher than could be expected; and there was one outstandingly bad performer—Canada—with a rate of productivity growth which was only one-half as high as the computed figure. There were two moderately poor performers—Italy and Denmark— with a deficiency of around 15 per cent, and three moderately good performers—Netherlands, Belgium and the United States— whose productivity record was 12–15 per cent above the average. As to the rest, four of them were strictly average—and this group comprises Japan, Germany, France and Austria—with deviations of less than 2 per cent from the regression line; and finally there was one *marginally* good performer, with a record that was 7 per cent better than the computed figure—the United Kingdom. If we award, as we must on this test, β to the strictly average performers and $\beta +$ to the moderately good performers, Britain, I think, must be rated $\beta? +$.

All this is subject of course to the statistical uncertainties inherent in all international comparisons, and many of these deviations are too small to be of much significance in judging a country's performance. But the interesting point about them is that with one notable exception—again Canada—they appear to be closely related to investment behaviour. The countries which invested a great deal in relation to their growth rate were the good performers, whilst the countries whose investment was small in relation to their growth rate were poor performers. If we measure investment behaviour by the incremental capital/output ratio (ICOR for short) we find that Norway, the best performer on the Verdoorn test, had the highest ICOR (over 5), all the good performers had over-average ICORs (over 3), all the average performers had average ICORs (around $2\frac{1}{2}$), and the poor performers had low ICORs (below 2).[1] (Canada was the one exception to this rule—a poor performer with a very high ICOR—but I am glad to be able to report that since the dates of this examination Canada has improved her showing quite considerably.) In other words, if we look for the effects of investment behaviour on growth, not in terms of the growth rate itself, but in terms of a country's performance according to the Verdoorn test, the figures make much more sense. But they also indicate that increasing returns is by far the more important cause of differences in productivity growth rates; differences in investment behaviour explain residual differences which are relatively less important.

I am not suggesting that the Verdoorn relationship applies *only* to manufacturing activities or that it applies to every manufacturing industry considered separately. But its application

---

[1] ICOR is defined here as the ratio between gross fixed investment in industry and the level of industrial production, divided by the growth rate of industrial production.

outside the industrial field is clearly far more limited. It certainly does not apply, on the evidence of the statistics, to agriculture and mining, where the growth of productivity has been much greater than the growth in production and where, in so far as any definite relation is shown, productivity growth and employment growth tend to be negatively related, not positively. This supports the classical contention that these are "diminishing returns" industries: the fact that this is overlaid by technological progress or the adoption of more capital-intensive methods may statistically conceal this, but it does not eliminate its significance. In some of the countries the relatively high rate of growth of productivity in agriculture is merely the passive consequence of the absorption of surplus labour in secondary and tertiary occupations, and not necessarily a reflection of true technological progress or of higher capital investment per unit of output.

There remains the tertiary sector, services, comprising such divergent items as transport, distribution, banking and insurance, catering and hotels, laundries and hairdressers, and professional services of the most varied kind, publicly and privately provided—which together account for 40–50 per cent or more of the total output and employment of the advanced countries. Over much of this field learning by experience must clearly play a role but economies of scale are not nearly so prominent and are exhausted more quickly. In the case of activities like research or education, the Adam-Smithian principle of the advantages of specialisation and of the division of labour must operate in the same sort of way as in industrial activities. But precisely in these fields it cannot be directly reflected in the estimates of productivity, since "output" cannot be measured independently of "input". In some fields in which output can be measured independently—as, for example, in transport and communications, statistical evidence shows no correlation between productivity growth and production growth. In yet others such as distribution, productivity—meaning sales per employee—tends to grow the faster the faster the rise in aggregate turnover; but in this case, it is merely a reflection of the changing incidence of excess capacity generated by imperfect competition, and not of true economies of scale. In other words, productivity may rise in automatic response to the rise in consumption caused by the growth of production in the primary or secondary sectors—just as the productivity of the milkman doubles, without any technological change, when he leaves two bottles of milk outside each door instead of one bottle.

It is the rate of growth of manufacturing production (together with the ancillary activities of public utilities and construction) which is likely to exert a dominating influence on the overall rate of economic growth: partly on account of its influence on the rate of growth of productivity in the industrial sector itself, and partly also because it will tend, indirectly, to raise the rate of productivity growth in other sectors. This will happen, or may happen, both in agriculture and in the distributive trades—in the first because it induces a faster rate of absorption of surplus labour; in the second because it secures a faster increase in the through-put of goods into consumption. And of course it is true more generally that industrialisation accelerates the rate of technological change throughout the economy.

IV

It remains to deal with the question of why it is that some countries manage to increase their rate of manufacturing production so much faster than others. The explanation, in my view, lies partly in demand factors and partly in supply factors, and both of these combine to make fast rates of growth the characteristic of an intermediate stage in economic development.

Economic growth is the result of a complex process of interaction between increases of demand induced by increases in supply and of increases in supply generated in response to increases in demand. Since in the market as a whole commodities are exchanged against commodities, the increase in demand for any commodity, or group of commodities, reflects the increase in supply of other commodities, and vice versa. The nature of this chain-reaction will be conditioned by both demand elasticities and supply constraints; by individual preferences or attitudes and by technological factors. The chain-reaction is likely to be the more rapid the more the demand increases are focused on commodities which have a *large* supply response, and the larger the demand response induced by increases in production—the latter is not just a matter of the marginal propensities in consumption but also of induced investment. Viewing this process from a particular angle—what determines the rate of growth of manufacturing output—it will be convenient to consider the problem in two stages: first, from the point of view of the sources of demand, and secondly from the point of view of the factors which govern potential supply.

Looking at the matter from the point of view of demand, this is fed mainly from three sources—from consumption, domestic investment and from net exports—by which I mean the net excess of exports over imports.

The behaviour of consumer demand depends on the changing structure of consumption associated with a rise in real incomes per head. It is well known that a *high* income elasticity for manufactured goods—as reflected in a growing proportion of consumer expenditure spent on manufactured products—is a characteristic of an intermediate zone in the levels of real income per head. At low levels of income a high proportion of both average and marginal incomes is spent on food. At very high levels of real income, the income elasticity of demand for manufacturers falls off, both absolutely and relatively to that of services: but for the continued appearance of new commodities, like washing machines or television sets, it would fall off more rapidly. In the middle zone in which this proportion is both large and growing, there is a double interaction making for faster economic growth: the expansion of the industrial sector enhances the rate of growth in real incomes; the rise in real incomes steps up the rate of growth of demand for industrial products.

This, however, is only part of the explanation. A more important source of growth in demand originates in capital investment. It is the peculiarity of a highly developed industrial sector that it largely provides the goods on which capital expenditure is spent, and thereby generates a demand for its own products in the very process of supplying them. Once a country attains the stage of industrialisation at which it largely provides for its own needs in plant and machinery and not just in consumer goods the rate of growth of demand for its products will tend to be stepped up very considerably, since the expansion of capacity in the investment sector by itself raises the rate of growth of demand for the products of its own sector, and thereby provides the incentives, and the means, for further expansion. Provided that entrepreneurial expectations are buoyant, and the process is not hampered by labour shortages, or shortages of basic materials, the very establishment of an investment goods sector makes for a built-in element of acceleration in the rate of growth of manufacturing output that could—theoretically—go on until technological constraints—the input/output relationships *within* the investment goods sector—impose a limit on further acceleration.

The third source of the rate of growth of demand arises from the changing structure of foreign trade. The early stages of industrialisation invariably involve reduced imports of manufactured consumer goods and increased imports of machinery and equipment. During this phase, therefore, the rate of growth of demand for domestic manufactures—which can be supposed to consist mainly of the so-called "light industries", generally textiles—rises faster than total consumption, on account of the substitution of home production for imports. But as the experience of many countries has shown, this phase of relatively rapid development tends to peter out as the process of import substitution of consumer goods is gradually completed. To maintain the rhythm of development it is necessary for the industrialising country to enter a second stage in which it becomes a growing net exporter of manufactured consumer goods. This is followed (or accompanied) by a third stage, marked by "import substitution" in capital goods, and for the reasons mentioned, it is likely to be associated with a fast growth rate, as the "heavy industries" develop out of relation to the growth of the rest of the economy. There is a fourth and final stage, at which a country becomes a growing net exporter of capital goods; it is at this last stage that "explosive growth" is likely to be encountered— when a fast rate of growth of external demand for the products of the "heavy industries" is combined with the self-generated growth of demand caused by their own expansion. It has been the passage into this fourth stage which I think mainly explains the phenomenal growth rates of post-war Japan. Fast though her growth of consumption has been, her growth due to the rise in the production of investment goods—both for home use and exports—was very much greater. But this again is a transitional stage: once the investment sector is fully developed, and once a country has acquired a reasonably large share of world trade in investment goods, the growth of demand is bound to slow down, as the broad historical experience of the older industrial countries has shown.

All this is looking at the matter from the demand side alone. The actual course of development may at any stage be slowed down, or interrupted by supply constraints; and as I shall argue presently, it is inevitable that sooner or later the rhythm of development should be slowed down on account of them.

Such supply constraints can take one of two forms: commodities or labour. As the industrial sector expands, it absorbs growing amounts of commodities (and services) produced outside the manufacturing sector: such as food and industrial materials produced by the primary sector (agriculture and mining); manufactured goods which it does not provide itself, or not in sufficient quantities and on which it is dependent on imports—this is probably relatively more important in the earlier stages of industrialisation, but as post-war experience has shown, there is a very large scope, even among the industrially highly developed countries, for trade in manufactured goods for industrial use, both finished goods and components. Finally, industrial growth generates demand for services of numerous kinds—like banking and insurance, lawyers, accountants and so on—and is thus responsible, in part at any rate, for the fast expansion of the "tertiary" sector. (Also, the growing use of durable consumer goods sets up a growing demand for repair and maintenance services.)

For an *individual* country—though not for the group of industrialised countries together—a commodity constraint generally takes the form of a balance of payments constraint: it arises because a particular rate of growth generates a rate of growth of imports which exceeds the rate of growth of exports. This is certainly true of countries in the early stages of industrialisation when the growth of industry, despite import-substitution, causes a substantial rise in *total* import requirements at a stage when the industrial development adds little, if anything, to the country's export potential. But it is also suggested that it may slow down the rate of growth of industrially advanced economies; and it is a widely held view that it has been a major constraint on the post-war economic growth of Britain.

It is certainly true that brief periods of relatively high growth during the last twenty years were invariably attended by a rapid growth of imports, resulting in balance of payments deficits; and it was the occurrence of these deficits, as much as the labour shortages and the resulting inflation, which forced the intro-duction of deflationary measures which brought these periods to an end. It is equally true that if the trend rates of growth in our exports had been higher, we could have sustained higher rates of growth of imports, and that if the rhythm of our develop-ment had been more even, imports would not have risen so fast as they did during the recovery phases. But this does not necessarily prove that the balance of payments was the *effective* constraint on our rate of economic growth. This would only follow if it could also be shown that with a faster rate of growth of exports, we could have achieved a higher rate of growth of manufacturing production, or else that we could have increased exports at a faster rate while keeping domestic investment and consumption rising at a lower rate. In the latter context it must be remembered that the volume of our exports has been pretty large in relation to the total volume of our manufacturing production; and while the share of our exports in world trade declined dramatically, the share of exports in our own manufacturing output remained remarkably steady. It is possible to interpret this by saying that it was the trend rate of growth of exports which governed the trend rate of growth of production, since any higher rate of growth of production would not have been compatible with keeping the balance of payments even, over a run of years. It is also possible to interpret this in the opposite way: that over a run of years it was the rate of growth of production of exportable goods which determined the rate of growth of our exports, and not the other way round.

The important question is whether, *apart* from balance of payments constraints, it would have been possible to increase our manufacturing output at a faster rate. Was the growth in production mainly governed by the growth in demand for manufactured products, or was it governed by supply-constraints, which would have frustrated a higher rate of growth of output, irrespective of the growth in demand?

v

And here we come back to the labour situation and to Verdoorn's Law. This as we have seen, suggests that a higher rate of growth of manufacturing output breeds higher rates of productivity growth, but not enough to obviate the need for a faster rate of growth of employment. In post-war Britain periods of faster growth in manufacturing industry invariably led to severe labour shortages which slowed down the growth of output and which continued for some time after production reached its cyclical peak—in fact, on almost every occasion, employment continued to rise after output had begun to fall. All this suggests that a higher rate of growth could not have been maintained unless more manpower had been made available to the manufacturing industry.

Indeed all historical evidence suggests that a fast rate of industrial growth has invariably been associated with a fast rate of growth of employment in both the secondary and the tertiary sectors of the economy. The main source of this labour has not been the growth of the working population, nor even immigration, but the reservoir of surplus labour, or "disguised unemployment" on the land. In the course of industrialisation there has been a continuous transfer of labour from the countryside to the urban areas in the course of which the percentage of the labour force in agriculture diminishes in a dramatic fashion. But the *longer* this process proceeds, the *smaller* the labour force remaining, the *less* it yields in terms of manpower availabilities in the secondary and tertiary sectors. Moreover, the process of transfer is bound to come to a halt once the gap between agricultural and industrial productivity is eliminated, and this becomes fully reflected in relative earnings. The United Kingdom, almost alone among the advanced countries, has reached the position where net output per head in agriculture is as high as in industry; though there is still a wide gap in relative wages which, I think, is mainly due to the fact that the fall in the demand for agricultural labour, owing to mechanisation, has outrun, over the last ten years, the rate of diminution in the agricultural labour force.

Table 3 shows, for the twelve countries, the rate of growth in

Table 3

RATES OF GROWTH OF LABOUR FORCE, AND THE RATE OF CHANGE OF
EMPLOYMENT IN AGRICULTURE, MINING, INDUSTRY AND SERVICES
(TWELVE COUNTRIES 1954–64): EXPONENTIAL GROWTH RATES

	Rate of growth of labour force	Rate of growth of employment[1] in agriculture and mining	Rate of growth of employment[2] in industry and services		
			Total	Industry[3]	Services[4]
Japan	1·5	−2.6	5·4	5·8	5·1
Italy	−0·1	−4·5	3·9	4·4	3·2
West Germany[5]	1·4	−4·1	2·8	2·7	2·9
Austria	0·2[6]	−3·6[6]	2·3	2·0	2·6
France	0·2	−3·5	2·2	1·9	2·4
Denmark[7]	0·8	−2·8	2·2	2·5	1·9
Netherlands	1·3	−2·0	2·3	1·9	2·7
Belgium	0·3	−4·4	1·9	1·5	2·3
Norway	0·3	−2·5	1·3	0·5	2·0
Canada	2·3	−2·8	3·5	2·3	4·3
U.K.	0·6	−2·3	1·1	0·6	1·6
U.S.A.	1·3	−2·4	1·8	0·8	2·4

[1] Including self-employed and unpaid family workers.
[2] Wage and salary earners.
[3] Manufacturing, construction and public utilities.
[4] Transport, distributive trades, financial and other services, public administration, etc.
[5] 1957–64.
[6] 1951–63.
[7] 1955–64.

Source. O.E.C.D. Manpower Statistics.

the total labour force, and the rate of change in employment in agriculture and mining, industry and the services; Table 4 shows the percentage composition in total employment between the three sectors in 1962–3.

One of the remarkable features of Table 3 is the uniform fall in employment in agriculture and mining in all countries; it varied between 2 per cent and 4½ per cent a year. In countries in which the agricultural labour force was still large, as a percentage of total, this meant a substantial annual addition to the labour force in industry and services—substantial both absolutely and in relation to the growth of the working population, which was relatively modest, in most countries—whilst in the countries where the size of the labour force in primary occupations was small—as in the United Kingdom and the United States—the rate of increase in employment in secondary and tertiary occupations was much smaller. As is shown in Table 3, the United Kingdom had the smallest rate of increase in employment in industry and services taken together, despite the fact that the rate of growth of her total labour force over this period was higher than that of five of the other eleven countries. The explanation is found in Table 4, which shows that Britain had the smallest proportion of the labour force in agriculture and mining.

Table 3 also shows that whilst the absorption of labour in the tertiary sector was substantial in all countries—at least of the

Table 4

PERCENTAGE COMPOSITION OF TOTAL EMPLOYMENT BETWEEN PRIMARY, SECONDARY AND TERTIARY OCCUPATIONS (TWELVE COUNTRIES, 1962–3 AVERAGE)

	Primary (Agriculture and mining)	Secondary (Manufacturing, construction and public utilities)	Tertiary (Services)[1]	Total
Japan	30·0	30·3	39·7	100
Italy	27·8	39·4	32·8	100
Austria[2]	23·8	40·6	35·6	100
France	21·1	37·0	41·9	100
Norway	20·0	35·5	44·5	100
Denmark	19·1	39·5	41·4	100
West Germany	14·1	47·9	38·0	100
Canada	12·9	32·7	54·4	100
Netherlands	12·0	42·3	45·7	100
Belgium	10·6	44·0	45·4	100
U.S.A.	8·9	30·7	60·4	100
U.K.	6·7	44·0	49·3	100

[1] Includes transport, distribution, financial and other services, public administration, etc.

[2] 1961.

Source. O.E.C.D. Manpower Statistics.

same order of magnitude as the increase in industrial employment—it tended to be relatively greater (in relation to the growth
of industrial employment) in the slow-growing countries than
in the fast-growing ones. This may be due to the fact that the
growth of labour requirements in services is less sensitive to
changes in the rate of economic growth than the growth of labour
requirements in industry. One could certainly think of several
reasons why this should be so—for example, the rise in the standard of educational and health services which tends to proceed
by its own momentum. It is also possible that the relatively high
rate of growth of employment in services is to some extent a
consequence of the instability in the demand for labour in manufacturing: in the case of Britain, it may have been a by-product of
the stop-and-go cycle. Since employment opportunities in services are less sensitive to short-period variations in demand than
manufacturing employment, it is possible that a kind of ratchet
effect has been in operation: there may have been a drift of labour
into services as a result of a fall in employment in manufacturing
in the "stop" phase, which was not reversed in the subsequent
"go" phase.

However that may be, it is clear that if our basic hypothesis is
correct, *all* countries will experience a slow-down in their growth
rates as their agricultural labour reserves become exhausted. It is
the existence of an elastic supply curve of labour to the secondary
and tertiary sectors which is the main pre-condition of a fast
rate of development. As Table 4 shows, some of the advanced
countries—such as Japan, Italy or France—still possess a large
agricultural labour force (of the order of 15–30 per cent) so that
they still have a considerable period of potentially fast growth
ahead of them. But the United States, Belgium and also Germany
are approaching the structural pattern of the United Kingdom.
In the case of Germany, the rate of growth of production and
employment in industry has already slowed down considerably
in the last few years. In the United States—which operated with
a high unemployment rate throughout the 'fifties—growth could
be accelerated quite considerably by the orthodox techniques of
Keynesian economics, but now that unemployment has fallen
to lower levels, the rate of growth is likely to slow down again,

though the United States is still far off from a situation of acute labour shortage.

Britain, having started the process of industrialisation earlier than any other country, has reached "maturity" much earlier—in the sense that it has attained a distribution of the labour force between the primary, secondary and tertiary sectors at which industry can no longer attract the labour it needs by drawing on the labour reserves of other sectors. There are disadvantages of an early start, as well as advantages—as is shown by the fact that some of the latecomers of industrialisation have attained higher levels of industrial efficiency even before they became fully industrialised.

But once it is recognised that manpower shortage is the main handicap from which we are suffering, and once our thinking becomes adjusted to this, we shall, I hope, tend to concentrate our efforts on a more rational use of manpower in *all* fields, and to limit the absorption of labour into those sectors in which—if I may use a Pigovian phrase—the marginal social product is likely to be appreciably below the marginal private product.

It is possible, looking further ahead, that the new technological revolution—electronics and automation—will so radically reduce the labour requirements in industry as to make it possible to combine fast growth with *falling* industrial employment. But there are no signs of this yet. If we take the technologically most advanced country, the United States, we find that her fast growth of manufacturing production over the last few years was associated with large increases in the volume of manufacturing employment—fully in line with what the Verdoorn equation would lead to us expect.[1]

Finally there is the question how far a mature economy could continue to reap the benefits of economies of scale, not through a fast growth in manufacturing industry as a whole, but through greater international specialisation. If the main hypothesis advanced in this lecture is correct, and economies of scale in industry are the main engine of fast growth, at least some of its

[1] In 1962–5 manufacturing output of the United States (as measured by the index of manufacturing production) increased by 6·7 per cent a year; the rate of growth of the volume of man hours of employment was 2·7 per cent. The regression equation at the bottom of Table 2 yields a computed figure of 2·4 per cent.

benefits could continue to be secured by concentrating our resources in fewer fields and abandoning others—in other words,
by increasing the degree of interdependence of British industry
with the industries of other countries.

APPENDIX A

THE ROLE OF MANUFACTURING IN ECONOMIC GROWTH

The significance of the relationship between the growth of manufacturing output and the growth of the G.D.P. shown in Table 1
has been tested (i) by reference to the relation of the growth of
non-manufacturing output (i.e. G.D.P. *minus* G.D.P. in manufacturing) to the growth in manufacturing production; (ii) by
relating the growth rate of G.D.P. to the *excess* of the growth
rate of manufacturing production over the growth rate of the non-
manufacturing sectors. The results are summarised in the following regression equations:[1]

(1) Rate of growth of non-manufacturing output (Y) on rate
of growth of manufacturing production (X)

$$Y = 1·142 + 0·550X, \quad R^2 = 0·824.$$
$$(0·080)$$

(2) Rate of growth of G.D.P. (Y) on the excess of the rate of
growth of manufacturing over the rate of growth of non-
manufacturing production (X)

$$Y = 3·351 + 0·954X, \quad R^2 = 0·562.$$
$$(0·267)$$

Both of these are statistically significant at the 99 per cent level
and thus confirm the generalisation derived from Table 1. A
comparison of regression (1) above with the regression in Table 1
shows that the exclusion of manufacturing output from G.D.P.
makes no appreciable difference to the structural relationship:
both the constants and the coefficients in the two equations are
very similar.

[1] The four regression equations in this section relate to the same group of countries,
and the same periods, as indicated in Table 1.

The significance of these findings has been further tested by examining the relationship between the growth rate of G.D.P. and the growth rate of agricultural production, mining, and the output of services.[1] No correlation was found between the rate of growth of G.D.P. and the rate of growth of either agricultural production or mining. As between G.D.P. and G.D.P. originating in "services" there is a highly significant relationship but of a different character, as shown by the following equation:

(3) Rate of growth of G.D.P. (Y) on rate of growth of G.D.P. in services (X)

$$Y = -0{\cdot}188 + 1{\cdot}060X, \quad R^2 = 0{\cdot}930.$$
$$(0{\cdot}092)$$

The fact that the coefficient is so near to unity, and the constant is negligible suggests that the causal relationship here is the other way round—i.e. that it is the rate of G.D.P. which determines the rate of growth of the "output" of services. It also confirms recent American studies[2] which suggest that, contrary to general belief, the income-elasticity of demand for services is not significantly greater than unity; the fact that most countries (as indicated in Table 3) had a higher rate of employment growth in "services" than in "industry" is not due to a high income-elasticity of demand, but to a lower rate of productivity growth in services. This latter finding is further confirmed by relating the rate of growth of output in "services" to the rate of growth of industrial production (manufacturing, construction and public utilities):

(4) Rate of growth of output in services (Y) on the rate of growth of industrial production (X)

$$Y = 1{\cdot}283 + 0{\cdot}597X, \quad R^2 = 0{\cdot}846.$$
$$(0{\cdot}0805)$$

This shows that the "real" output of services—as measured

[1] The term "services" comprises transport and communications; wholesale and retail trade; banking, insurance and real estate; ownership of dwellings; public administration and defence; health and educational services and miscellaneous services.
[2] Cf. Victor R. Fuchs, *The Growing Importance of the Service Industries*, New York, National Bureau of Economic Research, Occasional Paper No. 96 (1965).

in the national accounts of each country at constant prices—grows less than in proportion to industrial output, even though employment grows (in most cases) more than in proportion.[1]

APPENDIX B

THE VERDOORN LAW

The "Verdoorn Law" asserts that with a higher rate of growth of output, both productivity and employment increase at a faster rate, the regression coefficients with respect to each being of the same order of magnitude. This relationship was also investigated with regard to other sectors of the economy for which comparable data could be found in the O.E.C.D. statistics—i.e. public utilities (gas, electricity and water) and construction; agriculture and mining; transport and communications and "commerce" (the latter term includes the distributive trades, banking, insurance and real estate).[2] Owing to the lack of data, some countries had to be omitted in some of the estimates, and a somewhat shorter period taken; also, it was not possible to adjust the employment figures for changes in man hours outside the manufacturing sector. The results for each sector (including the manufacturing sector, already shown in Table 2) are summarised in the following set of regression equations:

Annual rates of growth of productivity (P) and of employment (E) on the rates of growth of output (X)[3]

---

[1] The only exceptions in the period considered (i.e. 1953–4 to 1963–4—though this would not be true of the more recent period, 1960–5) were the U.S.A. and Canada, where the output of services grew at a somewhat higher rate than industrial output.

[2] It was not possible to separate, on the employment statistics, the distributive trades from banking, insurance, etc. in more than a few cases; but the distributive trades account for much the greater part (around four-fifths or more) of the total output of this sector, and a similar proportion of employment.

[3] Since exponential growth rates have been used throughout, $P + E = X$, and hence the sum of the constants of the two equations should be zero, and the sum of the regression coefficients unity, irrespective of the nature of the correlations involved. However, since estimates of employment growth and of productivity growth have been separately rounded, the sum of these can vary from the total by one decimal point, which explains small deviations from the correct result in some of the pairs of regression equations.

Industry

(1) *Manufacturing*

$$P = 1 \cdot 035 + 0 \cdot 484X, \quad R^2 = 0 \cdot 826,$$
$$(0 \cdot 070)$$

$$E = -1 \cdot 028 + 0 \cdot 516X, \quad R^2 = 0 \cdot 844.$$
$$(0 \cdot 070)$$

(2) *Public utilities* (11 countries, 1953–63)[1]

$$P = 2 \cdot 707 + 0 \cdot 419X, \quad R^2 = 0 \cdot 451,$$
$$(0 \cdot 154)$$

$$E = -2 \cdot 690 + 0 \cdot 577X, \quad R^2 = 0 \cdot 609.$$
$$(0 \cdot 154)$$

(3) *Construction* (11 countries, 1953–63)[1]

$$P = -0 \cdot 543 + 0 \cdot 572X, \quad R^2 = 0 \cdot 810,$$
$$(0 \cdot 092)$$

$$E = 0 \cdot 552 + 0 \cdot 428X, \quad R^2 = 0 \cdot 702.$$
$$(0 \cdot 092)$$

Primary sector

(4) *Agriculture* (12 countries, 1953–63)[1]

$$P = 2 \cdot 700 + 1 \cdot 041X, \quad R^2 = 0 \cdot 812,$$
$$(0 \cdot 155)$$

$$E = -2 \cdot 684 - 0 \cdot 056X, \quad R^2 = 0 \cdot 013.$$
$$(0 \cdot 155)$$

(5) *Mining* (10 countries, 1955–64)[1]

$$P = 4 \cdot 0714 + 0 \cdot 671X, \quad R^2 = 0 \cdot 705,$$
$$(0 \cdot 153)$$

[1] For *public utilities* and *construction,* the equations relate to all countries listed in Table 2, except the Netherlands; the data relate to 1953–63, except for Austria (1951–61), Italy and France (1954–63), Denmark and Canada (1955–63). The same holds for *agriculture,* except that here the Netherlands (1953–63) is also included. The estimates on *mining* exclude Austria and Denmark; they relate to 1955–64, except for Netherlands where they relate to 1955–61.

$$E = -4\cdot0714 + 0\cdot329X, \quad R^2 = 0\cdot365.$$
$$(0\cdot153)$$

Tertiary sector

(6) *Transport and communications* (9 countries, 1955–64)[1]

$$P = 2\cdot314 + 0\cdot224X, \quad R^2 = 0\cdot102,$$
$$(0\cdot252)$$

$$E = -2\cdot314 + 0\cdot776X, \quad R^2 = 0\cdot576.$$
$$(0\cdot252)$$

(7) *Commerce* (9 countries, 1955–64)[2]

$$P = -1\cdot751 + 0\cdot953X, \quad R^2 = 0\cdot932,$$
$$(0\cdot098)$$

$$E = 1\cdot744 + 0\cdot056X, \quad R^2 = 0\cdot044.$$
$$(0\cdot098)$$

The regressions reveal an interesting pattern. In the case of construction and public utilities, the equations relating to both productivity and employment are similar to those in manufacturing, except that in the case of public utilities the constant term of the equations is much larger, and hence the significance of the relationship is less, than in the case of either manufacturing or construction.[3] One can thus conclude that the effects of economies of scale on the growth of productivity are significant not only for manufacturing industry, but for the industrial sector generally.

Agriculture and mining reveal a different picture. In each case, productivity growth shows a large trend factor which is

---

[1] In the case of *transport and communications*, the estimate excludes Austria, Denmark and Japan; the data relate to 1955–64, except for the U.S.A. (1955–63), France (1956–64) and West Germany (1957–64).

[2] *Commerce* includes G.D.P. originating in wholesale and retail trade, banking, insurance, real estate, at constant prices, and employment relating to the same category, except for Japan where the data on output and employment relate to wholesale and retail trade only. The estimate excludes Austria, Denmark and the Netherlands; it relates to 1955–64, except for Canada (1955–61), U.S.A. (1955–63), West Germany (1957–64) and France (1958–64).

[3] However, in the case of the construction sector there is a *negative* constant term of 0·5 per cent a year in the productivity equation, in contrast to manufacturing which shows a positive constant term of 1 per cent a year. The reasons for this are likely to be similar to those given below in the discussion of the equations for commerce.

various factors—summed up under the term "resource endowment"—which are themselves unexplained. Some areas are favoured by climate or geology; by the ability, vitality, ingenuity of their inhabitants, and by their thriftiness, and these innate advantages may be enhanced by good political and social institutions. Beyond suggesting that the right kind of human material is fostered by a temperate climate—in zones which are neither too hot nor too cold—and all of this owes a great deal to historical accidents and to luck, the theories which explain riches or poverty in terms of "resource endowment" do not really have anything much to offer by way of explanation.

Nevertheless one must agree that they go as far as it is possible to go in explaining that part of economic growth—and until fairly recently this was much the most important part—which consisted of "land based" economic activities, such as agriculture or mineral exploitation. These are clearly conditioned by climatic and geologic factors—the suitability of soil, rainfall, the availability of minerals, and so on. These provide the natural explanation why some areas are more densely settled than others; and why the comparative advantage in procuring different products (and which settles the nature of their external trading relations) should differ as between one area and another. No sophisticated explanation is needed why it is better for some areas to grow wheat and for others bananas; or why some areas which are lucky in possessing things with a fast-growing demand (such as oil or uranium) are fortunate, from the point of view of their growth-potential, in relation to others which possess minerals with a slow-growing or declining demand—coal, for example. We would all agree that some part of the interregional specialisation and the division of labour can be adequately accounted for by such factors.

It is when we come to comparative advantages in relation to processing activities (as distinct from land-based activities) that this kind of approach is likely to yield question-begging results. The prevailing distribution of real income in the world—the comparative riches or poverty of nations, or regions—is largely to be explained, not by "natural" factors, but by the unequal incidence of development in industrial activities. The "advanced", high-income areas are invariably those which possess a highly developed modern industry. In relation to differences in industrial development, explanations in terms of "resource endowment" do not get us very far. One can, and does, say that industrial production requires a great deal of capital—both in terms of plant and machinery, and of human skills, resulting from education—but in explaining such differences in "capital endowment" it is difficult to separate cause from effect. It is as sensible—or perhaps more sensible—to say that capital accumulation results from economic development as that it is a cause of development. Anyhow, the two proceed side by side. Accumulation is largely financed out of business profits; the growth of demand in turn is largely responsible for providing both the inducements to invest capital in industry and also the means of financing it.

We cannot therefore say that industries will be located in regions which are "well endowed" with capital resources for reasons other than industrial development itself. It was not the result of the peculiar thriftiness of the inhabitants of a region, or of a particularly high degree of initial inequality in the distribution of income which "induced" a high savings-ratio, that some regions became rich while others remained poor. The capital needed for industrialisation was largely provided by the very same individuals who acquired wealth as a result of the process of development, and not prior to it. The great captains of industry, like Henry Ford or Nuffield, were not recruited from the wealthy classes—they started as "small men".

Nor is there a satisfactory "location theory" which is capable of explaining the geographic distribution of industrial activities. The only relevant factor which is considered in this connection is that of transport costs. But transport cost advantages can help to explain location only in those particular activities which convert bulky goods—where transport costs are an important element, and where processing itself greatly reduces the weight of the materials processed. If say, two tons of coal and four tons of iron are needed to make a ton of steel, it is better to locate steel plants near the coal mines and the iron ore deposits; and if these are themselves situated at some distance from each other, it is best to locate the steel plants near both places, in proportions determined by the relative weight of the two materials per unit of finished product—i.e., in this example, two-thirds of the plants near the iron ore, and one-third near the coal mines— since this arrangement alone would ensure full utilisation of transport capacity in both directions.

But where the effect of processing in reducing bulk is not so important, the location of the processing activity may be a matter of indifference—whether it is near the source of the materials, near the market for the products, or anywhere in between. It is often suggested that such "footloose" industries tend naturally to develop near the market for their products. But this again is a question-begging proposition. Great urban conurbations are normally large centres of industrial activity—the "markets" are there where the "industry" is. The engineering industry in this country is highly concentrated in and around Birmingham— it is also a great "market" for engineering goods of various kinds. But it does not explain why either of these should be located there, rather than in some other place, say Leeds or Sheffield.

THE PRINCIPLE OF "CUMULATIVE CAUSATION"

To explain why certain regions have become highly industrialised, while others have not we must introduce quite different kinds of considerations—what Mydral[1] called the principle of "circular and cumulative causation". This is nothing else but the existence of increasing returns to scale—using that term in the broadest sense—in processing activities. These are not just the economies of large-scale production, commonly considered, but the cumulative advantages accruing from the growth of industry itself—the development of skill and know-how; the opportunities for easy communication of ideas and experience; the opportunity of ever-increasing differentiation of processes and of specialisation in human activities. As Allyn Young[2] pointed out

---

[1] *Economic Theory and Underdeveloped Regions,* London, Duckworth, 1957.
[2] "Increasing Returns and Economic Progress", *Economic Journal,* vol. xxxviii, December 1928.

in a famous paper, Adam Smith's principle of the "division of labour" operates through the constant sub-division of industries, the emergence of new kinds of specialised firms, of steadily increasing differentiation—more than through the expansion in the size of the individual plant or the individual firm.

Thus the fact that in all known historical cases the development of manufacturing industries was closely associated with urbanisation must have deep-seated causes which are unlikely to be rendered inoperative by the invention of some new technology or new source of power. Their broad effect is a strong positive association between the growth of productivity and efficiency and the rate of growth in the scale of activities—the so-called Verdoorn Law. One aspect of this is that as communication between different regions becomes more intensified (with improvements in transport and in marketing organisation), the region that is initially more developed industrially may gain from the progressive opening of trade at the expense of the less developed region whose development will be inhibited by it. Whereas in the classical case—which abstracts from increasing returns—the opening of trade between two regions will necessarily be beneficial to both (even though the gains may not be equally divided between them) and specialisation through trade will necessarily serve to reduce the differences in comparative costs in the two areas, in the case of the "opening of trade" in industrial products the differences in comparative costs may be enlarged, and not reduced, as a result of trade; and the trade may injure one region to the greater benefit of the other. This will be so if one assumes two regions, initially isolated from one another, with each having both an agricultural area and an industrial and market centre; with the size of agricultural production being mainly determined by soil and climate, and the state of technology; and the size of industrial production mainly depending on the demand for industrial products derived from the agricultural sector. When trade is opened up between them, the region with the more developed industry will be able to supply the needs of the agricultural area of the other region on more favourable terms: with the result that the industrial centre of the second region will lose its market, and will tend to be eliminated—

without any compensating advantage to the inhabitants of that region in terms of increased agricultural output.

Another aspect of assymetry between "land-based" and "processing" activities (which is basically due to economies of large-scale production) is that in industrial production, contractual costs form an important independent element in price-formation: competition is necessarily imperfect; the sellers are price-makers, rather than price-takers. Whereas in agricultural production incomes are derived from prices, in industrial production it is prices that are derived from, or dependent on, contractual incomes (i.e. on the level of wages).

As a result, the "exchange process"—the nature of the adjustment mechanism in inter-regional trade flows and money flows—operates differently in the two cases. In the case of trade between agricultural regions, the classical theory of the adjustment process is more nearly applicable. The price of agricultural commodities rises or falls automatically with changes in the balance of supply and demand; these price changes in individual markets will automatically tend to maintain the balance in trade flows between areas, both through the income effects and the substitution effects of price changes. Where the goods produced by the different regions are fairly close substitutes for one another, a relatively modest change in price—in the "terms of trade"—will be sufficient to offset the effects of changes in either supply or demand schedules as may result from crop failures, the uneven incidence of technological improvements, or any other "exogenous" cause. If the goods produced by the different regions are complements to rather than substitutes for each other, the adjustment process may involve far greater changes in the terms of trade of the two areas, and would thus operate mainly through the "income effects". But in either case, the very process which secures an equilibrium between the supply and demand in each individual market through the medium of price changes will also ensure balance between sales and purchases of each region.

In the case of industrial activities ("manufactures") the impact effect of exogenous changes in demand will be on production rather than on prices. "Supply", at any rate long-run supply, is normally in excess of demand—in the sense that producers would be willing to produce more, and to sell more, at the prevailing price (or even at a lower price) in response to an increased flow of orders. In this situation the adjustment process operates in a different manner—through the so-called "foreign trade multiplier". Any exogenous change in the demand for the products of a region from outside will set up multiplier effects in terms of local production and employment which in turn will adjust imports to the change in exports; on certain assumptions, this adjustment will alone suffice to keep the trade flows in balance.[1]

Some time ago Hicks[2] coined the phrase "super-multiplier" to cover the effects of changes of demand on investment, as well as on consumption; and he showed that on certain assumptions, both the rate of growth of induced investment, and the rate of growth of consumption, become attuned to the rate of growth of the autonomous component of demand, so that the growth in an autonomous demand-factor will govern the rate of growth of the economy as a whole.

From the point of view of any particular region, the "autonomous component of demand" is the demand emanating from *outside* the region; and Hicks' notion of the "super-multiplier" can be applied so as to express the doctrine of the foreign trade multiplier in a dynamic setting. So expressed, the doctrine asserts that the rate of economic development of a region is fundamentally governed by the rate of growth of its exports. For the growth of exports, via the "accelerator", will govern the rate of growth of industrial capacity, as well as the rate of growth of consumption; it will also serve to adjust (again under rather severe simplifying assumptions) both the level, and the rate of growth, of imports to that of exports.

The behaviour of exports on the other hand will depend both on an exogenous factor—the rate of growth of world demand for the products of the region; and on an "endogenous" or quasi-endogenous factor—on the movement of the "efficiency wages"

---

[1] The necessary assumptions are that all other sources of demand except exports are endogenous, rather than exogenous—i.e., that both Government expenditure and business investment play a passive rôle, the former being confined by revenue from taxation, and the latter by savings out of business profits.

[2] *A Contribution to the Theory of the Trade Cycle*, Oxford, 1950.

in the region relative to other producing regions, which will determine whether the region's share in the total (overall) market is increasing or diminishing. The movement of "efficiency wages" (a phrase coined by Keynes) is the resultant of two elements—the relative movement of money wages and that of productivity. If this relationship (the index of money wages divided by the index of productivity) moves in favour of an area it will gain in "competitiveness" and vice versa.

As regards the movement of money wages the one uncontroversial proposition that one can advance is that given *some* mobility of labour, there is a limit to the differences in the levels of wages prevailing between industrial regions, or between different industries of a region. Indeed, it is a well known fact that whilst the general level of money wages may rise at highly variable rates at different times, the pay differentials between different types of workers, or between workers doing the same job in different areas, are remarkably constant. This may be the result partly of the mobility of labour but also of the strong pressures associated with collective bargaining for the maintenance of traditional comparabilities.[1] But this means that the rates of growth of money wages in different regions will tend to be much the same, even when the rates of growth in employment differ markedly. On the other hand, under the Verdoorn Law, the rates of growth of productivity will be the higher, the higher the rates of growth of output, and differences in the rates of productivity growth will tend to exceed the associated differences in the rates of growth of employment.[2] Hence differences in the rates of productivity growth are not likely to be compensated by equivalent differences in the rates of increase in money wages.

---

[1] It has also been true in an international context that the comparative differences in the rates of growth of money wages in the different industrial countries had been smaller (in the post-war period at any rate) than the differences in the rates of productivity growth in the manufacturing industries of those countries, though the reasons why this has been so are not as yet well understood (cf. e.g. Kaldor, *Monetary Policy, Economic Stability and Growth*, Memorandum submitted to the Committee on the Working of the Monetary System. Principal Memoranda of Evidence, Vol. 3, pp. 146–153, London, H.M.S.O., 1960, at paras 22–3 and Table 1, reprinted in *Essays on Economic Policy*, vol. I, pp. 128–53).

[2] Recent empirical analyses of productivity growth in manufacturing industry suggest that a 1 per cent increase in the growth of output is associated with a 0·6 per cent increase in productivity and a 0·4 per cent increase in employment (cf. e.g.: *Economic Survey for Europe*, 1969, U.N. Geneva, 1970).

In other words, "efficiency wages" will tend to fall in regions (and in the particular industries of regions) where productivity rises faster than the average. It is for this reason that relatively fast growing areas tend to acquire a cumulative competitive advantage over a relatively slow growing area; "efficiency wages" will, in the natural course of events, tend to fall in the former, relatively to the latter—even when they tend to rise in both areas in absolute terms.

It is through this mechanism that the process of "cumulative causation" works; and both comparative success and comparative failure have self-reinforcing effects in terms of industrial development. Just because the induced changes in wage increases are not sufficient to offset the differences in productivity increases, the comparative costs of production in fast growing areas tend to fall in time relatively to those in slow growing areas; and thereby enhance the competitive advantage of the former at the expense of the latter.

This principle of cumulative causation—which explains the unequal regional incidence of industrial development by endogenous factors resulting from the process of historical development itself rather than by exogenous differences in "resource endowment"—is an essential one for the understanding of the diverse trends of development as between different regions. In reality, the influences and cross-currents resulting from processes of development are far more complex. The intensification of trade resulting from technological improvements in transport or the reduction of artificial barriers (such as tariffs between regions) has important diffusion effects as well as important concentration effects. The increase in production and income in one region will, as such, stimulate the demand for "complementary" products of other regions; and just as, in terms of microeconomics, falling costs generally lead to oligopoly rather than monopoly, so the principle of cumulative causation leads to the concentration of industrial development in a number of successful regions and not of a single region. These "successful" regions in turn may hold each other in balance through increasing specialisation between them—some area becomes more prominent in some industries and another area in some other industries.

Actually, in terms of national areas, Kuznets found that different industrialised countries are remarkably similar in industrial structure, at similar stages of industrial development. The tremendous increase in international trade in industrial products between highly industrialised countries since the Second World War was more the reflection of specialisation within industries than that between industries: it was mainly in parts and components and machinery for industrial use. For example, in the case of the motor car industry, whilst most developed countries have a developed and highly competitive motor car industry (and are large net exporters) there has been a huge increase in international trade in motor car components—with some countries supplying some part of a carburetter to everybody, and some other country doing the same for some other part of the engine, or the carburetter.

There are also important dis-economies resulting from excessive rates of growth in industrial activities in particular areas: the growing areas will tend to have fast rates of population growth (mainly as a result of immigration) with the associated environmental problems in housing, public services, congestion, and so on, and these at some stage should serve to offset the technological economies resulting from faster growth. But as is well known, many of these dis-economies are external to the individual producer and may not therefore be adequately reflected in the movement of money costs and prices. A counterpart to this are external economies in the slow growing or declining regions—in terms of unemployment of labour, or an under-utilised social infrastructure, which again tend to be external to the firm and hence inadequately reflected in selling costs or prices. There is some presumption therefore for supposing that, if left to market processes alone, tendencies to regional concentration of industrial activities will proceed farther than they would have done if "private costs" were equal to "social cost" (in the Pigovian sense) and all economies and dis-economies of production were adequately reflected in the movement of money costs and prices.

REGIONS AND COUNTRIES

Now consider some of the basic differences in the mode of operation of this principle—i.e. of "cumulative causation" as between different regions of a single country and as between different political areas.

There is, first of all, the fact that the inter-regional mobility of labour is very much greater than the international mobility of labour. As a result differences in regional growth rates cannot cause differences in living standards of the same order as have emerged in the last few centuries between more distant regions, separated by political and cultural barriers. Real earnings no doubt improve faster in the areas of immigration rather than in areas of emigration, but the very fact of easy migration limits the extent to which differences in regional growth rates will be associated with divergent movements in earnings per head. The fact that trade unions are nation-wide and collective bargains in most countries are on a national basis, is a further reason why the movement of real earnings in various regions broadly tends to keep in step.

A second and even more important fact is that a region which forms part of a political community, with a common scale of public services and a common basis of taxation, automatically gets "aid" whenever its trading relations with the rest of the country deteriorate. There is an important built-in fiscal stabiliser which arrests the operation of the export-multiplier: since taxes paid to the Central Government vary with the level of local incomes and expenditure, whilst public expenditures do not (indeed they may vary in an offsetting direction through public works, unemployment benefit, etc.), any deterioration in the export-import balance tends to be retarded (and ultimately arrested) by the change in the region's fiscal balance—in the relation between what it contributes to the central Exchequer and what it receives from it.

This "built-in" fiscal stabiliser—i.e. that a fall in exogenous demand leads to an increase in the public sector deficit, and thereby moderates the effect of the former on employment and incomes—operates of course on the national level as much as on the regional level; and it is one of the main reasons why a fall in exports does not generate a sufficient fall in the level of incomes to maintain equilibrium in the balance of payments through the adjustment in imports. But the important difference is that in the case of the region the change in the local fiscal balance is externally financed; in the case of the nation the balance of payments deficit causes a fall in reserves, or requires "compensatory finance" from abroad, which is by no means "automatic".

This is probably the main reason why there appears to be no counterpart to the "balance-of-payments problem" on the regional level. It is often suggested by the "monetary school" that the reason why a country with a separate currency gets into balance of payments difficulties, whilst a region never does, is because in the one case the "local money supply" is reduced in consequence of an excess of imports over exports; in the other case the monetary authorities offset the effects of the adverse balance on current account by "domestic credit expansion"—by replacing the outflow of money (resulting from the excess of imports) with "new" money. In my view this way of looking at the problem is putting the cart before the horse. The "replacement of the money" is simply a facet of the fact that the foreign trade multiplier is arrested in its operation through the induced fiscal deficit —possibly aggravated also by the fall in private saving in relation to private domestic investment (though in practice the latter factor may be quantitatively of less importance, since the foreign-trade multiplier will tend to induce a reduction in local investment, and not only in local savings). But exactly the same thing happens at the regional level—with the outflowing money being (at least partially) replaced by a larger net inflow from the Exchequer, which is a direct consequence of the "outflow"; but since it happens automatically as part of the natural order of things nobody kicks up a fuss, or even takes notice of it.

In these ways "regions" are in a more favourable position than "countries". On the other hand sovereign political areas can take various measures to offset the effect of an unfavourable trend in their "efficiency wages" which is not open to a "region"— i.e. by diverting demand from foreign goods to home goods, through varying forms of protection (tariffs and non-tariff barriers, such as preferences given in public contracts) and occasionally also—though usually only very belatedly, in extremities—through adjustment of the exchange rate.

Of these two instruments for counteracting adverse trends in "efficiency wages"—protection and devaluation—the latter is undoubtedly greatly superior to the former. Devaluation, as has often been pointed out, is nothing else but a combination of a uniform *ad-valorem* duty on all imports and uniform *ad-valorem* subsidy on exports. The combination of the two allows the adjustment in "competitiveness" to take place under conditions which give the maximum scope for obtaining the advantages of economies of scale through international specialisation. Protection on the other hand tends to reduce international specialisation, and forces each region to spread its industrial activities over a wider range of activities on a smaller scale, instead of a narrower range on a larger scale. The effects of protection in inhibiting the growth of industrial efficiency is likely to be the greater the smaller the G.N.P. (or rather the gross industrial product) of the protected area. It is no accident that all the prosperous small countries of the world—such as the Scandinavian countries or Switzerland—are (comparatively speaking) "free traders". They have modest tariffs, and a very high ratio of trade in manufactures (both exports and imports) to their total output or consumption.

It has sometimes been suggested—not perhaps very seriously—that some of the development areas of the U.K.—such as Scotland or Northern Ireland—would be better off with a separate currency with an adjustable exchange rate vis-à-vis the rest of the U.K. For the reason mentioned earlier, I do not think this would be a suitable remedy. However, we have now introduced a new instrument in the U.K.—R.E.P.[1]—which potentially could give the same advantages as devaluation for counteracting any adverse trend in "efficiency wages", but with the added advantage that the cost of the consequent deterioration in the terms of trade (the cost of selling exports at lower prices in terms of imports) is not borne by the region, but by the U.K. taxpaying community as a whole.

[1] The Regional Employment Premium.

For this same reason, perhaps, the drawback of R.E.P. as an instrument is that it would be politically very difficult to introduce it on a scale that could make it really effective. The present R.E.P. is equivalent to a 5-6 per cent reduction in the "efficiency wages" in the manufacturing sector of the development areas. Since "value added by regional manufacturing" is no more than a quarter, or perhaps a third, of the total cost of regional export-commodities (the rest consist of goods and services embodied that are mainly produced outside the region) the effect of a 6 per cent R.E.P. is no more than that of a 2 per cent devaluation (for the U.K. as a whole). It thus could have only one-fifth of the effect on "regional competitiveness" which the recent U.K. devaluation had on the U.K.'s competitiveness in relation to the rest of the world.

Development Area policy comprises a host of other measures as well, of which the differential investment grant is the most costly and the most prominent. In my view investment grants as an instrument are less effective for the purpose of countering adverse trends in competitiveness than subsidies on wages (and not only because they stimulate the wrong kind of industries— those that are specially capital intensive) but I would agree that this is an issue that requires closer investigation than it has yet received.

One further possibility can be considered. Given the limitation on the scope of development expenditures by the natural disinclination of the Central Government (or the Parliament at Westminster) to spend huge sums in subsidising particular regions, there is a case for supplementing Central Government sources from local sources—through more local fiscal autonomy. For example, if it were found (and agreed) that R.E.P. is an efficacious way of subsidising regional exports (I suppose this is far from agreed at the moment) and that this might have dramatic effects in terms of enhanced regional development in the long run, it could well be in the interest of the regions to supplement the centrally financed R.E.P. by the proceeds, say, of a local sales tax. Perhaps this is a dangerous suggestion since in practice the growth of locally financed subsidies might simply be offset by lesser subsidies from the Centre. It would be less "dangerous" however, if it was the Central Government which offered to raise the level of such subsidies—R.E.P. or even investment grants—on condition that a proportion of the cost should be raised by local taxation. Clearly, far more could be spent for the benefit of particular areas, if the areas themselves would make a greater, or a more distinct, contribution to the cost of such benefits. But these are thoughts for the distant future; long before they become practical politics we shall be deeply involved in the same kind of issues in connection with our negotiations to enter the Common Market.

13

THE ROLE OF INCREASING RETURNS, TECHNICAL PROGRESS AND CUMULATIVE CAUSATION IN THE THEORY OF INTERNATIONAL TRADE AND ECONOMIC GROWTH[1]

Traditional theory, both classical and neo-classical, asserts that free trade in goods between different regions is always to the advantage of *each* trading country, and is therefore the best arrangement from the point of view of the welfare of the trading world as a whole, as well as of each part of the world taken separately.[2] However, these propositions are only true under specific abstract assumptions which do not correspond to reality. Under more realistic assumptions unrestricted trade is likely to lead to a loss of welfare to particular regions or countries and even to the world as a whole—that is to say that the world will be worse off under free trade than it could be under *some* system of regulated trade.

Traditional theory emanated from Ricardo's doctrine of comparative costs which says that even if one country is more efficient in everything—has a higher productivity all round—it pays for it to specialise in those things in which its comparative efficiency is greatest and to rely for the rest on supplies from the less efficient countries. His famous example was the exchange of cloth for wine between England and Portugal; he supposed that Portugal had a higher output per man both in the production of wine and cloth than England but its productivity advantage was greater in wine production than in

[1] Originally published in *Économie Appliquée*, No. 4, 1981.
[2] The latter part of this proposition abstracts from the possibility that a particular country possesses some degree of monopoly power and thereby can turn the terms of trade in its favour by means of a tariff even after retaliation by other countries is taken into account.

cloth-making; hence Portugal would be better off if it specialised in producing wine and obtained cloth by way of trade with England.

This theory went through further important stages of development; some of it was due to J.S. Mill, some to Marshall and later, more importantly, to two Swedish economists, Ely Hecksher and Professor Ohlin. These two Swedish economists have shown that under certain assumptions (to which I shall return) differences in comparative costs can only exist if "resource endowment" or "factor proportions" of the different regions are different; such differences must be reflected in differences in relative factor prices, and the effect of trade must be to bring relative factor prices into a closer relationship to one another (each country exports goods which require larger quantities of those goods in which it is relatively well endowed). Samuelson in his well-known "factor price equalisation theorem" carried this doctrine a stage further in showing that on certain assumptions as regards the production functions, the effect of free trade must be to *equalise factor prices* in the different participating areas.

The implications of these theorems are very far reaching. For if they are true they would show:

(1) that the free movement of goods is a substitute for the movement of factors; and therefore

(2) trade brings about the same tendency to equalisation of factor prices (mainly wages and interest rates) as the free mobility of factors would cause (abstracting from the cost of movement in each case);

(3) from which it follows that trade must necessarily *reduce* the differences in real earnings per head between the different trading areas and in favourable circumstances (*i.e.* identical production functions which are "well behaved") eliminate them altogether.

However all this rests on artificial assumptions which are not always stated or even understood:

(1) That the "production functions" for different goods are the *same* in different countries—*i.e.* technology and the efficiency of its exploitation are the same everywhere.

(2) Perfect competition prevails throughout.

(3) Constant returns to scale (homogeneous and linear production functions) for all processes of production.

It is these two latter assumptions—which are themselves closely involved in one another—which are critical from the point of view of the theory. (Perfect competition can normally obtain only when costs of production are the same, however small or however large is the rate of production).

As soon as we allow for either diminishing returns (to transferable factors) and/or increasing returns due to economies of scale, the propositions will no longer hold.

Take the first case of *diminishing returns*. Suppose the amount of wine produced in Portugal is limited by the amount of land suitable for viniculture while only a limited amount of labour can be used with advantage on any one hectare of land. Production could then be limited by a *land-constraint*, not a *labour constraint*. If the maximum number of people who can be usefully employed on the land is smaller than the total number available to work, the remainder can only be employed in industry or services. In the absence of international trade, the people who are not wanted on the land will be engaged in making "cloth", in the ratio, say, of 1 yard of cloth = 10 litres of wine. In England on the other hand, 10 litres of wine cost the same as 10 yards of cloth. The opening of trade will mean that the price of *cloth* will fall so much, both in terms of money and in terms of wine, that it will no longer be profitable to produce cloth in Portugal—the Portuguese textile trade will be ruined. (This is not just an imaginary example: according to Friedrich List this is what *actually* happened as a result of the Methuen Treaty with Portugal of 1704). Now if all the workers freed from cloth-making could be employed in increasing the production of wine, in proportion to the increase in labour, all would be well: the real income of Portugal would be greater than before. Portugal would have *more* cloth and *more* wine to consume than in the absence of trade. However, if land is limited, this is not possible. Nor will it be possible to save the cloth-trade by reducing wages. For there is a minimum wage (in terms of wine) below which the cloth workers could not subsist. Hence the result might be that while Portugal will export more wine to England, the national real income of Portugal would shrink, since the addition to its wine output may not compensate for the loss of output of the cloth trade. Portugal could well end up by being a much poorer country than before—there would be less employment and less output.[1]

It will be readily seen that this could not have occurred under the rule of constant labour costs in both industries. but the same kind of conclusion emerges if one considers the existence not of diminishing returns in *agriculture* but that of increasing returns in *industry*.

The case of increasing returns has never been properly explored in economic theory—beyond the famous statement of Alfred Marshall (and of Cournot and Walras before him) that increasing returns lead to monopoly because some producers get ahead of their rivals and gain a cumulative advantage over the others whom they will drive out of business—hence increasing returns (or falling marginal costs) could not exist under conditions which prevail in a *competitive market*. When in the 1930s the new theories concerning the imperfection of markets suggested that this need not be—falling costs and competition can co-exist—economists in general shied away from exploring the consequences.

However, businessmen could never ignore the existence of diminishing costs. It is on account of the economies of large-scale production that a rising market share means success and a falling market share spells trouble. And it is on that account that in a growing market a business *cannot* stand still: it

---

[1] The example supposes that England can manufacture cloth much cheaper in terms of wine than Portugal and not solely on account of the unsuitability of the British climate for wine production. The example also supposes that England uses a technology in cloth production involving a smaller outlay of labour per unit of output, otherwise it could not sell cloth at a price which is below the *minimum* cost at which it can be produced in Portugal, even when wages are at the minimum quantity of wine on which workers can subsist (unless English workers can subsist on so much less wine than Portuguese workers, which is unliekly).

must grow if it wishes to survive.[1]

Owing to increasing returns in processing activities (in manufactures) success breeds further success and failure begets more failure. Another Swedish economist, Gunnar Myrdal, called this "the principle of circular and cumulative causation".

It is as a result of this that free trade in the field of manufactured goods leads to the concentration of manufacturing production in certain areas—to a *"polarisation process"* which inhibits the growth of such activities in some areas and concentrates them in others.

This is just what happened as a result of the Industrial Revolution and the transport revolution of the nineteenth century. Areas which were wholly isolated previously became drawn into the world economy. But one cannot say that the enlargement of markets brought about by these technological revolutions benefited *all* participating areas in the same way. The manufacturing industry of Britain (at first chiefly the cotton industry, later iron and steel and machinery) received an enormous stimulus through the opening of markets in Europe, in North and South America and then in India and China. But at the same time the arrival of cheap factory-made goods eliminated local producers (of hand-woven textiles and so on) who became uncompetitive in consequence, and it made these countries "specialise" in the production of raw materials and minerals which however could only offer employment to limited numbers of workers. As a result of this the countries dependent on the exports of primary products remained comparatively poor—the poverty was a consequence, not of low productivity of labour in their export sectors, but of the limited employment capacity of their "profitable" industries.

On the other hand, the "polarisation process" was counteracted by the successful spread of industrialisation to other countries. Ever since Britain started the Industrial Revolution in the closing decades of the eighteenth century there was the prospect that her new techniques based on the

---

[1] The only economist of the nineteenth century who fully recognised this was Karl Marx. In neo-classical theory, each firm has an "optimum size"; when the output of an industry grows, it is the *number* of firms, not the size of the existing firms, which increase.

factory system, of the use of new types of machinery and of new sources of energy would be sooner or later emulated by other countries. And so they were. In the second half of the nineteenth century the countries of France, Germany, Italy and many of the smaller countries of Western Europe began to industrialise behind the protection of newly erected tariff walls, and this happened also outside Europe, in the United States and still later in countries like Japan, India, the countries of Oceania, and many others. All this time the spread of industrialisation over wider and wider regions was counteracted by the "polarisation" effect which is nothing other than the inhibiting effect of superior competitive power of the industrially more efficient and dynamic countries, as compared to the others. The economic unification of Italy probably provides the best known example of the polarisation effect. Since the unification occurred at a time when the industries of the North of Italy were rather more developed than those of the South (though the difference was not very large—industrial productivity was 20–25 per cent higher in the North than in the South) it was quite sufficient for the free and guaranteed access of the Northern industries to the Southern markets to inhibit the development of the latter at the same time as it accelerated the industrial development of the North. The interaction between these forces—*i.e.* that of polarisation which leads to concentration of development in successful areas, and of imitation or emulation which leads to the *spread* of industrialisation into a wider range of areas—has never to my knowledge been properly explored.

The fact remains that all the countries which became industrialised (other than Britain which started off the process) did so with the aid of protective tariffs which were high enough to induce a substitution of home produced goods for imports. This was true of Germany (particularly after Bismarck's famous tariff of 1879), France, which abandoned the earlier free trade policy of the 1860s, Italy and most of the smaller European countries, with the possible exception of Sweden. It was also true of the United States, which became increasingly protectionist at the end of the nineteenth century, culminating in the McKinley tariff of 1900. In some cases (of which Japan is the most important example) the form of protection relied more on State subsidies, financed out of a tax on agriculture, than on import duties. But without some such instrument industrialisation could never have started. However, what distinguished the successful industrialisers from the others was the use of relatively moderate tariffs—no greater than was necessary to make domestic industries profitable—and a system of duties that was carefully designed in favour of those industries that had the capability of developing an export potential, and not just a substitute for imports. As against that, the less successful industrialisers were those who used a high degree of protection rather indiscriminately and who developed industries whose costs in terms of primary products were much too high to enable them to break into the world markets. (In many of these countries, *e.g.* the countries of Latin America, the emergence of many highly inefficient industries was not the result of a policy of protection introduced as a matter of choice, but more in the nature of a [largely unforeseen] by-product of widespread import prohibitions, which were introduced to conserve foreign exchange at a time when export earnings from their traditional exports collapsed during the Great Depression of the 1930s.)

The history of Britain since 1873 at any rate (if not earlier) provides an excellent example of both the need for, and the practical limits of, "restructuring" the economy in the face of adverse changes in the world market—of the loss of markets for the main export products in a succession of countries and of increasing import penetration in the home market, resulting from the industrialisation of other countries.

The main staple export of Britain in the middle of the nineteenth century consisted of cotton goods which supplied both European and overseas markets at prices with which local producers could not compete. This is shown by the fact that in 1850 the consumption of raw cotton in Britain was considerably larger than that of the rest of Europe put together. But cotton textiles, based on the modern methods of factory production, were also technically the easiest thing to establish, so that one country after another replaced Britain's exports by home-made goods. For a time, however, the full adverse effects of this development on the British economy were counter-balanced by the fact that each of these industrialisers simultaneously developed a demand for British-made plant and machinery. But in each case this was a transitional phenomenon since each of the successful industrialisers became self-sufficient in time in the machinery industry, and not just in the textile industry, and indeed some of these countries appeared as important competitors of Britain in third markets or even in Britain's home market, which remained wholly unprotected as a result of the strong intellectual heritage of the *laisser-faire* philosophy. Thus the change in the destination of British machinery exports gives a very good historical guide to the stage of industrial development of different countries. In the 1880s Germany was the most important market for British-made machinery; in the 1890s it was the United States and the 1900s it was Japan.

Up to a point the British economy showed a remarkable resilience and adaptability in the face of adverse conditions. As British goods were chased from one market after another— from pillar to post—successful efforts were made to develop new markets to compensate for the loss of the old ones. Thus the "centre of gravity" of British exports wandered from Europe to North America, thence to the Far East and Oceania, thence to India and the Near East, and finally to Africa (where at first South Africa was the most important customer; this role has now been taken over by Nigeria).

Corresponding to this there was also an adaptation of the structure of manufacturing industry. As late as 1913 Britain retained a huge export market in cheap cotton textiles (90 per cent of Lancashire's output was exported), which greatly diminished by the 1920s and entirely disappeared after World War II. On the other hand, exports of engineering goods, chemicals and vehicles expanded. There has thus been plenty of "restructuring" in British industry over the past hundred years, caused by the industrialisation of other countries. But this is a far cry from "full compensation". Britain's rate of economic growth slowed down a great deal: in the forty years before 1913 both manufacturing output and the GNP grew by around 2 per cent a year. This involved both lower employment growth and lower productivity growth, both absolutely and relatively to the then fast growing countries, chiefly Germany and the United States.

In the course of this development a continued loss in the U.K.'s export share was combined with rising import penetration, which meant that the share of manufactured goods in total imports rose from 5 per cent in 1860 to 25 per cent by 1900; and in the latter year some 19 per cent of the total domestic absorption of manufactures was represented by imports.

There was also a very large amount of disguised unemployment—lacking social insurance, support for the unemployment was limited to Trade Union members, but these related only to the labour force who had already been recruited into industry. For the rest emigration offered the only escape from starvation. There was mass emigration which amounted to 6 million from Britain alone in the last twenty-five years before World War I.

After World War I the industrial situation was never quite so bad again, because following the war (in the course of which many new industries were established which would not have been profitable under the pre-war régime of free trade) some of the newly established industries remained protected on the grounds of either being "infant industries" or being essential for national security. After an abortive attempt by a Conservative Government in 1923 a general protective tariff on industrial goods was finally introduced in 1932 with a general rate of 20 per cent *ad valorem*, and which amounted to 33⅓ per cent in the case of such industries as chemicals and steel. This was followed by quantitative import restrictions introduced during World War II, which were not lifted until the late 1950s.

This change of commercial policy gave a second "golden age" to British industry. In the five years 1932-1937 the production of manufacturing industry increased by nearly 8 per cent a year, and in 1937 it surpassed the previous peak of 1929 by no less than one-third. More significant still, if one takes the thirty-three years 1922-1955 there was a growth of industrial production of 4 per cent a year, or if the war years 1939-1946 (during which there was no overall increase in output) are omitted, by no less than 5 per cent a year. During that period import penetration was sharply reduced from 19 per cent in 1929 to 10 per cent in 1937, and to only 5 per cent in 1955. With the trade liberalisation in the late 1950s the rate of growth of manufacturing output slowed down and import penetration increased, while the U.K.'s export share continued to fall. By 1973 the share of imports in total domestic absorption exceeded the previous peak, and since then it has proceeded at an accelerated pace.

EXPLANATION OF DIFFERENTIAL PERFORMANCE

All this is explicable in Keynesian (or rather Harrodian) terms, but not in neo-classical terms—*i.e. not* in terms of a theory which assumes continuous full employment and a situation in which output in general is "resource constrained".

It was Harrod, not Keynes, who put forward the idea (in 1933)[1] that the level of fluctuations of industrial output (or rather the output of industrial countries) is to be explained by the principle of the "foreign trade multiplier", which at the same time provided the mechanism for keeping the balance of payments in equilibrium.[2]

Harrod assumed that exports form the exogenous component of demand, and this in turn means that they give rise to multiplier and accelerator effects (which form the endogenous components) and that in the absence of other leakages the sum of the incomes generated by this process will be such as to give rise to a volume of imports which matches the volume of exports.[3]

---

[1] *International Economics*, Cambridge Economics Handbooks, 1933.

[2] This proposition, underlying the principle of effective demand of Keynes, published three years later, did not receive the attention which it deserved. However some economists working in the field of the theory of international trade (in particular P. Barrett Whale, "The Working of the Pre-War Gold Standard" *Economica*, 1937, p. 18 and *Economica*, 1938, p. 90) recognised that Harrod's theory provides a far more convincing explanation of the workings of the gold standard in the nineteenth century than the classical or neo-classical theories which rely on gold flows (which were extremely small) or on relative price changes induced by movements of relative interest rates.

[3] This of course will only be true if:

If exports, E, generate induced expenditures of kE in the first round, k^2E in the second round etc. (with $0<k<1$)
and assuming that
imports $M = mY$, with $0<m<1$,
the condition of equilibrium in the balance of trade is

$$M = E. \tag{1}$$

This will be attained when total income, Y, equals the sum of exports plus the sum of the endogenous components of demand (comprising both investment and consumption) generated by such exports. This is given by:

$$Y = \frac{1}{1-k} E \tag{2}$$

Assuming $1-k = m$, this can be written:

$$Y = \frac{1}{m} E \tag{3}$$

The 'dynamised' version of this formula, as shown by Thirlwall,[1] is:

$$\dot{Y} = \frac{\dot{E}}{\pi} \tag{4}$$

where $\dot{Y}$ and $\dot{E}$ are the logarithmic growth rates of Y and E respectively, and π represents the income elasticity of demand for imports.

Thirlwall's paper shows that the simple formula (which is

(i) the Government budget is also in balance when foreign trade is in balance;

(ii) the induced investment generated by this process, together with any autonomous investment will balance the savings generated at the same level of income. (This latter adjustment may occur as part of the same process, if it is assumed that savings mainly come out of profits and that the profit margins charged by firms are themselves governed by the financial requirements of investment).

[1] A.P. Thirlwall, "The Balance of Payments Constraint as an Explanation of International Growth Rate Differences", *Banca Nazionale del Lavoro Quarterly Review*, March 1979, p. 45.

really a formula for showing the rates of growth of different countries consistent with the maintenance of equilibrium in their balances of payments) explains the post-war differences of growth rates among industrial countries remarkably well (*op. cit.* p. 51).[1]

Thus, while the balance of payments is a monetary constraint, which in theory can be adjusted by relative price changes, it appears that the growth rates of individual countries, constrained by their balance of payments, can be approximated without reference to movements in relative prices. If this is so, it

A comparison of the actual growth rate with that predicted from the dynamic Harrod Trade Multiplier

Country	%Δ in Real GNP(y)		%Δ in Export Volume $\dot{E}$		Income elasticity of demand for imports π	Predicted growth rate from the Harrod Trade Multiplier (%) $\dot{Y} = \dfrac{\dot{E}}{\pi}$	
	1951-73	1953-76	1951-73	1953-76		1951-73	1953-76
USA	3.7	3.23	5.1	5.88	1.51	3.38	3.89
Canada	4.6	4.81	6.9	6.02	1.20	4.84	5.02
West Germany	5.7	4.96	10.8	9.99	1.89	5.71	5.29
Netherlands	5.0	4.99	10.1	9.38	1.82	5.55	5.15
Sweden	–	3.67	–	7.16	1.76	–	4.07
France	5.0	4.95	8.1	8.78	1.62	5.00	5.42
Denmark	4.2	3.58	6.1	6.77	1.31	4.65	5.17
Australia	–	3.58	–	6.98	0.90	–	7.76
Italy	5.1	4.96	11.7	12.09	2.25	5.20	5.37
Switzerland	–	3.56	–	7.20	1.90	–	3.79
Norway	4.2	4.18	7.2	7.70	1.40	5.14	5.50
Belgium	4.4	4.07	9.4	9.24	1.94	4.84	4.76
Japan	9.5	8.55	15.4	16.18	1.23	12.52	13.15
UK	2.7	2.71	4.1	4.46	1.51	2.71	2.95
South Africa	–	4.97	–	6.57	0.85	–	7.73

Sources: Data for 1951-73 from Cornwall, *Modern Capitalism: Its Growth and Transformation*. Martin Robertson, 1977.

Data for 1953-76 from Kern, "An International Comparison of Major Economic Trends 1953-1976", *National Westminster Bank Quarterly Review*, May 1978.

Estimates of π from Houthakker and Magee, "Income and Price Elasticities in World Trade," *Review of Economics and Statistics*, 1969.

[1] With a Spearman rank correlation of around 0.8-0.9. In general the calculated growth rates are remarkably close to the actual growth rates which is the more notable since the empirical series (especially the estimates of income elasticities of demand for imports) are subject to considerable statistical error. The only important difference is Japan where the calculated growth rate is as much as 50 per cent higher than the actual rate, even though the actual rate is very much higher than that of the other countries in the sample. (See Table).

follows that it is variations in real incomes, not relative prices and exchange rates, which provide the more powerful force tending to adjust imports to exports. This provides empirical support for the validity of the Harrod trade multiplier (which in its pure form assumes the terms of trade to be constant).

The essence of the Harrod theory could be summed up in the following propositions:

(a) that the growth rate of output of any area or "region" is mainly propelled by the external demand for its products;

(b) that economic growth is thus always demand-induced and not resource constrained. This remains true even when regions are political entities, *i.e.* "countries". "Resources" such as capital and labour do not determine growth, partly because they are mobile[1] between regions, and partly because they are never optimally allocated (there are always economic sectors where labour is in surplus in the sense that its marginal productivity is zero or negative, as *e.g.* in agriculture); and partly because capital (in the sense of industrial capacity) is automatically generated as part of, and in consequence of, the growth of demand;

(c) import variations are mainly governed by *real* income variations rather than by price variations; real incomes however vary as a result of changes in the terms of trade as well as changes in domestic output; and finally

(d) the growth of a country's exports should itself be considered as the outcome of the efforts of its producers to seek out potential markets and to adapt their product structure accordingly. Basically in a growing world economy the growth of exports is mainly to be explained by the income elasticity of foreign countries for a country's products; but it is a matter of

---

[1] This is true of both capital and labour, and it is true also in the case of individual countries as well as individual regions or countries. It is easy to assume that a given country has an exogenously determined "resource endowment", at least in the shape of its labour force, but as post-war history has shown, immigration restrictions are almost invariably lifted when the demand for labour exceeds the supply from domestic sources. The migration of labour, both intra-national and inter-national, is not determined by earnings differences alone; given such differences, it is very much conditioned by the existence of employment opportunities at the receiving end.

the innovative ability and adaptive capacity of its manufacturers whether this income elasticity will tend to be relatively large or small.

As regards the industrially developed countries, normally high income elasticities for exports and low elasticities for imports go together, and they both reflect successful leadership in *product development*. Technical progress is a continuous process and it largely takes the form of the development of marketing of new products which provide a new preferable way of satisfying some existing want. Such new products, if successful, gradually replace previously existing products which serve the same needs, and in the course of this process of replacement, the demand for the new product increases out of all proportion to the general increase in demand resulting from economic growth itself. Hence the most successful exporters are able to achieve increasing penetration both in foreign markets and in home markets because their products go to replace existing products.

All this of course is a highly simplified picture. Price elasticities also matter for that part of trade which is in "traditional goods" like textiles, shoes etc. where product innovation and technical change is far less important. It is in these sectors that newly industrialised countries have traditionally achieved important and rapid gains in world trade. They did so because they were able to copy the technologies of the more advanced countries, but had the advantage of much lower wages. As Huftbauer pointed out,[1] the proper division of international trade in manufactures is not so much the traditional division between "capital intensive" and "labour intensive" trade, but between "low wage" trade and "technological lead" trade. The developed industrialised countries with high wages must be able to export goods in which they have a technological lead over others, either on account of the design and marketing of new products (such as computers, silicon chips etc.), or because of advanced manufacturing processes

---

[1] *Synthetic Materials and the Theory of International Trade*, London, 1966.

which yield comparatively high productivity. (On account of the importance of static and dynamic economies of scale a country which has a large home market may thereby acquire an automatic advantage also in exports. A good example is synthetic rubber production in which U.S. costs have traditionally been much lower than those of other countries, mainly because of the size of the U.S. home market.)

A new feature of the world economic development of the last ten years is that the newly industrialised countries became important exporters, not only in the so-called traditional products, but in technologically advanced products, particularly when these happened to be highly labour intensive (as e.g. all the electronic products based on the transistor or the silicon chip). At an earlier stage Japan achieved important advances as against all other countries in a number of fields, such as optics. Thus a number of semi-industrialised, low wage countries of South-East Asia, such as Hong Kong, Taiwan, South Korea and Singapore, acquired significant shares in the world market in the products of the latest electronic technology, but in general they did so as a result of the access to U.S., German or Japanese technology, whose leading firms have increasingly tended to develop subsidiaries in these countries in order to take advantage of low wages.

We may sum up our conclusions reached so far in the following way:

(i) The spread of industrialisation in developing countries, if successful, involves following an "outward strategy" which leads to the development of export potential and not just to import substitution, and which will inevitably involve reduced export shares, and increased export penetration of the older industrialised countries. However, the new industrial production of these countries will generate additional incomes which add to the general level of demand for industrial products (as well as for fuel and raw materials) and it will therefore stimulate the exports of older industrial countries, and not only their imports. (As we have seen, the beginnings of industrialisation of the present developed countries in the nineteenth century generally meant an increase, if only for a temporary period, of the demand for British machinery). There is no guarantee however that if we take the case of any arbitrarily chosen pair of countries, or even the whole group of "developed" and developing countries (such as, say, the 100 odd countries who are members of UNCTAD and the eighteen developed countries who are members of the OECD) that these two changes—the reduced export share of the older industrialised countries and the increase in total world demand—will fully offset one another. Taking any individual manufacturing exporter, the tendency to such an offset (which is the same as the tendency for a country to gravitate to a state of equilibrium in its external balance of payments) may well be brought about through variations in relative growth rates. In the short run the emergence of new sources of supply will tend to cause a rise in a region's (or a country's) propensity to import, which in itself will tend to reduce its domestic output and employment. In the longer run this is translated into a lower growth rate, either through a fall in the rate of growth of exports and/or a rise in the income elasticity of imports.

(ii) Both these factors would necessarily cause both employment and productivity growth to fall (on account of the so-called "Verdoorn Law"), if the rate of growth of *total* world trade (which is the same thing, of course, as the rate of growth of world demand) remained unchanged. However, as the growth of world trade will also be accelerated by the addition to the number of countries which have a relatively fast growing manufacturing output, the fall in the relative growth rates of the industrialised countries need not necessarily imply a reduction in their *actual* rates of growth. A good example of this is provided again by the experience of the United Kingdom. The period 1950–1970 witnessed a rapid fall in Britain's share of world trade from 24.6 per cent in 1950 to 10.8 per cent in 1970. At the same time the share of imports of manufactures in Britain's home market increased from about 5 per cent to 18 per cent. Nevertheless, these twenty years of "full employment" registered a higher growth rate of the GDP in Britain than in any previous comparable period of history. The explanation is of course that the decennial growth rate of world industrial production was also twice to two and a half times as high as in any earlier period of history of comparable length.

(iii) In the matter of both absolute growth rates of the GDP and the rate of diminution of her share in world trade in manufactures Britain fared much worse than any of the other industrially developed countries. The performance of these other countries was far more uniform. Japan owed her exceptional success both to a high foreign world income elasticity of demand for her exports and an exceptionally low income elasticity of demand for manufactured imports (which no doubt was assisted by various forms of restraints on the imports of manufactures). In the case of Italy, on the other hand, an exceptionally high rate of growth of exports was offset by an exceptionally high income elasticity of demand for imports with the result that her growth record was not much better than average. This seems to have been true also of West Germany, though in her case both the rate of growth of exports and the absolute value of the income elasticity of demand for imports was lower than in the case of Italy. In the U.K., as we have seen, a falling share of world trade (at least up to the early 1970s—since then her share appears to have remained constant) was aggravated by a steadily rising income elasticity of demand for imports. To a lesser extent the same combination explains the disappointing record (at least in comparison with earlier periods) in the manufacturing output of the United States. However, the differences in growth rates which resulted from such differences in market performance were not sufficient to avoid chronic imbalances in the balance of payments. The trade gaining countries (Italy apart) failed to raise their internal growth rates sufficiently to make their imports rise as fast as their exports. In the case of the trade losing countries such as the U.K. and the U.S., internal employment policies, operated mainly through fiscal measures, have kept both domestic employment and the overall growth rate higher than what would have been consistent with continuous equilibrium in their balance of payments. They failed to reduce their import growth sufficiently to match their unsatisfactory rate of export growth.

(iv) This led to the emergence of chronic surplus countries (such as Germany and Japan, and since 1973 the members of OPEC) which caused a balance of payments constraint on the growth of the other industrialised exporters whose growth rates and employment levels were reduced below the levels necessary for full employment of their indigenous populations. (In the case of the successful industrial exporters the maintenance of the growth rate required—up to 1973—an increasing supplementation of their indigenous labour force with foreign guest workers!) These balance of payments constraints, by keeping domestic output and employment levels below potential, had unfavourable repercussions on the growth of world demand and hence on the growth prospects of the developing countries.

At the moment the world suffers from an insufficiency of demand for industrial products which most industrial countries however are not in a position to remedy, because of the need to avoid deficits in their balance of payments. It does not follow therefore that free trade leads to the maximum development of trade: if it involves chronic imbalances it might lead to a situation in which the world economy is in a state of continued recession, which cannot be effectively counterbalanced by national policies of economic management. Most governments and economists are in constant fear lest the state of recession will lead to the haphazard introduction of protective measures to domestic industries, which on balance will cause a further shrinkage of world demand. This may well happen in the absence of a co-ordinated policy, but my own prescription would not be that we must stick to free trade (whatever the cost), but to introduce a system of *planned trade* between the industrially developing countries on a multilateral basis. This means an agreed pattern of surpluses and deficits in the trade of manufactures between the developed countries, so as to remove the balance of payments constraint on their internal expansion.[1]

---

[1] The French Government in the year preceding the legislative election, under the leadership of M. Barre, advocated something similar with their slogan "Croissance ordonnée des échanges". It is possible however that this was a temporary slogan for the sake of electoral popularity since not much was heard about these policies after the last French elections.

Contrary to the actual policies adopted—which put trade restrictions mostly on imports from low wage developing countries—I would allow such imports freely since these countries have an unlimited appetite for manufactured imports of capital goods, which is only restrained by their ability to pay for them. Contrary to the general view, therefore, it is not the imports coming from the developing countries, but the import penetration of goods produced in *developed* countries which threatens major industries of other developed countries (such as the motor car industry in Britain or the television industry in the U.S.) and which requires some system of regulation of trade if we wish to remove existing impediments for the expansion of production and employment in the industrialised countries of the world.[1]

LABOUR-SAVING AND LAND-SAVING TECHNOLOGICAL PROGRESS

The general conclusion which emerges is that, barring impediments caused by trade imbalances between developed countries (which could arise irrespective of the rate of industrialisation of the developing countries), there is no necessary conflict of interest between the accelerated industrialisation of the developing countries and the economic interests of the developed countries provided the developed countries pursue full employment policies and avoid trade induced balance of payments constraints among themselves. The developing countries, as I have said earlier, are not likely to be a cause of such constraint—at least not for a long time to come—since they are not likely, apart from the OPEC group, to generate chronic surpluses in the current account of their balance of payments. On the contrary, they are much more likely to follow a policy of matching increased exports by increased imports. However, a conflict is only avoided if world

---

[1] It also requires the recycling of OPEC surpluses—a function which has been performed up to now, not by official institutions such as the IMF, but mainly by American private banks, operating through the Euro-dollar market. While I have no time to develop this theme on the present occasion, I think I ought to mention that I would favour as an instrument of such planning the introduction of some licensing system for imports of manufactures which is directly linked to exports, so that imports and exports are kept in some agreed balance.

industrial production continually accelerates so that the emergence of each new centre of industry is a net addition to the existing rates of growth of the other industrial countries. The question I must now raise is whether this could actually happen, and if it does, whether it could be maintained?

It is time for us to pay attention to the basic fact that, while for reasons stated earlier, industrialisation is the essence of fast development leading to high incomes per head, manufacturing industry is a *processing* industry. It is dependent on supplies which are the products of Nature—broadly agriculture and mining—because industrial activity consists of processing the crude products of nature. Raw materials, fuel and food are the three main products of the primary sector, and these form the "essential inputs" of the secondary and tertiary sectors. Among these, food is not a direct input (except for the food processing industries) but an indirect one, since its availability is essential for the employment of labour in secondary (or processing) activities. Agriculture supplies the basic foods; it also supplies many industrial materials, such as cotton, wool or timber. Mining supplies fossil fuels, which are the main sources of energy, as well as all the metallic ores.

The past two hundred years have witnessed a tremendous acceleration of technological progress, and it has become a commonplace to say that the greatly accelerated population growth and the tremendous accumulation of capital over this period were the consequences of new technologies, and not its causes. But it is not always kept in mind that technological progress is basically of two kinds; it is either labour-saving or land-saving (or more accurately, natural resource-saving). Most inventions tend to have elements of both. It is critically important, however, whether on balance, the labour-saving or the land-saving aspect predominates.

"Land-saving" inventions must be interpreted in a broad sense as any new invention or innovation which enables more resources to be got out of a given natural environment. Indeed the increasing density of the world's population, which is such a major feature of human history from the very earliest times of which we have a record, was really a consequence of an endless series of land-saving inventions. Settled agriculture (created by the discovery of the possibility of raising crops by cultivation and of domesticating animals), as well as the invention of the wheel, which enabled materials to be carried for much longer distances and at a much smaller expenditure of energy, are perhaps the most important ancient examples. Taking the last two hundred years, I would say that the discovery of a cheap and rapid means of transport by land and sea was a very important "land-saving" invention, because it made it possible to exploit the natural resources of more distant areas. But so were important inventions which enabled the substitution of a new process or a new material for an old process, using a material which threatened to become scarce. The most important examples are the invention of the coking of coal, which made it possible to free iron-making from dependence on timber (in the form of charcoal) at the very time when on account of large-scale deforestation timber was threatening to impose a severe constraint on growth in the western world; or the discovery first of coal, and then of mineral oil, as a source of energy. I would regard the invention of high-yielding variants of crops as falling into the same category, or even the discovery of new oil fields—since oil, which exists under the ground, but the knowledge of which is unknown, comes to the same thing as if it were non-existent. Finally there are all the synthetic materials (fibres, plastics or rubbers) which enormously reduce the natural resource content of the materials produced.

The fact that the primary sector has taken up a steadily falling proportion of the value of world output and an equally falling proportion of the human manpower—so that it now requires in the most developed countries 5 per cent or less of the labour force to produce enough food for the remaining 95 per cent, as well as for themselves—is proof that the improvement in the "arts of cultivation" (to use Ricardo's own expression) was more "land-saving" than "labour-saving" in character. It is for that reason that the dismal spectre of economic progress being brought to a halt by the increasing scarcity of land—the classical ghost of the Stationary State, which was regarded as the ineluctable consequence of the Law of Diminishing Returns—

has never materialised, despite all the gloomy predictions from Adam Smith through Ricardo down to John Stuart Mill. Population increased rapidly with the increase in the means of subsistence—just as Malthus predicted; yet the labour force required to procure food became proportionately steadily smaller, instead of steadily greater.

Yet if you regard the world as a whole and not just any single region or country trading with others, it is surely true to say that it is the growth in the output of primary products (of food, fuel and raw materials) which governs the rate of economic growth generally, and not the rate of capital accumulation or some exogenous growth rate in the labour force. This view is of course in sharp contrast to the neo-classical view which regards the "natural rate of growth" of any closed economy (*i.e.* of any wholly self-contained region) as being determined by the growth of the labour force, plus the growth of *labour* productivity due to technical progress. This view, which dominates the thinking of most professional economists, abstracts from Nature as a factor of production (or rather as a "constraint") entirely. This is because modern economics developed from the viewpoint of the advanced industrial countries, which did not in the period under review suffer from such constraints, since they were always able to procure the primary products necessary for their industrial expansion through the discovery and development of new areas, and through the relative plenitude of natural resource-saving innovations. Yet if you were thinking not in terms of the viewpoint of developed countries, but from the viewpoint of the world population as a whole, it is by no means as evident that poverty and under-development are not basically due to scarcity of natural resources, rather than to the insufficient availability of capital goods. The accumulation of capital is an inevitable concomitant of the development of industrial production; industrial production in any one self-contained region is limited in its extent by the growth of the agricultural surpluses which provide both the wage goods necessary for industrial employment and the sources of outside demand, which mainly sustain the growth of industrial products. The fact that such a large part of the world's population is not in effective employment—*i.e.* it is either totally unemployed or it makes no effective contribution to output, since it merely participates in some form of work sharing, *i.e.* in work which could equally well be done by fewer hands—is surely due to the insufficiency of food, far more than to the fact that their labour is less efficient at industrial tasks or uses more antiquated or primitive technology. If all the hundreds of millions who make no real contribution to world production of any magnitude were to be brought into effective employment the saleable output of agriculture would need to be enormously enlarged and correspondingly there would have to be greatly enlarged supplies of all forms of energy and raw materials. (To give but one example, the 300 million cultivable acres of India occupy several hundred million agricultural workers, but 90 per cent of these could be withdrawn from the land if the land were capable of producing the surpluses that would provide employment opportunities for them outside agriculture).

In the case of many important raw materials such as copper, production could be considerably enlarged, but any such enlargement requires investment in new mines with a long gestation period. In the case of rapidly exhaustable materials, such as oil, it also requires a decision (which is certainly not made automatically through the market) of how far the growth of current consumption is to be restrained for the sake of the future.

Clearly the industrialisation of the developing countries will require either a rapid increase in the supply of basic materials and energy, or else their re-allocation between different countries. At present it is estimated that the richest 20 per cent of the world's population absorbs for its own use more the 80 per cent of the world's energy and raw material output. It also absorbs a disproportionate part of the world's food output, at least when measured by value.

This dilemma could only be avoided if future technical progress was reorientated from its current "labour-saving" bias to one with a "natural resource-saving" bias. This, it seems to me, is the most important contribution which the superior intellectual capital of the industrialised countries could make to safeguard the future and enhance the prosperity of mankind as a whole—both for the populations of the developing countries and of their own. It is no good inventing "silicon chips"—the new micro-electronic technology which is potentially capable of enormous labour-saving in all sectors of the economy—if we do not also invent ways in which the land-content or rather the natural resource-content of a unit of final product is reduced at the same time.

For the moment the required balance between natural resource-saving and labour-saving technical progress is not attained—as is shown by the fact that the backlog of unintegrated labour in the less developed countries is rising rather than falling, and indeed it is the imbalance between these two kinds of inventions which in my view forms the only true cause of "structural" unemployment.

However, the long-term outlook is not necessarily hopeless. We may have dramatic new inventions—such as new forms of nuclear energy through a fusion rather than a fission of atoms, which, as far as we can see, would ensure absolutely unlimited energy supplies. Or we may invent radically new ways of utilising solar energy directly, instead of indirectly through fossil fuels. We could invent forms of food production which would not require large tracts of land, and we may also invent new synthetic materials which could be made out of materials like nitrogen, which could be drawn from air. But at the moment the danger is that, as the result of new inventions, labour productivity may rise dramatically, but the growth of total output will be constrained by the scarcity of natural resources such as oil, which would create more inequalities and more tensions in the world than if these new forms of labour-saving technical progress had never been invented.

14

CAPITALISM AND INDUSTRIAL DEVELOPMENT: SOME LESSONS FROM BRITAIN'S EXPERIENCE[1]

UNTIL fairly recently economic theory of the orthodox kind had very little to contribute to an understanding of the most important questions which occupy the minds of historians and politicians: why some countries or regions of the world grow relatively fast whilst the others stagnate or grow only slowly. The division of the world into rich and poor areas is now known to be the cumulative result of differences in the compound rates of economic growth which only emerged with modern industrial capitalism—the so-called Industrial Revolution which started in England in the late eighteenth century. Up to that time—as far as one can tell—the rate of economic growth was very slow everywhere and the differences in the living standards of the inhabitants of the different areas were comparatively small. The differences in the endowment of natural resources of different parts of the globe were largely balanced by differences in the density of population of those areas —the innate advantages of the areas of high fertility tended to be offset by comparatively high population density—with the exception of the newly colonised areas of the Western Hemisphere or Oceania where the settlers brought with them a superior technology capable of providing far more food than was required for their own numbers.

But with the Industrial Revolution, particular regions began to grow at exceptionally high rates by past standards, whilst others were left behind. Fast economic growth was largely, if not exclusively, the result of the establishment of large-scale enterprises in manufacturing industry. The countries which have succeeded

[1] First published (in Spanish) in *Política Económica en Centro y Periferia (Ensayos en Honor a Felipe Pazos)*, eds. Diaz Alejandro, Teitel and Tokman, Fondo di Cultura Económica, Mexico 1976, and in *Cambridge Journal of Economics*, no. 1, 1977.

in becoming large centres of industry have become richly endowed with capital—both in terms of plant, machinery etc. and of human skills, resulting from education. But while capital is the most important condition or prerequisite of high efficiency production, one cannot *explain* differences in the wealth of nations in terms of differences in "capital endowment" of the different countries, in the same manner as one *can* explain differences in population density by reference to differing endowments of natural resources, such as climate, rainfall, geology, etc. For in contrast to natural resources which exist independently of human activities, "capital endowment" is necessarily the *result* of such activities. It is impossible therefore to separate cause and effect: it is just as sensible —indeed more enlightening—to say that capital accumulation has resulted from industrial development than that it was the cause of such development. For taking manufacturing activities as a whole, the growth of output and the accumulation of capital are merely different aspects of a single process. Capitalistic production is "production of commodities by commodities"; individual industrial activities make use of goods produced by other industrial processes as their inputs, and provide outputs which (in the great majority of cases) serve as the inputs of further processes. If all the various commodities were "non-durable"—i.e., if they were consumed, or rather transformed into other products, in a relatively short period—the gross output of industry per unit period could be looked upon both as the capital stock which serves as an aid to labour in production and as the product of that labour. The fact that some goods are durable does not create any basic difference: capital and output would still grow together at much the same rate so long as in the course of growth, the product-mix between durable and non-durable goods remained roughly the same.

A.   CAUSES OF THE RISE OF MODERN CAPITALISM

To explain why certain countries have become industrialised and in the course of it have become richly endowed with capital, and gradually developed relatively high standards of living, we must enquire why modern industrial capitalism developed *when* it did—and why it developed in England and not in some other country, say in France for example, which at that time was a much larger entity and just as advanced, or even more advanced, in culture and economic prosperity. And we must further explain why and how it spread to a limited number of other countries in the following two centuries.

This is a standard question which economic historians of every generation attempt to answer afresh in the light of the prevailing doctrines of economics and sociology. (It is a commonplace that each generation of economic historians rewrites history in the light of the latest prevailing theory.) Thus a generation ago it was fashionable, under the influence of Weber and Tawney, to emphasise the role of Protestant ethic in the development of modern capitalism. Protestantism generated a favourable attitude to trade and money-making, whereas in Catholic countries the acquisitive instinct was suppressed and the bourgeois tradesmen had a much lower social status than the bourgeois professional, such as a lawyer.

An even earlier view regarded the industrial revolution as the result of a number of important technological inventions in the eighteenth century which, by accident rather than any more basic cause, happened to have been first invented in England. The most important of these were Watt's steam engine; the invention by Abraham Darby of coke (and gas) from the heating of coal which made it possible to smelt iron without the use of charcoal (by this invention, at one stroke, Western civilisation was freed from the menace of economic decline through deforestation and the exhaustion of timber supplies); and finally, there were the vast improvements in labour productivity in the textile industry through the invention of a fast spinning machine (the so-called "spinning jenny") and a fast weaving machine (the "flying shuttle").

No doubt these inventions played a very important role. So did the triumph of the reformation—not so much on account of changes in psychological attitudes, or in the social status of commercial activities, but through the development of laws and institutions, which were favourable to the establishment of freedom of trading, both in goods and in property, and thus of competition and market-orientated enterprise.

B. THE FACTORY SYSTEM

But in themselves none of these developments would have transformed the productive powers of society and its rhythm of change as dramatically as they did had it not been for another change, which was a great social innovation which could by no stretch of the meaning of words be regarded as a "discovery" or "invention" in the sense of being the product of the progress of physical or engineering knowledge—I am referring to the introduction of the "factory system". It is worth pausing to inquire how this came about, and what were its principal consequences.

Though there is no settled view on these things, there were two important factors which in my view led to the introduction of this system in England in the closing stages of the eighteenth century: first, the rise of a powerful class of merchant-capitalists resulting from the development of overseas trade, following on the establishment of the American colonies, and also from the "glorious revolution" of 1689 which secured in England the political and institutional framework for the development of competitive market enterprise.

The second important factor was the agrarian revolution of the eighteenth century—also connected with important technical discoveries, in the form of new crops, new methods of ploughing and planting, and new methods of breeding animals—which was peculiar in that it meant the expropriation, not of feudal "absentee" landlords, but of the peasantry. It was therefore the very opposite of what happened in France during the Great Revolution when the peasants freed themselves of feudal dues and took effective possession of the land which they cultivated. In England, through many hundreds of special Acts of Parliament, the landowners took effective possession by depriving the peasantry of their traditional grazing land, and the opportunity to raise crops in open fields. The newly "enclosed" land was thus cultivated in much larger units, and by new techniques, mostly by commercially minded tenant farmers who rented the land from the landlords. This had two important consequences. First, it led to a dramatic increase in the "agricultural surplus": the proportion of output which was in excess of agriculture's own needs for food, seed and feeding stuffs, and which was then produced for sale in the markets. (The existence of such a surplus is an essential prerequisite of urbanisation.) Second, it led to large numbers of peasants losing their traditional means of support on the land and being forced to seek employment away from their native surroundings—by "selling their labour", as Marx put it.

Until about 1780, the capitalist merchant-manufacturer made his profit mainly by buying raw materials—wool from domestic agriculture and cotton from overseas—and getting the spinner, the weaver, the dyer, etc. to process these materials in their own homes and with the aid of their own equipment much as a small dress-maker who would make a dress out of materials supplied by her customers in her own home, on her own sewing machine, and at her own pace. The capitalist entrepreneur owned the circulating capital through all stages of processing and occasionally made advance payments to the cottage artisans on their work contracts. But the latter owned the *tools* of their trade—the spinning wheel or the shuttle—and controlled the speed and the regularity with which the work was performed.

Even without the invention of new and more costly instruments —assisted first by water power and later by steam power—it was obvious that, given the emergence of a fast-growing urban prole-tariat without independent means of livelihood, the cost of pro-cessing materials into finished goods could be greatly reduced by erecting large buildings—"factories"— and fitting them up with enough equipment to occupy a large number of workers, who were hired to work for a fixed number of hours a day under close super-vision: the workers would then be paid by the *hour*, or by the *day*, and not by the *piece*. This "factory system" had enormous advan-tages for the capitalist entrepreneur even without the possibility of using large and more complex machinery than the individual artisan could obtain or use with advantage. For it made the close supervision of work performance much easier and far more eco-nomical and thus got the maximum out of any given labour force. But it became *practicable* only when there were large numbers of workers thrown off the land seeking to be hired.

The long-term consequences of the introduction of this factory system were even more revolutionary, for they led to a tremendous acceleration in the rate of technical progress. For once the merchant-capitalists cottoned on to the idea of "manufacturing" by building factories, equipping them with plant and machinery and with workers to man them, a process of cumulative technological change had begun—a permanent technological revolution the end of which is still not in sight. For the very system of "factory production" gave a continued and powerful incentive to the invention and installation of "bigger and better machines" which were increasingly labour-saving and able to produce goods on an ever-increasing scale. It also gave a continuous incentive for the invention of new products, of new processes, and for increasing specialisation in the making of parts and components.

Before the factory system was invented profit-seeking or "profit-maximising" enterprise was largely confined to trade: in other words, to buying things from the producers and transporting them to places where they could be sold to the best advantage. The merchant-capitalist of the Renaissance was "dynamic" enough in the continued search for new sources of supply and of new markets (hence the voyages of discovery and the emergence of the great trading companies of India, the Far East and of the West Indies) but he did not become directly responsible for the production of raw materials or their processing into finished products which remained in the hands of peasants, handicraftsmen or skilled artisans: in other words, traditionally minded producers, working largely with their own tools and their own labour, resistant by nature to change or innovation.

But with the introduction of the factory system, the thought of making fortunes by making goods cheaper—by introducing new methods and producing on a large scale with the aid of power-driven machinery—opened up a new dynamic phase in which the individual enterprise continually enlarged its scale of operations by accumulating capital and hiring more and more workers; and where the profits available for plough-back into the business set the limit to the rate of growth of the individual enterprise. Since increasing returns (the economies of large-scale production) appeared virtually inexhaustible, each entrepreneur strove to accumulate capital as fast as possible in order to keep ahead of, or at least to keep pace with, his rivals.

C. THE ROLE OF DEMAND

In the view of some of the keenest contemporary observers—such as Ricardo, John Stuart Mill or even Marx (at some stage)—the pace of this feverish expansion "fed on itself". So long as labour was available—and an unlimited supply of wage labour appeared to be ensured, partly through the destruction of independent small-scale enterprise which attended this development and partly by the rapid increase in population attributed, in a Malthusian manner, to the very fact that the demand for labourers was increasing—it was taken for granted that an increase in production itself generated the increase in purchasing power to ensure that the market for the commodities produced by capitalist enterprise increased *pari passu* with the scale of production. Since in the market, commodities are exchanged against commodities, money is just a circulating medium—"supply creates its own demand" and "there is no amount of capital which may not be employed in a country, because demand is only limited by production".[1] The point has been made even more forcibly by John Stuart Mill: "All sellers are inevitably and *ex vi termini* buyers. Could we suddenly double the productive powers of the country, we should double the supply of commodities in every market; but we should, by the same stroke, double the purchasing power." Hence "there is no over-production; production is not excessive, but merely ill-assorted".[2]

However if the "capitalist sector" of the economy does not embrace economic activity of *all kinds* (and in *all areas*) but is mainly confined to "manufactures"—i.e. the processing of crude materials through the aid of wage-labour—the purchasing power generated by the additional production of the capitalist sector will not in itself be sufficient to match the increase in supply: for only a proportion of the incomes earned in the capitalist sector (whether in the form of wages, profits or rents) will be spent on goods produced within that sector; the rest will generate demand for the products of other sectors, mainly agriculture.

Now it is in this context that the Say–Mill method of reasoning leads one astray. Mill would have said that if production in the

---

[1] Ricardo, *Principles* (Sraffa, ed.), pp. 290–2.
[2] John Stuart Mill, *Principles*, Book III, ch. xiv.

industrial sector expands too fast relative to the agricultural sector, production becomes "ill-assorted": but the movement of prices that would accompany that event, together with the free mobility of labour and capital, would bring its own remedy. Agricultural prices would rise in terms of industrial prices; this would cause capital (and labour) to flow from industry to agriculture until the returns on investment were again equalised: when that happened, the necessary balance between the sectors would have been re-established, and the demand for each commodity (and hence the demand for *all* commodities) would again be in balance with the supply. This result moreover would not have been regarded as being dependent on agriculture responding to an increase in demand for its products by increasing the supply of agricultural commodities. Even if—on account of the Law of Diminishing Returns—the supply of agricultural goods were inelastic, the operation of competitive markets would still ensure that equilibrium between market demand and supply in individual *sectors* is restored through the movement in prices. If agricultural goods are scarce, relative to industrial goods, agricultural prices will rise in terms of industrial prices: this will mean a transfer of "real" purchasing power from industry to agriculture; and this process will go on until the producers in the agricultural sector are able (and willing) to buy all the goods which industry is capable of producing in excess of industry's *own* requirements for industrial goods, whether for purposes of consumption, or capital investment.

Now it has long been perceived, though somewhat dimly, that there is something basically wrong with this account of how a capitalist market economy works. But few economists have been able to show convincingly just what is wrong with it: *which* is the critical point in the argument where the reasoning goes astray. In my view it is at the stage where the argument presupposes that the terms of trade "will go on improving" in favour of agriculture (i.e. agricultural prices will *go on* rising in terms of industrial prices) until the "excess supply" of industrial goods is eliminated.

This cannot happen (or is unlikely to happen) simply because "industry" is not an independent form of activity: it consists of the *processing* of goods produced on the land—either directly, as when raw wool or raw cotton is made into finished textiles; or indirectly, when the food produced in agriculture serves as the means of employing labour in industry.

Since industrial wages in terms of food cannot fall below a certain minimum, the "value added" by manufacturing activities cannot fall in terms of agricultural products below a certain minimum either (at any given productivity of labour in terms of industrial goods) and this sets a limit to the extent to which agricultural prices can rise in terms of industrial prices. (If agricultural prices rise in money terms, this will invariably carry with it, as the experience of many Latin American countries has shown, a corresponding rise in money wages in industry, so that a rise in agricultural prices induced by excess demand may result in a general rise in prices, even though in the relevant sense, there is an excess supply, not an excess demand, for industrial products.)

Given this fact—i.e. that the supply of goods produced by the capitalist industrial sector is highly elastic at a particular price in terms of agricultural goods (meaning that at given terms of trade between industry and agriculture the quantity supplied is highly responsive to the quantity demanded) it follows that both the level and the rate of growth of output of the capitalist sector is dependent on the level, or rate of growth, of the effective demand for its products coming from *outside* the capitalist sector. The pace at which both output and employment can grow and at which industrial capital will accumulate will thus be dependent on the growth of exogenous demand. The capitalist sector, beyond a certain stage, cannot grow on its own, lifting itself by its own bootstraps.

This means however that "Say's Law" will not apply when one considers the economic relationships between the "capitalist" and the "non-capitalist" sectors of the world economy, or, what comes to the same thing in broad approximation, the relationship between "industry" and "agriculture". Since in most areas of the world the population density of rural areas is adapted to, and varies with, the "productive powers" of the soil, it is these "productive powers" and not the available supply of labour, which will determine how much will be produced at any given time in any given area. Labour is an essential factor in all agricultural production, but it will not (normally) be a "scarce" factor—there will be "disguised unemployment" which will ordinarily be large relative to the population of working age. Hence the withdrawal of labour from rural areas will not cause any reduction in the amount of output derived from the soil; indeed any sizeable reduction in the population will normally be associated with an increase in land, as well as labour productivity, owing to the consequential changes in the organisation of farms and in technology.

Hence the "opportunity cost" of labour to industry, in terms of agricultural products foregone, will be zero or negative, but its actual cost will always be positive—the worker cannot survive, let alone perform work, below a certain real wage in terms of food.

It is this factor which makes the supply of industrial products elastic in terms of agricultural goods (in the sense defined above), irrespective of whether there is "full employment" or not. And it is the basic reason why Say's Law does not apply to the processing part of economic activities looked at in isolation; why Ricardo's statement that "there is no amount of capital which may not be employed in a country because demand is only limited by production" is basically untrue, if the term "country" is taken to apply to any actual country, such as Britain. This is because the demand generated by incomes earned in production *in* Britain can never be sufficient to match the production that gave rise to those incomes, since part of the demand thus generated is for goods produced in other countries, i.e. for imports. On the other hand, part of the demand for goods produced in Britain comes from abroad, and this part can be taken to be given more or less independently of incomes generated by production in Britain. For a country which imports food and raw materials and exports manufactures the Ricardian mechanism showing the equalisation of price levels and of payments balances through changes in the international distribution of precious metals (or, what comes to the same thing under modern conditions, through changes in the exchange rate) may be unavailing in securing "full employment equilibrium" through a lowering of the price of exports in terms of imports, precisely because, owing to the downward rigidity of the level of wages in terms of imported goods, the *price* of exports (given

G

the productivity of labour) may not be reduced, or not lastingly reduced, beyond a certain level.

This is the basis of the doctrine of "foreign trade multiplier" according to which the production of a country will be determined by the *external* demand for its products and will tend to be that multiple of that demand which is represented by the reciprocal of the proportion of *internal* incomes spent on imports. This doctrine asserts the very opposite of Say's Law: the level of production will not be confined by the availability of capital and labour; on the contrary, the amount of capital accumulated, and the amount of labour effectively employed at any one time, will be the resultant of the growth of external demand over a long series of past periods which permitted the capital accumulation to take place that was required for enabling the amount of labour to be employed and the level of output to be reached which was (or could be) attained in the current period.

Keynes, writing in the middle of the Great Depression of the 1930s, focussed his attention on the consequences of the failure to *invest* (due to unfavourable business expectations) in limiting industrial employment *below* industry's attained capacity to provide such employment; and he attributed this failure to excessive saving (or an insufficient propensity to consume) relative to the opportunities for profitable investment. Hence his concentration on liquidity preference and the rate of interest, as the basic cause for the failure of Say's Law to operate under conditions of low investment opportunities and/or excessive savings; and the importance he attached to the savings/investment multiplier as a short-period determinant of the level of production and employment.

In retrospect I believe it to have been unfortunate that the very success of Keynes's ideas in connection with the savings/investment multiplier diverted attention from the "foreign trade multiplier" which, over longer periods, is a far more important and basic factor in explaining the growth and rhythm of industrial development. For over longer periods Ricardo's presumption that capitalists only save in order to invest, and hence the *proportion* of profits saved would adapt to changes in the profitability of investment, seems to me more relevant; the limitation of effective demand due to over-saving is a short-run (or cyclical) phenomenon, whereas the rate of growth of "external" demand is a more basic, long run determinant of both the rate of accumulation and the growth of output and employment in the "capitalist" or "industrial" sectors of the world economy.

From the point of view of any particular centre of industry (I use this term advisedly—in preference to "country") the growth of such "outside" demand is partly the result of increased "market penetration" (which means gains in trade achieved at the expense of producers in other industrial centres or of small-scale "pre-capitalist" enterprise) and partly it reflects the increased purchasing power of the agricultural sector due to a rise in agricultural productivity and the consequent rise in the marketable surplus. The rate of industrial growth will thus be dependent on the growth of "exports"—using that term in the specific sense of sales *outside* the particular industrial centre, as against sales *within* it.

Contrary to the traditional view which attributed the rate of industrial development in England to the rate of saving and capital accumulation and to the rate of technical progress due to invention and innovation, more recent evidence tends to suggest that Britain's industrial growth was "export-led" from a very early date. This is clearly shown by the timing of fluctuations in industrial output and investment which, both in the eighteenth century and since the early railway boom at any rate, were regularly preceded by fluctuations in the volume of exports.

Britain, being the first country to manufacture goods in factories on a large scale, was able to increase her exports at a fast rate, partly at the expense of other exporting countries (such as France) but largely by competing successfully with small local producers in other countries. The growth of exports of British-made cotton goods to India and China in the nineteenth century meant a severe shrinkage of local small-scale enterprise—the virtual disappearance of locally made handwoven cloth—without any compensation in the form of alternative employment opportunities for the people displaced. With the transport revolution, vast areas became accessible to trade, and regions previously self-contained were increasingly drawn into the network of the world economy. But while the growth of industries in Britain (followed by other countries of Western Europe) created new markets for temperate foodstuffs, tropical products and minerals, it also meant the increasing displacement of local small-scale industries, with the attendant increase in disguised unemployment and poverty.

D. CAUSES OF BRITAIN'S DECLINE

The third quarter of the nineteenth century—more precisely, the years 1846–73—saw the zenith of Britain's predominance in industrial production. This was the period in which Britain's share of world trade in manufactured goods was at its highest, and British exports showed the fastest growth.

From then on, Britain experienced a continuing loss of foreign markets caused by the industrialisation of other countries. A succession of countries—Germany, then France, then the United States, then the smaller countries of Western Europe, and finally Japan—went through the same succession of stages of industrial development, fostered in every case by protective tariffs and other forms of Government support. The first stage was the substitution of home production for imports in the so-called "light industries" (consumer goods) and then the development of an export potential in such goods; then the development of the so-called "heavy industries", or the capital goods industries—such as steel, engineering and shipbuilding—again, first to provide substitutes for imports in these categories and then to develop an export potential. Each of these countries provided at some stage a major market for British goods; indeed a large increase in the demand for British made plant and machinery accompanied the early stages of industrialisation in most countries—including that of the United States or Japan. But in each case this was a *transitional* phenomenon: as industrial development proceeded, each of these countries became not just self-sufficient but an important supplier of such goods in the world market, and thus an important competitor to Britain in third markets. So the destination of British exports was constantly shifting: the British machinery sold to Germany in the 1880s and to America in the 1890s went to Japan in the 1900s and to India, Australia and South Africa after the First World War. This meant that the rate of growth of British exports to the outside world became slow and uncertain: for a period of about sixty to seventy years, Britain succeeded in making up for the loss of exports in a succession of markets by the development of new markets in other places, supported by heavy British investment, as in the railways of India or Latin America. But the net outcome was not only that Britain's share in world trade kept on declining, but the rate of growth of her manufactured exports, and that of her manufactured production as a whole, remained considerably lower than that of the countries the industrialisation of which was of more recent origin.

Thus the very fact of being the country which gave birth to modern industry—the "arch-capitalist" country—which gave Britain such a strong competitive advantage over other countries in the first seventy-five years of the last century, actually turned into a serious handicap in the subsequent seventy-five years. This is because of two basic features of capitalism which are rarely emphasised or properly understood. The first of these is that in an unregulated market economy the *growth* of industrial production is strongly dependent on the growth of the market, which means demand originating from outsiders—the latter may come from the growth of her own agriculture or through exports to other countries. The second is the so-called "Verdoorn Law"—the strong correlation between the growth of output per worker and the growth of *total* output, which in turn is a reflection of "increasing returns" or the economies of large-scale production. As a result of the latter, the faster the "effective demand" for a country's industry is growing, the faster the rate of growth of productivity and of real income per head.

As the experience of the last hundred years has shown, the *successful* latecomers to industrialisation were able to attain much faster rates of growth both of "outside" sales and of total production than Britain achieved in the heyday of her industrial supremacy, and for that reason were able to overtake her, one after another, in a relatively short space of time. This is because, given the size and the rate of growth of the world market at any one time (including in that notion any particular country's "own" or "protected" market) the *successful* challenger who is able to increase its share in the world market is bound to have a faster rate of growth than that of the market as a whole and, *a fortiori*, of the country whose share in the world market is reduced in consequence.

There can be little doubt that throughout the nineteenth century and also in the present century, right up to the Second World War, Great Britain's economic growth was closely dependent on the growth of her exports. Given the fact that her share of the world market was bound to decline continually as a result of the industrialisation of other countries, whereas the share of the later industrialisers—at least of the "successful" industrialisers (on this more below)—was bound to increase over sustained periods, it was quite inevitable that both the growth of production and the accumulation of capital should be much lower in Britain than in the countries that were subsequently industrialised and became major competitors of Britain as exporters of manufactured goods. As the world was "catching up" with Britain in the development of modern capitalism, her opportunities for continued economic growth were continually threatened and became increasingly precarious.

Many economic historians have attributed the major cause of Britain's relative decline from the last quarter of the nineteenth century onwards to poor industrial management,[1] to the failure to keep up with the growth of modern technology in comparison to countries such as Germany and the United States which had a more advanced network of educational institutions in industrial technology. No doubt such factors played a role in the speed with which Britain lost markets to her more "dynamic" competitors. But so long as other countries were able to expand their industries under the umbrella of protective tariffs and thereby reduce the market for British goods through the process of "import-substitution" and through exports to third markets, Britain was bound to operate under a strong handicap, as the growth of both her industrial investment and her labour productivity lagged increasingly behind the others, steadily weakening her competitive strength, and for these basic disadvantages the exploitation of the international advantages and know-how of the London capital market, and the development of protected overseas markets under

---

[1] See, e.g., D. H. Aldcroft: "The Entrepreneur and the British Economy, 1870–1914", *Economic History Review* (2nd series), August 1964, pp. 113–34.

Imperial preference could offer but temporary and limited compensation.

E. THE POST-WAR ERA

The last twenty-five years have had a number of unique and unexpected features. There was an unprecedented boom in the world economy, sustained over several decades and interrupted only by short and minor setbacks. Due to the successive reductions in obstacles to trade—through the G.A.T.T. treaties, the creation of the Common Market and of E.F.T.A. and other preferential areas—there was an increasing interchange of industrial goods *between* the highly industrialised countries; both their exports and imports of manufactured goods increased at a faster rate than the total domestic production or consumption of such goods. This was in sharp contrast to the period 1880–1940, which was characterised by increased economic nationalism and industrial autarky: international trade in manufactures grew *less fast* than world industrial production. The post-First World War policies were more successful in exploiting economies of specialisation and large-scale production, and were attended by much faster rates of growth of the productivity of labour.

All fast-growing industrial countries had an even faster rate of growth of output in their manufacturing sector and this was associated with a rate of growth of *exports* of manufactures which in turn was considerably higher than the rates of growth of their *total* output of manufactured goods. This was true of nine of the eleven industrialised countries which account for 85–90 per cent. of total world trade in manufactures—the two exceptions being the U.S. and the U.K., whose joint share of world trade diminished from 40 per cent. to 20 per cent. in the last twenty years. (By contrast the share in world trade of the three trade-gaining countries—Germany, Italy and Japan—rose from 20 to 40 per cent., while the remaining countries maintained a more or less stable share of world trade in manufactures, the overall volume of which showed an almost uninterrupted accelerating trend.)

Thus the growth of all fast-growing countries appears to have been "export-led". The two conspicuous exceptions were Britain and the U.S., whose rates of economic growth, however, were also highly satisfactory by their own historical standards—though their growth was appreciably lower than that of the other advanced industrial countries of the post-war period.

In the case of Britain the adoption of Keynesian policies of economic management after 1945 meant that the growth of demand for industrial production, and therefore the level of industrial investment, was no longer *dependent* on the growth of export demand. The pursuit of "full employment policies" involved the substitution of "consumption-led" growth for "export-led" growth.[1] This meant that instead of having a chronic insufficiency of effective demand, manifesting itself in low investment and heavy unemployment, there was a chronic tendency for the growth of imports to outpace the growth of exports, leading to periodic balance of payments crises and consequent sharp reversals of domestic policies—the so-called "stop-go". Despite these periodic interruptions, the quarter of the century following the Second World War recorded a higher rate of growth in G.N.P., in output per head, and even in exports than any previous twenty-five-year period in British history. It appears paradoxical, but in the light of our analysis by no means surprising, that during the very period when Britain was consistently at the bottom of the "League tables" in terms of the rate of economic growth in relation to other advanced countries, she was at the top in terms of her *own* historical record. This was because despite its obvious limitations (particularly under a regime of fixed exchange rates) a deliberate policy of demand management through fiscal measures *did* ensure a certain rate of growth of industrial capacity and this in turn induced, as a by-product, a steady growth in the capacity to export which might not have occurred otherwise.[2]

In the case of the United States also, Keynesian policies of demand management, combined with a large increase in the scale of public expenditure in relation to the G.N.P., ensured a rate of growth of effective demand independently of exports which

---

[1] This distinction, and the consequential effects of the two kinds of growth on productivity etc. are set out at some length in my paper "Conflicts in National Economic Objectives", *Economic Journal*, March 1971, pp. 10–16, and reprinted in *Further Essays on Economic Theory*, pp. 155–75.

[2] The proportion of the G.N.P. devoted to industrial investment was more than twice as great as in the inter-war period. See R. C. O. Matthews, *Economic Journal*, September 1968, p. 559.

in the latter parts of the period was attended by a chronic and growing deficit in the balance of payments: though unlike Britain, the U.S., by virtue of the international position of the dollar, was never forced into the position of having to contract demand internally for the sake of the balance of payments.

It is an open question how far the growing payments deficit of the U.S.—which was largely a reflection of her own fiscal policies —was not itself a major contributory factor to the sustained expansionary climate of the world economy. Clearly this rapid progress would not have occurred without a rapid growth in the overall world demand for industrial goods—which involved in turn a rapid growth in the supply of food and basic materials absorbed by the industrial sectors. The rapid and sustained growth of agricultural yields was the most important and perhaps the least expected feature of this period. So far, despite growing forebodings of the shape of things to come, the growth, both of agricultural productivity and of raw material extraction—fuels, fibres and minerals—kept pace, or more than kept pace, with the demands of the industrial centres.[1]

This post-war period was conspicuous however for its failures as well as its successes; and the really intriguing question is why industrial capitalism failed to "take off" in so many countries when it succeeded in others.

In the pre-First World War period (and to a large extent also in the pre-Second World War period) a considerable part of the underdeveloped world had a colonial status—their development policies were governed by the colonial powers that ruled over them and whose interest dictated that they should develop as raw material producers and provide markets for the industrial goods which they themselves produced.

But with the disappearance of colonies there was no reason why the process of industrial development should not "take off" in these countries in much the same way as it did in say, Germany of the 1880s or in Japan of the 1920s.

Yet in a large number of countries industrialisation has not succeeded in raising productivity, employment and living stan-

---

[1] This was true at the time of writing. Since then the situation has changed as described in my 1976 paper. See *Further Essays on Economic Theory*, pp. 214-30.

dards in the dramatic manner of the "successful" developers of Western Europe or Japan. In a number of Latin American countries the tempo of economic growth originating in the industrialisation which began in the 1930s and was much stimulated during the Second World War, tended to peter out subsequently. In others, such as India and Pakistan, a succession of comprehensive development plans failed to bring about any significant improvement in living standards.

The single common characteristic of all these countries is that they failed to develop a significant volume of exports in manufactured goods. The stimulus to industrial production came from high tariffs or severe quantitative restrictions on imports. This made it profitable to develop home industries in substitution for imports, but since the exogenous component of demand for the products of industry was confined to the purchasing power of the agricultural sector, which was limited, and improved only slowly, the basis for a sustained growth of industrial production was lacking, once the opportunities for "easy" import substitution were exhausted.

Their failure to follow up the import-substitution stage with the export stage no doubt reflected the fact that the productivity of labour in industry, given the level of real wages in terms of foodstuffs and raw materials, had not risen to the point at which the costs of "value-added by fabrication" became low enough, in terms of unprocessed materials, to enable them to compete in the world market.

This is not just a matter of the *size* of the market in the individual country, but of the degree of concentration and dispersion in industrial development. There have been a number of small countries—from Switzerland to Hong Kong—who succeeded in becoming major exporters of industrial products by concentrating their industrial effort over a narrow field—i.e. by developing *certain* industries to the stage at which they have become major exporters before extending import-substitution to others. The secret of "successful" industrialisation thus appears to be an "outward strategy"—to develop the ability to compete in export markets in selected fields at a relatively early stage of development, and to keep the growth of export capacity in line with the growth of industrial activities.

PART IV

THE CHALLENGE TO EQUILIBRIUM THEORY

THE IRRELEVANCE OF EQUILIBRIUM ECONOMICS[1]

The purpose of my lecture today is to explain why, in my view, the prevailing theory of value—what I called, in a shorthand way, "equilibrium economics"—is barren and irrelevant as an apparatus of thought to deal with the manner of operation of economic forces, or as an instrument for non-trivial predictions concerning the effects of economic changes, whether induced by political action or by other causes. I should go further and say that the powerful attraction of the habits of thought engendered by "equilibrium economics" has become a major obstacle to the development of economics as a *science*—meaning by the term "science" a body of theorems based on assumptions that are *empirically* derived (from observations) and which embody hypotheses that are capable of verification both in regard to the assumptions and the predictions.

The word "equilibrium" in economics is used, of course, in all kinds of contexts—in Keynesian economics for example, or in theory of the balance of payments, and so on. I should therefore make clear that the notion of equilibrium to which I refer is that of the general economic equilibrium originally formulated by Walras, and developed, with ever-increasing elegance, exactness, and logical precision by the mathematical economists of our own generation, of whom perhaps the French economist, Gerard Debreu, is now regarded as the most prominent exponent.[2]

Taken at its purest and most abstract level, the pretensions of this equilibrium theory are modest enough. Although Debreu describes the subject-matter of his book as "the *explanation* of the

[1] Originally delivered as the Goodricke Lecture at the University of York, May 10, 1972. First printed in the *Economic Journal*, Vol. 82, December 1972.
[2] *Theory of Value, An Axiomatic Analysis of Economic Equilibrium*, Cowles Foundation Monograph no. 17, New York, 1959.

price of commodities resulting from the interaction of the agents of a private ownership economy",[1] it is clear that the term "explanation" is not used in the ordinary everyday sense of the term. It is intended in a purely logical and not in a "scientific" sense; in the strict sense, as Debreu says, the theory is "logically entirely disconnected from its interpretation". It is not put forward as an explanation of how the actual prices of commodities are determined in particular economies or in the world economy as a whole. By the term "explanation" Debreu means a set of theorems that are *logically* deducible from precisely formulated assumptions; and the purpose of the exercise is to find the minimum "basic assumptions" necessary for establishing the existence of an "equilibrium" set of prices (and output/input matrixes) that is (*a*) unique, (*b*) stable, (*c*) satisfies the conditions of Pareto optimality. The whole progress of mathematical economics in the last thirty to fifty years lay in clarifying the minimum requirements in terms of "basic assumptions" more precisely: without any attempt at verifying the realism of those assumptions, and without any investigation of whether the resulting theory of "equilibrium prices" has any explanatory power or relevance in relation to actual prices.

I. AXIOMATIC THEORY AND SCIENTIFIC HYPOTHESIS

It would take me too long to enumerate all these basic assumptions; it would also lead me away from my main argument. But unlike any scientific theory, where the basic assumptions are chosen on the basis of direct observation of the phenomena the behaviour of which forms the subject-matter of the theory, the basic assumptions of economic theory are either of a kind that are unverifiable—such as that producers "maximise" their profits or consumers "maximise" their utility—or of a kind which are directly contradicted by observation—for example, perfect competition, perfect divisibility, linear-homogeneous and continuously differentiable production functions, wholly impersonal market relations, exclusive rôle of prices in information flows and perfect knowledge of all relevant prices by all agents and

---

[1] *Ibid.*, p. vii, italics mine.

perfect foresight. There is also the requirement of a constant and unchanging set of *products* (goods) and of a constant and unchanging set of *processes of production* (or production functions) over time—though neither category, goods nor processes, is *operationally* defined: in other words, no attempt is made to show how these axiomatic concepts are to be defined or recognised in relation to empirical material.

While this pure theory is not *intended* to describe reality, it is put forward as the necessary conceptual framework—the necessary starting point—for any attempt at explaining how a "decentralised" system works; how individuals guided entirely by the market, or rather by price information, sort themselves out between different activities and thereby secure the maximum satisfaction both to themselves and, in the specific Pareto-sense, to society as a whole.

Indeed it is the deep underlying belief, common to all economists of the so-called "neo-classical" school, that general equilibrium theory is the one and only starting point for any logically consistent explanation of the behaviour of de-centralised economic systems. This belief sustained the theory despite the increasing (*not* diminishing) arbitrariness of its basic assumptions—which was forced upon its practitioners by the ever more precise cognition of the needs of logical consistency. In terms of gradually converting an "intellectual experiment" (to use Professor Kornai's phrase)[1] into a scientific theory—in other words, into a set of theorems directly related to observable phenomena[2]—the

---

[1] J. Kornai, *Anti-Equilibrium. On economic systems theory and the tasks of research*, Amsterdam, North Holland Publishing Co., 1971, p. 11.

[2] The difference between a scientific theory and an "axiomatic" theorem has been well put by Einstein:

"Physics constitute a logical system of thought which is in a state of evolution, whose basis cannot be distilled, as it were from experience by an inductive method, but can only be arrived at by free invention. The justification (truth content) of the system rests in the verification of the derived propositions by sense experiences."

"The skeptic will say: 'it may well be true that this system of equations is reasonable from a logical standpoint. But it does not prove that it corresponds to nature'. You are right, dear skeptic. Experience alone can decide on truth."

A. Einstein, *Ideas and Opinions*, New York, 1960, pp. 322 and 355 (quoted by Kornai, *op. cit.*, pp. 9–10).

The difference mainly resides in this. In the case of physics, any fundamental reconsideration of the basic "axioms" of the system is the result of observations which could not be made consistent with existing hypotheses. Examples (chosen at random) are the observation that the amount of radiation emitted by Pitchblende was greater than could be accounted for by the absorption of sunlight; that a stream of light

development of theoretical economics was one of continual *de*gress, not *pro*gress: the ship appears to be much further away from the shore now than it appeared to its originators in the nineteenth century. The latest theoretical models, which attempt to construct an equilibrium path through time with all prices for all periods fully determined at the start under the assumption that everyone foresees future prices correctly to eternity, require far more fundamental "relaxations" for their applicability than was thought to be involved in the original Walrasian scheme. The process of removing the "scaffolding", as the saying goes—in other words of *relaxing* the unreal basic assumptions—has not yet started. Indeed, the scaffolding gets thicker and more impenetrable with every successive reformulation of the theory, with growing uncertainty as to whether there is a solid building underneath.

Yet the main lessons of these increasingly abstract and unreal theoretical constructions are also increasingly taken on trust—as if in the social sciences, unlike the natural sciences, the problem of verification could be passed over or simply ignored. It is generally taken for granted by the great majority of academic economists that the economy always approaches, or is near to, a state of "equilibrium"; that equilibrium, and hence the near-actual state of the world, provides goods and services to the maximum degree consistent with available resources; that there is full and efficient utilisation of every kind of "resource"; that the wage of every kind and quality of labour is a measure of the net contribution (per unit) of these varying kinds and qualities of labour to the total product; that the rate of profits reflects the net advantage of substituting capital for labour in production, etc., etc.—all propositions which the *pure* mathe-

---

which passed through a glass and was directed at a mirror at some particular angle is not reflected by the mirror; or that there is a "reddening" of the spectrum observed in distant stars. In economics, observations which contradict the basic hypotheses of prevailing theory are generally ignored: the "theorist" and the "empiricist" operate in two isolated compartments and the challenge of anomalous observations is ignored by the theorist—as something that could be taken into account at the stage of "second approximation" without affecting the basic hypotheses. And where empirical material is brought into conjunction with a theoretical model, as in econometrics, the rôle of empirical estimation is to "illustrate" or to "decorate" the theory, not to provide support to the basic hypothesis (as for example, in the case of numerous studies purporting to estimate the coefficients of production functions).

matical economist has shown to be valid only on assumptions that are manifestly unreal—that is to say, directly contrary to experience and not just "abstract". In fact, equilibrium theory has reached the stage where the pure theorist has successfully (though perhaps inadvertently) demonstrated that the main implications of this theory cannot possibly hold in reality, but has not yet managed to pass his message down the line to the textbook writer and to the classroom.

Yet without a major act of demolition—without destroying the basic conceptual framework—it is impossible to make any real progress. There is, I am sure, a vague sense of dissatisfaction, open or suppressed, with the current state of economics among most members of the economics profession—as is evidenced, for example, by recent Presidential addresses to the Royal Economic Society and to section F of the British Association.[1] On the one hand it is increasingly recognised that abstract mathematical models lead nowhere. On the other hand it is also recognised that "econometrics" leads nowhere—the careful accumulation and sifting of statistics and the development of refined methods of statistical inference cannot make up for the lack of any basic understanding of how the actual economy works. Each year new fashions sweep the "politico-economic complex" only to disappear again with equal suddenness—who can now recollect the great revival of the quantity theory of money of three years ago, or the more recent belief that frequent fiscal adjustments, guided by the best forecasting techniques, can maintain the steady growth of the economy at its pre-determined growth potential, not to speak of the Phillips Curve? These sudden bursts of fashion are a sure sign of the "pre-scientific" stage, where any crazy idea can get a hearing simply because nothing is known with sufficient confidence to rule it out.

---

[1] E. H. Phelps Brown, "The Underdevelopment of Economics"; G. D. N. Worswick, "'Is Progress in Economic Science Possible?", *Economic Journal*, March 1972, pp. 9–20 and 73–86.

II. WHERE ECONOMIC THEORY WENT WRONG

The difficulty with a new start is to pinpoint the critical area where economic theory went astray. In my own view, it happened when the theory of value took over the centre of the stage—which meant focusing attention on the *allocative* functions of markets to the exclusion of their *creative* functions—as an instrument for transmitting impulses to economic change.

To locate the source of error with more precision, I would put it in the middle of the fourth chapter of Vol. I of the *Wealth of Nations*. The first three chapters are devoted to the principle of the Division of Labour. These explain that the larger the production, the lower real cost per unit tends to be, because the larger the production, the more efficient the modes of production that can be employed: the greater the specialisation and the sub-division into different processes. In the first chapter Smith gave numerous reasons for this basic law, beautifully illustrated by the example of pin-making. In the second chapter he explains the peculiarly human characteristic of the propensity to truck, barter and exchange one thing for another—"nobody ever saw a dog make a fair exchange of one bone for another with another dog"—which alone makes it possible to develop the division of labour through social co-operation. Indeed for Smith the existence of a "social economy" and the existence of increasing returns were closely related phenomena. And the third chapter, perhaps the most significant of them all, is devoted to the proposition "that the division of labour is limited by the extent of the market"—a theorem which Allyn Young, writing 150 years later (in a paper to which I shall refer more extensively presently), regarded as "one of the most illuminating and fruitful generalisations which can be found anywhere in the whole literature of economics".

But in the following chapter, after discussing the need for money in a social economy, Smith suddenly gets fascinated by the distinction between money price, real price and exchange value, and from then on, hey presto, his interest gets bogged down in the question of how values and prices for products and factors are determined. One can trace a more or less continuous development of price theory from the subsequent chapters of Smith through Ricardo, Walras, Marshall, right up to Debreu and the most sophisticated of present-day Americans.

The basic assumption of this theory is constant costs, or constant returns to scale. With Smith and Ricardo, this was implicit in the very notion of the "natural price" determined solely by costs of production (irrespective of demand). With the neo-classical school—in any rigorous formulation of it—it was explicit in the assumption of homogeneous and linear production functions which is one of the required "axioms" necessary to make the assumptions of perfect competition and profit-maximisation consistent with one another.[1] Though Marshall, through the notion of "external economies" and the use of the partial equilibrium technique, thought he could accommodate both increasing and decreasing returns to scale within the same analytical framework—an attempt which was shown to be logically faulty in Piero Sraffa's famous 1926 article on the Laws of Returns[2]—the general equilibrium school (as distinct from Marshall) has always fully recognised the *absence* of increasing returns as one of the basic "axioms" of the system. As a result, the existence of increasing returns and its consequences for the whole framework of economic theory have been completely neglected.

III. THE DOMINATING ROLE OF INCREASING RETURNS

Yet on an empirical level, nobody doubts that in any economic activity which involves the processing or transformation of basic materials—in other words, in industry—increasing returns dominate the picture for the very reasons given by Adam Smith in the first chapter of the *Wealth of Nations*: reasons that are

---

[1] This of course, embraces the classical case of increasing costs of production (in terms of labour and capital) due to the fixity of supply of land, provided the fixed factor earns its due rent. It is *not* consistent however with diminishing returns to scale—when *all* factors are increased in the same proportion, and the product increases in less than the same proportion—due, e.g., to "external diseconomies."

[2] "The Laws of Returns under Competitive Conditions", *Economic Journal*, December 1926, p. 535. To be fair, Sraffa's critique had more relevance to the "Marshallian school" at Cambridge (and particularly to Pigou) than to Marshall himself who always expressed considerable doubt about the applicability of the theory of "normal price" to the case of increasing returns. (See particularly Appendix H of the *Principles*.)

fundamental to the nature of technological processes and not to any particular technology.[1] One aspect of this is that *plant costs* per unit of output necessarily decrease with size in any integrated process of operation—such as a steel plant, a chemical plant, an electricity generator or an oil tanker—simply on account of the three-dimensional nature of space.[2] Provided the technical problems of construction can be solved, an increase in size is bound to bring further cost reductions since capacity is bound to increase faster than construction cost.[3] In the last decade, for example, there have been very large increases in the size of generating stations, of oil tankers and of the "optimal" steel plants, and there appears to be no reason why this process should come to a halt.

Another aspect, to which Allyn Young attributed major importance, is the break-up of complex processes into a series of simple processes, "some of which at least lend themselves to the use of machinery." He argued that the extent to which capital is used in relation to labour is predominantly a matter of the scale of operations—the capital/labour ratio in production is a function of the extent of the market rather than of relative factor prices.[4]

---

[1] As Smith emphasised in the first chapter, the opportunities for enrichment through a greater division of labour are far more important in manufactures than in agriculture: "The most opulent nations, indeed, excel all their neighbours in agriculture as well as in manufactures; but they are commonly more distinguished by their superiority in the latter than the former."

[2] For a discussion of this cf. G. C. Hufbauer, *Synthetic Materials and the Theory of International Trade*, Duckworth, London, 1966, pp. 46 ff. For a much earlier account of the same idea, cf. E. A. G. Robinson, *The Structure of Competitive Industry*, Cambridge, 1931, pp. 29–31.

[3] For example, the cost of construction of a cylinder (or a pipeline) may be assumed to vary with the size of the diameter, since $2r\pi$ will indicate the size of the surface to be covered per unit of length. The capacity of the cylinder will grow on the other hand as the square of the radius, $r^2\pi$. Since a larger cylinder will require a thicker steelplate, the material costs will increase more than in proportion, but the labour costs will increase less than in proportion. Assuming that labour and material costs *together* vary in linear proportion to r, and assuming that one wished to describe this relation in terms of a "production function" of the Cobb-Douglas type (i.e., with a constant elasticity of substitution of unity) the sum of the coefficients of the function would add up exactly to 2. See also Appendix on "Indivisibilities and Increasing Returns," below.

[4] "It would be wasteful to make a hammer to drive a single nail; it would be better to use whatever awkward implement lies conveniently at hand. It would be wasteful to furnish a factory with an elaborate equipment of specially constructed jigs, lathes, drills, presses and conveyors to build a hundred automobiles; it would be better to rely mostly upon tools and machines of standard types, *so as to make a relatively larger use of directly-applied and a relatively smaller use of indirectly-applied labour.* Mr. Ford's

Finally, there are the inventions and innovations induced by experience to which Adam Smith paid the main emphasis— what we now call "learning by doing," or "dynamic economies of scale". The advance in scientific knowledge in physics or in the science of engineering in the laboratory cannot by itself secure the innumerable design improvements that result from the repeated application of particular engineering principles. The optimum design for the steam engine or for the diesel engine or the sewing machine has only been achieved after many years or decades of experience: that for the nuclear power plant is still far away. The gain in design through experience is even more important in the making of plant and equipment; hence the *annual* gain of productivity due to "embodied technical progress" will tend to be all the greater the larger the number of plants constructed per year.[1]

It was left to Allyn Young to explore the main implications of Adam Smith's theorem on the manner of operation of economic forces in his famous article "Increasing Returns and Economic Progress", originally given as a Presidential address to Section F of the British Association in 1928.[2] On re-reading this paper after a lapse of many years, I feel convinced that it was so many years ahead of its time that the progress of economic thought has passed it by despite the attention it received at the time of its original publication. Economists ceased to take any notice of it long before they were able to grasp its full revolutionary implications. This was partly because Young was a man of exceptional

---

methods would be absurdly uneconomical if his output were very small, and would be unprofitable even if his output were what many other manufacturers of automobiles would call large." *Op. cit.*, below, p. 530, italics added.

[1] On all these aspects there is a rapidly growing volume of empirical evidence, which makes the neglect of increasing returns by the theoretical model-builders all the more surprising. Taking only more recent publications, there is, apart from the sources cited by Hufbauer, *op. cit.*, the Annex on "Industrial Profiles" to the *Manual of Industrial Project Analysis* issued by the O.E.C.D. Development Centre (the Manual, but *not* the Annex, was prepared by I. M. D. Little and J. A. Mirrlees) which shows very large scale-economies in every one of the 18 types of industrial activities, such as brick-making, sugar manufacture, meat packaging, ironfounding, etc. for which detailed estimates are given. C. F. Pratten found (*Economies of Scale in Manufacturing Industry* D.A.E. Occasional Paper No. 28, Cambridge University Press, 1971) that of 44 types of activities examined, the minimum efficient scale for a *single plant* is 100 per cent or more of total U.K. output in 7 cases, and in the range of 25–80 per cent in 10 other cases. (This does not take into account, of course, economies due to greater differentiation and subdivision of processes.)

[2] *Economic Journal*, December 1928, pp. 527–42.

modesty who underplayed, rather than emphasised, the full implication of what he was saying; his manner of exposition is suggestive, rather than compelling, and at times (as for example in the Appendix attached to the paper) obscure. It was partly also because its importance as a basic criticism of general equilibrium theory could not be appreciated at a time when that theory itself was not properly understood.

The consequences of abandoning the axiom of "linearity" and assuming that, in general, the production of any one commodity, or any one group of commodities, is subject to increasing returns to scale, are very far-reaching. The first and most important casualty is the notion of "general equilibrium" as such. The very notion of "general equilibrium" carries the implication that it is legitimate to assume that the operation of economic forces is constrained by a set of exogenous variables which are "given" from the outside and stable over time. It assumes that economic forces operate in an environment that is "imposed" on the system in a sense other than being just a heritage of the past—one could almost say an environment which, in its most significant characteristics, is independent of history. These critical exogenous features of the "environment" include Pareto's "tastes and obstacles"—the preferences of individuals as consumers, the transformation functions of factors into the products and the supply of resources—at any rate of "ultimate resources" —which are thus transformed. The notion of general equilibrium also assumes that the nature of the functions and of the social institutions—in particular the markets—are such that any given constellation of such exogenous variables will inevitably lead the system, possibly through a succession of steps, to a state of rest characterised by unchanging prices and production patterns over time: in other words that whatever the initial situation, the system will converge on a *unique point* the exact nature of which, both as regards the price system and the output system, can be deduced from the "data". Continuous economic change on these assumptions can only be conceived as some kind of "moving equilibrium" through the postulate of an autonomous (and unexplained) time-rate of change in the exogenous variables of a kind that is consistent with "continuous equilibrium" through time—such as a given rate of shift per unit of time in the production function of the so-called "Harrod-neutral" type or in the supply or resources: an exogenous rate of growth in the labour force and/or in the rate of increase in "capital"—though the very meaning of the latter concept has given rise to insoluble problems.

IV. THE THEOREM OF ENDOGENOUS AND CUMULATIVE CHANGE

Once, however, we allow for increasing returns, the forces making for continuous changes are *endogenous*—"they are engendered from within the economic system"[1]—and the actual state of the economy during any one "period" cannot be predicted except as a result of the sequence of events in previous periods which led up to it. As Young put it, with increasing returns "change becomes progressive and propagates itself in a cumulative way".[2] Further, "no analysis of the forces making for economic equilibrium, forces which you might say are tangential at any moment of time, will serve to illumine this field, for movements away from equilibrium, departures from previous trends, are characteristic of it".[3]

The basic consideration underlying Young's analysis is surprisingly the same as that underlying Say's Law. If one takes an all-inclusive view of the economic process, economic activity ultimately consists of the exchange of goods against goods; this means that every increase in the supply of commodities enlarges, *at least potentially*, the market for other commodities. (The qualification "potentially", as we shall see, is very important and distinguishes Young's views from that of Say or Mill.) Hence the "extent of the market" depends on the division of labour almost as much, according to Young, as the division of labour depends on the extent of the market; and [quoting Young again] "modified . . . in the light of this broader conception of the market, Adam Smith's dictum amounts to the theorem that the division of labour depends in large part upon the division

---

[1] Young, *op. cit.*, p. 530.
[2] *Op. cit.*, p. 533.
[3] *Op. cit.*, p. 528.

of labour. *This is more than mere tautology.* It means that the counter forces which are continually defeating the forces which make for economic equilibrium are more pervasive and more deeply rooted than we commonly realise."[1]

Myrdal, writing twenty-five years later, called this the "principle of circular and cumulative causation".[2] But neither Young nor Myrdal expressed the consequences in the radical form stated by Hicks[3] who said that "unless we can suppose . . . that marginal costs generally increase with output at the point of equilibrium" . . . "the basis on which economic laws can be constructed is shorn away". The words "economic laws" and "at the point of equilibrium" are of course question-begging. The issue is whether such laws (and "economic equilibrium") exist or not. In the scientific sense, the postulate of the existence of such "laws" is refuted if they can be logically shown to be valid only under assumptions that are contrary to observed phenomena.

The whole issue, as Young said, is whether an "equilibrium of costs and advantages" is a meaningful notion in the presence of increasing returns.[4] When every change in the use of resources —every reorganisation of productive activities—creates the opportunity for a further change *which would not have existed otherwise*, the notion of an "optimum" allocation of resources— when every particular resource makes as great or greater contribution to output in its actual use as in any alternative use— becomes a meaningless and contradictory notion: the pattern of the use of resources at any one time can be no more than a link in the chain of an unending sequence and the very distinction, vital to equilibrium economics, between resource-creation and resource-allocation loses its validity. The whole view of the economic process as a medium for the "allocation of scarce means between alternative uses" falls apart—except perhaps for the consideration of short-run problems, where the framework of social organisation and the distribution of the major part of available "resources", such as durable equipment and trained or educated labour, can be treated as given as a heritage of the

---

[1] *Ibid.*, p. 533. My italics.
[2] *Economic Theory and Underdeveloped Regions*, London, Duckworth, 1957.
[3] *Value and Capital*, Oxford, 1939, pp, p. 88–9.
[4] *Op. cit.*, p. 535.

past, and the effects of current decisions on future development are ignored.[1]

Young saw clearly that the combination of Say's Law with Adam Smith's theorem is not enough in itself to ensure that change is progressive and "propagates itself in a cumulative way". Something more is needed linking the effects of changes of production to demand: something that would ensure that an increase in supply emanating from any particular part of the economy has a stimulating effect, and not a depressing effect, on production in other parts. Given that factor, the process of economic development can be looked upon as the resultant of a continued process of interaction—one could almost say, of a chain-reaction—between demand increases which have been induced by increases in supply, and increases in supply which have been evoked by increases in demand. Lacking a theory of income generation such as was supplied by Keynes in the General Theory eight years later, he thought that the necessary additional condition to ensure a continued chain reaction is to be found in the nature of reciprocal demand and supply functions—in other words, in the elasticity of Marshallian "offer curves", when the "commodities exchanged are produced competitively, under conditions of increasing returns". According to Young, when the demand for each commodity is elastic, "in the special sense that a small increase in its supply will be attended by an increase in the amounts of other commodities which can be had in exchange for it" progress is bound to be cumulative for "under such conditions an increase in the supply of one commodity *is* an increase in the demand for other commodities, and it must be supposed that every increase in demand will evoke an increase in supply. The rate at which any one industry grows is conditioned by the rate at which other industries grow, but since the elasticity of demand and supply will differ for different products, some industries will grow faster than others. *Even with a stationary population and in the absence of new discoveries in pure and applied*

[1] The only respect in which market prices have an indispensable "allocative" function to fulfil is that involved in the distribution over time of the use of *exhaustible* natural resources (i.e., in the decision how far the current use of such resources should be restricted for the sake of the future) and it is notorious that it is in this respect that the price mechanism fails completely in making any allowance for the probable higher scarcity of such resources in the future.

science (as contrasted with such new ways of organising production and such new 'inventions' as are merely adaptations of known ways of doing things, made practicable and economical by an enlarged scale of production) *there are no limits to the process of expansion except the limits beyond which demand is not elastic and returns do not increase.*"[1]

V. THE ROLE OF DEMAND AND THE TWO KINDS OF "INDUCED INVESTMENT"

If the above passage has not received the attention which it deserved, it was, I believe, mainly because of the obscurity surrounding the meaning of "elasticity of demand" in the particular context. Clearly what Young intuitively perceived was that the pre-condition of cumulative change is that the rise in production of any one commodity *a*, should be associated with an increase in demand for all other commodities. He thought that this condition will be satisfied when the elasticity of demand for commodity *a* is greater than unity, since in that case the sales-receipts (or income) of the producers of *a* will be the greater the larger the production.

A little reflection will show however that if by "elasticity of demand" we mean something which is a reflection of the elasticity of substitution of consumers—in other words, of the elasticity of "flow" demand, as defined below—the increase in purchasing power of the producers of commodity *a* following upon the rise in the production of *a* must have been the result of a *diversion* of expenditure in favour of *a* and against other commodities. The rise in incomes of the *a* producers must therefore be offset by reduced incomes of the producers of some other commodities. It is possible that if the elasticities of substitution are high, and income elasticities are all positive, the elasticities of demand for all commodities, *taken individually*, should be greater

---

[1] Young, op. cit., p. 534, italics mine. In a footnote attached to the beginning of the above passage, Young also says that "if the circumstance that commodity *a* is produced under conditions of increasing return is taken into account as a factor in the elasticity of demand for *b* in terms of *a*, elasticity of demand and elasticity of supply may be looked upon as different ways of expressing a single functional relation". This almost suggests the view that the elasticity of demand for some commodities is a reflection of the elasticity of supply of other commodities.

than unity. But this is not enough to produce a chain reaction of rising demand followed by rising production, followed by rising demand, and so on, unless *total income* measured in terms of money is rising as well, which in turn presupposes that *total* expenditure, and not just the expenditure on a particular commodity, rises in response to a rise in production.

In order to show how an increase in the production of a commodity may involve the generation of additional incomes which in turn generates additional demand for other commodities and thereby becomes a "chain" in a continuous sequence, we must first of all take into account the fact that there are two kinds of demand (and supply) in a market: a "flow" demand and a "stock" demand: the former is the demand and supply of "outsiders" (i.e., producers and consumers), whereas the latter represents the demand (or supply) originating from *inside* the market.

In pure theory the existence of this "stock" demand or "inside demand" is ignored. In a state of equilibrium, production and consumption, or "flow"-demand and "flow"-supply, are necessarily equal in each market, and in the rarefied world of Walrasian perfection where markets are *continually* in equilibrium, the question of how the market responds to "disequilibria" does not arise because all such "disequilibria" are ruled out—all equilibrating adjustments are assumed to be instantaneous, either because changes are timeless or because all changes have been perfectly foreseen.

However, the markets of the real world are not in continuous equilibrium in this sense; there are, or can be, persistent differences between production and consumption which are reflected in increments or decrements in stocks. The impact effect of any undesigned or unexpected rise in production (due to a bumper harvest, for example) must be a rise in stocks; any subsequent adjustment in flow-demand or supply due to consequential price-changes requires time to materialise. For that reason, competitive markets are inconceivable without intermediaries—merchants or "dealers"—who are both buyers and sellers at the same time (at different prices) and who carry stocks so as to make "a market" that enables producers to sell and consumers to buy.

The size of the difference between their buying and selling prices (normally called the "dealer's margin") depends both on the degree of perfection of the market in which they operate and on the amount of "processing" or "transformation" performed by them. This may consist of pure merchanting activities—such as transportation, breaking bulk, packaging, etc.—and could also include varying degrees of physical transformation through manufacture. But what differentiates a merchant from other economic agents (such as a "producer") is that his natural response to "outside" influences is to vary the size of his stock— to absorb stocks in the face of excess supplies and to release stocks in the face of excess demand. The merchants' function in other words is to create and preserve an "orderly" market which they can only do through their willingness to act as a shock-absorber: through their readiness to enlarge their commitments when prices are sagging, and to curtail commitments when they are rising. The very notion of "merchanting" or "commercial" activities involves therefore the assumption that there is a certain elasticity of demand for *holding* stocks by the traders: an elasticity which is ultimately governed by the traders' expectations concerning prices and selling opportunities in the future. In a paper published many years ago I called this factor the "elasticity of speculative stocks" in a market[1] though the term "speculative" was perhaps a misnomer. It is true of course that traders only carry stocks in the expectation of making a profit, and therefore any inter-temporal transfer of goods could be called a form of "speculation," though it is fundamentally no different from any geographical transfer; and since the transportation of goods takes time, merchanting activities normally involve transfers of both kinds.[2]

---

[1] "Speculation and Economic Stability", *Review of Economic Studies*, October, 1939, p. 7 (reprinted in *Essays on Economic Stability and Growth*, London, Duckworth, 1960, p. 30), and above, Chapter 6.

[2] Any kind of merchanting activity—buying things with a view to their subsequent re-sale—is "speculative" in the sense that it involves the assumption of risks: by carrying stocks, traders *deliberately* take an "open position". Hence an increase in investment in stocks which occurs in response to an increase in supplies, though "induced", is a form of "voluntary" investment and not "involuntary". On the other hand, an increase in stocks which occurs as a result of a disappointment in sales-expectations—failure to *close* a position at the time and to the extent expected—may be regarded as "involuntary investment", in the sense that the addition to

It is a hen-and-egg question whether historically it was the growth of commerce which continually enlarged "the size of the market" and thereby enabled increasing returns to be realised, or whether it was the improvement of techniques of production and the improvement in communication which led to the growth of commerce. In the process of the development of capitalism the two operated side by side. And it involved a tendency for a continual rise in the *value* (and not just the volume) of stock carried by traders in the markets, which meant in turn that the growth of production resulting from any favourable change on the supply side led to a growth in incomes which in turn generated an increase in effective demand for commodities.

The essential element missing from Young's presentation, and which can only be supplied on the basis of Keynesian economics, is the addition to incomes resulting from the accumulation of capital (in other words, from investment expenditure) combined with the induced character of such investment which arises more or less as a by-product of changes in the organisation of production.[1] It operates moreover in two different ways. In the really "competitive" markets, such as those for most primary products, which approximate the economist's notion of perfect competition (where individual buyers and sellers are faced with infinitely elastic demand and supply curves, and where increasing returns *cannot* be operative, at any rate at the level of the individual producer) the stocks which are essential for the functioning of the market are carried by merchants who are independent both from the producers and the consumers; it is their ability to act as a buffer—to absorb stocks in the face of a short-term excess of supply and vice versa—which will lead to induced

---

stocks *ex-post* must have been greater than that planned *ex ante*. However, any step which implies an increase in commitments—the "opening" of a position—may be assumed to be deliberate, even when in response to events which may have been unforeseen.

[1] On re-reading Young in the light of Keynes, one is tempted to quote Keynes' account of Marshall's view that " . . . those individuals who are endowed with a special genius for the subject and have a powerful economic intuition will often be more right in their conclusions and implicit presumptions than in their explanation and explicit statements. That is to say, their intuitions will be in advance of their analysis and their terminology. Great respect, therefore, is due to their general scheme of thought, and it is a poor thing to pester their memories with criticism which is really verbal." (*Economic Journal*, September 1924, p. 235, note, reprinted in *Essays in Biography*, p. 232.)

investment in the face of a rise in production: provided that the merchants' expectation of future prices makes it appear profitable for them to increase the *value* of their stocks (and not only their volume) when prices sag in the face of excess supply.[1] In the markets for commodities in which increasing returns are important, and which, for that very reason, are only "imperfectly" competitive—as is the case with manufactures—the producers carry their *own* stocks and adjust the rate of their production in response to changes in their sales (or in the state of their "order book") and there will be "induced investment" in response to an *increase* in demand and the associated depletion of stocks. Such induced investment will partly take the form of circulating capital—that is to say, of an increase in the value of goods in process that is inevitably associated with the rise in production— and partly of fixed capital, in so far as the rise in current sales causes a revision of expectation of future sales.

It may seem paradoxical that "induced investment" should result from both increases in supply and increases in demand, but there is nothing necessarily inconsistent in this, provided there is asymmetry in market organisation between the two kinds of commodities, primary products and manufactures, an asymmetry which is imposed on the system by the differing incidence of the theorem of the "division of labour" between industry and agriculture—a feature of life which was already noted by Adam Smith. If, in the first approximation, one regards the essential division in economic activities as that between manufacturing activities and land-based activities (agriculture and mining) which provide the inputs (the food and raw materials) for manufacturing activities, and if we suppose that the quasi-automatic process of growing diversification and technological improvement resulting from the growth of activities—in other words increasing returns in the broad sense—is mainly a feature of the latter

---

[1] Strictly speaking, there should be a net demand effect in real terms whenever there is an increase in the volume of stocks carried in relation to turnover (and not only when there is a rise in the total value of stocks) since any such increment implies a rise in investment (in real terms) in relation to output. However, when the merchants' elasticity of demand for increasing the stock-turnover ratio is less than unity—so that a 1 per cent increase in the volume of stocks carried requires more than a 1 per cent reduction in price—the purchasing power of producers will diminish in consequence of a rise in production, while the (theoretically) more-than-offsetting rise in the real purchasing power of consumers will be slow to percolate through the system.

rather than the former, then the process of endogenous self-sustained growth requires both a certain *inelasticity* of expectations concerning *prices* (in regard to primary products) and also a certain *elasticity* of expectations concerning the *volume* of sales (in regard to manufactures). Induced investment reflecting the "acceleration principle" is a property of the latter; induced investment reflecting the price-stabilising effect of the operation of traders is a property of the former.[1]

And it requires, above all, a monetary and banking system that enables capital investment to increase in response to inducements, so as to generate the savings required to finance additional investment out of the *addition* to production and incomes. This is the real significance of the invention of paper money and of credit creation through the banking system. It provided the pre-condition of self-sustained growth. With a purely metallic currency, where the supply of money is given irrespective of the demand for credit, the ability of the system to expand in response to profit opportunities is far more narrowly confined.

VI. SOME CONCLUSIONS

To end, we can do little more than to sketch some of the main consequences of this marriage of the Smith-Young doctrine on increasing returns with the Keynesian doctrine of effective demand. I should like to make three observations.

First, the sharp distinction made by Keynes between a "full employment" situation where real income is confined by resource-endowment, and an unemployment situation where it is limited by effective demand, disappears in the presence of increasing returns. Except in a purely short-term sense, total output can never be *confined* by resources. At any one time, there is, or there may be, a maximum potential output for the world as a whole resulting from past history which has determined the existing network of institutions and organisations, the different kinds of plant and equipment available and their geographical distribu-

---

[1] In post-Keynesian models of cycles and growth (such as, for example, Hicks, *A Theory of the Trade Cycle,* Oxford, 1950) the only kind of "induced investment" considered was the demand-induced kind—the kind relevant to the manufacturing sector. The other, induced by excess supply, was completely neglected.

tion, as well as the distribution of the available labour in all the different areas and their educational endowments and skills. Over a period, there may be a maximum *rate of growth* of output determined by the maximum rate of growth of production in some key sectors of the economy (such as the food-producing sectors) which limits the sustainable rates of growth of the other sectors. If that happens, it must be on account of the scarcity of natural resources, and the impossibility of substituting capital goods for natural resources at more than a certain speed, on account of an insufficiency of land-saving innovations. But if we take an inclusive view, neither labour nor capital can limit either the level, or the rate of growth, of production over a longer period. Capital accumulation can always be speeded up— or rather it automatically *gets* speeded up, with a faster growth of production. In the case of labour, there is no such thing as an "optimal" distribution of the labour force—with each man making a greater contribution to output in his existing employ- ment than in any alternative employment—since every re- organisation of production resulting from overall expansion or new investment will mean the transfer of some of the labour force to new employments where its contribution to production will be greater than before. Just as Young emphasised that the adoption of more roundabout methods of production, due to an increase in the size of the market, and the adoption of more capital-intensive processes, are different facets of the same thing, so in the case of labour, no valid distinction can be made between an increase in the effective labour supply due to a rise in numbers employed and that due to a rise in productivity secured by a re-deployment of labour.

Second, it is evident that the co-existence of increasing returns and competition—emphasised by Young and also by Marx, but wholly excluded by the axiomatic framework of Walrasian economics—is a very prominent feature of de-centralised economic systems but the manner of functioning of which is still a largely uncharted territory for the economist. We have no clear idea of *how* competition works in circumstances where each producer faces a limited market as regards *sales* and yet a highly com- petitive market as regards *price*.

H

Third, it is evident from our analysis that the "self-sustained growth" of decentralised economic systems, largely directed not by exogenous factors, but by the growth and the constellation of demand, is a fragile thing which will only proceed in a satisfactory manner if a number of favourable factors are present simultaneously: such as merchants who are ready to absorb stocks in the short run rather than allow prices to fall too far—because experience has taught them that market prices have some long-run stability—and manufacturers who respond to the stimulus of growing sales with an expansion of productive capacity, because experience has taught them that over a period markets are growing and not stable. It also requires a "passive" monetary and banking system which allows the money supply to grow in automatic response to an increased demand for credit.

In the nineteenth century, with the background of rapid technological change, particularly in transport and communications, all these factors seem to have been present. In the present century, continued growth seems to have owed more to active government intervention—in the primary producing areas, through government-operated buffer stocks for commodities; in the industrialised countries, through "Keynesian" fiscal policies; both of which secured the continued growth of *real* purchasing power (i.e., of effective demand in real terms and not just in money terms) without which economic growth would quickly grind to a halt.

APPENDIX

ON INDIVISIBILITIES AND INCREASING RETURNS

In an article published in the *Economic Journal* in 1934 I wrote that

" . . . it appears methodologically convenient to treat all cases of large-scale economies under the heading 'indivisibility'. This introduces a certain unity into analysis and makes possible at the same time a clarification of the relationships between the different kinds of economies. Even the cases of increasing returns where a more-than-proportionate increase in output occurs merely on account of an increase in the amounts of the factors used, without any change in the proportions of the factors, are due to indivisibilities; only in this case it is not so much the 'original factors,' but the specialised functions of those factors, which are indivisible."[1]

This proposition was later criticised in some detail by E. H. Chamberlin[2] while my own view was subsequently defended by Tjalling C. Koopmans.[3] I did not participate in this subsequent controversy since the question of whether increasing returns are "fundamentally" due to indivisibilities or not, did not then appear to me a matter of great moment. Recently, however, on reading Professor Koopmans' defence of my 1934 views, I have come to the conclusion that I ought to make a belated apology to the memory of the late Professor Chamberlin and acknowledge that he was basically right in his main contention—even though I was not persuaded by his arguments at the time.

The point is of more than semantic interest since if indivisibilities were the sole cause of increasing returns, there would always be some level of production at which such scale economies were exhausted and "optimum scale" production reached. Moreover, the prevalence of competition could itself be taken as an indication that the effects of "indivisibilities" are not such as to prevent optimum-scale production prevailing for a sufficiently small fraction of total output to be consistent with a reasonable approximation to perfect competition.

As was shown above, not all causes of increasing returns can be attributed to indivisibility of one kind or another and there is no reason to suppose that "economies of scale" become inoperative above certain levels of production. There is first of all the steady and step-wise improvement in knowledge gained from experience—the so-called "dynamic economies of scale" which

---

[1] "The Equilibrium of the Firm", *Economic Journal*, March 1934, p. 65, reprinted in *Essays on Value and Distribution*, p. 39, and above, Chapter 2.

[2] "Proportionality, Divisibility and Economies of Scale", *Quarterly Journal of Economics*, February 1948, reprinted as Appendix B to the sixth edition of *The Theory of Monopolistic Competition*, Cambridge, Mass., 1948.

[3] *Three Essays on the State of Economic Science*, New York, McGraw-Hill, 1957, pp. 150–2.

have nothing to do with indivisibilities. But even in the field of "static" or "reversible" economies, there is the important group of cases which I described above as being due to the three-dimensional nature of space—i.e., the fact that the capacity of, say, a pipeline can be quadrupled by doubling its diameter while the costs (in terms of labour and materials) are more nearly related to the diameter than to its capacity. There is nothing "indivisible" about tubes or pipelines as such: technically, it may be just as easy to make tubes of a relatively small or a relatively large dimension and there can be a continuous range of sizes in between; the existence of a non-linear relationship between costs and capacity is inherent in the nature of *space*, and there is nothing "indivisible" about space as such. Moreover, this "space principle" applies equally to non-durable items (like plastic containers or paper bags) no less than to durable equipment (like steel pipes).

Professor Koopmans mentions the case of the pipeline explicitly but misses the point of the example:

> "I have not found one example of increasing returns to scale in which there is not some indivisible commodity in the surrounding circumstances. The oft-quoted case of a pipeline *whose diameter is continuously variable* can be seen as a case of choice between alternative pieces of capital equipment, differing in diameter, used to carry oil from Tulsa to Chicago, say. *No matter what diameter is selected, one entire pipeline of the requisite length* is needed to render this service. Half the length of the line does not carry half the flow of oil from Tulsa to Chicago."[1]

There is a clear misunderstanding here as to the relevance of the indivisibilities involved to the existence of increasing returns. This has nothing to do with the *length* of the pipeline but only with the *width* of the pipeline: the "indivisibility" on the other hand (as Koopmans says) relates to the length and not the width. Increasing returns arise because the capacity of a pipeline of *unit length* to carry oil—i.e., the maximum volume of throughput

[1] *Op. cit.*, p. 152, n. 3. Italics mine.

per unit of time—increases with the square of diameter, whereas the cost of production is a linear function of it. If a pipe of 5 feet diameter can transmit 5,000 tons per hour, a pipe with 10 feet diameter will transmit 20,000 tons per hour, and so on. Professor Koopmans' method, if I understand him correctly, is to treat pipelines of differing diameters as different "commodities", so that the choice of a pipeline with a particular diameter comes to the same as the choice of a particular "linear activity", or process of production. He regards every produced commodity which has the characteristic that "the ratios of inputs into their manufacture to outputs from their use cannot be reproduced at a smaller scale" as undergoing a "qualitative change" with every change in the ratio of inputs to outputs.[1]

However, each of these "linear processes" would only be relevant for a *particular* output,[2] and there is also an underlying functional relationship between outputs and inputs which may show perfect continuity but which is basically non-linear. This underlying relationship links the quantity of oil transmitted per hour as the "output" and the labour, materials, etc., involved in constructing the pipeline and all other associated outlays as the "inputs".

Professor Koopmans agrees with Chamberlin that his definition of "commodities" makes the whole issue a tautological one[3] but he believes that nevertheless the indivisibility has the right "intuitive connotations":

" . . . the reproach of tautology has been levelled against many propositions of economic theory. What matters is that a model which differs from the linear activity analysis model in that it omits the proportionality postulate or at least excepts from it all activities involving certain commodities seems to express those aspects of reality that have been recognised as responsible for increasing returns to scale. Such a model

---

[1] *Op. cit.*, pp. 151–2.
[2] Defined in this case as the *throughput* of oil (at any particular point) per unit of time.
[3] Although the statement, quoted earlier, that he has not "found a single case in which there is not some indivisible commodity in the surrounding circumstances" would suggest that he regarded the proposition as a factual one, and not as a logical (tautological) one.

may therefore be a suitable vehicle for a first exploration of this phenomenon, and on the suitability of prices as guides to allocation. So far, mathematical difficulties have been the main obstacle to such an exploration."[1]

The significance of all this depends on what is meant by the "suppression of the proportionality postulate". At one end, it may mean nothing more than the introduction of discontinuities which may rob the analysis of some of its elegance and simplicity, but without destroying the existence of a convex "Pareto-frontier" of some kind. At the other end, it may mean that the whole notion of a Pareto-optimal equilibrium and of the price mechanism as a means of bringing about an "optimal" resource-allocation becomes illegitimate.

Allowance for indivisibilities means that for activities involving certain commodities there is a minimum scale of output, and the activity can only be "attained" at integral multiples of that minimum scale. If in an actual economy the level of output of any one final commodity is some multiple of the minimum output of the "best" available technique for producing it, the existence of indivisibilities will simply mean that the "efficiency frontier" becomes a "jagged surface" instead of a smooth one, but yet remains convex in the large.

However, if at any actual level of output the "best" available technique for that output is less efficient than that available for a somewhat larger output—if, in other words, there is a whole hierarchy of activities not all of which are feasible or attainable at any point of time—the choice among "activities" becomes primarily a matter not of prices but of the scale of production. With every enlargement of production new "activities" become profitable which could not have been employed earlier, whilst the introduction of such new "activities" leads to the invention of further "activities" which have not been "known" earlier.

Since (as was argued above) the demand for any particular product or group of products is a reflection of the level of production of other products, this means that any re-allocation of resources which enlarges the range of feasible activities comes

[1] *Ibid.,* p. 152.

to the same as an "outward shift" in the production frontier. The problem then becomes not just one of "solving the mathematical difficulties" resulting from discontinuities but the much broader one of replacing the "equilibrium approach" with some, as yet unexplored, alternative that makes use of a different conceptual framework.

WHAT IS WRONG WITH ECONOMIC THEORY[1]

There is a widespread and growing dissatisfaction with prevailing economic theory in numerous quarters in England. It has even reached such respectable pillars of the economic establishment as the President of the Royal Economic Society and the British Association, as shown by their recent (1971) Presidential addresses. I do not believe that this wave has yet reached America in its proper dimensions—except perhaps at the graduate student level, and among a few rather isolated critics or heretics—but I have little doubt that some day it will. For primarily because the logical system of general equilibrium theory has been more thoroughly explored by American economists of the mathematical school of the post-war generation than anywhere else— clarifying in detail the number and kind of postulates required to establish its conclusions and their precise implications—they (or rather their pupils) should also be the first to perceive that the result of that great exercise has ended in a "cul-de-sac": it made the theory a less usable tool than it was thought to have been in its early and crude state before the full implications of general equilibrium had been so thoroughly explored.

My basic objection to the theory of general equilibrium is not that it is abstract—all theory is abstract and must necessarily be so since there can be no analysis without abstraction—but that it starts from the wrong kind of abstraction, and therefore gives a misleading "paradigm" (or scenario?—the now fashionable word in America) of the world as it is: it gives a misleading impression of the nature and the manner of operation of economic forces.

[1] A Political Economy lecture given at Harvard University, April 29, 1974 and published in the *Quarterly Journal of Economics*, August 1975.

In this connection there is not, in my view, a single, overwhelming objection to orthodox economic theory: there are a number of different points which are distinct though interrelated. Some of my Cambridge colleagues are "monists" in this respect: they believe that there is a single basic, logical objection to the theory of marginal productivity which is alone sufficient to pull the rug out from under the neo-classical value theory. I am referring to the difficulty of isolating or measuring the change in the quantity of capital when the inventory of capital goods changes—which makes it impossible to regard capital as a quantity, *per se*, irrespective of the actual forms in which it is embodied at any one time, and makes it impossible to attribute to capital a marginal productivity of its own. But there are other things to object to that in some ways are even more misleading than the application of marginal productivity theory to the division between wages and profits, which has been the main subject of discussion.

I

The first of these is that economic theory regards the essence of economic activities as an *allocation problem*—"the allocation of scarce resources among alternative uses"—to use Lord Robbins' famous definition of the subject matter of economics. This means that attention is focused on what are subsidiary aspects, rather than the major aspects, of the forces in operation. The principle of substitution (as Marshall called it) or the "law of variable proportions" or of "limited substitutability" is elevated to the central principle on the basis of which both the price system and the production system are explained; and it is implied that the world is one where elasticities of substitution are all-important. This approach ignores the essential complementarity between different factors of production (such as capital and labour) or different types of activities (such as that between primary, secondary and tertiary sectors of the economy) which is far more important for an understanding of the laws of change and development of the economy than the substitution aspect. Indeed, it is, I think, the concentration on the substitution

I

aspect which makes "pure" equilibrium theory so lifeless and motionless: it purports to "explain" a system of market-clearing prices which are the resultant of various interactions: it cannot therefore deal with the problem of prices as signals or incentives to change. Attempts have been made to graft growth and development to equilibrium theory, but they have not succeeded in transforming it into a seqence analysis in which the course of development is dependent on the path of evolution.

Perhaps the best way I can illustrate this point is by asking the question: *Is Say's Law valid, and if not, just what is wrong with it?* This is a very old question, hotly debated already in the early 19th century, if not earlier, and ever since then (until Keynes came along) it was the hallmark of all true economists to have understood the reasons why competitive markets necessarily bring about a situation in which all scarce resources are fully utilised.

The reason, in essence, is a very simple one. The laws of supply and demand state that in any competitive market, say, for the *j*th commodity, there is a "market clearing" price, characterised by

$$d_j = s_j,$$

where d_j and s_j respectively are the *maximum* quantities that buyers are willing to buy or sellers to sell, at those prices (not just sales $\equiv$ purchases).

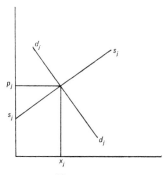

FIGURE I

At p_j buyers are ready to buy and sellers to sell x_j or any quantity *less than x_j*.

If this is true of any one market, it must be true for all, $j = 1 \ldots n$ ($0 < n < \infty$), in the markets for resources, as well as commodities. Hence if all markets are in equilibrium, all resources must be utilised, and production in total must be supply-constrained, or resource-constrained; it cannot be *demand*-constrained.

Or, put in other words, since taking all markets together it is commodities which are exchanged against commodities, there is no sense in saying that the production of commodities can be limited by demand. As Ricardo said, "there is no amount of capital which may not be employed in a country, because demand is only limited by production".[1] Or, John Stuart Mill made the point more forcibly—"All sellers are inevitably and *ex vi termini* buyers. Could we suddenly double the productive powers of the country, we should double the supply of commodities in every market, but we should, by the same stroke, double the purchasing power." Hence, "production can be ill-assorted, but it can not be excessive".[2]

Keynes thought he found the answer to this compelling bit of logic by postulating, in effect, that in one particular market, the market for savings, the price is not, or need not be, "market clearing" (owing to liquidity preference) and if it is not, there is another mechanism, that of the multiplier, to bring about equality in that market—equality between savings and investment (or the supply and demand for savings). But that mechanism operates by varying the amount of production in *general*. It leads to a situation which is *not* resource-constrained.

However, there is a more basic reason why Say's Law is wrong: a reason that might apply equally in a barter economy, and not just a money economy, or in an economy where there is no capital market because people save directly in "real terms" by accumulating stocks of their own produce—e.g., the farmer who accumulates corn so as to increase further corn output, or the steel producer who saves by ploughing back steel into the business so as to increase steel capacity. All we need to assume is the

---

[1] Ricardo, *Principles* (Sraffa ed.) Cambridge University Press, 1951, p. 290.
[2] J. S. Mill, *Principles of Political Economy*, London, 1849, vol. II Book III, ch. XIV, §2–§4.

absence of constant returns to scale in terms of transferable resources as a general or universal rule (applicable to *all* productive activity).

Suppose we take a simple two-sector model, consisting of *A* and *B* sectors, of agriculture and industry. And let us assume that *land* exists as a specific factor in agriculture—i.e. land is required for agricultural production but not (or not in significant amounts) for industrial production. Industrial production consists of the *processing* of basic materials produced by agriculture, for example, transforming raw cotton or wool into finished textiles, shirts or suits (or for that matter, iron ore extracted from the soil into steel and machinery) with the aid of Labour, which also requires food, which is the wage-good par excellence. Hence agriculture (and mining) produces both direct and indirect inputs for industry—basic materials and food.

If agriculture is subject to the Law of Diminishing Returns, agricultural output may be constrained by land and the available technology which limit the number of workers who may be effectively employed in agriculture.[1] The rest could only be effectively employed in industry.

Supposing that the employment of all the available labour in industry (and assuming adequate capital for their employment in the form of physical equipment at the prevailing technology) would lead to a relative "over-production" of industrial goods (and services)—relative to the available supply of *agricultural* goods—Mill would have said that this is a case of production becoming, or threatening to become, "ill-assorted". But the movement of prices that would accompany this event would bring its own remedy. Agricultural prices would rise in terms of industrial prices, and this process will go on until the excess supply of

---

[1] Though the classical economists (and of course, the neo-classical economists) reasoned as if agricultural production were simultaneously constrained by the supply of both land and labour, it is in fact unlikely that in any given situation (i.e in a given state of technology) the land/labour ratio will be such as to permit effective "full employment" for both labour and land. Since there is only a limited range within which these two factors are substitutes for one another at the margin, the likelihood is that either the land constraint or the labour constraint will be operative, i.e. that there will be too much labour (relative to land) or too much land (relative to labour) though for reasons given below, it would be vain to look for evidence for this by asking which of these two resources has a zero price.

industrial goods—which is the same as the excess demand for agricultural goods—is eliminated. Even if agricultural output were wholly inelastic owing to the shortage of land, the very rise in prices would be sufficient: for it would transfer purchasing power from industry to agriculture, and this transfer will go on until the agriculturists are willing and able to buy all the goods which industry is capable of producing (in excess of industry's own requirements for investment and consumption).

There must be *some* price, therefore, at which the excess supply of *B* (or excess demand for *A*) disappears: to suppose otherwise is to assume that industrial goods would remain in excess supply even at a zero price. And this formal conclusion (as I already said) is not dependent on the supply of agricultural products being elastic, which would be the case if the land shortage did not impose a constraint on output.

Now the error in this reasoning is that it ignores the peculiar character of labour as a commodity or resource, the price of which cannot be regarded as being determined by supply and demand in the same way as the price of other resources, such as land, for example.

Whatever the supply of labour (or the potential supply of labour) in relation to demand, the *price* of labour in terms of food cannot fall below a certain minimum determined by the cost of subsistence, whether that cost is determined by custom or convention or by sheer biological needs. (The food-value of wages tends to be very rigid downward in all communities at some *attained* level.) Ricardo and Mill (just as Adam Smith and Marx) were fully aware of this point, but they had not thought out its consequences in terms of Say's Law.[1]

---

[1] Or rather they assumed that the dependence of population on capital (through a Malthusian process) will ensure that the labour supply in existence will be no greater than can be employed at a positive profit. Mill in particular argued that as capital accumulates, and population grows in consequence of it, profits would fall on account of the operation of the Law of Diminishing Returns in agriculture and this would cause "all further accumulation of capital to cease"—implying (without putting the point explicitly) that this itself will limit the size of the labour force to the numbers that can be effectively employed in the given natural and technological environment. It was for this reason, I presume, that Mill made the statement that "low profits, however, are a different thing from deficiency of demand; and the production and accumulation which merely reduce profits, cannot be called excess of supply or of production." But what if the absorption of the unemployed involved a negative profit? This latter possibility as far as I know was never considered. Yet there is no reason

If wages (or minimum wages) can be taken as given in terms of food, the prices of manufactured goods (or rather the "value added" by manufacturing activities) are equally constrained, and this constraint may prevent both markets from being in equilibrium simultaneously.

The supply price of industrial goods is given by the equation

$$p = (1 + \pi)\bar{w}l,$$

where p = prices of industrial goods per unit, in terms of agricultural prices

$\bar{w}$ = wages per man, ditto

l = labour required per unit of output (inverse of productivity)

π = profits as a share of output

and this will *not* be a "market-clearing" price, so long as the supply of labour exceeds the demand; or so long as there is a low-earnings "subsistence" sector of the economy which enables people to survive without being effectively employed or effectively contributing to output.

This has important consequences.

(1) First, the level of $\bar{w}$, cannot be less than earnings in the subsistence sector; but otherwise it is by no means tied to it: the *optimal* wage to a capitalist employer may be a great deal higher owing to the dependence of the efficiency of work-performance on food intake. The poorer the country, the higher $\bar{w}$ is in relation to earnings in the subsistence sector. (A. Smith, Ricardo, Mill and all classical economists assume a *constant* food wage—i.e., an infinitely elastic supply curve of labour to industry.) Hence one cannot say that the relative price of industrial and agricultural goods is determined by marginal rates of substitution between the two sectors. There is no such thing as a

---

why the density of population resulting from the Malthusian Law (and which operates so as to keep income per head at a bare subsistence level) should coincide with the highest population density at which the whole of the labour force can still be effectively employed—i.e. which is consistent with a positive marginal product of labour in agriculture. (See Mill, *op. cit.*, Book III, ch. XIV, §4, and Book IV, ch. IV, *passim.*)

"production frontier" showing output combinations, a maximum *A* for any given *B*, or vice versa, reflecting the allocation of resources between sectors. For each sector accumulates its own capital as it expands its own output; and labour which is common to both has a positive marginal product only in industry, not in agriculture.[1]

(2) Secondly, the fact that the price of "value-added" by manufacture cannot be reduced or compressed in terms of basic products (if basic products rise in money prices, as they do now, it results in general inflation rather than in a fall in industrial prices in terms of primary products) is the equivalent of a "fixed price" situation (as Hicks called it)[2] where production is determined by demand, or rather by the exogenous components of demand which in turn determine, through the usual multiplier and accelerator effects, the endogenous components of demand. (Hicks called the relationship of endogenous to exogenous demand the "super-multiplier"—to allow for induced investment as well as induced consumption.)[3] Hence it is the income of the agricultural sector (given the "terms of trade") which really determines the level and the rate of growth of industrial production, according to the formula:

$$O_I = \frac{1}{m} D_A,$$

where O_I = industrial output

  D_A = demand for industrial products coming from
       agriculture

  m = share of expenditure on agricultural products in
     total industrial income.

---

[1] It will be readily seen that this conclusion is critically dependent on the existence of diminishing returns (in terms of capital and labour) in agriculture. For assuming that agriculture were subject to constant returns to scale, the excess supply of industrial goods at a given price-relationship would cause a transfer of labour and capital into agriculture until the excess demand for agricultural goods is eliminated and "full-employment output" would cease to be "ill assorted". Hence the postulate of constant returns to scale (in terms of transferable resources) as a universal rule applicable to all "processes" or "activities" (which is a common axiom of the general equilibrium theory) is sufficient to ensure a Walrasian equilibrium which is truly resource-constrained.

[2] *Capital and Growth*, Oxford, 1965, chs. vii–xi (pp. 76–127).

[3] *A Contribution to the Theory of the Trade Cycle*, Oxford, 1950, p. 62.

This is really the doctrine of the foreign trade multiplier, as against the Keynesian savings/investment multiplier. In both cases multipliers arise on account of a "fixed-price" situation: the liquidity preference rate of interest in the one case, and the fixed real wage giving a cost-determined supply price for industrial products in the other case. In some ways I think it may have been unfortunate that the very success of Keynes' ideas in explaining unemployment in a depression—essentially a short period analysis—diverted attention from the "foreign trade multiplier", which, over longer periods, is a far more important principle for explaining the growth and rhythm of industrial development. For over longer periods, Ricardo's presumption that manufacturers and traders only save in order to invest, so that the amount and/or the proportion of savings would adapt to changes in the opportunities for, or profitability of, investment, seems to me more relevant than the Keynesian assumption for explaining the true constraints on the growth of production and employment in the "capitalist" industrial sector.

II

(3) Added to this is the second major point I want to make at this point—albeit only briefly—and this concerns the existence of *increasing returns to scale* or falling long-run costs, in industry. This was first emphasised by Adam Smith in the first three chapters of the *Wealth of Nations,* and subsequently emphasised by English economists of the Ricardian school and by Marshall; while in the United States (in a more isolated way) by a single great economist, Allyn Young.

Marshall's falling long-run supply curve, unlike the ordinary supply curve, is a schedule of *minimum* quantities, not *maximum* quantities: see diagram opposite. At p_j manufacturers are willing to supply x_j or any amount *larger than* x_j but not *less than* x_j.

Neither Marshall, nor anyone else, has ever succeeded in reconciling this assumption with neoclassical value theory— which is the reason perhaps why, according to Hahn and

Matthews,[1] it has received so little consideration in recent economic literature.

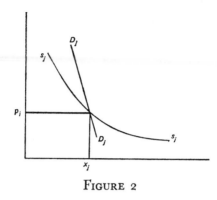

FIGURE 2

There are three important consequences that I would like to emphasise here. The first, which was emphasised by Allyn Young is that with increasing returns "change becomes progressive and propagates itself in a cumulative way".[2] There can be no such thing as an equilibrium state with optimum resource allocation, where no further advantageous reorganisation is possible, since every such re-organisation may create a fresh opportunity to a further re-organisation. There can never be full employment in the sense of "efficient" or Pareto-optimal full employment, and the very distinction between changes in the *quantity* of resources, and changes in the *efficiency* with which they are used, becomes a questionable one.

Second, the accumulation of capital becomes a by-product, rather than a cause, of the expansion of production—indeed it is only one aspect of it. Again, as Young emphasised, it is the increase in the scale of activities that makes it profitable to increase the capital/labour ratio: the larger the scale of operations the more varied and more specialised the machinery which can be profitably used to aid labour. As Young said, "It would be wasteful to make a hammer just to drive a single nail; it would

---

[1] "The Theory of Economic Growth: A Survey", *Economic Journal*, Vol. LXXIV, December 1964, p. 833.
[2] Allyn A. Young, "Increasing Returns and Economic Progress", *Economic Journal*, December, 1928, p. 533.

be better to use whatever awkward implement lies conveniently at hand".[1] The form which increasing returns normally takes is that the productivity of labour rises with the scale of production while that of capital remains constant. The best proof of this resides in the fact that while the capital/labour ratio increases dramatically in the course of progress (and varies equally dramatically at any given time between rich and poor countries) these differences arise without corresponding changes in the capital/output ratio. (For example, comparing the U.S. with India, the capital/labour ratio is of the order of 30:1, while capital/output ratio is around 1:1.) Paul Samuelson emphasised as the central proposition of neo-classical value theory (placed in italics in his well-known textbook) "Capital/labour up: interest or profit rate down: wage rate up: capital/output up".[2] These propositions are *only* true in a world of homogeneous and linear production functions, where an increase in capital relative to labour increases output less than proportionately. In reality this is not so—higher wages rates in terms of product are associated with higher capital/labour ratios but are *not* associated with higher capital/output ratios. (This is to my mind an even more important "pull on the rug" than the discovery of the possibility of "double-switching" of techniques.)

Third, for the same kind of reason for which increasing returns lead to a monopoly in terms of microeconomics, industrial development tends to get polarised in certain "growth points" or in "success areas" which become areas of vast immigration from surrounding centres or from more distant areas—unless this is prevented by political obstacles. As the post-war experience of European countries (e.g. Germany, France, Switzerland) has shown, the emergence of a labour shortage need not hold up the further fast development of a successful industrial area, since such political obstacles tend to be removed when it becomes profitable to import foreign labour.

But this process of polarisation—what Myrdal called "circular and cumulative causation"—is largely responsible for the growing

[1] *Ibid.*, p. 530.
[2] P. A. Samuelson, *Economics—an Introductory Analysis,* Seventh ed., New York, 1967, p. 715.

division of the world between rich and poor areas which, in per capita terms at any rate, still appears to be widening. It would be foolish to pretend that we understand *all* the causative influences which make the industrialisation of *some* parts of the world so much more successful than that of others. But I am sure that a better understanding of the nature and mode of operation of market forces making for change and development will increase our powers of control for counteracting inherent trends toward greater inequality as between the different regions of the globe.

EQUILIBRIUM THEORY AND GROWTH THEORY[1]

1. INTRODUCTION

My purpose is to explain why I regard prevailing economic theory, as taught in the regular textbooks in most of the universities of the Western World, as thoroughly misleading and pretty useless—in terms of the theory's declared objective of explaining how economic processes work in a decentralised market economy. It is useless for formulating nontrivial predictions concerning the effects of policy measures or other changes.

Section 2 is a brief discussion of what I consider to be the basic assumptions of equilibrium theory. Section 3 is a discussion of what is wrong with these assumptions—why these hypotheses are misleading as a starting point for making generalisations about the behaviour of the economic system. Finally, Section 4 is a brief outline of the postulates needed for an alternative approach—a "non-equilibrium theory"—which I should like to call a "growth theory", because it would be primarily concerned with the manner of operation of the (both exogenous and endogenous) forces in a market economy making for continuous change and development.

2. THE MAIN CHARACTERISTICS OF EQUILIBRIUM THEORY

The basic characteristics of existing equilibrium theory are:

(1) It is permeated by a basic dichotomy between "wants" and

---

[1] Originally published in M. Boskin (ed.), *Economics and Human Welfare: Essays in Honour of Tibor Scitovsky* (Academic Press, 1977).

"resources", "tastes" and "obstacles" or "ends" and "means". (One could equally say, with Bentham, between "pleasure" and "pain".)

(2) It follows from the basic assumption that men have given "wants" or "needs", which in a basic, though not precisely definable, sense are given by man's nature, independently of the social environment and of the social institutions created for satisfying them, that the essence of "economic activities" is regarded as that of allocating "scarce means which have alternative uses" (Robbins, 1932). The price system, the market mechanism, and the legal institutions, property rights, contracts, etc., are regarded as social instruments for "resource allocation". Under *ideal* conditions, individuals, whether in their capacity as producers or consumers, by acting rationally but quite independently of each other—that is to say, by acting so as to maximise something—bring about an "optimum" allocation of resources which secures the highest or maximum satisfaction to each member of society in the specific Pareto sense of no one being capable by any change in his *own* arrangements, *i.e.* in his own set of decisions concerning production or consumption, of making himself *better off* without making some others, or at least one other person, *worse off*. *A*'s pleasure is maximised subject to *B*'s being given. So everyone is as well off as he could be subject to everyone else's satisfaction being given.

(3) "Wants" are satisfied by the consumption (or destruction) of "goods" (including non-material services). Goods are produced out of labour, natural resources, and goods; *i.e.* to a large extent, goods are produced out of each other, and only a proportion of goods produced in any year are destined to satisfy wants in that year. The goods which are available at any point of time, or over an interval of time (such as a year) for the purposes of producing goods, together with the labour and natural resources so available, are called "resources".

(4) The essence of equilibrium theory consists of stating, in a comprehensive manner, the properties of such a Pareto equilibrium—having demonstrated that on certain basic "axioms" such an equilibrium can be assumed to exist. The necessary axioms include, first of all, that the supply of

resources (the total amount of each kind that is available) is given "exogenously" in some sense—though what the precise meaning of exogeneity is when one tries to clothe the skeleton and think of "resources" as concrete objects as they appear in reality, and not just as mathematical symbols in a system of equations, has never been satisfactorily resolved.

(5) For the purpose of demonstrating the existence of such an "equilibrium", it is also assumed that the productive relationships—the "transformation functions" or "production functions"—are universally *known* and of a *given* number; equally, there are a *known* and *given* number of different goods.

(6) Equally, the distribution of the *ownership* of resources among individuals is given exogenously.

(7) Similarly, the preference functions of each individual are assumed to be given and invariant over time, and invariant also with respect to the preferences of other individuals.

One can draw a distinction between the axioms necessary for a Pareto-optimal resource allocation to exist, and the additional assumptions required for supposing that a *market economy* will tend to function in such a way as to bring about (fully, or with a certain degree of approximation) an equilibrium allocation of resources. In order to show that the market mechanism will function in this way, it is necessary to suppose further that:

(a) transformation functions must be *linear*; there is an absence of increasing returns (or economies of scale), *i.e.* production is equally efficient, irrespective of the scale of production;

(b) competition must be *perfect*—each individual "transactor" can sell anything or buy anything in unlimited amounts without affecting market prices, and therefore prices are the only type of information required for individual decisions; and

(c) there is *perfect knowledge* of all relevant prices by all "transactors" (or "economic agents");

(d) there is also "perfect foresight" in the sense that over time the experience of individuals serves to *confirm* (and not to contradict or "disappoint") the expectations in the light of which they made their decisions in the past.

The real purpose of all these assumptions is to show that there is at least one set of prices which, *if established in the markets*, would leave everyone content to go on as they are—that it would not be in anyone's interest to revise their decisions (or "plans") concerning their *own* activities in the sphere of production and consumption. But this in itself is not sufficient to show that markets will operate so as to approach an equilibrium of this description from any arbitrarily given starting point. For, if transactions are conducted at non-equilibrium prices, this in itself will alter the conditions of equilibrium—it will come to the same as a change in the distribution in the ownership of resources between different individuals. (It can also affect conduct by creating false anticipations.) Hence, in the pure Walrasian model, it is assumed that the system of equilibrium or market-clearing prices is established *before* any transactions are made, by a process of *"tatônnement"*,[1] which is the same as assuming that the markets *are* in equilibrium, without showing how they got there. Nor has it been demonstrated that this equilibrium is a stable one; *i.e.* that it would maintain itself in the face of chance disturbances.

Moreover, the whole approach is necessarily "static" in the sense that it assumes that the forces operating in the economy can be characterised in terms of a *unique* point (or a predetermined point) on which any *changing* system converges and at which all forces making for change are exhausted—in other words, to a state in which the various forces hold each other in balance in such a way as to establish an unchanging routine. Once the system attains equilibrium, it remains in it forever.

Now all human societies are in a process of continual change—a change which differs from the continual biological change of ecological systems in nature only in that it is far

---

[1] The meaning of the French word *"tatônnement"* according to *Petit Larousse* is *procéder avec hésitation*. In Walras, it means a cautious approach to business which enables people to discover the right prices *before* transactions are made.

speedier and takes more spectacular forms. Within the framework of equilibrium theory, there are two ways in which attempts have been made to introduce change into the system while preserving the notion that it is in continuous equlibrium:

(1) The first is the assumption that there are "markets" at which purchases and sales can be made not only for the current period but for *all* future periods as well; decisions then depend on prices in both the current and all the "future" markets; the system is in intertemporal equilibrium when, at the ruling prices, both the "spot" and "future" market supplies and demands are in equilibrium for *all* future periods and not only for the current period. The purpose of this approach is to establish that on certain axioms, such an equilibrium price system for all "commodities" (with each "commodity" having a time suffix for the date of its availability) exists. The real world admittedly bears only a very limited resemblance to this model, since apart from some specific commodities for specific periods in the near future, such futures markets do *not* exist.[1]

(2) The other approach is to assume that changes are only due to purely exogenous factors which proceed in time wholly independently (or at least *largely* independently) of economic decisions which depend on prices; and the price system operates so efficiently as to produce an optimal allocation of resources for each period taken separately. In other words, the system is in continuous equilibrium, even though the quantity of available resources and technological knowledge is changing over time—for, in each period, the system produces a Pareto-optimal allocation for the quantity of resources and the knowledge of technology *pertaining to that period*.

The trouble with that approach is that there is nothing in the theory to explain how the system gets into equilibrium and what happens when it is out of equilibrium. The "production

---

[1] Also it would be a mistake to equate the markets in "futures" in the real world to the "dated" markets of equilibrium theory. The "futures" markets of the real world relate to transactions between hedgers and speculators: they do *not* attempt to match supplies and demands accruing at particular future dates.

frontier" which is supposed to shift at some exogenous rate in time is meaningful only if the system is actually *on* the frontier and not *within* it. For any movement of the system *toward* the frontier increases capital as well as output, and therefore changes at least one of the parameters which define the "frontier".[1]

3. WHY EQUILIBRIUM THEORY IS WRONG

The Walrasian equilibrium theory is a highly developed intellectual system, much refined and elaborated by mathematical economists since World War II—an intellectual experiment, as Kornai (1971) called it. But it does not constitute a scientific hypothesis, like Einstein's theory of relativity or Newton's law of gravitation, in that its basic assumptions are axiomatic and not empirical, and no specific methods have been put forward by which the validity or relevance of its results could be tested. The assumptions make assertions about reality in their implications, but these are not founded on direct observation and, in the opinion of practitioners of the theory at any rate, they cannot be contradicted by observation or experiment.

The effects of complementarity

My first criticism of this approach is that it concentrates on subsidiary aspects and not the main aspects of market processes. Equilibrium theory elevates the "principle of substitution" (as Marshall called it) to be the "be-all" and "end-all" of all economic activity—the main explanatory principle of the forces which operate on the economy. "Resources" are limited substitutes (or substitutes at the margin) both as regards production and consumption, hence profit maximisation and utility maximisation are essentially substitution problems—a problem of equating prices to marginal rates of substitution in production and consumption. This is misleading because it ignores the essential complementarity between different kinds

---

[1] This point is considered further below.

of products and different kinds of activities, and the nature of the market impulses which result from this complementarity. Take, for example, capital and labour. These are essentially complementary to each other; this aspect is far more important than the fact that they are also "substitutes" in some respects—*i.e.* that enterprises can be induced by relative price changes to use more or less mechanised techniques of production involving greater or lesser amounts of "capital" per worker.

The French Physiocrats and English classical economists were of course conscious of this complementarity; they regarded the role of capital accumulation as one of raising production by increasing the level of employment of the economy (so as to increase the amount of labour that is effectively utilised in production) and not for the purpose of substitution of "capital" for "labour" in relation to labour already employed.

Another example is the interdependence of different kinds of economic activities as is shown in the distinction between the primary, secondary, and tertiary sectors. Industrial (or manufacturing) activities—which are "secondary"—consist of the processing or refinement of crude products which are the output of the so-called "primary" sectors, agriculture and mining. They depend on agriculture also for food which is the consumption-good or wage-good par excellence. Hence, an increased availability of primary products is a necessary precondition for increased industrial output; in the same way, an increase in industrial activity necessarily increases the demand for primary products. The same is true of "tertiary" services: the scale on which they can be provided is dependent on the output of both the primary and secondary sectors.

In equilibrium theory, if the economy is assumed to possess two industries such as manufactured goods A and food products B, the available resources are supposed to be divided between them, depending on consumer preference. The nature of neoclassical general equilibrium in the simplest case of two factors and two industries is shown in Fig. 1. The locus of "efficient combinations" is given by the "production frontier" A-B. This assumes that factor supplies X and Y, as well as the transformation functions for *A* and *B*, are given. Ignoring (for the purpose of our argument) the difficulties in the way of representing collective preferences by indifference curves, point *P** can be said to represent the "equilibrium" position at which the two kinds of products are produced in the most preferred ratio, and at which output (A^*, B^*) is at a maximum, given the resource constraints.

Figure 1

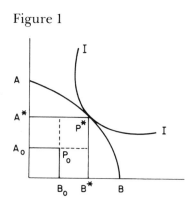

But this is a false way of looking at things. The two industries do not make use of the same resources and, insofar as they do, these resources are not, in any meaningful sense, allocated between them.

Labour is common to all activities, but there is always "surplus labour" in agriculture—labour can be withdrawn without any adverse effect on output and normally with a favourable effect. (This can be expressed by saying that normally the marginal product of labour working on the land is zero or negative. The reason is that the density of population living on the land is generally such that output actually produced does not require the *effective* employment of more than a fraction of the labour force available.) There is no such things as "full employment of labour" except as a short-term phenomenon in a given area (or locality).

Equally, capital cannot be regarded as a *given* quantity which is allocated between the two sectors. On the contrary, each sector generates (or "accumulates") its own capital in the course of its own expansion.

The growth of output and the growth of capital, in the sense of the increase in the stock of goods (or stock of durable goods) serving the purposes of production, are not two different things but merely two different *facets* of the same process; neither is prior to the other nor a precondition of the other. It would be better to say that they are the same thing viewed from two different aspects. Fisher (1906) was the first economist to my knowledge who emphasised this by saying that the stock of goods existing *at a given moment of time* is "capital"; the flow of goods accruing *over a period of time* is "income".

It is true that the competition between the owners of capital to seek the most-profitable activities brings about a certain tendency to equalisation in the rate of return; but this is not because capital "flows" between the various sectors in any real sense, but because the rate of accumulation of capital in each particular sector varies positively with the rate of return of that sector, so that sectors with higher rates of profits will expand relatively fast in relation to other sectors and this tends to bring their relative prices, rates of profit, and hence rates of accumulation down, so that the *profile* of the rate of expansion of different sectors tends to approach a structurally determined pattern, determined primarily by technical relationships and also by the income elasticities of demand of consumers. (In reality, at any one time the high rates of profit are made in the so-called "growth industries" resulting from dynamic change.)

But the main point to bear in mind is that under favourable conditions (of which I shall say more later), the expansion of any one sector tends to stimulate (via a demand effect) the expansion of the others; so that production, under favourable conditions, escalates by a kind of chain reaction—each sector receives impulses through market phenomena, and transmits impulses in turn.

The market is thus not primarily an instrument for *allocating* resources. It is primarily an instrument for transmitting impulses to change; it would be truer to say that the market mechanism creates or generates resources than that it allocates them. (There is, of course, also an allocative aspect, but I think this should be regarded as subsidiary and not the primary or most important aspect, and, as Kornai (1971) has recently shown, the markets can perform their allocation functions through a "stock-adjustment" mechanism which is not primarily guided by prices and which is capable of functioning irrespective of prices.)

The implication is that the so-called "equilibrium position" (or the locus of all such positions, such as the "production frontier" shown in Fig. 1) cannot be derived from a study of "data" independently of the actual position in which the economy finds itself at any given time. For, suppose that the initial position of the economy at $t = 0$ is P_0, yielding outputs A_0, B_0. Since these outputs serve as the commodity inputs of the processes of production (and are not use-goods destined for personal consumption), any movement of the system toward optimal allocation necessarily enlarges the quantity of resources available to the economy and therefore changes the position of the production frontier. Since P_0 was a non-optimal position by definition (*i.e.* a position at which the marginal rates of substitution of the factors in the two industries were *not* equal), any movement of the system toward "equilibrium"—*i.e.* to the northeast of P_0—will increase the amount of resources available to at least one of the two industries, if not both. Hence, if P^* was assumed to be the optimum position of annual output when starting from an initial position P_0, it could no longer be the optimal position if one started from any intermediate point such as P_l, with $A_l > A_0$ and $B_l > B_0$ as outputs. This means that the position of the frontier can be defined only if the state of the economy is actually *on* the frontier to start with. Otherwise, one cannot define the frontier except by reference to some *particular* starting point; and any movement of the system toward the frontier from that starting point will necessarily shift the "frontier" itself outward. The optimal output cannot be defined except by reference to the quantity of capital; but the quantity of capital cannot be defined except by reference to output, since output and capital are fundamentally only different ways of looking at the same thing.[1]

Thus the first thing which is wrong with the paradigm of equilibrium theory is thinking of a "given" quantum of resources which are "scarce" and always fully utilised, and which are effectively allocated between different uses. This view permeated the classical school of Ricardo and his followers as well as the neoclassical economists, and it is at the basis of Say's law, *la théorie des debouchès*. The latter is best expressed in Mill's (1848, p. 95) dictum that "there is no over-production; production is not excessive, but merely ill-assorted." If agriculture can employ only a limited number of men (because of the shortage of land), the rest could be employed only in industry and services. If this meant an "overproduction" of industrial goods and services relative to agricultural goods, industrial prices[2] would fall in terms of agricultural prices (agricultural prices will rise in terms of industrial prices, which is the same thing). This will mean a transfer of "real" purchasing power from industry to agriculture, which will go on until the producers in the agricultural sector are able to buy all the goods which industry is capable of producing in excess of industry's own absorption of such goods, whether for purposes of consumption or capital investment. Hence, the price mechanism of competitive markets, which causes a *fall* in the prices of goods in excess supply and a *rise* in prices of goods in excess demand, will always bring about a set of prices at which *all* markets are cleared—to say that demand can never be sufficient to match the potential supply for any or all

---

[1] Adherents of the neoclassical theory may object that this is no more than a "complication", since under the assumption of homogeneous and linear functions the increase in output associated with an increase of capital will be less than proportionate to the increase in capital, so that after a certain number of steps (or a certain number of time periods) the actual frontier will eventually be reached even if that frontier will by then have become far removed from what it appeared to be at the starting date. But this proposition critically depends on the assumption of linear homogeneity of the production functions which ensured that any increase in capital per man will increase output per man less than proportionately. If one abandons the assumption of linearity and allows for increasing returns, it is no longer true—in which case one could equally hold *either* that the frontier will forever remain an unattainable goal *or* that the distinction between an actual historical situation and the equilibrium situation ceases to have a definite meaning.

[2] The same holds for the prices of services provided by the tertiary sector, but for simplicity we shall neglect the existence of the tertiary sector in this analysis.

commodities is the same as saying (according to the Say-Mill view) that the supply would still exceed the demand if the price of any or all commodities fell to zero.

However, this view ignores the peculiar nature of labour, the price of which can never fall to zero—however much the potential supply exceeds the demand in the labour market. Since industrial activities—the processing of crude products of agriculture and mining—invariably require labour, the value added by manufacturing activities cannot fall below a certain minimum (given the productivity of labour in terms of industrial goods), and this minimum sets a limit to the extent to which agricultural prices can rise in terms of industrial prices. But this is the same as saying that in normal circumstances supply cannot equal demand *simultaneously* in both the market for agricultural goods and the market for industrial goods. If the agricultural market is in equilibrium in the sense that the maximum which the sellers are prepared to sell at the prevailing price equals the maximum which the buyers are willing to buy at that price, the industrial market will *not* be in equilibrium in that sense, since the amount actually produced and supplied may be smaller than the amount that would be supplied at the prevailing price, if sufficient demand existed at that price. It is therefore wrong to suggest that the actual output of the economy is determined by the availabilities of resources— capital, labour, and land—which will then be fully utilised irrespective of the structure of demand. If agricultural output is limited by the scarcity of land and not be the availability of labour, and the price of industrial goods in terms of agricultural products is dependent upon the minimum wage which must be paid to labour, then industrial production will be limited by demand and not by the available resources, while the amount of capital available to industry will necessarily vary *pari passu* with the level of industrial production; in other words, capital will also be limited by demand.

This is the intellectual basis of the doctrine of the "foreign trade multiplier", according to which the production of an (industrial) country will be determined by the *external* demand for its products, and will tend to be that multiple of that demand which is represented by the reciprocal of the proportion of *internal* incomes spent on imports. This doctrine asserts the very opposite of Say's law; the level of production will *not* be confined by the availability of capital and labour; on the contrary, the amount of capital accumulated, and the amount of labour effectively employed at any one time, will be the resultant of the growth of external demand over a long series of past periods which permitted the capital accumulation to take place that was required for enabling the amount of labour to be employed and the level of output to be reached which was (or could be) attained in the current period.

Keynes, writing in the middle of the Great Depression of the 1930s, focused his attention on the consequences of the failure to *invest* (due to unfavourable business expectations) in limiting industrial employment *below* industry's attained capacity to provide such employment; and he attributed this failure to excessive saving (or an insufficient propensity to consume) relative to the opportunities for profitable investment. From this came his concentration on liquidity preference and the rate of interest as the basic cause for the failure of Say's law to operate under conditions of low investment opportunities and/or excessive savings, and the importance he attached to the savings/investment multiplier as a short-period determinant of the level of production and employment.

In retrospect, I believe it to have been unfortunate that the very success of Keynes's ideas in connection with the savings/investment multiplier diverted attention from the "foreign trade multiplier" which, over longer periods, is a far more important and basic factor in explaining the growth and rhythm of industrial development. For, over longer periods, Ricardo's presumption that capitalists save only in order to invest, and hence the proportion of profits saved would adapt to changes in the profitability of investment, seems to me more relevant; the limitation of effective demand due to oversaving is a short-run (or cyclical) phenomenon, whereas the rate of growth of "external" demand is a more basic long-run determinant of both the rate of accumulation and the growth of output and employment in the "capital" or "industrial" sectors of the world economy.

Increasing returns

The second major objection (which in some ways is connected with the first) concerns the assumption of linear-homogeneous production functions, *i.e.* the neglect of increasing returns to scale. Here again classical economists show an insight and awareness that is lacking in the neoclassical school. Adam Smith, as is well known, attributed primary importance to the proposition that the efficiency of production—*i.e.* the productivity of labour—depends on the division of labour, and the division of labour in turn depends on the size of the market. He devoted the first three chapters of the *Wealth of Nations* to an exposition of this basic law, and he regarded the existence of a "social economy"—one in which men devote themselves to producing particular things for the market and obtain the commodities they require largely through exchange. Smith's view was that the degree of specialisation in particular processes or in particular portions of processes is constantly enlarged through an increase in the size of the market: the processes of production used when 20,000 pins can be sold daily are very different from the processes used when the daily demand was only for a few hundred pins. Hence productivity expands as the market expands, but the increase in productivity resulting from a larger market in turn enlarges the market for other things and by the same token causes productivity to rise in other industries. As Young (1928) said in a well known article:

> "Adam Smith's famous theorem amounts to saying that the division of labour depends in large part upon the division of labour. This is more than mere tautology. It means that the counter forces which are continually defeating the forces which make for economic equilibrium are more pervasive and more deeply rooted than we commonly realise" (p. 533).

Young said that with increasing returns "change becomes progressive and propagates itself in a cumulative way" (p. 533).

Indeed, these cumulative forces—which Myrdal (1957) called "the principle of circular and cumulative causation"—largely explain the polarisation of the world between the rich and the poor countries that occurred during the last two centuries. Owing to increasing returns, industries tended to be developed in particular growth centres, and in their development they inhibited the growth of industrialisation in other areas. The country which became rich and attained high incomes per head was a country which became "well endowed" with capital and in which therefore the capital/labour ratio became very high. But this capital was largely accumulated out of reinvested profits in consequence of increasing demand, and the ability to use so much capital in relation to labour is very largely a reflection of the scale of activities and not of the relative price of capital and of labour. As Young (1928) emphasised, it would be absurd to suppose that it would "pay" to make a hammer just to drive a single nail, or to furnish a factory "with an elaborate equipment of specially constructed jigs, lathes, drills, presses and conveyors to build a hundred automobiles". It was the increase in the size of the market (not the savings or the rate of interest paid on loans) which made it possible to use so much more capital per worker. The best proof of this resides in the fact that, while the capital/labour ratio increases dramatically in the course of progress (and varies dramatically in the same period between rich and poor countries), these enormous differences (of the order of 30:1 or 50:1) in the capital/labour ratio are quite uncorrelated with differences in the capital/output ratio. If production functions were as neoclassical theory supposes—as is assumed, for example, by Samuelson (1967) who emphasised as the central proposition of neoclassical theory that "*capital/labour up: interest or profit rate down: wage rate up: capital/output up*"—the capital/output ratio would be all the higher the higher the capital/labour ratio.[1]

In fact, the universal experience has been that whether one takes cross-sectional studies, as between different firms in the

---

[1] In fact, it is easy to calculate on the basis of a Cobb-Douglas-type production function that if the capital coefficient of the function is one-third and the labour coefficient two-thirds, doubling the cpaital/labour ratio would involve the increase the capital/output ratio by one-half.

same industry or of the same industry in different countries, or takes a time-series analysis of the movement of labour productivity and of the capital/labour ratio over time, there is no evidence at all to show that high labour productivity—which is almost invariably associated with a correspondingly high capital/labour ratio—is associated with any increase in the amount of capital per unit of output. If anything, the contrary appears to be true. The capital/output ratio in more advanced countries, such as the United States which has the highest capital/labour ratio and the highest output per man, is *lower* than in countries at a low level of industrial development, such as India.

Neoclassical economists attempted for a time to reconcile these phenomena by introducing the *deus ex machina* of a "Harrod-neutral" technical progress which proceeds at an exogenous rate in time. Since technical progress is incapable of being independently measured, this of course was equivalent to making the whole theory untestable or vacuous. Moreover, technical progress is supposed to proceed at some exogenous rate in time, whereas the phenomena to be explained—the high correlation between the capital/labour ratio and of output per man, and the absence of any correlation between these two factors and the capital/output ratio—applies equally to cross-sectional comparisons of firms and industries and to time comparisons. The observed phenomena are, of course, capable of a much simpler explanation: the existence of increasing returns to scale, which makes it possible to use more and more capital with an increase in the scale of production, without encountering diminishing returns. If the use of more specialised machinery is economical only with higher levels of output, there is no reason why a rise in labour productivity should be associated with any fall in capital productivity, but with that explanation, the whole neoclassical value theory clearly goes out of the window.

4. AN ALTERNATIVE APPROACH TO GROWTH THEORY

Most abstract economic models postulate a "closed system", but they apply the conclusions reached to open systems, such as national economies, without being fully aware of the inconsistencies involved in this procedure. "Foreign trade" has always been treated as a special branch of the subject; for the general analysis of prices and markets, it was usual to assume a closed economy, defined by given resources, commodities, markets, etc., which are self-contained.

There is no such really closed system except the world economy as a whole, and, to capture the really important aspects of the economic mechanism, one ought to use a paradigm which embodies the significant features of the world economy as a unit as a starting point in the basic theoretical model before tackling the more complicated models required for particular non-self-sufficient "regions" or "countries".

In a first approximation, one should consider the world economy as consisting of two vital sectors: the production of primary goods (food and raw materials) and the production of "secondary" goods (industry—the processing of crude materials into manufactured goods, whether for industrial use or for final consumption).[1]

Primary production is agriculture (including forestry and fisheries) and mining. These are "land-based" activities in the sense that natural resources play a vital part in the ease or difficulty of their performance—*e.g.* climate, the nature of the soil, and what is beneath the surface in the form of minerals. In some languages, such as German, such activities are referred to as "archproduction" (*Urproduktion*). This conveys the idea that this is the *fond et origine* of all human activities—everything else comes from there; it also conveys the idea that production at any time is governed by the *productivity of the soil*—which is not just a matter of nature but of the state of technology and the amount of capital expended in the past—and not by the productivity of *labour*. For, however essential labour is in all such activities, there is always more labour (and generally much more labour) available than can be *effectively* used on any given area of land. This is because the density of population in any

---

[1] The tertiary sector—services of all kinds—could be ignored in a first approximation.

given area is itself a function of the productivity of the soil—the more food is produced, the more people there will be. Since the output of the soil is a constraint on the labour force, one cannot, at the same time, assume that the labour force is the effective constraint on production—only one of these constraints is likely to "bite" at any one time. And there can be no doubt that with rare exceptions—such as when a region is invaded by new settlers bringing with them a much superior technology capable of producing very much more food per acre of land, as was the case with the first European settlers in America or Oceania—it is the Malthusian constraint which is the critical one, and not the labour constraint. Hence, there is generally disguised unemployment in the rural areas of the world, and economic development essentially consists of tapping these labour reserves. In the course of development, the proportion of population in agriculture diminishes in a dramatic fashion. (In pre-war Bulgaria it was 90 per cent; in present-day Britain it is less than 3 per cent.)

Secondary production converts crude materials into finished goods in two ways—through direct inputs, such as raw wool or cotton made into clothes, and through the food consumed by industrial labour, which is an "indirect" input.

It is important to emphasise that the potential supply of labour to industry is *unlimited*; since the transfer of labour from the primary to the secondary sector (allowing for international as well as intranational migration) can be limited only by the rate at which such labour can be absorbed or utilised, it cannot be constrained by the size of potential supply. (This is true even when international migration is inhibited, so long as capital and enterprise can move across political frontiers.)

But while the supply of labour to industry is practically unlimited, the price paid for the use of that labour cannot fall below a certain amount in terms of primary goods. For wages must cover a certain minimum means of subsistence, irrespective of the size of excess of the supply of labour over demand. Moreover, it is the peculiarity of industrial labour, in modern days of high organisation and even in the ancient days preceding modern industrial capitalism, that the supply price of labour *in terms of food* contains a strong conventional element; wages tend to have a downward rigidity in terms of food prices, around the "attained" or "customary" level, at any rate in free (non-slave) societies, even when that level bears no recognisable relationship to subsistence needs in some biological or calorific sense.

This makes the prices of industrial goods in terms of agricultural products—the terms of trade between industry and agriculture—virtually independent, except in very short periods, of the supply/demand situation in agriculture. (That is to say, agriculture is not likely to obtain *better* prices in terms of industrial goods in times of scarcity. It is less clear that it does not obtain *worse* terms as a result of superabundance, but I believe that over longer periods the latter proposition is like to be true as well.) Hence, the level of prices of processed goods in terms of foodstuffs is determined by three factors $\bar{w}$, l, π, and given by the formula

$$p = (1 + \pi)\bar{w}l$$

where p is the price of manufactured goods in terms of food, $\bar{w}$ the wage of labour in terms of food, π the share of profits in terms of food, and l the labour requirements per unit of output $= 1/(\text{productivity})$.

There are important asymmetries in the position of these two sectors:

(1) Primary output can be assumed to grow at a certain rate owing to technological progress in land-saving inventions (whether in the form of new crops or new means of planting, new fertilisers, cheapening transport, or the discovery of new substitutes, *e.g.* synthetics, requiring fewer natural resources). All these have in common is the fact that they are land saving—*i.e.* they allow more to be extracted from a given natural environment. However, the exploitation of new technology requires capital investment; capital investment is a matter partly of the size of the surplus over the consumption needs of the primary sector, and partly of the terms on which

industrial goods can be obtained in exchange for primary products—in other words, on the terms of trade p. Hence, the rate of growth of primary output will be all the greater the more favourable are the terms of trade to agriculture. This is projected by the downward-sloping nature of the $\dot{A}/A$ curve in Fig. 2.

(2) With regard to industry, as was argued earlier, there is a minimum supply price below which no production would be forthcoming; this at the point k where $p = \bar{w}l$. Industrial production can grow only if some part of the output is "ploughed back" in the form of industrial investment. To the extent that this happens, $p > k$, the excess $(p - k)/k$ being equal to the share of output which is "retained" by the sector for the purpose of investment by the sector. In industry, therefore, investment "finances itself" since it generates equivalent profits (excess of p over k) automatically. If, in addition, part of the profits are consumed (profits generate consumption), $p - k$ will be that much larger.

Figure 2. $\dot{A}/A$ is the growth rate of agricultural production, $\dot{B}/B$ the growth rate of industrial production.

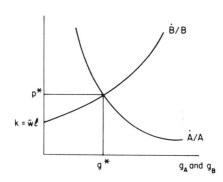

(3) This means that, in the case of *secondary output*, the *supply price* of industry curve $\dot{B}/B$ starting from $k = wl$ will rise in a functional relation to $g_B = \dot{B}/B$ (Fig. 2).

There should exist at any one time a point at which $g = g_A = g_B$ and (abstracting from consumption out of industrial products) $p = (1 + \text{n})\bar{w}l = (1 + gv)\bar{w}l$. Whether this point is reached and, if reached, maintained over time, is a complex problem which I cannot enter into here. But *supposing* the system does have a tendency to settle at p^* and will grow at the rate g^*, this itself will vary with time, since, owing to economies of large-scale production and labour-saving (as distinct from land-saving) technical progress, $dl_t/dt < 0$, $\dot{B}/B$ will shift downward with time, hence p_t will be falling with t, and g_t will be rising. With both labour- and land-saving technical progress and a *given* real wage in terms of food (or primary products), economic growth should not only be continuous but would show a tendency to continual *acceleration* (at any rate when exhaustible resources are ignored).

(4) However, there is no *need* for this to happen in this way. Real wages need not be constant at $\bar{w}$; $dw_t/dt > 0$ is quite possible, owing to all kinds of things—monopolistic or oligopolistic price policies by industrial firms, or the pressure exerted through trade unions.

A special case is $dw_t/d_t = -dl_t/d_t$, in which p_t will be constant over time and g_t will be constant ($dg_t/d_t = 0$). But $dw_t/d_t > -dl_t/d_t$ cannot be excluded either, in which case $dg_t/d_t < 0$: with wages rising faster than productivity in industry, the equilibrium growth rate will tend to diminish.

(5) In any case, we can assume that the rate of expansion of industrial capacity is "induced": the "accelerator principle" governs the rate of capital accumulation in the industrial sector. At any given p_0, the growth of "outside" demand proceeds at the rate g_0 and this induces, by a multiplier/accelerator process, a corresponding rate of capital accumulation and of the growth of output in industry.

(6) Hence in *this* model, industrial growth is dependent on the exogenous components of demand for industry—that part of the demand which comes from "outside" the industrial sector: the growth of its exports (even though this may only amount to a small fraction of the total output or demand—the rest will tend to be resonant with it). Hence *industry* will determine what the terms of trade will be, since p will depend on factors endogenous to the sector; but the growth of

purchasing power of the primary sector (which is the same as its growth of output $\dot{A}/A$) will determine the growth rates of both; and $\dot{A}/A$ is itself a function of p.

All this, of course, is a tremendous oversimplification, deliberately neglecting numerous complicating elements. But the main message to be drawn is that if one assumes that markets function so as to be consistent with expansion—which means that an increase in supply of A will increase the purchasing power of the A sector for B products and vice versa—the rate of growth will ultimately depend on the growth of foodstuffs and basic materials, which is itself dependent on p as shown by some such relationship as the $\dot{A}/A$ curve in Fig. 2.

So, finally, it is the progress of land-saving inventions— including here the continued invention of new substitutes for existing materials and sources of energy—which not only sets the limit to growth, but in the long run governs the rate of growth.

All this is true if we regard world industrial output as a single entity. To analyse the divergent trends in the growth rate of different regions and countries, we must go further and consider the competition between different industrial areas. Owing to the economies of large-scale production and of spatial (geographical) concentration, industrial growth tends to be concentrated in urban areas: the growth of industry and of urbanisation are closely related. But any *particular* region may have a rising, constant, or falling share in the total world market for "industrial goods" (including its own "protected" market). In the course of time, new industrial centres emerge and displace, or narrow, the market for the older centres. The fast-growing countries *gain* in competitiveness, for their "efficiency wages", $w_t l_t$, fall in relation to those of areas which grow more slowly—whose market share is diminishing.

In industrial growth, owing to increasing returns, Myrdal's principle of "cumulative and circular causation" operates. Success breeds success; regions or "countries" whose industrial exports increase faster than world net exports have a faster rate of economic growth; this tends to depress the rate of growth of the regions whose share of world trade is diminishing in consequence. Industrialisation is the key factor in economic development. All rich countries with high incomes per capita are industrialised countries. Myrdal's principle explains why rapid growth tends to be concentrated among a relatively small number of "successful" areas, and also, why, within that fortunate group of areas, the relative wealth and standard of living are subject to continuous change—poorer areas with lower efficiency wages overtake areas which were initially richer, but, owing to higher wages in relation to their productivity, are unable to stand up to the competition of others. Both the growing polarisation of the world between developed and underdeveloped, or rich and poor countries, and the remarkable shifts in the relative positions of individual "rich" countries are, in my view, to be explained by the same basic principle.

REFERENCES

Fisher, I. (1906). *The Nature of Capital and Income*. New York: Macmillan.
Kornai, J. (1971). *Anti-Equilibrium*. Amsterdam: North-Holland Publ.
Mill, J.S. (1848). *Principles of Political Economy*, Vol. II. London: John W. Parker.
Myrdal, G. (1957). *Economic Theory and Underdeveloped Regions*. London: Duckworth.
Robbins, L.C. (1932). *An Essay on the Nature and Significance of Economic Science*, p. 12. London: Macmillan.
Samuelson, P.A. (1967). *Economics—An Introductory Analysis*, 7th ed., p.715. New York: McGraw-Hill.
Young, A.A. (1928). "Increasing Returns and Economic Progress". *Economic Journal* (December).

PART V

DOMESTIC AND INTERNATIONAL ECONOMIC POLICY

18

A NEW LOOK AT THE EXPENDITURE TAX[1]

THERE has been a revival of interest recently in the idea of replacing personal income tax by a personal expenditure tax. As one who explored the idea more than a quarter of a century ago,[1a] and later had a share in getting it adopted (albeit not very successfully) in India and Ceylon, I feel it incumbent on me to say how far my position on the issue has changed, and how far I subscribe to the various schemes recently advocated on both sides of the Atlantic.[2]

The basic issue of income versus expenditure as the ideal measure of taxable capacity can be discussed at various levels.

To some economists, of whom Irving Fisher is the most famous, the real meaning of income is a flow of personal satisfactions or more accurately that part of it which is derived from the consumption (or destruction) of things which have an exchange value, the sum of which can be expressed in terms of exchange value (or purchasing power).[3] Looked at in this way, the measure of the aggregate flow over a time interval is consumption, and not

---

[1] Based on a talk given at a Brookings Conference on *Income versus Expenditure Taxes* in Washington, October 1978.

[1a] *An Expenditure Tax*, London, Allen and Unwin, 1955.

[2] Cf. J. E. Meade and associates, *The Structure and Reform of Direct Taxation*, Report to the Institute of Fiscal Studies, London, Allen and Unwin, 1978; J. A. Kay and M. A. King, *The British Tax System*, Oxford, 1978; *The Expenditure Tax*, by James Griffin on behalf of the Advisory Commission on Intergovernmental Relations, Washington D.C., 1974; U.S. Department of the Treasury, *Blueprints for Basic Tax Reform*, 1977; William D. Andrews, *A Supplemental Personal Expenditure Tax*, to be published by the Brookings Institution, Washington D.C.; David F. Bradford, *The Case for a Personal Consumption Tax*, ditto; M. J. Graetz, *Implementation of a Progressive Tax on Consumption*, ditto; S. O. Lodin, *Progressive Expenditure Tax—An Alternative?*, Stockholm, 1978.

[3] There are innumerable kinds of satisfactions—such as friendship, divine worship, the contemplation of beautiful objects, love in its various forms, etc.—which cannot be bought and sold and must therefore be left out of account.

what is usually regarded as income, which is consumption plus net saving. According to Fisher, net saving over a period is nothing else but the discounted value of the *increment* to the flow of future satisfactions resulting from decisions made in the current period; and the addition of the discounted value of future satisfactions to the (undiscounted) sum of current satisfactions involves double counting. Saving is an addition to future satisfactions; it should not therefore also be counted as part of present satisfactions as well.

As against that is the Haig-Simons conception of income as "the net increment of economic power between two points of time". Here the basic notion is the addition, over a time interval, to an individual's command over society's scarce resources, irrespective of how much or how little of it he chooses to exercise for the purpose of current consumption.

On the Haig-Simons view it is a man's command over scarce resources which is the measure of his "economic power", and this in turn is the proper yardstick for assessing his capacity to contribute to the expenses of society.

There is no particular virtue, however, in measuring this power by its annual increment rather than its total at a given moment. An annual wealth tax which assesses individuals according to their power of command over resources as such may therefore appear a more reliable measure than an income tax which takes account of the current increment of economic power only.

There are, however, at least two reasons why historically a tax based on income appears the more natural (and reasonable) measure of taxable capacity than a tax based on the sources of income.

One is that "power of command" over resources has different implications according to whether or not a man's wealth consists of things that can be disposed of at a moment's notice, so that he is free to exercise that power at any time—whether for the satisfaction of personal needs or whims, the exploitation of an opportunity to make a profitable investment, or in ways that add to his influence over his fellow men or to the esteem in which he is held. At one extreme is the case where a man keeps the bulk of his wealth in gold or other precious metals or in bank accounts that can be withdrawn on demand or at short notice. It would be universally agreed that the taxable capacity of such individuals cannot be measured by their income, however defined. At the other extreme is the man who holds a life interest in an entailed estate which he cannot dispose of; his true command over resources is confined to the value of the produce of the land. Even if the land is not entailed, the owner of it in a predominantly agricultural community would not regard it as a disposable asset; the actual measure of his command over resources (or his "wealth") is the harvest from the soil, not the soil itself. In a modern capitalist community where physical assets are to a predominant extent "owned" by legal personalities—by companies, public or private—with the corollary that an individual's ownership consists of negotiable titles to wealth, in the form of stocks and shares, the distinction between "disposable" and "non-disposable" wealth is blurred. In this latter case, the annual yield (in the form of interest and dividends) on such "financial assets" may vary for all kinds of reasons as between different "titles" which are in no relation to the relative advantages which their possession confers on the owners. In this case an annual wealth tax may give a far more reliable measure of taxation in accordance with "economic power" than a tax levied on interest and dividends.[1]

A second reason is that the wealth residing in personal earning power—which has no market value because it cannot be alienated, any more than entailed land—cannot, as such, serve as a measure of taxable capacity. Hence in regard to the economic benefits derived from work-performance, there is no alternative to income as a measure of "economic power". On the other hand it is desirable that the taxable capacity derived from material possessions and from personal earning power should be assessed on a comparable basis, particularly since many individuals derive "economic power" from both sources simultaneously and a progressive system requires that incomes from all sources should be aggregated. This can only be accomplished through a personal income tax; though the imposition of a progressive tax on income from all sources does not exclude a supplemental tax on material

---

[1] Though this is less certain in relation to a comprehensive income tax which includes capital gains as income.

wealth, which can be justified on the ground that the possession of disposable assets endows its owners with an additional "economic power" which has no equivalent in the case of those whose sources of income are non-disposable (or inalienable).

As I think I made clear in my book, I found the Haig-Simons conception of taxable capacity intellectually more appealing than the Fisherian conception—except on the ground of social ethics which suggests that it is better to tax people on the basis of what they take out of the common pool than on the basis of what they put into it. However, from the point of view of distributive justice this is not a decisive consideration. I came to the advocacy of an expenditure tax mainly on account of the difficulties of finding a definition of income that gives proper effect to the Haig-Simons conception; and the impossibility, in terms of legislative and administrative practice, of approximating such notion of income for tax purposes, even if a theoretically satisfactory definition were found.

The Haig conception, as Simons has shown,[1] is identical with the sum of consumption and net saving. All the difficulties with income tax concern the problem of taxing "net savings" in a comprehensive manner that is just and fair as between individuals in different circumstances. As Simons so convincingly argued, capital appreciation—an increase in the market value of a man's properties—is a form of saving and no different in nature from an increase in the value of assets of the same magnitude which results from an addition to the stock of assets, such as the purchase of bonds and shares out of current income. Indeed, an appreciation in the value of ordinary shares may be no more than the equivalent of the savings made in the form of retentions by companies on behalf of their shareholders. In an ideal system therefore capital gains should be treated in the same way as other forms of income; moreover, to be just between different taxpayers, capital gains should be taxed as they accrue, and not only when the assets are realised. However, it is generally agreed that the annual taxation of unrealised capital appreciation would be an administrative nightmare. For that reason even the most ardent advocates of a comprehensive income tax stop short of advocating it.

[1] Henry Simons, *Personal Income Taxation* (Chicago, 1938).

But the basic difficulties with the notion of net saving do not lie with the realisation criterion (which involves, in effect, a reduction in the effective rates of taxation as compared with savings made out of "ordinary" income, and one which varies for wholly accidental reasons between different taxpayers) but on the question whether the appreciation in the value of financial assets is in the nature of an *accrual* (which is invariably a *process* in time) or whether it is the result of a re-valuation of future prospects (which normally occurs at a *point* in time). An increase in value which has its counterpart in an increment of assets (i.e. that which enters into "saving" in the sense defined for national income purposes) is clearly in the nature of an *accrual*. But a revaluation of existing assets (which is not part of "saving" as defined for the purposes of national income calculations) can nevertheless be an addition to an individual's "economic power", if it represents an increase in his command over goods and services. In assessing the taxable capacity of different *individuals* the notion of saving cannot be restricted to accruals only—any more than one can say that a business earns a true profit only by making more shoes, not from selling more attractive or fashionable shoes for which it is able to charge a higher price.

However, this is not true of *all* re-valuations, and it is not possible—in theory, let alone as a matter of practical administration—to isolate the genuine kind from the non-genuine kind. If two taxpayers spend equal amounts over the same period, they can be *presumed* to have had the same real consumption—though in times of inflation this statement will only be true within limits, since one person's expenditure-basket may have shown a larger rise in prices (between two points of time) than another person's. Nevertheless the extent of arbitrariness thereby introduced is limited and could be safely disregarded for practical purposes. But when it comes to net saving, two persons who show the same net amount of saving in terms of money—irrespective of whether the saving represents a transfer of funds from an income account to a capital account (i.e. the purchase of additional shares out of income) or merely the appreciation in the value of shares already held—will not normally have gained equally in terms of "economic power". In times of inflation allowances should be made for the reduced purchasing power of money, if only because any given rate of inflation will have differing implications for different taxpayers according to their individual circumstances. Thus when the rate of inflation is, say, 10 per cent. a year and two taxpayers have both made in a particular year a net saving of £100 in terms of money, the net addition to "economic power" would be negative to a person who had £2000 to start with, but positive to the man who started with less than £1000. The appropriate adjustment for inflation is not a simple matter of the indexation of net saving; the proper allowance depends not only on the rise in prices in a given period, but on the relationship of the current accrual of wealth to the volume of a person's possessions at the beginning of the period.[1]

As I have shown in my book, the same kind of problem arises when capital values change owing to a change in the rate of interest (rather than in the expectation of future yields or earnings) and this in turn is analogous to the re-valuation which is the result, not of a change in the rate of interest, but of a change in the (subjective) uncertainty surrounding the expectations of future earnings which are discounted.

I therefore came down in favour of the expenditure tax principle not just because of the loopholes and defects in existing systems of income tax but because of basic limitations of the income concept which make it impossible to give practical effect to the Haig-Simons conception, no matter how the tax laws are framed. In that sense my advocacy of an expenditure tax was that of a second best. If "spending power" is measured by actual spending, there is an injustice in the allocation of the tax burden as between misers and spendthrifts. But if it is assumed (which I

[1] It is for this reason that partial indexation of certain forms of gain (which is the only adjustment that appears practicable) by "writing up" the costs of assets by some price index may create more inequities between taxpayers than would exist without it. It would be unfair to index gains without also indexing losses; to do this adequately would require an annual valuation of *all* assets (including cash, bank deposits, etc.) and not only those which happen to be bought and sold in a particular year. As numerous writers pointed out, so long as inflation persists, the taxation of capital gains (measured in money terms) includes an element of a wealth tax, and serves as some kind of substitute for the latter. The wealth tax element will not be a too large one so long as the yield of the capital gains tax amounts to no more than a small proportion of the value of privately owned wealth. The fact that the tax falls mainly on those whose capital is appreciating most (since there is bound to be a fairly strong correlation, at any rate over a run of years, between capital appreciation and realised capital gains) is thus not necessarily a "distributional evil"—even in times of inflation.

think is not an unreasonable assumption) that different individuals' propensity to spend does not vary much because of differences in tastes and temperaments (as Pigou called it), but mainly because of objective factors that a tax system can make allowance for—for example, the number of dependents—a tax based on actual spending may give a better approximation of true spending power than any practically feasible tax on income.

There is no need, however, to opt for one to the exclusion of the other; and as I argued in a later work,[1] in a society composed of individuals who draw benefits in many forms from widely different sources, a system of personal direct taxation based on a number of criteria (such as income, expenditure, capital gains, net wealth, the receipt of gifts and inheritances) may give a more reasonable or more reliable allocation of taxation in accordance with taxable capacity than a system based on a single criterion only.

Such a "multiple-criteria" system would have two practical advantages. First, it would make it very much easier to operate a personal expenditure tax on a "cash flow" basis—i.e. by the method of measuring expenditure as the difference between cash received from all sources and all non-taxable outlays. (All advocates of a graduated personal expenditure tax, at least from Irving Fisher onwards[2] agree that the only practical way of ascertaining how much a person spent over a period is by taking what a person had at the beginning of the period, adding his cash receipts during the period and subtracting what he was left with at the end, including in the latter the net purchases during the year of capital assets of all kinds.) However this depends on the tax authorities receiving regular and comprehensive information on cash received from all sources—from the sale of assets, from depletion of cash and bank balances, borrowings, business withdrawals, gifts and inheritances, as well as the receipts which rank as "income payments" and are thus liable to tax under present law. Though in principle it would be possible for the tax authorities to request all this information for the purposes of the expenditure tax only (just as is done now when the

---

[1] *Indian Tax Reform, Report of a Survey* (New Delhi, Ministry of Finance, Government of India, 1956), reprinted in Volume 8 of these Essays.
[2] Cf. I. Fisher, "Income in Theory and Income Taxation in Practice", *Econometrica* (1937).

Revenue requires a "wealth statement" in the so-called "back-duty" cases) in practice it is difficult to imagine that all this information would be readily forthcoming, unless the information would be readily forthcoming, unless the information was required for the purposes of assessment of some tax—such as the annual wealth tax, the tax on capital gains (which already involves reporting on the purchases of all capital assets), a gift and inheritance tax, as well as an income tax.[1]

A second advantage of a multiple-based system is that it would make it easier to introduce the expenditure tax, not as a complete replacement of income tax, but as a supplemental tax which would replace the higher rates of income tax (i.e. something corresponding to the old surtax) and not the basic-rate income tax. For reasons given in my book there are important advantages in this procedure, not least of which is that it would make the transitional problems of changing over to the new system less serious than they would be otherwise.[2] Another advantage is that while there are numerous incongruous concessions to savings in the existing tax legislation (in the form of life assurances, super-annuation and mortgage relief, as well as various kinds of subsidies on investment) it is only in the higher ranges of wealth or income that these concessions become really anomalous, since they make it possible for the wealthier taxpayer to claim tax relief on purely fictitious savings which are offset, or more than offset, by dis-savings out of capital or capital gains. The expenditure of the typical wage and salary earner is far more closely geared to his taxable income: hence the exemption of savings in his case (with the exception of mortgage relief) does not make so much difference in the *relative* burden of taxation as between different individuals. Since such savings (mainly contractual) are a relatively small proportion of income, their exemption goes to reduce the yield of any given tax schedule without greatly changing the distribution of taxation between taxpayers. In the higher income ranges, however (and particularly in the case of incomes

---

[1] As I recommended in my Indian tax report, the liability to all these taxes could be assessed on the basis of information given in a single comprehensive return.

[2] The recent U.S. advocates of an expenditure tax, particularly Professor William D. Andrews, came down in favour of a supplemental tax, and so did the Meade Report. (Cf. his paper "A Supplemental Personal Expenditure Tax" in the forth-coming Brookings publication.)

derived from capital), these various concessions produce highly anomalous results.

What I feel about the recent advocates of the change-over from income to expenditure as the basis of personal taxation—on both sides of the Atlantic—is the same as what I now think about my own writing of twenty-five years ago. They both show a lack of awareness (or at least of sufficient awareness) of the political and sociological problems involved in closing tax loopholes. A highly distorted and loophole-ridden income tax is compared with an expenditure tax drawn up on the right principles and free of distortions and of anomalous concessions resulting from political pressures.

In fact, as the example of India shows, it is just as easy to make a mockery of an expenditure tax as it has been with progressive income tax. The Expenditure Tax Bill, introduced by the Finance Minister, the late T. T. Krishnamachari, in 1957, was so severely mauled in its passage through the Lokh Saba (the Indian Parliament) that the outcome was a joke—incapable of enforcement, and a sheer waste of time for the tax administration. The particular provision which crippled the tax in the case of India was that the liability to the tax was tied to a minimum income limit and not a minimum expenditure limit. All that was necessary to avoid any liability to the expenditure tax was to manipulate income so that the critical limit was not attained at least in those years in which a sizeable expenditure tax liability would have been incurred. And as everyone knows it is not difficult to avoid having an excessive income. In addition the Act contained a long series of exemptions—such as expenditure on marriages, on medical expenses, the purchase of cottage industry products, etc., which have no counterpart in the income tax laws. There is little doubt that if the tax had not been withdrawn fairly soon after its introduction these loopholes would have become wider.[1]

If, as has been argued, "the current political climate is not hospitable to the taxation of capital or an increase in the taxation of capital gains", why is it supposed that it is hospitable to the

[1] For my contemporary views on the Indian tax reform introduced following my recommendations, cf. my paper *Tax Reform in India* originally published in the *Economic Weekly*, Bombay, January 1959, and reprinted in Volume 3 of these Essays.

introduction of a progressive expenditure tax? The very idea of such a tax was *unanimously* rejected by the Finance Committee of the United States Senate, and this was during a particularly critical phase of World War II (in September 1942) with the tax intended for the duration of the war only.

There are, as is well known, many millionaires in the United States, in England and in other countries who manage to avoid payment of income tax—because they can avoid having a *net* taxable income—who yet live in great luxury and manage to become steadily richer as well. It would be easy to conceive of changes in the tax laws that would make these people just as liable to taxation as the man in the street. Since this is not done there must be powerful political reasons for it; and these reasons would be just as powerful whether the attempt to create a genuine system of progressive taxation were made through a supplemental expenditure tax or through a reform of the income tax.[1]

The strongest political argument in favour of a supplemental expenditure tax is that it removes (or at least it greatly weakens) the case which is so frequently made against progressive taxation on the grounds that it reduces the funds available for savings of those taxpayers who, on account of their high incomes, are alone in a position to save a substantial part of their incomes. If net savings are exempt from taxation (or taxed only at a low rate) it cannot be said that the well-to-do are deprived through taxation of the means to save.

However, this argument is not as strong as it appears—not if one believes (as I do) that the market mechanism always generates sufficient profits to finance the investment that entrepreneurs decide to undertake. An expenditure tax, by encouraging savings and discouraging spending of the well-to-do, will not thereby cause more investment to be undertaken unless there are other

[1] Indeed there is a group of American economists who use one of the arguments in favour of the expenditure tax principle—i.e. that it avoids the double taxation of savings—for advocating the abolition of *all* taxes on profit, interest and dividends and turning the existing income tax into a wage tax. The argument is that all capital is the fruit of past saving; it must therefore have suffered taxation *already* when it was first accumulated out of taxed income; and the simplest way to avoid the double taxation of savings is not to exempt net savings when they are made, but to exempt the fruits of savings. Since all extant capital must have been "saved" by someone sometime, this, according to this view, "justifies" exempting all unearned income from taxation altogether (see David Bradford, *The Case for a Personal Consumption Tax*, op. cit.; also *Blueprints for Basic Tax Reform*, Department of the Treasury, Washington D.C., 1977).

incentives (of a monetary or fiscal kind) which ensure that there is more investment *pari passu* with the reduced spending of the well-to-do. But assuming that such instruments are available, and appropriate policies of economic management are followed by the Government, much the same distribution of resources between investment and luxury consumption could be secured (in principle) under the one system as under the other.

MONETARY POLICY, ECONOMIC STABILITY AND GROWTH[1]

1. The present memorandum deals almost exclusively with basic issues concerning the role of monetary and credit policy in the maintenance of stability in prices and incomes, rather than with questions concerning the technique of monetary management. My excuse for putting forth a paper devoted to elementary propositions is the prevalence of confused thinking in this particular field even among eminent authorities. Yet without a basic understanding of the processes through which changes in the amount of money in circulation influence the level of expenditure and the general level of prices, it is impossible to arrive at any sound judgment concerning the merits of particular methods of monetary management.[2]

I. THE MODUS OPERANDI OF MONETARY POLICY

The Supply of Money and the Level of Expenditure

2. It cannot be emphasised too strongly that there is no direct relationship in a modern community between the amount of money in circulation (whatever definition of "money supply" is adopted in this connection) and the amount of money spent on goods and services per unit of time. To proceed from the one to the other it is necessary to postulate that changes in the supply of money leave the frequency with which money changes hands (the so-called "velocity of circulation of money") unaffected, or at least that any consequential change in the velocity of circulation is limited to some predictable fraction of the primary change in the supply of money. There are no valid grounds however for

---

[1] A memorandum submitted to the Committee on the Working of the Monetary System on June 23, 1958.
[2] The present memorandum is restricted to the internal aspects of monetary policy. Its external aspects (questions of the exchange rates, the sterling area system, convertibility, capital movements, etc.) are outside its scope.

any such supposition. The velocity of circulation of money (or what comes to the same thing, the ratio which cash balances bear to the volume of turnover of money payments, per unit of time) is not determined by factors that are independent either of the supply of money or the volume of money payments; it simply reflects the relationship between these two magnitudes. In some communities the velocity of circulation is low, in others it is high, in some it is rising and in others it is falling, without any systematic connection between such differences or movements and the degree of inflationary pressure, the rate of increase in monetary turnover,[1] etc. Such differences can only be explained in terms of historical developments rather than psychological propensities or of institutional factors, while the movements in the ratio can only be accounted for by the varying incidence of the policies pursued by the monetary authorities. In countries where the authorities pursue a restrictive policy, the ratio tends to fall, and *vice versa*. Thus in the U.K. there has been a spectacular rise in the velocity of circulation, particularly since 1955, which fully compensated for the failure of the money supply to expand *pari passu* with the rise in prices and in money incomes. The "money supply" has been kept constant (indeed it has been slightly falling) while the annual percentage rise in the money value of the national product has been as great or greater than in previous years when the money supply was rising. It could not seriously be maintained that this change in the velocity of circulation was in any sense an *independent* phenomenon which happened to coincide in time with the change in monetary policy. It was simply a reflection of this policy: if the supply of money had not

[1] According to the statistics published by the International Monetary Fund, the ratio of the money supply (currency plus deposit money) to the gross national product varied in the latest available year (1957 or 1956) from 54 per cent. in Switzerland, 46 per cent. in Belgium, 38 per cent. in Brazil and 36 per cent. in France to 30 per cent. in the U.S., 27·5 per cent. in the U.K., 18 per cent. in Germany and 13 per cent. in Mexico. In the period since 1951 this ratio fell in some countries, and rose in others, but there was no systematic connection between these movements and the rate of increase in the money value of the G.N.P., or that and the initial magnitude of this ratio. The ratio fell in some relatively "inflationary" countries (e.g. in the U.S. from 37 to 30 per cent., in the U.K. from 36 to 27·5 per cent., in Mexico from 16 to 13 per cent.) as well as in some "non-inflationary" countries (e.g. in Switzerland from 62 to 54 per cent.). It rose in some relatively "non-inflationary" countries (e.g. in Germany from 14 to 18 per cent., in Belgium from 40 to 46 per cent.) as well as in some "inflationary" countries (in France from 31 to 36 per cent. and in Brazil from 35 to 38 per cent.).

been restricted, the increase in the velocity of circulation would not have taken place and it is a matter of doubt, to say the least, whether the course of prices and incomes would have been any different. At any rate the *impact* effect of any change in the money supply is not on the level of payments at all, but on the velocity of circulation.[1]

3. Those who maintain the opposite view (the adherents of the "quantity theory" of money) argue that the social and institutional factors which determine the frequency of recurring payments of various kinds (the frequency of wage and salary payments, the frequency of settlement of business accounts, etc.), together with the uncertainty concerning the exact timing of these payments lead to individuals and businesses having a certain "desired" cash balance in relation to turnover which is substantially independent of the supply of money. It is a mistake to assume, however, that given the normal frequency of various kinds of payments the maintenance of any given *flow* of payments requires some definite quantity of monetary media. Outstanding cash balances invariably contain large amounts held for purely speculative purposes, or out of the "precautionary" motive (i.e. as hedge against unforeseen delays in the inflow of prospective receipts) as well as the so-called "transaction balances" proper, i.e. those arising automatically as the result of differences in the relative time frequency of receipts and out-payments. These latter, in turn, can be reduced considerably through "synchronising" payments and receipts, and through the creation of money substitutes of various kinds. As the experience of Germany and other countries during the great inflations has shown, the economic system in case of need can be "run" on a very small fraction of its normal cash requirements. (In Germany in 1923 money in circulation amounted to less than $\frac{1}{2}$ per cent. of the current level of incomes, expressed at annual rates.) Obviously this cannot be attained without considerable inconvenience; and the resulting rise in the rate of interest paid on short loans is the measure of the extent of this inconvenience. The experience of various countries indicates that when the ratio of cash to turnover is at more normal

---

[1] Failure to recognise this vitiates much of recent thinking on monetary matters. Cf. e.g. the *First Report of the Council on Prices, Productivity and Incomes*, (1958) particularly chap. v.

levels (i.e. in the range of 20–50 per cent. of the annual value of G.N.P.) the "inconvenience" caused by changes in the ratio is not very great—i.e. considerable changes in the money supply in relation to the national income can take place without inducing spectacular changes in interest rates.

The Effect of Changes in Interest Rates on the Level of Expenditure

4. Yet it is through the consequential changes in interest rates that we must look for the effects of changes in the money supply on the demand for goods and services.[1] In theory a rise in interest rates should lead to a postponement of postponable expenditures by both businesses and personal consumers, as well as to some more or less permanent reduction in the rate at which capital expenditures are incurred. Thus a rise in interest rates should cause businesses to reduce the ratio of the stocks of materials and finished goods which they carry in relation to turnover—in much the same manner as their cash payments-turnover ratio—but here the "interest-elasticity" is likely to be much smaller, since economising on physical stocks may involve heavy costs in the form of higher transport charges, losses due to delays in production, etc., and not just "inconvenience."[2] To achieve any substantial reduction in the rate of investment in stocks far greater changes in (short-term) interest rates would have been required than have taken place since 1954.

5. The effect of a rise in interest rates on short-term investment is in any case a temporary one: if the rise in interest rates is successful in inducing traders to reduce their stocks in relation to turnover, it will restrain the pressure of demand as long as this process of adjustment is going on; once the adjustment is completed, the restraining effect of a higher interest rate on the level of expendi-

---

[1] Where the loan market is imperfect (as it is with an oligopolistic banking system) interest rates may not fully reflect the pressure of the demand for loans, owing to the policy of "credit rationing" adopted by the banks. In this case, however, unsatisfied borrowers willing to pay higher rates are likely to turn to other financial institutions willing to cater for their needs. (The mushroom growth of hire-purchase finance houses, for business as well as personal purposes, was a direct consequence of the policy of the "credit squeeze" imposed on the clearing banks after 1955.)

[2] The policy of the "credit squeeze" in the U.K. since February 1955, while it involved a substantial change in the size of cash balances held in relation to turnover, did not cause any contraction in the size of physical stocks in relation to turnover: the (real) rate of investment in stocks, in each of the three years 1955 to 1957 was substantially higher than in the preceding three years.

ture is exhausted. This means that it is hopeless to expect a downward adjustment in stocks induced by credit policy to compensate (more than temporarily) for inflationary pressures emanating from other sectors—from, say, a chronic insufficiency of savings in relation to investment in fixed capital, the budgetary deficit, or the export surplus.[1]

6. The effect of higher interest rates on long-term investment may be more lasting, but here again, only drastic and spectacular changes in interest rates can be counted on to exert a marked effect on capital expenditure. The reasons for this are as follows:

(i) The interest rate relevant to long-term investment is the long-term rate whose movement is sluggish in relation to changes in the short-term rate. (This is on account of the fact that both unusually high and unusually low short-term rates are regarded as temporary by the market; hence a change in the short-term rate normally induces a change in the long-term rate in the same direction but of a considerably smaller magnitude.)

(ii) Such increases in the long-term rate as occur in response to a rise in the short rate are only regarded as temporary since the market assumes that bond prices are depressed on account of the high money rates, and will recover with any reduction in the latter. Hence the rise in the long-term rates will not have the same discouraging effect on capital expenditure as it might have if the current long rates were expected to be permanent, and if it were not open to investors to finance long-term capital expenditure with short-term borrowing on the prospect of being able to borrow over long-term on more advantageous terms later on.[2]

(iii) There is normally a considerable gap between the prospective rate of profit obtainable on direct investment and the market rates of interest on money loans. This gap serves (in Ricardo's words) as "compensation for the [farmers' and manufacturers'] trouble and the risk which they must necessarily encounter in employing their capital productively." However,

[1] It is a different matter when the acceleration of stock accumulation or the reverse is the source of instability. This could in principle be compensated for by correctly timed and correctly scaled variations in the terms of short term credit. Cf. paras. 27-30 below.

[2] The very fact that in times of high money market rates the yield of irredeemable bonds may actually stand lower than the bill rates or the bond rates on loans with most maturity is a clear indication that the market expects a fall in the long term rates in the future.

this compensation for risk and trouble is not something rigid, and when the rate of profit exceeds the rate of interest by a considerable percentage (as, for example, when the prospective rate of profit is 15 per cent. and the rate of interest only 5 per cent.), moderate changes in the rate of interest may have no appreciable effect on investment decisions. It must be remembered that in times of rising prices the rate of profit is higher (as will be shown in paragraph 11 below, the annual percentage increase in the price level may be regarded as a flat addition to what would have been the ruling rate of profit with a stable price level) and therefore the gap between the rate of profit and the rate of interest may be abnormally large.[1]

(iv) It must be remembered that in times of full employment, or even of approximately full employment, the capacity of the investment goods industries may exert a far more important limitation on the level of capital expenditure than the cost of borrowing or the availability of particular forms of finance. Thus the rate of building and constructional activity may be confined by the availability of building and constructional labour; expenditure on plant and equipment may be limited by lengthening delivery periods on new contracts.[2] In such situations the range of projects whose execution would be influenced by changes in the cost of borrowing or in the availability of loans might be unusually narrow, and be largely confined to cases where the terms of lending can be regulated by quantitative rules, and where the borrower cannot easily find alternative sources of finance. Such is the case with consumer purchases of durable goods (motor-cars, etc., as well as houses) which can be regulated

[1] The taxation system also operates so as to reduce the sensitivity of investment decisions to changes in interest rates. For what matters from the point of view of the entrepreneurs is the excess of the prospective net rate of profit on investment (net after income tax and profits tax) over the net rate of interest on loans (net of income tax). With a given gross rate of profit the excess of the net rate of profit over the net rate of interest will of course only be reduced (with a rate of income tax of 50 per cent.) by one-half of every percentage point rise in the gross rate of interest.

[2] One of the assumptions of traditional economic theory is that any such limitation would cause a rise in prices and profit margins of capital goods which in turn would reduce the gap between profit rates and interest rates to normal levels. However, when a considerable sector of the economy operates under oligopolistic conditions with "administered" prices, an excess demand can overhang the market for long periods without being eliminated through price inflation. Since a particular investment project consists of a number of complementary expenditures, it is possible moreover that the demand for the products of the competitive sectors is held down by the availability of complementary goods produced by oligopolistic sectors.

by laying down terms (such as a legal minimum of down-payments) for the granting of hire-purchase credit and mortgage finance.[1]

Summary of Above Argument

7. The argument up to this point may be summed up as follows:

(i) Changes in the money supply do not exert any direct influence on the level of monetary demand for goods and services as such, but only through the consequential changes in interest rates which are induced by them. (ii) The magnitude of these consequential changes in interest rates for any given percentage change in the money supply depends on the extent of inconvenience (or, conversely, increased convenience) involved in any corresponding change in the average ratio of cash balances to monetary turnover. Except where this ratio is abnormally small, the elasticity of interest rates with respect to change in the cash balance ratio may only be a moderate one. (iii) Since the regulatory effect of monetary policy essentially resides in the effect of changing interest rates on expenditure, it is more efficacious to concentrate on the regulation of interest rates directly (through open market operations in the money market and/or the gilt-edged market) than indirectly through pressure exerted on the supply of bank credit.[2] (iv) Relatively moderate changes in interest rates may have no certain or predictable effect on either consumer

[1] Whether this kind of regulation is the most suitable method of limiting consumer demand is a different question. As against the discouraging effects of either taxation or consumer rationing (by means of building licences, for example) the effects of hire-purchase or mortgage-finance regulations are confined to a particular class of buyers who are dependent on loans for their purchases.

[2] It is erroneous to assume that the quantitive regulation of credit by the clearing banks will have the same effect as a corresponding change in short-term interest rates. This would only be true if the clearing banks were the sole source of short-term credit which of course is by no means the case. Apart from the existence of other types of financial institutions, there is the extension of "trade credit" of varying kinds, of which the involuntary (or at least partially involuntary) credit represented by the debtor's delay in settling account is the extreme example. As a recent analysis of the accounts of 3,000 quoted companies has shown, the *net* amount of trade credit outstanding of the 3,000 companies exceeded by a considerable margin the total amount of their bank credits in 1953; moreover the growth of the *net* trade credit (excess of trade debtors over trade creditors) in the five years prior to 1953 was $2\frac{1}{2}$ times as large as the increase in bank overdrafts and loans. Trade credit received in 1953 by these companies exceeded their bank overdrafts 5 times; trade credit granted $6\frac{1}{2}$ times. (Cf. *Company Income and Finance, 1949-53*, N.I.E.S.R., 1956, Table 5. Unfortunately no figures are yet available to record the effect of the "credit squeeze.")

expenditure or on business expenditure. This is particularly true in times of full employment and inflation when factors other than finance inevitably play an important role in limiting capital expenditures: it may be also important in times of large-scale unemployment and deflation when interest rates are already near their minimum practicable level, and cannot be reduced much further through open market operations.

The Undesirability of Unstable Interest Rates

8. None of this is intended to suggest that increases in interest rates are ultimately ineffective in curbing expenditure. When the prospective rate of profit on new investments is around 15 per cent., a rise in the (irredeemable) gilt-edged rate from 3 to 5 per cent. or even to 6 per cent. might prove ineffective in eliminating an excess pressure of demand. But nobody would suggest that a rise in the yield of Consols to 15 per cent. would not exert a tremendous deflationary impact. Hence provided the authorities are prepared to take sufficiently drastic steps in raising interest rates, it should always be possible to eliminate inflationary tendencies due to an excessive pressure of demand; and if they had sufficient elbow room for lowering interest rates (which may not be the case) they might be equally effective in countering deflationary tendencies through reductions in interest rates. But it is impossible to devise tests which would enable the authorities to judge, in any given situation, how great a change is required; and for reasons advanced above it is useless to look for such tests in the resulting changes of the quantity of money in circulation.

9. There is fair agreement among economists that if monetary and credit policy was to be relied on as the principal instrument of control, changes in interest rates would have to be far more drastic than those recently applied.[1] The reason generally advanced for the reluctance of the authorities to impose more

---

[1] This concerns the effects of changes in the Bank Rate and the money market rates on internal inflationary and deflationary tendencies. Actually, it is a matter of doubt how far changes in the Bank Rate in recent years were prompted by considerations of domestic inflation rather than by the state of the reserves. From the point of view of its external effects there can be little doubt that an increase in the Bank Rate proved an effective device on almost every occasion for bringing to a halt a speculative drain on the pound.

drastic changes in interest rates is the Government's own vulnerability to such changes on account of the existence of a massive short-term Government debt (much of it owed abroad) and the constant need to refinance a large volume of bonded debt which matures every year. This must undoubtedly reduce the relative attractiveness of the Bank Rate instrument as an economic regulator. I believe however that even if these factors were not present (on the supposition, for example, that the whole of the outstanding Government debt were repaid by means of a once for all capital levy) it would still be impossible to stabilise the level of demand by means of credit policy alone without highly undesirable consequences in other directions. Reliance on monetary policy as an effective stabilising device would involve large and rapid changes in the level of interest rates and, in consequence, a high degree of instability in bond prices in the capital market. But the relative stability of bond prices is a highly important feature of an effectively functioning capital market, and of the whole credit mechanism in a capitalist economy. If bond prices were liable to vast and rapid fluctuations, the speculative risks involved in long-term loans of any kind would be very much greater than they are now, and the average price which investors would demand for parting with liquidity would be considerably higher. The capital market would become far more speculative, and would function far less efficiently as an instrument for allocating savings—new issues would be more difficult to launch, and long-run considerations of relative profitability would play a subordinate role in the allocation of funds. As Keynes said, when the capital investment of a country "becomes a by-product of the activities of a casino, the job is likely to be ill-done." In addition, since average rates of interest are bound to be considerably higher, the rate of profit required to make investment attractive in the long run would also have to be higher; to achieve this effect Government policies would have to aim at stimulating consumption at the same time as they restrained investment. By the force of circumstances rather than by design, a Government relying on credit control for combating inflationary tendencies would be bound to stimulate consumption rather than investment in times of inadequate demand (for political as well as for technical reasons) and would thus gradually transform the economy into one of high consumption and low investment—with all its undesirable consequences on the long-run rates of economic growth.[1] Those who argue in favour of credit policy as the main economic stabiliser frequently overlook the fact that the increased instability of interest rates which is a necessary precondition for the effective use of monetary policy as an economic regulator can only be bought at the cost of making the *average* level of long-term interest rates considerably higher than what it would be if interest rates were relatively stable.

The Dangers of a Régime of Stable Prices

10. High rates of interest are not necessarily inconsistent with sustained economic growth *provided the inflationary trend of prices is maintained*. As the examples of various Latin American countries show, when the price level rises by 10 per cent. a year or more, interest rates of 10 or 15 per cent. are perfectly consistent with the high rates of investment required to sustain a 3–5 per cent. annual rate of growth in the real national income. But the objective of those who favour credit restriction as an instrument of economic control is not the maintenance of a steady trend of price inflation, but the attainment of price stability; and when the potential rate of growth is low the latter may only be reconciled with high interest rates (or indeed, with any attainable level of interest rates, high or low) at the cost of economic stagnation.

11. In a steadily growing economy the average rate of profit on investments can, in the first approximation, be taken as being equal to the rate of growth in the money value of the gross national product divided by the proportion of profits saved.[2] Thus if the rate of growth of the money national income is 6 per cent. a year and if the proportion of profits saved (defined as the excess of profits earned over property owners' consumption) is 40 per cent. (or, alternatively, if the national income grows at 7·5 per cent., and the proportion of profits saved is 50 per cent.) the average rate of profit will be 15 per cent. To keep the process of investment going, the rate of profit must exceed the (long-term) interest

[1] Cf. paras. 11-12 below for a further consideration of this point.
[2] For the derivation of this formula, cf. *Economic Journal*, December, 1957, pp. 604-11 and 613-14.

rates by some considerable margin—a margin that is all the greater
the higher are the taxes on profits and income. Though nobody
knows what the required minimum margin is, at a guess I would
put it at 6–10 per cent. gross or 3–5 per cent. net (of taxation), so
that a 15 per cent. profit rate is consistent with long-term interest
rates of 4–7 per cent. or less. The rate of growth of the money
national income is the sum of the rate of growth in production
and the rate of growth of prices. Assuming that the 6 per cent.
rate of growth in the gross national product in money terms is
composed of a 3 per cent. per annum growth in production and a
3 per cent. per annum rise in prices, a régime of complete price-
stability would cut the average rate of profit on investment by
one-half—i.e. to 7·5 per cent. in the above example. This in turn
would only be consistent with continued investment and expansion if the long-term rate of interest were down to 1–2 per cent.
If the rate of interest were higher than this, the process of accumulation would be interrupted, and the economy would relapse into
a slump. To get it out of the slump it would be necessary to stimulate the propensity to consume—by tax cuts, for example—which
would raise the rate of profit and thus restore the incentive to
invest. If by such means the proportion of profits saved were
reduced to one half—from 40 per cent. to 20 per cent.—the rate
of profit would again be 15 per cent., assuming that the level of
output, and thus the national income at constant prices, continues
to grow at 3 per cent. a year. But the share of savings in income,
and thus the share of investment in output, would be only half as
high as before, hence the rate of growth of the national product
would necessarily become less than it was—with the share of
investment in output at one half of its previous level it may be
reduced to, say, 2 per cent. a year. This in turn would imply a
rate of profit of 10 per cent., possibly necessitating a further
stimulus to consumption, a further cut in the investment coefficient, a further fall in the rate of growth of production, and
so on.

12. The moral of this is that it is dangerous for a weakly-
progressive economy to aim at a régime of stable prices (let alone
at a régime of falling prices!) since when the rate of growth of
production is low (on account of a stagnant working population,

a low rate of technical progress, or both) stable prices are only consistent with low rates of profit which may be insufficient to maintain the inducement to invest, unless the latter is stimulated by measures which cut down the ratio of investment to output and thereby reduce still further the rate of growth of production. Thus in the United Kingdom the rate of growth of the "real" gross national product in the period 1950–7 was 3 per cent. a year. Thanks to inflation, the gross national product at current prices grew at a rate of 7·5 per cent. a year. If inflation had been entirely avoided, the average rate of profit on new investment would have been 60 per cent. lower, that is to say, 6 per cent. instead of 15 per cent. (which we assumed for the purpose of this exercise, but which was probably not far off the truth). In Germany on the other hand, in the period 1950–7 the rate of growth of the gross national product at constant prices was 8·5 per cent. and at current prices 11·5 per cent. a year. This explains why Germany was able to combine average rates of profit of 20 per cent. or more with a reasonable stability of prices, and why interest rates on commercial loans could rise to 10–12 per cent. without discouraging investment. Indeed, if German prices had been falling by 1–2 per cent. per annum, instead of rising (owing to a failure of money wages to rise as fast as productivity) the rate of profit would still have been high enough to keep the process of expansion going. In the light of this the objective of stable or falling prices may well be regarded as a luxury which only fast-growing economies can afford.[1] (We shall return to this in paragraphs 23–25 below.)

---

[1] The *First Report of the Council on Prices, Productivity and Incomes* spent some time in considering the relative merits of rising, stable and falling prices (chap. iv), without any mention of the effect of stable or falling prices on the rate of profit, and the added difficulty in maintaining the incentives to invest at a lower rate of profit. This omission is the more surprising since one of the distinguished members of the Council, Professor Sir Dennis Robertson, was one of the first economists to have perceived this point in his early writings (cf. "The Case for a Gently Rising Price Level" in *Money* (Cambridge, 1922), pp. 122–8). According to Mr. D. H. Robertson (as he then was) a régime of gently rising prices gives a "fillip to production [which] by adding to the flow of goods serves to moderate the very rise in prices which gives it birth" (p. 123), whereas "it is tolerably certain that a price-level continually falling, even for the best of reasons, would prove deficient in those stimuli upon which modern society, whether wisely or not, has hitherto chiefly relied for keeping its members in full employment and getting its work done" (p. 125).

Credit Policy and the Creation of Uncertainty

13. Before we leave the subject of the *modus operandi* of monetary policy we must mention yet another argument in favour of credit policy, as an instrument of economic control. Its advocates would not dispute the undesirable effects of highly fluctuating interest rates; they would argue, however, that the psychological effects of changes in the Bank Rate are far more important than its technical effects; hence the policy could be made effective, even if applied in moderate doses, provided these come "at the right moment" and have the right kind of impact on business psychology. Allied to this is the further argument that frequent use of the Bank Rate mechanism keeps the business world guessing concerning the ultimate intentions of the monetary authorities: and this uncertainty makes businesses responsive to "signals" communicated by the authorities through changes in the Bank Rate, even if, on the basis of a strict calculation of costs and returns, the resulting changes in interest rates would not have affected their conduct. These arguments were frequently used in support of a return to a flexible Bank Rate policy in the early 1950's, but they have been much less prominent recently; and the reason, I believe, is that the expectations that were originally entertained concerning the psychological effects of even moderate changes in the Bank Rate have so demonstrably been proved wrong by subsequent experience. It is fairly generally recognised now that the purely psychological effects of the changes in credit policy which started in February 1955, and which were accompanied by a rising crescendo of warnings and exhortations by the Chancellor of the Exchequer in the course of that year and the following year, were negligible. This does not prove, of course, that the psychological effects of such changes would be equally unimportant on other occasions, but it does show that these effects are completely unpredictable, and hence no reliance can be placed on them.[1]

---

[1] Indeed, it is questionable how far the whole view which regards the deliberate creation of an atmosphere of uncertainty as an effective means of making the economic system amenable to control is a legitimate one. This is a complex question, which cannot be gone into here in detail; but it should be evident that any simple view on this matter is likely to be one-sided. On the one hand, the existence of uncertainty, and the prevalence of a variety of opinion which is associated with it, clearly increases the power of the monetary authorities to determine the rates of interest ruling in the

II. MONETARY POLICY AND THE PROBLEM OF STABILITY

14. It follows from the above reasoning that monetary and credit policy represents, at best, a crude and blunt instrument for controlling inflationary and deflationary tendencies in the economy which should be employed only in circumstances in which, and to the extent to which, no superior instruments of control are available. In order to discover what, if any, these circumstances are it is necessary to review briefly the nature of the various problems confronting the monetary and financial authorities.

(i) Excessive Pressure of Demand

15. First, there is the problem of an excessive pressure of demand for resources of all kinds which must be a reflection of the expenditures on capital account exceeding the planned savings on income account (of individuals, businesses, and public authorities). The manifestations of this are: (a) abnormally long, and lengthening order books in many industries; (b) an acute shortage of labour in the majority of industries;[1] (c) a faster rate of increase of business profits than of wages and salaries; (d) a deteriorating relationship between exports and imports, due to a rising volume of imports, or a falling volume of exports or some combination of both. The remedy must be sought either in a reduction of capital expenditure or in an increase in planned savings; and, from the point of view of the national interest, there is generally a strong presumption in favour of policies which increase savings (i.e. reduce consumption) as against policies which involve a reduction of investments. Unless therefore the excess pressure of demand is due to some sudden spurt, showing manifest instability in the level of business capital expenditures (of which more below), the appropriate instrument of control is to be found not

market through open market operations. On the other hand, the prevalence of uncertainty reduces the extent to which businessmen's decisions are based on neatly balanced calculations of gain or loss, and thus the extent to which such decisions are responsive to changes in interest rates.

[1] In an industrially developed economy such as Britain manufacturing capacity is *normally* more than sufficient for the employment of the available labour force (even without resorting to double shift or treble shift working in the great majority of industries) so that the effective bottleneck limiting production is a shortage of labour, rather than of capacity.

in monetary but in fiscal policy—the more so as the latter is more predictable and immediate in its operation than the former.[1]

(ii) *Unbalanced Growth*

16. Secondly, as a variant of the former, there is the problem of an excessive pressure of demand in certain key sectors of the economy, due to an unbalanced (or disproportionate) development between the different sectors, which can persist even if the pressure of demand in general is not excessive in relation to available resources. The standard example of this is the failure, in many underdeveloped countries, of the increase in the supply of "wage-goods," particularly of foodstuffs, to match the growth of incomes generated by production. This leads to a constant upward pressure of the price-level of wage-goods, involving periodic upward revisions in money wage-rates which in turn make the rise in costs and prices general throughout the economy and keep up the upward pressure on the prices of wage-goods.

17. This particular combination of a demand-generated inflation of food-prices with a cost-generated inflation of industrial prices is peculiar to underdeveloped countries and is absent in developed countries which either generate food-surpluses (like the United States, Australia, New Zealand or Canada) or else possess the buying power to satisfy their excess food requirements through purchases in the world market (like Britain, Western Germany, Belgium or Switzerland). But a somewhat analogous situation may arise when the growth in the capacity of the export industries of "developed" countries fails to keep pace with the requirements of additional imports which result from the growth of production and incomes in the economy in general. (It is arguable, e.g. that a policy of holding back the expansion of

[1] A rise in total taxation relative to public expenditure will always increase total net (planned) savings, though by less than the increase in public savings (since a rise in taxation will be associated with *some* reduction in private savings). The relevant measure of the *change* in public savings is the *change* in the "overall" deficit (or surplus). A change in the "above the line" surplus will make no (immediate) contribution to the relief of inflationary pressure if offset by a simultaneous change in the below-the-line deficit. There are situations, however, in which changes in public capital expenditure reflect opposite changes in private capital expenditure (as, for example, when an industry is nationalised and hence its investment is transferred from the private to the public sector) and in which therefore the change in the surplus on current account gives a better indication of the change in the net income-creating effect of Government operations.

production was forced on Britain in the last few years on balance-of-payments considerations—i.e. on account of the fact that expansion would have raised imports, whilst the capacity of the export industries would not have permitted any corresponding increase in exports.) In such cases overall measures of control, whether through credit policy or fiscal policy, may be inappropriate or insufficient, and the remedy may have to be sought in selective controls of various kinds (as e.g. control over the allocation of investments; the forced expansion of investment in the critical sectors, or food rationing when the driving force behind the inflation is the inadequacy of food supplies, etc.), by means of which the tendencies to disproportionate development can be counteracted or compensated for.

(iii) Wage Inflation

18. Thirdly, there is the case when the driving force behind the inflation is an excessive rate of increase in money wages. To be sure, a continued rise in money wages is invariably involved in every *process* of inflation, since if money wages did not rise, the rise in the price-level could not continue beyond a certain point, whatever the nature of the forces underlying the price rise. But a distinction can be drawn—blurred though it is in a range of border-line cases—between a situation in which the rise in wages *reflects* the forces making for the rise in prices and one in which the rise in wages *causes* the rise in prices to take place—i.e. in which the rise in wages is primary and the rise in prices secondary. In the former category belong the cases (*a*) when the upward revisions in money wages can be shown to be clearly related to a prior rise in the cost of living index, as a result of which real wages fell appreciably below some previously attained level; (*b*) when the rise in wages is mainly the result of the competitive bidding for labour by employers, rather than the demand for higher pay by the workers enforced through collective bargaining. In the second category fall those situations in which the rise in the general level of wages is mainly the outcome of the struggle of wage-earners in different industries and occupations to secure an improvement, or to prevent a deterioration of, their earnings relative to the wages paid in other occupations—in other words,

where the rise in the general wage level is largely a by-product of countervailing pressures acting on the scale of relative wages. In the latter situation the rise in prices is mainly the consequence of the rise in costs (matched by the increase in monetary demand resulting from the rise in incomes) and not of the excessive pressure of demand pulling prices upwards. A wage inflation of the first category is but a particular aspect of the "demand inflation" discussed above, and calls for the same remedies. A wage inflation of the second category, however, is not one that can be expected to be cured by restrictions of demand—not unless the restriction is carried to the point of such heavy unemployment that the wage-earners in any particular industry are unable to hold out for higher wages on account of the competition of unemployed workers.[1]

19. Some economists hold that the wage inflation of the post-war period was mainly the reflection of a demand-inflation—of the competition between employers for scarce labour—and would not have taken place if demand had been damped down to more reasonable levels. They cite as evidence for this the fact that in a number of post-war years the rise in earnings was greater than the rise in wages—which provides some indication that the actual wage rates paid in a number of industries were above the negotiated levels. Even if it is admitted that in times of acute labour shortage wages tend to rise above the negotiated levels, it does not follow that the rise in the negotiated levels themselves would have been avoided or lessened if the pressure of demand had been smaller (and it must be remembered that the rise in the official wage rates accounted for much the greater part of the total increase in wages). Equally it does not follow that if the rise in official wages had been smaller the element of "wage slide" (the excess of actual wages over negotiated wages) would have been substantially greater.

20. Other economists would agree that the wage inflation is of

---

[1] It is sometimes asserted that with a tight credit policy employers will be unable to grant wage increases or to pass on higher wage costs in higher prices and will therefore offer far greater resistance to demands for higher wages. This is clearly fallacious. Tight credit policy, if sufficiently severe, will force employers to reduce their rate of investment, and possibly even to disinvest. But neither their willingness to grant wage increases, nor their ability to pass on higher costs in the form of higher prices will be *directly* affected by it—any such effect will be indirect, and dependent on a prior reduction in the scale of operations.

the second category rather than of the first. They would maintain, however, that a fairly moderate reduction in the level of economic activity might reduce the pressure for wage increases sufficiently to prevent the rate of increase in wages exceeding the rate of increase in productivity. Assuming that there is a "breakeven point"—for wages—at a level of unemployment which is not too large (say, of the order of 2–3 per cent.) it is argued that the loss of production due to a lower level of activity would not be large either; and provided the economy could be kept growing and productivity rising in the same way as under conditions of full employment, the long-run benefits in increased economic and monetary stability would be bound to outweigh the once-for-all cost in terms of lower output.

21. As will be suggested in the following paragraph, there is no evidence to show that a moderate degree of unemployment would suffice to reduce the rate of increase in money wages to levels consistent with cost and price stability. But assuming that this would in fact be the case there is still the question whether it would be possible to run an economy at a consistently moderate level of unemployment; and whether such under-employment equilibrium would be consistent with a satisfactory rate of growth of production year by year. In the first place, there is the question whether an under-employment equilibrium where the general level of production is limited by effective demand, and not by the scarcity of available resources, is at all stable except under conditions in which the level of production is stationary. For when the forces making for economic expansion are powerful enough to cause the level of production to grow from year to year, they will be powerful enough also to cause an expansion of activity which eliminates non-frictional unemployment. Contrariwise, when the restraints on demand are powerful enough to prevent an increase in activity to the full employment level, they will be powerful enough also to put a damper on investment and on the growth of productivity. For these reasons it may not be possible to run a growing economy at half-cock. In the second place, there is the question whether the prospective rate of profit in an economy of stable prices would be attractive enough (relative to the market rate of interest) to keep the process of investment and expansion going.

22. Table I (in the Annex) summarises the experience with regard to money wages, the cost of living, industrial production and productivity over the last six years of twelve mainly industrial countries, arranged in descending order of magnitude of wage inflation. On the evidence of these figures there appears to be little connection between the magnitude of the wage inflation, and changes in the cost of living or apparent changes in productivity; nor does there appear to be any close relationship between the level of unemployment and the rate of increase in money wages. Thus the rate of increase in money wages was approximately the same in the United Kingdom as in Denmark and Austria, though in the former non-agricultural unemployment was most of the time around 1·3 per cent., while in the latter two countries it was around 5 per cent. The fact that ten out of these twelve countries experienced wage increases of around 30–50 per cent. in the six years, or say 5–7 per cent. per annum, rather tends to suggest that there is a certain inherent momentum in the rise of the wage level in an advancing industrial community which is fairly insensitive to changes in living costs or the growth of productivity. Thus Germany (with 48 per cent.) and the United Kingdom (with 43 per cent.) had a fairly similar experience with wage inflation although the rise in the cost of living was 6 per cent. in Germany and 29 per cent. in the United Kingdom, whilst the rise in productivity was 31 per cent. in the former and only 11 per cent. in the latter. The fact that three of the countries near the top of the scale (France, Sweden and Norway) were countries of a very low rate of unemployment, whereas the three countries at the bottom of the scale (Italy, the United States and Belgium) had relatively high rates of unemployment lends some support to the view that wage increases tend to be rather more moderate with unemployment rates of 3–5 per cent. than with unemployment rates of 1–1½ per cent. But even with the latter group, the rise in wages was greater than what would have been consistent with price stability, and there were countries such as Germany, Austria and Denmark which combined high rates of wage inflation with relatively high rates of unemployment.[1]

[1] In the U.K. there were only two years since the war when the percentage of increase in wages was 3 per cent. or less and it is of some significance that these were 1949 and 1950 when Sir Stafford Cripps' policy of wage restraint and dividend

23. The common feature of all these countries has been that they were *expanding economies* during the period under consideration: their investment sufficed for an expansion of productive capacity, and the system operated so as to produce a growth in demand (in real terms) adequate to match the growth in the capacity to produce. The fact that most of them show annual wage increases in excess of 5 per cent. per annum may be no accident therefore: if the argument in paragraphs 11 and 12 above is correct, a 5–6 per cent. annual increase in the money value of the gross national product—which presupposes a similar rate of increase in the total wages bill—is necessary in order to secure a rate of profit on investment high enough to maintain the process of capital accumulation and continued expansion.

24. In the circumstances of Britain in the 1950's annual wage increases of this order were not consistent with the stability of the price-level since the growth in total production was only of the order of 3 per cent. If, however, our reasoning in paragraphs 11 and 12 is correct, it would have been futile to compress the growth in aggregate money incomes to 3 per cent. a year: since at that rate full employment and economic growth might not have been maintained.

25. The basic malaise of the British economy is thus seen to have been the slow rate of growth in productivity and total production. Given this basic limitation, a certain degree of inflation (in my opinion) could not have been avoided—or rather, it could only have been prevented at the cost of jeopardising the modest annual improvement actually attained. The unsatisfactory rate of economic growth since 1951—as Table I shows, the United Kingdom has shown by far the lowest rate of growth of productivity during the period—is variously attributed, by different authorities, to the "overloading" of the British economy, to excessive outlays on defence, on foreign investment or on the social services; to the effects of the "new" monetary policy itself in putting a brake on expansion just as it was gathering momentum;

limitation was in operation (see Table III). Apart from these there was only one year, 1954, when the percentage rise in weekly wages was below 5 per cent., and there were four years, 1951, 1952, 1955 and 1956, when it reached 8 to 9 per cent. In the last two of these years, 1955 and 1956, the rise in wages proceeded at record levels despite the fact that the policy of tight money and credit squeeze were in operation.

and finally, to the low "technical dynamism" of those in charge of British industry, and the lack of compulsion (due to the absence of effective competition, etc.), to introduce technical improvements.

26. My own view would incline towards the latter explanation. No doubt productive investment in Britain has been highly inadequate in relation to her competitors, such as Germany, Japan, France or Italy (the extent of this inadequacy is understated by comparisons of overall percentages of investment since U.K. investment tends to be more concentrated on "unproductive" fields such as housing) but it is difficult to treat this as more than a symptom of the malaise. If British entrepreneurs had been keener on expansion and innovation, the resources for the needed additional investments could no doubt somehow have been found; it was certainly not the lack of financial resources which held them back.[1] In an economy where labour is fully employed, and where the expansion of the working population is small, the level of industrial investment tends to be limited by the speed of adaptation to new techniques—by the rate at which technical change can be absorbed into the economic system. It would go beyond the scope of this paper—and also, I believe, of the Committee's terms of reference—to examine the historical, sociological or institutional factors which make the majority of British businessmen less alert and more sluggish in their reactions than some of their competitors in other countries. But it is here, I feel, rather than in the operation of the monetary and financial system, or in the strength of the competing claims on the national resources, that we must look for the basic cause of our unsatisfactory rate of economic progress.

(iv) Fluctuations of Investment in Stocks

27. Finally, there is the problem of the instability in demand due to fluctuations in investment, particularly investment in stocks. As the official national income estimates show, the varia-

---

[1] The 3,000 quoted companies mentioned in the footnote to para. 7 (which represented over two-thirds of the total paid-up capital of all public companies) held financial assets (cash, marketable securities and tax reserve certificates) of over £1,400 million in 1953, whereas their annual expenditure on fixed assets was only around £450 million.

tion of investment in stocks has been the really unstable element in the British economy since the war. These variations have largely reflected changing expectations concerning price movements and they were largely responsible (in the period 1948–52 at any rate) for the instability in the balance of payments. While the average amount of these investments has been relatively small (in relation to investment in fixed capital) the annual swings have been relatively large; and it can be said that until the re-establishment of a flexible monetary policy at the end of 1951 the Government had no real weapon at its disposal for controlling the rate of investment in stocks which was in any way analogous to the instruments of control of fixed investment, such as the licensing system and accelerated depreciation allowances, not to speak of taxation of various kinds for controlling consumption. Indeed, it is difficult to conceive of a technique for stabilising the rate of investment in stocks other than the institution of buffer stocks or credit policy. The operation of buffer stocks requires international action in most cases. But within limits at any rate it should be possible to stabilise *national* investment in inventories through credit policy. High short-term interest rates, subject to the limitations mentioned in paragraph 4 above, discourage investment in stocks, and vice versa. A sudden restocking boom such as that which followed the outbreak of the war in Korea, is invariably associated with a sudden increase in the demand for bank overdrafts. If through appropriate measures of control such an expansion can be prevented, the rise in inventory investment would undoubtedly be curbed; indeed, with sufficiently stringent measures of financial discouragement, it might be prevented altogether.

28. There are two conclusions to follow from this argument. The first is that the function of credit control should be sought in stabilising investment in stocks (i.e. in offsetting spontaneous tendencies to instability in inventory investment), and not in the control of investment in fixed capital or the control of consumption which can far more appropriately be secured by other instruments. Hence, it is the regulation of short-term interest rates which is important, and not the variation in bond yields—since manufacturers and traders are unlikely to borrow on long term for increasing their investment in liquid assets, though they sometimes

operate the other way round. Secondly, while the quantitative control of bank credit may prevent, or at least hinder, increased investment in stocks by that part of the business community which is dependent on bank credit, it will not have the same discouraging effect on carrying stocks as a general increase in short-term interest rates.[1] This is partly because as we have seen (paragraph 7, note 1) the limitation of advances by the clearing banks may lead to increased trade-credit or increased lending by other financial institutions; partly also because putting pressure on one sector of the trading community—i.e. the one dependent on bank overdrafts—cannot be as effective as an inducement extended to all. I am a little dubious therefore of the various suggestions—i.e. the reintroduction of Treasury Deposit Receipts or a variable minimum liquidity ratio—for operating credit policy "on the cheap," so to speak, which aim at making credit control effective without invoking the variation of short-term borrowing or lending rates.

29. This is not to suggest that varying the short-term interest rate is a sensitive or dependable instrument. In times when price expectations are very volatile (and this in turn can only ensue from past experience of instability) the changes in interest rates required to compensate for the changing inducements to hold stocks may have to be pretty severe. The actual change in the amount of investment of both fixed and circulating capital in the ten years 1948–57 is shown in Table II. This shows that in the quinquennium 1948–52 variations in stock investment were appreciably greater than in the quinquennium 1953–7. The greater stability of short-term investment in the latter period might at first be regarded as an achievement of credit policy; however, as Table III shows, world prices were remarkably stable in the period 1953–7 whereas they were highly unstable in the period 1948–52. The incentives to instability which existed in the former period were thus absent in the latter and it is therefore not possible to say how much credit is to be given to the new credit policy—

[1] If the loan markets were perfect an increase in the severity of credit rationing by the clearing banks would automatically induce a general rise in short-term interest rates. Owing to imperfections in the market, however, the two are by no means equivalent to one another and it is quite possible that the former policy should discourage potential borrowers without discouraging inventory investment by potential lenders.

how the new policy would have coped with the kind of situation which emerged in 1951 and 1952 and which has not recurred in later years.

30. The best guarantee against vast political fluctuations of investment in stocks is an international buffer stock scheme which would confine fluctuations in world commodity prices within moderate limits. Failing this monetary policy can and should be used to moderate these fluctuations though one cannot feel entirely confident of the promptness and efficacy with which it can be made to operate.

ANNEX

Table I

WAGES, PRICES, PRODUCTION AND PRODUCTIVITY IN SELECTED
COUNTRIES IN 1957

(1951 = 100)

Country	Wages	Cost of Living	Industrial Production	Productivity[1]	Percentage of non-agric. unemployment 1957[2]
Japan	169	121	231	174	2·5
France	158	118	145	145	0·7
Sweden	149	124	117	117	1·2
Norway	148	124	134	128	1·3
Germany	148	106	172	131	3·4
Austria	144	126	151	132	5·1
United Kingdom ..	143	129	118	111	1·3
Denmark	142	118	115	115	4·8
Netherlands	138	115	138	131	1·4
Italy	138	113	155	142	11·1[3]
U.S.A.	130	108	119	121	4·3
Belgium	130	107	119	118	3·5

[1] Ratio of Percentage Change in Manufacturing Production to Percentage Change in Manufacturing Employment.

[2] Unemployment outside agriculture as percentage of wage and salary earners outside agriculture.

[3] Percentage of occupied labour force outside agriculture.

Source: I.M.F. International Financial Statistics, June 1958.
E.C.E. Economic Survey for Europe in 1957, chap. II, table 6.
U.N. Monthly Bulletin of Statistics.

Table II

CHANGES IN FIXED CAPITAL FORMATION AND IN PHYSICAL
INCREASE IN STOCKS AS COMPARED WITH PRECEDING YEAR,
UNITED KINGDOM, 1948–57

(£ million)

	1948	1949	1950	1951	1952	1953	1954	1955	1956	1957
At 1948 prices Fixed capital formation										
Private (est.)	– 70	50	40	– 60	– 30	80	160	160	80	80
Public (est.)	190	90	40	70	60	100	– 10	– 40	10	40
Total	120	140	80	10	30	180	150	120	90	120
Physical increase in stocks										
Private (est.)	– 230	– 170	– 60	330	– 350	80	90	130	– 130	(100)
Public (est.)	50	60	– 190	260	– 40	10	– 150	60	60	(20)
Total	– 180	– 110	– 250	590	– 390	90	– 60	190	– 70	(120)
At current £'s Fixed capital formation										
Private	–	55	60	20	50	110	205	275	190	170
Public	230	95	60	170	170	140	– 20	15	85	100
Total	230	150	120	190	220	250	185	290	275	270
Physical increase in stocks										
Private	– 190	– 170	– 60	480	– 575	175	140	185	– 165	145
Public	35	60	– 215	305	50	– 100	– 215	90	90	30
Total	– 155	– 110	– 275	785	– 525	75	– 75	275	– 75	175
Balance of Trade	390	100	80	– 570	670	– 120	40	– 210	320	– 10

Estimates in brackets are provisional

Source: C.S.O.

Table III

PERCENTAGE CHANGES IN PRICES COMPARED WITH PREVIOUS YEAR
IN THE UNITED KINGDOM

	1948	*1949*	*1950*	*1951*	*1952*	*1953*	*1954*	*1955*	*1956*	*1957*
Board of Trade Wholesale Prices .. U.N. World	14	5	14	22	3	—	1	3	3	1
Exports (sterling prices) Imports—goods	8	3	22	19	−3	−5	−1	—	2	3
and services Wage Rates	8	2	16	28	−5	−8	—	5	−1	2
(weekly) .. Retail Prices	5	3	2	8	8	5	4	8	9	5
(C.S.O.) ..	8	3	3	9	9	3	2	5	5	4

Sources: Annual Abstract of Statistics.
U.N. Bulletin of Statistics.

THE NEW MONETARISM[1]

THE Keynesian Revolution of the late 1930s has completely displaced earlier ways of thinking and provided an entirely new conceptual framework for economic management. As a result, we think of day-to-day problems—of inflationary or deflationary tendencies, unemployment, the balance of payments or growth—on different lines from those of economists of earlier generations. We think of the pressure of demand as determined by autonomous and induced expenditures, and we seek to regulate the economy by interfering at various points with the process of income generation: by offsetting net inflationary or deflationary trends emanating from the private sector or the overseas sector by opposite changes in the net income generating effect of the public sector. Previously, economists had thought of the level of demand—the volume of spending—as being directly determined by the supply of money and the velocity of circulation, and thought of regulating the level of expenditure mainly by monetary controls.

For the last twenty or thirty years we have felt we have much better insight into the workings of the market mechanism than our predecessors, and felt much superior to them. However, we now have a "monetary" counter-revolution whose message is that during this time we have been wrong and our forbears largely, if not perhaps *entirely*, right; anyhow, on the right track, whereas we have been shunted on to the wrong track. This new doctrine is assiduously propagated from across the Atlantic by a growing band of enthusiasts, combining the fervour of early Christians with the suavity and selling power of a Madison Avenue executive. And it is very largely the product of one economist with exceptional powers of persuasion and propagation: Professor Milton

[1] A public lecture given at University College, London on 12 March, 1970 and originally published in the *Lloyds Bank Review*, July 1970.

B

Friedman of Chicago. The "new monetarism" is a "Friedman Revolution" more truly than Keynes was the sole fount of the "Keynesian Revolution". Keynes's *General Theory* was the culmination of a great deal of earlier work by large numbers of people: chiefly Wicksell and his followers, Myrdal and Lindahl in Sweden, Kalecki in Poland, not to speak of Keynes's colleagues in Cambridge and of many others.

The new school, the Friedmanites (I do not use this term in any pejorative sense, the more respectful expression "Friedmanians" sounds worse) can record very considerable success, both in terms of the numbers of distinguished converts and of some rather glittering evidence in terms of "scientific proofs", obtained through empirical investigations summarised in time-series regression equations. Indeed, the characteristic feature of the new school is "positivism" and "scientism"; some would say "pseudo-scientism", using science as a selling appeal. They certainly use time-series regressions as if they provided the same kind of "proofs"as controlled experiments in the natural sciences. And one hears of new stories of conversions almost every day, one old bastion of old-fashioned Keynesian orthodoxy being captured after another: first, the Federal Reserve Bank of St. Louis, then another Federal Reserve Bank, then the research staff of the I.M.F., or at least the majority of them, are "secret", if not open, Friedmanites. Even the "Fed" in Washington is said to be tottering, not to speak of the spread of the new doctrines in many universities in the United States. In this country, also, there are some distinguished and lively protagonists, like Professor Harry Johnson and Professor Walters, though, in comparison to America, they write in muted tones and make more modest claims, which makes it more difficult to discover just what it is they believe in, just where the new doctrine ceases to be a matter of semantics and becomes a revelation with operational significance.

ELEMENTS OF NEW DOCTRINE

What are the essential propositions of the new doctrine? For this, it is no good turning to the "moderates", who do not really say anything, or to the "extremists"—like Messrs. Andersen,

Jordan and Keran of St. Louis—who both vulgarise and discredit the new creed by the blatant simplicity of their beliefs and the extravagance of their claims. One must turn to the archpriest, Friedman himself, and such of his close disciples, like Meiselman, Anna Schwartz and Philip Cagan, who can be relied on to follow the master closely and interpret him correctly.

The essential elements of the creed can, I think, be summarised in the following four propositions:

(1) Money alone matters in determining *"money things"*, such as the *money* G.N.P., the level and the rate of changes of *money* prices, and the level and the rate of change of *money* wages. *Per contra,* other things—such as fiscal policies, taxation, trade union behaviour, etc.—do not (or do not really) matter.

(2) Money cannot change *"real"* things, except temporarily, and in the manner of throwing a spanner into the works—a "monkey-wrench into the machine", to use Friedman's more homely expression[1]—at the cost of painful adjustments afterwards. There is a unique real equilibrium rate of real interest, a unique real equilibrium real wage, an equilibrium level of real unemployment. By monkeying around with money, these things can temporarily be made to change—interest reduced, unemployment cut, the real wage cut (or raised, I am not sure which)—only by making, in each case, reverse changes (abnormally high interest rates, abnormal unemployment, etc.) the inevitable sequel.

All this part of the Friedman doctrine is closely reminiscent of the Austrian school of the twenties and the early thirties—the theories of von Mises and von Hayek—a fact which so far (to my knowledge) has received no acknowledgment in Friedmanite literature. (Very few people these days know the works of the Mises–Hayek school; unfortunately, I am old enough to have been an early follower of Professor von Hayek, and even translated one of his books, and there is nothing like having to translate a book, particularly from the German language, to force you to come to grips with an argument.) Friedman differs from von Mises and von Hayek in being more liberally spiced with the new empiricism. On the other hand, he misses some of the subtleties of the Hayekian

---

[1] "The Role of Monetary Policy", *American Economic Review*, March 1968, p. 12.

transmission mechanism, and of the money-induced distortions in the "structure of production".

(3) While the money supply alone determines money expenditures, incomes and prices, it does so with a time lag which is, unhappily, not a stable one. It can vary, for reasons yet unknown, between two quarters and eight quarters. This is what the regression equations show.

(4) Hence, while control of the money supply is the only powerful instrument of control, it is hopeless for central banks to pursue a positive stabilisation policy by varying the money supply in a contra-cyclical manner. Indeed, their attempts to do so may have been the very cause of the cyclical instabilities in the economy which they aimed to prevent. Hence, the best thing for stability is to maintain a steady expansion of the money supply of 4–5 per cent. (in the latest version, the ideal has come down to 2 per cent.) and, sooner or later, everything will fall into line. There will be steady growth without inflation.

All this is argued not, like the Keynesian theory, in terms of a structural model which specifies the manner of operation of various factors. The results are based on direct and conclusive historical evidence; on statistical associations which appear—to the authors —so strong and clear as to rule out other interpretations. The actual mechanism by which exogenous changes in the supply of money influence the level of spending—how the money gets into circulation, whom it is received by, whether the recipients treat it as an addition to their spendable income or to their wealth, or whether it comes into existence in exchange for other assets without augmenting either wealth or income—is hardly considered by the orthodox Friedman school. It is significant perhaps that when Friedman in his latest essay does attempt a graphic description of how an increase in the money supply leads to a rise in prices and incomes, the money is scattered to the population from the air by a helicopter.[1]

The basis of all this is the "stable demand function for money", derived from empirical observations over longer and shorter periods; with varying definitions of money, and varying time lags between changes of money and income, where the choice of the

---

[1] Cf. Friedman, *The Optimum Quantity of Money*, London, Macmillan, 1969, pp. 4 ff.

time lag, and the choice of the definition of what is "money", are both determined by the criterion of the best statistical "fit" (in terms of R^2 and "t" values) of the regression equation. It is sometimes expressed in terms of a "money supply multiplier" which is clearly implied by the "stable demand function", though the empirical values of the "multiplier" are not consistent with a unity elasticity in the demand for money (*i.e.*, an equi-proportional relationship between the change in money and that of money income) which the quantity theory postulates; sometimes in terms of a relationship between changes in the money supply and changes in consumption expenditure, together with the demonstration that the money multiplier invariably "outperforms" the Keynesian multiplier. (This latter contention, for what it is worth, has been shown to be dependent on arbitrary and inappropriate definitions of "autonomous" expenditures in a Keynesian model.[1])

Friedman interprets his empirical findings in a strict Walrasian (or Marshallian) manner, as an indication that "people" wish to keep a constant proportion of their real income (or their permanent real income) in the form of money, a proportion which is not (very) sensitive to interest rates. But who are "the people" in this connection? Are they the wage- and salary-earners, who, between them, account for 70 per cent. of the national income, but hold, at any one time, a much lesser proportion, perhaps 10 to 20 per cent., of the total money supply? Or are they the "rentiers", whose "portfolio selection" and "portfolio shifts" are much influenced at any time by short-term expectations, as well as by the relative yields of various types of financial assets? Or are they businesses, for which holding money is just one of a number of ways of securing liquidity—unexploited borrowing power, unused overdraft limits and so on being other ways—and for which the state of liquidity is only one of a number of factors that influence current expenditure decisions?

RELATION OF MONEY TO G.N.P.

Before we consider these contentions further, one might pause

---

[1] Cf. Ando and Modigliani, "Velocity and the Investment Multiplier"; De Prano and Mayer, "Autonomous Expenditures and Money"; together with Replies and Rejoinders, *American Economic Review*, September 1965.

to ask whether there is anything surprising in a "stable money" function.

Clearly, in a broad sense the "money supply", however defined, correlates with the money G.N.P.—so does everything else: consumption, investment, wealth, the wage-bill, etc. All these things move over time, normally upwards, and in any time series the movement of any one item is bound to be highly correlated with the others. Thus Richard Stone demonstrated years ago that for the U.S. economy in the inter-war years *all* principal items of income and expenditure (eighteen of them) were closely correlated with three independent factors, which he identified as the G.N.P., the change in the G.N.P. and a time trend.[1]

The important questions to ask are:

First, does a high correlation indicate a causal relationship either way? Does it imply that the supply of money determines the level of income, or the other way round? Or are both determined simultaneously by a third factor (or factors)?

Second, does the existence of a strong statistical association imply that by controlling one of the variables, say the money supply, one can induce a predictable variation in the other? In other words, would the "money multiplier" survive if it were subjected to serious pressure?

In the U.K., the best correlation is undoubtedly found, not between the so-called "money supply" and the G.N.P., or that and consumers' expenditure, but between the quarterly variation in the amount of *cash* (that is notes and coins) in the hands of the public, and corresponding variations in personal consumption at market prices.[2] This, of course, was broadly known long before multiple regressions were invented (or computers to calculate them with ease). Every schoolboy knows that cash in the hands of the public regularly shoots up at Christmas, goes down in January and shoots up again around the summer bank holiday.

[1] R. Stone, "On the Interdependence of Blocks of Transactions", *Journal of the Royal Statistical Society, Supplement*, 1947.

[2] Thus, for 83 observations in the period 1948–69, the R^2 is ·884, the "cash multiplier" 2·3, the "t" value 3·7, *after* allowing for seasonality. The "cash multiplier" is 6·1, the "t" value 9, the R^2 is ·494, without correction for seasonality. Even better sounding results can be attained by relating the change in expenditure to both current and lagged changes in the cash supply, lagged for each of the four quarters, which yield positive and negative multipliers in regular sequence—which only goes to show what "t" values and R^2s are worth. (For equations, see Appendix on p. 493.)

Nobody would suggest (not even Professor Friedman, I believe) that the increase in note circulation in December is the cause of the Christmas buying spree. But there is the question that is more relevant to the Friedman thesis: Could the "authorities" prevent the buying spree by refusing to supply additional notes and coins in the Christmas season?

Of course, most people would say that it would be quite impossible to prevent the rise in the note circulation without disastrous consequences: widespread bank failures, or a general closure of the banks as a precautionary measure. If I were asked to advise, I would say that it could be done by less dramatic means: by instructing the banks, for example, not to cash more than £5 at any one time for each customer; by keeping down the number of cashiers, so as to maintain reasonably long queues in front of each bank window. If a man needed to queue up ten times a day, half an hour a time, to get £50 in notes, this would impose a pretty effective constraint on the cash supply.

But would it stop Christmas buying? There would be chaos for a few days, but soon all kinds of money substitutes would spring up: credit cards, promissory notes, etc., issued by firms or financial institutions which would circulate in the same way as bank notes. Any business with a high reputation—a well-known firm which is universally trusted—could issue such paper, and any one who could individually be "trusted" would get things on "credit". People who can be "trusted" are, of course, the same as those who have "credit"—the original meaning of "credit" was simply "trust". There would be a rush to join the Diners Club, and everyone who could be "trusted" to be given a card would still be able to buy as much as he desired.

The trust-worthy or credit-worthy part of the population—the people who can be trusted *not* to spend in excess of what they can afford to spend—would thus live on credit cards. The rest of the population—the mass of weekly wage-earners, for example, who have no "credit", not being men of substance—would get paid in chits which would be issued in lieu of cash by, say, the top five hundred businesses in the country (who would also, for a consideration, provide such chits to other employers). And these five hundred firms would soon find it convenient to set up a clearing system of their own, by investing in some giant computer which would at regular intervals net out all mutual claims and liabilities. It would also be necessary for the member firms of this clearing system to accord mutual "swops" or credit facilities to each other, to take care of net credit or debit balances after each clearing. When this is also agreed on, a complete surrogate money-system and payments-system would be established, which would exist side by side with "official money".

CHARACTERISTICS OF MONEY

What, at any time, is regarded as "money" are those forms of financial claims which are commonly used as means of clearing debts. But any shortage of commonly-used types is bound to lead to the emergence of new types; indeed, this is how, historically, first bank notes and then chequing accounts emerged. To the extent that no such new forms have emerged recently—in fact, they are emerging, though not as yet in a spectacular way—this is only because the existing system is so managed as to make it unnecessary, with the "authorities" providing enough money of the accustomed kind to discourage the growth of new kinds. They thereby also condition our minds into thinking that money is some distinct substance, a real entity, whose "quantity" is managed and controlled quite independently by the monetary authority.

Of course, within limits, the ultimate monetary authority can and does exercise control over the volume of borrowing, because it can control interest rates, particularly at the short end, through open market operations, far more powerfully than other operators, and because, within limits, it can control the volume and direction of lending by the clearing banks, which have such a powerful role in the system as suppliers of credit. But, as the Radcliffe Committee has shown, when credit control is operated as an independent instrument—as a substitute for fiscal policy, and not as a complement to it—any forceful initiative by the monetary authorities weakens their hold over the market by diverting business from the clearing banks to other financial institutions. The post-war experiments in monetary policy caused a lot of disorganisation—"a diffused difficulty of borrowing", in the words of Radcliffe, with firms having to borrow money from unaccustomed sources, or else to delay paying bills so as to achieve a better synchronisation between receipts and outlays—but with little discernible effect on spending. When the central bank succeeds in controlling the quantity of "conventional money", lending and borrowing is diverted to other sources, and the "velocity of circulation", in terms oi conventional money, is automatically speeded up.

VELOCITY OF CIRCULATION

Friedman's main contention is that the velocity of circulation, in terms of conventional money,[1] has been relatively stable. That may well be, but only because, in the historical periods observed, the supply of money was unstable. In other words, in one way or another, an increased demand for money evoked an increase in supply. The money supply "accommodated itself" to the needs of trade: rising in response to an expansion, and vice versa. In technical terms, this may have been the result of the objective of "financial stabilisation", of maintaining the structure of interest rates at some desired level, or the so-called "even keel policy", of ensuring an orderly market for government debt.[2]

[1] The precise meaning of "conventional money" differs from author to author (and from country to country); in the U.K. context it is usually defined as cash plus clearing bank deposits (both current and deposit accounts) in the hands of the public.

[2] A great deal of the current discussion on the importance of "money" is devoted to the issue of the "interest elasticity" of money balances—i.e. to the question of how the ratio between the "money supply" (as conventionally defined) and the national income can be expected to vary with changes in interest rates. Evidence of a low-interest elasticity is supposed to support the "monetarist school", while a high-interest elasticity is supposed to lend support to the "Keynesian" view. In fact, it does neither the one nor the other. The interest-elasticity of the demand for money really concerns a different issue: the power of the monetary authorities to vary the money supply in an exogenous manner. The *less* prepared the public is to absorb more cash in response to a reduction in interest rates, or to release cash in response to a rise, the *less* possible it is for the monetary authorities to expand the "money supply" relative to demand, or to prevent it from rising in response to a rise in the public's demand. This is because the authorities' sole policy instrument for changing the "money supply" is the buying and selling of financial assets in exchange for money; this presupposes that such sales or purchases can be effected in reasonable amounts without creating violent instabilities in the financial markets. Hence, the more Friedman and his followers succeed in demonstrating the insensitiveness of the demand for money to interest rates, the more they denigrate the role of money as an autonomous influence on the economy. The "stable money function" is evidence, not of the "importance of money", but only of the impotence of the authorities in controlling it. If it required a 50 per cent. fall in Consols to effect a 5 per cent. reduction (or to prevent a 5 per cent. rise) in the amount of money held by the public (i.e., assuming an interest elasticity of 0·1), any *autonomous* regulation of the "money supply" would in practice be rendered impossible by the exigencies of the financial and banking system. Those who hold that an "excess supply"

More fundamentally (and semi-consciously rather than in full awareness) it may have sprung from the realisation of the monetary authorities, be it the Federal Reserve or the Bank of England, that they are in the position of a constitutional monarch: with very wide reserve powers on paper, the maintenance and continuance of which are greatly dependent on the degree of restraint and moderation shown in their exercise. The Bank of England, by virtue of successive Acts of Parliament, has a monopoly of the note issue, at least in England and Wales. But the real power conferred by these Acts depended, and still depends, on maintaining the central role of the note issue in the general monetary and credit system; and this, in turn, was not a matter of legal powers, but of the avoidance of policies which would have led to the erosion of this role.

The explanation, in other words, for all the empirical findings on the "stable money function" is that the "money supply" is "endogenous", not "exogenous".

This, of course, is the crux of the issue, and it is vehemently denied by the monetarist school. They base their case on two kinds of evidence:

---

of money under these circumstances would *directly* increase spending forget that, barring helicopters, etc., the "excess supply" could never materialise.

One of the main contentions of the Friedman school is that, whenever the central bank changes the money supply by open market operations, say, by selling bonds in exchange for cash, it does not follow that the individuals who buy the bonds which the central bank sells will reduce their holding of money correspondingly—they may continue to hold the same amount of money, and economise instead on the buying of "goods". In this way, it is contended, a reduction in the money supply will have a "direct effect" on the demand for goods, and not only an "indirect effect", via the rate of interest. But there is a confusion here between "stocks" and "flows". The amount of money held by an individual is part of his *stock* of wealth; if he buys additional bonds, and this purchase represents an addition to his total stock of wealth, and not merely a substitution between one form of holding wealth and another (i.e. he continues to hold the same amount of money, *plus* a larger amount of bonds) this is only another way of saying that the individual bought the additional bonds out of income (i.e. out of foregone consumption), which in plain language means that he was induced to save more as a result of the opportunity of buying bonds on more attractive terms. No one has ever denied that monetary policy operating through changes in interest rates (or through direct controls over the volume of bank lending) could have an effect on the propensity to save as well as on the inducement to invest. But, unless the monetarists assume a high-interest elasticity in the propensity to save, and attribute the major influence of monetary action to this factor (in which case this should be made explicit), they *cannot* be saying anything different from Keynes—i.e. that the effects of "monetary action" on the level of demand depend on the effects of the consequential changes of interest rates (or, what comes to the same thing, of credit rationing by the banks) on the level of investment.

(1) The first is the time lag. Peaks and troughs in the money supply (in the U.S., at any rate) have regularly preceded peaks and troughs in G.N.P., though with a variable lag of two to six quarters, and one that tended to shorten in the post-war era to one quarter or less.[1] If the money supply changes first, and the level of income (or business activity) afterwards, it is contended that the one that came first must have been the *cause* of the other.

(2) The second is the contention that in the U.S., at any rate, banks are always "loaned up", more or less. Hence, the "money supply" (which includes bank deposits, as well as notes and coins held by the public) is fairly closely related to "high-powered money"—to the so-called "monetary base", which is under the sole control of the Federal Reserve, and who exercise their power, wisely or foolishly, but quite autonomously.

In my opinion, neither of these arguments *proves* that money plays—in the U.S., let alone in the U.K.—the causal role: that the "money supply" governs the level and the rate of growth of money incomes or expenditures.

THE TIME LAG

With regard to the time lag, it is now fairly generally admitted that it does not prove anything about the nature of the causal relationships. If one assumed a purely Keynesian model where expenditure decisions govern incomes, and if one assumed a purely passive monetary system—with reserves being supplied freely, at constant interest rates—it would still be true that the turn-round in the money supply would precede the turn-round in the G.N.P., for much the same reasons for which the Keynesian multiplier invariably involves a time lag.

Suppose the initiating change is a decision of some firms to increase their inventories, financed by borrowing. The first impact is to cause some other firms whose sales have increased unexpectedly to incur some involuntary disinvestment. It is only when that is made good by increased orders that productive activity is expanded; any such expansion will cause higher wage outlays,

---

[1] Richard G. Davis, "The Role of the Money Supply in Business Cycles", *Monthly Review of the Federal Reserve Bank of New York*, April 1968, p. 71.

which in turn may involve further borrowing. The ultimate effects on income involve further increases in productive activity arising from the expenditure generated by additional incomes. There is every reason for supposing, therefore, that the rise in the "money supply" should precede the rise in income—irrespective of whether the money-increase was a cause or an effect.

There may be other explanations which would need to be investigated, such as the contra-cyclical behaviour in the fiscal balance which, particularly in the U.S., has been a very important feature of the scene, especially in the post-war years. I am referring to the so-called "built-in fiscal stabiliser", which means that the fiscal deficit automatically rises in times of declining activity and automatically falls in times of rising activity. Owing to lags in tax collection, particularly in taxes on corporate profits, this operates so that the maximum swings occur sometimes after the turning point in economic activity.

Now, it is well known that changes in the government's net borrowing requirement are the most important cause of changes in the money supply. This is only partly due to the fact that the government's own balances are excluded from the "money supply", so that any depletion of such balances automatically augments the money supply. Partly it is due to the fact that the government is the one borrower with unlimited borrowing power: an increase in government borrowing, whether due to a decline in tax receipts, a rise in expenditure, or both, involves an increase in the money supply as an automatic result of a "passive" monetary policy, which supplies reserves as part of a policy of stabilising interest rates or simply to ensure orderly conditions in the bond market.[1] Moreover, since, in the U.S. at any rate, the government's borrowing requirement is largest when the economy is depressed, it occurs at a time when the Federal Reserve system is least inclined to follow a "tough" credit policy; whilst in times when it wishes to

[1] As Hawtrey has repeatedly emphasised, in the case of private borrowing the maintenance of orderly conditions in the bond market invariably involved some policy of "credit-rationing" or rather "issue rationing" by the issuing houses, who made sure that the volume of issues for public subscription at any one time was no greater than what the market could absorb. This is his explanation for the long-term rate of interest being largely a "conventional phenomenon". (Cf., e.g., *A Century of Bank Rate*, London, 1938, pp. 177 ff.) But there is nothing equivalent to this in the case of *government* borrowing.

restrain the expansion of credit, the government itself is likely to be in surplus. Hence, the large observed fluctuations in the money supply, preceding in time the business cycle, may merely be a reflection of the operation of the built-in fiscal stabiliser.

An interesting bit of evidence for this view is the abnormal behaviour of the money supply following the Korean War, when the money supply peaked about a year after, not in the year preceding, the peak of the post-Korean boom. A possible explanation is that the rise in government expenditure (and the deficit) followed on this occasion the sharp rise in activity, which was induced, no doubt, by the large rise in military procurement but which had been reflected in a sharp increase in federal expenditure only some time later on, when the bills came to be paid.

CHANGES IN MONEY SUPPLY: U.S. EXPERIENCE

This brings me to Friedman's second contention and the one on which he would himself lay the most emphasis: that in the United States, at any rate, changes in the money supply have been "exogenous" and were largely determined by autonomous policy decisions of the Federal Reserve Board. Since Friedman and Anna Schwartz have written a book of eight hundred pages to prove this point,[1] it is not easy to deal with their massive evidence in a few sentences. None the less, I shall try but will confine myself to some key issues and to some general observations.

In the first place, while the correlation between the "monetary base" (defined above) and the "money supply" was good in general, it was not sufficiently good to be able to regard changes in the one as being the equivalent of changes in the other. In particular, it appears that on occasions when the Federal Reserve went out of its way to increase reserves (as in the 1929–39 period), the reaction on the total money supply was small. Moreover, the effects of changes in the "monetary base" on the "monetary multiplier" were consistently negative in all periods.[2]

---

[1] *A Monetary History of the United States*, 1867–1960, National Bureau of Economic Research, Princeton University Press, 1963.

[2] Cf. Keran, "Monetary and Fiscal Influences on Economic Activity—The Historical Evidence", *Review of the Federal Reserve Bank of St. Louis*, November 1969, Tables VII and VIII.

More important than this, the variations in the "monetary base" are themselves explained by factors—such as the desire to stabilise interest rates, or to ensure government debt financing (the so-called "even keel" objective[1])—which makes the "monetary base" automatically responsive to changes in the demand for money. In other words, if variations in the money supply were closely related to changes in the "monetary base", this is mainly because the latter has also been "endogenous", as well as the former.

Friedman himself regards the monetary history of the Great Contraction, 1929–33, as the ultimate test of his basic contention. It is worth quoting the critical passage in his Presidential Address to the American Economic Association[2] at some length:

"The revival of belief in the potency of monetary policy was fostered also by a re-evaluation of the role money played from 1929 to 1933. Keynes and most other economists of the time believed that the Great Contraction in the United States occurred despite aggressive expansionary policies by the monetary authorities—that they did their best, but their best was not good enough. Recent studies have demonstrated that the *facts* are precisely the reverse: the U.S. monetary authorities followed highly *deflationary* policies. The quantity of money in the United States fell by one-third in the course of the contraction. And it fell not because there were no willing borrowers—not because the horse would not drink. It fell because the Federal Reserve System *forced or permitted* a sharp reduction in *the monetary base*, because it failed to exercise the responsibilities assigned to it in the Federal Reserve Act to provide liquidity to the banking system. The Great Contraction is tragic testimony to the power of monetary policy—not, as Keynes and so many of his contemporaries believed, evidence of its impotence."

I cannot understand the reference to the "sharp reduction in *the monetary base*" in the above passage, which is absolutely critical to the argument. According to Friedman's own figures,[3] the

---

[1] Keran, *op. cit.* Table VI.
[2] "The Role of Monetary Policy", *American Economic Review*, March 1968, p. 3. (My italics.)
[3] Friedman and Schwartz, *op. cit.*, Table B–3, pp. 803–4.

amount of "high-powered money", which is Friedman's own synonym for the "monetary base" (i.e. currency held by the public plus member bank reserves with the Federal Reserve) in the U.S. increased, not decreased, throughout the Great Contraction: in July, 1932, it was more than 10 per cent. higher than in July, 1929, whereas it was held constant in the three previous years (1926–9). The Great Contraction of the money supply (by one-third) occurred *despite* this rise in the monetary base. This was partly because the ratio of currency held by the public to bank deposits rose substantially. This is attributed by Friedman to a confidence crisis: the public's diminished confidence in the banks. But it is important to observe that this dramatic rise in the ratio of currency held by the public to bank deposits was never reversed subsequently. In July, 1960, it was still at approximately the same level as in July, 1932, which in turn was nearly twice as high as in July, 1929. If it was a matter of confidence in the banks, why was it not reversed in the subsequent thirty years? The fact that the currency–deposit ratio was at its highest during the war years, 1944–5 (when it stood 45 per cent. *above* the July, 1932, level), suggests rather that the main explanation may lie elsewhere—in the change in the pattern of expenditure between goods (or assets) normally paid for in cash and those normally paid for by cheque, which was due partly to the fall in the volume of financial transactions in relation to income transactions (this would explain why the deposit–currency ratio rose so much during the years of the Wall Street boom[1]) and partly also to the rise in the share of wages and fall in the share of property incomes during the slump.

The other reason was the fall in the ratio of bank deposits to bank reserves—in other words, a rise in commercial bank liquidity by some 27 per cent. between July, 1929, and July, 1932—which *may* have reflected prudential motives by the banks, but may also have been the consequence of an insufficient demand for loans—

---

[1] The demand for money is usually considered as a function of income and wealth; this is legitimate on the assumption that the volume of money transactions is itself uniquely related to income and wealth. However, in times when people make frequent "switches" in their portfolios, and the volume of financial transactions is large relative to the total value of assets, it is inevitable that the amount of money held by speculators as a group should also relatively be large, even if no one individual intends to hold such balances for more than a short period.

of the horse *refusing* to drink (particularly the fall in the demand for loans for speculative purposes). There is nothing in these figures, in my view, to support the far-reaching contentions which I have just quoted and, in a complex issue of this kind, I would put far more trust in the "feel" and judgment of contemporary observers, like Keynes or Henry Simons, than in some dubious (and tendentious) statistics produced thirty years later.

I have also perused the one hundred and twenty pages devoted to the Great Contraction in the book on the monetary history of the U.S. and, while I would agree that he makes out a good case for saying that the policy of the Federal Reserve, particularly after Britain's departure from the gold standard, was foolish and unimaginative, and that the succession of bank failures in the course of 1932 might have been avoided if the Federal Reserve had followed more closely the classic prescription for a financial panic of Mr. Harman of the Bank of England in 1825 (quoted by Bagehot)[1]—of lending like mad on the security of every scrap of respectable looking paper—I do not believe that it would have made all that difference. In particular, I do not believe that the Great Depression (with all its tragic consequences, Hitler and the Second World War) would not have occurred but for Governor Benjamin Strong's untimely retirement and death in 1928. Indeed, I am not sure whether Governor Strong's policies in the years prior to 1928 might not have contributed to the financial crisis following the crash in 1929. For he kept the volume of reserves— the supply of "high-powered money"—rigidly stable in the years 1925–9. This occurred at a time when the U.S. economy and the national income was expanding, with the result that the banking system became increasingly precarious: the ratio of bank deposits to bank reserves, and the ratio of deposits to currency in the hands of the public, rose well above the customary levels established prior to the First World War, and to very much higher levels than these ratios have ever attained subsequently.[2]

Indeed, the best answer to Friedman's main contention is provided by Friedman himself, in comparing U.S. and Canadian

---

[1] Bagehot, *Lombard Street*, London, 1873, pp. 51–2; quoted in Friedman and Schwartz, *op. cit.*, p. 395.
[2] Friedman and Schwartz, *op. cit.*, Table B–3, pp. 800–8.

experience during the Great Contraction.[1] In Canada, there were no bank failures at all; the contraction in the money supply was much smaller than in the U.S.—only two-fifths of that in the U.S., or 13 against 33 per cent.—yet the proportionate contraction in money G.N.P. was nearly the same. The difference in the proportional change in the money supply was largely offset by differences in the decline in the velocity of circulation: in the U.S. it fell by 29 per cent., in Canada by 41 per cent. This clearly suggests that the relative stability in the demand for money is a reflection of the instability in its supply; if the supply of money had been kept more stable, the velocity of circulation would have been more *unstable*.

This last statement may appear to be in contradiction to Friedman's empirical generalisation according to which the movement in the velocity of circulation in the U.S. has historically been positively correlated with movements in the money supply— the velocity of circulation was at its most stable when the money supply was most stable. But the two propositions are not inconsistent, which shows how easy it is to draw misleading conclusions from statistical associations. If one postulates that it is the fluctuation in the economy that causes the fluctuations in the money supply (and not the other way round), but that the elasticity in the supply of money (in response to changes in demand) is less than infinite, then, the greater the change in demand, the more *both* the supply of money and the "velocity" will rise in consequence. If the supply of money had responded less, the change in velocity would have been greater; if the supply of money had responded fully, no change in velocity would have occurred (under this hypothesis).

WHAT ABOUT BRITAIN?

In this country, at least since the Second World War, it is even less plausible to argue that the "money supply" is under the direct control of the monetary authorities, regulated through the rate of creation of bank reserves. Clearly, it is not controlled through the 8 per cent. minimum cash ratio, for there is an agreement between the Bank and the clearing banks to supply sufficient reserves to

[1] *Ibid.*, p. 352.

validate this ratio week by week without any window-dressing. Nor can it be said that the "money supply" is controlled by the agreement of the clearing banks to observe the 28 per cent. prudential liquidity ratio, since there are numerous ways open to the banks to maintain this latter ratio which do not involve recourse to central bank credit.

What, then, governs, at least in the U.K., the changes in "money supply"? In my view, it is largely a reflection of the rate of change in money incomes and, therefore, is dependent on, and varies with, all the forces, or factors, which determine this magnitude: the change in the pressure of demand, domestic investment, exports and fiscal policy, on the one hand, and the rate of wage-inflation (which may also be partly influenced by the pressure of demand), on the other hand. This basic relationship between the money supply and G.N.P. is modified, however, in the short period by the behaviour of the income-expenditure relation (or, as I would prefer to call it, the receipt-outlay relation) of those particular sectors whose receipt-outlay relation is particularly unstable—in other words, whose net dependence on "outside finance" is both large and liable to large variations, *for reasons which are endogenous, not exogenous, to the sector.* This is true, of course, to a certain extent of the business sector, though business investment in fixed capital and stocks has not been nearly as unstable in the last twenty years as it was expected to be in pre-war days. But it is chiefly true of the public sector, whose "net borrowing requirement" has been subject to very large fluctuations year by year. I am convinced that the short-run variations in the "money supply"—in other words, the variation relative to trend—are very largely explained by the variation in the public sector's borrowing requirement.[1]

Over the last five years we have witnessed a dramatic change in the rate of increase in the money supply: it fell from 9·8 per cent. in 1967 to 6⅔ per cent. in 1968 and to only 2·9 per cent. in 1969. The last of these years has also witnessed a dramatic turn-round

---

[1] In fact, a simple regression equation of the annual change of the money supply on the public sector borrowing requirement for the years 1954–68 shows that the money supply increased almost exactly £ for £ with every £1 increase in the public sector deficit, with "t"=6·1, R^2= ·740, or, in fashionable language, 74 per cent. of the variation in the money supply is explained by the deficit of the public sector *alone.* (See Appendix.)

in the balance of payments. This is regarded as a "feather in the cap" for the monetarists, who point with pride to the effectiveness of monetary policy—not in stopping wage and price inflation, for this unfortunately has not happened—but at least in restoring a healthy balance of payments. They forget that the same period witnessed an even more dramatic turn-round in the net borrowing requirement of the public sector—from over £2,000 million in 1967–8 to *minus* £600 million in 1969–70. The recent "credit squeeze" is not really a "credit squeeze" but a "liquidity squeeze". It is a direct consequence of a big fall in the receipt-expenditure relationship of the business sector which, in turn, was a reflection of the big improvement in the receipt–expenditure relationship of the public sector, only partially offset by the (more recent) improvement in the outlay–receipt relationship of the overseas sector.

What, if anything, follows from all this? I have certainly no objection to Friedman's prescription that the best thing to do is to secure a steady expansion of x per cent. a year in the money supply. But I doubt if this objective is attainable by the instruments of monetary policy in the U.S., let alone in the U.K. If it is ever attained, it will be because, contrary to past experience, we shall succeed in avoiding stop-go cycles emanating from abroad, or from the private business sector, or, what is more likely, from the very changes in fiscal policy which aim to compensate for other instabilities; and if, by some combination of incomes policy and magic (but more by magic), we shall also succeed in keeping the rate of increase in money wages in both a stable and a reasonable relationship to the rate of growth of productivity.

SOME REGRESSION EQUATIONS

I *Regression Equations relating Changes in Consumers' Expenditure in the U.K. to Changes in Currency in Circulation held by the Public.*

Data: Quarterly changes in £ millions; 1948 II—III to 1969 II—III

Notation: $\triangle C$ = Change in Consumers' Expenditure

$\triangle N$ = Change in average currency in circulation with the public;

$$\left.\begin{array}{l} d_1 \\ d_2 \\ d_3 \\ d_4 \end{array}\right\} \begin{array}{c}\text{Dummy variables} = 1 \text{ for quarter} \\ \text{to quarter changes}\end{array} \left\{\begin{array}{c} \text{I— II} \\ \text{II—III} \\ \text{III—IV} \\ \text{IV— I} \end{array}\right\}, 0 \text{ otherwise.}$$

Standard deviation in brackets; R^2 unadjusted; s = standard error (adjusted for degrees of freedom).

Lags in quarters denoted by negative subscripts.

Results:

$$\triangle C = -65\cdot99 + 6\cdot127\,\triangle N \qquad\qquad R^2 = 0\cdot494$$
$$\quad\quad (24\cdot23)\quad (0\cdot681) \qquad\qquad\qquad\quad s\ = 183\cdot8$$

$$\triangle C = 170\cdot35 - 166\cdot77\,d_2 + 3\cdot71\,d_3 - 476\cdot48\,d_4 +$$
$$\qquad\quad (38\cdot78)\quad (29\cdot74)\quad (40\cdot57)\quad (49\cdot83)$$
$$2\cdot350\,\triangle N \qquad\qquad\qquad\qquad\qquad R^2 = 0\cdot884$$
$$(0\cdot636) \qquad\qquad\qquad\qquad\qquad\qquad s\ = 89\cdot5$$

$$\triangle C = 5\cdot77 + 3\cdot855\,\triangle N - 2\cdot565\,\triangle N_{-1} + 2\cdot725\,\triangle N_{-2} -$$
$$\quad (23\cdot52)\ (0\cdot639)\qquad (0\cdot411)\qquad\quad (0\cdot417)$$
$$5\cdot640\,\triangle N_{-3} + 4\cdot220\,\triangle N_{-4} \qquad\qquad R^2 = 0\cdot878$$
$$(0\cdot417)\qquad\quad (0\cdot644) \qquad\qquad\qquad s\ = 94\cdot62$$

$$\triangle C = 96\cdot84 - 31\cdot51 d_2 + 37\cdot54 d_3 - 310\cdot88 d_4 + 2\cdot624\,\triangle N -$$
$$\quad (49\cdot17)\ (63\cdot52)\quad (69\cdot18)\quad (68\cdot15)\quad (0\cdot672)$$
$$2\cdot062\,\triangle N_{-1} + 1\cdot528\,\triangle N_{-2} - 2\cdot205\,\triangle N_{-3} + 1\cdot947\,\triangle N_{-4}$$
$$(0\cdot706)\qquad\quad (0\cdot699)\qquad\quad (0\cdot702)\qquad\quad (0\cdot665)$$
$$R^2 = 0\cdot920$$
$$s\ = 78\cdot33$$

II *Regression Equations showing the Relationship of Changes in the Money Supply in the U.K. to the Public Sector Borrowing Requirement.*

Data: Annual figures in £ millions, relating to calendar years.

Notation: $\triangle M$ = increase in money supply.

P = Net acquisition of financial assets by the public sector.

Standard deviation in brackets.

Results:

(1) Period 1954–68

$$\triangle M = -299 \cdot 1 - 1 \cdot 035 P \qquad\qquad R^2 = 0 \cdot 740$$
$$(0 \cdot 170) \qquad\qquad\qquad s = 210 \cdot 2$$

(2) Period 1960–68

$$\triangle M = -246 \cdot 3 - 0 \cdot 979 P \qquad\qquad R^2 = 0 \cdot 714$$
$$(0 \cdot 231) \qquad\qquad\qquad s = 212 \cdot 1$$

CONFLICTS IN NATIONAL ECONOMIC OBJECTIVES[1]

Economics, at least since Adam Smith, has been concerned with understanding how the economic system works in order to discover by what kind of policies it could be made to work better. More wealth, and a more even distribution of wealth, have always been regarded without question or argument as the main objectives of national economic policy. But up to fairly recently—up to the Second World War in fact—the tasks of economic policy were mainly thought of as the creation of a framework of laws and institutions which provided the best environment for the operation of market forces, and not as any direct manipulation of those forces.

THE FOUR MAJOR OBJECTIVES OF POST-WAR POLICY

Since that time the notion of "economic policy objectives" has acquired a new precision—one could almost say a new meaning—and governments have come to be judged by performance criteria which they would have strongly disclaimed in earlier days. The best evidence for this is that policy objectives have come to be expressed in quantitative terms—as "targets." Successive post-war Chancellors have announced a *full-employment* target, expressed in terms of an average percentage of unemployment which is not be to exceeded (3 per cent by Mr. Gaitskell in 1950): a *balance of payments* target, expressed in terms of a current surplus of so many millions (such as the £300 million put forward by Mr.—now Lord—Butler in 1952); a *growth*

---

[1] Originally delivered as Presidential Address to Section F of the British Association at Durham, September 1970, and printed in *Economic Journal*, vol. LXXXI March 1971.

target (4 per cent by Mr. Maudling in 1964 and in the National Plan of 1965) and a *wage-increase or incomes policy* target (by Sir Stafford Cripps in 1949; by Mr. Selwyn Lloyd in 1962; Mr. Maudling in 1964; Mr. Brown in 1965; by legislation in 1966, etc.).

Though the status of such official targets was never clearly defined, the very fact of their announcement was an outward manifestation of a deep-seated change in public attitudes in regard to the powers and responsibilities of Government in the economic sphere. It has come to be taken for granted—by the leaders of both of the major political parties, as well as by the public—that Governments can, and should, assume responsibility for the "management of the economy"; and that "successful management" comprises the simultaneous attainment of at least the four major objectives.

The fact that these have come to be accepted as mandatory objectives of policy—i.e., as ends that the public can legitimately expect from its Government—was the most important political result of the intellectual revolution engendered by the publication of Keynes' *General Theory of Employment*. The important message of that work was the idea that in a market economy the total amount of goods and services produced is not (or not normally) determined by the amount of scarce resources at its disposal, and the efficiency with which they are utilised, but on certain features of the process of income generation which tend to establish an equilibrium level of effective demand that will limit the amount produced, irrespective of potential supply.

Keynes' theory has shown how the economy can be managed so as to secure the full utilisation of resources, in particular the full employment of labour, mainly by Government action in the fiscal and monetary field, without any radical change in the framework of institutions of a market economy. This idea had a tremendous appeal, the more so since war-time experience has demonstrated how quickly, given sufficient demand, unemployment could be made to disappear; and the pressure of public opinion created by that experience was undoubtedly responsible for the famous declaration of the war-time Coalition Government which stated that "the Government accept as one of their primary aims and responsibilities the maintenance of a high and stable level of employment after the War."[1]

Once that responsibility had been assumed, it was quite inevitable that successive post-war Governments should also assume responsibility, or at least be *held* responsible, for the other vital aspects of the performance of the economy necessary to make a full-employment policy viable, in particular for ensuring a satisfactory balance of payments, and for ensuring a "reasonable stability of wages and prices." Both of these "associated requirements" figure quite prominently in the 1944 White Paper, which may be regarded—along with Beveridge's book on Full Employment, published in the same year[2]—as the original blueprint from which all post-war policies of economic management have evolved. In the matter of price stability, the White Paper states quite categorically that "increases in the general level of wages must be related to increased productivity." In the matter of the balance of payments it emphasised that "to avoid an unfavourable foreign balance we must export much more than we did before the war."

However, there was little understanding of the difficulties which were to arise in the attempt to achieve all these objectives simultaneously, or of how Government policy was to be conducted if they were not attained, or if the various objectives came into open conflict with one another.

On the question of the balance of payments, the White Paper stated, somewhat surprisingly, that "the state of our foreign balance depends very largely upon the behaviour of persons and Governments outside our jurisdiction" and suggested that the best way to make sure that we shall be able to export enough to pay for our imports is to ensure, by means of international agreements (of the type of Bretton Woods and G.A.T.T.— neither of which were then in existence), "conditions of international trade which will make it possible for all countries to pursue policies of full employment to their mutual advantage." There was no hint of a suggestion that the maintenance of full employment might prove incompatible with a continued equili-

---

[1] Cf. White Paper on *Employment Policy*, Cmnd. 6527, May 1944.
[2] W. H. Beveridge, *Full Employment in a Free Society* (London, 1944).

brium in the balance of payments under a regime of fixed exchange rates, even when prices and wages were kept "reasonably stable" and when the world economy was expanding.

On the question of price and wage stability, the White Paper stated that "it will be essential that employers and workers should exercise moderation in wages matters," and "that condition can be realised only by the joint efforts of the Government, employers and organised labour." But it offered no suggestion of the kind of institutional arrangements that would be needed if the determination of wages and prices were no longer to be left to the impersonal forces of the market.

TARGETS AND INSTRUMENTS

In the language of present-day econometrics, the failure of post-war Governments to pursue a policy consistent in terms of its declared objectives could thus be primarily attributed to an insufficient orchestration of instruments—of not having enough separate policy instruments at hand to secure the simultaneous attainment of the various objectives. It is a well-known principle of the modern theory of economic policy, first put forward by Professor Tinbergen,[1] that in order to secure a stated number of objectives the Government needs to operate at least an equal number of different policy instruments—it is only in exceptional circumstances that the same instrument can secure the attainment of more than one "target" simultaneously. If demand management (through fiscal policy) is used to secure the target level of employment, another instrument—which can only be thought of in terms of an incomes policy—is needed to secure the target rate of wage increases; and yet a further instrument—a flexible exchange rate—to secure the target balance of payments. If in addition the Government wishes to secure a target rate of productivity growth it needs yet further instruments to secure a more effective utilisation of resources.

On a formal theoretical plane one could thus assert that the

---

[1] J. Tinbergen, *On the Theory of Economic Policy* (Amsterdam, 1952), Chapters IV and V. Also J. E. Meade, *The Balance of Payments, Mathematical Supplement* (Oxford, 1951), pp. 28–9.

basic cause of our failures was that of trying to achieve too much with too little freedom of action—of failing to grasp the full implication of the principles of economic management. On a more realistic plane, I think one must recognise that the limits on the degrees of freedom of Governmental policy were set by political, social and ideological constraints which inhibited action in certain fields; the intellectual failure to recognise the need for them was a symptom, rather than the cause, of the inhibition. The tremendous resistance which Governments have invariably put up to devaluation—even in circumstances where such an adjustment was plainly in accord with both the letter and the spirit of the Bretton Woods agreement—has, I am sure, far more deep-seated causes than simply a failure by Ministers or officials to make a proper study of the writings of Professor Tinbergen. As recent events have shown, the resistance can be almost equally strong when the required adjustment involves revaluation (as in the German case) rather than devaluation. Equally, the resistance to an incomes policy by economists and politicians of both the right and the left had more to do with a refusal to accept its social and political implications than with the uncritical acceptance of the econometric studies of Professor Phillips which confirmed many of our economists in the more comfortable view that, provided monetary and fiscal policy is properly conducted and the pressure of demand is not allowed to exceed certain limits, wage and price inflation will automatically be contained by the forces of the market.

As a result of the extraordinary stresses and strains of the last few years—on an international plane, and not only in this country —there has been a distinct improvement, and there is now a much greater consensus of opinion on the need for such instruments than existed before. It is now more widely accepted that adjustments in the exchange rate are a legitimate, indeed an indispensable, part of the international "adjustment process"—for keeping the system of international payments in reasonable balance— and the I.M.F. has been charged with the task of putting forward suggestions for greater exchange-rate flexibility within the general framework of the system. It is also far more generally acknowledged—even by Conservative Prime Ministers—that the process of inflation is "cost-induced," not "demand-induced," with the evident implication that it can be tackled only by an incomes policy—though I must confess, I am no more clear than others by what kinds of institutional arrangements such an instrument could be effectively operated. Can it be based on anything less than the creation of a social consensus on what constitutes a fair system of pay differentials on a national scale, and if so, is there a way of bringing this about?

As the problem of an incomes policy raises sociological and political issues that are outside my competence, and as it is a problem that is common to all industrial countries, and not specific to Britain, I do not propose to consider it today in any detail. Instead I shall devote the rest of this address to the other major problem of economic management—the question of exchange-rate policy. Here my contention is not merely that we should have used this instrument more often and more readily to avoid the periodic interruptions to our economic growth on account of balance-of-payments crises, important and unwelcome though these have been. My basic contention, which I propose to develop at some length, is that by choosing the control of the pressure of demand through fiscal management as the centrepiece of action, we have opted, quite unintentionally, for the creation of an economic structure which has involved a slower rate of growth in our productive potential than was both possible and desirable.

My main criticism of the philosophy underlying the White Paper, and of the post-war policies of economic management that were built on it, is that it treated the problem of full employment and (implicitly) of growth as one of internal demand management, and not one of exports and of international competitiveness.

This was the result of the failure of the economists who were responsible for laying out the groundwork of the new policy to examine, or to appreciate, the true implications of the Keynesian model of under-employment equilibrium, elaborated in terms of a "closed economy," to an "open economy" such as Britain. As I was one of the economists engaged in laying out the groundwork—in a memorandum prepared for Sir William

Beveridge's working group in 1943[1]—I would like to state that I feel I am as much responsible for that failure as any other economist of the time. And by the word "failure" I do *not* mean— as will become evident in the concluding part of this address— that the policy was fundamentally wrong, in the sense that Britain would now be better off if it had never been invented or adopted. This is far from the case. What I do mean to suggest is that it was very much a policy of the "second best"; and that after twenty-five years of experience it is time to re-examine its foundations to see whether for the future we cannot replace it with something better.

A LOOK-BACK TO THE 1920s

As I have no time to develop the argument in terms of basic theoretical models, I propose to demonstrate my point by asking what would have happened if the principles of demand management, as laid down in the White Paper, had been applied to deal with the pre-war unemployment problem. For this purpose it is best to start with the 1920s, when the rest of the world was prosperous, and world trade expanding, whilst in Britain, starting from 1921, unemployment, except for brief periods, had never fallen below a million and a quarter, or 10 per cent of the labour force.

I propose to begin by quoting at some length from an internal Treasury minute that has recently come to light, written by Winston Churchill as Chancellor of the Exchequer in February 1925 in connection with the discussions that were going on inside the Government concerning the return to the Gold Standard. (It is worth quoting this document at some length, partly as a tribute to the intuition and intelligence—in hitherto unsuspected directions—of one of our greatest national leaders, but also because in analysing what would have been the right answer to Churchill's queries one comes to grips with what was wrong with our pre-war policies, and by implication, also with our post-war policies.) Churchill wrote:

[1] "The Quantitative Aspects of the Full Employment Problem in Britain", published as Appendix C to Beveridge's *Full Employment in a Free Society* (London, Allen and Unwin, 1944), pp. 344–401 and reproduced in *Essays on Economic Policy*, I, pp. 23–82.

"The Treasury have never, it seems to me, faced the profound significance of what Mr. Keynes calls 'the paradox of
unemployment amidst dearth'. The Governor shows himself
perfectly happy in the spectacle of Britain possessing the
finest credit in the world simultaneously with a million and a
quarter unemployed . . . *This is the only country in the world
where this condition exists.* The Treasury and Bank of England
policy has been the only policy consistently pursued. It is
a terrible responsibility for those who have shaped it, unless
they can be sure that there is no connection between the
unique British phenomenon of chronic unemployment and
the long, resolute consistency of a particular financial policy.
. . . It may be of course that you will argue that the unemployment would have been much greater but for the financial
policy pursued; that there is no sufficient demand for commodities, either internally or externally to require the services
of this million and a quarter people; that there is nothing for
them but to hang like a millstone round the neck of industry
and on the public revenue until they become permanently
demoralised. You may be right, but if so, it is one of the most
sombre conclusions ever reached. On the other hand I do not
pretend to see even 'through a glass darkly' how the financial
and credit policy of the country could be handled so as to
bridge the gap between a dearth of goods and a surplus of
labour; and well I realise the danger of experiment to that
end. The seas of history are full of famous wrecks. Still, if I
could see a way, I would far rather follow it than any other.
I would rather see Finance less proud and Industry more
content."[1]

Today, with almost a half century of experience and of progress
in economic theory behind us, we can see "through a glass
darkly" rather better than either Churchill or his official advisers were able to do in 1925.

Most economists would now agree that fiscal policy, combined with credit policy, could have been so handled as to

[1] Minute of February 22, 1925, quoted in D. E. Moggridge, *The Return to Gold,
1925* (Cambridge University Press, 1969), p. 54. Italics not in the original.

eliminate (at least gradually, even if not immediately) unemployment, and that such a policy would *not* have involved a "vicious and cumulative inflation" that would have gone on until money "ceased to be acceptable as value."[1] On the other hand, any such policy which raised production and employment through a stimulus to domestic demand would have involved an increase in imports relative to exports; this would have brought a downward pressure on sterling on the exchanges, and would have made it quite impossible to return to the Gold Standard.

Indeed, there was no way of pursuing a full-employment policy in Britain in the 1920s consistently with a return to the Gold Standard at the pre-war parity of $4.86. As a result of the deflationary policies adopted on the recommendation of the Cunliffe Committee (which regarded the restoration of the Gold Standard as the most important national economic objective) and the rise in the sterling exchange rate, British exports failed to recover: in 1924 the volume of exports was only 72 per cent of pre-war, whilst imports had regained the pre-war level;[2] British exports performed very badly even in relation to continental European countries, who were only just recovering from the war.[3] Unemployment was largely concentrated in the traditional export industries—steel and engineering, shipbuilding, textiles and coal. The only possible way in which this heavy unemployment could have been absorbed would have been through higher exports, which in turn would have required abandoning the Gold Standard objective and opting instead for a floating rate—for the "managed currency" advocated by Keynes in 1924.[4]

The truth that was hidden from Churchill and his official advisers in 1925—and was evidently not perceived even by the authors of the White Paper twenty years later—is that the main autonomous factor governing both the level and the rate of

[1] Cf. the official reply to Churchill's minute quoted by Moggridge, *op. cit.*, p. 55.
[2] *The British Economy, Key Statistics* 1900–1966 Table B (London and Cambridge Economic Service).
[3] Cf. A. Maddison, "Growth and Fluctuations in the World Economy, 1870–1960", *Banca Nazionale del Lavoro, Quarterly Review*, June 1962, Tables 25 and 27.
[4] Keynes, J. M., *A Tract on Monetary Reform* (London, 1924), Chapters IV and V. Keynes' proposal was that the Bank of England should announce fixed buying and selling prices for gold (or dollars) every Thursday, but that it should have freedom to vary these rates up and down at weekly intervals, in the same way as the Bank rate.

G

growth of effective demand of an industrial country with a large share of exports in its total production and of imports in its consumption is the external demand for its exports;[1] and the main factor governing the latter is its international competitiveness, which in turn depends on the level of its industrial costs relatively to other industrial exporters. Since the level of money wages is bound to be sticky in a downward direction, and is not greatly influenced by world prices in an upward direction, the degree of competitiveness, given the relationship of wage-rates and productivity levels of different industrial countries, depends largely on the exchange rate.[2] Moreover, owing to the existence of increasing returns to scale in manufacturing industries, any initial advantage in terms of export competitiveness tends to have a cumulative effect, since the country which is able to increase its manufactured exports faster than the others also tends to have a faster rate of growth of productivity in its export industries, which enhances its competitive advantage still further. The task of maintaining competitiveness through the choice of a favourable exchange rate is therefore of the highest importance to an industrial country from the point of view of its long-run

[1] According to all recent evidence, external influences, operating through export demand, determined both the timing and the scale of fluctuations in the British economy throughout the nineteenth century; with the possible exception of the 1901–14 period (which has special features) the level of domestic investment has generally followed the movement of exports. Cf. Appendix A of W. H. Beveridge's *Full Employment in a Free Society* (prepared in collaboration with Mr. Harold Wilson), particularly pp. 294–305; Sayers, R. S., *The Vicissitudes of an Export Economy: Britain since 1880*, the Mills Memorial Lecture (Sydney, 1965); *A History of Economic Change in England, 1880–1934* (Oxford, 1967), part. Chapters 2 and 3; Ford, A. G., "British Economic Fluctuations, 1870–1914", *Manchester School*, June 1969, pp. 99–130.

[2] This is not to deny that the rate of increase in money wages—with or without an incomes policy—is influenced by the cost of living, so that money wages will tend to rise faster as a result of a falling exchange rate and rising import prices; if the movement of wages is controlled, or moderated, by an incomes policy a flexible exchange rate will put a greater strain on this instrument. But there is no reason for supposing that the "efficiency wages" of a country, in terms of international currency, cannot be permanently lowered by a downward adjustment of the exchange rate, even though the change in the exchange rate necessary to secure a given reduction in "efficiency wages" will be greater than it would be if money wages did not react to the change in the cost of living. It must also be borne in mind that the change in "efficiency wages", or in the terms of trade, that is necessary to achieve a given increase in the volume or the rate of growth of exports, comes to the same whether it is achieved by a change in internal costs (*i.e.*, in the level of wages), or a change in the exchange rate, or some combination of both. There is no net national cost in "devaluation" that is not equally involved in some alternative policy—such as "freezing" wages by incomes policy for long enough (relatively to other countries) while productivity is rising—which secures the same improvement in "efficiency wages" and in exports.

growth potential and not only on account of its short- or medium-term effect on the level of employment.

STATIC AND DYNAMIC ASPECTS

The "orthodox" Keynesian of the 1930s, in looking at the problem of the 1920s, would not have quarrelled with the view that a full-employment policy would have been incompatible with the return to the Gold Standard; he would have argued, however, that the adoption of a floating rate, or a "managed currency," would not have been sufficient in the absence of further measures to deal with the problem of insufficiency of demand due to excessive saving, unless the exchange rate were kept low enough to yield a large export surplus—that is to say, by generating sufficient overseas investment to make up for the lack of home investment.

However, this problem takes on an entirely different aspect if it is considered in a dynamic setting and not, as the original Keynesian models of the 1930s, in a purely static one. If we consider the problem in terms of the *growth rates* of demand, and not just in terms of the *levels* of demand, we can no longer treat the level of domestic investment as being autonomously determined; industrial investment will be all the greater the faster the demand for the products of industry is growing and the more fully its existing capacity is utilised. Professor Matthews has shown in a recent paper that the important difference between the full-employment level of effective demand of the post-war period and that of the under-employment situation of the pre-war period was mainly in the level of investment (particularly in industrial investment) in relation to full-employment output; it was not due to a more "expansionary" fiscal policy.[1] On Hicks' principle of the "super-multiplier,"[2] any given (exogenous) rate of growth of demand will generate a certain ratio of

---

[1] R. C. O. Matthews, "Why Has Britain Had Full Employment Since the War?", *Economic Journal*, September 1968, pp. 555–69. However, in my own view (as will be argued below) the true effects of Keynesian policies adopted since the war lay in the repercussions of maintaining a certain rate of *growth* of demand on the incentive to invest; they cannot be adequately discerned in terms of a "static" analysis which considers only the changes in the composition of the *sources* of demand.

[2] J. R. Hicks, *A Contribution to the Theory of the Trade Cycle* (Oxford, 1950), p. 62.

investment to output (including both "autonomous" and "induced" investment) that will be all the greater the higher the rate of growth of demand: for any given savings ratio, therefore, there is some rate of growth of export demand which, at any given fiscal balance, will generate sufficient domestic investment to balance full-employment savings. (This will be true even when account is taken of the fact that, under full-employment conditions, not only the volume of savings, but the ratio of savings to income, would have been higher, because a lower exchange rate would have secured higher profits in the export trades; it would also have brought about in the export trades, and, through the multiplier effects, in the economy generally, a higher degree of utilisation of capacity, and hence a higher share of profits in output.)

It is quite possible therefore that if we *had* adopted a "managed currency" in the 1920s (i.e., the system that was actually in operation in 1932–35, when the exchange rate was free to vary, but the actual movements of the rate were heavily influenced by official intervention) and if the exchange rate had been purposively managed with a view to maintaining an appropriate rate of growth of exports, we should thereby have secured both sufficient exports to give us a satisfactory balance of payments and sufficient domestic investment to secure both full employment and a satisfactory growth of capacity; and this could have been achieved without any drastic change in budgetary conventions and without producing any undue surplus in the balance of payments (because of the additional imports which would have been generated).

Since world trading conditions are constantly changing, and our own state of export competitiveness is much under the influence of the rise of new industrial exporters, it cannot, of course, be supposed that any constant exchange rate (in terms of gold or dollars) would have secured a steady rate of growth of exports over time—unless money wages had moved in the highly implausible manner (implicitly assumed by the then prevailing theory) so as to compensate for any net change in the demand for labour. The exchange rate would have had to be varied in the light of experience, though there is no reason to suppose that such adjustments would have been only in one direction. For reasons which I shall consider in more detail presently, our productivity growth would have been accelerated as well, and it might occasionally have been necessary to raise the exchange rate in order to prevent the demand for exports from rising faster than desirable.

The ideal rate of growth of exports, from a long-run point of view, is that which maximises the rate of growth of the real national income. What that rate is depends partly on the effects of a higher rate of growth of exports and of investment on the rate of productivity growth, and partly on its effects on the terms of trade. A higher rate of growth of exports (just as a higher volume of exports at any given time) necessarily involves *less* favourable terms of trade, at least in "commodity" terms (not necessarily in "factorial" terms); it also involves (up to a point at any rate) a higher "underlying" growth rate of the G.D.P.; the theoretically optimal target is therefore the one which secures that particular underlying growth rate of productivity at which the rate of growth of real income (taking into account the terms of trade) is the highest.[1]

It does not follow, of course, that this ideal, or "target," rate of growth of exports would be the same as the one required to secure the equality of domestic savings and domestic investment at full employment (or, what comes to the same thing, a zero balance on current account); nor is this necessarily a desirable condition, since a certain proportion of domestic savings will be required to finance overseas investment, and it is therefore desirable to aim at a *surplus* on current account. Hence reliance on exchange-rate policy to secure the desirable rate of growth of exports does not mean that fiscal policy will play a purely "neutral" rôle; the instrument of fiscal policy would still be required to secure that fiscal balance (which may be positive or

---

[1] I would hesitate to hazard a guess of what this "ideal" rate of growth of exports would have been in the circumstances of *post-war* Britain. It would almost certainly have been higher than the attained rate of growth of manufactured exports of 2½ per cent a year in the period 1951–66; it would most probably also have been lower than the rate of growth of the volume of world trade in manufactures over the same period, which was 7 per cent a year. In other words, it would have involved a more gently falling trend in the United Kingdom share of world trade as compared with the recorded fall from 22·5 per cent in 1951 to 12·9 per cent in 1966.

negative) which reconciles, over a run of years, the optimal rate of growth of exports and of the G.D.P. with the maintenance of a "target surplus" in the current balance of payments.

CONSUMPTION-LED GROWTH AND EXPORT-LED GROWTH

I am not suggesting that in the circumstances of the war or the immediate post-war period this type of policy of "demand management" would have been a practicable alternative to the policies outlined in the 1944 White Paper—even if its advantages had been seen, which they clearly were not. First, though we had actual operational experience with floating exchange rates, we had, in effect, abandoned that system already in 1935 with the Tripartite Agreement, and the interval of time between that and the outbreak of the war was far too short for the ill consequences of its abandonment to be fully appreciated. Second, we were living in a world where trade was almost wholly regulated by quantitative controls, and where the world was hungry for goods—the problem was how to set aside enough resources for exports, not how to sell them. Third, as the White Paper emphasised, international agreements that would make it possible to dismantle controls and get the world economy expanding on the basis of free multilateral trade rightly appeared to be the major long-term interest of Britain as a trading nation. The Bretton Woods Agreement, which held out the hope for a return to this system on the basis of fixed exchange rates and currency convertibility, and which provided the finance (albeit on a rather meagre basis) to start it off, was an essential keystone of this policy; and although (as is clear from the Parliamentary debates) many people felt misgivings, in general, most people felt that the advantages of assuming the obligations of Bretton Woods greatly outweighed the risks.

Since then a quarter of a century has elapsed. We must be free to reconsider our future policies in the light of that experience, particularly our experience of the difficulty of getting an adequate growth of exports even in a period in which world trade was rapidly expanding. The actual policies of economic management that we have been operating up to now—which relied on internal demand management through fiscal measures and a system of fixed exchange rates, making use of exchange-rate adjustments only in extreme situations of severe crisis—can be seen to suffer from a number of disadvantages, both from the point of view of their operational efficiency in the short-term and from their structural effect on economic growth in the long-term.

Though the intention of the policy has been to give priority to the growth of exports and investment, the very fact that the policy aimed at regulating the pressure of demand by internal measures—by stimulating or restraining personal consumption—meant, in the circumstances of the United Kingdom, that personal consumption expenditure took over the rôle of the "prime mover" of the economy.[1] This is because in a capitalist economy private business investment is largely demand-induced: it responds little to direct incentives (such as interest rates, tax incentives or subsidies); it is far more effectively influenced through the control of final demand. Hence both fiscal measures and monetary measures (credit control) operated on the economy primarily by controlling the *rate of change* of consumer expenditure.

This meant that as a result of demand management personal consumption has taken over the rôle of exports as the autonomous factor governing the rate of growth of demand; hence both the level of investment and the composition of investment have mainly been controlled by the growth in consumption; the growth of capacity in the various industries has been governed by the structure of demand of domestic consumers, and not (or not mainly) by the growth of world demand for different products. Since investment has not directly been induced by exports,

---

[1] I am not suggesting that the regulation of the pressure of demand by fiscal measures would in *all* circumstances lead to this result; one can conceive of the use of fiscal measures, the main effect of which was to accommodate an excessive rate of growth in exports which would otherwise have caused inflation through an excessive pressure of demand (as, e.g., in the case of Germany in recent years). But in those circumstances it was not fiscal policy but the growth of exports itself which was primarily responsible for ensuring continued growth and full employment; fiscal policy made it possible to maintain a growth of exports that was in excess of the economy's growth potential (at the cost of an unwanted and growing export *surplus*); it was not an instrument for ensuring growth in circumstances in which the exogenous growth in export demand lagged behind the growth potential.

the growth of exports itself mainly depended on the growth of capacity of the various industries, reflecting the growth, and the pattern, of domestic consumption.

In the case of an industrialised country which is an "open economy," such "consumption-led" growth has several disadvantages as against "export-led" growth.

First, the Government is bound to take a cautious line in deciding on the permissible rate of growth of consumer demand, since any large stimulus to demand would lead to a disproportionate rise in investment, which in the short run would overspill (both in the form of stockbuilding and investment-goods purchases) into imports and cause a sudden rise in the trade deficit. (In a closed economy, or an economy controlled by import licences, an investment boom is restrained by capacity shortages until it can be accommodated—hence the Government could take a less cautious line in deciding on the permissible rate of growth of demand.)

Second, the caution dictated by the first consideration will mean that the incentive to invest will be weak, and hence the level of investment, as a proportion of output, will be low; this in turn will mean that fiscal policy, though cautious on the rate of growth of demand, will nevertheless operate so as to permit consumption to take up a high share of total demand if full employment is to be maintained. Hence, as an unintended consequence of the policy of managing the pressure of demand, a structure of final demand will be generated in which consumption will take up a high proportion, and investment a relatively low proportion, of total output; this factor alone (on account of the effects of capital investment on the rate of technological progress) will make for a relatively low rate of growth of productivity and a low "underlying" growth rate.

The main structural weakness of "internal demand management" with a fixed exchange rate—in an economy in which the exogenous growth in export demand is insufficient to match the growth potential—is that it provides no effective instrument for transferring resources from consumption to investment. Reducing consumption through higher taxes or stricter control of consumer credit will release resources, but it will weaken the incentive to invest at the same time; and may result in *less* investment, not more. Post-war Governments have constantly been plagued with the dilemma whether to restrain consumption, so as to provide more resources for investment and exports, or to allow a relatively free rein to the growth of consumer demand, so as to ensure the growth of capacity (and the growth of efficiency) that is vital to exports. With export-led growth this dilemma does not arise—consumption can be restrained in order to release resources; the growth of foreign demand will provide the incentive to utilise them effectively—not only through higher exports but in increasing the capacity of the export industries.[1]

Third, the pattern of the rate of growth of output and output capacity will reflect the pattern of final consumer demand, which gives far less scope for realising the productivity gains resulting from increasing returns. There is now a very considerable body of evidence to show that manufacturing industries exhibit strongly increasing returns, while other economic activities (agriculture, mining or services) do not.[2] Hence the rate of growth of productivity in the manufacturing industries will be the greater, the higher the rate of growth of production; the overall rate of productivity growth in the economy will be the greater, the faster manufacturing output rises in relation to the rest of the economy, and the larger the share of productive resources (both labour and capital) engaged in manufacturing activities.

On the evidence of the latest input–output estimates of the National Income Blue Book, only about 30 per cent of personal consumption expenditure generates income in manufacturing industry; the corresponding figure in export demand (for goods and services) is 70 per cent. Hence consumption-led growth involves far less increase in the demand for manufactured goods than export-led growth; as a result, the growth in the manu-

---

[1] Special problems may arise from any large or sudden stimulus to exports in connection with the fact that the industries (such as engineering) which provide the most important source for higher exports are also those which produce the plant and machinery necessary for an expansion of their own capacity—if they are asked to do too much of the one they cannot do enough for the other. (The 1949 devaluation proved largely abortive in its effects, mainly because soon after the event the engineering industries became overloaded with rearmament orders, leaving little scope either for higher exports or faster growth of capacity.)

[2] For the latest published estimates cf. E.C.E. *Economic Survey for Europe for 1969*, Part I (Geneva, United Nations, 1970), Chapter III.

facturing sector will be smaller, relatively to the rest of the economy, at any given rate of growth; with the consequence that, at a given ratio of investment to output, the rate of productivity growth will be lower.[1]

For both of these latter reasons—a high investment ratio and a high share of manufacturing in the growth of output—export-led growth generates a higher "underlying growth rate" than consumption-led growth. Of these two, the latter factor may be of quantitatively far greater importance, and though some of its effect will be temporary—i.e., will be confined to the phase in which the structure of the economy is adjusted to a higher rate of growth of the autonomous component of demand, and in which therefore both exports and investment grow at a *faster* rate than the G.D.P. as a whole—some of it will be permanent. Owing to the indefinite scope for technological progress through a continual increase in specialisation, and the subdivision of productive processes—the main reasons for continued economic progress adduced by Allyn Young in his famous Presidential address to the British Association forty-two years ago[2]—the rate of productivity growth will remain relatively high in the manufacturing sector, even when all sectors grow at the same rate. Also the "temporary" phase during which productivity growth in the economy should rise at a still faster rate relates to a period of structural change which, judging by the experience of other countries, may extend over several decades.

Fourth, since with "consumption-led" growth the growth of exports will follow the growth of productive capacity rather than lead it, while the growth of imports will be simultaneous with the growth of domestic consumption and investment (and may even precede it), the policy of internal demand management is likely to create a situation of inherent precariousness in the balance of payments—with the growth of imports always tending to exceed the growth of exports. This makes the task of policy-makers far more difficult; the success of the policy is more critic-

[1] According to the findings of the E.C.E. (*op. cit.*), the United Kingdom has been the country with one of the largest "negative residuals" in the relationship between the growth of manufacturing production and the stage of development, as measured by the level of G.D.P. per head.

[2] "Increasing Returns and Economic Progress", Glasgow meeting, September 1928 (*Economic Journal*, December 1928).

ally dependent on the accuracy of short-term forecasts—on the likely movement of exports, imports, consumption and investment in the near future, resulting from *existing* policies—with the result that inevitable errors in short-term forecasting force the Government to sudden and unforeseen counter-measures of a far too violent character. With export-led growth, the Government has far more elbow room to allow the effects of such errors to be reflected in fluctuations in the export–import balance—which means spreading this effect on the world economy as a whole, rather than making the home economy bear the full brunt of the consequential adjustment. Hence when demand management is founded on exchange-rate policy, and not on fiscal policy, the success of the policy is likely to be less dependent on the accuracy of short-term forecasts, and the problem of successful economic management is less difficult.

Thus the main cause of our post-war difficulties can be traced to a mistaken orientation in our general policies of economic management which made success more difficult to achieve operationally and which also made the reward of successful management a relatively meagre one.

But in saying this I do not wish to imply that the post-war attempt at "managing the economy" was a failure in the sense that we would have been better off without it. On the contrary, I am convinced that in comparison to the restoration of the pre-war system of *non*-management—which would have meant operating under a system of fixed exchange rates combined with a "neutral" fiscal policy—we have achieved higher employment and also more stability of employment; a higher level of investment, a faster rate of economic growth and also a faster trend rate of growth of exports. The reason for this is that the managed growth of the domestic market ensured a *certain* rate of growth of industrial capacity, which also induced, as a by-product, a steady growth in our capacity to export. Without it we might well have had not only more unemployment but also far less investment and, in consequence, an even worse export performance. Consumption-led growth is clearly preferable to economic stagnation—which might well have been the alternative if the autonomous growth of exports had not in itself been sufficient to keep up an adequate level of investment. But while our post-war policies may have thus served to mitigate, not aggravate, the long-term adverse trends in our international competitiveness due to the continued emergence of new industrial rivals, they have failed to come to grips with the basic problem, and have failed to devise policies for countering these trends effectively.

If we enter the Common Market, and the Community proceeds with its plans for currency integration and not just customs integration, our economic dilemmas are likely to become much greater. For not only shall we be precluded from employing the instrument of a managed exchange rate but our existing instrument of ensuring a continued growth of domestic demand through fiscal policy will itself be far more difficult to operate. Unless we manage to become the fast-growing industrial centre of the Community—a difficult prospect, if we start off by being the slow-growing area—we may be faced with the same problem of declining total demand and employment as our development areas have had during the last twenty years, and with no more ability to counter it by local policies, without external assistance.

The obstacles to gaining international acceptance for a policy of a "managed floating rate" may not now be as great as they would have been a few years ago—particularly if it were accompanied by an assurance that the policy will be so operated as to keep the growth of exports to a target rate that is a reasonable one in the light of the rate of growth of world trade as a whole. But it would be dangerous to underestimate the serious internal problems which the adjustment from "consumption-led growth" to "export-led growth" would involve—a far more difficult problem than if one had started from a situation of heavy unemployment, as in the 1920s.[1] The adjustment to the 1967 devaluation had to be accompanied by severe increases in

---

[1] Most countries who have successfully followed "export-led" growth, and attained relatively fast rates of growth of manufacturing output, started from a position of heavy "disguised unemployment" (rather than open unemployment) in the form of vast labour reserves in agriculture and services, which made it possible for them, through the growth in total industrial employment, to provide more resources for exports and investment, without restraining the growth of domestic consumption. This is not possible in a "mature economy", with near-full-employment, such as Britain. I have discussed the manpower aspects of the growth process in an earlier paper, *Causes of the Slow Rate of Economic Growth in the United Kingdom* (reprinted on pp. 282-310 above).

taxation (as well as cuts in the Government's expenditure programmes) in order to release resources; the share of exports in the G.D.P. rose (in terms of constant 1963 prices) from the pre-devaluation figure of about 21 to 25 per cent in 1969; with export-led growth, this ratio would have to rise still higher. And while, with a tremendous effort, we have managed to release resources for the turn-round in the balance of payments, we have not yet adjusted the economy for the rise in investment (particularly of manufacturing investment) required to sustain a higher rate of growth. The ratio of consumption to G.D.P. in Britain is still appreciably higher, and that of investment lower, than in all the industrialised countries with higher trend rates of growth. The adjustment to an export-led growth with a higher underlying growth rate would require therefore holding back the growth of consumption for a further period—with all the political unpopularity which such a policy entails.

INFLATION AND RECESSION IN THE
WORLD ECONOMY[1]

The first twenty-five years after the end of the Second World War were an exceptional period of economic growth and prosperity in the leading industrial countries, marked by fast-rising living standards, very low levels of unemployment and—omitting the Korean War period, the effects of which were over by 1953—by the absence of instabilities of the pre-war kind, whether of production or prices. I think I can safely say that almost no one *expected* this to happen, since it was in such marked contrast to the course of events after World War I. This time there was no post-war slump.

True, during the whole of this period there was a continued increase in prices—the ideal of *complete* price stability (as measured, say, in terms of an index of consumer prices) was, as far as one can tell, not attained anywhere. But for a long time the rate of inflation (as measured by consumer prices) remained moderate, and until the closing years of the 1960s it showed no clear tendency to acceleration. In the fourteen years 1953–67 it averaged in 11 leading industrial countries just over 2 per cent a year.[2] And it was confined to, or at least originated in, the industrial sectors of the advanced countries: the world price of foodstuffs and basic

---

[1] Presidential address to the Royal Economic Society, delivered on 22 July, 1976, and printed in the *Economic Journal*, vol. 86, December 1976.

[2] The 11 countries comprise the United Kingdom, United States, France, Germany, Italy, Netherlands, Belgium, Sweden, Switzerland, Canada and Japan. The rate of increase in consumer prices tended to be rather higher (between 3 and 4 per cent a year) in some of the fast-growing countries—like Japan, Italy, France and Sweden—and rather less (between 1 and 2 per cent) in the United States and Canada. (In Germany, Belgium and Switzerland it was around 2 per cent; in the United Kingdom and the Netherlands around 2¾ per cent.)

materials (again omitting the Korean episode) remained, on the average, remarkably stable.[1]

But from about 1968 things began to change. The rise in labour costs per unit of industrial output began to accelerate in all the main industrial countries, though at differing rates. There was an increasing strain on the international payments system which led to the general abandonment of the system of fixed exchange rates in 1971. This was followed by rapidly rising commodity prices in the course of 1972 and 1973,[2] which preceded the sudden fourfold rise in oil prices following the Arab–Israeli war. The rise in commodity prices was followed in turn by an inflation in wage settlements which served to augment the general rate of increase of prices. There resulted an unprecedented inflation in consumer prices in all countries. In the two years 1973–5 it averaged 26 per cent for *all* O.E.C.D. countries, ranging (for the two-year period) from 44 per cent for the United Kingdom and 39 per cent for Japan to 13 per cent for Germany and 17 per cent in Switzerland.

Nothing of this kind has ever occurred before in peace-time—I mean an inflation of that magnitude encompassing not just one or two countries, but *all* the leading industrial countries of the world. The other unique feature of this inflation was that it was accompanied by a marked recession in industrial production. World industrial production, which rose at a fairly steady rate of 6–7 per cent a year throughout the sixties and by 8 per cent a year in 1971–3, was stagnant in 1974 and *fell* by 10 per cent in 1975, accompanied by unemployment levels which had not been encountered since the 1930s.

This combination of inflation and economic recession is a new phenomenon, the explanation of which presents an intellectual challenge to economists.

In my view it would be futile to look for a single basic cause—such as the increase in the money supply in all countries, or

---

[1] The U.N. index of the export prices of primary commodities in terms of U.S. dollars was virtually the same in 1970 as in 1950. In the intervening period (again, abstracting from Korea) it had a gently falling trend up to about 1962, and first a stationary, then a gently rising trend thereafter.

[2] The U.N. index of primary commodities excluding fuels rose (in dollar terms) by 58 per cent in the two years 1971–3 and a further 26 per cent in 1974, so that the index doubled in three years.

universal cost-push resulting from collective bargaining—and it would be wrong to suppose that the great acceleration of inflation of the last few years was the inevitable sequel of the long creeping inflation which preceded it.

THE PRIMARY SECTOR AND THE INDUSTRIAL SECTOR

In order to show this I think it is necessary to disaggregate economic activities more than is generally done in macro-economic analyses (whether of the Keynesian or the monetarist variety) by distinguishing between the "primary sector" of the world economy on the one hand and the "secondary" and "tertiary" sectors on the other hand. These sectors are largely complementary to each other—the primary sector provides the indispensable basic supplies for industrial activities in the form of food, fuel and basic materials; the secondary sector processes the materials into finished goods for investment or consumption, while the tertiary sector provides a variety of services which are ancillary to the other sectors (such as transport or distribution, or professional expertise of various kinds) as well as services which are an independent source of enjoyment (such as theatrical performances).

While no great problems are likely to arise on account of the tertiary sector, both the industrial sector and the primary sector can become sources of inflation, but of a different character—differing both in the nature of the causal mechanism and in the general economic consequences.

Continued and stable economic progress requires that the growth of output in these two sectors should be at the required relationship with each other—that is to say, the growth of the saleable output of agriculture and mining should be in line with the growth of demand, which in turn reflects the growth of the secondary (and tertiary) sectors.

However, from a technical standpoint there can be no guarantee that the rate of growth of primary production, propelled by land-saving innovations, proceeds at the precise rate warranted by growth of production and incomes in the secondary and tertiary sectors. To ensure that it does is the function of the price mechanism, more particularly of relative prices, or the "terms of trade" between primary commodities and manufactured goods. The more favourable are the terms of trade to agriculture and mining, the more current technological advance will be exploited through new investment, and the faster the growth of output. If the growth of primary production runs ahead of the growth of industrial demand, the terms of trade will move in favour of industry: this, in theory, should stimulate industrial growth and thereby the demand for primary commodities, whilst retarding the growth of production of primary commodities.

Since the "terms of trade" is the *ratio* of two kinds of prices, of primary commodities and manufactured goods, we must look at the nature of the markets for commodities and for industrial products respectively more closely before we can say how efficiently this mechanism works. In the field of primary production the market price is given to the individual producer or consumer, and prices move in direct response to market pressures in the classical manner described by Adam Smith. Changes in prices act as "signals" for the adjustment of production and consumption in the future. In industry, on the other hand—at least in a modern industrial society where the greater part of production is concentrated in the hands of large corporations—prices are "administered", i.e. fixed by the producers themselves, and the adjustment of production to changes of demand takes place independently of price changes, through a stock-adjustment mechanism: production is reduced in response to an accumulation of unsold goods, and raised in the face of a depletion. Industrial prices (in contrast to the prices of primary products) are not "market clearing", since normally the typical producer operates at less than full capacity; he can increase production without incurring higher costs per unit, and indeed, frequently benefits from reduced costs resulting from a greater volume of production. Such "administered prices" are cost-determined, not "market determined"; they are arrived at by applying various percentage additions to direct labour and material costs on account of overheads and profits. Neither profit margins nor labour costs in the industrial sector are particularly responsive to changes in demand.

This means that the burden of any maladjustment between the growth of primary production and the growth of manufacturing activities is thrown almost entirely on the commodity markets, the behaviour of which is erratic owing to the large influence of speculative expectations on the holding of stocks, as well as on account of the price-inelasticity of demand, and of the time-lags involved in the adjustment of supply to price changes. When the growth of production exceeds the growth of consumption (as was the case in the 1920s) the immediate effect is an accumulation of stocks, which, with favourable expectations concerning the growth of future demand, may go on for years with only moderate changes in prices. This happened in the years 1925–9, during which, according to the League of Nations index, end-year stocks of primary products rose by no less than a third with only a moderate fall in prices.[1] When the boom did break, prices fell catastrophically—by more than 50 per cent in three years—and this, so far from stimulating the absorption of commodities by the industrial sector, had the very opposite effect: the fall in demand for industrial products coming from the primary producers, and the fall in investment by the industrial countries in primary production—in opening up new areas, etc.—more than offset any stimulus to industrial demand on account of the rise in real incomes of the urban workers resulting from the fall in food prices; the rapid fall in commodity prices ushered in the greatest industrial depression in history.

The above is an illustration of a more fundamental proposition that *any* large change in commodity prices—irrespective of whether it is in favour or against the primary producers—tends to have a dampening effect on industrial activity; it retards industrial growth in both cases, instead of retarding it in the one case and stimulating it in the other. There are, as I shall now show, two reasons for this. It is partly a consequence of the fact that whilst a *fall* in commodity prices tends to be an effective instrument in moving the terms of trade against the primary producers, a *rise* in commodity prices is not likely to be nearly as effective in moving the terms of trade in their favour. It is partly

[1] Quoted by Lewis in "World Production and Trade, 1870–1960", *The Manchester School*, 1952, p. 128.

also a consequence of an asymmetry in the behavioural consequences as between a gain and a loss of real income, the result of
which is that any sudden shift in the distribution of world income,
caused by a change in the terms of trade, is likely to have an
adverse effect on industrial demand (in real terms).

The important cause of the first asymmetry is that while commodity prices are demand-determined, industrial prices are cost-
determined, and because of that the rise in commodity prices has
a very powerful inflationary effect operating on the *cost* side. The
rise in the price of basic materials and fuels is passed through the
various stages of production into the final price with an exaggerated effect—it gets "blown up" on the way by a succession of
percentage additions to prime costs which mean, in effect, an
increase in cash margins at each stage. This causes (initially) a
rise in the share of profits in the value added by manufacturing
which in itself is a powerful factor (in countries where trade union
power is strong) in causing pressure for wage increases. Added to
this is the price-induced rise in wages caused by what Sir John
Hicks called "Real Wage Resistance"—the reluctance of workers
to accept a cut in their standard of living[1] (which is not paralleled
by similar reluctance to accept a rise). For these reasons a swing
in the terms of trade in favour of the primary producers is not
likely to last for long. The industrial sector with its superior
market power, resists any compression of its real income by
countering the rise in commodity prices through a cost-induced
inflation of industrial prices.

Moreover—and here we come to the second reason mentioned

---

[1] *Lloyd's Bank Review*, October 1975, p. 5. According to Professor Milton Friedman
and his followers, this "real wage resistance" is in itself evidence of an excessive demand
for labour—of unemployment being less then some "natural rate"—because at a
higher level of unemployment the desired real wage—the real wage *ex-ante*—would
have been less and the *ex-post* real wage (owing to higher "marginal productivity")
would have been greater. I am sure, however, that in all this the monetarists are
barking up the wrong tree. The *ex-post* real wage is smaller, not greater, at higher levels
of unemployment—both because of short-term increasing returns ("Okun's Law")
and of social overheads which cause a disproportionate part of any increase in output
to be available for wage-earners' consumption, whereas the "desired real wage" is
mainly governed by the attained standards of living of the working population and is
not much affected if at all by the level of unemployment. The inflation in industrial
countries was not the result of excess demand, either for labour or for the products of
labour: if anything, it was the result of an excess demand for primary products
(food and raw materials), which is quite a different thing (cf. Hicks, *op. cit.*; H. G.
Johnson, *Lloyd's Bank Review*, April 1976, p. 14).

above—the inflation itself has a deflationary effect on the effective demand for industrial goods in real terms, partly because the rise in the profits of producers in the primary sector is not matched by a rise in their expenditure—this was particularly marked on the present occasion through the vast accumulation of financial assets by the oil producers—and partly because the governments of most, if not all, of the industrial countries are likely to react to their domestic inflation by fiscal and monetary measures which reduce consumer demand and put a brake on industrial investment. Thus the rise in commodity prices may well result in a wage/price-spiral type of inflation in the industrial sectors which in turn causes industrial activity to be restricted. The latter tends to eliminate the shortages and thereby reverse the trend in commodity prices. A good example of this has been the U.S. inflation of 1972–3, which was clearly cost-induced but not wage-induced; it was caused by the rise in commodity prices (with wage rises trailing behind the rise in living costs) and which led to strongly restrictionist monetary policies in order to counter the inflation, which in turn brought about a considerable economic recession. (Somewhat later similar restrictionist policies were adopted by governments of other leading countries, such as Germany and Japan.)

If the above analysis is correct, the market mechanism is a highly inefficient regulator for securing continuing adjustment between the growth of availabilities and the growth in requirements for primary products in a manner conducive to the harmonious development of the world economy.

The emergence of commodity surpluses which should, in principle, lead to accelerated industrialisation may have a perverse effect by diminishing effective demand for industrial products. Similarly the emergence of shortages which should accelerate the growth of availabilities of primary products through improvements in the terms of trade may lead instead to an inflation of manufacturers' prices which tends to offset the improvement in the terms of trade, and by its dampening effect on industrial activity, worsens the climate for new investment in both the primary sector and the industrial sector.

In retrospect, the remarkable thing was that the great post-war boom in the industrial countries could go on for so long with so few interruptions and with a background of stable commodity prices (ignoring the sharp but short-lived commodity boom during the Korean War) right up to the early 1970s. The main reason for this was that the progress of land-saving agricultural technology proceeded much faster than in any previous period of history.[1] This led to large surpluses in the main grain producing and exporting countries, the normal price effects of which, however, were obviated by government price-support policies in all the main producing countries, combined with stock-piling policies for strategic purposes. These price-support policies secured a steady growth of agricultural incomes and provided an important primary source for the growth of demand for manufactured goods.

REASONS FOR THE "CREEPING INFLATION"

However, while export prices of primary products were stable (or rather fluctuated around a stationary trend) the export prices of manufactures were slowly rising, due to the "creeping inflation" of the industrial countries to which I have already referred. On looking back at this period—say the period extending from 1953 to 1967—I do not think that either of the two standard theories of a wage-induced inflation, the "cost-push" due to the collective bargaining process or the "demand pull" due to excessive tightness in the labour market, provides the key to an explanation.

The explanation which I think is much nearer the mark is to be found in the powerful social forces which make for constancy in relative earnings in different trades and occupations[2] as a result of which the increase in wages obtained in certain "leading" or

---

[1] Sir Arthur Lewis, writing in 1952 (*op. cit.* p. 13) predicted that the growth in world food production in the decade 1950–60 was likely to be in range 1·3–2 per cent per annum; though he held that owing to various adverse circumstances the lower figure was more likely. He put the possible growth of world manufacturing production as 3·9–5 per cent, depending on the availabilities of raw materials and the success of economic management in avoiding slumps. As it turned out, world manufacturing production (according to U.N. estimates) increased by 6⅔ per cent a year (on the average) in the decade 1950–60 and also in 1960–70, while world food production increased by 2·7 per cent a year in both decades. (In the three years 1970–3, however, it fell to 1·6 per cent a year.)

[2] For evidence, see in particular *Problems of Pay Relativities*, Advisory Report No. 2 of the Pay Board (Cmnd. 5535, 1974).

"key" sectors tends to set the pace for the *general* rate of wage increases in the economy combined with the tendency for wages in the so-called "dynamic sectors"—where the rate of productivity growth is appreciably *above* the average—to rise at the rate which tends to be *less* than the rate of productivity growth in those industries, but appreciably *more* than the rate of productivity growth in other sectors.[1]

In an economy dominated by large corporations price competition is not so prompt or effective as to compel firms which experience exceptional reductions in costs (owing to the introduction of new products, or new processes, or a fast increase in selling volume, or both) to pass on the full benefit to the consumer in the form of lower prices *pari passu* with the reduction of costs. The very existence of this situation leads to wage increases that are, in a sense, unnecessarily large—i.e. they are governed by what the employer can *afford* to pay (without compromising his competitive position) and not by what he *needs* to pay, in order to obtain the necessary work force.[2]

---

[1] For empirical support for this proposition see Eatwell, Llewellyn and Tarling, "Money Wage Inflation in Industrial Countries", *Review of Economic Studies*, October 1974, pp. 515–23, particularly Table III, p. 520.

[2] The above account of what causes wage increases to exceed productivity increases in capitalist economies is one particular version of the "leading-sector" hypothesis which I personally favour but which cannot be regarded as firmly established to the exclusion of others. Another version, more in accord with traditional thinking, attributes this rôle to the particular firms or sectors which show a fast rate of expansion in the number of their employees either because it is a case of a new firm which has to recruit its labour force, or of firms the demand for the products of which has shown a sudden rise (as a result, for example, of the abolition of HP restrictions) and which therefore are anxious to recruit additional labour by the offer of higher pay. Yet another version asserts, contrariwise, that the "leading sectors" are found in those industries where the workers have been compelled to allow a deterioration of relative earnings because (owing to falling demand for their products, or exceptional productivity gains, or both) there was a prolonged shrinkage in the labour force; when this comes to an end, their bargaining position improves, enabling them to "catch up" so as to regain their previous position. (This version is tailor-made to fit the British case where coal miners set the standard for wage increases for several years in succession.) Yet another variant of this theory is the so-called "Swedish theory of inflation" according to which the prices in the export and import competing industries (broadly the manufacturing industry) are set by world prices, and the rate of wage increases in these sectors—which are also the "dynamic sectors" with a high rate of productivity growth—are then applied to the so-called "sheltered" industries whose rate of productivity growth is much smaller. It is doubtful, however, whether the Swedish theory is applicable to an economy like the United Kingdom where the domestic prices of industrial products are much less under the influence of world prices, and still less to the United States, whose foreign trade is small in relation to domestic trade. (For an account of the "Swedish" theory see Edgren, Faxen and Odhner, *Wage Formation and the Economy*, London, Allen & Unwin, 1973.)

This explanation is heavily dependent on the hypothesis that the percentage rate of wage increase demanded and obtained in the great majority of settlements in any particular period are imitative in character: they are motivated by the desire to maintain the position of any particular group of workers relative to other groups, rather than to secure some given absolute improvement in the standard of living. There have been a number of studies tending to show that custom and tradition form a strong element in pay differentials between groups of workers who are in close contact with one another; and since any particular group is closely related to some other group which in turn is more closely related to a third, there is a kind of chain reaction by means of which any particular standard for wage increases communicates itself through the influence of the principle of "fairness" or "comparability" which is the great social force behind the (long-term) constancy of such differentials. Lacking any objective and universally accepted criteria of "fairness", this attribute attaches itself to differentials which have been hallowed by custom and therefore the mere passage of time tends to reinforce them.[1]

YEARS OF THE WORLD-WIDE WAGE EXPLOSION, 1968–71

An analysis on the above lines of the long creeping inflation of 1953–67 clearly cannot account for the sudden acceleration of the rate of increase in wages and prices in the years 1968–71—years during which the movement of commodity prices, though upward, was still relatively moderate. For reasons which are still in dispute the rate of increase in wages took a sudden spurt in a large number of industrial countries more or less simultaneously; it happened in the course either of 1968–9 (as in Japan, France, Belgium and

[1] The fact that in 1975–6 the voluntary incomes policy of a uniform increase of £6 a week, without any regard to differences in earnings, has so largely succeeded, does not necessarily weaken the above argument. An incomes policy, provided it is *believed* to be generally observed, sets a new criterion of "fairness" which temporarily displaces the traditional criteria—in much the same way as equality of consumption achieved through comprehensive rationing is the most promising way of gaining approval to austerity in war-time. If the incomes policy is maintained for a limited period only, the old differentials will re-assert themselves on its termination; if, however, the policy could be maintained (possibly in a relaxed form) for a whole series of years, this might exert a permanent effect on the scale of pay differentials which are considered "fair".

the Netherlands) or of 1969–70 (as in Germany, Italy, Switzerland and the United Kingdom). In the United States the process began earlier but was far more moderate, the annual rise of hourly earnings in manufacturing having reached a peak rate of 6 per cent between 1967 and 1968; whilst the annual increase in earnings reached double figures in all Western European countries and Japan by 1970.

There is a school of thought which attributes all this to a demand-inflation in the United States caused by the Vietnam War which communicated itself, through international prices or else through the demand pressures induced by unrequited balance of payments surpluses (the counterpart of growing U.S. deficits) to other countries,[1] but this explanation seems to me implausible for several reasons. First, since the rate of wage and price inflation in the United States was more moderate than that of Europe or Japan it is difficult to attribute the rise in international prices to the internal inflation in the United States. Second, to assume that the American balance of payments deficit created additional demand pressures in other industrial countries implies that the pressure of demand in those countries did increase in those years and the wage explosion could be regarded as a consequence of increased demand pressure on the labour market. While this may have been the case in some countries, it was clearly not the case in others. For example, it would be very difficult to explain the British wage explosion in late 1969/1970 by additional pressure of demand—since it occurred at a time when unemployment was relatively high and, as became evident in the course of 1970, the economy was moving into a recession.[2]

I find the alternative explanation put forward by the O.E.C.D. and others[3]—which regards the basic cause as increased trade-union militancy mainly attributable to the sharply rising deductions from the pay packet for payment of income tax and

---

[1] See William Nordhaus, *The Worldwide Wage Explosion*, Brookings Papers on Economic Activity, no. 3, 1972.

[2] For a detailed analysis see John Williamson and Geoffrey Wood, "The British Inflation: Indigenous or Imported?" *American Economic Review*, September 1976, pp. 520–31.

[3] See for example, Jackson, Turner and Wilkinson, *Do Trade Unions Cause Inflation?*, D.A.E. Occasional Paper, Cambridge, 1972.

insurance contributions—more plausible.[1] This hypothesis still leaves unexplained why the wage explosion occurred at that particular time and not earlier—since the trend of an increasing share of income being deducted at source for tax and insurance contributions has proceeded for more than a decade—or why the explosion should have occurred more or less simultaneously in so many different countries. For this there is no fully satisfactory explanation on present evidence—any more than for the social forces which caused simultaneous outbreaks of student revolts in America and all over Europe in 1968—or the wave of revolutions which swept Europe in February and March 1848. In all these cases there had been long-smouldering resentment and dissatisfaction which, when matters came to a head in one country, caused the rapid spread of the eruption to others.

THE EXPLOSION OF COMMODITY PRICES

The acceleration of wage inflation was associated with a far more rapid increase in the price level of manufactured goods in international trade. Thus the U.N. index of prices in world trade of manufactures in dollar terms rose by 1 per cent a year between 1953 and 1968, and by 5 per cent a year during 1968–71.

The slow and steady rise in the price of manufactured goods involved a corresponding deterioration in the terms of trade of primary producers; the cumulative deterioration amounted to 24 per cent between 1953 and 1971, all but 3 per cent of which occurred in the period 1953–68. This was because during the three years when the price of manufactured goods increased fast, the prices of primary products also rose, though at a lesser rate.[2]

---

[1] As the O.E.C.D. has shown, there has been a steady fall in the proportion of privately financed consumption to total private consumption in all the main O.E.C.D. countries throughout the period 1955–69 with an accelerating trend from 1966–7 onwards. (See *Expenditure Trends in O.E.C.D. Countries 1960–80*, O.E.C.D., July 1972, charts B and E and table 12.) This was partly to be accounted for by higher public expenditure on goods and services, but mainly by increased social transfers reflecting an increased scale of social service benefits and welfare services.

[2] The above figures are derived from the U.N. index of primary commodities excluding fuels, divided by the U.N. index of export prices of manufacturers in world trade (all in dollar terms). It is arguable, however, that the slow deterioration in the primary producers' terms of trade over the 18-year period was more apparent than real, since the price-indices take no account of the increase in real purchasing power

The real explosion of commodity prices began in the latter half of 1972 and there can be little doubt that much of it was in anticipation of shortages, since the end-of-season stocks of the main agricultural commodities did not show a big fall until 1973. World wheat stocks fell to less than half their normal level in 1973 (with no significant improvement in 1974 and 1975). This was mainly the result of unexpected purchases by the U.S.S.R. following the failure of their 1972–3 harvest and in later years; and the slowness of the Americans in realising that, after so many years of burdensome surpluses, they were now entering an era of prolonged shortages. Though food presents a special case, the sharp rise in the prices of fibres, and later of metals, in 1973 and early 1974 does seem to indicate that the rate of absorption of commodities threatened to outrun the growth of availabilities at the rate of growth of world industrial activity of over 10 per cent a year experienced in the latter half of 1972 and the first half of 1973.

But this was not the only factor at work. To an unknown extent the currency upheavals following the formal suspension of the gold convertibility of the dollar, together with general inflationary expectations, must have induced a great deal of commodity buying as an inflation-hedge—in the same way as the outbreak of the Korean War 25 years earlier led to the rapid rise in commodity prices in anticipation of shortages which in the event did not materialise. That boom (which increased commodity prices by some 50 per cent) collapsed within a year or so. In the present instance there was a remarkable correlation between movements in the price of gold and of *The Economist*'s index of commodity prices which followed much the same time-path.[1]

After commodity prices had thus doubled or trebled came the big rise in the price of oil with consequences that are well known. The subsequent world-wide industrial recession caused some commodities—metals and industrial materials—to fall back in price with almost equal rapidity, only to rise again, since

---

resulting from the appearance of innumerable "new" industrial goods (like new types of tractors or fertilisers, washing machines or television sets) which greatly enlarged the range of goods available for purposes of consumption or investment.

[1] Cf. the diagram on page 106 of the O.E.C.D. *Economic Outlook*, December, 1973.

February 1976, with even greater rapidity—with the first signs of renewed industrial expansion.[1]

The price of food had fallen only moderately from its 1974 level and is now rising again. Yet the level of employment in the industrialised countries is still far from restored to pre-recession levels; production is also lower, at least in relation to trend. And the terms of trade of commodity producers *other than* oil appear to be not much better in terms of manufactures than in 1970; if their need to purchase oil is taken into account, they are probably worse.

The danger now is that the rise in commodity prices will bring in its train a new inflationary wave in the industrial countries, causing the repetition of the same kind of process as we experienced in 1974 and 1975, but starting from much higher levels of unemployment. The very jumpiness of commodity prices shows that they are increasingly under the influence of inflationary expectations.[2] The absence of any stable monetary medium which would serve as a hedge against inflation may well come to mean that any revival of demand will lead to spectacular increases in commodity prices, fed by speculation; and the problem of keeping inflation at bay will increasingly be at the centre of preoccupations of *all* industrialised countries, with untoward consequences in terms of waste of resources and unemployment.

It would be premature to conclude, however, that the terms of trade required to secure an adequate rate of growth in the supply of primary products will prove to be incompatible with the maintenance of price stability in the industrial world. For all past experience has tended to show that when prices in commodity markets are stabilised (by means of official market intervention of some kind) the very stability of prices thus created, by reducing the subjective risks of producers and investors, is likely to call forth greatly enhanced supplies. Hence under a regime of stable

---

[1] *The Economist* index of commodity prices in dollar terms has risen by nearly 30 per cent since February 1976 and is now (July 1976) above its previous peak in May 1974.
[2] Without being a "monetarist" I do believe in the importance of inflationary expectations; but unlike the monetarists, I believe they are mainly of importance in markets where speculation is important—i.e. in commodity markets, and not in the labour market or the market for goods with cost-determined prices.

commodity prices the terms of trade adjustment that may be required for securing adequate supplies in the long run, when brought about slowly and gradually, is likely to be one that the industrial sectors of the world are well capable of accommodating.

THE MONETARY SOLUTION TO WORLD ECONOMIC GROWTH

The primary need is to strengthen the adjustment mechanism between the growth of supply and demand for primary products. This requries that governments (or international bodies) acting singly or in concert should be prepared to carry much larger stocks than private traders are willing to carry on their own; and be ready to intervene in markets in a price-stabilising manner.

For reasons given earlier the duration and stability of the post-war economic boom owed a great deal to the policies of the United States and other governments in absorbing and carrying stocks of grain and other basic commodities both for price stabilisation and for strategic purposes. Many people are also convinced that if the United States had shown greater readiness to carry stocks of grain (instead of trying by all means throughout the 1960s to eliminate its huge surpluses by giving away wheat under PL 480 provisions and by reducing output through acreage restrictions) the sharp rise of food prices following upon the large grain purchases by the U.S.S.R., which unhinged the stability of the world price level far more than anything else, could have been avoided.

I remain convinced—as I have been for a long time—that the most promising line of action for introducing greater stability into the world economy would be to create international buffer stocks for all the main commodities, and to link the finance of these stocks directly to the issue of international currency, such as the S.D.R.s, which could thus be backed by, and directly convertible into, major commodities comprising foodstuffs, fibres and metals. Assuming these buffer stocks cover a sufficiently wide range of commodities, their very existence could provide a powerful self-regulating mechanism for promoting growth and stability in the world economy.

Assuming the system starts off in the right circumstances when commodity surpluses are about to develop, and the intervention of the buffer stock authorities serves to prevent a recession in commodities by accumulating stocks, they would have a far-reaching effect in influencing the rhythm of development. The value of the commodities bought by the authorities would represent a net addition, in terms of international currency, to the incomes of the producers. The addition to world investment would have a powerful multiplier effect—it would increase the export demand for industrial goods which in turn would stimulate industrial investment; the process thereby set in train would tend to increase the rate of absorption of commodities until it comes into balance with the rate of production. If it went beyond this point, the mechanism would go into reverse—the sale of commodities by the buffer stock authorities would cause a contraction of demand for industrial goods (for the incomes of primary producers would now fall short of consumers' outlay, and hence there would develop a net adverse balance on current account of the industrial countries); it would thereby again operate in the direction of restoring balance—through a downward adjustment of the rate of absorption of commodities by the industrial countries to limits set by the availabilities of primary products. The system of buffer stocks would thus substitute the mechanism of income-stabilising variations in stock accumulation for the crude mechanism of rising and falling commodity prices—which latter, as we have seen, operates slowly and wastefully, and tends to set up perverse and unnecessary cycles in world industrial activity.[1]

Moreover, it is yet to be demonstrated that a monetary system consisting of paper currencies convertible only into each other can ever succeed in keeping their value stable in terms of commodities. Though the role of gold has been purely ephemeral ever since the 1920s, the formal though distant link embodied in the Bretton Woods system sufficed to maintain the illusion that dollars were as good as gold, and that commodities have a (long-run) *normal* dollar price, around which their market prices

---

[1] Looking at the matter from another angle, a system of this kind would enormously enhance the effectiveness of monetary policy. For the international monetary authority would then come to regulate the supply of basic money (or "very high powered money") through open market operations in commodity markets (and thereby ensure that such operations have a direct and powerful effect on demand and on incomes) and not in the market for high-grade substitutes for money (such as Treasury bills) the income effects of which are both slow and highly uncertain.

fluctuate. The formal demonetisation of gold, as subsequent events have shown, has greatly weakened this stabilising force in the markets, and I do not believe that the regulation to the money supply, when "money supply" means current account deposits and other forms of liquid financial assets, could ever be an adequate substitute for direct convertibility of money into commodities or that without such convertibility we could, in an unregulated market economy, create a monetary medium that is adequate for maintaining stability whilst giving a free rein to the forces of economic expansion.

THE ROLE OF COMMODITY PRICES IN ECONOMIC RECOVERY[1]

INTRODUCTION

The economic model which in my view is most likely to highlight the central problems facing the world economy, is the one which looks upon the economic activities of the world as consisting of two large complementary sectors. One is the primary sector, which supplies food, raw materials and energy, all of which depend upon man's powers to exploit for his own use the natural resources of the planet. The other main sector is the so-called secondary sector, which consists of the production of finished goods out of the products of the primary sector. In a simple approximation we could refer to these two sectors as "agriculture" and "industry". But not all primary products are agricultural; there are all the minerals and forms of energy such as coal and oil which are the result of mining. What is common to all of them is that they are "land-based" activities in the production of which natural resources (or simply "land" to use the classical expression) play an important role. Industry on the other hand is dependent on the flows of supplies of primary products, for the conversion of which it requires increasing amounts of labour and capital. However, the availability of labour and capital for industrial purposes cannot really be regarded as an effective limitation in itself except for short periods. The conversion capacity of the numerous industries of the world can be treated as given at any one moment, as the heritage of the past, but over longer periods it can be increased

---

[1] Originally published in *Lloyd's Bank Review*, July 1983, and reprinted in *World Development*, May 1987.

almost indefinitely, since on a global scale there are no practical limits to the increased employment of labour, while the accumulation of capital through additional investment is but a facet of the increase in industrial production and a more or less automatic consequence of the increase in demand for manufactured goods.

The classical economists, Adam Smith and his followers, were undoubtedly on the right track when they made their predictions on the assumption that while the law of increasing returns applies in industry (because the productivity of labour depends on the division of labour and the latter in turn depends on the size of the market), the law of diminishing returns applies in agriculture, because the most favourable opportunities are exploited first, and any further enlargement of production implies exploiting the less favourable or less adaptable resources of nature. Hence their underlying pessimism based on the existence of ultimate limits to primary production which must bring all economic growth sooner or later to an end.

Yet nowhere were the predictions of economists so completely falsified as in the prophecy of Malthus and Ricardo that with the growth of world population more and more of the world's labour and capital resources would be required to be devoted to agriculture, leaving less available for industry and services. On the contrary, the last two hundred years witnessed, despite the enormous population explosion, a spectacular diminution of the share of economic resources devoted to agriculture and mining.

There can be no guarantee that this favourable trend will continue. That it was so completely unforeseen was due to the failure to recognise that land-saving or natural-resource-saving technological progress was so much more important quantitatively than the labour-saving technical progress in the manufacturing industries. This account gives a partial view, however, since the world production of primary commodities has not grown as fast as would have been required to raise the living standards of the world population at the same rate as those of the industrially developed countries which comprise only one-third, or perhaps only one-quarter, of humanity. In fact, elimination of the backwardness and low living standards of the Third World would require a manifold increase in the production of energy, metal-containing minerals, agricultural raw materials and food. This is only another way of saying that the ultimate factors governing the permissible rate of growth of the world economy are to be found in the growth of the availabilities of primary products and not in the availabilities of labour or capital; and given this rate, industrial growth tends to get polarised (or concentrated) in a minority of fast-growing areas owing to the cumulative effects of static and dynamic economies of scale.

THE MARKET MECHANISM

According to standard economic theory, it is the function of the market mechanism to ensure that the long run compatibility between the growth of availabilities of primary products and the growth of industry is maintained. In the absence of economic planning by governments or by international organs, the mechanism consists of price variations in primary commodities relative to industrial goods, induced by market forces. If industrial requirements race ahead, primary product prices will rise, and this will check industrial growth and at the same time stimulate "agricultural" growth. In the converse case, the terms of trade move against "agriculture", and the adjustment will work in a contrary direction.

The functioning of this mechanism in the present century (though not perhaps in the nineteenth century) was increasingly impaired by the fact that primary product prices (until the 1930s at any rate) were determined in highly competitive markets, whereas industrial products were marketed under monopolistic conditions with producers setting their prices mainly by reference to costs. In the latter case, the response of supply to demand took place not through the agency of price changes, but as a direct result of the so-called stock-adjustment principle. Manufacturers expanded or contracted their rate of production according to whether the flow of new orders exceeded or fell short of what was required to keep stocks in a normal relation to turnover.

The highly competitive markets in basic commodities on the other hand rely on variations in *prices* for keeping demand and supply aligned to one another, both in the short run and in the long run. In the short run it was the function of middlemen (the merchants or professional traders operating in every market) to cover the gap arising from short-period differences between the flow of absorption and flow of accrual of commodities, by keeping a variable stock reserve which provided a source of additional supply in case of excess demand and of additional demand in the case of excess supply.

The efficiency of this mechanism, however, depended crucially on the professional traders' willingness to absorb stocks or to release stocks in response to variations in market prices that were not unduly large. This in turn depended on the traders having a *firm* expectation of a long run normal price for each commodity, deviations from which would be considered as temporary. The firmer or the more certain the expectation of a normal price for, say, wheat, based on normal costs of production, the greater was the traders' willingness to increase their stocks in response to a fall in prices and *vice versa*. It is important to remember that the whole system depended for its smooth functioning on induced variations in (privately held) stocks—a condition which may have been more valid in the nineteenth century than in the present century. Long before the outbreak of World War I and far more in the period between the two World Wars, commodity markets functioned in an increasingly unsatisfactory manner—that is to say, they functioned only through very large short-term variations in prices which were reversed within a few months. Thus Keynes, writing in 1938, calculated that on the *average* of the previous 10 years the difference between the highest and lowest prices in *the same year* in the case of rubber, cotton, wheat and lead amounted on *the average* to 67 per cent.[1] In the post-World War II period

---

[1] "The Policy of Government Storage of Foodstuffs and Raw Materials", *Economic Journal* (September 1938), pp. 449-60.

the volatility of commodity prices in the free-market commodities was greater than before the War, as the calculations of Mr St. Clair Grondona have shown.[1] While between 1950 and 1970 the index of the prices of international traded basic materials, as compiled by the UN, remained constant in dollar terms, there were sharp fluctuations up and down with changes in the rate of growth of industrial activity, and of course much sharper fluctuations in *individual* commodities such as sugar. And since 1971, as Professor Sylos Labini has recently shown,[2] the prices of raw materials became far more sensitive to variations in world industrial production than they were before. Whereas in the period 1950-71 the rise and fall of raw material prices coincided with corresponding changes in the growth rate of world industrial production, but the percentage range of variations in prices was somewhat smaller than that of industrial production, *after* 1971 the extent of price fluctuations in percentage terms was nearly three times as great (see Figure 1).[3] Thus the sharp rise in prices in 1972-74 was followed by an almost equally sharp fall in 1974-75, which was again abruptly reversed when world industrial production recovered in late 1975 and in 1976; in fact there can be little doubt that the sharp rise in raw material prices in 1976 (and again, following another sharp fall, in 1978) was the main factor which nipped world industrial recovery in the bud. These extraordinary changes reflected changing expectations concerning the future rate of inflation, far more than varying pressures of demand coming from outside the markets, and this is best seen by the close correlation between movements in the gold price and commodity prices which doubled and quadrupled in a couple of years only to be halved again in the next couple of years. Until recently, with deepening world-wide recession, the terms of trade of commodity producers were less

[1] St. Clair Grondona, *Economic Stability is Attainable*, London 1975.

[2] Labini, "On the Instability of Commodity Prices and the Problem of Gold", paper presented to the World Conference on Gold, Rome, February 1982.

[3] Professor Labini's calculations are shown in Figure 1. Professor Labini also calculated the regression equations of the rates of change of commodity prices ($\dot{R}M$) as a function of the rate of variation in industrial production ($W\dot{I}P$) for the periods 1958-71 and 1972-80. For the first period the regression equation is: $\dot{R}M = -5.1 + 0.9\ W\dot{I}P$. For the second period it is $\dot{R}M = +9.1 + 2.4\ W\dot{I}P$.

favourable than at any time since the 1930s.[1]

Figure 1. Industrial production and the prices of raw materials

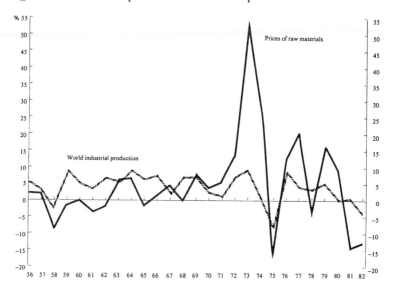

Source: Compiled by Prof. Sylos Labini from various issues of *International Financial Statistics Yearbook*, IMF, and *Main Indicators*, OECD.

STABILISATION SCHEMES

The efficiency of commodity markets as we have seen very largely depends on the traders' belief in the long run stability of the "normal price" of each commodity. Once this belief is

---

[1] In the more recent period the high volatility of commodity prices was aggravated by the policy-induced volatility of interest rates—a consequence not of economic forces, but of the spread of "monetarist" ideologies, and the attempts by Governments to set targets to the growth of the money supply, and to vary interest rates so as to secure some degree of conformity with these targets. Thus according to Nordhaus ("Chaos and Confusion in the International Economy Today", prepared for the Seminaire de reflexion sur l'économie mondiale, Paris, May 1982), since 1979 the volatility of monthly changes in interest rates in the United States rose by a factor of six at the short end, and a factor of 2½-4 at the long end of the capital market. This was reflected, in greater or lesser degrees, in corresponding increases in volatility of interest rates and of spot exchange rates of other countries. Thus some countries such as Japan preferred to keep interest rates relatively stable at the cost of more violent movements in the spot exchange rate; others, like the members of the EMS (European Monetary System) or Britain preferred to allow their interest rate to fluctuate with US rates. This of course was an additional source of instability, with adverse effects both on investment and on international trade.

impaired or destroyed by the instability of *actual* prices, the traders' subjective appreciation of the risks incurred in holding stocks is increased, with the result that they require a higher expected compensation for any departure—upwards or downwards—from their normal commitments (their normal stock/turnover ratio). But this means, in turn, that any variation in the carry-over of stocks from period to period will be associated with an even greater variation of prices, which in turn will have further repercussions on the traders' willingness to take risks. Thus unregulated commodity markets, contrary to the generally held belief, represent a highly wasteful and primitive instrument for aligning the supply and demand for commodities. In fact, as a result of experience, the demand for commodity price stabilisation schemes became increasingly widespread even before the collapse of world commodity prices after the 1929 crash.

In the course of the 1930s, most countries introduced schemes for securing "remunerative and stable prices" for the producers of the main agricultural crops, chiefly food-grains. One of the first of these schemes was the agricultural price support program of the Roosevelt Administration in the United States, which set the pattern for national schemes in all those countries which had exportable surpluses and which could not therefore be adequately protected by import duties. The Common Agricultural Policy (CAP) of the EEC was a development in direct line with these earlier measures; it was the first of its kind which aimed at securing a uniform set of agricultural prices in a number of countries—the members of the EEC—simultaneously, but did so by methods of local market intervention that gave the appearance of a "common price" without the reality of free competition between relatively low-cost and relatively high-cost areas.

It was intended, first of all, as a subsidy to farmers through the stabilisation of prices at a remunerative level. I do not wish to go into the defects of its basic conception, which have already been frequently analysed. Here I would stress its two advantages which have not been so widely recognised.

(1) The first is the great advantage of guaranteed prices in improving agricultural productivity. This is equivalent to a large reduction in costs, or in the cost of borrowing, which makes it profitable to the producers to carry investments a great deal farther than they would have done otherwise. The introduction of a guaranteed price has thus a productivity-raising effect as such—this was found equally to be the case among temperate or tropical foodstuffs (*e.g.* the effect of the introduction of marketing boards in West Africa, etc.); and also under schemes in which the price was stabilised by direct market intervention, or through deficiency payments to the farmers who sold in a free market below the guaranteed price (as under the postwar British scheme which was in force prior to the UK joining the Common Market).

(2) The second relates to the effects of steadily rising purchasing power of the agricultural community on the demand for manufactured goods. The rate of growth of the secondary, or manufacturing sector, mainly depends on the rate of growth of the demand for its products coming from *outside* the sector—whether this is export demand, or demand coming from the agricultural sector *within* a country. If the growth of demand from "agriculture" is speeded up, then the growth of demand within the industrial sector will also be speeded up—through induced investment as well as consumption—by a kind of "tuning-fork" effect. Hence, provided agricultural prices are maintained in a reasonably stable relationship with industrial prices, agricultural price fixing carried out through market intervention will speed up the rate of expansion of both "agriculture" and industry.

This will certainly be true if the net sums spent on market intervention (which correspond to the net acquisition of commodity stocks by the international agency) are treated as capital expenditures financed by borrowing and not as current expenditures financed by taxation. For if it is the latter—as is the case with the CAP—the expansionary effects of the policy are (partly if not wholly) rendered nugatory through additional taxation.

Finally, if the policy results in the accumulation of stocks—as is often the case with the CAP through the accumulation of butter mountains, beef mountains and so on—it is no good trying to get rid of these stocks by selling them at a discount in the world market, for this latter policy will also set up negative effects on the generation of incomes outside the EEC area that may nullify, partially at least, the expansionary effects of the policy.

A NEW INTERNATIONAL AGENCY

The net effect of these considerations is that the principles of the CAP ought to be extended so as to make it truly international—in other words, world-wide—and not confined to producers of a favoured group of countries; and that the net expenditure on market intervention resulting in the acquisition of stocks should be treated as investment and not as current expenditure, and financed as such.

In other words there ought to be a new international agency, on the lines recommended by Keynes during the last war, for world-wide price-stabilisation by means of buffer stocks for as many commodities as possible. Keynes's war-time plan for an international agency for stabilising commodity prices (alongside his plan for an International Clearing Union—which came into existence, in a much emasculated form, in the Bretton Woods Agreement of 1944) has only become known some years ago, with the release of war-time Government papers under the 30 years' rule and their subsequent publication in Keynes's *Collected Writings*.[1] He named this agency International Commodity Control, which would set up buffer stocks for all the main commodities, operated for each particular commodity by a subsidiary organisation run on identical principles and subject to the central control of the General Council of the main body. Unlike his proposals for an International Clearing Union, this plan was never seriously considered at the international level, though Keynes and some of his fellow economists (such as Roy

---

[1] Ed. D. Moggridge, Vol. XXVII, 1980, pp. xiii and 539.

Harrod and Dennis Robertson) regarded it as of the utmost importance for securing stability and prosperity in the postwar world. Both schemes went through a succession of drafts as a result of discussion inside the government machine, and they largely overlapped with one another. The first draft of the Clearing Union plan is dated early September 1941; the first draft of the buffer stock plan 20 January 1942; a succession of further drafts of both schemes followed in quick succession in the first half of 1942. The various versions of the buffer stock plan make it clear that Keynes's ideas advanced considerably since his first article on the topic in the *Economic Journal* of 1938.[1] Both went through detailed consideration by both official and ministerial committees, but the buffer stock scheme ran into far more opposition from the Ministry of Agriculture and (more surprisingly) from the Bank of England, who considered the proposals "to be far too *laisser faire* inasmuch as they still allow a place for private trading", thereby displaying, in Keynes's view, a "bias towards rigidly controlled State trading on Russian lines." In a minute to Sir Richard Hopkins of 15 April 1942, Keynes wrote: "I can only plead guilty of aiming at a plan which does take a middle course between unfettered competition under *laisser-faire* conditions and planned controls which try to freeze commerce into a fixed mould."[2]

It is assumed that the net expenditure on this scheme represents a net addition to world investment, which would be ensured if and only if the expenditure of the Commodity Control Agency were directly financed by the issue of new international currency, in other words, by SDRs. The great advantage of such a scheme is that it would provide a most powerful stabilising device to the world economy, which would oeprate so as to secure the highest sustainable rate of economic growth to the world as a whole, *i.e.* the highest rate of growth of

---

[1] Cf. *Economic Journal* (*op. cit.* in n. 1 on p. 536).

[2] *Ibid.*, pp. 110-11. The Minister of Agriculture, Mr Hudson, and his Permanent Secretary, Sir John Fergusson, were the most vociferous opponents, and they had the support of Sir Frederick Leith-Ross. They were all convinced that nothing but output restriction, enforced through export and import quotas, could solve the problem of commodity surpluses. In their view Keynes's buffer stock scheme gave all the *wrong* incentives since, by guaranteeing a floor, price, it gave a strong stimulus for increasing production instead of diminishing it.

world industrialisation which the growth of availabilities of primary products permit.[1] This would happen because whenever the increase in the supply of primary products was in excess of the growth of requirements (as governed by the prevailing rate of growth of world industrial production), there would be an increase in investment in stocks which would automatically generate an increase in the rate of growth of demand for industrial products and would have large multiplier effects; in the converse case, an excessive growth of industrialisation would automatically be damped down by a decrease in investment in stocks which would cause the growth of demand for industrial products to be slowed down, since the industrial sector's outlay on primary products would come to exceed the receipts of producers.

In other words, under a buffer stock regime—assuming that it is worldwide in scope and sufficiently comprehensive as to the range of products included—the task of aligning the growth of world industrial production to that permitted by the growth of availabilities of primary products would take place, not through price variations but through variation in the rate of investment in stocks of the International Commodity Control Authority.

The "alignment" of the two sectors would thus take place, not by changes in the terms of trade, but by income variations—or rather by induced changes in the rate of growth of industrial output and incomes.

A comprehensive buffer stock scheme of the kind advocated by Keynes would not rule out adjustments of relative prices as between different commodities, nor would it guarantee the *complete* stability of the average level of prices in terms of the international currency unit into which the range of commo-

---

[1] Contrary to generally held beliefs, the rate of growth of industrial production is *not* confined by the available "supplies" of Labour and Capital in any particular country or region and their exogenous growth rate over time. As the postwar experience of Germany and most other Western European countries have shown, when home and foreign demand for manufactured goods reaches the point where the growth in production threatens to be confined by shortages of domestic labour, the latter will be augmented by the importation of guest workers from labour-surplus areas. Similarly the accumulation of capital will automatically be stepped up with the growth of industrial production—indeed the one is but an aspect of the other. There are limits in any given situation to the possible speed of adaptation and adjustment; but this is a quite different thing from saying that the growth of industrial output will be *determined by* the (exogenous) rate of growth of labour and capital resources.

dities included in the scheme would be convertible. But the adjustment of prices would be circumscribed by carefully laid down rules, relating the movement of the stock/turnover ratio of a particular commodity deviating from the average in excess of a permitted range of variation; and the adjustment process would need to follow rules prescribing a graduated change in successive steps extending over a period. However, since such individual adjustments due to deviations from the *average* change in stocks can take either direction, the consequential variations in the price level of basic commodities in general are not likely to exceed a fairly narrow range in terms of international currency units (SDRs). A buffer stock scheme linked to the issue of SDRs would thus provide the world with a basic money unit which can be guaranteed to be stable in terms of basic commodities.

And this in itself would be a tremendous achievement— indeed it would largely deal with the problem of chronic worldwide inflation. In any one country inflation occurs because of (i) the rise in commodity prices which now occurs regularly as a result of even a moderate recovery in demand, but which leads to a revision of expected future prices[1] and thereby greatly increases the volatility of prices (*i.e.* the amplitude of price fluctuations);[2] (ii) the rise in commodity prices, by increasing the cost of production of manufactured goods, increases the cost of living, which in turn tends to raise the rate of increase of money wages, thereby adding further to the rise in costs and prices.

---

[1] This is only another way of saying that it leads to purely speculative *in*vestment in commodities (by traders and speculators) which cause the price rise to become exaggerated instead of being moderated (as in the normal case) by speculative *dis*investment.

[2] It is sometimes suggested that the volatility of commodity prices would be reduced if the spreading of risks through "hedging" were made more readily available through increased facilities for buying and selling "futures" for each commodity, for a whole series of future periods. In my opinion this is a mistaken view, because while such development would make the spot price in any market more narrowly dependent on the "futures" prices, there is no reason to suppose that the volatility of movement in the "futures" market would be any less (and therefore the movements in the spot price would vary less), and there is evidence for the view that it would be greater than in the absence of futures markets. Greater scope for "hedging" risks must generate a correspondingly greater volume of "speculative transactions" (or "movement trading") and that assumes greater, not lesser, deviations from the "normal" price. (See an illuminating article by Colchester ("Protection from Chicago", *Financial Times*, 4 February 1983, p. 7.

Hence a rise in commodity prices (at any rate above a certain limit) causes inflation in the industrial countries for two separate but connected reasons: (1) because the rises in raw material prices are passed through the various stages of processing and distribution (magnified by the customary percentage addition for profit) to the prices paid by the final buyer; (2) because the increase in the cost of living caused by (1) leads to additional wage increases which further magnify its inflationary effect. It is the difference between the two types of market structures—the cost-determined character of industrial prices and the market-determined character of commodity prices—which might cause a "spiral effect" in the course of which the rise in prices becomes general and self-perpetuating without providing thereby any large change in the *average* of the relative prices of the two groups over any given period.

The critical factor in the generation of the inflation of the 1970s was President Nixon's suspension of the convertibility of the dollar into gold on August 15, 1971. Although at the time it was regarded largely as a formality (indeed it was welcomed by many economists as a necessary move to re-establish more appropriate exchange rates and to reduce the imbalance in the international flow of payments), in fact, as it became evident later, it had fateful and unexpected consequences, given the special role of the dollar in the world economy in the postwar period.

This role emerged as a (largely unforeseen) consequence of the mode of operation of the Bretton Woods Agreement[1] elevating the dollar into a universally accepted reserve medium which increasingly replaced the role of gold in the international payments system. As US dollars were the scarce currency *par excellence* both in the 1930s, and in the initial postwar years, the central banks of the world were quite happy to hold dollar balances which yielded an interest income in preference to gold which did not, in the secure expectation that inter-country

---

[1] Under the accepted rules of interpretation of the statutes of the IMF, the dollar became the universally accepted "intervention currency" among the members of the IMF, which meant that any country was deemed to have fulfilled its obligations under the treaty if it maintained *in its own market* the parity of its currency in terms of the US dollar.

balances could be "cleared" by payment in dollars. This meant, in turn, that for many years almost the whole annual increment in monetary gold out of new production was absorbed (with some reluctance) by the US Treasury.

But as time went on, and the official dollar balances of foreign countries came to exceed the US gold reserve by the early 1960s, countries became gradually more reluctant to increase their dollar holdings; and some countries, like France, insisted on converting any increment in their dollar balances into gold. This unwillingness increased considerably when, as a result of the Vietnam War, the rate of US inflation reached 5-6 per cent a year (instead of the previous postwar average of 1-1.5 per cent), while the US balance of payments which was adverse on "basic transactions" from the end of the 1950s, became increasingly adverse on current account as well. The Washington agreement of March 1968 provided temporary relief through the agreement of a number of major countries to accept dollars in payment from other countries and not seek to increase their holdings of gold. But with the rise in the rates of inflation which was worldwide,[1] the demands of dollar-holders for conversion into gold intensified to the point at which the total suspension of convertibility became necessary.

The effect of this step was to destroy the belief, still held by professional traders in various markets, in the long run stability of the *dollar* price of particular commodities. This, as we have seen, is a vital element in ensuring the satisfactory functioning of markets which requires that professional traders (just like jobbers on the Stock Exchange) behave in the opposite way to outsiders: ready to sell when outsiders are buying, and *vice versa*. There is evidence that President Nixon's move unleashed

---

[1] This occurred prior to any major change in commodity prices as a result of the inflationary rise in wage rates in a large number of countries in 1968 and 1969, the precise causes of which are uncertain. It may have been the reaction to the "événements" in France in June 1968, when a general strike led to the Government agreeing to a universal increase in wage rates by 15 per cent, the effects of which rapidly spread to other countries (much as the February revolution in Paris in 1848 led, within a very short time, to revolutionary outbreaks all over Europe) given the increased aggressiveness of trade unions after many years of full employment. This meant that the annual rise in the dollar price-level of manufactured goods moving in international trade, which hovered around 1-1.5 per cent throughout the postwar period, rose to 5 per cent a year after 1968.

inflationary expectations and led to speculative investment in commodities or commodity futures as an inflation hedge. Such speculative investment extended to "soft" commodities (such as cocoa, coffee, tea and sugar) where there was no evidence of a reduction in stocks due to excess consumption, as well as to nonferrous metals like tin and copper, where there was an apparent excess of consumption over current production in 1972-73. That a great deal of the rapid rise (and subsequent rapid fall) in commodity prices was due to the perverse effects of speculation is shown by the similarity, both in extent and timing, of movements in the gold price and in the index of commodity prices.[1]

Of course a scheme of the kind advocated here does not in itself guarantee the absence of inflation in the prices of industrial products due to a rise in "efficiency wages"—*i.e.* money wages increasing in excess of the increase in the productivity of labour. However, the very existence of an international reserve currency which is stable in terms of commodities would exert a strong dampening effect on wage-induced inflations. This is because if one country allows its "efficiency wages" to rise at a faster rate than others, it will face an unfavourable balance of payments on current account; it will therefore be tempted to devalue (in terms of SDRs) so as to ease the balance of payments constraint on employment, which in turn would serve to lower industrial prices in terms of SDRs. It would also turn the terms of trade against any devaluing country more powerfully than at present, which in turn would be bound to exert a moderating effect on excessive wage claims.

But with the present volatility of commodity prices, any expansionary move is likely to generate inflationary tendencies (due to the rapid and disproportionate rise in commodity prices) and thus tempt Governments of all political hues to seek safety in fiscal austerity and thereby aggravate the stagnation in the world economy.

---

[1] Cf. OECD, *Economic Outlook*, Paris, December 1973, p. 106.

CONCLUSIONS

An international buffer-stock scheme (on the lines worked out by Keynes[1]) appears to me the most promising avenue for getting out of the rut into which capitalist market economies have fallen,[2] for two main reasons:

(1) It is essential if market economies are to resume sustained economic expansion without generating unacceptable inflation due to the consequential rise in commodity prices, resulting from speculative influences of a perverse character, and to enable the changes in stock to be carried which are necessary to tide over short-period differences between absorption and accrual of commodities without any large deviation of the current price from the "normal" price.

(2) It is essential in order to resume investment in new capacity in primary products on an adequate scale. With wildly fluctuating prices, the risks of investment in additional capacity are greatly enlarged, particularly for commodities like copper or oil, where investment in new capacity has a long gestation period.

If the argument advanced in this paper is correct, and economic growth in the long run depends on the growth of availabilities of the essential "inputs" of the industrial sector, in food, industrial raw materials and energy, the prime condition is to secure stable world prices for such commodities through a new international reserve currency that is *de facto* convertible into commodities.

This, I am sure, was the thought behind Keynes's advocacy of

---

[1] Cf. Moggridge (ed.) (*op. cit.* in n. 1 on p. 541).

[2] The scheme advocated here falls short of an International Commodity Reserve Currency (advocated by Benjamin Graham in the 1930s), a detailed version of which was submitted to the first UNCTAD Conference in 1964, in the names of A.G. Hart, J. Tinbergen and myself. The basic conception of that scheme was an international currency convertible into a fixed *bundle* of commodities, each unit of the bundle consisting of so much wheat, so much rice, tobacco, copper, wool etc.—altogether 30 commodities comprising some 90 per cent of the total value of commodities moving in international trade. However, on closer inspection, a scheme of this kind revealed inherent problems of its own which are absent in the case of a simpler scheme consisting of separate buffer stocks being operated for the various commodities: also, it would have been highly complicated to operate.

an International Commodity Control. His proposals have thus the same intended effect as the more recent proposals for a "Common Fund"—even though the latter is not linked to the creation of a new international currency convertible into commodities. However, since the latter scheme originated with the "developing" countries (members of UNCTAD), it had the same cool reception which Keynes's ideas received from the British establishment during the War. Nobody seems to have understood that, while the proposal was promoted by the developing countries, its adoption was in the vital interest of the "developed" or industrialised countries, since it is a precondition for securing adequate long-term investment necessary for sustained industrial growth.[1]

[1] The very large expenditures incurred on prospecting and developing new oil fields since the war would not have been possible if oil had fluctuated in price in the same way as copper or tin. The fact is that, prior to OPEC, a stable price was secured thanks to the control over distribution and marketing by the seven major international oil companies. Since 1973, the world price mainly depended on the fixed price charged by OPEC's "price-leader", which is Saudi Arabia (owing to her large share in total world production). Recently, there was a threat of a collapse of oil prices due to reduced demand which (in my opinion) was rightly received with a great deal of misgiving, even by the large oil-importing countries: since they realised that in the long run they are likely to fare worse under a regime of fluctuating oil prices than under a regime of stable prices, even though the latter would be a relatively high one in terms of industrial goods.

INDEX OF NAMES

SUBJECT INDEX